Penguin Books

SO-ACI-054

THE PENGUIN NEW LITERARY HISTORY
OF AUSTRALIA

This publication has been assisted by The Australian Bicentennial Authority, to celebrate Australia's Bicentenary in 1988 and by the Literary Arts Board of the Australia Council the Federal Government's arts funding and advisory body.

A joint project of the Association for the Study of Australian Literature and Penguin Books.

This publication has been assisted by The Australian Bicentennial Authority to celebrate Australia's Bicentenary in 1988 and by the Literary Arts Board of the Australia Council, the Federal Government's arts funding and advisory body.

A joint project of the Association for the Study of Australian Literature and *Australian Literary Studies.*

THE PENGUIN NEW LITERARY HISTORY
OF AUSTRALIA

GENERAL EDITOR
Laurie Hergenhan

EDITORS
Bruce Bennett, Martin Duwell, Brian Matthews,
Peter Pierce, Elizabeth Webby

Penguin Books

Penguin Books Australia Ltd
487 Maroondah Highway, PO Box 257
Ringwood, Victoria, 3134, Australia
Penguin Books Ltd
Harmondsworth, Middlesex, England
Viking Penguin Inc.
40 West 23rd Street, New York, NY 10010, USA
Penguin Books Canada Limited
2801 John Street, Markham, Ontario, Canada, L3R 1B4
Penguin Books (N.Z.) Ltd
182-190 Wairau Road, Auckland 10, New Zealand

First published by Penguin Books, Australia 1988

Typeset in Times by Allset Graphics Pty. Ltd.
Made and printed in Australia by Australian Print Group, Maryborough, Victoria.

CIP

The Penguin new literary history of Australia.

Bibliography.
Includes index.
ISBN 0 14 007514 3.

1. Australian literature—History and criticism. I. Hergenhan, L. T. (Laurence Thomas), 1931-
II. Bennett, Bruce, 1941-   . III. Association for the Study of Australian Literature.
IV. Title: Australia literary studies. V. Title: New literary history of Australia.

A820'.9

DEDICATION

To the Memory of Barry Andrews (1943-1987)

Note on Tribal Affiliations

Both Kath Walker and Colin Johnson have changed their names into a traditional form using a tribal affiliation. Kath Walker is now Oodgeroo Noonuccal and Colin Johnson is now Mudooroo Narogin.

Note on Pounds, Shillings and Pence

There were 12 pennies (d.) in one shilling (s.), and 20 shillings in one pound (£). A guinea was worth £1 1s.; a sovereign was a coin worth £1. When Australia changed to decimal currency in 1966, $2 was equal to £1.

Contents

GENERAL INTRODUCTION LAURIE HERGENHAN

GENERAL INTRODUCTION

LAURIE HERGENHAN

Why a 'new' literary history of Australia when there has been no lack of histories, including recent ones? The short answer is that Australian works have generally remained unadventurous and slow to change in their approaches to writing literary history. 'Content', rather than the various ways in which this can be constructed, has been what counted.

Authors have been more adventurous than the critics. The supposed lack of an indigenous history—the idea that for Australians history is what happened overseas—is a colonial legacy. Henry Lawson, Henry Handel Richardson, and Thomas Keneally, for instance, reacted against the way this was even embedded in the educational system. But instead of being a cultural handicap, this myth of Australian emptiness has driven many of our writers, from Marcus Clarke and others before him, both to reclaim and to recreate an indigenous past. There is a need for independence, which takes the form of escape from an imposed, subordinate history. This tension is common to all post-colonial cultures, including South American; it has been a main source of the creative vitality in their literatures, and at no time more so than recently.

In Australia the preoccupation with 'old tales of a young country', or even more ambiguously, of a 'young old country' has become a means both of constantly revising the past and of asserting a difference from the colonising country, as in novels of Miles Franklin, Eleanor Dark, Xavier Herbert and Patrick White. The result is a range of books which deal with history—poems, novels, plays, autobiographies, documentaries, and so on—as well as works in other media, especially painting (as in Nolan's historical series), and more recently in film and television. Aboriginal literature is different and prior, and as *The Penguin New Literary History of Australia* shows, its two main concerns have been to conserve a long past through oral literature and, latterly, to write Aborigines back into the history of Australia, as in recent novels and poetry by Colin Johnson and Kath Walker, and the plays of Jack Davis. The rewriting of history in literature has thus involved the rewriting of *literary* history, notably so when Furphy's *Such is Life* reacted against Kingsley's *Geoffry Hamlyn.*

In contrast to the literature, histories of it have usually taken the form of 'surveys' or 'outlines'—both depending on potted comment on authors. Histories of Australian literature have been more concerned to document, to reorder and to revalue the literature than to rewrite its history by finding approaches appropriate to its distinctive but diverse nature. Most histories have imitated or adapted European models, not creatively but so as to confirm dependence. There is need, then, for different approaches. *The Penguin New Literary History of Australia* aims to be innovative to show that the actual writing of such history needs to be reconceived: that approaches to the past do not simply reveal, they help to create it. For history is not simply a record of 'what happened'; it involves competing, recounted versions of the past. Some versions get suppressed: they do not get written, or alternatively they are neglected or discredited in favour of received versions. This new history does not pretend to solve all the problems, but it does aim to open up possibilities and to uncover some of the difficulties.

There has been a remarkable lack of debate in Australia about the writing of literary history. It is revealing that no history has been really controversial, except for *The Oxford History of Australian Literature* (1981). Unfortunately that controversy provided more an occasion for airing pent-up dissatisfactions with the state of criticism in Australia and for fighting old battles than for debating literary historiography. H. M. Green's landmark, two-volume history (1961) is innovatory not in its methodology but in its widening of conceptions of what constitutes Australian literary texts and in its wealth of information. These achievements have given it enduring value.

An essential element of *The Penguin New Literary History* is its consciousness that it is written out of the present, and that the needs of the present must cause us to reassess ways of looking at the past, though the one should not impose itself on the other. The present is not, of course, fixed and views of it—and from it—vary greatly. The present that the *The Penguin New Literary History of Australia* is written out of is the late 1980s and it has been influenced by changes in criticism dating from the 1960s. Recent histories have ignored or played down these changes and the role of the present in constructing the past. Each generation writes its own literature and should produce its own literary histories.

What, then, is the nature of the present out of which *The Penguin New Literary History of Australia* is written? Sacvan Bercovitch, editor of a much more ambitious and revisionary history than this, a forthcoming literary history of America in five volumes, sees the main shift in post-1960s criticism in America as the decay of consensus and the growth of 'dissensus', a seeming 'babel of contending approaches'. Bercovitch claims that consensus about both terms in the phrase 'American literature' has 'broken down, worn out, or at best opened up'.

There are parallels with the Australian literary situation. The concepts of 'Australian literature' which have underwritten previous histories, consciously or not, have been a limiting pair of dualities. These have been described in various ways but are both, in effect, sides of the same coin. On the one hand is a colonial or post-colonial nationalism; on the other is an internationalist view. The first seeks to promote and to test the new local product in relation to the older literatures (mainly English and European). The second is conservative and defensive: it invokes 'universal' (i.e. European) standards so that claims for the local writing are kept properly modest.

These dualities have hardened into adversary stances, but they are in fact different symptoms of the same post-colonial uncertainty and need for recognition. The twin concerns have pre-empted and dominated discussion, leaving little space for other views to be raised. Hence literary histories have not encouraged a variety of voices, or relativity of viewpoint—as opposed to a belief in centralising uniformity and absolute, canonical values—which are needed to break down European dominance. 'Who's on whose margins?', a basic question recently asked in connection with women's ethnic literature in Australia, is of wider concern, influencing many aspects of our literature.

In both history and criticism the adjective 'Australian' has often overshadowed its subject 'literature' and narrowed readings of it. 'Australian' has either been equated with a version of national identity that becomes a determining measure of value, as in A. A.

Phillips' *The Australian Tradition* (1958), or it has been equated with a parochialism that needs to be kept in check, as in parts of *The Oxford History*. (The latter is not the homogeneous work some critics have reduced it to.) Since the 1960s, national identity has often been seen differently. It is regarded as both more a problematic and a changing concept, and hence it is no longer such a dominating preoccupation. On the other hand, internationalism is now also seen in less simple terms; it involves exclusions and emasculating standardisations.

Another change since the 1960s, inside and outside Australia, involved not simply an expansion of what constituted literary texts but new ways of reading them based on the realisation that neither the text, nor the reading, is value-free, and hence culture-free. Such readings seek out ideological elements or codes to show how diverse texts play a part in asserting power, of supporting some values at the expense of others, often in concealed ways. And literary histories, including this one, are no exception. This critical development derives partly from the political upheavals of the 1960s—especially the Vietnam protest—which deeply affected Australian literature, and encouraged the recognition that considerations of race, class, gender, regionalism and politics are necessary parts of literary criticism. At the same time, there was more awareness of the means by which social forces, not simply individual talent and taste, influence the production and consumption of literature.

If the terms 'Australian' and 'literature' have been reassessed, so has 'history'. Historiography has been a lively field of debate and at the same time a source of competing approaches for historians, such as Manning Clark, Geoffrey Blainey, Geoffrey Serle, Anne Summers and Miriam Dixson. Historians have taken more account of literature than literary critics have taken of history. There are signs of change, however, in David Carter's recent suggestion that

> the most informative and provocative of books on Australian literature over the last decade or so have been written *not* by literary critics but by historians—or, at the very least have been written not *as* literary criticism but as history.

He instances such books as John Docker's *Australian Cultural Elites* (1974), David Walker's *Dream and Disillusion* (1976), Drusilla Modjeska's *Exiles at Home* (1981) and Sylvia Lawson's *The Archibald Paradox* (1983). G. A. Wilkes' *The Stockyard and the Crocquet Lawn* (1981) could also have been added. Another notable example of the impact of history on literary studies is the rediscovery of nineteenth-century literature in journal articles. But the problems which historians have grappled with have had little effect on *literary* historiography. Problems of writing history have included the following: conceptions of cause and effect have become complicated to the point of breakdown, so that narrative history seems no longer viable or at best restrictive; it is difficult to make generalisations about an unstable 'reality'; it is difficult to write history 'from below' instead of around 'great' names and events; boundaries between high and low culture are dissolving; and there is the complex role of ideology to be allowed for.

If new possibilities are to be opened up for Australian literary history, such problems together with changes in literary criticism have to be taken into account; it is not to be expected that all the problems will be solved or all the changes endorsed. Expression of these new possibilities has been a main aim in the planning and writing of *The Penguin New Literary History of Australia* and the format was designed by the editors to accommodate them, and to expose diverse areas to a variety of viewpoints. Multiplicity of authorship does not of course necessarily produce pluralism but the editors have encouraged it through the *History's* general structure. The chapters were designed to provoke new kinds of questions and to encourage diversity. The editors worked out the format and the briefs for each chapter, but they encouraged contributors to be exploratory and to make changes. The contributors responded to varying degrees and in their own ways. Hence *The Penguin New Literary History of Australia* aims for flexibility rather than strict orderliness of organisation.

It also aims to reach a wide audience, and a mixed one, by introducing some readers to Australian literature and at the same time interesting the knowledgeable. A previous Penguin Books publication, *The Literature of Australia* (1964, rptd 1982), edited by Geoffrey Dutton, was the first popular history of Australian literature, if one uses 'popular' in the best sense of being widely read. Its accommodating eclecticism gave it an openness which contrasts with Grahame Johnston's *Australian Literary Criticism* (1962), a collection of revisionist essays. Johnston's introduction is anti-nationalist and judgemental and his aim was to establish a critical canon; this can be seen as part of the politics of gaining academic recognition for Australian literature and establishing control over it. Not so long afterwards canon formation came under critical fire.

The Penguin New Literary History of Australia is closer in spirit to Dutton's work. It departs, however, from the two main forms which Dutton and Johnston represent: on the one hand the broad survey, comprehensive and annalistic, and on the other hand the selective, judgemental account. Some degree of selection and survey must enter into any history. *The Penguin New Literary History of Australia* aims at as broad a coverage as possible. The emphasis is not, however, on description but on the kind of account which links things together; consequently it uses examples and allusions rather than giving a book by book review. The contemporary section (Part V)—and several other chapters—aims to be more inclusive and open in order not to set limits on an expansive new field, still very close to us. While there are separate chapters on Aboriginal literature, on language, culture and women's writing, these are among subjects which recur throughout the book.

To open up questions about literary history, and to avoid the flatness of a survey, the editors of *The Penguin New Literary History of Australia* have opted for a greater range of chapters and variety of contributors than is usually found in literary histories, and all of the thirty-four chapters have been kept short. But it has not been assumed that pluralism is inherently 'redemptive'. The pluralistic approach has its own limitations and forms of closure: it can encourage fence-sitting, and it can give the misleading impression that everything has been talked about.

Similarly, this is not the exclusive kind of history centring around outstanding names. While *The Penguin New Literary History of Australia* avoids the judgemental, it does include evaluation: but the evaluations are made on a variety of grounds and as part of its exploratory spirit, not as judgements handed down on books and authors. So while some books necessarily get more attention than others, the approach is different from the mountains-down-to-foothills perspective, a geographical metaphor common in Australian literary history. Comment on outstanding writers, such as Christina Stead, Patrick White, Joseph Furphy and Barbara Baynton, will be found not in any one place but in a number of contexts on the understanding that is can be revealing to view an author in this way. For those who prefer to focus on the individual author, many studies are available. Here we pursue diversity, rather than centralising attention and power on a few selected authors.

The format of *The Penguin New Literary History of Australia* is designed to prevent arbitrary divisions, especially the kind of divisions into periods predetermined by metaphors of progress or evolution, which abound in Australian and other post-colonial histories. Divisions into periods of roughly fifty years have been made, but these are not in themselves part of any overall scheme. The chapters are not seen as having impassable borders; they are not seen as part of a linear chronological progress. Similarly, genres such as poetry, fiction, drama, as well as other forms, including popular literature, are not treated as fixed categories and are generally not separated from one another into different chapters. Instead, the emphasis is on making connections between forms and individuals works. For instance, Chapter 16, 'Dreams, Visions, Utopias', provided an opportunity to make bedfellows, at least experimentally, of those apparently doomed always to be separated: Lawson the social realist; Brennan the 'metaphysical' writer; the reformist Catherine Helen Spence; William Lane, who can be considered as combining both aspects; and the bardic utopian, O'Dowd. Similarly, chapters 13-15 on melodrama, romance and realism show a new approach; they treat popular genres not in a formalistic sense but as literary expressions of ideology and culture. Chapter 23 breaks down the simplified image of social realism, and examines its diversity; it uncovers the hidden problems which social realism poses both about itself and other forms of literature. Writers who have been previously neglected, such as Catherine Helen Spence and William Lane, will receive more attention as well as appearing in a number of contexts.

The format is also flexible in balancing narrative and analysis. Recurrent chapters on production and on literary perceptions of Australia are more chronological than others and give a general idea of the influence of these changing aspects of context. The various ways in which a culture perceives itself involve its relation to other cultures, and also reactions to views of itself from 'outside'. Such perceptions have always been important. As Bernard Smith has commented, 'Australian culture has been a complex web from the beginning', and this includes Aboriginal and white cultures and their interactions. *The Penguin New Literary History of Australia* accordingly emphasises the importance of both contemporary and early literature, whereas some histories have skimped one or the other.

Chapters on the production of literature have been included because of redefinitions of its importance. Production, or 'the marketing of the literary imagination', to borrow the title of Chapter 18, involves economic and socio-political forces; these forces influence what society thinks of as 'literature' and how it is read; they govern such matters as authors' earnings (or the lack of them), publication outlets, the publishing industry, copyright, audiences, and the values which inform all of these. Much of the work on production in *The Penguin New Literary History of Australia* is pioneering, for this kind of study is still comparatively new. Changes in the production of literature and in perceptions of what constitutes literature are closely related. This can be seen in attempts to change the relationship between the local product and the overseas 'centres'. The very concept of centres and peripheries has been called into question; it constitutes a problem for post-colonial countries.

The aims of this history could not have been realised if it had had to include substantial biographical or bibliographical information. Fortunately, neither is necessary, for as the Appendix shows there has been an extraordinary flowering since the 1960s of bibliographies and guides. By way of comparison, such aids were available at an earlier period for Carl Klinck to rely on in the compilation of *The Literary History of Canada* (1965).

> We have to remember that there is no one, single, correct kind of criticism, no complete criticism. You only have different kinds of perspectives, giving them, when successful, different kinds of insights. And at one historical moment, one kind of insight may be more needed than another.

This comment by Robert Penn Warren sums up the spirit of *The Penguin New Literary History of Australia.* This work addresses aspects of 'the historical moment'—the 1980s—as well as addressing the past. The task is a challenging one; any attempt must necessarily be inconclusive, given the diverse perceptions of both the present and the past. But it is important to continue to question them.

Notes

The endnotes to Chapter 5 include documentation of the Australian literary histories and critical works referred to specifically or in general in this introduction. Additional works referred to are: Sacvan Bercovitch, 'The Problem of Ideology in Literary History', *Critical Inquiry*, 12 (Summer 1986); Sacvan Bercovitch (ed.), *Reconstructing American History* (1986), which includes a chapter by Werner Sollors, 'A Critique of Pure Pluralism'; Carl F. Klinck (ed.), *Literary*

History of Canada (1965); 'Robert Penn Warren' in *The Paris Review Interviews,* introd. by Malcolm Cowley (1958); David Carter, 'Tragical-comical-historical-political: Criticism and the Cold War in Australia', *Meridian,* 5 (1986); Sneja Gunew, 'Migrant Women Writers: Who's on Whose Margins?' in C. Ferrier (ed.), *Gender, Politics and Fiction* (1985).

PART I

Chapter 1

AUSTRALIAN LITERATURE AND AUSTRALIAN CULTURE

BRUCE CLUNIES ROSS

European culture arrived in Australia with a gun and a whistle. Three days after the First Fleet sailed into Botany Bay, Captain Watkin Tench of the Marines went ashore with a party which encountered some Aborigines. The white men displayed their clothing. The Aborigines, comfortably naked in the midsummer heat of the New South Wales coast, were amazed, and signified a wish to know the sex of the invaders. Evidence of masculinity was presented—Tench refrains from explaining how—at which the Aborigines broke into immoderate laughter. It may have been this display of uncalled-for mirth which caused the white men to demonstrate a more powerful weapon, for the next day they went ashore and discharged a gun at a target set up in a tree. The Aborigines retreated, but on hearing one of the sailors whistle the tune of *Malbrouke*, cautiously returned. When Tench reported this incident to La Perouse, who had also arrived in Botany Bay, the French navigator told him that the same melody had a calming influence on the natives all over the Pacific region. In any case, it had a sinister aptness. It was a tune of French origin, popular at the end of the eighteenth century, with words in various languages. With adjustments for a different syllabic distribution and a slight variant in the last phrase, it is still current in the English-speaking world as the tune of 'For he's a jolly good fellow' or, at a more lugubrious tempo, 'We won't go home till morning, we won't go home at all!'

For centuries before this encounter, Europeans had been speculating about the antipodes, or the unknown south land, that lay just beyond the limits of their navigational and ship-building ingenuity. The idea of a topsy-turvy world of wonders at the opposite pole of the globe was a commonplace which inspired writings like

The Antipodes (1636), a play by Ben Jonson's servant Richard Brome, where, amongst other natural inversions,

> All wit, and mirth and good society
> Is there among the hirelings, clowns and tradesmen;
> And all their poets are puritans.

If this is not earthly perfection, there were those like Pedro Fernández de Quirós who imagined it could be attained in the south land. In 1606 he claimed it for the Holy Spirit and tried to establish a community devoted to the principles of pure religion, served by a new order of holy knights, at a place he prematurely called New Jerusalem. It proved to be located not on the southern continent, but on an island of Vanuatu, which still bears the name Espiritu Santo.

Just over twenty years later, events occurred on an island on the opposite side of the continent which belied de Quirós' faith in human perfectability. There, on the barren Albrohos archipelago, the treasure-laden Dutch ship *Batavia*, bound for the Indies, was wrecked, and a gang of mutineers misappropriated the treasures, donned some of the finery they found in the cargo, and instituted a reign of terror over the other survivors, enforced by random murder. Since they were at the very edge of the known world, they can hardly have anticipated the arrival of the rescue party which caught them in the act. The culprits were tried and executed on the spot, except for two of the youngest, who were marooned on the west coast of the southern continent and enjoined to establish contact with the native inhabitants. Nothing has been heard of their fate; their punishment foreshadowed by a century and a half that of thousands of other convicts transported to Australia, and they were the first of a succession of Europeans who disappeared into the continent without a trace.

The poet and novelist Randolph Stow once pointed out how these two events in the early seventeenth century—the de Quirós venture and the wreck of the *Batavia*—prefigured a pair of preoccupations which became prominent in Australian culture: the idea of Australia as prison or place of exile, and the idea of Australia as paradise. They also illustrate two opposite attitudes to nature and civilisation; on the one hand the belief that human beings will fulfil the perfect ideal of which they are capable when they are removed from the temptations and corruptions of civilisation and placed in an unspoilt, natural world; on the other, the belief that civilisation is a restraint on barbarity and improvement on nature; if it is removed, human beings revert to savagery.

These two ideas have also had a marked influence on culture in Australia. As long as it was seen as an empty space, roughly defined by a few discontinuous lines on the charts of early mariners, it was the paradisal or utopian dream that predominated, though the journals of mariners who had actually discovered stretches of the coastline before Captain Cook failed to substantiate these specu-lations. Jonathan Swift certainly knew of these when he ridiculed currently fashionable conceptions of human nature through the figures of houyhnhnms and yahoos, whose country he located some-where in the region of the unknown south land, an invention deeply appreciated but never equalled by Australian satirists.

From about the time of *Travels into Several Remote Nations of the World* by Lemuel Gulliver (1726) or soon afterwards, the South Pacific, including the still hypothetical southern continent, became, as Professor Bernard Smith has shown, the object of European scientific enquiry. New methods of description and classification associated with the Linnaean system and with the projects of the Royal Society (also ridiculed in *Gulliver's Travels*) were developing just as explorers stood on the threshold of this region. It therefore offered an ideal field for scientific investigation where everything was unknown and waiting to be described. Moreover, the discoveries that were made were unexpectedly different from anything previously recorded, and a splendid reward for scientific curiosity. They sometimes even seemed to confirm old fantasies about the antipodes.

The scientific impulse persisted after the settlement of the country. It led to Darwin's visit and influenced a tradition of humane scientific writing which began with the explorer's journals and continued through Darwin's observations of Australia in *The Voyage of the 'Beagle'* (1832) to such books as *The Red Centre* (1936) by H. H. Finlayson, *Flying Fox and Drifting Sand* (1938) by Francis Ratcliffe and *A Million Wild Acres* (1981) by Eric Rolls. Scientific description was often the primary object of the visual arts in the early days of European settle-ment. Bernard Smith has traced its impact and shown how it combined with the prominent influence of Turner in the misty landscapes of Conrad Martens, one of the artists who sailed with Darwin of the *Beagle*. It is apparent also in the remarkable desert landscapes and views of the explorers painted by the artist and scientist Ludwig Becker on the Burke and Wills expedition, which prefigure uncannily the work of such modern painters as Sidney Nolan and Arthur Boyd.

6 BRUCE CLUNIES ROSS

The scientific mode of observation continued to influence Australian artists, up to the work of Fred Williams (1927-1982) and the contemporary painters John Olsen and John Wolseley, as Gary Catalano has recently observed. The same tradition had an important impact on poetry in Australia, from Barron Field's facetious lines on the kangaroo to the preoccupation of the Jindyworobaks and modern poets such as Judith Wright and Les Murray with naming and describing an environment for which no adequate European poetic formulations exist, and thereby taking possession of the country imaginatively.

The primarily scientific object of Captain Cook's voyage during which he discovered the east coast of Australia is apparent even from the name of Botany Bay, the destination of the first convict fleet. However, although Europeans introduced current scientific attitudes to Australia, together with the strain of visionary speculation which continued to flourish as long as the interior of the continent remained a mystery, there was a third cluster of preconceptions, perhaps more prominent at the time of settlement, which has continued to influence Australian culture. This is evident even in the writing of Watkin Tench, who as a captain of the Marines might be considered a typical representative of the scientific spirit. In his *Narrative of the Expedition to Botany Bay* (1789), he reflected on the departure of the First Fleet from the Cape of Good Hope:

about noon, on the 12th of November (1787) we weighed anchor, and soon left far behind every scene of civilization and harmonized manners, to explore a remote and barbarous land, and plant in it those happy arts which alone constitute the pre-eminence and dignity of other countries.

Quite apart from its mention of distance, which Professor Geoffrey Blainey demonstrated was to become a major determinant of Australian history and culture, this observation is remarkable, considering that the primary object of the voyage was to remove from the scene of European civilisation a consignment of convicts who presumably threatened its 'harmonized manners'. The very phrase, and the idea which pervades the whole passage, is redolent of neo-classical civilisation, which one of its chief proponents, Edward Gibbon, still alive and rewriting his memoirs, regularly described as 'humane' and 'polite', invoking the Latin *humanus* and *politus,* which could mean 'refined' or 'civilised', and as the etymology of *politus* suggests, imply the idea of civilisation as polish.

The major achievements in literature and philosophy of this phase of civilisation in Britain were over by the last decades of the eighteenth century when Australia was settled, and most of its major figures except Gibbon were dead. Australia inherited its fag-end, as it had filtered down to conventional assumptions and thoughts in the minds of middle-ranking officers in the services and modest government officials charged with establishing a prison in the wilderness. However, neo-classicism, with its insistence on decorum and proportion, persisted in architecture and the fine arts; it is apparent in some of the first pictures painted in Australia, and if these are any guide, in attempts to reduce the landscape to some kind of order, but most of all in the simple, well-proportioned buildings of early New South Wales and Van Diemen's Land.

Australia was settled at a critical stage for European civilisation. A year after the arrival of the First Fleet in New South Wales, a revolution broke out in France which all those who shared the long-established traditional values recognised as the beginning of the collapse of their civilisation. At the same time, the principles of reason, order and decorum on which it was based were being questioned by writers and intellectuals who valued spontaneity and subjective experience. Distance isolated Australia from these currents, so that the concept of civilisation which influenced its foundation became set, a process which was assisted by the rigidly hierarchical structure of the penal colony. Thus, though early New South Wales was a sink of iniquity, it was also, potentially, a haven from social and intellectual disturbances in Europe.

This in itself has continued to be an influential idea in Australia. It resurfaced, for example, in Norman Lindsay's attempt in the early decades of this century to save Australian culture from the decadence of modern art by reverting to earlier stages in European civilisation, and importing a healthier blend of wide-eyed seductive nymphs, coarse satyrs and swashbuckling tavern brawlers. However, in the colony's early years a few people were able to create, within certain constraints, an imitation of eighteenth-century European civilisation. This is evident in the style of life adopted by the colonial gentry, which exemplified some of the neo-classical pastoral ideals, and in early poems and paintings, like Thomas Watling's view of Sydney Cove in 1794, with its two bewigged officers in their dress uniforms engaged in polite conversation in the centre of the picture.

They are not really incongruous in the context of the painting, which, as Bernard Smith has shown, is composed according to the conventions of picturesque landscape in the eighteenth century. Yet its conventional mode does not prevent it from being a revealing glimpse of the beginnings of civilisation in Australia. The bush—or desert, as Tench would have called it—has not been eliminated. It is present in the trees in the right and left foreground which frame a landscape already harmonised with rows of buildings and straight lines of cultivation to form a decorous background for the two figures embodying civilisation. They are apparently oblivious of the group of Aborigines in the shadows around the fire on the left of the picture.

The painting thus hints at a disjunction between the concept of civilisation and the concept of culture which continues to divide Australians. In fact, the slippery word 'culture' did not evolve its cluster of familiar modern senses until long after the foundation of the penal colony in New South Wales. Tench, for example, would not have attached any cultural significance to the whistling of *Malbrouke*; the educated people among the early arrivals, whether they were warders, or convicts like Watling, had no idea of culture which was not contained in their idea of civilisation, which in itself implied a notion of human improvement.

The settlement of Australia by Europeans can be seen, partly, as a way of working out, or testing, this idea. In the beginning a few were able to realise some of its ideals in the new land, but altogether, it failed to give Australians an adequate grip on the environment (to paraphrase Judith Wright). The continuance of life in the new country, if it was not to be permanently distorted by a sense of exile or relegation, required something which would make it familiar, and give the inhabitants imaginative possession of their place—a complex problem in itself, since a sense of place in Australia entails a sense of its relation to Europe, from which its culture principally derives. It was out of this need that Australian culture evolved, and this produced an awkward disjunction between the idea that civilisation improves the human state and the idea that culture supplies a fundamental imaginative need. Such things as grand opera alone, in whatever quantity, will not effect an improvement if they fail to satisfy this need, as Bennelong was perhaps the first to discover when he cast off his fine clothes and returned to the bush.

The history of civilisation in Australia is thus a record not only of its limited successes, but of the way its limitations and darker sides emerged at the frontier, in its impact on the Aborigines, for example. This suggests a need to revise it by reference to a more comprehensive, if elusive, idea of culture. There has been a recurrent debate about this in Australia, which still persists, as can be seen from a recent exchange in the journal *Australian Cultural History* between Eugene Kamenka, representing culture as an international civilising force, and Jim Davidson representing it as a kind of imaginative comprehension of region and nation.

The equation of culture in Australia with European civilisation has an ambivalent legacy. On the one hand, it inspired an arcadian or pastoral idea of the country, evident early in the paintings of the John Glovers, father and son, and still present a century or more later in the squatter's vision at the end of William Baylebridge's unconvincing *An Anzac Muster* (1921, 1962) and in a much finer novel about World War I, *When Blackbirds Sing* (1962) by Martin Boyd. Not surprisingly, since Martin Boyd traced his ancestry from the colonial gentry of Port Phillip, that novel closes with Dominic envisaging his Australian farm as a 'quiet place' and haven from European violence.

On the other hand, the main effect of regarding Australian culture as European civilisation transported has been to instil a sense of exile into Australians, since on this view, culture by its very nature is a reminder of Australia's isolation. The cry of the cultural exile is heard forcefully in the opening of A. D. Hope's poem 'Australia' (1939), in which images of nature are employed to suggest cultural barrenness and philistinism, implying an opposition between nature and culture which is qualified and complicated by the famous closing lines which opt for Australia, despite its faults.

A sense of exile instilled particularly by what the phantom Australian poet of the 1940s, Ern Malley, called 'Culture as Exhibit', along with the complementary awareness of a disparity between culture and nature, gave rise to a double vision. Whatever its advantages, in endowing Australians with imaginative flexibility through familiarity with things they may never have experienced—like snow at Christmas, the resurgence of life in spring, and thatched cottages—it has obstructed the imaginative assimilation of the country and set Australian artists the problem of reforming artistic traditions and conventions inherited from Europe to engage with an environment for which they were not always well fitted.

From the beginning, civilisation in Australia embodied a fundamental anomaly; it was built upon convict labour. While this had certain advantages for the rapid establishment of colonial estates, it had obvious drawbacks. A major reason for transporting the convicts in the first place was to enhance the quality of British civilisation, yet ladies and gentlemen in Australia lived in daily familiarity with the magpie-suit, the chain gang, the triangle and the gallows. They inhabited an open prison where public floggings and hangings were frequent, and sometimes they were the witnesses to even worse horrors. After his execution for murder,

> the body of Morgan was ordered to be hung in chains on the island Matte-wan-ye. This spectacle, shocking to the refined mind, served as an object of ridicule to the convicts, and terror to the natives, who though, hitherto, particularly partial to that spot, now totally abandoned it, lest the malefactor should descend and seize them, in the same way as their superstitions prompted them to imagine spirits did.

An appreciation of the progress of civilisation in Australia no doubt depended upon the degree to which the refined minds repelled by sights like this were inured to the ordinary brutalities of life in the penal colony.

The convicts (except for a few, like Watling, Francis Greenway and Thomas Griffiths Wainewright) may have lacked civilisation, but they possessed a culture. Watkin Tench would have discounted its significance, though he still mentioned the convicts' 'flash' or 'kiddy' language which was sometimes so obscure that it required the presence of an interpreter in the courtroom. This in itself is remarkable testimony to the strength, as well as the difference, of convict culture. Its traces may be hard to discern, because it was transmitted orally, yet some of them are probably quite close to the surface of Australian life, in the accent, rhythms and idioms of Australian speech and in certain male attitudes towards authority, women and other men. The convicts are responsible for introducing the early folksongs, which in their tunes show the signs of normalisation associated with urban music and the music hall, but in their words illustrate the process of adaptation which civilised writers were unable to make at such an early date. The verses of 'Frank the Poet' manage to encompass the terrible experiences of convicts imaginatively, with, in places, the grim humour which was no doubt invaluable for his survival. They are remarkable, too, in projecting an utterly different vision of early Australia from that to be found in the work of any of the convict painters.

The convict inheritance blended with the oral cultures of immigrant workers, who sometimes arrived in families or larger groups from distinct regions of Britain, to form a distinctive *corpus* of Australian folklore in which, as W. Fearn-Wannan observed, 'new strains of lore, custom, legend and folk-wisdom born of experience in a vastly different environment were grafted on to an already complex oral inheritance'. This process brings us close to the sources of the 'Australian legend', currently the subject of revision by critics who sometimes overlook the fact that whatever the inadequacies of its stock of types and images, the fundamental reason for its importance is that it embodies the earliest attempts to adapt a culture derived from Europe to the Australian environment (even if not always successfully). It counterbalances the influence of civilisation in Australia, and provides a fount of vernacular literature. Les Murray's recent *Oxford Book of Australian Verse* (1986) is, amongst other things, an implicit reassessment of the significance of the demotic tradition.

The *Bulletin* writers of the 1880s and 1890s were the first to exploit this tradition, taking an example, perhaps, from a few poems by Adam Lindsay Gordon. By their time, almost a hundred years after its foundation, Australian society and culture had changed considerably. The rigid structure of the penal settlement had broken down as a result of the emancipation of convicts, free immigration, the growth of a native-born population and the extension of settlement to other centres around the Australian coast. In the cities— particularly in Sydney and Melbourne—cultural circles evolved around periodical journals and literary coteries. These were inevitably concerned with the transmission of European and mainly British literature and ideas, just as the early theatres were concerned with the presentation of imported plays, yet at the same time they fostered the development of local writers like Marcus Clarke.

By the time of some of the new settlements the climate of ideas had shifted completely in Britain, so that whereas New South Wales and Van Diemen's Land might be regarded as experiments in penology, South Australia, founded in 1836, was an experiment in religious equality and Edward Gibbon Wakefield's theory of systematic colonisation. There are similarities between Wakefield's concept of civilisation and that of the first colonists in New South Wales, but whereas the penal colony was an operation to remove undesirable elements from the civilised world, Wakefield envisaged colonisation as a way of extending civilisation. South Australia was founded in a spririt of liberal optimism consistent with the culture of 'moral enlightenment' which, as Michael Roe has shown, developed in eastern Australia around the same time, and influenced the course of art and ideas for the rest of the nineteenth century. This was the antipodean counterpart of a general concern with self-improvement, coupled with the hope that this would achieve a better future, which permeated the English-speaking world in the nineteenth century. It can be detected in the writing of some of the English romantics, and was later developed by John Ruskin and William Morris. In the United States, it was evident in the work of such writers as Emerson, Thoreau and Whitman, who were influential in nineteenth-century Australia.

The utopian speculations which formed a part of this nineteenth-century tradition generally located the ideal realm at, or beyond, the edge of civilisation, in the New World. Coleridge and Southey, for example, imagined their pantisocracy on the banks of the Susquehanna. However, the poet Charles Harpur, from whom Roe borrowed the term 'moral enlightenment', and who was its leading exponent in Australia, did not have to imagine the New World. He was actually there; closer even than his contemporaries in the United States of America to the possibility of realising the European vision of Utopia in its new-found dominions. His work reflects yet another way in which Australian culture involved the working out of a European idea. Harpur was one of the earliest Australian artists to express the hope of future perfection and the disappointment which attends its inevitable defeat. The alternation, and even new conjunction, of these two states is, as many critics have noticed, a prominent preoccupation in Australia. Repeated often enough the cycle instils that other Australian characteristic, stoical resignation.

Harpur made the most resolute attempt in the nineteenth century to encompass Australia imaginatively. He was in a position to experience the romantic poet's awe in the presence of wild scenery and dramatic effects of nature, and the poems by which he is remembered are compelled by his response to the Australian wilderness. He shared this vision with the mid-century painters Conrad Martens, Eugene von Guerard, Nicholas Chevalier and William Piguenet, and together they conveyed something of the gloom—or what Marcus Clarke called 'weird melancholy'—which was supposed to characterise Australian nature. This was partly because as romantics they depicted mountain scenery with its tenebrous effects, and either excluded human figures, or included them on a scale where the landscape overwhelmed them. However, this scenery was not hard to find in their day, when the frontier included tracts of heavily wooded ranges which have since been cleared. We cannot dismiss their vision of Australia as a romantic invention. Rather, it might be suggested, they discovered in Australia scenes which conformed to current European preconceptions, just as later, the Heidelberg painters, and then the mid-twentieth-century landscape painters, discovered different aspects of Australia that satisfied different preoccupations. They were not inventing Australia. Their work illustrates the impact on imaginations stocked from European sources of experience in the borderland between civilisation and the unknown world. What appears to be romantic or surrealist at the centre of civilisation may take on a realistic quality at the periphery. The so-called 'magic realism' of Latin American fiction has taught us that. There has always been a similar strain in Australian culture though it is yet to be clearly discerned. It is apparent in the landscapes of Russell Drysdale, in Randolph Stow's novel *Tourmaline* and in other literature and painting of the 1940s and 1950s. These typically antipodean visions which result from the translation of European culture to the southern world should not be confused with the surrealism which writers like Murray Bail have derived from recent American or European writing.

Despite Harpur's acquaintance with the work of the English romantic poets, and admiration for Coleridge, he made no attempt to reform the language of poetry as they had done. As the mainly self-educated son of convicts, he was probably aware of the popular ballad tradition, but the songs which might have delighted Wordsworth and Coleridge left no impression on him. Although his little-known satiric poetry uses a vernacular style, he derived his poetic language mainly from his reading of English poets, especially the blank verse of Milton and the heroic couplets of the Augustans. The result is a verse that lacks tonal definition. Yet Harpur saw himself as an essentially Australian poet and his sentiments prefigured those of the nationalist writers in the 1880s and 1890s.

Nationalism was a prominent movement in the arts and culture in many parts of Europe during the nineteenth century. It inspired artists in Scandinavia, Russia and Ireland, for example, and it was often associated with an interest in folklore. The *Bulletin* writers who drew on vernacular sources—the ballad and the yarn—may not have been directly influenced by any of this, but their work forms an Australian counterpart to it. Whatever the limitations or implicit contradictions in their vision of Australia and the typical Australian (and these remain matters of controversy), they introduced the Australian voice and idiom into literature, and therefore gave their local readers that shock of recognition which occurs only in transplanted cultures when the double vision they instil is suddenly resolved into a single familiar image.

The Heidelberg painters, their contemporaries, produced a similar impact by drawing not on any local sources, but on the European tradition of *plein air* painting to capture the distinctive qualities of light and colour in the regions where they painted. Recent criticism has focused upon their bush genre pictures, like Tom Roberts' *Shearing the Rams* (1890), but this emphasis obscures the fact that they painted a varied range of subjects, including the cities, the beaches and harbours, and the outer suburban bushland. The overwhelming effect of most of these paintings, including genre pictures like Roberts' *The Breakaway* (1890-1) or McCubbin's *The Lost Child*, is the way they register and fix effects of light. This sets them apart from the work of photographers and black-and-white illustrators who shared some of their subjects, and may have provided some of their iconographical sources.

In an interesting passage in his introduction to the *Bulletin Story Book* (1901), A. G. Stephens commented on the way in which European preconceptions of landscape interfered with an appreciation of Australian scenery, and suggested that 'Verlaine's Cult of Faded Things' was more appropriate to Australian tones and colours. However, he pointed out (in a passage replete with diction and images which would not have been out of place in *The Yellow Book*):

> there are not wanting adumbrations of the Beauty of Australia,—glimpses of the secret enchantment in which this strange, feline land—half-fierce, half-caressing—holds those who have listened to the gum-trees' whispered spells or drunk the magic philter of landscapes flooded with Nature's opiate-tints.

The Heidelberg painters did reveal the beauty of Australia even as we were deforming it. They generally depicted the cultivated landscape, or settlers in the process of subduing it, and in this they were drawing on the European tradition of pastoral landscape painting which suggests a harmony between nature and human beings. Theirs was a rough, frontier version of this idyll which had much in common with Paterson's 'vision splendid on the sunlit plains extended'. Henry Lawson, as is well known, disputed this vision.

The argument about the city and the bush which broke out in the pages of the *Bulletin* was a variant of an ancient opposition in European culture, which became the focus of a complex and unresolved debate in Australia. Recent cultural historians and critics have been troubled by the evolution of a rural legend, or image, in a community which even by the 1890s was highly urbanised. This is neither surprising nor inappropriate; the majority of Australians may live in cities or suburbs, but the country is hardly humanised, let alone urbanised, at all. About two-thirds of it is still designated on maps as of 'no significant use' and the urban centres of population form only a discontinuous fringe around the coast. It would have been more surprising had Australians evolved an urban legend or image, for such phenomena are products of the imagination, the faculty which, by its very nature, enables human beings to transcend the constraints of their immediate circumstances. A sense of place, for example, is only one of the components of the Australian legend which involves the interaction of actual perception with memory and imagination.

Recent critics of the Australian legend rest their arguments on the assumption that the city and the bush are exclusive alternatives, and thus they deny the distinctive interplay of geography and civilisation in Australia, but legends and images need somehow to balance both aspects. The poet Les Murray has advanced an idea which preserves this balance. It is based on a distinction between the 'Athenian' model of civilisation, which is hierarchical, and centred on the city, and the 'Boeotian' model, in which the transactions between town and country do not relegate one to the other. Murray's poetry is, among other things, an illustration of the possibilities in Australia of the 'Boeotian' alternative to the internationally dominant 'Athenian' model.

The work of the nationalists, both painters and writers, confirmed the prominent role of place and environment in Australian culture. Its impact is apparent in all the arts, as well as in a lot of folklore about such things as the country beyond the black stump. The composer Percy Grainger, who was brought up in Melbourne in the 1880s and 1890s, always regarded himself as an Australian nationalist, and in an early notebook he set out a plan for an 'Australian Bush Style' which was 'to embody the veiled weirdness of the unopened continent'; a vision which parellels the 'greatest of the Muses' in Victor Daley's poem 'The Muses of Australia': 'the Desert Muse . . . veiled from head to feet'. Grainger's serious compositions, from the irregular rhythms of his *Hillsongs,* begun around 1901, to the free music machines he was working on at the end of his life, were attempts to create a music which would express the compelling power of the natural environment. Other composers have felt a similar impulse, which culminated in music like the *Irkanda* and *Sun Music* series by the contemporary composer Peter Sculthorpe, who apparently believes that Australia is essentially a visual country.

The nationalist movement of the late nineteenth century inspired a home-grown alternative to imported culture and demonstrated that a distinctive Australian culture could be built on the vernacular traditions which had evolved in the first century of settlement. However, these sources were limited. Percy Grainger realised that they were a key to the kind of nationalist music he wanted to create, but since the melodies of almost all Australian folksongs remained fixed in the normalised versions in which they had arrived, and inevitably evoked their Irish, Scottish of English sources, there was no musical equivalent to the vernacular ballad texts. Grainger tried to supply the lack, and lay the foundation for the creation of an Australian art-music, with what he intended as popular compositions, such as *Australian Up-Country Song, Marching Song of Democracy, The Gum-Suckers' March,* and *Colonial Song,* which Sir Thomas Beecham, unaware of Grainger's intention, considered the worst musical composition he had ever heard. However, Grainger's comprehensive conception of art was rare, and during his lifetime his ideas remained almost unknown in Australia, or were misunderstood and ridiculed.

The connection which the nationalist writers of the 1890s had established with vernacular sources proved hard to sustain. The writers who tried to carry on the tradition were imbued with the hope that Australia would be a better, as well as a different place—as Bernard O'Down put it, 'A Delos of a coming Sun-God's race'—for the utopian element in nationalist culture had not expired with the labour defeats at the end of the century or the collapse of William Lane's foredoomed Paraguayan experiment. However, their hopes were dissipated in what they regarded as the increasing conformism and materialism of Australian life, for which they blamed the cities, or more specifically, the suburbs. Thus they turned away from the popular culture around them, which they condemned, often rightly, for its mass-produced triviality, and idealised the past. Their resistance to European—and later American—cultural developments was apparent not only in the concerted hostility to modern art in Australia, but also in opposition to such forms of popular culture as jazz, which in fact, through the inspired work of Ade Monsborough and

Dave Dallwitz, developed a distinctly Australian accent for a brief period in the 1940s and early 1950s. By this time, artists—particularly those associated with the periodical *Angry Penguins*—had begun to take a renewed interest in popular culture, and this became one element in the artistic resurgence in Australia after World War II. It was associated with the challenge from artists anxious to introduce the possibilities opened up by modern art in Europe and the United States, and with a critical reappraisal of the nationalist movement.

The images of Australia and Australians, based on the bush, the pastoral workers and the concept of mateship, all of which were prominent in the first phase of Australian nationalism in the 1890s, were severely criticised in what may be regarded as its second phase, in the 1970s. Some of the criticisms were insistently doctrinaire or obtuse, but they also revealed hidden facets of Australian culture, notably through questioning the almost exclusive masculinity of the images, which displace the important role which women have taken in Australian culture, and especially literature, almost from the beginning. Recent writing about the sexual imbalance in the Australian culture, and the way women have imagined themselves in relation to the dominant stereotypes, has recast Australian cultural history in a new light.

However, the nationalist movement was under attack long before this. Judith Wright considered it 'a dubious legacy that we may take another century to outgrow', and went on, 'The proliferation of political demagogy and the cult of the unreal bush-hero nationalist hid the beginning of the twentieth century in a mist of bad writing.' Another poet, Ian Mudie, in 'The Australian Dream' (1943) revealed the delusory quality of the nationalist perception of Australia through its refusal to take into account the destruction of the natural environment and of Aboriginal culture.

Mudie's poem was informed by an idea about Australian culture developed in the 1930s and 1940s by the Jindyworobaks, a group of mainly South Australian poets often misrepresented by critics who claimed that the movement aimed to base Australian culture on Aboriginal culture. The Jindyworobaks were interested in the Aborigines, and if white Australians are now able to recognise the grim impact of their civilisation on the Aboriginal inhabitants of the country, the Jindyworobaks are partly responsible. However, their central idea, that the language and conventions of poetry inherited from Britain had to be reconstructed to incorporate the values of the local environment, was not very different from one discovered by

Barron Field, who aspired to be the first poet to write about Australia. In a passage published in 1825, he explained how the 'common consent and immemorial custom of poetry' connected 'all the dearest allegories of human life' to the passsage of the seasons. Since nature in Australia disrupted this connection, Field yearned for England, but the Jindyworobaks, a century later, wanted to achieve a harmonious relationship between culture and environment, and realised that Aboriginal culture embodied it. This was an example from which they could learn, not by imitation, but by coming to understand and accept the conditions which environment imposes on those who live in it. The Jindyworobaks' interest in Aboriginal culture had been preceded, about a decade before, by the painter Margaret Preston, though it is doubtful if any of them were familiar with her work.

The typical landscape of Jindyworobak poems was the harsh desert of inland Australia. Sir Arthur Streeton, the most seductive of the landscape painters of the Heidelberg school, had imagined this, and planned an expedition into it, but apart from pioneering work of Ludwig Becker, it was not prominent in Australian painting until it was discovered by Hans Heysen, around the time the Jindyworobaks were developing their ideas. From then on it became a dominant image of Australia, and the movement of the artist's imagination inward, towards the heart of the country, can be traced schematically from Streeton, through Heysen's paintings of northern South Australia, to the works of Drysdale and Nolan, in which the desert landscape takes on symbolic implications.

The use of typical Australian landscapes symbolically is apparent not only in the work of painters, but in that of writers like R. D. FitzGerald, Judith Wright, Patrick White, Randolph Stow and Thea Astley and a number of composers from Percy Grainger to Peter Sculthorpe and Richard Meale. It began as a kind of home-grown innovation which merged, particularly through the work of the painters associated with the periodical *Angry Penguin*, with the strains of expressionism and surrealism which eventually broke through the resistance to modern art in Australia.

The imagined landscape at the heart of Australia remains a compelling influence on Australian culture and a valid symbol, often endowed with the traditional associations of deserts, as places of visionary revelation or sterility and emptiness. In the latter sense, it is becoming commonplace. The satirist Barry Humphries recently told an interviewer that he was 'always conscious of the desert inside Australia, of the vacuum in the heart of it', echoing Patrick White's observations thirty years before about the 'Great Australian Emptiness'.

The idea that Australian culture is spiritually vacuous, as well as Philistine, would have dismayed earlier artists like Harpur, some of the nationalists, or Grainger, who, however they felt about the indifference their own works inspired, entertained hopes for a humane society founded on reason rather than religious belief. The outcome, in the eyes of many of their successors, was simply a more materialistic society. The suburbs came to exemplify this vision, and in a range of writings after World War II, like Robin Boyd's *Australian Ugliness* (1960) and a host of similar jeremiads, or some of Patrick White's novels, stories and plays, or the satirical sketches of Barry Humphries, suburban life became an object of ridicule, and a negative image of Australia. Its counterpart was a preoccupation with the need for spiritual understanding which is prominent in the work of Patrick White and other post-war writers.

The negative images of Australia in post-war culture may have been exaggerated for the purpose of satire, but they were not unfounded. A succession of events, like the trial of Max Harris in the wake of the Ern Malley hoax in 1944, the legal attack on William Dobell's Archibald prize-winning *Portrait of an Artist* (1944), the prosecution for obscenity of the novelists Robert Close and Lawson Glassop in 1945 and 1946, the outcry against the public pronouncements of the Sydney philosopher John Anderson, the founder of the only original school of thought in Australia, the indifference to the first exhibition, in 1948, of Nolan's Kelly paintings, and to the work of his colleague, Albert Tucker, and the public outrage when the Adelaide gallery purchased Drysdale's *Woman in a Landscape* (1948), combined with the strict and complicated censorship which prevailed until the early 1970s, indicate the pressure of conformity. Unfortunately this narrow-mindedness sometimes provided support for those who upheld a principled opposition to modern art and the decadence they associated with it. Yet at the same time, it provided the necessary contrastive background for the eccentrics, clowns or ratbags intermittently thrown up by Australian culture. Barry Humphries is perhaps the most notable of these.

The decades between the Ern Malley hoax in 1944 and the performance of Peter Sculthorpe's *Sun Music I* at the Commonwealth Arts Festival in London in 1965 were sufficiently restrictive to drive a number of artists and intellectuals into exile, yet they were far from being culturally sterile, as is sometimes assumed. On the contrary they were decisive years, when a distinctive Australian culture was created by Russell Drysdale, Albert Tucker, Sidney Nolan, Arthur Boyd and other painters of the Angry Penguins school, by such writers as Judith Wright, Francis Webb, Patrick White, Randolph Stow and Christopher Koch and finally, by a school of innovative Australian composers, including George Dreyfus, Peter Sculthorpe and Richard Meale. They were also the years when Christina Stead, working abroad, was creating her finest novels, though they remained almost unknown in Australia. Much of this work is notable for the way it adapted the modes of modern art to local and vernacular traditions, to produce new, ambivalent or critical, evocations of Australia. Sidney Nolan's Ned Kelly paintings exemplify this and also illustrate the way artists at the time were recreating legends out of the Australian environment and its past. These often involved the search for some kind of visionary experience through the human encounter with the landscape, in which the figures of explorers, bushrangers, pioneers and Aborigines were prominent. Altogether, this was a consolidation of Australian culture in the face of vociferous, but ultimately ineffectual opposition.

Contemporary Australian culture rests on this achievement which was produced while the country was being transformed by post-war immigration from Europe and rapid improvements in communication which altered, but did not eliminate, the influence of distance on Australia. The cities around the coast are now closer to the rest of the world than ever before, and their culture is more like the urban Western civilisation anywhere on the globe. However, Australia is still the place where civilisation runs out. The culture which Europeans introduced continues to be shaped by a sense of being at the edge of things, with the double vision this produces, though the external point of reference is now often the United States, rather than Europe. One result of the outward view of the metropolitan culture around the coast is a widening of the gap between the city and the bush, which sometimes goes along with a literal-minded, not to say ungeographical, insistence that Australia is an urban country *tout court*.

This has been an issue in the debates about Australian history and identity which have been a prominent element in the self-confident culture which has evolved since the early 1970s. A renewed interest in the Australian, rather than the European, past is evident in a variety of ways, from the costumed versions of Old Colonial Australia which have been erected for tourist purposes, to the serious exploration, by both scholars and creative writers, of regional history. Certain aspects of the past which had dropped out of sight have been recovered, notably the history of the Aborigines, which is an inextricable counterpart to the history of Europeans in Australia. Australians cannot now avoid coming to terms with the ancient Aboriginal heritage and their part in destroying it, though this remains a contentious matter.

Nevertheless there are signs that it is impinging on white Australian culture in a new way. George Dreyfus' *Sextet for Didjeridu and Wind Quintet* (1971) requires for its performance a communion between an Aboriginal musician inprovising according to one tradition, on an instrument without parallel in Western music, and five wind-players reading from a score. Les Murray's *Buladelah-Taree Holiday Song Cycle* (1977) matches the rhythms and conventions of Professor R. M. Berndt's translation of the Wonguri-Mandjigai *Song Cycle of the Moon Bone* with the intonation and idioms of Australian speech to suggest, thematically as well as stylistically, a parallel between Aboriginal and white Australian customs. Both works offer clues to the way the continent is shaping our culture.

The environment remains a dominant factor in Australia, as a recent book, *An Intimate Australia* (1985), by Gary Catalano acknowledges. He cites a number of examples, including the poetry of Les Murray and the paintings of John Olsen, along with the work in landscape gardening of Edna Walling, the architecture of Kevin Borland and Alistair Knox and the photography by Marion Hardman and John Richards to suggest that we are entering into the landscape, and living with it more intimately than previously. If that is true, it is not because we are civilising it, but because we are accepting its terms.

Transplantation to Australia transformed European civilisation and called some of its basic assumptions into question. The British-derived culture which evolved was a new blend, in which elements submerged by the relegatory nature of European civilisation became prominent again. This provided the context for a local vernacular tradition. Moreover, in Australia, Europeans encountered a resistant environment, and two hundred years of engagement with this have exposed the limits of civilisation, just as they are becoming apparent everywhere else in the world. This partly explains the quality of excitement in recent Australian culture, evident in films like *The Last Wave* (1977), for it is the fact that two-thirds of the country remain almost untouched by European civilisation—'set aside for mystic poetry'—which is now a case for hope.

Notes

Geoffrey Serle's *From Deserts the Prophets Come: The Creative Spirit in Australians* (1973, rev. 1987), remains the best introduction to the subject. However, the discussion of culture in Australia goes back beyond Francis Adams' *The Australians, A Social Sketch* (1893), to the beginning of European settlement. Some of the early documents are collected in Manning Clark (ed.), *Select Documents in Australian History*, vol. I (1950), Russel Ward and John Robertson (eds), *Such Was Life: Select Documents in Australian Social History,* vol. I (1969), John Barnes (ed. with commentaries), *The Writer in Australia, 1856-1964* (1969) and Bernard Smith (ed.), *Documents on Art and Taste in Australia* (1975). There has been a lot of informal writing about Australian culture, of which the books of Keith Dunstan, *Wowsers* (1968), *Knockers* (1972), and *Ratbags* (1979), are typical. The 'state of Australia' books, and jeremiads of the 1950s and 1960s include Robin Boyd, *The Australian Ugliness* (1960, rev. 1968) and *The Great Australian Dream* (1972), Donald Horne, *The Lucky Country* (1964), Craig McGregor, *Profile of Australia* (1966), Ronald Conway, *The Great Australian Stupor: An Interpretation of the Australian Way of Life* (1971), and Ian Moffitt, *The U-Jack Society* (1972). Censorship is discussed fully in Peter Coleman, *Obscenity, Blasphemy, Sedition* (1965), Enid Campbell and Harry Whitmore, *Freedom in Australia* (1966) and Geoffrey Dutton and Max Harris (eds), *Australia's Censorship Crisis* (1970).

There are chapters on culture in W. K. Hancock's *Australia* (1930), and C. Hartley Grattan (ed.), *Australia* (1947). Civilisation is a pervasive theme in Manning Clark's *History of Australia,* 6 vols (1962-87), and Geoffrey Blainey's *The Tyranny of Distance* (1966) is rich in cultural implications. Other formal discussions of Australian culture include Peter Coleman (ed.), *Australian Civilization* (1962).

Serle was able to depend on several specialised studies: H. M. Green, *A History of Australian Literature, Pure and Applied,* 2 vols (1961; revised Dorothy Green, 1985), Bernard Smith, *Australian Painting* (1962), Roger Covell, *Australia's Music: Themes of a New Society* (1967), Robin Boyd, *Australia's Home* (1952), Morton Herman, *The Early Australian Architects and Their Work* (1954), and J. M. Freeland, *Architecture in Australia* (1968). Related books include Bernard Smith's *Place, Taste and Tradition* (1945), and his *European Vision and the South Pacific 1788-1850* (1960; 2nd edn, 1985), Geoffrey Dutton (ed.), *The Literature of Australia* (1964; 2nd edn,

1976), Robert Hughes, *The Art of Australia* (1966; rev. 1970). Three books were influential on Australian cultural historiography: Vance Palmer, *The Legend of the Nineties* (1954), Russel Ward, *The Australian Legend* (1958; 2nd edn, 1966), and A. A. Phillips, *The Australian Tradition* (1958; 2nd edn, 1966; reissued with an introduction by Harry Heseltine, 1980). Judith Wright's *Preoccupations in Australian Poetry* (1965) and Brian Elliott's *The Landscape of Australian Poetry* (1967) are important and comprehensive studies.

The journal *Australian Cultural History* has published a range of interesting essays, and the older journals along with new ones like *Island Magazine* and the *Journal of Australian Studies*, regularly include relevant articles. For the significance of many journals see Bruce Bennett (ed.), *Cross Currents: Magazines and Newspapers in Australian Literature* (1981). Major formal studies of crucial periods in the history of Australian culture are David Walker's *Dream and Disillusion* (1976) and Richard Haese's *Rebels and Precursors* (1981). John Docker's *Australian Cultural Elites: Intellectual Traditions in Sydney and Melbourne* (1974) is an essay in cultural politics; R. W. Connell in *Ruling Class, Ruling Culture* (1977) applies the methods of academic sociology.

Specialised studies have continued with books like Frank Callaway and David Tunley (eds), *Australian Composition in the Twentieth Century* (1978), David Stratton, *The Last New Wave* (1980), on the Australian film revival, and Scott Murray (ed.), *The New Australian Cinema* (1980).

The range of Australian cultural history has broadened recently, partly through the influence of the work of the historian Ian Turner. His *Cinderella Dressed in Yella* (on Australian children's rhymes and games, 1969), was revised with June Factor and Wendy Lowenstein (1978), and after his death, Leonie Sandercock and Stephen Murray-Smith edited a selection of his essays, *Room for Manoeuvre* (1982). Specialised studies include Eric Watson, *Country Music in Australia* (1975), Andrew Bisset, *Black Roots, White Flowers: A History of Jazz in Australia* (1979), Vane Lindesay, *The Inked-In Image: A Social and Historical Survey of Australian Comic Art* (1979) and W. Fearn-Wannan, *Australian Folklore: A Dictionary of Lore, Legends and Popular Allusions* (1977).

Australian culture appears in a new light when viewed from the angle of women, as was revealed by two books during the 1970s: Anne Summers, *Damned Whores and God's Police* (1975) and Miriam Dixson, *The Real Matilda: Women and Identity in Australia,*

1788-1975 (1976). For more detailed references to relevant women's studies see Appendix 1.

The allusions to Watkin Tench are from his *Narrative of the Expedition to Botany Bay* (2nd edn, 1789), one of the books studied by Ross Gibson for his *Diminishing Paradise* (1984), which should be read in conjunction with Alan Frost's criticism of it, 'On Finding "Australia": Mirages, Mythic Images, Historical Circumstances', *Australian Literary Studies*, 12 (1986). Werner P. Friedrich, *Australia in Western Imaginative Prose Writings* (1967) includes translations from documents relating to the voyage of De Quiros. These are edited by Celsus Kelly, *La Austrialia Del Espiritu Santo* (1966). The story of the *Batavia* disaster is told in Henrietta Drake-Brockman, *Voyage to Disaster* (1963). Randolph Stow's account of it is 'The Southland of Antichrist: The *Batavia* Disaster of 1629', in Anna Rutherford (ed.), *Common Wealth* (1971).

Bernard Smith's *European Vision and the South Pacific* is supplemented by Marjorie Tipping (ed.), *Ludwig Becker: Artist and Naturalist with the Burke and Wills Expedition* (1979) and Sandra McGrath and John Olsen, *The Artist and the Desert* (1981). The neo-classical impulse is the subject of Robert Dixon's *The Course of Empire: Neo-Classical Culture in New South Wales 1788-1860* (1986). The pastoral idea of Australia discussed in Coral Lansbury's *Arcady in Australia* (1970) is criticised by Alan Frost, 'What Created, What Perceived? Early Responses to New South Wales', *Australian Literary Studies*, 7 (1975).

The description of the hanging of the body of the convict Morgan is in George Barrington, *The History of New South Wales* (1810). Convict influences on Australian English are discussed in G. W. Turner, *The English Language in Australia and New Zealand* (1966), W. S. Ramson, *Australian English: An Historical Study of the Vocabulary, 1788-1898* (1966) and W. S. Ramson (ed.), *English Transported* (1970).

Early Australian culture is discussed by Michael Roe, *The Quest for Authority in Eastern Australia 1835-1851* (1965), K. S. Inglis, *The Australian Colonists* (1974), David Denholm, *The Colonial Australians* (1979), and G. A. Wilkes, *The Stockyard and the Croquet Lawn* (1981), a general reassessment.

Ian Turner's *The Australian Dream* (1968), is an anthology tracing utopian visions of Australia. Critical discussions of the nationalist period can be found in Humphrey McQueen, *A New Britannia* (rev.

edn, 1975), the introduction to Leon Cantrell (ed.), *The 1890s* (1977), John Carroll (ed.), *Intruders in the Bush: The Australian Quest for Identity* (1982), and Richard White, *Inventing Australia* (1981), as well as in Sean Glynn, *Urbanisation in Australian History, 1788-1900* (2nd edn, 1975) and Graeme Davison, *The Rise and Fall of Marvellous Melbourne* (1979). Leigh Astbury's *City Bushmen: The Heidelberg School and the Rural Mythology* (1985) amplifies a couple of generalisations offered at the end of Davison's book without making them any more convincing.

The work of the Heidelberg school is discussed by Alan McCulloch, *The Golden Age of Australian Painting* (2nd edn, 1977). Early photography and its influence on the painters is discussed by Peter Quartermaine, 'The Lost Perspective; Australian Photography in the Nineteenth Century', in Quartermaine (ed.), *Readings in Australian Arts,* Michael Cannon, *An Australian Camera 1851-1914* (1973), Keast Burke, *Gold and Silver: Photographs of Australian Goldfields From the Holtermann Collection* (1973), and Astbury's *City Bushmen.* A. G. Stephens' observations on Australian light and scenery can be found in his introduction to the *Bulletin Story Book.*

Les A. Murray's essay on Athenian and Boeotian civilisation appears in *The Peasant Mandarin* (1978), his essay on the Aboriginal element in his work in *Persistence in Folly* (1984). Percy Grainger's nationalistic ideas are discussed by Kay Dreyfus and Janice Whiteside, 'Percy Grainger and Australia', *Meanjin,* 41 (1982) and in Covell, *Australia's Music.* There is a cogent discussion of Australian music by Andrew D. McCredie, *Musical Composition in Australia* (1969). Peter Sculthorpe's views on Australia and music are related by Michael Hannan, *Peter Sculthorpe: His Music and Ideas, 1929-1979* (1982).

Judith Wright's views on nationalism are in chapter 5 of *Preoccupations in Australian Poetry.* The movement led by William Lane to found a New Australia in Paraguay is described by Gavin Souter, *A Peculiar People: The Australians in Paraguay* (1968).

Documents relevant to the Jindyworobak movement can be found in Brian Elliott (ed.), *The Jindyworobaks* (1979). The quotation by Barron Field is from Brian Elliott's *Landscape of Australian Poetry.* Vincent Buckley discussed the development of the symbolic associations of the landscape in 'The Image of Man in Australian Poetry', *Essays in Poetry, Mainly Australian* (1957). The quotation by Barry Humphries is from his interview with Jim Davidson, *Meanjin,* 46

(1986); Patrick White's observation is from 'The Prodigal Son', *Australian Letters,* 1 (1958). The concluding quotation is from Les Murray's poem 'Louvres', in *Selected Poems* (1986).

Chapter 2

ABORIGINAL LITERATURE

STEPHEN MUECKE; JACK DAVIS
AND ADAM SHOEMAKER

A: ORAL: *STEPHEN MUECKE*

Oral production remains the major means of cultural transmission and maintenance for Aboriginal peoples in Australia. This 'literature', to use the term loosely, is vast and diverse, spanning not only the continent and its 200 or so language families, but also the range of contemporary and traditional cultures; from Radio Redfern in central Sydney to initiation ceremonies, from the lyrics of country and western songs to the *Djanggawul* song cycle of Arnhem Land.

In all this diversity, what is to count as Aboriginal oral literature? It is not a simple matter of establishing a body of canonical texts, excluding the vast majority of other texts because they seem trivial. One has to make systematic distinctions, recognising cultural differences all the way from Esperance to Torres Strait, between popular and sacred texts, narratives and songs. And while certain features of a general, common nature can be found across Australia, these cultural works are characterised for the most part by diversity, specificity and difference.

And there are contradictions in the use of the term 'literature' for these texts. By virtue of the category 'oral' we would seem automatically to exclude the printed word from this field of study, yet it is through the printed word that most white Australians come to know about Aboriginal oral texts.

There is a general tendency to think of Aboriginal oral production as a kind of historical backdrop to contemporary work in Australian literature, whether Aboriginal or not. It is a view of history which sees the spoken word giving way to the more powerful written word and disappearing into the depths of time. It is a view of the history of Australian literature which comes dangerously close to repeating the story of colonial Australian domination of Aborigines which led to them being 'wiped out', erased from the slate of history. One can respond to this familiar history with an assertion: that Aboriginal 'Oral Literature' is alive and well, that its response to colonialism was not one of acquiescence, but one of fighting back with words, making stories in order to come to terms with the structure of colonial economy and law and the place Aborigines were supposed to occupy in it; of articulating suffering; of satirising the various figures of the colonial administration and the pastoral industry.

An almost irresistible idea for the historical scenario is to give Aboriginal oral literature a primeval status by equating it with 'the very land itself', as timeless, undivided and arcadian. Borrowings from Aboriginal oral productions can then be used to underpin certain strands of nationalist writing in Australia (see for example the Jindyworobaks, p. 18). Now while it can be demonstrated that Aboriginal oral works *do* evolve, especially in response to new social conditions, that ceremonies, songs and dances have been and still are traded across wide areas of the northern and central parts of Australia in the form of 'cults', it is nevertheless the case that there is an Aboriginal practice of stressing the immutability and continuity of their traditions as well as the eternal and intimate associations that these literary traditions maintain with the land. However, this relationship with the land is of a quite different sort from that experienced by white settlers, as can be imagined, and as the different literatures demonstrate.

As a first example, let us look at a text from Central Australia, from A. Glass and D. Hackett, *Pitjantjatjarra Texts* (1969):

1. *story nga:-nya early day-ngkatja*

   story this   early day-pertaining to

   This story is about the early days.

2. *wati-ya minyma-tara nyina-payi wantu-ma:lpa nikirpalya*

   man-they woman-also   would be   clothes-without   naked

   Men and women used to be naked with no clothes.

3. *kuka kutju-ya ngalku-payi ra:pita malu yimiya-tara*

   meat only-they would eat   rabbit   kangaroo emu-too

   ngalku-payi panakaninytjara-tara pu-ngkula

   would eat   goanna-too   hitting

   They would only kill and eat meat; rabbit, kangaroo, emu and goanna too.

4. *paranyina-payi-ya kapi kutjupa-ngka-ya katuri-ngkula matju-nkupayi*

would sit around-they   water another-at-they   having got up   would put

They would sit around and then go and pitch camp at another water-hole.

5. *nyina-rayilku-ya kapi piti pulka-la-ya nyina-rayilku katuri-ku-ya*

would stay-they   water hole big-at-they   would stay   would get up-they

    kapi pa:lyukati-nyangka-ya pirkili-ku kutitja-ku

water having fallen-they   clay pan-to   would go

    paranga-lkulayinma

would eat around

They would stay at a big water hole and when it had rained, they would go to a clay pan and eat around there.

As a story about 'early days' (note the use of the English phrase in the original, as well as 'story'), this text represents a reconstruction of traditional life, seen by 'the white man'. Traditional life is seen, for instance, in terms of nakedness which was a missionary obsession. More importantly, the text shows the way in which foreign elements are introduced into a picture of Aboriginal life 'before the advent of the white man'. In the third paragraph the rabbit (ra:pita, now a food staple in parts of central Australia) makes an appearance as a traditional item of food, along with the goanna, kangaroo and emu. This is not so much an historical inaccuracy on the part of the storyteller, as an assertion of *continuity*. It is not so relevant for this man to 'date' the appearance of the rabbit, but to absorb this foreign element in a picture of Aboriginal life. This is in accordance with other aspects of Aboriginal literary production in which certain verb forms, tenses, indicate the eternal, the unchanging relation of man to his environment. Compare for example, the first lines of the Goulburn Island Song Cycle (1976):

bili   ŋaii bunbuwam milgari njinadugan djamurbunara

because it   make   forked stick put   rafter

    gurururu bugu-damalajuman

floor post   make roof like sea-eagle nest[1]

baima   malwi ŋaiiŋa guruwilin jalmaŋ

always there Place   it (camp) Place   Place

Erecting forked sticks and rafters, posts for the floor, making the roof of the hut like a sea-eagle's nest;

They are always there, at the billabong of the goose eggs, at the wide expanse of water.

'Baima', 'always there' is the form indicating an eternal present typical of the ideology of the Dreaming, an ideology which always tries to establish an homology between *what happened in the past* when the culture heroes, god-like beings, created the features of the country, and *what is happening now,* as the people sing and dance, recreating by re-enactment these same features, laws and language forms. These are cultures which, for the most part, stress continuity even in the face of change; this represents an attitude towards the new which contrasts strongly with European modernism and its tendency to celebrate novelty.

Significant also in these two texts is the role of place and place-names. This is yet another way of reinforcing links with the land. In the Goulburn Island song the places are named (and poetically translated by Berndt), while Fred Murray prefers to indicate the movement from place to place which represents Aboriginal nomadism. His story, like many other Aboriginal stories, utilises a formula of coming and going and collecting food on the way, an alternating storytelling pattern (We got up, collected food and went to A. We went to sleep, we got up, collected food and went to B, and so on). When these places are named, there are important functions operating in the oral text. One is cultural transmission of information; the story functions mnemonically to remind or teach people about food-gathering routes where seasonal abundance and scarcity called for fairly precise movements of people. A parallel function can also be the mythical one, that the route also represents the route followed by an ancestor being; the storytellers may see themselves as repeating the actions of these mythical Others.

It is an important part of traditional storytelling practice that travel provides the occasion for storytelling or singing. Not only do special festivals, meetings of different groupings of people from the one tribe or different tribes, provide the occasion for 'corroborees' (song and dance which may include quasi-theatrical representations), but also a group of people travelling across the country tends to allow for the arrival at a place to be the occasion for the production of a specific story. People collecting stories have often found the narrator expressing the desire to go to a place so that the 'full version' of the story can be told.

The personnel for the production of particular stories or songs is organised according to kin relations. Not just anybody can tell a story, because the body of culturally significant texts is distributed among tribal members according to individuals' custodianship of particular places in the country, associated laws and ritual objects, as well as songs and stories. And as a group travels each member can take over a leading role for the evening's entertainment or ceremony because they are present in his or her 'country'.

Wide divisions of responsibility also exist between men and women, as groups, who have different roles to play in ceremony, and strategies of exclusion from each other's 'business'. Children also are excluded from knowing sacred texts, until of course they come of age and these exclusive texts are progressively introduced to them and they learn them by heart. Again, this initiation procedure, or education, typically involves a tour around an appropriate stretch of country.

It is worth considering, in this respect, the powerful content of an account of an initiation given by an Aranda man to T. G. H. Strehlow in the 1930s (1947):

The old men sat assembled in a circle. They beckoned me in, told me to sit down in their midst. They began to chant.

They sang of the wanderings of the worrupuntja boys who came to Emiana and thence flew to Tukulja. I listened in silence. The old men continued singing. They sang of the boys, how they were plagued by flies, how they wandered amongst white-blossoming ti-tree bushes, over flowering herbs and flourishing grasses, and how they frolicked on the wide plain bordering the Emiana creek.

The boys desired to perform a ceremony. They wished to decorate themselves. They tore off their finger-nails from their thumbs and first fingers; they used the spurting blood to glue on the ceremonial down.

The old men seized my hand. They all struck up the chant-verse:

With fierce eyes, with glowing eyes,
they seize the thumb;
With fierce eyes, with glowing eyes,
they rip off the nail.

An old man produced a sharp kangaroo bone *(ntjala)*. He stabbed my thumb with it, pushed the bone deeply underneath the nail. He drew the point out; the rest kept up the chant. He thrust it under the nail in a different place. He gradually loosened the thumb-nail.

It was slippery with blood. I almost shrieked with pain; the torment was unbearable. I have not forgotten it; the pain was not slight; it was exceedingly great.

This text is interesting for our understanding of Aboriginal oral literature in a number of respects. Firstly it shows the close parallel associations with the *word* (the song), the *body* of the initiate and the actions of the culture heroes of the particular *country* which the initiate is inheriting.

Secondly, the text is not oral; it exists now only in the written form which represents Strehlow's translation. Strehlow, by the way, is one of the few Europeans who has grown up speaking an Aboriginal language fluently, and his *Songs of Central Australia* is one of the monuments in the study of Aboriginal oral literature. However, traces of what might have been the structure of the original text remain: for instance there is the repetition within lines 1 and 4, and the repetition of those same lines, which frames the progression of the action in the other two lines. It is a feature of oral literatures generally that in both narrative and song repetition functions to slow down and emphasise the amount of information which must be absorbed by a listener or produced by a narrator in a given amount of time. There is a further example of repetition in the last sentence of the text, the formula of *inversion of meaning* which has been noted as an Aboriginal rhetorical form in many parts of the continent.

While Strehlow's text thus retains some aspects of the formal structure of Aboriginal oral literature, it is still very much an English text. His is a familiar mode of rewriting for his generation, that is, he and writers like K. Langloh Parker, Roland Robinson, and Bill Harney have translated and summarised, altering the syntax to an English model for written, not spoken, language. The consequences for the 'feel' of a narrative or poetic style are thus enormous; one tends to read for content alone, and in some instances having to side-step the overlay of a Westernisation of those contents. In many of these rewritings custodianship of material was not taken into account, in a virtual defiance of Aboriginal copyright, and in some instances 'sacred' stories were rewritten as cautionary or 'quaint' stories for children. This was part of a general racist formation in which Aborigines themselves tended to be patronised by church, welfare and pastoral employers.

Here is the English style of K. Langloh Parker: 'Mullian the eaglehawk built himself a home high in a yaraan or white gum-tree. There he lived apart from his tribe, with Moodai the opossum his wife . . .' (1953). It can be contrasted with an Aboriginal narrator Paddy Roe whose English has been transcribed precisely, with pauses indicated by the spacings into lines (1983):

Well this fella used to look after the trough he had —
oh he had childrens too—
he had childrens—
he had about five or six children—
and a old lady—
mother for the children—
old man—

Clearly a tape-recorder and a certain linguistic technique have shaped this text in a way different from the first text, but the repetitions and clause structures are more typical of oral literatures anywhere in the world; the information is introduced progressively. Transcription, in this instance, displaces translation as a strategy for rewriting, and the authorship and identity of the Aboriginal narrator is retained.

If one wished to set up a classification of Aboriginal oral literature, one of the primary distinctions would be between *public* and *sacred* texts. Sacred narratives and song cycles are usually reserved for initiates of one or the other sex, while public ones are usually conceived of as belonging to everyone in the community and as having an entertainment rather than a ritual function. *Song cycles*, like the Goulburn Island one quoted briefly above, involve the progression from place to place, from event to event, in the song of mythical or legendary beings. These songs tend to be collectively produced, with musical accompaniment, perhaps with different roles for male and female singers. There are also individual songs of a public nature, often known as *tabu djabi*, which have a particular songman or woman as their acknowledged creator. They are concise and often deal with delightful scenes, like love-play or unique social events. Here is one called 'Aeroplane, Miracle in the Sky', from Western Australia, translated by Carl von Brandenstein (1974):

janari punura milaŋgulba kardipulu
pagarrbala wirnda jambinba
jirrigula jirrigula
maŋuṅpirdijaba purpurkurra karlamanu
marnda maŋuṅba tibalandalba
punuwaganiga kardaliara
'erraplane' pagarrbala ŋaḏuruḏuru.

From the south a wonderful glint
Steers through the sky

cutting across

Passing   passing.
A mysterious secret with a shimmering tip,
A secret of steel.
It can be turned around in flight
You can see through its double wings—
'Erraplane'—buzzing in the sky.

This song also points to a new category in Aboriginal literature, those pieces dealing with 'early times' or contact history. Legendary or heroic tales have emerged about the people who fought against colonisation, and at the same time these stories are the expression of a people who even today are negotiating through literature to come to terms with a totally different environment from which they tend, in any case, to be excluded.

Maureen Watson is a contemporary poet and storyteller who has sought to maintain tradition by shunning as much as possible the printed word. She performs her stories at schools, as well as making good use of Aboriginal community radio outlets. The important Central Australian Aboriginal Media Association has also spearheaded an Aboriginal move into the contemporary media of radio, television and video which provide the occasions for the broadcasting of both traditional oral genres as well as more contemporary productions in Aboriginal English. These use country and western or rock and roll as musical vehicles for song lyrics with sentimental, romantic or political emphasis.

This short chapter has not been able to do justice to the immense range of traditional and contemporary oral literature in Aboriginal Australia. It is clear that urgent decisions will have to be made concerning the preservation of Australia's Aboriginal heritage. But if 'preservation' means translating or transcribing, publishing and promoting, then we must ask to what extent the literature will remain *oral*. Such literature is solely an artefact of the social conditions under which it is produced; kinship, nomadism and the hunter and gatherer economy are the basis of the traditional oral forms. These can only be preserved by supporting a whole way of life and keeping intact the country with its sacred sites. And in the security of their traditional countries some Aborigines are beginning to use oral sources for the production of educational and literary materials, just as their colleagues in more urban environments are making creative use of audiovisual media, and contemporary Aboriginal writers are moving between the two; scriptwriting for film and television, and at the same time going to oral sources for themes and techniques.

Notes

General anthropological texts often contain chapters on art and literature, for example R. M. and C. H. Berndt, *The World of the First Australians* (1968). T. G. H. Strehlow's *Songs of Central Australia* (1971) has been signalled as a monumental achievement in the analysis and presentation of one oral literature, and his *Aranda Traditions* (1947) is also worth consulting. The Berndts' *Djanggawul* (1952) is an important translation of an Aboriginal song cycle and R. M. Berndt's *Love Songs of Arnhem Land* (1976) was cited as was C. G. von Brandenstein's *Taruru* (1974). K. Langloh Parker *(Australian Legendary Tales,* 1953), Bill Harney *(Tales from the Aborigines,* 1959), and Roland Robinson *(Aboriginal Myths and Legends,* 1966) are representative of the traditional school of collection and rewriting of Aboriginal literature from oral sources, while Paddy Roe's *Gularabulu* (ed. S. Muecke, 1983) is in the newer style of transcription from tape. L. Hercus and P. Sutton (eds.), *This is What Happened* (1986) is a useful collection of original narratives of contact with Europeans.

B: WRITTEN: *JACK DAVIS AND ADAM SHOEMAKER*

In January 1987, a significant but largely unreported event took place in Australia's national capital. The first national Black Playwrights' Conference and Workshop was held in Canberra over a two-week period; five new plays were performed and the conference culminated with an awards banquet which recognised recent Black Australian achievement in all dramatic fields, including film, television and stage.

Twenty years earlier this event would have been unthinkable. The first Aboriginal play ever performed was Kevin Gilbert's *The Cherry Pickers,* presented at the Mews Theatre in Sydney in 1971. Since that time, a handful of Aboriginal dramatists—Gilbert, Robert Merritt, Gerry Bostock, Eva Johnson and Jack Davis—have firmly established Black Australian theatre in the domestic and overseas market. For example, Bostock's *Here Comes the Nigger* was excerpted in *Meanjin* in 1977 after a successful Sydney season; Merritt's *The Cake Man* (1978) has been on national tours, has been televised (in condensed form in

1977) and had a two-week sell-out season at the World Theatre Festival in Denver, Colorado in 1982. *The Cake Man* and Davis' plays *Kullark* (1982) and *The Dreamers* (1982) are now set texts in the secondary school syllabuses of New South Wales, South Australia and in tertiary institutions throughout Australia.

In 1984 Eva Johnson's *Tjinderella*—much more than a phonetic parody of the Cinderella fairy tale—was one of the highlights of the Adelaide Festival, and two years later Davis' *No Sugar* (1986), received standing ovations at the World Theatre Festival which was held in conjunction with Expo 86 in Vancouver, British Columbia. Meanwhile, Merritt's script for the critically acclaimed feature film *Shortchanged* was nominated for best original screenplay at the 1986 Australian Film Institute awards.

This catalogue of achievements is significant. It shows that Aboriginal drama and Aboriginal literature as a whole are now recognised as far more than a counter-cultural curiosity. It also shows that Black Australian writing has been—and to some extent still is— more appreciated abroad than in Australia itself. At the same time the gathering momentum of playwriting has been paralleled by work in other literary genres, especially poetry and the novel. Finally, fewer than half of the Aboriginal plays written to date, and all the dramatic works of Kevin Gilbert, have yet to be published, a situation which is unfortunately true of Black Australian writing of all types. For example, there are at least fifty currently practising Aboriginal poets in English (let alone the wealth of oral poets in the traditional and tribal sphere), yet only about twenty of those writers are in print.

Thus, while Aboriginal writing has gained a foothold in the Australian literary camp over the past two decades, it is still to a large extent unknown and invisible to most Australians. The works discussed here provide some small idea of the potential of Black Australian writing, a potential which depends upon a process of discovery. One of the most striking of these discoveries is that Aboriginal people did not first begin to write during the economic boom and cultural magnanimity of the 1960s. As opposed to the continuum of oral literature discussed in the first half of this chapter, Black Australian writing in its printed form had a dateable beginning which was not in the 1960s, but forty years earlier. The true father of Aboriginal literature was David Unaipon of the Point McLeay mission in South Australia, a brilliant, complex and eccentric man who produced a significant body of work starting in the 1920s.

Born in 1872, Unaipon was an Aborigine of many talents: he could read and speak Latin and Greek, he was a habitual inventor and took out numerous patents in fields as various as ballistics and helicopter flight; he was an accomplished organist and a polished public speaker. He was a prolific writer who produced not only sermons and religious treatises but a vast, eclectic body of stories with Aboriginal themes. These stories, entitled 'Legendary Tales of the Australian Aborigines' comprise several hundred pages of Christianised legends, religious fables and anthropological notes, all of which are held in manuscript and typescript in the Mitchell Library. Four of these were published in booklet form by the Aborigines Friends' Association in 1929 and that publication—the first by an Australian Aborigine—is a fascinating synthesis of quasi-documentary traditional tribal material and Scripture, as well as symbolism more characteristic of fairy tales.

For example, Unaipon's story 'Release of the Dragon Flies, by the Fairy Sun Beam' is an unusual mixture of the Biblical and the biological. Here, frogs stand guard over captive water grubs in a 'beautiful and enchanting' place that arouses 'feeling and emotions of sacred fear'. Furthermore, Unaipon is overtly didactic: 'Then a guilty conscience smote them one and all; for the wrong they did unto the helpless, harmless water grubs who did need the help; the strong should give.'

It is possible to interpret such stories allegorically if one assumes that Unaipon is equating the water grubs with his Aboriginal brethren, allegedly held against their will on the Point McLeay mission. However, there are no simple equations in Unaipon's case; in fact, in an address entitled 'An Aboriginal Pleads for His Race' published in 1928, he outlines the view that separate institutions are essential for Aboriginal advancement:

> The white man must not leave the aborigine alone. We cannot stand in the way of progress . . . If some sort of reserve were possible, in which only the good influence of civilisation could be felt, a new civilised race could be built up. With a gradual process of introducing Christianity and all the best civilisation can give, the aborigine would come up fully developed. It might take two generations, perhaps more, but eventually we would be able to take our stand among the civilised peoples.

As a result, there is internal tension throughout most of Unaipon's work. It is the pressure resulting from the efforts of a brilliant and inventive Black Australian who tries to distance himself from what he views as the 'primitive' aspects of his Aboriginality while at the same time posing as an expert on traditional Aboriginal customs. The tension often produces stylistic strain which is hardly surprising and is certainly socially significant. As that of the first published Aboriginal author, Unaipon's work is both fascinating and challenging and deserves republication as well as a thorough critical examination.

Although Unaipon published several stories in mission magazines during the 1930s and 1940s and produced a brief autobiography in 1951, no other Black Australians followed him into print until Kath Walker in the early 1960s. One can only speculate concerning the explanation for this delay. It may be that Unaipon was such an unusual and distinctive genius and that few people of his intellect are born in any race in any generation. Also, until the 1950s and 1960s Aboriginal education was, generally speaking, very rudimentary and almost entirely vocational. Another reason was that poverty stricken Aborigines were far more concerned with survival than with creative expression in a Western format.

Nonetheless, even during those years the basis was being laid for the literary achievements of the 1970s and 1980s: Jack Davis was writing down sketches of poems on scraps of paper while he worked as a stockman in Western Australia and, as the 1960s began, Kath Walker was becoming increasingly involved in the political movement for Aboriginal advancement. Her first collection of poetry, *We Are Going* (1964), was a landmark publication. It was the first contemporary and readily accessible example of Black Australian writing to appear in print and it sold extremely well, as did her following volume, *The Dawn Is At Hand* (1966).

The enthusiasm for Walker's poetry in the marketplace was not echoed by most critics, who took her to task for indulging in juvenile rhythm and rhyme and unsophisticated clichés. This indictment was parochial and overlooked her achievement. It certainly did nothing to stem the sales of Walker's books, which have been some of the most frequently translated works in modern Australian literature. One of Walker's main aims was to reach a wide audience and to speak clearly and directly to that audience on behalf of the Aboriginal people.

There is no doubt that she has succeeded. Her collection *My People* (1981), which brings together poems from all of her previous books as well as several new pieces of prose and poetry, is the comprehensive Walker text. In it one finds the whole range of the author's verse, from impassioned occasional poems such as 'Acacia Ridge' to her most famous and most anthologised 'We Are Going'. Although one can argue in a restrictive, technical fashion that Walker's rhymed poetry is sometimes flawed, direct and poignant, free verse is definitely her forte:

Let no one say the past is dead
The past is all about us and within . . .
A thousand thousand camp fires in the forest
Are in my blood
Let none tell me the past is wholly gone

('The Past')

While it is true that part of Walker's significance to Aboriginal literature lay in the fact that she was both a pioneer and a success, her best verse stands on its own independent of such external considerations.

Considering Black Australian writing, one is initially preoccupied with those who break new ground: the first Aboriginal novelist, the first Black playwright, the author of the first Aboriginal best-seller. There is the temptation to invest Black Australian writing with significance merely because it is something different, an indication of the expanding horizons of Australian literature. But to stop at this point is to do Aboriginal authors an injustice—it is not simply the fact of their writing which is noteworthy, but the style, content and talent of that writing.

Aboriginal literature in English is in part fascinating because of its relative newness, but it is worthy of serious public and critical attention for a number of significant reasons. Almost all Black Australian writing has a strong socio-political dimension, even when this aspect is only implicit or allusive. In addition, Aboriginal writers transform Australian history in many of their works; for example, Colin Johnson's novel *Doctor Wooreddy's Prescription for Enduring the Ending of the World* (1983) is a creative revision of the accepted history of race relations in Tasmania. Aboriginal literature stems from an oral tradion which in longevity dwarfs Western literature and which influences the form, style and dialogue of contemporary Black Australian writing. Black literature gives non-Aboriginal readers a view of the contemporary face of a prior and foreign culture in their midst, with distinctive attitudes towards authority, sexual relations, identity and humour. Finally, Aboriginal literature is a post-colonial manifestation of what has been termed the Fourth World. Even if Aboriginal poets have never had contact with North American Indians or Swedish Laplanders, their verse can be said to share more with the poetry of those minority groups than with the literature of the dominant Euro-Australian culture.

These aspects of contemporary Black writing are not exhaustive but they do illustrate that the *corpus* of work being produced is far more than counter-cultural. It is, rather, pro-Aboriginal; a reflection of a strong and adaptive Black culture in modern Australia.

Many Aboriginal writers are also political activists. A significant number consider that their most successful work is what could be considered creative propaganda. Kevin Gilbert stands out in this regard: his poetry is often stark and accusatory and in *People Are Legends* (1978) he censures exploiters of the Aboriginal situation:

> Our fare is ashes, damper, stew or mungulmay
> They eat real flash all on our cash
> up there at D.A.A.
>
> ('Visiting Head Office, Canberra')

Gilbert just as forcefully condemns Aborigines who allegedly betray their brethren ('Selling out our people/While our people die') but he controls the bitterness effectively. Moreover, Gilbert is not a one-dimensional writer; he has written lyrical love poems and displays an impressive feel for ribald, humorous dialogue in his two unpublished plays, *The Cherry Pickers* (1970) and *Ghosts in Cell Ten* (1979). There is often a sexual and sardonic side to this humour in his poetry too, as when Gilbert images the figurative emasculation of Aboriginal men:

> Dear director of Aboriginal Grants
> My association needs $55,000 bucks
> To purchase silky black ladies pants
> A quota to cover each area, the Territories—
> State by state
> To conceal from the prying eyes of the world
> The Aborigines poor buggered fate
>
> ('Granny Koori')

Gilbert's activism and his writing are complementary. Like Kath Walker, he feels that his literature has a representative role, and he has stated: 'I've adopted writing as a means of voicing the Aboriginal situation . . . There is the need to educate White Australians to the present situation of Aboriginal people.' Like others who have followed his approach—the poets Lionel Fogarty *(Kargun,* 1980, *Yoogum Yoogum,* 1982, and *Ngutji,* 1984 *Kudjela,* 1983) and Gerry Bostock *(Black Man Coming,* 1980)—Gilbert intends to shock and to challenge complacency.

Colin Johnson became the first Aboriginal novelist with *Wild Cat Falling* (1965). Although that book is an interesting treatment of the prison motif which later partly inspired Archie Weller's *The Day of the Dog* (1981), the beatnik idiom of *Wild Cat Falling* has dated significantly, and Johnson's subsequent novels *Long Live Sandawara* (1979) and *Wooreddy* display far more confidence and also focus upon Aboriginal history. In fact, in *Wooreddy,* Johnson re-casts the alleged extermination of the Tasmanian Blacks by defining the White invaders as *num* or 'ghosts' who have harnessed the malevolent power of the ocean, while the land-locked Aborigines are at the mercy of these evil spirits. Much of the novel's use of myth and symbolism centres around the violent clash of opposites—good and evil, black and white, fire and water—which finally leads the protagonist to a revelation concerning potential reconciliation at the close of the work. Above all, *Wooreddy* underlines the fact that despite physical death, the spirit of Aboriginal pride and resistance lives on:

> The real Doctor Wooreddy had disappeared before they could get to him and inflict further humiliation upon him . . . The yellow setting sun broke through the black clouds to streak rays of light upon the beach. It coloured the sea red.

The historical theme is important in Aboriginal literature, as it is in Johnson's novels. Whether it is in Kevin Gilbert's extended critique *Because A White Man'll Never Do It* (1973), or his fine collection of interviews, *Living Black* (1977), in Robert Merritt's play *The Cake Man* or in the poetry of Jim Everett, Maureen Watson and Gerry Bostock, or in Jack Davis' plays *Kullark* (1979), *The Dreamers (1982)* and *No Sugar* and *Barungin: Smell the Wind* (1988) the events, recollections and atmosphere of the past are inescapable.

It is Davis' particular talent for bringing to life the history of relationships between Aborigines and Whites with immediacy that has made his contribution to Black Australian literature such a major one. This point was brought home when *The Dreamers* was invited to Portsmouth in England, in May 1987 to be performed at exactly the same time that the re-enactment of the launch of the British First Fleet was taking place. Davis' play provided a suitably ironic counterpoint to the beginning of what Aboriginal Australians term 'the invasion' by highlighting the poverty and dispossession which afflicts many contemporary Aborigines as a result of that historical event. It is as true for *The Dreamers* as it is for *No Sugar* that, as one viewer wrote to the *West Australian*:

> Since the play itself, which embodies much humour as well as good theatre, also says something politically and socially penetrating about Australia, it will create at least as honest an image of our country overseas as any other aspect of our external relations.

That mixture—of skilful drama, socio-political commentary and humour—is characteristic of all of Davis' plays. For example, in *No Sugar* the Chief Protector of Aborigines, A. O. Neville, admonishes one of his charges with the words 'Munday, let me give you a piece of advice: sugar catches more flies than vinegar'. But this suggestion is totally inappropriate to a situation in which, as the play's title indicates, the Aborigines have 'no sugar', both literally and figuratively:

> There is a happy land,
> Far, far away.
> No sugar in our tea,
> Bread and butter we never see.
> That's why we're gradually
> Fading away.

In Davis' plays, as in a number of other Black Australian works, writers attempt to rectify what are seen as incorrect interpretations by White Australians of post-contact history. Some—particularly Johnson—wish to encourage Black pride in indigenous heroes of the past while others wish to emphasise the longevity and dignity of their people's history in Australia. For all of these authors, Aboriginal history is firmly bound up with contemporary Aboriginality.

One of the most potent and distinctive ways in which Aboriginal writers image the past is by drawing increasingly upon the atmosphere and rhythms of traditional Black oral narrative in their works. For example, in *Wooreddy* Johnson intersperses poetry which has cadences and repetitions reminiscent of oral literature. Similarly, the preliminary verse in his *The Song Circle of Jacky* (1986) emphasises the continuum of oral narrative from past to present which such 'cross-over' works represent:

Jacky him been sit listening to the wind;
Jacky him been walk listening to the wind;
Jacky him been sit talking to the wind;
Jacky him been walk following wind.

A further variation on the theme is exemplified by the poetry of
Tutama Tjapangati, which is founded on a phonetic synthesis of his
tribal language (Pintupi/Luritja) and English (1981):

Ohhh,
too much/little bitta cheeky bug
kapi purlka/walpa purlka/ohhh! ebbrywhere!
jitapayin WOOF! gone. Pinished!

Davis extends this process to his plays, incorporating entire phrases
from the Western Australian *Nyoongah* language in *The Dreamers* and
No Sugar. For example, in the latter, Jimmy falls into a reverie
thinking of food and says *'Mirri-up, mirri-up. Allewah koorkantjerri
gnuny nooniny dininy, woort dininy'* ['Hurry, hurry, Watch out sheep,
I'm going to cut your throat']. The point is not only that the White
reader is being offered a bilingual insight into Aboriginal Australia but
also that in performance, the White theatregoer must rely upon an
understanding of mime rather than solely of dialogue. Plays such as
those of Davis are stating quite clearly that Black Australian culture is
different and distinctive and that, while it is not inaccessible to non-
Aborigines, some effort is required in order to reach an understanding
of it.

The same salutary effort is required when one reads the work of
Archie Weller, but for different reasons. The cruel violence which
Weller details is foreign to most readers, even if it is commonplace to
the poverty-stricken Aborigines and poor Whites whose story he tells.
Reading Weller, one has to remind oneself that the brutality and
oppression which he penetrates so skilfully is a daily occurrence in
Australia. Perhaps more than any other Black Australian author,
Weller provides an insight into contemporary Aboriginal views of
authority, sexuality, humour and mores. For example, behind the
description of Doug Dooligan's frenzied life in his 1981 novel *The
Day of the Dog* is the potent philosophical observation that, 'Laughter
takes away the pain of most things. That is why Tiny and so many of
the People always laugh, because they have the pain of failure that
sometimes becomes too much.' Similarly, the narrator of 'Fish and

Chips' in Weller's collection of stories *Going Home* (1986), observes, 'We all laugh about that now: the night the munadj took Jimmy away; because, really, laugh is all we *can* do about it.'

Elsewhere in *Going Home*, Weller's dialogue is so forceful as to seem tape-recorded at source:

> 'Who's your mates? Who was drivin'? What was the girl's name? How old was she, sonny? Do you know what carnal knowledge is all about? What's your name, arsehole? You 'ad the gun, eh, Jesse James? Well, who did then? Where did you get all this beer and grog, matey? By Christ, you're in the shit now.'
>
> ('One Hot Night')

Weller's work illustrates the fact that Black Australian writing has become increasingly confident throughout the 1980s. One indication of the distance it has already come is the fact that a comprehensive anthology of Black writing has already been assembled. It presents the work of over twenty Aboriginal authors in all literary fields. Black Australian authors are also convinced of the wider significance of their writing; as Robert Merritt has put it, 'We need to be the generals in a peaceful cultural revolution.' In the same vein, Jack Davis has said, 'Black writers are the most important thing we've got.' Prominent land rights activist Mick Miller also emphasises the importance of authors as Black role models:

> In years to come, they're going to be standing out there for everybody to see—Aboriginal people to see—that we have somebody out there who is just as good as anybody else in the country.

As the overseas success of Aboriginal drama has already illustrated, that domestic recognition may well be preceded and hastened by foreign accolades. Until that time and after it, Aboriginal writers will continue to be one of the most poignant and effective voices for their people.

Notes

The quotations is this section are taken from a variety of sources. Robert Merritt's observation is extracted from Mary Colbert's article 'Flint-splitter of identity' in the *National Times on Sunday* (16

November 1986) while Robert Merritt, Jack Davis and Mick Miller are all quoted from unpublished interviews.

In the case of Aboriginal literature, primary sources are not always published nor readily available. For example, Kevin Gilbert's unpublished plays, *The Cherry Pickers* (1970) and *Ghosts in Cell Ten* (1979), are accessible only in manuscript at the National Library of Australia, Canberra (ms. no. 2584). Similarly, David Unaipon's 'Legendary Tales of the Australian Aborigines' can be found only in manuscript and typescript at the Mitchell Library, Sydney (ms. nos A1929-A1930). A number of works by Black Australians are simply not available in their entirety at this stage; these include Gerry Bostock's play 'Here Comes the Nigger' and Eva Johnson's 'Tjinderella'. To date, only excerpts of the former have been published, in *Meanjin,* 36 (1977).

A number of important examples of Black Australian writing are published but out of print. In this category are such works as Unaipon's *Native Legends* (1929) and *Australian Aborigines: Photographs of Natives and Address* (1928). Contemporary Aboriginal literature is often not accessible nationwide; for example, Maureen Watson's collection of poetry and short stories, *Black Reflections* (1982), was printed in pamphlet form primarily for local use in South Australia. In addition, much Black Australian literature appears in rare or little-known publications such as Aboriginal community newsletters, which are maintained systematically only by the library of the Australian Institute of Aboriginal Studies, Canberra. The AIAS is also one of the few sources for the entire series of the Aboriginal journal *Identity* which, for the decade between 1971 and 1981, was one of the most important vehicles for emerging Aboriginal writing.

The first major journal to devote an entire issue to Aboriginal literature was *Meanjin*, 36 (1977). K. L. Goodwin's *A History of Australian Literature* (1986) contains a concise resumé of Aboriginal writing.

Apart from some journal articles there are few critical books dealing with Black Australian literature; the most important produced thus far are *Aboriginal Writing Today* (1985), a collection of papers from the first national conference of Aboriginal writers, edited by Jack Davis and Bob Hodge, and *Connections* (1988) edited by Emmanuel Nelson. The first full-length critical study of Black Australian literature is Adam Shoemaker's *Black Words, White Page* (1988). The first comprehensive anthology of Aboriginal writing, *Paperbark* (1988), edited by Jack Davis, Stephen Muecke, Colin Johnson and

Adam Shoemaker, has the most thorough and up-to-date bibliography covering all genres of published Black Australian literature and commentaries on it, although *Black Words, White Page* contains more references to unpublished material as well as interviews.

Chapter 3

AUSTRALIAN ENGLISH

ARTHUR DELBRIDGE

The notion that Australian literature is written not in English but in Australian English ought by now not to be controversial. But to some readers it probably is. The linguistic argument is that the name 'English language' represents a highly abstract language system which is realised in different communities in different ways, in the form of dialects. Each dialect has the same status as any other. The delicacy of the analysis controls any estimation of the number of dialects in use in any given area. Each dialect is likely to be distinguished from others in a wide range of language features produced over time in response to local physical and social pressures. There is no area, no community, for which 'the English language' is the dialect; in this sense there is no such thing as pure English but only London English, or Oxford English, or Scottish English, or (if you lump a number of these together) British English, which is itself in contrast, at the same national level of abstraction, with American English, Jamaican English, Australian English, and so on. English is an aggregation of Englishes. Australian English is that one of them which has evolved here in Australia, under the pressure of the physical and social forces which have made Australia—forces which include some of the other Englishes.

Australian English may, on one classification, be lumped in with British, American, Canadian and New Zealand Englishes because they are all native varieties. That is, they evolved through a relatively undisturbed succession of native speakers, speakers for whom English is the mother tongue. Looked at this way, Australian English may be defined as that dialect of English which is spoken by native-born Australians. On the other hand, Australian English—though it is like

47

American and New Zealand English—is unlike British English in that it began with the transportation of a British people to a new country where its evolution has gone on, more or less unaffected by other languages already established in the new location. Australian English may be classified as a transported native English.

All the native Englishes are in contrast with the non-native Englishes, developed in countries where the local English speakers have at some stage not been English speakers: they have learnt the language as a second language (or third or fourth). Historically, most non-native varieties originated from contact with an influential group of transported (or visiting) English speakers who had come as conquerors, or governors, or in some other ultimately influential role. On this view it would be clear that post-colonial immigration to Australia has led to the use of some non-native varieties of English here, though with a strong tendency to converge with Australian English, and some interaction between the native and non-native varieties.

The languages of the Aboriginal people cannot realistically be regarded either as transported or as migrant languages. They alone in Australia can properly be described with the single epithet 'Australian'. When scholars refer to Australian languages they mean the languages of the Aboriginal people.

In terms of number of users of English worldwide, Kachru's summary claims that 'at present there are 266 million native speakers and 115 million non-native speakers . . . if the current trend continues, there will soon be more non-native than native speakers of English'. The total for the native varieties is made up of (in millions): British 55, Australian 13, New Zealand 3, American 182, Canadian 13. The non-native total, on the same count, comprises Asia 60, Africa 20, West and Central Europe 15, USSR 10, Western Hemisphere 10. So Australian English looks like a rather minor variety.

But if one believes that all dialects have equal status as language systems serving the needs of those who use them, the numbers become quite unimportant. It is the use made of a dialect within the community of its users, and in communication with communities having different dialects, that determines its value. For any dialect, its literary use, whether oral or written, is a major source of value.

Australian literature is often numbered among 'the new literatures in English'. This is understandable for a country now celebrating its bicentenary. But it is not so easy to estimate the age of Australian English itself. Distinctively Australian words appeared very soon after

1788—indeed the name of one Australian animal got immediate currency as early as 1770, when Captain Cook first sighted the 'leaping quadruped' and identified it by the name *kangaroo* which he believed (rightly or wrongly) to be the local Aboriginal name. The post-1788 harvest of new names reflects the difficulty settlers had in identifying and classifying the novelties of land-form, flora and fauna that confronted them. The names themselves came from their familiar British dialects or from the bewildering array of unwritten Aboriginal languages with which the early settlers had only very imperfect and ill-informed contact. Make-shift and confusion are the sources of many early Australian words and uses, and have since given both linguists and folk-etymologists much to speculate on.

Why (for example) is an Englishman called a *pommy*? how did we come to call a sheep *jumbuck*? why *station* for a sheep- or cattle-run? why *she-oak* for a casuarina which is not an oak at all? why *jackass* for a kookaburra? There are well-founded answers to some such questions, but for many of them one must wait for systematic and more extensive research to be completed.

The growth of a local vocabulary reflecting both the physical and the social conditions of the new colony was the first manifestation of Australian English. By the end of the nineteenth century the Australianisation of the vocabulary was so extensive as to encourage E. E. Morris to produce a dictionary with the title *Austral English, A Dictionary of Australian Words, Phrases and Usages* (1898). Morris claimed to have entered in his book 'all the new words and new uses of old words that have been added to the English language by reason of the fact that those who speak English have taken up their abode in Australia, Tasmania, and New Zealand'.

Some of his critics thought he had concentrated too much on the novelties of Australian flora and fauna, to the great neglect of distinctive and characteristic Australian colloquialisms. Morris' emphasis was on how transportation to Australia had altered English, a very different emphasis from that which Noah Webster almost a century earlier had given to his descriptions of the English transported to America. Six years after the American War of Independence ended Webster wrote in the first of his *Dissertations on the English Language* (1789):

> As an independent nation our honour requires us to have a system of our own, in language as well as government. Great Britain, whose children we are, and whose language we speak, should no longer be our standard. For

the taste of her writers is already corrupted, and her language is on the decline. But if it were not so, she is at too great a distance to be our model and to instruct us in the principles of our own tongue.

Australia has never had a similarly bold and authoritative declaration made of the independence of its language; and our novelists, even in the twentieth century, have often felt obliged to provide glosses on local lingo for the benefit of British publishers and readers. For example, Rolf Boldrewood in *The Crooked Stick, or Pollie's Probation* (1895) writes:

> 'They heard he was to be in the coach from Orange on a certain day, and made it right to stick it up and give him a lesson.'
> 'What's sticking up?'
> 'Well, sir, by what one hears and reads, it is what used to be called "stopping" on the Queen's highway in England.'

Even well into the twentieth century, when the sense of national identity is beginning to be explicit, and there is much more bravado in the display of colloquialism which foreign readers might find obscure, the glosses are still there. In Glassop's *We Were the Rats* (1944) Gordon, an Australian soldier in Tobruk, tells his mates he believes in 'amassing smash'.

> 'Smash?' asked Clive. 'What's that?'
> 'Smash, dough, fiddlies, coin, tin, hay, oot, shekels, sponduliks,' says Gordon. 'I'm still the highest paid member of this company.'

The display of our funny-peculiar words has been a familiar preoccupation of Australian fiction.

So, Australia has seen a continous lexical development, with borrowing, adaptation and extension. And some invention! John Norton had no doubts about the origin of *wowser.* 'I invented the word myself,' he said. 'To me, John Norton, alone belongs the sole undivided glory and renown of inventing a word, a single, simple word, that does at once describe, deride, and denounce that numerous, noxious, pestilent, puritannical, kill-joy push—the whole blasphemous, wire-whiskered brood.'

There is an indirect inventiveness in the (predominantly male) game of rhyming slang: Adrian Quist for pissed, drunk; Werris (Creek) for Greek; Captain Cook for look; and Old Jack Lang for rhyming slang itself.

But it would be hard to make a case for anything unique in the way the lexicon of Australian English developed: it used its inherited stock of word forms and processes; it borrowed from other languages, and has exchanged words with other varieties of English. It has expanded to meet the needs of its community, and it always reflects the characteristics of its users or of any image of a set of Australian characteristics that may emerge, or be invented and projected.

It is in this reflection, naturally, that Australian English is most distinctive. Whether the image is of the Australian as the wild colonial boy, or as workingman, bushman, mate, 'digger', heroic lifesaver, sportsman, bohemian, ocker or suburban commuter—all male images, only lately becoming genderless, if only by the -*person* suffix—there is a reflection of each image in our established colloquial phraseology, and its occasional variants. Australians recognise themselves in their various roles and moods in expressions like

> getting off at Redfern, stone the crows, dog's disease, emu parade, fair crack of the whip, come the raw prawn, rattle your dags, spine bashing, two-bob lair, Queen Street bushie (or Pitt Street farmer, or Collins Street cocky), poke borak, paddock basher, mad as a cut snake (or as a meat-axe, or as a gum-tree full of galahs), have kangaroos in the top paddock (like 'bats in the belfry'), hump the bluey, on the bludge.

But although these are distinctively Australian and to a degree characteristic of Australian talk, it would be foolish to imagine that Australian English is different only at the colloquial end of the style range. It is different also in much of what Robert Burchfield calls 'the common core' of the vocabulary of English. For example, the Australian use of *creek* and *station* is clearly different in some senses from British and American usage. Although Morris' *Austral English* covered the distinctive Australian names for flora and fauna and showed a limited interest in Australian talk up to the end of the nineteenth century, it was not until 1981 that a dictionary was written with Australian usage as its point of focus, with a comprehensive word list in which all aspects of meaning and form were taken from the use of English in Australia, and with Australian English as the basis of comparison with other national varieties of English. This was the *Macquarie Dictionary*, a dictionary which holds up the mirror not to British English, or to American English, but to Australian English in the full range of its uses.

If the development of an Australian vocabulary has been continuous from Captain Cook on, the same cannot be said for the emergence of an Australian phonology and style of pronunciation. It is not easy to say just when the 'Australian accent' began.

Spoken Australian English is different from both British and American English in some general ways: it has had a much shorter history; it has developed in a period of population mobility; although it displays an interesting range of personal and social variation, it is remarkably uniform throughout the whole continent and entirely lacking in clearly differentiated regional dialects; with few exceptions, those who have felt the need to comment on it have commented unfavourably, even if it is their own English they are criticising. Indeed, attitudes to the Australian accent have been an important component of 'the cultural cringe'. Among students of the accent it has generally been agreed, despite interest in topics like the rate of utterance, rhythm, lip and jaw movement, and a supposedly tell-tale voice quality, that what is most characteristic is the pronunciation of the vowels. There is a spectrum of vowel pronunciation which is different from any that may be found in Britain or America. This spectrum may be divided into three unequal parts, with General Australian in the middle and Cultivated and Broad Australian as minority varieties at either end. Broad, General and Cultivated represent three stages in a progressive retraction of vowel quality, throughout the whole vowel range. The Cultivated variety is usually seen as the prestige form of Australian English, and the Broad (unfairly) as fitting the stereotypes of country or urban ockers. In recent years both ends have begun to converge on General Australian, which has thus strengthened its position as typical Australian, to be heard in board-rooms, courts and conferences as much as at beaches and in the work-room. Even so, most Australians show no difficulty in moving up from Broad to General or Cultivated for occasions that seem to demand some elevating of their normal speech style. Since the three varieties are phonologically identical, or nearly enough so for the differences not to be a significant source of misunderstanding, it is not surprising that the relative homogeneity of Australian English is simply taken as a fact of life.

But how could such linguistic homogeneity have developed from the circumstances of the 1788 settlement? Among the first convicts, soldiers and administrators there was certainly dialect diversity now unnaturally brought into one close settlement. The dialects of London, the home counties and the Midland cities predominated, and there is no reason to believe that the expatriate convicts would have lost their British accents under the colonial influences of the penal settlement. Indeed some early fiction writers like Alexander Harris and James Tucker attempted to represent dialect differences in the dialogue of their characters:

> 'That be's so loike our Tummas's slop! Whoi, I could a'most ha' sworn to it, b' the patch on the back.'

and

> 'But if id's raaly raping you want, I'll give you a pound an acre for all you'll cut of this saam whate.'

and

> 'Vell, and vere have you been to all this vile? Vy didn't you come 'ere sooner than this ere?'

West country, Irish, or Cockney—all were thus differentiated in *Ralph Rashleigh* (written 1845, published 1952), to choose but one example.

The first signs of a new accent emerging from the transported dialects are found among the 'Currency' children, those born in the colony as the first generation of Australians.

> The children born in these colonies and now grown up speak a better language, purer, more harmonious than is generally the case in most parts of England. The amalgamation of such various dialects assembled together seems to improve the mode of articulating the words.

So wrote James Dixon in 1822 after a visit to New South Wales, the first to comment specifically on the locally born youth as different in speech from their transported parents. How long it took for the new accent to develop is uncertain, though it is significant that by the time the number of Irish convicts became substantial, in the 1830s, there was apparently no Irish dialect influence, certainly no lasting one, on the speech of the Australian-born of the colony, either then or later. When in 1887 Samuel McBurney came to describe the pronunciation of English in Australia, his analysis of its most distinctive features was basically the same as Professor A. G. Mitchell's, made in the 1940s.

So, from the early nineteenth century, Australian English has been the medium of the Australian community, sufficiently distinctive both in vocabulary (though hardly distinctive at all in grammar) to have become an established national variety of English. In the census figures for the year 1901, 77 per cent of the total population were persons born in Australia. Another 18 per cent had been born in the British Isles. Australia was thoroughly monolingual; English was its language, and its few immigrant languages, like its Aboriginal languages, counted for little. By contrast, Australia at its bicentenary is both generally and officially recognised as a multilingual, pluralistic society, with about 140 different community languages, all brought here, sooner or later, by immigrants, as English itself had been. By 1983, 17.3 per cent of Australians aged over four years had as their first language a language other than English. Although the position of English as the national language is strongly maintained, the other community languages have in various degrees secured roles in social, commercial, educational and political life that make significant contributions to Australian culture. The consequences of language contact and language isolation have become a contributory theme in fiction and biography written in English, and there is a small body of Australian or expatriate work written in one or other of the community languages other than English. The linguistic effects of multiculturalism on Australian English have so far not been great— certainly not nearly so great as the effects of the world-wide communication explosion, in press, radio, film and television. But it is perhaps early days to talk, even allowing for the established fact that the second-generation youths of migrant families use English much more extensively than their parents and grandparents do, especially if they were born here or arrived from abroad at an early age.

Contact between Australian English and the Aboriginal languages also has literary consequences, both for Aboriginal writers and for any writers whose themes include life contact between Aborigines and other Australians. Since 1788, many Aboriginal languages have become extinct, and the number of speakers of those surviving much reduced. Colin Yallop has listed twenty-five extant languages each having more than 250 speakers (though none have much more than 3000 speakers). These twenty-five have a reasonably good chance of survival, either because they are being used in bilingual school programs or because they are otherwise cared for and promoted by institutions such as the Australian Institute of Aboriginal Studies in Canberra, and the School of Australian Linguistics in the Northern Territory. Many Aborigines, especially those in urban areas, no longer speak any Aboriginal language, but a variety of Australian English. But in several areas of Australia, Aboriginal languages are in use in schools, in bilingual programs in which children learn the skills of reading and writing in a language they know, as a preparation for coping with English, which as the national language will be essential to them as they proceed with schooling and look forward to opportunities in the wider community.

Meanwhile in northern Australia language contact between Aborigines and whites has produced both pidgins and creoles. (A pidgin is a language which has developed as a standard means of communication between two groups neither of whom speaks pidgin as their mother tongue. A creole is a pidgin which eventually becomes the first language of a community.) Australian pidgins show the combined influence of simplified English, particular Aboriginal languages, and pidgins developed earlier in other places. There are well-established creoles in the Torres Strait Islands and Cape York, in the Roper River region and in the north of Western Australia. A language such as the Roper River creole is felt by its speakers to be quite distinct from English, despite its English borrowings. It is in some respects more complex grammatically than English. Yallop cites its pronominal system, for example, in which elements of English origin such as *mi* and *yu* are exploited to yield a rich set of distinctions including *yunmi* (a dual inclusive, for 'you and I'), *mintupala* (dual exclusive, for 'we two, not you'). *yunmalapat* (plural inclusive for 'we, including you') and *milapat* (plural exclusive for 'we, not you'). Speakers of this creole who also speak English recognise a clear difference between the two and rarely mix them. Naturally the systems and complexities that linguists are aware of in such languages, produced originally as contact languages, are not so apparent to literary writers whose main linguistic interest may be restricted to creating dialogue between white and Aborigine, or betweeen Aborigine and Aborigine that is not a parody and that remains intelligible to readers.

It is arguable that in holding up the mirror to Australians at talk and presenting the result as literary dialogue or monologue (whether in verse or prose) our writers have demonstrated most clearly their attitudes to Australian English and to the sense of national identity that it may embody. Writers, like the rest of the community, have been part of a protracted linguistic tug-of-war between freedom and discipline.

At any one time there is uncertainty about who is on which side.

But broadly the discipline team includes those who see a paramount value in standards and standardisation in language, who see moves away from an assumed British standard as distortion and treachery, needing to be disciplined by education, in the interests of purity of language, accuracy of expression and the conservation of language values. Its captains have declared its aims and beliefs and the troops have echoed them:

> Teachers must do their utmost to check this development away from standard English, not necessarily because it is a development away, but because it is neither graceful nor useful.
> (S. H. Smith, Director of Education in N.S.W., reported in *Evening News*,
> 20 December 1920).
> We would define Australian-English as that pleasant oral communication which is audible and instantly apprehended by reason of its clear enunciation and rate of articulation; which is expressed in correct grammatical form and is free from solecisms; it has the vowel quality and absence of nasality associated with a person of respectable attainments and the inflections are such as do not provoke a sense of antagonism or resentment in the auditor by virtue of such speech.
> ('Womerah', *Sydney Morning Herald*, 28 December 1933.)

The freedom team, on the other hand, takes a more pluralistic, laissez-faire stand. Its academic leader, Professor A. G. Mitchell, startled Australia in the 1940s with the view that 'There is Nothing Wrong with Australian Speech' (*A.B.C. Weekly*, 12 September 1942). At about the same time Sidney J. Baker wrote a well-known book, *The Australian Language*, in which he followed the example of H. L. Mencken, who only twenty-odd years earlier had declared the independence of American English in an even better-known book, *The American Language*. From the 1940s on the recognition of Australian English as Australia's own variety of English, available and adequate for all purposes, has grown stronger, in education, in publishing, in broadcasting and in the world of entertainment.

But it has been a phoney war, fought over the wrong issues. The Australianness of Australian English is inevitable, and writers in this variety as in any other have to make individual choices about both freedom and discipline in the use of language, choices that are determined by writers' own perceptions of their subject matter and of their readers. Henry Lawson presumably recognised a duty to some of his readers when he wrote, in one bit of dialogue:

'I always had a pup that I gave away or sold and didn't get paid for or had "touched" (stolen) as soon as it was old enough.'

The addition of the gloss was a self-imposed discipline. But he felt free (in writing 'He was an innercent old cove') to respell *innocent* in a way that held the mirror up to the rather slow syllabic utterance of the Australian bush character who speaks this bit of the dialogue.

There is a developing sense of national identity in Australian literature that becomes both visible and inwardly audible in the dialogue which represents Australian talk. The earlier nineteenth-century novelists would try their hand at dialect, as we have seen, but were uneasy with local colloquialism. For in Australia, as in England and America, bookishness was in the air. The school-marm stood looking over the shoulders of Cooper and Irving in America, Boldrewood and Furphy in Australia; even Henry Lawson too, and especially his editors and literary advisers. The revolt against bookishness, when it came, often produced dialogue which the inward ear of the reader rejects: it rejects the grammar of the overlong sentences, the concentrated display of curiosities of the language. The writer's interest in a background of community speech habits can so easily displace interest in individual character and action:

Well, then, it seems to me that all you have to do is yarn along and make us come alive just as we blooming well were. Let us drivel and meander like life itself. You don't need to swell your head with shaping destiny or interpreting life according to those new-fangled blokes who never baked a damper, or felled a tree, or rode a buck-jumper, or killed a snake or a beast, or tanned a hide, or broken in a team of bullocks, or knocked up a coffin for a mate out of stringybark, or drank water out of their hats. You just set us down on paper like we were without any of your own shennanakin!

(Preface to Brent of Bin Bin, *Ten Creeks Run*, 1930.)

One waits until early Patrick White to find dialogue which by contrast has the characteristics of real talk, the looseness of grammatical structure, the idioms, the rhythm that the inward ear responds to with a shock of recognition, whether or not it has tell-tale lexical Australianness in it. One waits until the 1970s to find dialogue not a vehicle of linguistic display but subservient to other communicative behaviours, as in David Ireland's *The Glass Canoe* (1976) for example:

The King and Mick had their own language.

'Honestly.'

'Truly.'

'No worries.'

'Well—'

'Fair enough.'

They were agreed on the plan of campaign.

And one waits till the 1980s for the suburban pubs of *The Glass Canoe* to step back into social obscurity, and for the novelists' Australian cities to become more international, more anonymous (in the way that multi-storey office blocks are anonymous) and for the social dialect though not unAustralian to be not aggressively Australian either. In Peter Carey's *Bliss* (1981), for example, the dialogue is the intense, understated talk of city people who are seen by their language to be under strain, to be contemplating violence without explicitly planning it. It is not colourful language, not language devoted to the glorification of Australian folkways; it is a dialogue of apparent realism that is pointed, intentional, relevant, crystallising situation, expressing character, advancing plot; in ways that (for Australian readers at least) present Australian speech that can be immediately recognised as faithful and proportionate.

Notes

Since about 1970, the study of language variation has been one of the chief occupations of linguists all over the world. Naturally, English has been a favourite topic, especially since so much of the world's population seems to want to learn English as a second language. But which English? Braj Kachru's book *The Other Tongue* (1982) makes a good presentation of the leading themes of this field of study. The place of Australian English among world Englishes has not had much particular attention, even though its importance as a single native English in a south-east Asian area full of non-native Englishes is beginning to be felt in the countries of our area. The study of Australian English itself has till lately concentrated on the 'Australian accent' and on innovations of vocabulary, especially at the colloquial end of the style spectrum. The work of A. G. Mitchell laid the foundations for the study of Australian phonology and pronunciation, as in A. G. Mitchell and Arthur Delbridge, *The Speech of Australian*

Adolescents (1965) and *The Pronunciation of English in Australia* (1965). A representative of more recent work, considerably more sophisticated in techniques and concepts, is B. Horvath, *Variation in Australian English* (1985). This work takes account of the effects of post-1940 migration to Australia, as does Michael Clyne's *Australia Talks: Essays on the Sociology of Australian Immigrant and Aboriginal Languages* (1976). The study of Aboriginal languages is now vigorously pursued, even though lost opportunities cannot be made up. Although there are several comprehensive accounts of work done in this field, the one most accessible to the general reader is by Colin Yallop, *Australian Aboriginal Languages* (1982), on which the present chapter leans heavily, and gratefully. A report of a Senate Standing Committee on Education and the Arts, entitled *A National Language Policy* (1984) is the source of information given here on the so-called 'community languages' of Australia. Australian English is now well served by its own dictionaries, such as the *Macquarie Dictionary* (1981), the *Macquarie Thesaurus* (1984), and G. A. Wilkes, *Dictionary of Australian Colloquialisms* (1978). A dictionary on historical principles is in press, prepared under the editorship of W. S. Ramson.

Chapter 4

AUSTRALIAN HUMOUR

DOROTHY JONES AND BARRY ANDREWS

To define a national humour is perhaps impossible. Jokes, bandied around from country to country through many retellings assume their own form of local colour, so that distinctions between the humour of one nation and another eventually come to depend on subtle differences of tone, nuance and language. An Australian soldier crouching in a foxhole while enemy tanks bear down, says to his mate, 'You go that way, Digger, and I'll go this way, and we'll surround 'em.' The humour, which lies in the ironic acceptance of a losing situation and balances on the edge of a barely evident self-parody, is different in tone from the joke about an Irish constable who, when asked how he managed to arrest so many offenders at once, replies, 'It was surrounded them moiself I did, Sorr.' Australian humour is characterised, not so much by content, as by a special configuration of attitudes. Irony predominates, and individuals manipulated by circumstances, or a destiny they are unable to control, wryly resign themselves to their own powerlessness.

Patrick White considers the black humour and satire he himself favours are relatively recent developments prompted by the growth in cosmopolitanism after World War II. While his kind of Australian satire may be a largely twentieth-century phenomenon, drawing substantial nourishment from Britain and Europe, there have been significant traditions of verse satire and black-and-white art which have their roots in colonial culture, and a long established tradition of Australian humour originating from the early days of European settlement. Significantly, White begins his meditation in *Flaws in the Glass* (1981) 'The Better Classes—the Lower Classes; the English— the Australians', for such clashing perspectives have proved important in the development of our humour. Shirley Hazzard in *The Transit of Venus* (1980) describes how, to someone entrenched within the English establishment, 'Australia required apologies, and was almost a subject for ribaldry', while the joke about an Australian in London who, mistaking an Englishman walking ahead for a friend from home, slaps him on the back crying 'How are you, ya' old bastard', reveals further complexity in the relationship between the two countries. The embarrassed Australian explains that 'in Australia we all call each other bastard', only to receive the cold English reply, 'Well you all *are*, aren't you?' Despite their nationalistic fervour, Australians have felt, and perhaps still feel, lingering doubts about their own legitimacy as a nation. Our humour is deeply rooted in the disjunctions of colonial life—English and Currency, upper class and lower class, old hands versus new chums, the bush versus the city, and an assertively male view of the world which sought to render women peripheral. These are contained within a still larger disjunction, the confrontation between European settlers and a land which seemed to undermine and deny all their expectations.

When perceived from this divided perspective, one's local habitation, and events occurring there, are readily transformed into myth. The narrator in Lawson's 'Hungerford' recounts his perplexity over information he has received:

> At least, I believe that's how it is, though the man who told me might have been a liar. Another man said he was a liar, but then *he* might have been a liar himself—a third person said he was one. I heard that there was a fight over it, but the man who told me about the fight might not have been telling the truth.

Peter Carey's *Illywhacker* (1985) opens with an air of spurious authority as Herbert Badgery asserts he is a hundred and thirty-nine years old:

> I am a terrible liar and I have always been a liar. I say that early to set things straight. *Caveat Emptor.* My age is the one fact you can rely on, and not because I say so, but because it has been publicly authenticated.

Such utterances provide material from which legends spring. The Adelaide dentist who narrates Murray Bail's story 'The Drover's Wife' appropriates the central figure of Russell Drysdale's painting (and by implication Lawson's heroine) with a similarly authoritative air: 'The woman depicted is not the Drover's Wife. She is my wife.' But the woman and the region she inhabits elude his grasp: 'it could easily be Queensland, West Australia, the Northern Territory.' She belongs to a landscape where he feels lost and from which he retreats into a narrow suburban existence she still overshadows, even though it cannot contain her: 'Hazel—it is Hazel and the rotten landscape that dominate everything.'

In his version of 'The Drover's Wife', Frank Moorhouse presents a lecture delivered by Franco Casamaggiore, an Italian student of Commonwealth literature, supposedly defining an Australian 'insider' joke presented by Lawson, Drysdale and Bail. Proclaiming as 'historical fact' that a total absence of women in pioneering time led outback workers to take refuge in mateship and discover sexual solace in 'the maternal bulk of the merino sheep, with its woolly coat and large soft eyes,' he insists that in all three works of art the drover's wife is really a sheep. Moorhouse mocks academic pretensions along with narrowly defined notions of Australian literary culture, while showing how intangible in essence that culture may prove for an outsider. Documents clustered at the story's end—letters of protest or inquiry and cartoons—simultaneously dissolve and augment the literary myth. This is further deconstructed by Barbara Jefferis who responds to Moorhouse with a story narrated by the drover's wife herself, delivering opinions on Mr Lawson, Mr Drysdale, the dentist and Franco Casamaggiore:

> Women have a different history. Someone ought to write it down. We're not sheep or shadows, or silly saints the way Mr Lawson would have. There's more to us. More to me than any of them have written, if it comes to that.

Bush tradition plays an important part in Australian humour, even in the work of many contemporary urban writers, like Frank Moorhouse, who has recently declared, 'much of my inner landscape as a person and a writer came from, or used, the days of settlement, the Desert, the Outback—The Bush.' Marcus Clarke describes 'the subtle charm of this fantastic land of monstrosities' where the 'phantasmagoria of that wild dream-land termed the Bush interprets itself', and tall tales with their deadpan accounts of grotesque impossibilities were one means of coming to terms with such strangeness. Fantasies were generated in gatherings where, as Lawson writes in 'Stragglers', men 'tell lies against each other sociably ... and every true Australian bushman must try his best to tell a bigger outback lie than the best bush liar'. Tales were told of the fabulous Speewah station where everything was larger, more abundant, more spectacular, and sometimes more disastrous than anywhere else. So many men worked there that the cook and his assistant had to row out in a boat to sugar the tea, while the station hands were gargantuan figures like Crooked Mick who used Ayers Rock to stone the crows. Fantasising the hardships of bush life endows with heroic stature those who endure them, and stories revolve around characters who perform miraculous feats of mastery, like Dal Stivens' creation, Cabbage-tree Ned, who 'shot so straight he could knock the eye off a snail at a hundred yards' and 'shot so far he used salt bullets so the game would keep until he got up to it'.

Fantastic exuberance, however, is frequently offset by irony to invest much of our humour with a characteristically dismissive quality. An old-timer, in response to a patronising inquiry about his longest droving trip, replies, 'From Cape York to Hobart son, and we walked them all the way', while one Australian parliamentarian is reputed to have interrupted a long-winded colleague in mid-speech with a note saying, 'Pull out, dig. The dogs are pissing on your swag!' Although such reductivism succeeds in pricking pretensions, it can also represent a denial of individual aspiration with its possiblity of personal triumph or command over circumstance. Outsiders of various kinds are mocked by demolition experts to reinforce group solidarity. Outback workers used new-chum jokes to test and reject newcomers, often portrayed as upper-class Englishmen, so that the humour also tended to express the feelings of class conflict. It is no accident that new chums like the lisping effeminate Charles Harold Vane Somers Golightly in Alfred Dampier's *Marvellous Melbourne* (1889) are stock figures of the nineteenth-century Australian popular theatre. Banjo Paterson represents animosity between English new chum and Australian bush worker as a physical combat when Saltbush Bill distracts the jackeroo by picking a fight which he deliberately loses, so his mob can graze on the squatter's grass unhindered:

> And the tale went home to the public schools of the pluck of the English swell,
> How the drover fought for his very life, but blood in the end must tell

while Saltbush Bill repeats the yarn, 'How the best day's work that he ever did was the day he lost the fight.' Similar humour is generated by the interaction between country and city dwellers. According to Judith Wright, opposition between city and rural values has often been perceived as a conflict between vice and virtue. But from a city-dweller's point of view, this moral contrast readily modifies into an idealised vision of life outback which has proved significant in creating films like *Dad and Dave Come to Town* (1938) or *Crocodile Dundee* (1986) for city audiences, who relish the irony directed against them from the bush.

The ironic stance sometimes takes the form of an unhurried casualness, so strikingly exemplified by Paul Hogan as 'Crocodile' Dundee or as promoter of Australian beer and tourism. Les Murray's name for this quality is 'sprawl':

> Sprawl is the quality
> of the man who cut down his Rolls-Royce
> into a farm utility truck, and sprawl
> is what the company lacked when it made repeated efforts
> to buy the vehicle back and repair its image.

As Murray goes on to point out, sprawl invests life with a certain scope, magnitude and generosity of spirit:

> Sprawl is doing your farming by aeroplane, roughly,
> or driving a hitchhiker that extra hundred miles home.

But excessive casualness can also produce a chilling detachment from the lives and concerns of others, as in the story of two men travelling outback in a buggy startled by a bullet whistling through the air to pass safely between them. Two station hands come running to ask if they noticed the shot, the one with the rifle explaining he had a bet that he could put a bullet between them without touching either. When one of the travellers exclaims, 'Supposin' the bullet had gone though me head,' the marksman replies, 'Oh well, I'd have lost me bet.'

In a land where hopes of prosperity were frequently negated by geography and climate, aspirations and hope readily gave way to an enervating sense of failure expressed with grim irony or the shoulder-shrugging resignation of such typical sayings as 'no worries' and 'she'll be right'. A waterside worker drinking with a writer from the *Bulletin* in a pub in Wyndham, Western Australia, is recorded as saying:

So you are up here to write about us . . . Put this in mate.
Cambridge Gulf is the arsehole of the world, and
Wyndham is 65 miles up it!

His comment reveals that blend of protest, resignation and pride which sets the tone of so much Australian humour—protest at a harsh environment and its alienating effect on the individual, resignation to the impossibility of change, and pride in being able to endure it all. The resignation however, lends itself to parody. The sombre acceptance of death by the Sick Stockrider and the Dying Stockman established a tradition which has accommodated dying shearers, bagmen, aviators, bargehands and fettlers as well as Rolf Harris' popular song of the 1960s, 'Tie Me Kangaroo Down, Sport':

Tan me hide when I'm dead, Fred,
Tan me hide when I'm dead;
So we tanned his hide when he died, Clyde,
And that's it hangin' in the shed!'

Similarly, protest at an intractable environment is parodied in John O'Brien's famous poem 'Said Hanrahan', in Chad Morgan's hillbilly chronicle of catacylsm 'The Fatal Wedding', and in Elizabeth Jolley's 'Neighbour Woman on the Fencing Wire':

So you've bought this place well let me tell you straight away your soil's no good all salt even a hundred and sixty feet down and up on the slopes is outcrops of granite and dead stumps of dead wood nothing'll grow there we know we've tried what the crows don't take the rabbits and bandicoots will have . . .

Just as in the tall story absurd fantasy is balanced against undercutting irony, so in graphic art and comic fiction a sense of bleak confrontation between individuals and intractable circumstances often erupts into outbursts of riotous disorder. The most famous cartoon produced in Australia appeared in *Smith's Weekly* during the Depression and depicted two workmen, one hanging from a girder high above a city street, while the other, grabbing his mate round the ankles in an attempt to save himself and pulling down his trousers in the process, looks upwards overcome with laughter as the first man implores, 'For gorsake sake stop laughing—this is serious!' Although it embodies the notion 'you can't win' (which Vane Lindesay the historian of black-

and-white cartoons, has seen as the essential theme of Australian graphic humour), this is offset by the anarchic absurdity of indecent exposure in public with its accompanying emotions of embarrassment and derision. The explosions of farce, anarchy or absurdity, however, generally subside, leaving everything much as it was before. It is a similar pattern to the way so many nineteenth-century bush workers punctuated long spells of abstinence with spectacular bouts of drunkenness—a refuge against the harshness of daily existence and a means of anarchic protest against it.

In Lawson's 'The Loaded Dog', Dave Regan, Jim Bently and Andy Page, attempting to extract gold at Stony Creek, are pitted against a starkly alienating landscape. Rock is blasted away to reveal still greater emptiness, 'an ugly pot-hole in the bottom of the shaft', and a yield of useless rubbish, 'half a barrow-load of broken rock'. Fishing in the creek proves equally unrewarding, and the 'formidable bomb' Andy hopes will blast fish from the water is, like the 'rich reef' believed to exist in the vicinity, another deluding fantasy of the imagination. Riot and anarchy enter the story when Tommy the retriever runs off with the cartridge in his mouth, letting the fuse catch fire. The inevitable explosion is anticipated in wild scatterings of people—first with Andy, Jim and Dave, then with Dave, the dog still joyfully pursuing him, runs into the local pub and sends the drinkers flying out—and finally erupts with the gathering of neighbourhood dogs violently dispersed into the scrub. Tommy represents both vital energy and the mindless absurdity of existence, his lashing tail equated with the live fuse of the cartridge 'swishing in all directions and burning, and spluttering and stinking'. Although his mad spurt of energy is potentially lethal, it nevertheless challenges the bitter, unyielding pattern of the men's daily lives. Everything eventually settles down to normal, but for a brief period the empty, desolate location of Stony Creek bursts into life. Often in comedy, the collapse of formal order into anarchy provides a saturnalian release, charging ordinary life with renewed energy, but the outbursts of anarchic disorder characterising so much Australian humour are generally less celebratory, not so much a reaffirmation of order as reminders of how precariously it is maintained.

John Docker, pointing to a 'carnivalesque' element in Australian culture where accepted social and family hierarchies are often over-turned, refers to 'our fertile tradition of admired outlawed figures'. In 'Waltzing Matilda', the swagman hero defies the forces of authority represented by squatter and troopers. But it is surely significant that the swagman drowns, and that only a ghostly voice utters defiance from the billabong. Would the song be so dearly cherished had he triumphed over the squatter and escaped with his stolen jumbuck? Although Australians appreciate irreverence, its implications make them nervous. Even that young larrikin, Ginger Meggs, is firmly ensconced within a safe, coherent middle-class world. Outside the home he is often at odds with but ultimately accepts the values of his gang—and the gang is violent, anti-intellectual, deals harshly with nonconformists, duplicating authority structures found in society at large. An older larrikin, C. J. Dennis' Ginger Mick, 'a man uv vierlence . . . an' 'andy wiv a brick', who sees no reason to fight 'so toffs kin dine / On pickled olives', ends up at the front in World War I, revelling in a sense of national identity—'the reel, ribuck Australia's ere'. Although he boasts that class distinctions have become meaningless, merged in a larger patriotism, he tries 'fer a stripe to fill in time', is made a corporal 'cos they trust me', and wins the epitaph 'gallant gentleman'. The rebel, although absorbed within the social hierarchy, must be killed off because his existence is impossible back home: 'Yeh'll ave to face the ole tame life'.

Oral culture contributes significantly to our humour, and much Australian idiom reveals wry irony, blended or contrasted with fantasy and riotousness, generally expressed through energetic outbursts of abuse and profanity. In early convict usage, bread which contained more chaff than flour was a 'scrubbing brush', and 'wearing a red shirt' described a back lacerated from flogging. A black eye was a 'Botany Bay coat of arms', freed convicts were 'Botany Bay swells', and the rocky outcrop in Sydney Harbour where recalcitrant convicts were kept in solitary confinement on a diet of bread and water was named Pinchgut Island. Similar irony pervades modern prison slang, where a regular employee is a 'cut-lunch commando', payday is 'eagle shit day' and a policewoman is a 'dickless tracy'. Our vernacular really comes into its own in flights of abuse where irreverence and anarchic energy have full reign, as in Ned Kelly's Jerilderie letter of 1879 when he denounces

> the brutal and cowardly conduct of a parcel of big ugly fat-necked wombat headed big bellied magpie legged narrow hipped splay footed sons of Irish Bailiffs or English landlords which is better known as officers of Justice or Victorian Police . . .

The same spirit was displayed by a St Kilda supporter at a VFL match denouncing the referee as 'You rotten bloody commo poofter mongrel bastard', or by the Captain of the Push in the invective he unleashes in the famous bawdy poem as he curses the Bastard from the Bush.

Australians early developed a reputation for swearing. Alexander Majoribanks in his *Travels in New South Wales* (1847) was horrified by the constant use of the word 'bloody', calculating that one bullocky would, through a fifty-year life of swearing, 'have pronounced this disgusting word no less than 18,200,000 times'. It becomes clear how deeply rooted in a profane vernacular much Australian humour is when reading the work of nineteenth-century writers. Lawson resorted to dashes, to euphemisms like 'blanky' or 'crimson', while Furphy in *Such is Life* (1903) used an elaborate code to indicate just which word readers should have in mind at any particular point. Skilful manipulation of the profane vernacular was crucial to the success of Roy Rene, perhaps our greatest stage comic, just as nowadays it is fundamental to the routines of comedians such as Kevin Bloody Wilson. In Gough Whitlam's address to the Canberra branch of the Australian Labor Party in 1974 there is an enjoyment similar to that which Furphy must have experienced in manipulating the subtle range of nuances certain expletives can assume:

> I do not mind the Liberals, still less do I mind the Country Party, calling me a bastard. In some circumstances I am only doing my job if they do. But I hope you will not publicly call me a bastard as some bastards in the Caucus have.

A reputation for profanity has also inspired in some Australians a curious mixture of conscious pride and self-mockery. Such usage may be disarmingly innocent, as in Randolph Stow's *The Merry-Go-Round in the Sea* (1965) when Rob Cordan as a child asks Harry the rouseabout whether 'shit' is a dirty word: ' "Shit," said Harry, dropping the axe, "where did you kids pick that up?" ' In theory swearing is deplored while indulged in freely and almost unconsciously at all levels of our society, so that a parliamentarian can assert in the House of Representatives: 'I never use the word "bloody" because it is unparliamentary. It is a word that I never bloody well use.'

Australian humour, like our culture, has tended to be heavily male-oriented, and many characteristic jokes, colloquialisms and one-liners have been generated within the male group. Olga Masters reveals a keen ear for the different ways men and women shape their stories, as she describes how men waiting in a barber's shop eagerly observe a chance meeting between a fellow customer and his former lover:

> Grace had something to show old Charlie, no doubt about that! The only
> difference was he had seen it before. He'd love to see it again though,
> simply love to see it, make no mistake about that! They got the story
> ordered and ready for the first group of yarning males they could join.

Women, perceived as at best outsiders, and at worst the enemy, have
been the butt of innumerable jokes: 'No kids, dogs or women in this
bar.' In *The Glass Canoe* (1976) David Ireland reveals the resentment
many women have felt at their peripheral status, as he portrays the
hostility of wives and girlfriends toward the regulars drinking at the
local pub. After one of the drinkers has died and the others have
attended his funeral, a woman comes into the bar holding something
in her hand:

> 'Listen to me, you useless lot! I'm Missus Mott. We had Fred's funeral
> today. When he was alive he spent all his time with you always down here
> in the pub, so you can have him now!'

And she scatters her husband's ashes over the startled drinkers.
Women, often represented as 'God's police', are identified with the
forces of domestic respectability which the world of male solidarity
delights to challenge. In Lennie Lower's *Here's Luck* (1930) the hero
Jack Gudgeon, abandoned by his wife, forms a precarious alliance
with his eighteen-year-old son, and in a series of drunken binges they
set about demolishing the family home, a deeply symbolic destruction
recorded with mingled triumph and despair. Female sexuality is a
further threat to male camaraderie and achievement. Barry Oakley's
satiric hero in *A Salute to The Great McCarthy* (1970) fights a losing
battle against the oppressive power of various father figures who
frustrate his career as a footballer, but it is women who ultimately
undermine him—'Lois inhuman, Vera obsessed, Miss Russell in a state
of earnest dedication'—and marriage to the rich bitch Andrea eventually destroys his sporting career. 'Bums to mums', the instruction of
sporting coaches that team members refrain from sex the night before
a match, is more a demand for ritual purity than a genuine requirement for top performance.

Women attempting to enter or assert themselves within the male
world are dismissed as monstrous and absurd. The heroine of *Crocodile Dundee*, rejecting Dundee's assertion that, as a sheila, she cannot

cope in the bush on her own, is nearly devoured by a crocodile as punishment for her attempt at independence. Like St George rescuing his princess from the dragon, her bushman protector despatches the crocodile by plunging that very phallic knife through its head. The beast represents not only the perils theatening the heroine but with its cavernous fanged mouth, the very image of a *vagina dentata*, it also symbolises female dominance and self-assertion. In sequels to *On Our Selection* Dave's ferocious mother-in-law gets the better of Dad in what amounts to a stand-up fight and Steele Rudd derides Sarah and Nora Rudd as dried-up old maids. Sarah is even mocked for restricting male freedom by her not unreasonable desire to impose rudimentary standards of politeness on her family as she checks Joe for drinking milk straight from the jug or for throwing rather than passing the bread. More recently, suburbia, not the bush, has become the prime domain of termagants like Sarah Meggs or Patrick White's Mrs Jolley and Mrs Flack. Edna Everage, embodiment of prurient puritanism and repressive social control, whose career has escalated from housewife to superstar, is perhaps the greatest domestic monster of all—a destroyer, responsible for her husband Norm's 'dicky prostate', little Kenny's homosexuality and the domestic neurosis suffered by daughter Vamai, 'the fattest anorexic in the world'.

Barry Humphries' creation reflects the deep hostility to women so persistently present in Australian culture. How do women respond to assumptions that Sarah Rudd and Edna Everage are their representatives? Sumner Locke's answer to 'Dad' Rudd was 'Mum' Dawson who in *Mum Dawson, 'Boss'* (1911) and other selection sketches has no option but to manage her layabout husband. As for Edna, Dorothy Hewett in *Bon-bons and Roses for Dolly* (1976) has created Ollie, alter ego of her heroine Dolly, who carries around with her a puppet, a limp, life-size rag doll, representing her husband, addressed as Mate. But the satire, as savage as anything in Humphries, is directed not at women but at the social conditions and expectations which make monsters of them:

> But I was a bit of a girl in the ol'days, wasn't I, Mate? I had a figure all right. Marilyn Monroe of the twenties. And so fertile. Nothing wrong with my plumbing. Aborting meself every month with the knitting needle for a while there. I remember I useta keep them in the fridge to show you when you come home. Upset you a bit the first coupla times, specially when you could tell the sex. You went quite pale. You always did have a queasy stomach, Mate.

Mary Leunig reveals in her cartoons how the suburban home, so frequently perceived as restricting male freedom, is even more imprisoning for women. Her housewives, snapped at by ferocious domestic appliances and furniture red in tooth and claw, endure desperate mutilation there.

In graphic art humour and satire often merge, while words and pictures frequently complement one another. Elizabeth Webby has pointed out a causal connection between word and picture to account in part for the prevalence of colonial verse satire: before local newspapers and magazines were illustrated, satire in Australia might be said to have begun with the 'pipes', the anonymous, scurrilous verses which were occasionally circulated in Sydney during the early years of settlement and lampooned government figures such as Hunter, King and Macquarie. The authors, where known, were mainly free subjects such as Wentworth but one famous convict satire against the forces of authority passed into oral tradition and survived into the twentieth century: 'A Convict's Tour to Hell', a tour of the underworld by 'Frank the Poet', where he discovers that not only notorious penal administrators such as Logan and Darling are suffering grievous punishment:

> Cook who discovered New South Wales
> And he that first invented gaols
> Are both tied to a fiery stake
> Which stands in yonder burning lake
> Hark do you hear this dreadful yelling
> It issues from Doctor Wardell's dwelling
> And all those fiery seats and chairs
> Are fitted up for Dukes and Mayors
> And nobles of Judicial orders
> Barristers, lawyers and recorders.

At the end of the poem, just after Frank is admitted into Heaven, he wakes to find he has been dreaming. 'A Convict's Tour to Hell' was probably written at Stroud in northern New South Wales in 1839, which would place it at the beginning of a decade regarded as a high point in Australian satiric writing. Robert Lowe's 'Songs of the Squatters' and satires on the ill-advised Gladstone colony in Queensland, William Foster's 'The Devil and the Governor' (anti-Gipps) and 'The Genius and the Ghost' (anti-transportation), some of Charles Harpur's most pungent satire, and Edward Kemp's *A Voice from*

Tasmania (1846) were all published in the 1840s, when a range of political issues provoked the colonists of New South Wales and Van Diemen's Land. A second peak might be found in the decade or so before Federation. Henry Kendall's final volume of verse, *Songs from the Mountains* published in 1880, originally contained 'The Song of Ninian Melville', which within a few weeks was expunged to prevent a feared legal reaction and replaced with 'Christmas Creek', a sentimental tribute to the explorers. The suppression of 'The Song of Ninian Melville' is emblematic perhaps of the process by which the public poetry of the nineteenth century subsequently became a hidden tradition, with a corresponding undervaluation of the satiric dimension in the work of Harpur, Kendall and subsequent writers such as Lawson and Daley.

The year 1880 also saw the founding of the *Bulletin*, which in its first couple of years had as theatrical and society columnist Theodore Argles, 'the Pilgrim', of whom the *Bulletin*'s co-founder John Haynes wrote, 'There never was a more polished satirical writer in Australia.' Had he lived longer, the Pilgrim must surely have faced stiff competition from later *Bulletin* writers. These included John Farrell, who helped promote the journal's opposition to cant and humbug and whose long poem 'My Sundowner' is an underestimated Gothic parody. There were also Lawson, Paterson and the other contributors (themselves satirised in David McKee Wright's recently available 'Apollo in George Street') to the *Bulletin* verse debate of 1892 over the right way to represent bush life. Another challenger was Victor Daley, the Pilgrim's best mate in the early 1880s, who, as the century ended, was still confronting the *Bulletin* management and the limitations of Australian culture in poems such as 'Corregio Jones' and 'Narcissus and Some Tadpoles'. And just as in our day Patrick Cook creates political satire through a variety of media—cartoon and performance as well as column and script—so the *Bulletin*, in its heyday, assailed its targets through such columns as 'Pepper and Salt' and 'Aboriginalities' and through its cartoons and illustrations (which also helped to consolidate black-and-white art in Australia) as well as by means of the verse satires which it published. Its most prolific cartoonist was Livingston Hopkins, 'Hop', who contributed 19,000 drawings to the journal and whose satiric interpretation of the politicians, symbolic figures like the Little Boy from Manly (a representation first of New South Wales, later Australia) and allegorical animals did much to explain the *Bulletin* credo. His contemporaries and successors included David Low and Will Dyson, who both won an international reputation as political cartoonists, and several who were on hand to contribute to that other great Australian comic paper *Smith's Weekly* when it began publication in 1919.

Philip Neilsen has suggested in *The Penguin Book of Australian Satirical Verse* (1986) that there is in the twentieth century no longer a sense of satiric verse as a separate genre and that satiric verse has become absorbed within the mainstream of poetry. If this is so perhaps it is why writers such as Dennis, Goodge and even Lower and Stivens tend to be classified as 'humorists'. Is there a contemporary Australian satirist? David Foster, whose rich and savage indictment of imperialism, *Moonlite* (1981), has been followed by other satiric novels such as *Plumbum* (1983) and *Dog Rock* (1985), is one, yet for other Australian writers the label is confining; what can more accurately be said is that their work, like that of Harpur and Kendall, has a satiric dimension. And the targets? Frequent aim is taken at suburbia in its various manifestations, from the gentle melancholy of David Malouf's 'Safe behind lawns and blondwood doors, in houses / of glass. No one throws stones' to the sharp-edged attacks of A. D. Hope on a society where sexual passion—'Time payment calculating / Upon the bedroom suite'—is stifled in a 'box of brick', and brides roll off the assembly line, 'a miracle of design':

> He will find every comfort: the full set
> Of gadgets; knobs that answer to the touch
> For light or music; a place for his cigarette;
> Room for his knees; a honey of a clutch

Despite the existence of much barbed Australian satire, the most important distinguishing characteristic of our humour is irony. It may be goodhumoured dismissal, as in the story told by one Australian academic of how, when he was a young man, the battered old car he was driving ran out of petrol, and he discovered to his dismay he had only two shillings on him. Putting as good a face on things as possible, he drove into a service station and asked firmly for two bob's worth of petrol, to receive the reply, 'What are you trying to do? *Wean* the bastard?' Often the effect is considerably bleaker, as in the story of an old bagman tramping across a station property when the owner appears and offers him a lift in his utility truck only to receive the response, 'No flamin fear! You open yer own gates.' The bagman may represent an attitude of sturdy independence, or he may signify a figure isolated and driven in upon himself to the point of apathy and greatly limited capacity to respond to experience.

Alongside the bleak, reductive note in Australian humour is an element of fantasy and exuberance expressed in the exaggerations of the tall story and the inventiveness of our idiom. Exclamations about weather so hot it's a hundred in the waterbag, or drought country you couldn't flog a flea over, contain within them the seeds of more elaborate inventions like the story of a stockman who sent his dog after a strayed bullock, waiting patiently for years until the animal returned with a boot in his mouth, the leather marked with the brand on the hide of the lost beast. Abuse and invective also generate their own kind of comic energy—'May your chooks turn into emus and kick your dunny over'—and the abundant profanity of vernacular speech, with its mingled exuberance and defiance, can have a similar effect.

Generally, however, while bleak irony and anarchic exuberance are played off one against the other, in the end, irony prevails. A fatalistic vision of life infused with protest culminating in an outburst of disorder which changes nothing is the basic pattern of Australian humour. Fatalism undermines protest, so that no matter how vigorous or absurd the eruptions of comic disorder, everything remains as it was before. For all its deflationary, irreverent quality, Australian humour is usually an acknowledgement of the status quo.

Notes

The Australian idoms cited in the chapter are taken from Sidney Baker, *The Australian Language* (1966), Bill Hornadge, *The Australian Slanguage* (1980), Nancy Keesing, *Lily on the Dustbin* (1982), G. A. Wilkes, *A Dictionary of Australian Colloquialisms* (1978), and, for the prison slang, Ryan Aven-Bray, *Ridgey Didge Oz Jack Lang* (1983). Hornadge is also a source for several of the jokes, and some of the other humorous stories and sayings are taken from Baker and from the compilations of the folklorist Bill Wannan, including *The Australian* (1958) and *The Great Australian Book of Insults* (1982). Vane Lindesay's *The Inked-In Image* (2nd edn, 1979) which discusses 'For gorsake stop laughing' is a major survey of Australian cartoons. *The Golden Years of Ginger Meggs* (1978) reprints a selection of that comic strip from 1921-52, and Mary Leunig's work is collected in *There's No Place Like Home* (1982) and *A Piece of Cake* (1986). 'The Dying Stockman' can be found in Ron Edwards' *The Big Book of Australian Folk Song* (1976). *Australian Film 1900-77* (1980) by Andrew Pike and Ross Cooper is the standard reference work on the Australian cinema. A sample of the routines of comedians such as Roy Rene is included in *The Australian Stage: A Documentary History* (1984), edited by Harold Love. *Nellie Melba, Ginger Meggs and Friends*, Susan Dermody, John Docker and Drusilla Modjeska eds (1982) has a chapter on Ginger Meggs by Barry Andrews, while John Meredith and Rex Whalan have written the biographical *Frank the Poet* (1979). Sylvia Lawson's *The Archibald Paradox* (1983) and Patricia Rolfe's *The Journalistic Javelin* (1980) are indispensable for a study of the *Bulletin*.

Among the quotations and sources not already identified, the quotations from Lawson are taken from Colin Roderick's edition, *The Master Story-Teller: Prose Writings* (1984); Murray Bail's 'The Drover's Wife' appears in *Contemporary Portraits and Other Stories* (1975), Frank Moorhouse's in *Room Service* (1985), and Barbara Jefferis' in the *Bulletin*, 23-30 December 1980; Moorhouse talks of the influence of the bush in his *A Steele Rudd Selection* (1986); Marcus Clarke's comments on the bush form part of his preface to the 1876 edition of Adam Lindsay Gordon's *Sea Spray and Smoke Drift*.

The major sources for the Speewah tales, which are an important element in the humour of the *Australasian Post*, are Alan Marshall's *How's Andy Going?* and Bill Wannan's *Crooked Mick of the Speewah* (both 1956); Cabbage-tree Ned appears in Dal Stivens' *Ironbark Bill* (1955); 'Saltbush Bill' is included in *Singer of the Bush: A. B. 'Banjo' Paterson Collected Works, 1885-1900*, Rosamund Campbell and Philippa Harvie eds (1983); Judith Wright contrasts city and rural values in *Preoccupations in Australian Poetry* (1965); Les Murray's 'The Quality of Sprawl' is included in *The People's Otherworld* (1983), John O'Brien's 'Said Hanrahan' in *Around the Boree Log* (1921), Chad Morgan's 'The Fatal Wedding' in *Sheilas, Drongos, Dills & Other Geezers: 20 Chad Morgan Greats* (EMI Play 1006), Elizabeth Jolley's 'Neighbour Woman on the Fencing Wire' in *The Penguin Book of Australian Women Poets*, Susan Hampton and Kate Llewellyn eds (1986), and Ned Kelly's Jerilderie Letter in Graham Seal's *Ned Kelly in Popular Tradition* (1980); John Docker, adapting Bakhtin, points to a carnivalesque element in Australian culture in 'Antipodean Literature: A World Upside Down?', *Overland*, 103 (1986); the quotations from C. J. Dennis are taken from *Selected Verse* (1956), Alec Chisholm ed., the St Kilda supporter's abuse appears in Leonie Sandercock and Ian Turner, *Up Where, Cazaly? The Great Australian Game* (1981); 'The Bastard from the Bush' is published in Don Laycock's anthology *The Best Bawdry* (1982).

The fight between Dad and Dave's mother-in-law, Mrs White, and the derision of Sarah and Norah Rudd, occur in *Sandy's Selection* (1904) and *Back at Our Selection* (1906); the Edna Everage quotations are from *The Humour of Barry Humphries* (1984), comp. John Allen, and *Dame Edna's Bedside Book* (1984); Elizabeth Webby discusses illustrated periodicals in *Cross Currents*, (1981) ed. Bruce Bennett (1981), and has also compiled a bibliography of Australian poetry before 1850 (1982); John Haynes' assessment of Argles appears in *The Archibald Paradox*; 'Apollo in George Street' is discussed by Michael Sharkey and published in *Australian Literary Studies*, 12 (1986); David Malouf's 'Suburban' is included in *Bicycle and Other Poems* (1970); A. D. Hope's 'The Brides' and 'The Lingam and the Yoni' in *Collected Poems, 1930-1965* (1966).

There is extensive incidental discussion of Australian humour in histories of Australian literature and culture but few discrete studies; one such, and a source for this chapter, is Dorothy Jones' 'Winning and Losing: Australian Humour', in *Comic Relations: Studies in the Comic, Satire and Parody* (1985), Pavel Petr, David Roberts and Phillip Thomson eds. Similarly, there are only one or two general anthologies of humour including Bill Wannan's *A Treasury of Australian Humour* (1960), although Barry Humphries (*The Austral Book of Innocent & Garden Verse*, 1968), Geoffrey Lehmann (*Comic Australian Verse*, 1972) and Philip Neilsen (*The Penguin Book of Australian Satirical Verse*, 1986) have compiled verse anthologies (Humphries of unintentionally comic verse) and the surveys by Lindesay above and Ryan (*Panel by Panel*, 1979) contain numerous examples of humourous graphic art. *Meanjin*, 2 (1986) is a special issue of that journal devoted to Australian humour; it includes a story by Peter Mathers, one of the regrettable omissions from this chapter. Others include Henry Savery, Daniel Deniehy, Xavier Herbert and the radio coverage of humour. Also, although this chapter has sought to examine the role of women as objects and creators of Australian humour, this subject requires more extensive exploration than space here has permitted.

Chapter 5

FORMS OF AUSTRALIAN LITERARY HISTORY

PETER PIERCE

How fixed the commonplaces of Australian literary history are: the achievements of the national literature have been linked, and confused, with social change; political chronologies have been muddled with literary ones; the organic metaphor ('coming of age') has been persistently employed as though it was a method of causal explanation; the election, or suppression, of certain authors has been a feature of bitter sectional disputes concerning the canon of Australian literature, a corollary of which is the resuscitation of 'forgotten' authors and periods. Most importantly, a nationalist interpretation—whether endorsed or regretted—has dominated the writing of literary history here.

Accordingly, it might seem best to begin this analysis of the earnest hopes and tiresome vendettas that have distinguished Australian literary historiography with Frederick Sinnett's 1856 essay, 'The Fiction Fields of Australia'. That would be an instructive mistake. Several years before Nathaniel Hawthorne disingenuously complained—in a preface to *The Marble Faun* (1860)—of the paucity of materials for romance fiction in America, 'a country where there is no shadow, no antiquity, no mystery, no picturesque and gloomy wrong', Sinnett conceded that Australian novelists to come (for the fields he surveyed as yet had yielded little) would be

> quite debarred from all the interest to be extracted from any kind of archaeological accessories. No storied windows, richly dight, cast a dim, religious light over any Australian premises . . .

The catalogue of absences (in itself one of the key commonplaces of Australian literary commentary) sprily continued, though in a spirit that implied—not dearth—but the many opportunities that lay before Australian authors to whom these meretricious contrivances were not available. The literary history that Sinnett wished would come into being was one not bothered by immediate lack of genius (after all, 'It is only once in many years that there steps forth from among the many millions of the British people a novelist able to break new ground') nor one that was 'too Australian' (he complained of the tendency towards 'travel books in disguise'). Sinnett's hopes were notably unrealised. Complaints of the non-arrivals of 'Austral Miltons' or premature discoveries of them distinguished the literary histories that followed his. So did the impulse to discern and invent national qualities for the national literature.

Sinnett concluded his essay by goodhumouredly remarking that

> we believe it is found among farmers generally that nothing stimulates agriculture more than the exhibition of good specimens of agricultural produce, and we hope like benefit may be produced by like means with respect to cultivation of a less material kind.

Here the organic metaphor is playfully employed. In *Southern Lights and Shadows* (1859), Frank Fowler spoke seriously of 'the precious and malleable stuff' in the Australian soil which ought to be able to fertilise a literary crop. Many decades later, literary historians were more in earnest about the organic metaphor (or less aware that they were using it) than Sinnett apparently was. Thus John K. Ewers, surveying *Creative Writing in Australia* (1945) observed that 'the Novel Begins to Grow Up'; Heddle and Millington described *How Australian Literature Grew* (1962); Tom Inglis Moore traced 'the development of the national literature' from 'a period of infancy' towards 'national maturity' in *Social Patterns in Australian Literature* (1971); Eunice Hanger declared that 'the realistic play came of age in Australia with the success of Ray Lawler's *Summer of the Seventeenth Doll*' (she did so in an essay in the first edition of the collection of essays edited by Geoffrey Dutton, *The Literature of Australia*, 1964).

How is it possible to account for the pervasiveness of this metaphor in literary historiography? In his conclusion to *A Literary History of Canada* (1965), Northrop Frye urged that 'Cultural history . . . has its own rhythms. It is possible one of these rhythms is very like an organic rhythm.' In his essay 'Literature, History and Literary History' (1976), Brian Kiernan argued that the romantic movement fostered early expectations of a national literature in Australia, while later in the nineteenth century, evolutionary ideas were applied to the 'prospects' of a new literature in Australia; gauges of its progress were eagerly sought. There is a political aspect to this issue as well. Many commentators, seeking with difficulty contexts in which to read, remember and foretell Australian literature, have accepted the imperial assumption that colonial literatures on the periphery of metropolitan (in this case British) culture make a progression in literature parallel to a desirable one in politics. That is, they eventually come of age. Such a patronising assumption underlies what A. D. Hope decreed as a law of the development of national literatures (in his essay, 'A Second-Rate Literature', 1954), collected in *Native Companions* (1974): that a first stage of slavish emulation of the parent literature is succeeded by the stridencies of nationalist assertion, then at last by the arrival on the international stage. The contamination of a *literary* history by such political analogies and time-spans as the organic metaphor uses is one of its problems. Refusal to allow the career of the metaphor (and the literature) to continue logically to senescence and death is another. But it is the durability of the metaphor as a device of pseudo-explanation of literary history in Australia that is most important. The connection between Australian nationalism and the national literature was supposed to be at stake. This why G. B. Barton is a truer, though less amusing progenitor of Australian literary history than Frederick Sinnett.

Barton's *Literature in New South Wales* and *The Poets and Prose Writers of New South Wales* were published in 1866 as Australian contributions to the Paris Exhibition. Barton hoped that his histories would allow readers 'to form an exact idea of the progress, extent and prospects of literary enterprise among us'; would 'constitute a bibliographical account that might be practically useful'; would 'throw some light, from a new point of view, on our social history' and finally 'preserve the memory, and give some notion of the achievement of men whose names could hardly be expected to survive their generation'. The two books are essentially literary annals, rather than literary history. They present the names, some biographical details and selected quotations from the works of several dozen authors. Not that Barton's books are quaint relics of the pre-history of literary historiography in Australia. A good deal of *The Oxford History of Australian Literature* (1981), a work conventionally divided into 'Fiction', 'Poetry' and 'Drama' sections each by a different author, together with a bibliography, consisted of sketchy, chronological listings of authors, strewn with evaluations.

The vexed matter of the 'double standard' of critical judgement of Australian literature (that is, the application of a less rigorous standard of judgement to Australian than to European literature) was foreshadowed in Barton's comparisons with 'the productions of the Mother Country'. Much later, the danger of 'an involuntary lowering of standard' of literary judgement would exercise H. M. Green in *An Outline of Australian Literature* (1930). Barton's earnest measurement of the progress of Australian literature looked forward to nationalist literary historiography, as did his hope that literary history might illuminate social history.

Editors and historians of Australian literature from Barton's day until the end of the nineteenth century tended to conceive their chief responsibility as the introduction of the novelties of that literature both to a local and to an international public. Hybrid works of criticism, biography and anthology resulted, in the manner of Barton's *The Poets and Prose Writers of New South Wales*. (More than a century later, James McAuley's *A Map of Australian Verse* (1975) would be such a hybrid, though an elegant one.) Douglas Sladen prefaced *A Century of Australian Song* (1888) equivocally:

> Australia is the country of the future . . . This volume is essentially the work of people who have meditated in the open air and not under the lamp; and if its contents sometimes want the polish that comes only with much midnight oil, they are mostly a transcript from earth and sea and sky, and not from books.

Most of the rest of Sladen's preliminaries gave brief accounts of the lives of the authors whose works he included. These were attended by circumspect critical judgements. Sladen showed himself to be sensible both of the effects of conditions of publication—'the task of the editors of the great weekly papers'—of 'the character of Australian poetry' and of the influence of recent English and American poets. Some of the latter, he noted, had been mediated by Gordon and Kendall.

A decade afterwards, and still equivocally, Henry Gyles Turner and Alexander Sutherland considered the extent of *The Development of Australian Literature* (1898). They opened with a lament which—in a later year—would have been regarded as cringing:

> even if our history had been pregnant with the sublimest material, instead of hopelessly commonplace, we have, by the very nature of our surroundings, been precluded from developing the local Motley or Macaulay.

Their survey of Australian poetry commenced with a version of the organic metaphor, though one which had drifted some distance from talk of fertile soils and mineral wealth, towards a more pessimistic view of the ecology of Australian literature:

> There are little verdant oases, even in this wilderness, where genuine poetic aspirations and cultured poetic insight work together for good, and blossom into sweet song.

Like Barton's two works in their cautious solicitude for Australian literature, Turner's and Sutherland's study also anticipated salient features of the later course of literary histories of Australia. Biography mingled with criticism, and nervous comparisons were made with European literary tradition. They wrote of some lines by Thomas Heney that 'To apply the majestic style of Homer to such as the following is to court failure'. The lumping of disparate authors into manageably labelled groups was another frequent practice in *The Development of Australian Literature*. Thus A. B. Paterson, Henry Lawson, John Farrell and Edward Dyson were said to have 'all graduated in the same school, that of journalism, and the Sydney *Bulletin* was their nursing mother'. For the first time, Ada Cambridge, Rosa Praed and Jessie Couvreur ('Tasma') were coerced into association (though Turner and Sutherland also recognised Mary Gaunt and Ethel Turner among women writers of the late nineteenth century). Such lumping of authors, under various descriptive titles, continues to be the resort and bane of single-volume histories, as in Ken Goodwin's *A History of Australian Literature* (1986).

The remainder of the study by Turner and Sutherland—and its larger part—comprised biographical sketches of Adam Lindsay Gordon, Henry Kendall and Marcus Clarke. Here is Australian literary history in perhaps its dominant mode—as *catalogue raisonné*. The last of the biographical sketches attested to the eerie ability of Australian literary historians (then and now) to influence one another's judgements, to concur about narrowing the terms of debate, whatever differences of evaluation there might be. Sinnett's complaint of antipodean absences, drained of its humour, is behind Turner's remarks on the fiction of Clarke:

> Romance cannot consort with newness. A country without an ivy-clad ruin cannot rear a people who may be expected to believe in ghosts; and the

lone watcher in the moated grange, with its moss-coated flower-pots, would be terribly *de trop* in a weather-board hut with a paling fence.

The lonely, maverick refutation of such a view would come with P. R. Stephensen's *The Foundations of Culture in Australia* (1936):

> for us, each decade of our history is packed with love and legend and significant national experience. A decade of our own history is more important to us than a century of history from elsewhere.

From one aspect, H. M. Green's *An Outline of Australian Literature* (1930) and his *A History of Australian Literature* (1961) which followed it much later, are a culmination of nineteenth-century Australian literary historiography. Green's influence in the present century is then the more pointed and ironic. In the first chapter of his *Outline*, Green was categorical: 'The literature of a country is obviously an expression of characteristic qualities of its life.' Since this much was obvious to him, Green addressed the term 'Australian literature' with an amiable circularity: 'every work which can be considered a genuine expression of any aspect of Australian characteristics or ideals has been treated as Australian'. Green listed some of these national 'qualities' which 'seem to exist in solution, strong or weak, in most Australian literary work'. After vague references to 'vigour and freshness, crudity'—predictable features of the literature of a young country—Green concentrated on 'certain other qualities which are only in part literary': 'an independence of spirit, a kind of humorous disillusion, a careless willingness to take a risk, a slightly sardonic good nature and a certain underlying hardness of texture.'

The influence of Green's *Outline* on works so seminal and controversial in their turn as Russel Ward's *The Australian Legend* (1958), and on the whole climate of the historiography of Australian literature, cannot be exaggerated. Green's insistence on the inseparability of Australian national qualities (as he perceived them, sentimentally perhaps) from the history of the national literature that he sought to write signally influenced the discussion thereafter of that literature and its relations with the wider history of Australia. The much touted, if imprecisely conceived split between 'radical nationalists' and 'universalists' or 'New Critics' (as John Docker polemically and inaccurately called them in *In a Critical Condition*, 1984) which coincided with political fissures in Australian society of the 1950s was a major issue of debate arising from Green's contentions, although it should be remembered that these had been anticipated by the American critic Hartley Grattan in his *Australian Literature* (1929). In the first camp were ranged Vance Palmer, Ward, A. A. Phillips, Geoffrey Serle, Docker; in the second, Vincent Buckley, Leonie Kramer, G. A. Wilkes, H. P. Heseltine. Despite attempts at revision and redirection of debate on Australian literary history, the terms that Green crystallised have not been significantly disturbed.

The contribution of Green's contemporary, P. R. Stephensen, also needs emphasis. *The Foundations of Culture in Australia* ventilated and anticipated the main channels of debate about literary history in this country after World War II, whose advent Stephensen had dreaded despite his ambivalence concerning its possible consequences. Stephensen insisted on the relationship between literary achievement and the political climate; decreed the need for a national literary canon—'the talismanic works which endow us with a national idea'; supported a democratic and nationalist orientation and temper in Australian literature (without dismissing as malign international influences upon it); and promoted—though the words would be Palmer's—'a legend of the nineties'. These were the major matters upon which Australian literary historians have divided since the 1950s. The division has been fuelled less by extra-literary, political animosities—themselves a pale parallel of the Cold War—than by a history of intra-mural disputes concerning the nature and status of Australian literature.

Since World War II, contributions to Australian literary history have had in common their piecemeal form. Thus Buckley's *Essays in Poetry, Mainly Australian* (1957), Phillips' *The Australian Tradition* (1958), Grahame Johnston's *Australian Literary Criticism* (1962), the two editions (1964, 1976) of Dutton's *The Literature of Australia*, Hope's *The Cave and the Spring* (1965), Chris Wallace-Crabbe's *Melbourne or the Bush* (1974) and Fay Zwicky's *The Lyre in the Pawnshop* (1986) were all collections of essays and reviews. Numbers of these pieces had first appeared in the literary journals established in Australia during and after World War II: *Southerly* in 1939, *Meanjin* in 1940, *Overland* in 1954, *Quadrant* and *Westerly* in 1956. Other essays had been delivered as Commonwealth Literary Fund lectures, notably by A. A. Phillips, whose *The Australian Tradition* (1958) supported the deliberately combative assertion of its title with detailed readings of Australian authors, for example in the essay titled 'The

Craftsmanship of Henry Lawson'. The place of publication had a notable influence on all these contributions to Australian literary history, whether the authors' supposed orientations were radical-nationalist or conservative-Eurocentric. It may also account for their often impressionistic, evaluative temper, irrespective of which side of presumed ideological chasm the essays come from; and it may explain their relative lack of coherent connection when they were published together in book form.

One book with a strikingly misleading reputation for coherence was Palmer's *The Legend of the Nineties* (1954). This alleged classic of the radical-nationalist tradition was both a series of pen portraits (in the old Turner-Sutherland fashion) and a revisionary consideration of whether indeed there had been a *locus classicus* of Australian literary nationalism in the 1890s. Like Green and Phillips, Palmer was not an academic: the more ironic then that their books made unrivalled contributions to subsequent academic debate about Australian literary history. In one response to Palmer, Wallace-Crabbe's essay 'The Legend of "The Legend of the Nineties"' (1982), the suggestion was made that Palmer's title unjustly credited his book with the promotion of such a legend when he was in fact ambivalent towards it. Certainly that memorable title has been a handy prop to the anti-nationalist manoeuvres of such literary historians as G. A. Wilkes, for example in his essay 'The Eighteen Nineties' (1958) and in *Australian Literature: A Conspectus* (1969).

The *Conspectus* was part of the extensive body of postwar revisionary literary history that has been written in Australia (much more extensive, in fact, than the histories published during the nineteenth century and up until World War II by Barton and others, which were presumably the works being revised). Some consideration of the work of several critics can indicate how limited in extent and unexpectedly alike in method these purportedly revisionary literary histories and relevant critical articles have been—for example Wilkes (in the so-called 'universalist' corner); Docker (upholding the old radical-nationalist values and indicting 'the "New Critics"... who fall on the other side of the great divide but are equally desirous of owning the whole continent'); and Wallace-Crabbe (nationalist/neutralist perhaps).

Moreover, these revisionary literary histories are participants in the melodramatic ethos of recent Australian literary history. In this they are true to the melodramatic genius of the national literature—not only in drama but in fiction, from Clarke to Patrick White and

Thomas Keneally and Christina Stead. Here the popular 'play'—running so much to the satisfaction of the actors and small audience that its script scarcely changes—is the story of the persecution and dispossession of the nationalists by the oppressive tolerance of the silky aggression of the Eurocentrics. This literary historiographical melodrama apes the conflicts of convicts against their gaolers, bushrangers against squatters. The 'manners' with which each side conducts its discourse are exaggerated to fit the stereotypes: vernacular speech opposes the accents of Oxbridge. Each side is—of course—less coherent than it has been in the interests of the other to pretend. Crucially, the historical methods of each have a resemblance that there is no interest in disclosing. This melodrama has had a long run. The stasis of Australian literary historiography is a symptom and a consequence of it.

Eventually one of G. A. Wilkes' main achievements as a literary historian may be seen as the investment of the radical nationalist position with more coherence than it had ever itself desired. The second chapter of Wilkes' *Conspectus* was titled 'The Nationalist Period (1880-1920)'. Wilkes concluded (as in similar ways had Palmer and Phillips) that 'the nineties began to have a glow and a radiance about them that even now is hard to dissipate'. But what had created that glow? In his earlier essay 'The Eighteen Nineties', Wilkes mentioned G. A. Taylor's *Those Were the Days* (1918) and Jose's *The Romantic Nineties* (1933). In that essay he spoke of 'another inflating process at work'—the effects on later estimations of the 1890s of 'anecdote and recollection'. From this flimsy evidence that the 1890s had been erected into a crucial literary period (and ignoring Stephensen's contribution), Wilkes moved directly to Palmer's *The Legend of the Nineties*. Wilkes said that it showed how 'the period has become the embodiment of an Australian "myth"', further muddying the waters with the last word. Then he proceeded with the familiar annotated catalogue of the Australian writers in the 'Nationalist Period'. Paterson was installed as the poet of 'the heroic conception of Australia and the Australian that in the nineties became a living myth'. It lived—in the *Conspectus*—by virtue of smooth assertion rather than an argument that admitted qualifications. The 'conventional view of the 1890s' was partly of Wilkes' own construction: he did indeed make a 'myth' (the word that he preferred) of 'the legend of the nineties' in order to belabour the allegedly uncritical 'inflating' proponents of the legend. Few of the so-called proponents were given names.

Wilkes explained that one of the intentions of *The Stockyard and the Croquet Lawn* (1981) was to examine the connections between social and literary histories of Australia, which Barton had hoped for and upon which H. M. Green had insisted. Wilkes regarded as hegemonic the interpretation of 'Australian cultural development . . . in terms of emergent nationalism'. This interpretation, he suggested, proceeded by 'the antithesis of the genteel and the robust, the refined and the crude, the old world and the new, and the contest between them for mastery'. In the course of Australian literary historiography, the habit of 'antithesis' has been tenaciously maintained. As Wilkes justly notes, dualistic and antagonistic perspectives on Australian cultural development have been endemic: colonial and national, national and international, utopian and vitalist (Buckley), vulgarity and refinement (D. R. Burns), land and language (Goodwin) and Wilkes' own ironic contrast of stockyard and croquet lawn. These embattled dichotomies reveal more of the melodramatic temper of Australian literary histories. So many depend upon the perception that one system of value and allegiance is threatened and they choose to define the adversary in as starkly opposed terms as possible. They imply what a fragile, endangered property the national self and some critics' sense of Australian literature, the subject they are professing, are felt to be. This melodramatic taking up of exaggerated positions has had the effect of postponing ways of writing literary history that might eschew dichotomy; might study the subject more purely in literary terms, or in ones less trenchantly politicised.

When he considered the matter of Australian literary history, Chris Wallace-Crabbe declared that 'the lack I feel most strongly is that of good biographies'. The way to deal with the absence of materials to enable effective, or revisionary literary history, he contended, was to supply better texts, more secondary studies, more facts. The genial positivism of this remedy for present stasis had affinities with a Marxist observer of the national literature.

Calling also for more and other facts, names and texts, John Docker attacked the Leavisites and New Critics, whom he carelessly conflated—Buckley, Wilkes, Kramer, Heseltine—because they dominated the critical high places: university syllabuses, literary journals, received literary wisdom. All he was able to advocate was the teaching of a revised syllabus, which would challenge the 'metaphysical' bias, the genteel preferences that he reckoned to have been dominant. Rather than Henry Handel Richardson and Martin Boyd (heroine and hero of the fiction section of *The Oxford History of*

Australian Literature), Docker advanced the claims of Fergus Hume and Louis Stone. His enterprise certainly articulated resentments about the demeanour of academic departments of English: it contains much polemic against the 'universalists' (or New Critics, or metaphysicals . . . melodrama favours incontinent abuse). If one disregards this, one sees affinities with Wilkes, Wallace-Crabbe and the authors of the *Oxford History* in Docker's concern with reclassifying, re-ordering, sometimes adding to the objects for literary historical study.

Consideration of the most recent crop of Australian literary histories confirms the impression that impasse had been reached a while ago, that no thorough-going revision of that history has yet been managed, that old verities, old cruxes of argument are still the preferred terrain. Ken Goodwin's *A History of Australian Literature* (1986) offered comparative contexts with other Commonwealth literature and in general tarted up the old wares well, but without being able to disguise the fact that this was another *catalogue raisonné*. The collections, basically of literary essays, by Dorothy Green, *The Music of Love* (1984) and Fay Zwicky, *The Lyre in the Pawnshop* (1986), contained many locally illuminating arguments, but attempted no cohesive history of Australian literature; this reflected their miscellaneous, uncoordinated origins. Peter Fitzpatrick's excellent survey, *After 'The Doll': Australian Drama Since 1955* (1979), still had the air of treating a genre that has been regarded as not belonging to mainstream literary history in this country. Graeme Turner's *National Fictions* (1986) sought to describe similarities in the narrative procedures of Australian novels and film. With metaphorical boldness, Ross Gibson's *The Diminishing Paradise* (1984) traced how preconceptions of a paradisal *terra australis* were attenuated by experience, until the early explorers gained acquaintance with somewhere closer to purgatory. But the metaphor, of course, is the organic one, describing a progress from adolescent hope to middle-aged disillusion. At least Gibson recognised the importance of these two stages of being, two attitudes to Australian culture, two elements of another of the prevailing dichotomies.

A more coherent recent history (though also a set of essays) was H. P. Heseltine's *The Uncertain Self* (1986). This was the culmination of a long career of revisionist writing, whose earliest landmark had been the essay 'Australian Image: The Literary Heritage' (published in *Meanjin* in 1962). There Heseltine contended that 'Australian literature is historically a Romantic and post-Romantic phenomenon . . . it came much *earlier* than European literature to deal with a number of key themes of late Romantic awareness.' Thus he proposed an international rather than a parochially nationalist context for a history of Australian literature. The dramatic story that he went on to relate was neither one of vernacular, sardonic rebelliousness (the revenge of the stockyard) nor one of exemplary progress towards national maturity. Rather, it was something more melodramatic in its extremity, more lurid and contemporary than other literary historians of Australia had allowed; presided over by Nietzsche, rather than 'Saint Henry—Our Apostle of Mateship' (the title of another of Heseltine's revisionary essays of the 1960s). He argued that

> the fundamental concern of the Australian literary imagination [is] to acknowledge the terror at the basis of being, to explore its uses, and to build defences against its dangers. It is that concern which gives Australia's literary heritage its special force and distinction, which guarantees its continuing modernity.

In the literary history of Australia, proclaimed 'new directions' have been discouragingly lacking in novelty or—as in the case of Heseltine's essay—have represented challenges that have not been accepted. No comprehensive, and few convincing, efforts have been made to assimilate such overseas critical fashions of the 1970s and 1980s as semiotics and deconstruction to the writing of Australian literary history, although Turner's *National Fictions* was a salutary beginning. Ironically, 'new historicism' may have been present in Australia before America, as the contextual studies by literary historians such as Ken Stewart, Elizabeth Webby and Laurie Hergenhan among others indicate. Such work has found its place most often in *Australian Literary Studies*. Elsewhere the melodrama continues, as much a debate over the manners with which national literature should comport itself as a revisionist scrutiny of its contents. Fuelling the melodrama is a deep fear of dispossession, of losing either the tenuous culture which has developed in this continent, or coming adrift from the parent, European culture. This is why the desire that a national literature (exhibiting national qualities, however these have been defined) has been so strenuously held by some, so contemptuously dismissed by others. The literary histories of Australia that invent different issues of debate, that abandon residual insecurities concerning the value of local materials (insecurities implied by the dichotomising habit and the melodramatic temper of debate) remain to be written.

Notes

Readers should consult the sources listed and also the Appendix for histories of Australian literature and associated information. The most comprehensive literary history is H. M. Green's *A History of Australian Literature* (1961), since revised by Dorothy Green (1985). Its largest successor has been *The Oxford History of Australian Literature* (1981), edited by Leonie Kramer. The survey by E. Morris Miller and Frederick T. Macartney, *Australian Literature, From its Beginnings to 1950* (1956) remains valuable. Commentaries on literary criticism that also treat literary history are Brian Kiernan, *Criticism* (1974) and H. P. Heseltine's contribution on 'Criticism' to *The Oxford Companion to Australian Literature* (1985). The latter is a particularly useful guide to the miscellaneous ways and places in which historical and critical judgements of Australian literature have appeared. That literary history in Australia has often been ventured in piecemeal form, as collections of essays, has been noted above. Besides those by such individuals as A. A. Phillips, Vincent Buckley, A. D. Hope, Chris Wallace-Crabbe, Fay Zwicky and H. P. Heseltine, there have been collections by diverse hands, notably the two editions of *The Literature of Australia* (1964, 1976), edited by Geoffrey Dutton; *Australian Literary Criticism* (1962), edited by Leon Cantrell and *Considerations* (1977), edited by Brian Kiernan.

Treatments of the histories of single genres have not been numerous. They include Vincent Buckley, *Essays in Poetry, Mainly Australian* (1957); Judith Wright, *Preoccupations in Australian Poetry* (1965); D. R. Burns, *New Directions in Australian Fiction* (1975) and—for drama—Leslie Rees, *A History of Australian Drama* (1973; rev. 1978); Margaret Williams, *Drama* (1977) and Peter Fitzpatrick, *After 'The Doll': Australian Drama Since 1955* (1979). No extensive comparative literary history has been written here. There have been suggestive essays comparing Australia with America but the only book-length study, Joseph Jones', *Radical Cousins* (1976), confined itself to several nineteenth-century authors. Thematic studies have also been few, but include J. J. Healy, *Literature and the Aborigine in Australia* (1978); Ross Gibson. *The Diminishing Paradise* (1984) and Laurie Hergenhan's study of convict fiction, *Unnatural Lives* (1983).

Reflections on the relative lack of variety of forms of Australian literary history, for instance on the unexpected similarities of approach of G. A. Wilkes' two books, *Australian Literature: A Conspectus* (1969) and *The Stockyard and the Croquet Lawn* (1981) to John

Docker, *In a Critical Condition* (1984) have been few, but include Peter Pierce, 'How Australia's Literary History Might be Written' *(Australian Literary Studies*, 11, 1983), upon which this chapter has drawn. There is as yet no extended survey of Australian literary historiography such as Richard Reising ventured of its American counterpart in *The Unusable Past* (1986).

PART II

Part II

Chapter 6

PERCEPTIONS OF AUSTRALIA BEFORE 1855

ALAN FROST

The European idea of Australia began to form thousands of years before the Westerners knew the dimensions and nature of the geographical entity they were imagining. The Greeks had some idea of a 'south land'; and about AD 150 the Alexandrine geographer Ptolemy gave it the general outline it retained for twelve hundred years, when he wrote of an 'unknown' southern land 'which encloses the Indian sea and which encompasses Ethiopia south of Libya'. When, after the Dark Ages, European interest in the world again increased, Ptolemy's *Geography* was the standard text; and it contributed significantly to the idea of a great southern continent, *Terra Australia Nondum Cognita*. As fully elaborated by mid-sixteenth-century geographers, this continent covered the antarctic regions and extended into the temperate zones of the Atlantic, Indian and Pacific Oceans, with two large capes ('Beach', 'Maletur') running towards the equator in the vicinity of the East Indies.

As a consequence, variously, of theoretical argument, geographical confusion, experience of the East and the Americas, and simply the desire to have it so, Europeans saw this mysterious land as one of great wealth and plenty. Gerard Mercator described Beach as a land of gold, and Maletur as one of spices. Seeking support for yet another expedition to discover it, Quirós told the king of Spain that *Terra Australis* was the 'fifth part of the Terrestriall Globe' and in extent twice the size of the Spanish empire; that it was an earthly paradise offering spices and precious metals; and that its people were numerous, simple in their habits, and awaiting the saving grace of Christian conversion. One hundred and fifty years later, Alexander Dalrymple thought that its extent was greater than that of 'the whole civilised part of Asia, from *Turkey* to the eastern extremity of *China*'; and that the 'scraps' from its inhabitants' economy 'would be sufficient to maintain the power, dominion, and sovereignty of *Britain*, by employing all its manufactures and ships'.

Such were the idealists' conceptions of *Terra Australis*. During their great expansion into the world, as they probed the oceans, arrived at known lands and traced the outlines of unknown ones, Europeans were progressively forced to contract their ideas, to pare them of fanciful embellishments, to face a distinctly more mundane reality. The tracks they pioneered across the southern hemisphere's wastes of water showed that there was no continent of such vast extent as the Renaissance cosmographers drew; and the islands they came to offered no such riches. As one Spanish official complained, in his 1567-8 voyage Mendaña found 'no specimens of spices, nor of gold and silver, nor of merchandise, nor of any other source of profit, and all the people were naked savages'. And the seventeenth-century Dutch reconnaissances of the northern, western, and southern coasts of the finite New Holland revealed a generally desolate region offering no items of trade. Cook's 1770 voyage certainly revealed a more fertile eastern coast, but again it was one not distinguished by plenitude of fruits, spices, minerals or jewels. Hawkesworth's version of Cook's and Banks' descriptions was quickly summarised in a plethora of geographical publications; and by the mid-1780s it was common knowledge that 'New South Wales' was 'rather barren than fertile; yet in many places the rising grounds are chequered by woods and lawns, and the plains and vallies covered with herbage'.

Nonetheless, residual expectations continued to give the real southern continent something of the cast of the earlier imaginary one. Those who proposed the planting of a convict colony at Botany Bay saw the region as one of great possiblity, with James Matra writing that 'the climate and soil are so happily adapted to produce every various and valuable production of Europe, and of Both the Indies', and Sir George Young echoing this perception.

When the decision to colonise was taken, commentators elaborated it. Alexander Dalrymple raged against the placing of convicts in a good climate where they would soon have '*every object* of *comfort* or *Ambition* before them'. Another pundit told the readers of the *St James Chronicle* that 'all South Wales is formed of a Virgin Mould, undisturbed since the Creation', and he looked forward to the 'capital Improvement' soon to be wrought there by European agriculture and pastoralism. As the First Fleet proceeded towards its destination, the experience of other colonisations reinforced such perceptions. '[This] is situated in a fine Climate, & Yields most of the necessarys of Life, and some of its Luxuries', Daniel Southwell wrote home from the Cape of Good Hope; 'We have good hopes of B.ʸ Bay—it being in Nearly the same Latitude.'

But if the British public in the mid-1780s entertained images of a bountiful southern region, the colonists going there carried with them a heavy burden of derisory jokes and gibes. Sometimes, the humour was cheerful:

> They go to an Island to take special charge,
> Much warmer than Britain, and ten times as large:
> No customs-house duty, no freightage to pay,
> And tax-free they'll live when in Botany Bay.

More often, though, the perception of colonists 'raising human pine-apples and spices . . . on the dunghill of [their] vices' was laced with that condescension which a well-founded sense of rectitude allows:

> If the Botany Bay Colony should thrive and become a Civil Government, what a pleasant thought it must be to have Judges, who were reprieved at the Gallows, and Justices who picked pockets—to have Counsellors who have pleaded for their lives, and Lawyers who have set all laws at defiance—to see Housebreakers appointed to protect the Property of the Public, the Highwaymen entrusted with its cash—to see Rioters employed to Keep the peace, and Shoplifters to regulate their markets.

Though it readily gave rise to such humour, there was a serious side to Botany Bay, for the British also knew that hardship, danger, and death were the likely companions of exile to so distant a land. In January 1787, mentioning the rumour that the settlement was to be at Norfolk Island rather than Botany Bay, the *Bath Chronicle* observed: 'It is very little difference to the bulk of the destined wretches which of those remote places they are bound for. We believe that the first land that two-thirds of them will reach will be the bottom of the Sea.' The difficulties of the first years of colonisation gave substance to this perception. 'We expected to find a beautiful country', reported one disillusioned officer after six months at Port Jackson,

> as well as to rest ourselves from our fatigues, at least for two or three years; but you will be as much surprised, as we were disappointed, when I

assure you that there is not a spot of ground large enough for a cabbage garden, fit for cultivation, within several miles of [Sydney], and barely fresh water sufficient to supply our present wants.

Two years on, when the colonists were still struggling to establish agriculture and had not yet been resupplied from Britain, John White wrote bitterly of a 'country and place so forbidding and so hateful as only to merit execration and curses'. 'Botany Bay is as far from the Cape of Good Hope as Jamaica is from England', the *Morning Post* reported about the same time, 'so that in case of failure of provisions, the next news that arrives will probably be, that half the new Settlers have been carried off by famine'. The reports of the heavy mortality on the Second and Third fleets reinforced this image of Botany Bay as a place of penury, isolation and death. Put into a fit of romantic melancholy by reading Tench's *A Complete Account of the Settlement at Port Jackson in New South Wales* (1793), the youthful Robert Southey decided that whether he 'linger [ed] out existence in England in America or among the convicts of New Holland' was 'a matter of indifference'; and he filled his 'Botany Bay Eclogues' with the nostalgia of exile:

> Once more to daily toil, once more to wear
> The livery of shame, once more to search
> With miserable task this savage shore! . . .
>   Welcome ye wild plains
> Unbroken by the plough, undelved by hand
> Of patient rustic; where for lowing herds
> And for the music of the bleating flocks,
> Alone is heard the kangaroo's sad note
> deepening in distance. Welcome wilderness,
> Nature's domain! for here, as yet unknown
> The comforts and the crimes of polish'd life,
> Nature benignly gives to all enough,
> Denies to all a superfluity . . .
> On these wild shores the saving hand of Grace
> Will probe my secret soul, and cleanse its wounds,
> And fit the faithful penitent for Heaven.

Overshadowing these images of isolation and death, though, was that of the colonists' collective depravity. 'A dreadful Banditti', the Home undersecretary described the convicts privately; and the founding governor knew the majority of them to be thieves, 'indolent and not cleanly', with most of the women possessing 'neither virtue nor Honesty'. All too frequently, events on the way to and in the colony confirmed such perceptions. 'We shall not starve, though seven-eight of the colony deserves nothing better', Phillip observed in April 1790.

Thereafter, for forty years, as convict transport after convict transport unloaded its human cargo, as rum flooded into the colony, as a succession of governors strove to impose order and developed an ever broader range of secondary punishments to deal with recidivists, 'Botany Bay' became the shorthand term for a society stained by convict corruption, one marked by that depravity and lawlessness which decent society finds unconscionable. Three missionaries described to William Wilberforce in 1799 how in New South Wales they had

to contend with the depravity and corruptions of the human heart, heightened & confirmed in all its vicious habits by long and repeated indulgences of inbred corruption—each one following the bent of his corrupt mind and countenancing his neighbour in the pursuit of sensual gratifications.

Ten years later, Governor Macquarie was shocked to find immorality still rampant. 'There can be but one opinion,' Sydney Smith stated firmly in 1819:

New South Wales is a sink of wickedness, in which the great majority of convicts of both sexes become infinitely more depraved than at the period of their arrival ... It is impossible that vice should not become more intense in such [a] society.

The establishment, from the mid-1820s onwards, of those places of fearful secondary punishment fed this perception.

Buttressed by Biblical and genetic notions of the sins of the fathers being visited upon the children, the idea that the societies of New South Wales and Van Diemen's Land suffered from 'the lamentable taint of [their] original formation' permeated the British public's thinking in the 1830s. Howick's 1833 Parliamentary pronouncement that the quarrel between the exclusives and the emancipists represented 'a constant struggle ... between those who had been once convicts, or who were the descendants of convicts, and those who were wholly untainted' summed up the prevailing attitude. If the most colourful public statement of this attitude was Major James Mudie's *The Felonry of New South Wales* (1837), the most serious and influential was the Molesworth Committee's report (1838). Tendentiously drawn up with the aim of ending transportation, this sifted testimony and statistics to show that New South Wales was the most crime-ridden and degenerate of European societies. Because it pandered to prejudice, this view had great force and longevity. John Hood aptly observed in *Australia and the East* (1843):

> From the extreme distance of this country from England, little was known by those unconnected with its export and import trade, of its real state, or of its rapidly-increasing importance; and I am satisfied that I do not err in saying, that until within these ten years, few in Britain had any knowledge of it at all, or any ideas concerning it, except as connected with *Botany Bay*—the receptacle of the 'superfluity of naughtiness' of the empire.

As Hood's informed and sympathetic account recognised, there always had been another side to life in the Australian colonies, even if this side came to public view but slowly. It is doubtful, for example, if the early colonists ever found the environment nearly as hateful and forbidding as John White and many modern commentators would have us believe. That Europeans found life in Australia a bitter struggle for existence is a romantic notion, beloved of those who, looking back, find it impossible to imagine the past otherwise, but whose reasons for so imagining are not largely historical ones. Of course there were strangenesses in the landscape about Sydney, and of course the colonists had to adjust expectations and cope with unexpected circumstances; but the way in which the educated among them habitually perceived themselves and their endeavour was rather neo-classical than romantic.

In its purpose to bring order out of (both geographical and human) chaos, early colonisation was neo-classical in impulse. As the editor of *The Voyage of Governor Phillip to Botany Bay* observed,

> There are few things more pleasing than the contemplation of order and useful arrangement arising gradually out of tumult and confusion; and perhaps this satisfaction cannot any where be more fully enjoyed than where a settlement of civilized people is fixing itself upon a newly discovered or savage coast. The wild appearance of land entirely untouched by cultivation, the close and perplexed growing of trees,

interrupted now and then by barren spots, bare rocks, or spaces overgrown with weed, flowers, flowering shrubs, or underwood, scattered and intermingled in the most promiscuous manner, are the first objects that present themselves; afterwards, the irregular placing of the first tents which are erected for immediate accommodation, wherever chance presents a spot tolerably free from obstacles, or more easily cleared than the rest, with the bustle of various hands busily employed in a number of the most incongruous works, increases rather than diminishes the disorder, and produces a confusion of effect, which for a time appears inextricable, and seems to threaten an endless continuance of perplexity. But by degrees large spaces are opened, plans are formed, lines marked, and a prospect at least of future regularity is clearly discerned, and is made the more striking by the recollection of the former confusion.

The drive for order here described was always the dominant one in the young colony. Phillip strove to weld the convicts into a viable society; and numbers of these steadily came to see the benefits it offered—in August 1789, on their suggestion, he appointed twelve worthy convicts to form a 'Night Watch' to inhibit the thieving from dwellings and gardens. So successful were they that David Collins was able to remark a few months later, 'it possibly might have been asserted with truth, that many streets in the metropolis of London were not so well guarded and watched as the small, but rising town of Sydney, in New South Wales'. It was a point to which Peter Cunningham amusingly drew attention thirty-five years later, when he wrote in *Two Years in New South Wales* (1827):

Elbowed by some daring highwayman on your left hand, and rubbed shoulders with by even a more desperate burglar on your right, a footpad perhaps stops your way in front, and a pickpocket pushes you behind, all *retired* from their wonted vocations, and now peacefully complying with the tasks imposed upon them, or following quietly up the even path pointed out by honest industry. But nothing will surprise you more than the quietness and order which prevail in the streets, and the security wherewith you may perambulate them at all hours of the night . . .

As well as the desire to punish for transgression, transportation to Australia always turned on the Enlightenment and neo-classical premises that a change in environment might allow criminals to reform, and make themselves into a moral and useful society. As the founding governor told his charges, their sentences of transportation offered them the opportunity, not only 'to expiate their offences', but also to become 'good, and even opulent men, as many of the first settlers in the western world [i.e. America] had been convicts like themselves'. This duality of purpose continued to inform the system as it developed over the next forty years, even in its severer aspects: the various gradations in the female factories and Sir George Arthur's Van Diemen's Land, for example, existed not only to punish, but also so that convicts might advance through them towards 'reclamation'. Wedgwood's famous medallion, with its allegory of 'Hope encouraging Art and Labour, under the influence of Peace, to pursue the employments necessary to give security and happiness to an infant settlement', and its title of 'Etruria 1789' elaborated these premises strikingly.

Useful as they may be as means of categorising, though, the terms 'neo-classical' and 'romantic' spread a distorting haze about the historical landscape. In and about Sydney in the early years of colonisation (and the same is true of the other Australian ventures), reality was not literary and aesthetic but rather immediate and palpable. The colonists needed food and shelter if they were to survive; they needed social order, so as not to succumb to a barbarism that would engulf them completely and remove their endeavour from time. They needed freedom from labour and want if they were to raise families successfully; they needed leisure if they were, eventually, to develop those pursuits their culture considered 'civilised'.

So Phillip set his charges to clearing ground, fencing, and planting; to erecting tents, and then huts and public buildings; to laying the lines of a town; to exploring for better land; to building a second town at Parramatta; to building roads and bridges; to creating farms in outlying districts. Simultaneously, he strove ceaselessly to reduce lawlessness, to replace it with social cohesion. The first three years were difficult, what with many of the convicts being unwilling to work, with meagre agricultural returns, illness, and diminished effort as a consequence of reduced rations, with recalcitrance and crime, drought, and no new supplies from Europe until the Second Fleet arrived in June 1790. But by the autumn of 1791, a good harvest, improved behaviour from the convicts, and a trickle of supplies from India and the East Indies had shown the founding governor that the tide had turned in their favour. 'Tho' this Colony is not exactly in the state in which I would have wished to have left it', he reported, 'another year may do much, & it is at present so fully established, that I think there cannot any longer be a doubt but that it will, if Settlers are sent out, answer in every respect the end proposed by Government.' When he left the colony in December 1792, he knew that he had won the battle for its survival.

In winning this battle, Phillip had done, necessarily, a good deal more: he had set in train a massive transformation of the continent. For thirty years, this transformation was confined to the Cumberland Plain and to the regions about Hobart and Launceston (Port Dalrymple), but by the end of Phillip's time there was no doubting its import and eventual effect. When Malaspina's officers went up the harbour to Parramatta in March 1793 they saw

> along both shores . . . farms with residences of some of the colonists. Corn, wheat, and barley, though not too abundant, were giving signs of an attractive harvest. More flourishing certainly was the potato, which promised a less doubtful future. The fruit trees, vegetable patches, and especially the lemon and the grapevine, gave new stimulus to the common activity and aspirations. Finally, the first young livestock, though very few in number, of cattle, sheep, and horses, gave good hopes for combining, in this new centre of national wealth, English energy and policy with a climate and soil not unlike that of our own Andalucia.

The regenerating convicts, they observed, were transforming 'a rough and uncultivated country into a pleasant garden. It had been in existence for hardly five years and yet had the appearance of an old establishment'.

By the early 1800s, it had become clear that New South Wales produced things European abundantly: grains, fruits, animals—and people. As convicts arrived and stayed in their thousands; as men found more abundant means of livelihood than they had previously known; as, against previous experience, women found positive benefits to wifehood and motherhood, the convicts produced children in unexpected numbers. In an age when theories of baleful miasmas dominated medical thinking, New South Wales was soon renowned for its benign 'climate', in which adults lived longer than elsewhere, and children flourished. Unravaged by the usual scourges, these children lived: in 1807, children numbered 1830 and constituted a quarter of the white population of New South Wales, and the colony's bounty freed them from the necessity of unremitting labour from the age of five or six. Quickly the perception grew that this 'rising generation' was the key to the colony's future well-being. The children's parentage and freedom combined to make it imperative that they be inculcated with moral values, so that the authorities established schools where clergy and dames instructed them, another circumstance that also contributed to social order.

By 1810, New South Wales had reached a pitch of progress quite unexpected from a colony of thieves and prostitutes. Ordinary men and women enjoyed less taxing working conditions and ate better than their fellows in Britain. Some ex-convicts had become rich. So, too, had a number of free merchants and civil and military officers. Sydney had a prosperous air. 'A person coming into Sydney cove would think himself in the midst of a large city,' Dr Arnold wrote in early 1810:

> This town is large but not closely built every house having a garden, & the streets which are about a mile long are strait & wide, some of the houses are very magnificent and large, but the greater number are cottages . . .
>
> Fruit is in great plenty here there being thousands of acres planted with peach trees, fruit of which they make cider of, or feed their pigs with. There are also, apples, pears, oranges, lemons, plums, strawberries, melons &c.

Behind Sydney was the Cumberland Plain, with its agricultural holdings, its herds of cattle and (increasingly) sheep. As William Charles Wentworth described it, in 1819, about ten miles inland 'you are at length gratified with the appearance of a country truly beautiful. An endless variety of hill and dale, clothed in the most luxuriant herbage, and covered with bleating flocks and lowing herds.'

To a lesser extent, but distinctly nonetheless, Van Diemen's Land then exhibited the same transformation, with settlers beginning to push up the Derwent Valley and down the Tamar Valley from the developing ports of Hobart (founded 1803-4) and Port Dalrymple (1804). These settlements, too, were renowned for their healthy climate which, 'coming nearer to [that] of England [than the New South Wales one] is most productive of vegetable food, and of good Kinds'. Visiting these southern regions in 1811, Governor Macquarie found that though the settlers' dwellings were too often 'mean and badly built', the country was 'beautiful rich and picturesque', with 'the soil of the farms in general . . . excellent', and with 'every appearance of plentiful and abundant harvest'. Revisiting the island in 1821, he found Hobart to have 420 houses and 2700 European inhabitants, with settlers now cultivating some 10,600 acres (4300 hectares) and possessing some 29,000 cattle and 182,000 sheep.

In 1823, the British government legislated to establish separate administration in New South Wales and Van Diemen's Land. By this time, the colonists in both regions had achieved a level of general prosperity sufficient to attract free settlers. In 1823, 543 persons migrated from Britain to these regions, as did 780 in 1824, 903 in 1826, 1056 in 1828. At the time of the 1818 census, there were 25,142 Europeans on the Cumberland Plain, another 7670 in the Bathurst, Argyle, Illawarra and the Hunter River districts, and 3000-odd in places of secondary punishment or chain gangs. There were 18,408 persons in Van Diemen's Land. It was widely acknowledged that, in general, all social classes among the settlers—convict, ex-convict, labourer, small and great landholder or capitalist—lived better than their counterparts in Britain.

Contemporaries noticed that the first generation of native-born white colonists were taller and slimmer than their parents, and fairer of complexion; and that they saw themselves as 'currency' rather than 'sterling'. According to Peter Cunningham, the men announced this separate identity by wearing moleskin trousers and cabbage-tree hats, the women by their bad teeth and early fecundity; and both sexes together by eschewing the profligate ways of their parents. They also saw the colonies as their 'home'. William Charles Wentworth, for example, wrote in 1817, on the occasion of his studying law in England, that it was 'by no means my intention . . . to abandon the Country that gave me birth'. A few years later, he and Charles Tompson and Charles Harpur sought to create a local nurturing landscape of the imagination, when they described the Nepean-Hawkesbury region in ways similar to those in which, a generation earlier, Wordsworth had evoked the Wye Valley and the Lake District. It was inevitable that a term emerge for this separate identity. Suggested by Flinders and promoted by Macquarie, in the 1820s 'Australia' came into general use as the name of the continent, 'Australians' as that of its inhabitants. In 1824, for example, Wentworth titled his paper the *Australian*. The same year, the Macarthurs helped form the Australian Agricultural Company. In 1827, Cunningham wrote of the 'Australian' continent; and in this year, too, Tompson repeatedly characterised himself and his friends as 'Australians'.

It is tempting to see these things as signs of an emergent nationalism, but it is probably wrong to do so. At this time, however much the Currency lads and lasses saw themselves as different from their British counterparts, they and their parents also saw themselves as British people living in the antipodes. Tompson himself made this essential point when he also observed, 'if I know my own heart, *I solemnly avow my loyalty to my king and the British constitution; nor do I ever wish to see any other usurp its sway.*' And even as they pointed to the divergences in local culture, observers of the 1820s and 1830s stressed the essential 'Englishness' of the colonisations, a characteristic appearing variously in the speech, dress, and manners of the inhabitants, in the furnishings of their houses and the flowers of their gardens, in their workings of the land, and in the way of life of those among them who aspired to the status of 'gentry'. It was—and is—a paradox to tease the heart.

The one group which stood outside this general picture was the Aborigines. From the first manifestly uninterested in much of the Europeans' 'civilisation', these often also resisted white encroachment vigorously. However much circumstances may have differed at the centres of European settlement, the history of culture contact in Australia between 1788 and the 1840s is largely one of violence at the peripheries. In 1792, when the Sydney Aborigines were moving freely about the township, there was trouble in the Parramatta district. When, in the late 1790s, this area had become more peaceful, there were fierce clashes on the Hawkesbury floodplains. When, in the 1810s and 1820s, the whites had gained the ascendency on the Cumberland Plain, there was extreme violence in Van Diemen's Land, as settlers expanded sheep runs and cut the Aborigines' migration trails as well as disrupted their food supplies. In the later 1830s, when there was quite a deal of peaceful interaction on the Bathurst Plains, there were such frontier incidents as the Myall Creek massacre. The history of the other European settlements shows a similar pattern. At Swan River in the 1830s, for example, Stirling found it practically impossible to constrain the colonists in outlying districts.

The depiction in colonial paintings of the Aborigines literally 'beyond the pale' reflects this reality. William Westall's *A View of Port Jackson* (1802), for example, shows a naked Aboriginal family in an open, rocky space by a fire, with only a bark humpy for shelter, with a glimpse of the European settlement in the distance across an arm of the harbour. Duparc's engraving after Lesueur, *Vue de la partie meridionale de la ville de Sydney* (1803-7), and John Eyre's *Sydney from the West side of the Cove* (c.1806), the one showing Aborigines on Bennelong Point, the other placing them amid the Rocks, in either case separated from the European township by rows of paling fences, reflect the motif's definitive form, which was often repeated in the next thirty years. Indeed, we may see it as one of the most distinctive iconographical features of colonial painting.

Closely related to this image of a people knowing nothing of civilisation was that of the male Aborigines as skilled and savage hunters: see, for example, *Hunting the Kangaroo* and *Smoking out the Opussom*, in *Field Sports of the Native Inhabitants of New South Wales* (1813). Sometimes, as in Petit's and Lesueur's delicate images of the coastal Aborigines of Tasmania, and Glover's more robust ones thirty years later of those of the interior, we find less stereotyped depictions; but in general, in the first fifty years of colonisation, the Europeans found the Aborigines quite mysterious in their otherness. James Wallis's *Corroboree at Newcastle* (c.1817) conveys the sense of sinister primitiveness that Europeans so often attached to the dark denizens of the bush.

Nonetheless, the situation was not unrelievedly one of mutual fear and violence. At the centres of European settlement, where those in authority might better know events, maintain humanitarian attitudes and enforce the law, good relations might obtain. In March 1793, for example, Malaspina's officers found to their surprise

both Boys and Girls received and cared for with great attention in the houses of the principal persons of the colony. Both men and women . . . have been admitted to the dining room [in our presence], and have enjoyed delicacies from the same table. At times we heard entire families salute us in English. Sometimes we saw Aborigines dancing and singing in the principal streets about a fire the whole night, without anyone disturbing them.

And in the 1810s, however paternalistic they were, Macquarie's attempt to make farmers of some Aborigines and his annual greeting of the tribes of the Cumberland Plains again showed a better side of European culture.

Desirable as it certainly was, such peaceful contact also had its drawbacks, for it led to the raising of prejudice in the whites and the progressive degradation of the Aborigines. As well as Dampier's image of 'the miserablest People in the World', the First Fleet officers had carried with them ideas of the Aborigines as noble savages, which they quickly lost in the face of the blacks' distance, lack of hygiene, and personal violence. In describing the Aboriginal men's habit of beating the women severely, for example, Tench sighed:

A thousand times . . . have I wished, that those European philosophers, whose closet speculations exalt a state of nature above a state of civilization, could survey the phantom, which their heated imaginations have raised: possibly they might then learn, that a state of nature is, of all others, least adapted to promote the happiness of a being, capable of sublime research, and unending ratiocination: that a savage roaming for prey amidst his native deserts, is a creature deformed by all those passions, which afflict and degrade our nature, unsoftened by the influence of religion, philosophy, and legal restriction.

Extended contact showed the whites that the Aborigines simply would not live in a steady, 'civilised' way. Children whom the Europeans nurtured from an early age returned to the bush at puberty. Bennelong had the benefit of a governor's patronage and an educative journey to England, but he too shed his clothes on his return to the colony, and gave himself over to fighting. The Aborigines would not provide for the future, either by cultivating or by storing food. They would not provide themselves with shelter from the elements, and neither would they work. Daniel Paine observed in 1796 that they had as yet derived

no benefit from Civilization although our Settlement has been formed near ten years amongst them they have no Idea of profiting by the Example of our Settlers to sow Corn for a sure Provision. They have neither Hut or Habitation but the Clefts of the Rocks and Hollow trees excepting such as intrude themselves into the Houses of our People and intrusion it may justly be termed for nothing but the Inclemency of Weather or hunger makes them Visitants for they will not attempt to assist you by working.

Progressively, too, Aborigines in contact with the Europeans lost their tribal culture and came to depend on the white one. By the beginning of the nineteenth century, those about Sydney had fallen into prostituting their women, drinking, and brawling for the amusement of the whites. Cunningham offered the pathetic story of 'King' Boongaree who in the 1820s was in the habit of donning a gold-laced blue coat with epaulettes and a cocked hat, and rowing out to meet incoming ships, bidding '*massa* welcome to *his* country', and soliciting 'the *loan* of a *dump*, on pretence of treating his sick *gin* to a cup of tea, but in reality with a view of treating *himself* to a porringer of "Cooper's best", to which his Majesty is most royally devoted'.

Charles Rodius' *Scene in a Sydney Street* (1834), showing Aborigines dressed in cast-off European clothes drinking and fighting, captured this sad decline well. It was one repeated at all other European settlements.

Because of their refusal to live carefully and to follow civilised ways, in the general European outlook the Aborigines quickly came to have a status little apart from that of the higher animals. They were 'the most irrational and ill formed Human beings on the Face of the Earth', Daniel Paine remarked in 1796. In 1810, Dr Arnold wrote of their having been at the time of European settlement

> men so little civilized that they knew not even the use of cloathing, who lived upon the flesh of their neighbours, Whose only superiority above the brute consisted in their use of the spear, their extreme ferocity and their employing fire in the cookery of their food.

Occasionally, as in Robert Mudie's *The Picture of Australia* (1829), there was a recognition that European colonisation had dispossessed and degraded the continent's original inhabitants, but by the 1830s the prevailing white attitude was that evinced by the *Australian* on the occasion of New South Wales' fiftieth birthday: 'Fifty years since, the untutored savage was Australia's Monarch—barbarism of the most wretched and degrading description desolated the land—and everything bore a wild and antedeluvian appearance.' Some of the more enlightened of the white administrators, such as Bourke, Gipps and Stirling, did try to check the consequences of this view, but there was little they might do to diminish its sway.

At first, life in the Australian colonies seemed to offer Europeans limited opportunity only. 'To men of small property, unambitious of trade, and wishing for retirement, I think the continent of New South Wales not without inducements,' Tench wrote in mid-1788, when prosperity was still a hope for the future. Seven years later, when it had begun to appear, Mrs Macarthur desired that her children might 'see a little more of the world, and better learn to appreciate this retirement'. Into the 1820s, as settlement consolidated on the Cumberland Plain and began in Van Diemen's Land, this was the image which prevailed. While 'New South Wales does not appear to promise such a boundless field for colonisation as was at one time expected', James Losh wrote in 1820, it 'has many and great advantages for an industrious settler with a moderate capital'. A few years later, Peter Cunningham urged anyone who might possess a capital of £1200, who

> sees little chance of improving in England, and possibly with a rising family, whom he has but slender hopes of putting in a way either to realize an independence or even to secure a respectable livelihood; a man so situated, if he should resolve on endeavouring to brighten his prospects by emigration, will ... find New South Wales the best of all the newly colonized countries he can possibly fix on; for the purpose of turning that capital, when devoted to agricultural purposes, to a beneficial account.

Yet only fifteen years later, the Australian colonies generally had become in the public mind a land that offered almost boundless possibilities to convicts and ex-convicts, to free labourers, to small farmers, to large landowners, to small and large capitalists. What gave rise to this extraordinary change in perception was the pastoral expansion of the 1820s and 1830s. As Robert Mudie, Peter Cunningham, and many others pointed out,

> The enticements which Australia holds out to the intended settler are, a boundless extent of soil, unappropriated by any other people for purposes of cultivation, that soil situated in latitudes having such a range as to be adapted to the growth of every useful vegetable, and the rearing of every useful animal; and, great part at least, enjoying a climate much better adapted to the constitution and health of Europeans than any other country to which Englishmen resort for the purpose of settling.

In England the mere possession of land constituted wealth. This was not so in Australia. Much of the continent is not suited to intensive agriculture; rather, what it is suited to (particularly in the southern, first settled regions) is the grazing of sheep. Wakefield, however, promoted a scheme partly applied in South Australia and Western Australia whereby the proceeds of the sale of large holdings were to be used to sponsor the migration of a working class which could be engaged in extensive agriculture. In 1840, when this notion had almost brought about the failure of the new colonisations, Gipps commented tellingly:

> In a Colony like Demerara, where land is used for scarcely any purpose but cultivation, and cultivation too of the most expensive sort, the theory might perhaps be practically applied; but, to a pastoral country like Australia, it is evidently altogether inapplicable.

By this time, the eastern colonies were in the grip of the mania 'to put all into four feet', but it had taken some time for British and colonial authorities, and the colonists themselves, to see in which direction the Australian future lay. Though early efforts by such as the Macarthurs, Marsden, and Alexander Riley pointed the way, not until J. T. Bigge's 1823 report had recommended a pastoral future for New South Wales and Van Diemen's Land did local and imperial authorities act to permit settlers to realise it. Then, Major Thomas Mitchell surveyed New South Wales, and the colonial administrations fixed limits of location in 1826, 1829, and 1835. Rapidly, settlers spread westwards and southwestwards beyond the Blue Mountains; and as their sheep multiplied and British demand for their wool continually increased, they pushed further. As Gipps again observed,

> as well might it be attempted to confine the Arabs of the Desert within a circle, traced upon their sands, as to confine the Graziers or Woolgrowers of New South Wales within any bounds that can possibly be assigned to them; and as certainly as the Arabs would be starved, so also would the flocks and herds of New South Wales, if they were so confined, and the prosperity of the Country be at an end.

The situation was similar in Tasmania, with pastoralists taking up all suitable land by the late 1820s, and, in the early 1830s, with their flocks burgeoning, looking eagerly about for new pastures. In 1835 Batman and Fawkner reconnoitred and settled the Port Phillip district on behalf of groups of graziers; and Mitchell's 1836 probe into 'Australia Felix' soon brought squatters from the northern colony into this region too. By 1838, graziers were droving flocks to the South Australian colony, and settlers were deserting the struggling Swan River one for the greener pastures of the East.

By the end of the 1830s, the colonies' export of wool to Britain had reached 41,000 bales; and the future seemed to offer limitless possibility. After his 1836 expedition, Mitchell wrote in the *Sydney Herald*:

> it has been in my power, under the protection of Providence, to explore the vast natural resources of a region more extensive than Great Britain, equally rich in point of soil, and which now lies ready for the plough in many parts, as if specially prepared by the Creator for the industrious hands of Englishmen.

In May 1840, this paper announced the results of the Leslie brothers' exploration of the Darling Downs, commenting that 'the discovery of this splendid new land would gladden the hearts of the stockholders'. A dozen years later, Conrad Martens set forth images of spreading herds and flocks in the works recording his journey to Brisbane and its hinterland.

The pastoral expansion, together with the wealth it brought to the colonies, powerfully supported the idea that civilisation was being born again in the antipodes. New South Wales possessed 'vast and daily increasing resources' and a 'large population of free Englishmen', Lytton Bulwer pronounced in 1832, so that it might well receive 'the stream of our stifled and damned up state of civilization'. In 1843, John Hood saw that, 'considering its short existence, and the materials out of which it was reared', there was nowhere else a colony 'that has so benefited, by its trade and otherwise, the parent from which it sprung; while, at the same time, it has created a political and social existence for itself, with a rapidity unexampled in the annals of colonisation'.

The drought and the accompanying depression of the early 1840s temporarily dampened this optimism, but by the end of the decade it was resurgent again. It gave rise to very significant free migration: 31,626 persons reached New South Wales in the 1830s, and 28,414 in 1848 and 1849. Together with the natural increase in the colonies, this migration caused settlement to spread ever more widely, as people proceeded further and further into the interior in search of land or work. And as this happened, another Australian reality began to emerge.

Initially a town term for 'unenclosed and uncultivated country', by the 1840s 'the bush' was being generally applied to the margins of established settlement. In 1844, Gipps pointed out:

> We see here a British Population spread over an immense territory, beyond the influence of civilization, and almost beyond the restraints of Law. Within this wide extent, a Minister of Religion is very rarely to be found. There is not a place of Worship, nor even a School. So utter indeed is the destitution of all means of instruction, that it may perhaps be considered fortunate that the population has hitherto been one almost exclusively male. But Women are beginning to follow into the Bush; and a race of Englishmen must speedily be springing up in a state approaching to that of untutored barbarism.

As the governor saw, 'bush' life was not the same as that of the earlier settled, and distinctly more fertile, regions. In *A Voice from the Far Interior of Australia* (1847), a 'Bushman' sounded a number of those notes—of isolation, loneliness, death, drought, flood, fire—that later writers would make into the characteristic Australian bush ballad. But this story, and that of the goldrushes, belongs elsewhere.

Notes

The quotations in this chapter come from a variety of sources. The principal unpublished ones are the documentary collections of the Mitchell and Dixson Libraries, Sydney, which have been comprehensively mined for F. C. Crowley, *A Documentary History of Australia*, vol. 1: *Colonial Australia 1788-1840* (1980). *Historical Records of New South Wales* (1892-1901) and *Historical Records of Australia*, series 1 (1914-25) also print a mass of papers, both official and unofficial. Most of the paintings cited are reproduced in, variously, Cedric Flower, *The Antipodes Observed* (1974), James Gleeson, *Colonial Painters 1788-1880* (1971), and Susanna Evans, *Historical Sydney as seen by its Early Artists* (1983).

The various essays in Glyndwr Williams and Alan Frost (eds), *Terra Australis to Australia* (1988) offer details of European conceptions of the southern continent from classical times to the end of the eighteenth century. See also T. M. Perry, *The Discovery of Australia* (1982).

The images of Botany Bay appear in letters of the time, and in such contemporary publications as newspapers. Robert Hughes', *The Fatal Shore* (1987) reveals the historical basis of these images; and F. G. Clarke, *The Land of Contrarieties* (1977) shows their continuance into the 1830s and beyond.

The 'human pine-apples' quote is from Coleridge's 1824 poem 'The Delinquent Travellers'.

Phillip's unpublished and published letters, and the First Fleet narratives by Collins, Hunter (Phillip), Tench and White offer contemporary accounts of the founding of the New South Wales colony. Alan Frost's, *Arthur Phillip, 1783-1814: His Voyaging* (1987) gives a modern one. Lloyd Robson, *A History of Tasmania*, vol. 1, (1983) describes the progress of European settlement in Van Diemen's Land. B. H. Fletcher, *Colonial Australia before 1850* summarises the early histories of the other colonies.

Portia Robertson, *The Hatch and Brood of Time* (1985) is a rich study of the first generation of native-born white Australians. It and J. B. Hirst, *Convict Society and its Enemies* (1983) provide reliable views of New South Wales society in the period 1810-40.

G. A. Wilkes, *The Stockyard and the Croquet Lawn* (1981), and Robert Dixon, *The Course of Empire* (1986) are two recent works to examine questions of colonial culture and nationalism.

Glyndwr Williams, '"Far more happier than we Europeans": reactions to the Australian Aborigines on Cook's voyage', *Historical Studies*, 19 (1981) describes early European attitudes to the Aborigines. Henry Reynolds, *Frontier* (1987) and *The Other Side of the Frontier* (1982) give details of the clash of Aboriginal and European cultures. Daniel Paine's views appear in his *Journal* (1983).

The various letters printed or quoted from in *The Macarthurs of Camden* (1914) and J. J. Eddy, *Britain and the Australian Colonies 1818-1831* (1969), together with such contemporary accounts as those by Wentworth, Cunningham, Mudie, Macarthur and Hood, show the range of attitudes to life in the colonies. Gipps' despatches are printed in *Historical Records of Australia*.

S. H. Roberts, *The Squatting Age in Australia 1815-1847* (1935) describes—sometimes rather romantically—the pastoral expansion. Darren Baillieu's *Australia Felix* (1982) presents a miscellany of contemporary reports. See also J. G. Steele (ed.), *Conrad Martens in Queensland* (1978).

R. B. Madgwick, *Immigration into Eastern Australia 1788-1851* (1937) studies the European peopling of the continent.

Chapter 7

WRITERS, PRINTERS, READERS: THE PRODUCTION OF AUSTRALIAN LITERATURE BEFORE 1855

ELIZABETH WEBBY

In 1842, the *Sydney Morning Herald* in the course of some observations on 'Colonial Authorship' noted that local writers rarely produced anything longer than a letter to the newspapers:

> partly by want of ability, partly from the heavy expense of printing in Sydney, and partly from the great apathy of the public, which in the few cases where parties have 'written a book', has left the whole edition upon the shelves of the bookseller.

As this extract suggests, the production of literature is a complex business requiring, at the least, three interdependent parties: the writer, the printer and the reader. Without the writer, there is nothing to print or read. Without the printer, the writer cannot reach an audience. Without readers, the efforts of both writer and printer are merely ink marks on paper.

Each of these parties, and the ways in which they interrelate, is influenced by geographical, economic, political and cultural features particular to their time and society. In this chapter, and the parallel ones for later periods, some of the various and changing factors affecting the writing, publishing and reception of Australian literature will be examined. An account of the historical context in which a literature is produced should lead to a greater understanding and appreciation of its special qualities and achievements.

In early Australia, as in all colonial societies, the most important influence on the production of literature was the relationship with the parent culture. As the *Herald's* reviewer noted, Sydney's writers, printers and readers usually did not interrelate in the ideal way.

Australian readers were dependent on local writers and printers only for such prosaic and everyday literary articles as government regulations and newspapers. Imported books and magazines were preferred to the local product partly because they were cheaper. Since all the material needed for printing had to be imported, it cost at least twice as much to print a book in Australia as in England. English publications also had the charm of the known amidst the unknown. A favourite vignette of writers describing bush life in mid-century Australia was the squatter's table with its copies of *Punch* and the *Illustrated London News*. And, of course, imported books were believed to be of superior quality.

Fortunately for them and us, most of those writing in and about Australia in these first decades of white occupation were not dependent on local printers and readers. In Britain and Europe, these same decades saw vast improvements in printing technology and the rise of a mass reading public, both consequences of the Industrial Revolution. The birth of European Australia was, therefore, extremely well chronicled. John Ferguson's *Bibliography of Australia* (1941-86) now takes five volumes to cover the period 1784 to 1850, listing over 2000 items for the years to 1830 alone. Most of these were printed outside Australia, for non-Australian readers. An analysis of Ferguson's listings in terms of place of publication shows the very gradual growth of printing in Australia.

The British government was sufficiently conscious of the spirit of the age to send a printing press to Australia with the First Fleet. Initially, however, no-one could operate it. The first surviving Australian imprints—broadside instructions to watchmen and constables—date from 1796. The first book, printed in Sydney in 1802, was also made up of government orders. By 1829, however, the number of items listed by Ferguson as printed in Australia is almost equal to the number printed elsewhere. Twenty years later, slightly more than half the items for 1849 have Australian imprints.

The majority of Ferguson's listings are, of course, items of Australiana rather than Australian literature. Besides government proclamations and parliamentary statutes, one finds reports of missionary, agricultural and other societies, auction catalogs, emigrant handbooks and a host of other items which, even under the most flexible definition, would not be regarded as 'literature'. Where Ferguson lists over 2000 items for the years to 1830, Grahame Johnston's *Annals of Australian Literature* (1970) lists only 28, and even then includes many items not often thought of as literature. If

Johnston had used a narrower definition of literature, restricting it to poetry, fiction and drama, he would have been left with only seven items, five of verse, two of fiction, for the period 1788 to 1830.

Interestingly, six of these seven more 'purely' literary works were printed in Australia, forming the majority of the nine Australian imprints listed by Johnston for the period to 1830. This difference between the place of publication of what H. M. Green has defined as 'pure' and 'applied' literature becomes even more apparent when one examines Johnston's *Annals* for the whole period to 1855. Of the 98 items listed, one-third are poetry, fiction or drama, and just over one-third were printed in Australia. Again, there is a high degree of overlap between these thirds, with all the drama and nearly all the poetry being printed in Australia. So was the earliest fiction, though few of the items after 1840. Conversely, most of the non-fiction, the accounts of first settlement, later works of travel and exploration, histories, biographies and autobiographies, were published outside Australia, usually in London.

These correlations have a fairly simple explanation. As has been seen, there was no printing in Australia before 1796, so all the earlier works had to be sent to London. They were also, naturally enough, non-fiction, written for an English market eager for knowledge of the newest outpost of Empire. Ferguson lists 32 items published in 1789, most of them accounts of the First Fleet voyage and the early months of settlement. Indeed, nearly one-third of the entries are for Watkin Tench's *A Narrative of the Expedition to Botany Bay* (1789) which in this year alone went through three editions in London, two in Paris and one in each of Dublin, New York, Amsterdam and Frankfurt. Tench's popularity is easily explained by his lively prose style and vivid pictures of life in the new settlement. His later *A Complete Account of the Settlement at Port Jackson* (1793) remains the most readable of the early narratives. In some cases, as H. M. Green demonstrated with respect to *The Voyage of Governor Phillip to Botany Bay; with an Account of the Establishment of the Colonies of Port Jackson and Norfolk Island* (1789), English editors rewrote and 'improved' the material sent from Australia. Such editorial tampering was to remain a problem for Australian writers throughout the nineteenth century.

Initially, even books intended for Australian readers had to be printed in London. Of the seven eighteenth-century titles listed in the *Annals*, six are settlement journals including, besides Tench and Phillip, important early accounts by John White, John Hunter and

David Collins. The seventh is Richard Johnson's *An Address to the Inhabitants of the Colonies, Established in New South Wales and Norfolk Island* (1794). Johnson had arrived with the First Fleet as chaplain to New South Wales. By 1792 his health was failing and his parish daily increasing, so he wrote his *Address* in an attempt to reach those of his flock he could not meet personally. First, however, it had to be sent to London, be printed, and then come back to Australia, a long-distance sermon indeed.

By 1818, these sorts of delays were no longer necessary. The first general literary work to be printed in Australia, Thomas Wells' *Michael Howe, the Last and the Worst of the Bushrangers of Van Diemen's Land* (1818) was sold in Hobart for five shillings a copy. Even at this high price, there was enough interest in such a topical and local work for a second edition to be required. The often criticised apathy of Australian readers towards local publications needs, then, some qualification. It clearly depended a lot on the kind of book or magazine they were offered. Since the local market was so small, most general works capable of attracting wide interest continued to be sent to Britain, particularly if the author wished to make rather than lose money by their publication.

Although little detailed research has yet been carried out on the history of Australian publishing, it seems clear that virtually all the literary works published in early Australia were produced at their authors' expense. Some of them were private printings as we now understand that term: works intended not for sale but for circulation among friends and relatives. One example is Barron Field's *First Fruits of Australian Poetry* (1819), a small pamphlet which has achieved perhaps unfortunate notoriety as the first volume of poetry to appear in Australia. Contemporary and later writers, including Patrick White, have had much fun at the expense of Field's choice of title and his parents' choice of first name. Rejoicing in their own irony, they often seem to have missed Field's. His witty and whimsical verses can be much better appreciated if seen as intended for the amusement of a small circle of literary friends rather than as a claim for bardic pre-eminence. Such patriotic assertions were the prerogative of native-born poets, like W. C. Wentworth in his *Australasia* (1823) and, particularly, Charles Harpur.

At least one early novel also seems to have been printed with no intention of sale. For many years the authorship of *The Guardian: A Tale, by an Australian* (1838), the first novel to be printed in Sydney, was one of the great mysteries of early Australian literature. As often, it was solved not by those who had been puzzling over it for years but by a person working on something completely different. While researching a biography of the pioneer pastoralist and politician Terence Aubrey Murray, Gwendoline Wilson discovered that his sister, Anna Maria Bunn, had written *The Guardian*. Her conclusion that Mrs Bunn wrote the novel after her husband's premature death in order to make money, is, however, not consistent with publishing practices in Sydney during the period. Nor is it true that Mrs Bunn's authorship remained secret from her son William until her deathbed. In a diary kept in 1845 when he was fifteen, William noted that he had 'read Mamma's "Guardian"' though unfortunately he did not bother to record his opinion of it. Perhaps Anna Maria Bunn wrote *The Guardian* as a consoling occupation after her husband's death and her family thought sufficiently highly of it to pay for its publication. It was, however, never offered for sale.

While Field's poetry and Anna Maria Bunn's novel have sufficient literary merit to be regarded as private rather than vanity publications, the latter were certainly not unknown in early Australia. Most of the volumes of poetry, including several not listed in the *Annals*, could fairly be described by this term, and it particularly applies to Beverley Suttor's *Original Poetry* (1838). This lavishly produced volume, illustrated with an engraved portrait of the author in romantic pose, attracted about as much newspaper attention as the 1838 Jubilee celebrations, and far more than any of the seven much worthier 1838 publications listed by Johnston. Suttor became so notorious that the artist who had engraved his portrait made more money by selling sixpenny caricatures of him as 'The Ass That Thought Himself a Lion'.

Today the plays published in this period, mainly neo-classical tragedies such as Samuel Prout Hill's *Tarquin the Proud* (1843), may also seem nothing more than vanity publications. Contemporaries, who rechristened Hill 'Sprout' Hill, possibly agreed. Terry Sturm has, however, convincingly argued for the cultural value of plays and other literary works which have been overlooked subsequently because of their non-Australian content. Tragedies like David Burn's 'The Queen's Love' (1842; first produced 1845) published in his *Plays and Fugitive Pieces* (1842), can be seen as demonstrating the continuities between British and Australian culture and asserting that high art was possible even in the antipodes.

Only a few brave, or foolhardy, writers dared to assert that not only was high art possible in Australia, it was possible on Australian subjects. Chief of these was Charles Harpur who, particularly during the early stages of his career, deliberately attempted to write epics and tragedies using Australian material. Since Harpur was undoubtedly the finest Australian writer of this period, his publishing history is a telling example of how high printing costs and apathy towards local writers could sometimes thwart those with true literary ability. Though there was a ready English market for non-fiction and, later, fiction about Australia, Australian poets usually had no hope of publication outside Australia. As a native-born Australian, with convict parents and a far from sycophantic nature, Harpur was unable to draw on a wealthy patron or a wide circle of well-to-do friends to support his publications. Although he managed to publish two fairly substantial volumes and a number of smaller ones during his lifetime, the volume of collected poems Harpur worked on for years could never be financed. After his death in 1868, Mary Harpur raised money for a collection but the volume that eventually appeared in 1883, heavily edited by another hand, failed to sell.

During his life, Harpur's reputation suffered not only from the widespread belief that Australian material was literary anathema but from the factionalism of colonial society. Harpur sided with radicals such as W. A. Duncan of the *Weekly Register* and the young Henry Parkes in efforts to combat the power of the squattocracy and win greater freedom and independence for Australia. Inevitably, this ensured that his poetry did not get a good reception in more conservative circles. A similar pattern in reverse can be seen in the reviews of Charles Tompson's *Wild Notes, from the Lyre of a Native Minstrel* (1826). Like Harpur, Tompson had been born in Australia of convict parents, but seems to have had better success in winning friends. Over 200 of them subscribed to his volume of poems, printed by Robert Howe of the then leading conservative paper, the *Sydney Gazette*. The *Gazette* gave Tompson's poems lavish praise; its more radical rival the *Sydney Monitor* was much less impressed. This exchange went backwards and forwards for several months, ending with a writer to the *Monitor* claiming on 29 October 1827 that 'the public voice goes with me, of which presumptive evidence may be seen on the shelves of the Australian Stationery Warehouse'. This example seems to offer further evidence of apathy to local writers, but, given the political context, how much faith can be placed in it?

Certainly, not everyone in Sydney was apathetic. On 27 February 1845, the *Colonial Literary Journal* published what purported to be an overheard debate on the subject of 'colonial' or, as the more patriotic of the debaters insisted, 'Australian' literature. When his opponent raised the usual objections about the lack of suitable material, American literature was cited as a model and the assertion made that there was ample material 'in the town, in the bush, among sheep stations, homesteads, squatters, blackfellows, kangaroos and parrots'. Despite the reference to America as an example of what could be done by colonial literatures, it is worth remembering that nineteenth-century American writers themselves had to contend with similar doubts and prejudices.

The belief that new countries lacked the depth of culture and length of history required for the higher literary genres would seem to explain why most of those attempting poetry and tragedy set their works outside Australia. With the exception of Harpur and a few others, Australian subjects tended to be the preserve of those using more popular forms such as comic and satiric verse and prose, pantomime, melodrama and the novel. One of the most prolific early satirists was Laurence Halloran who, it was claimed, was writing verses against the governor even on his deathbed. Though Halloran several times called for subscribers to his volumes of poetry, none was published in Australia. The same fate befell his son Henry, even though his verse was more plentiful and less vituperative than his father's.

As the example of the Hallorans demonstrates, much of the literature produced in early Australia never got into print in volume form. So the 98 items listed by Johnston for the years to 1855 represent only a small fraction of that written during the period. Two of Johnston's items, Michael Massey Robinson's 'Odes' and Henry Melville's 1834 melodrama 'The Bushrangers', were in fact published not as separate volumes but in a newspaper and a magazine respectively.

Literary publication in Australia should then be dated not from 1818, the year of the first general book, but from 1803, the date of the first newspaper, the *Sydney Gazette*. From almost the first issue its editor and printer, George Howe, was including original poetry and, more occasionally, original essays, sketches, stories and reviews. Most early Australian newspapers featured a 'Poet's Corner', sometimes filled with selected verses, more often with original ones, in addition to the political satire printed by many. By 1855, thousands of original poems had been printed in Australian newpapers and magazines, together with hundreds of prose works, including several serialised novels, and a few plays.

While some writers, such as Charles Tompson, were able to collect their poems and publish them in a more durable form, most had to accept the ephemerality of newsprint, even to endure, as a writer to the Sydney *Colonist* for 8 June 1837 lamented, the sight of their literary production being used to wrap a pound of sausages. Few women writers, in particular, were able to share with Anna Maria Bunn the luxury of a private printing. The Mitchell Library holds a manuscript volume of poetry, 'The Vase', prepared for publication by Eliza Hamilton Dunlop, one of the first whites to take a serious interest in Aboriginal literature. Many of her poems were published in Sydney newpapers but, in the absence of a volume, her name is not recorded in the bibliographies or literary histories. Nor is that of Mary Bailey, a highly educated woman from a wealthy background, who published several volumes of poetry in England before following her clergyman husband to Tasmania. Though she continued writing, and published dozens of poems in Hobart papers, she was evidently unable to afford the high cost of colonial printing and, as the wife of a convict, could not draw on a circle of friendly subscribers.

Much of the writing done by women during this period was never, of course, intended for publication. Though there is now no way of knowing how many letters were written or diaries kept, of those that have survived, many of the most interesting were written by women. Some have subsequently found their way into print, including *Georgiana's Journal* (1934), the poet Hugh McCrae's edition of the diaries and letters written by his grandmother in Port Phillip during the 1840s and 1850s, and *Annabella Boswell's Journal* (1965).

Women were also prominent among the travel writers who, following in the tracks of the earlier governors and explorers, continued to cater for the avid English and European interest in Australia. Some of the liveliest accounts of life in Australia during this period may be found in Louisa Anne Meredith's *Notes and Sketches of New South Wales* (1844) and *My Home in Tasmania* (1852) and Ellen Clacy's *A Lady's Visit to the Gold Diggings of Australia* (1853). Of works in this style by men, the most readable are G. C. Mundy's *Our Antipodes* (1852) and William Howitt's *Land, Labour and Gold* (1855).

The fact that, of these four, all but Mundy wrote fiction as well as non-fiction, points to the difficulty of trying to make rigid distinctions between varieties of prose. In 1856 the critic Frederick Sinnett complained that most Australian novels were merely 'books of travel in disguise'. He might equally have observed that the best travel books, biographies and autobiographies have many fictional elements. Grahame Johnston, for example, lists Alexander Harris' *Settlers and Convicts* (1847) as a novel and Charles Cozens' *Adventures of a Guardsman* (1848) as autobiography. Yet many others have read Harris' text as non-fiction, Cozens' as fiction. Both, like Charles Rowcroft's highly popular novel *Tales of the Colonies* (1843), were written in England at a time when Australia was beginning to be perceived as a land of promise rather than exile. So all, naturally enough, were written with an eye on the potential market of intending settlers. Today, rather than worrying too much about how they might be classified and evaluated, these texts should be enjoyed for their intrinsic qualities as pieces of writing and for the insights they provide into aspects of life in various parts of early Australia.

While criticising novels by Howitt, Rowcroft and Harris, Sinnett singled out Catherine Helen Spence's *Clara Morison* (1854) for special praise. Spence, of course, was also writing for the English market. Her subtitle, *A Tale of South Australia During the Gold Fever,* signals its appeal to the next major source of overseas interest in Australia. Spence's account of the diggings is, however, limited to 'letters home'; the historical interest of *Clara Morison* is heightened by its rarity in concentrating not on the male gold seekers but on the women left behind to carry on as well as they can. The depth of characterisation praised by Sinnett is largely a result of Spence's decision to focus on interior adventures rather than the external ones favoured by male writers. As early as 21 March 1829, the *Hobart Town Courier* had defined the staple subjects of Australian fiction as 'Exploits against the natives, the apprehension of bushrangers, extraordinary narratives of all kinds'. If gold-digging and dying explorers and bushmen are added, one has the staple subjects of most nineteenth-century melodramas and narrative poems as well.

Spence's failure to stick to the staple male subjects suggests one reason why her novels, and those of other nineteenth-century women writers, have generally not been seen as part of the Australian literary tradition. The publishing history of *Clara Morison* is also a paradigm of what was to befall many later texts written in Australia but, of necessity, published in England. Spence entrusted the manuscript of the novel to a friend who was visiting England. He managed to find her a publisher, even, indeed, one willing to pay £40 for the privilege. But, as Spence later recorded with understandable indignity, 'as it was too long for the series, I was charged £10 for abridging it'.

Though later writers do not appear to have suffered the same financial penalties, their texts were often similarly cut and amended by English editors and publishers. The present century was well advanced before writers living in Australia could regularly expect to correct the proofs for works being published in England.

One of the most remarkable novels written in Australia during this period was not known to Sinnett since it remained in manuscript until 1929 and did not appear in full until 1952. *Ralph Rashleigh*, apparently written by a convict called James Tucker at Port Macquarie during the 1840s, was, in another example of the slipperiness of concepts of fiction and non-fiction, initially taken to be a convict memoir. Accordingly, what was read as its inappropriately over-heavy and literary style was severely cut and rewritten for the English edition of 1929. After much painstaking research, Colin Roderick was able to demonstrate that *Ralph Rashleigh* (1952) was a work of fiction and arrange for publication in its original form. Many other works mangled by English editors are still awaiting scholarly rescue.

Ralph Rashleigh contains a detailed account of plays performed by convicts at Emu Plains penal station in the 1820s. Besides this novel, Tucker is thought to have written several plays, of which the comedy *Jemmy Green in Australia* (1955) has survived. Since convicts were supposedly barred from Sydney theatres, the even more prolific convict playwright Edward Geoghegan had his works produced anonymously or under names of others. In a letter written to the Colonial Secretary, Deas Thomson, on 16 September 1846, Geoghegan listed seven plays written in the last four years, 'Besides several poetical addresses—the remunerations I have received for *all* of which has been under £6!!!' While most of these plays, in the contemporary fashion of English theatre, were adaptations of popular novels such as Dickens' *Pickwick Papers* (1837), they included the local musical comedy *The Currency Lass* (produced 1844; published 1976). Just as Australian booksellers stocked English rather than Australian authors, so most of the plays performed in Australia during this period originated in England or Europe. Theatre audiences seem generally to have been delighted by the few works with local reference. Certain popular nineteenth-century forms, especially the Christmas pantomime, demanded local and topical reference in both scenery and text. As early as 1845, an entirely Australian pantomime, 'Harlequin in Australia Felix', was performed in Geelong. Though few authors of these popular pieces could afford to have them published the texts of some have survived in the New

South Wales Archives. Unfortunately for posterity, the same licensing laws, which required new plays to be submitted for approval, were not in operation in Tasmania or South Australia. Knowledge of the original plays produced there is limited to the details that can be found in newspaper reviews and playbills.

As this last example indicates, to appreciate fully the range of literary production in early Australia one needs to go beyond the items listed in bibliographies, beyond those published only in magazines and newspapers, even beyond those which still survive in manuscript in libraries and archives. Though we may never be able to know these lost works in the same way as others, awareness of them, when added to the amount which has survived, should help to question prevailing notions of pre-goldrush Australia as a cultural desert. When contemporaries spoke of the slow progress of Australian literature, they were using a definition of literature which included history and biography but excluded comic and satiric verse, popular drama, all types of fiction and, of course, letters and diaries. Many later critics and literary historians have used different but equally narrow definitions, such as including fiction but excluding non-fiction. They have also frequently used narrow definitions of 'Australian' insisting, for example, that only what were seen as 'distinctively' Australian works or works set or published in Australia could be included.

But during the nineteenth century the place of publication had little to do with a work's 'Australianness'. Indeed, the more 'Australian' works, such as travel books, novels and explorers' journals tended to be published in London, the least, such as serious poetry and verse tragedies, in Australia, since there was no English market for them. The demographic and economic factors which produced this pattern also ensured that the fact of publication in Australia had more to do with an author's financial state than literary ability. Only by allowing for these factors, and extending our definition of literature to include not only so-called non-fictional and popular forms but unpublished works and those published in periodicals, can we begin to comprehend the literature of early Australia.

Notes

Besides Ferguson's *Bibliography*, Johnston's *Annals* and H. M. Green's *A History of Australian Literature* (2 vols, 1961), this chapter draws heavily on E. Morris Miller, *Australian Literature from its beginnings to 1935* (2 vols, 1940) and *Pressmen and Governors* (1952) and Elizabeth Webby, 'Literature and the Reading Public in Australia', unpublished Ph.D. thesis, University of Sydney (4 vols, 1971).

The *Sydney Morning Herald*'s remarks on colonial authorship appeared on 17 April 1842 in a review of John Lang's *Legends of Australia* (1842). Adverse reviews of Field's poetry include one in the *Sydney Gazette* for 25 November 1826. In Patrick White's *The Solid Mandala* (1966), the repressed Waldo Brown reads a paper on Barron Field to the Beecroft Literary Society.

Further information on Anna Maria Bunn can be found in Gwendoline Wilson, *Murray of Yarralumla* (1986); William Bunn's diaries are in the Mitchell Library. Beverley Suttor is discussed in Elizabeth Webby, 'Mr Beverley Suttor Publishes his Poems and Gets Laughed At', *The Push from the Bush*, 10 (1981).

Terry Sturm discusses early Australian plays in 'Drama', in L. Kramer (ed.), *The Oxford History of Australian Literature* (1981). Other detailed accounts of early drama and theatre include Eric Irvin, *Theatre Comes to Australia* (1971) and Harold Love (ed.), *The Australian Stage: A Documentary History* (1984).

For a fuller discussion of Charles Harpur, see chapter 9. Early attitudes to Australian literature are discussed in Elizabeth Webby, ' "Parents Rather than Critics": Some Early Reviews of Australian Literature', in Leon Cantrell (ed.), *Bards, Bohemians and Bookmen* (1976). On nineteenth-century attitudes to American literature, see for example, Fenimore Cooper, *Notions of the Americans* (1828).

Laurence Halloran's death was described in a letter from the Sydney solicitor George Allen, 7 April 1831, now in the Mitchell Library. Halloran called for subscribers to his *Poems* in the *Sydney Gazette* on 22 July 1824 and 21 May 1828. A complete list of original poems printed in surviving pre-1850 Australian newspapers and magazines may be found in Elizabeth Webby, *Early Australian Poetry* (1982). A few of Eliza Dunlop's poems have been reprinted in *The Aboriginal Mother and other poems* (1981); see also the entry on her in *Australian Dictionary of Biography*, vol. 1 (1966). Information on Mary Bailey may be found in the entry on her husband William in the same volume and in Miller's *Pressmen and Governors*. For Louisa Anne Meredith see the biography by Vivienne Rae Ellis subtitled *A Tigress in Exile* (1979).

Sinnett's 'The Fiction Fields of Australia' first appeared in the *Journal of Australasia*; it has been reprinted in John Barnes (ed.), *The Writer in Australia* (1969). Details of the publication of *Clara Morison* come from Spence's *Autobiography* (1910). Later texts to be considerably edited for the English market include the English edition of Marcus Clarke's *His Natural Life* (1875) and Miles Franklin's *My Brilliant Career* (1901). On 4 November 1932, in a letter to her mother now in the Palmer papers in the National Library, Nettie Palmer noted that Vance Palmer could have greatly improved his novel *Daybreak* (1932) if he had had the proofs to correct.

Roderick's researches are outlined in his introduction to the Australian edition of *Ralph Rashleigh* (1952). Geoghegan's letter is now in the New South Wales Archives. A list of all known nineteenth-century Australian plays is included in Eric Irvin's *Australian Melodrama* (1981).

Chapter 8

PUBLIC AND PRIVATE VOICES: NON-FICTIONAL PROSE

ROBERT DIXON

It is often assumed that the best early Australian writing was contained in explorers' journals, in official and semi-official records, and in the published 'descriptive accounts' of colonial life. Since the early 1970s, however, there has been a remarkable rediscovery of colonial letters and diaries, many from manuscript sources, and many written by women. This is a major shift in the way we have chosen to see ourselves and our history. Letters and diaries tend to record private experience rather than public events; they replace a world that is public, officially and masculine with one that is personal, domestic and, more often than not, feminine. But language does not function as the transparent medium of personal expression. Even in apparently personal documents like letters and diaries, it participates in the public sphere, actively shaping our most private perceptions. This is often most apparent when different types of documents— letters and sermons, or diaries and explorers' jounals—are read together, rather than in isolation. The non-fictional prose of the colonial period is therefore most appropriately seen as a complex network of writing in which a variety of disparate and opposing positions—public and private, masculine and feminine, official and domestic—are constructed and contested.

Although many First Fleet writers were naval and military officers, their voices tend to be distinctive, and even subversive of official views. The 'official' account of the First Fleet was *The Voyage of Governor Phillip to Botany Bay* (1789). It was not written by Phillip himself, but 'compiled from Authentic papers' by the publisher, John Stockdale. The text presents an officially acceptable interpretation of the settlement, admonishing the convicts for their 'habitual indolence' and 'general profligacy of manners', but acknowledging the progress and achievements of Phillip's administration. Other publications, however—even those by naval and military officers—reflect a diversity of experience and opinion. Private accounts flooded in from the new colony and were widely reproduced by the British press. A 'Letter from an Officer at Sydney', printed in the *Morning Post* of 23 April 1789, described New South Wales as 'the outcast of God's works'. At Botany Bay, there was 'not a spot of ground large enough for a cabbage-garden fit for cultivation', and the author believed that the country in general 'will never answer the intentions of Government'. So disparate were public and private reports that Banks attempted to prevent the publication of Captain Watkin Tench's *A Complete Account of the Settlement at Port Jackson* (1793)—still regarded by many historians as an official or 'semi-official' account—on the grounds that his earlier book, *A Narrative of the Expedition to Botany Bay* (1789), 'very widely misrepresented the circumstances in which the new Colony at Port Jackson then was'.

A second feature of these eighteenth-century accounts is the way in which conventional ideas and vocabulary were challenged by the actual contact with the new land and its Aboriginal people. Despite the influence of the Royal Society on the literary training of military and naval officers, their prose is not an objective rendering of a clearly perceived reality. Like the first generation of colonial poets, they brought with them a stock of neo-classical ideas about nature and society which influenced their perceptions and their writing. David Collins' description of the manners and customs of the Aborigines in *An Account of the English Colony in New South Wales* (1798) is widely regarded as a model of the empirical method of observation and description. Collins clearly believed himself to be employing a scientific method when he remarked that 'in describing their customs and in detailing their language, I have chosen to mention only those facts about which, after much attention and inquiry, I could satisfy my own mind'. Yet his remarks on many aspects of their customs indicate that he observed them within the framework of commonplace eighteenth-century ideas about 'savage life'. Lord Monboddo's influential classification of the natives of New Holland as 'Examples of Men Living in the Brutish State' is reflected in Collins' observations of their language and culture: 'To exalt these people at all above the brute creation,' he remarked, 'it is necessary to show that they had the gift of reason.' The influence of philosophical and even poetic ideas on the representation of

Aboriginal people is also evident in Captain John Hunter's *An Historical Journal of the Transactions at Port Jackson and Norfolk Island* (1793). His account of 'a native woman of Pitt Water', which accompanies the frontispiece, suggests a sincere personal response to his contact with the Aboriginal woman coloured by classical notions of primitive life recalled from his reading of Lucretius and Cicero.

The emergent romantic theme of personal sensibility is displayed in the convict artist Thomas Watling's *Letters from an Exile at Botany-Bay to his Aunt in Dumfries* (1794), where it assumes a disruptive and transgressive role. Watling creates the persona of a melancholy artist whose refined feelings are offended by the conditions of penal servitude, and his '*Il penseroso* gloom' is signified by the rhetorical excess of his prose: 'There are, thank God, no fetters for the soul: collected in herself, she scorns ungenerous treatment, or a prostitution of her perfections.' But Watling also seeks to distance himself from the very language he uses, as if to assert an essential self that remains untouched by penal discipline, just as it remains distinct from the public life of language:

> Never did I find language so imperfect as at present, nor letters to give so little satisfaction; for the former cannot shadow my feelings, nor the latter yield me more than pensive melancholy reflection.

In the network of writing produced by the convict system, the excesses of sensibility are brought under control by neo-classical rhetoric. Indeed, the official documentary record can leave an impression that, for many, private experience was little more than an object of public inspection. The official prose of Governor Macquarie (1810-21) demonstrates that intervention in the private sphere was one of his priorities. His proclamation of 24 February 1810, which deals with the suppression of immorality and vice, approaches the style of allegorical personification common in eighteenth-century poetry, and revived in New South Wales by Michael Massey Robinson. Within the text, 'HIS EXCELLENCY the GOVERNOR' becomes a figure of almost sublime abstraction, engaged in a public contest with 'Immorality', 'Vice' and '*Illegal Cohabitation*'.

An Address to the Inhabitants of the Colonies, Established in New South Wales (1794), by the Anglican chaplain, Richard Johnson, demonstrates a similar examination of private conduct in the religious literature of the period. In the imagery and rhetorical point of view of his address, Johnson conflates his own position as priest and penal official with that of God. He has been appointed over the convicts 'to watch, as one who must give an account'; at the same time they are warned that 'the eye of God is particularly upon you'. The metaphor of personal inspection implicit in the first part of the sermon receives a chilling elaboration in the second, when Johnson threatens to enter their very homes:

> Were I to visit your different places and huts, I fear I should find some of you . . . indulging themselves in mere sloth and idleness, others engaged in the most profane and unclean conversation, and others committing abominations, which it would defile my pen to describe.

When illiterate convicts and subordinate officials do enter the documentary record, their voices tend to be distorted by the context. Most convicts encountered written language only when petitioning government, and for these rare occasions there were professional letter writers and even prepared petition forms. Petitions tend to reflect purely formal expressions of repentance and self-worth, and reveal little of the personal lives of the convicts. Surviving convict letters confirm that even those who could write tend to reproduce the ideology of penal discipline in their most private thoughts. One of the earliest surviving letters by a convict woman ends with the comment, 'All our letters are examined by an officer, but a friend takes this for me privately.' Elizabeth Mitchell's petition to Governor Brisbane in 1822 indicates her willingness for government to inspect, judge, and then intervene directly in her domestic affairs. Upon her arrival in the colony, Elizabeth 'became acquainted with one William Freeman'. Five years later, her daughter Hannah arrived in Sydney and immediately began an affair with her mother's husband. It was 'the painful duty of Petitioner to endeavour to depict a Scene of Depravity scarce ever evinced or recorded by the Case History of this Colony'. Having 'scrutinized and watched' her daughter, Elizabeth discovered a 'Criminal Intercourse' that she was powerless to prevent, and appealed to the governor to remove Hannah from the colony, 'as well as Society in General'.

Transcripts of evidence provide another striking example of the effects of language and ideology on the individual voice. In *Uphill All the Way: A Documentary History of Women in Australia* (1980), Daniels and Murnane cite the example of John Hutchinson, Superintendent of the Hobart Female Factory, giving evidence before the Committee Inquiring into Female Convict Discipline, 1841-3:

I took the keys and went to the ward in question and allowing myself some time to identify if possible by their voices those who were disorderly and looking in at the window I saw five Prisoners now present dancing perfectly naked, and making obscene attitudes towards each other . . . in imitation of men and women together.

In giving evidence, individuals tend to become caught up in the process of inquiry, and as the 'I' offered by the narrative point of view becomes the 'eye' of disciplinary inspection, inmates become case studies in abnormal or criminal conduct. For those denied a voice, 'obscene attitudes' were often the only form of speech available. The inmates of the Female Factory responded in this way to a visit by the lieutenant-governor and chaplain: 'they all with one impulse turned round, raised their clothes, and smacked their posteriors with loud report'.

The sense of the private or family sphere, so absent in the network of writing associated with penal life, is everywhere apparent in writing of 'respectable' society. In the case of 'respectable' women, in particular, the family and the home are the place from which they speak. Middle-class women were taught the art of letter writing at an early age, often by a governess, and were expected to compose readable accounts of domestic life for the benefit of friends and relatives at home. Gentlewomen whose letters and diaries survive from this early period include the wives of governors—notably Elizabeth Macquarie and Eliza Darling—and the wives of churchmen and the civil and military officers, such as Elizabeth Marsden, Elizabeth Hassall, Elizabeth Macarthur, Mary Ann Piper, Elizabeth Paterson and Christiana Brooks. The best and most extensive letters of this group were written by Elizabeth Macarthur, the wife of the leading free settler. The Macarthurs moved to Rose Hill in 1793 and settled at Elizabeth Farm, which Elizabeth was to regard as her home for the rest of her life, even after the completion of Camden Park in the 1830s. Although she successfully managed her husband's pastoral interests for many years, she typically places herself at the centre of her domestic environment: 'I write to you now from our own House . . . I thank God we enjoy all the comforts we could desire'; and, 'It is now our winter season, & I am now sitting round a wood fire, with other dear members of the Family circle.' In 1816, Elizabeth assured her friend Eliza Kingdon that 'there is a sufficiency of pleasant, agreeable persons to visit and be visited by, to satisfy one who is not ambitious to have a very numerous visiting acquaintance'.

When the letters of Elizabeth Macarthur are read alongside the records of the penal system, it becomes apparent that the private sphere is an ideological construction of the period, not an objective historical fact. This is often most clear when the private sphere is penetrated by those outside influences from which it seeks to set itself apart. On 20 February 1830, Sophy Dumaresq wrote to her childhood friend Mrs Winn describing the daily routine of her life in Sydney. The letter is disrupted by a long digression—for which she later apologises—complaining of a convict servant who was too drunk to dress Sophy's infant son. Sophy's voice has its source deep within the experience of family life. Yet so profoundly do the disciplinary relations of the public sphere penetrate the private, that the very woman who dresses her baby must be 'placed under my observation', judged as 'abominable', and finally 'committed to the Penitentiary'. 'Ever since,' she adds, '[I] have dressed & undressed him myself.'

The domestic themes of women's writing form a marked contrast to the subject matter of published works on the colony. In the years following the Napoleonic wars, widespread economic distress and political uncertainty in Britain made emigration increasingly attractive, and the 1820s saw the first great influx of free immigrants. The majority were people of capital, attracted by Australia's obvious potential for pastoral settlement. The period was heralded by William Charles Wentworth's *Statistical, Historical, and Political Description of the Colony of New South Wales* (1819). Joseph Lycett's *Views in Australia* followed in 1824, James Atkinson's *An Account of the State of Agriculture and Grazing in New South Wales* in 1826, and Peter Cunningham's *Two Years in New South Wales* in 1827. Although differing in style, subject and purpose, these books reflect a generally optimistic vision of Australia's future. Wentworth acknowledged that one aim of his book was 'to divert from the United States of America to [Australia's] shores, some part of that vast tide of emigration, which is at present flowing thither from all parts of Europe'. Cunningham believed that 'England has already erected one immense empire in America, and founded, it is to be hoped, another considerable one in Australia'. The theme of continental destiny was fuelled by geographical speculations about a transcontinental river that would facilitate the spread of agriculture and commerce across the nation, and received its most rhetorical expression in Wentworth's account of the country west of the Blue Mountains.

Writers and artists alike responded with enthusiasm both to the

settled pastoral regions and the newly discovered interior of
Australia. Bush travel, bivouacking, kangaroo hunting and other
masculine themes suggest the beginnings of a frontier mythology
based partly on a comparison with the American experience, but also
directly emerging from life in Australia. Cunningham noted that the
'natural forest' was ideally suited to field sports:

> It is really delightful to ride through these open spots, where there is
> scarcely a tree you would wish to see cut down, so much do they beautify
> the prospect; while, if a kangaroo or an emu should start up in your path,
> you enjoy a clear and animated view of the chase, until the dogs finally
> surround and seize upon their victim.

James Atkinson's book is illustrated by three engravings showing an
exploring party bivouacking in the bush, a theme that recurs in the
work of other artists travelling on the pastoral frontier, such as
Augustus Earle and Joseph Lycett. 'Excursions are frequently made
by the more enterprising Settlers,' he observes,'. . . sometimes merely
for the sake of gratifying their curiosity.'

The imagery of pastoral wealth and the emergent mythology of the
frontier were developed in the journals of inland exploration, which
also contributed to the growing interest in Australia as a field for
emigration. When John Oxley set off on his expedition to discover
the termination of the Lachlan River in 1817, he was issued with a
set of instructions which derived ultimately from the Royal Society's
instructions to mariners, and stressed the essentially scientific
objectives of exploration: Oxley was to keep a journal, and to
describe 'the general appearance of the country' as 'circumstantially'
as possible. Quite apart from its scientific and political objectives,
however, Oxley's expedition also acquired an heroic dimension, and
his *Journals of Two Expeditions into the Interior of New South Wales*
(1820) catered to the growing interest in narratives of frontier
adventure. His description of Bathurst's Falls on the River Apsley, for
example, announces an awakening pride in the sublimity of the
Australian wilderness, and forms a suitable backdrop for the
increasingly heroic figure of the inland explorer.

Thomas Mitchell's *Three Expeditions into the Interior of Eastern
Australia* (1838) is the culmination of this epic phase of inland
exploration. In organising his journal, Mitchell deployed the episodes
of landscape description and narrative interest in a carefully
organised pattern of quest and discovery modelled partly on the

Lusiads of Camões, a sixteenth-century Portuguese epic poem on the history of discovery, which Mitchell translated into English in 1853. His description of Australia Felix exploits the imagery of the natural sublime as a fit setting for the heroic explorer as 'the harbinger of mighty changes'. Despite its apparently scientific purpose, the journal of inland exploration had become a stage for the projection of the romantic masculine persona:

> It seemed to me that even war and victory, with all their glory, were far less alluring than the pursuit of researches such as these; the objects of which were to spread the light of civilization over a portion of the globe yet unknown, though rich, perhaps, in the luxuriance of uncultivated nature, and where science might accomplish new and unthought-of discoveries; while intelligent man would find a region teeming with useful vegetation, abounding with rivers, hills, and vallies, and waiting only for his enterprising spirit and improving hand to turn to account the native bounty of the soil.

Like so much early Australian writing, Mitchell's book projects a view of colonisation that silences alternative voices whose presence is nonetheless evident beneath the surface of the text. This process may be observed in Mitchell's engraving and description of the Aboriginal warrior Cambo, which forms the frontispiece to *Three Expeditions*. Mitchell met Cambo in the Hunter Valley, and immediately recognised in him a fine 'specimen' of the Aboriginal warrior in his first contact with white men. As Mitchell sketched him 'the stout heart of Cambo was visibly overcome', and it was with difficulty that he acquired sufficient fortitude to allow Mitchell to finish the sketch. In the process of representation, the discourse of exploration expunges Cambo's Aboriginal identity, transforming him from a brave warrior in the midst of his tribe into an isolated, nervous and defeated man.

The literature of the frontier also played a direct role in constructing an image of femininity. John Curtis' *Shipwreck of the Stirling Castle* (1838), for example, uses the history of Mrs Fraser to 'convey a moral lesson'. Underlying the simple narrative of shipwreck and rescue are parallels with God's delivery of Israel and Christ's delivery from the wilderness. The island upon which Mrs Fraser and her party are stranded is described as a place where faith is tested by Providence and the 'figurative promises' of the Bible are 'literally exemplified'. The woods are a 'thorny vale' and the natives demons in human form. Mrs Fraser is inserted into this place of testing as an exemplum of the Victorian domestic virtues, a 'doating and affectionate wife', a woman 'influenced by conjugal felicity'. After the death of her husband, she is subjected to increased interference by the Aborigines, whose attentions on more than one occasion reduce the pious Curtis to silence. But Mrs Fraser's Christian and feminine virtues allow her to survive these abominations, and to draw the party as a whole back from the brink of barbarism. The author is finally moved to pay tribute to this devoted young wife who is 'faithful unto death': 'Well may we exclaim . . . "Lovely woman is a treasure."'

Despite the prominence of explorers' journals in the modern understanding of colonial culture, the triumph of the nomad tribe was contested by a number of women writers whose voices have been rediscovered since the rise of women's history in the 1970s. It is therefore interesting to find Emma Macpherson complaining of the dominance of the masculine point of view in the preface to her book *My Experiences in Australia, By a Lady* (1860):

> While [books by male authors] contained a large amount of information relative to Australia interesting and valuable to the statesman, the man of science, the merchant, and the emigrant, still, perhaps, they give but little notion of every-day life in the colonies, as it would appear to a lady's point of view.

Although Emma Macpherson claimed to have discovered the 'lady's point of view', it is the early books of Louisa Anne Meredith— *Notes and Sketches of New South Wales* (1844) and *My Home in Tasmania* (1853)—that represent the best work of this kind. The preface to *My Home in Tasmania*, in particular, suggests that the style of her books represented a deliberate commitment to the centrality of domestic and private life as a source of judgement:

> Lest the minute, perhaps trifling, detail, entered into in some parts, may seem inclining towards the egotistical, I should perhaps remark that I have been induced to adopt a more personal narrative, and to identify ourselves with the simple realities around us.

The book ends with a long, detailed description of the built domestic environment of Riversdale, the home in which it was written, as seen by the author in a series of prospects as she sits at her writing table finishing her book: 'From the front window of our dining-room window, where I now sit, I look through the verandah . . . From our side window . . . we look up the public road, through the district.' Mrs Meredith referred to this descriptive convention as the 'veranda-diorama'. Veranda dioramas and formal descriptions of domestic interiors are a recurring feature of writing by nineteenth-century women, and have their counterpart in women's sketchbooks, where it was also common to paint interiors of rooms, or views of the garden and surrounding country from verandas and windows. These conventions reveal a great deal about the way colonial women constructed their sense of self in the process of writing, and suggest the increasing importance of the home and family in Victorian ideology. The points of view made available by these conventions place the female subject at the physical centre of the domestic environment, which becomes a point of reference from which to judge the public world.

Only rarely did male writers seek to define their own subjectivity in relation to an observed domestic environment, and when they did they tended to handle the descriptive convention in fundamentally different ways from women. In a letter to his wife, written from Sydney in 1824, G. T. W. B. Boyes, for example, described the appearance of his cottage in Pitt Street. Boyes had come to the colony in search of a competency that would enable him either to rejoin his family at home, or to bring them out to join him in the colony. His description locates the cottage away from the sphere of public life: 'Nearly at the top, and quite on the highest part, of Pitt Street—stands on the left side of the road and a little retired from it, a white cottage.' The pronouns in the sentences that follow clearly reveal both the positions from which the description is written, and that from which it must be read: 'After opening the gate and advancing five paces you are upon the stone floor of the veranda . . . What a pretty place I am making of it.' The reader is then guided deeper into the inner rooms of the home, and the passage ends with a frank statement of the connection between writing and desire: 'When half blinded with reading or writing at night I stretch my limbs upon that simple widowed pallet—bolt up the shutters of my eyes and dream about you.' In its authorial point of view, and in the position it constructs for the reader, Boyes' letter therefore reproduces the oppositions between masculine and feminine, public and private, that were an increasingly important feature of Victorian life. It locates the female reader as an object of male desire, and places her forcefully amidst the other decorations of the private sphere, to which the male author may retire from the cares of public life. The letter is therefore more than simply an exercise in wish-fulfilment: it is a moment in writing where the Victorian ideology of the separation of the spheres may be observed shaping the privacy of desire.

The rediscovery of letters and diaries that began in the 1970s has continued into the 1980s, bringing new texts and new themes to the centre of Australia's cultural history. Important texts to be published, or republished, include the journal kept by Annie Baxter on the Macleay River during the 1830s and 1840s; the letters of Christina Cuninghame and Penelope Selby at Port Phillip in the 1840s; the diaries of G. T. W. B. Boyes and the journal of Elizabeth Fenton in Tasmania; the letters of Sophy Cooke in South Australia in the early 1850s; and the letters of Eliza and Thomas Brown at York in Western Australia during the period from 1841 to 1852. While the centrality of domestic life is confirmed, the importance of other activities has also become clearer, notably the satisfaction many pioneer women derived from economically productive labour. Annie Baxter and Penelope Selby, for example, both write of their pride of achievement in running the household dairy and poultry yard, while Sophy Cooke worked in a retail store in Adelaide. Another major theme to emerge is the abundant energy of Australia's pioneer women, so often suppressed or undervalued by their own culture. Christina Cuninghame's remarks are a striking illustration of this point:

> I feel as if I could roam the world over, and should like of all things to set out on a voyaging round it, and stop at every place I ever heard of to have a peep. We can see the sea from our window . . . and when I see the white sails, and the vessels rising on the waves, I do so long to be in one . . . I assure you this newly acquired restless disposition is very inconvenient, for of all places this is one where moving about is, to Ladies, most difficult, and I see little prospect of our getting further than this windy dusty Melbourne for many a long day.

In contrast to Thomas Mitchell, who could project his ambition on to the face of a continent, or through a published book, Christina had to content herself with the more modest outlet of a private letter to a friend, and with viewing her world from the wrong side of the window.

Notes

Contrasting histories of the period are R. W. Connell and T. H. Irving, *Class Structure in Australian History* (1980), and J. B. Hirst,

Convict Society and its Enemies (1983). Bernard Smith, *European Vision and the South Pacific* (2nd ed., 1985), Ross Gibson, *The Diminishing Paradise* (1984), and Robert Dixon, *The Course of Empire* (1986), discuss the literary, artistic and intellectual background; Henry Reynolds, *The Other Side of the Frontier* (1981) and Ian Donaldson and Tamsin Donaldson (eds), *Seeing the First Australians* (1985) discuss the Aboriginal response, and the representation of Aborigines; Don Charlwood, *The Long Farewell* (1981) surveys the literature of emigration and includes primary sources; Paul de Serville, *Port Phillip Gentlemen* (1980) draws extensively on Port Phillip letters and diaries and includes a comprehensive bibliography; Alan Frost discusses the literature of the First Fleet in 'On Finding "Australia"', *Australian Literary Studies*, 12 (1986); Robert Sellick discusses the literature of exploration in Ian Donaldson (ed.), *Australia and the European Imagination* (1982). Michel Foucault's *Discipline and Punish* (trans. 1977) offers a stimulating model for discussing 'the network of writing' in a penal society.

Useful discussions of women's history include Kay Daniels, 'Women's History', in G. Osborne and W. F. Mandle (eds), *New History: Studying Australia Today* (1982); Kay Daniels, 'Feminism and Social History' in *Australian Feminist Studies*, 1 (1985); and Elizabeth Fox-Genovese, 'Placing Women's History in History', *New Left Review*, (May-June 1982), which includes discussion of the ideology of the separate spheres.

Anthologies of women's writing include Kay Daniels and Mary Murnane (eds), *Uphill All the Way* (1980); Lucy Frost (ed.), *No Place for a Nervous Lady* (1984); Helen Heney (ed.), *Dear Fanny* (1985); and Maggie Weidenhofer (ed.), *Colonial Ladies* (1985). (These are the sources of quotations by Elizabeth Mitchell, Elizabeth Macarthur, Sophy Dumaresq and Christina Cuninghame.) Kay Daniels, Mary Murnane, and Anne Picot (eds), *Women in Australia* (1977) is the primary bibliographical guide for further research.

Modern editions of individual collections of letters and diaries include Graham Abbott and Geoffrey Little (eds), *The Respectable Sydney Merchant: A. B. Spark of Tempe* (1976); David Adams (ed.), *The Letters of Rachel Henning* (1966); Peter Chapman (ed.), *The Diaries and Letters of G. T. W. B. Boyes* (1985); Peter Cowan (ed.), *A Faithful Picture: The Letters of Eliza and Thomas Brown* (1977); Morton Herman (ed.), *Annabella Boswell's Journal* (1981); H. W. Lawrence (ed.), *The Journal of Mrs Fenton* (1901); Sibella Macarthur Onslow (ed.), *Some Early Records of the Macarthurs of Camden* (2nd ed, 1973); George Mackaness (ed.), *Some Private Correspondence of the Rev. Samuel Marsden and Family* (1942) and *Some Private Correspondence of Sir John and Lady Franklin* (1947); Hugh McCrae (ed.), *Georgiana's Journal* (1983); George Fletcher Moore, *Diary of Ten Years Eventful Life of an Early Settler in Western Australia* (1884); Pamela Statham (ed.), *The Tanner Letters* (1981); Irene Taylor (ed.), *Sophy Under Sail* (1969); Dorothy Walsh (ed.), *The Admiral's Wife: Mrs Phillip Parker King* (1967).

Chapter 9

COLONIAL TRANSFORMATIONS: WRITING AND THE DILEMMA OF COLONISATION

ELIZABETH PERKINS

Australian writing before 1855 was concerned with the responsibility of presenting a new natural and social environment in the forms and images then available for representing reality, and readily recognised and appreciated by readers in Britain and the colonies. It was too early for innovation. While the colonists were clinging to and cautiously assessing the relevance of the culture they brought with them, it was a radical act to effect any change in the written forms of that culture.

The one certainty, that the culture was colonial, was subject to opposing and ambivalent interpretations. Although it was a culture tainted by punishment and exile, it also promised new freedoms and responsibilities. Another more subtle ambivalence presented an even greater problem. The writing of the period often reflects the dilemma of colonisation, in which making a new home for the body and spirit involves destroying much of what is discovered and loved in the new environment. Colonists found beauty as well as deprivation in the strange country. Even the convict writer James Tucker paused in the middle of a harrowing narrative to present the same charming pastoral scenes, and vistas of awe-inspiring grandeur, as the free colonial advocate Alexander Harris found in the Nepean district of New South Wales. The recognition of colonial beauty was the first horn of the dilemma, for the mere presence of the beholder was an invasion and an assurance of future destruction.

For some it was not only an economic necessity but a moral responsibility to bring ordered civilisation to the landscape. But among these colonists were many who also felt the keenest sympathy with a primal beauty that they believed to be virtually untouched by its Aboriginal inhabitants. The settlers were disturbed by an Aboriginal civilisation they could not understand, even when they recognised its virtues; the worst settlers were contemptuous and could see only savagery. The most humane white settlers seldom lost the patronising attitude of Ensign Trevor in Charles Rowcroft's *The Bushranger of Van Diemen's Land* (1846): 'Sterne, was right . . . these black people have souls after all.'

The other horn of the dilemma was the colonists' recognition that for all the civilised gifts they brought, they were destroying the soul of the land and the soul of its people. Philosophy and religion suggested that the primitive represented chaos in need of order, and original sin in need of redemption: but the primitive also represented innocence and a source of imaginative creation. The colonial dilemma could only be accepted, if not resolved, by a philosophy and religion that replaced polarities of good and evil, chaos and order, with a belief in predestined evolution, where evil meant regression or wilful opposition to enlightenment. The transcendental philosophies and Nonconformist emphasis on individualism and self-reliance characteristic of the religious, social and political beliefs of English and American liberal protestantism, especially that of the Unitarian movement, underlie much colonial writing. Three figures who, together with the convict James Tucker, now seem most representative of colonial writing—the poet Charles Harpur, the prose writer Alexander Harris, and the South Australian novelist Catherine Helen Spence—were deeply influenced by spiritual individualists like Bunyan, W. E. Channing, Emerson and Carlyle. Even the constraint of colonial government was an incentive to writing, since it stood as an opponent against which liberal idealism and self-reliance could react. As writing took shape, it is not surprising that neo-classical structures and devices assisting control of form are often found expressing liberal and visionary ideals.

A balancing of the principles of guidance and natural growth is seen in the narrative style and the moral purpose of *Quintus Servinton* (1830-1), the first novel written and published in Australia. The story purports to be a narrative of real events and does cover much of the life of the author, Henry Savery, transported to Van Diemen's Land for forgery. Introduced and concluded by a distanced narrator, it insists on its own artifice by formal diction and sentence structure and a sprinkling of type names like Knowall, Briefless and Trusty. The title page, however, asserts that it is 'A Tale founded upon Incidents of Real Occurrence', and other names resemble those of real people, Quintus referring to Savery's position as the fifth surviving son of his family. *Quintus Servinton* begins and ends with an idealised portrait of Quintus and his wife Emily as grandparents living in rural peace in Devonshire, so that the novel is not only Savery's apologia, but an attempted reconciliation with his wife, who, as Emily, is given the moderation and wisdom that Quintus lacks. It exists now as a colonial novel urging balance and moderation in human conduct, the story of a man whose instability is partly ascribed to his parents' failure to recognise Rousseau's principle that "all the little ones' must be treated as individuals. The text represents a wishful vision of the unhappy author who never did regain his wife and respectability.

Balance is also the guiding ethic of the first-person narrator in *Settlers and Convicts or Recollections of Sixteen Years' Labour in the Australian Backwoods* (1847) by 'An Emigrant Mechanic', Alexander Harris. Harris does not claim that the account is autobiographical, although much of what is seen and done probably fell within the author's experience. The narrative presents aspects of the colonial dilemma with an immediacy which seems heightened because the ideal colonist is only half aware of his plight. The narrator shows his moral sensibility, commonsense and 'even mind' in everything from his relief of a dying prostitute in Sydney and his relationship with his wife and the Aborigines, to the handling of his cattle and his sawyer's tools. For the time, the account has a democratic temper, and the narrator believes that 'Human nature is the same from the throne to the gunyah'. His appreciation of the landscape frequently invokes the sublime and the effect of natural grandeur on the human presence:

> The effect of these vast avenues, particularly before the grass is worn away, and all but the mere opening remains in its primitive and natural state, is singularly fine and striking; perhaps the term sublime would not be too strong to apply to the effect . . . there, if the air be clear and you catch sight of some other traveller a mile away, the sense of his *conspicuous littleness* is irresistible; and this the next act of reflection can scarcely fail to transfer to yourself.

To be an appreciative, awed presence in this landscape, the settler has already encroached upon it. The narrator's trade, that of a sawyer who knows and loves timber, yet destroys forests in the act of building human settlements, is a simple but powerful image of the colonial dilemma.

Like the rest of humanity, the Aborigines are a subject which the narrator observes and contemplates. Although he acknowledges the fierceness of inter-tribal battles, he finds that in general the Aborigines are in harmony with their environment and that their language is 'exceedingly soft and euphonious'. He understands their bitterness against settlers who steal the land from mere wantonness, not from the pressure of necessity, and if he is disappointed that the Aborigines do not understand liberal democratic theories about 'capital and labour, and pauperism and emigration', he acknowledges their right to want nothing more or less than the complete removal of white settlement.

The colonial dilemma is also acutely present in Harris' novel *The Emigrant Family: or, The Story of an Australian Settler* (1849), which takes up the same principles of prudence, conservation and self-reliance as *Settlers and Convicts* recommends to the colonial working-man, but also emphasises the opportunities open to the native-born and migrant landowner and employer. In *The Emigrant Family*, romantic relationships between characters allow the pairing of similar and the reconciliation of unlike sensibilities to achieve balanced or harmonious couples. The recognition of dissimilarity includes the story of the Jewish father and daughter, Lazarus and Rachel Moses, and the tragic fall of the Negro overseer, Martin Beck. The central importance of Beck is recognised in the title of the second edition published in 1852 as *Martin Beck: or, The Story of an Australian Settler*.

Even the novel's structure depends on laws of action and consequence, and its moral code centres on the virtues of a balanced sensibility, equable temper, rational analysis and an 'even mind'. The emigrant Lieutenant Bracton appoints Beck as overseer on his newly acquired property. Failing to transform traditional English farm management to suit colonial conditions, Bracton allows the avaricious Beck to bring him to the edge of ruin as he attempts to acquire by wealth the status denied by his colour. The emigrant Bracton family is counterbalanced by a colonial-born brother and sister, Reuben and Mary Kable, who, significantly, have no parental figures of authority and need none. Like *Settlers and Convicts*, the novel may be read as an examination of the use and abuse of social, political and moral authority, and it is critical of government measures which interfere with the self-reliant native-born and settlers.

Both the Kables and the Aboriginal characters are called 'natives'. Reuben Kable confronts the colonial dilemma head on in a long speech addressed to Katharine Bracton, who, representing in an idealised form the perfectly harmonious development of womanly goodness, is here a figure of justice and charity. Having posed the question, 'Shall we hold the land or resign it?' Kable argues the moral right of white necessity against Aboriginal neglect of the land and their adequate means of subsistence: 'To suppose that the tribes which have disappeared have done so through scarcity of animals on their hunting grounds, is what no one acquainted with the country would do.' Katharine listens attentively but makes no comment. In *Settlers and Convicts* Harris insists through a hypothetical Aboriginal speaker that hunting grounds have been stolen by greedy white settlers, so that whatever Kable argues, Harris' work leaves the dilemma unresolved.

In *Ralph Rashleigh or The Life of an Exile* (1844-5; 1952), the formality of the eighteenth-century picaresque novel is sharpened by the irony of the authorial voice, ascribed to the convict James Tucker. Tucker's attitude to penal servitude in a new, promising country is understandably ambivalent. Although some of the events Rashleigh experiences have a stark immediacy, they are usually also presented as 'adventures' which befall 'our exile', 'our rambler' or 'our adventurer', even when he lives under harsh constraint as a convict or traverses the colony as the unwilling confederate of bushrangers.

After a rash and imprudent youth, Rashleigh enters the rigours of the Emu Plains convict settlement and becomes a model of prudence, sobriety and resourcefulness, whose experiences and sufferings present a pageant of the convict system and small farm settlement. Rashleigh is a figure constructed by a narrator whose sensibility is not as tender as Rashleigh's but whose critical irony and moral outrage are more pronounced, giving the text a presence suited to the needs of a convict writing from within the system. Sympathy is provoked by Rashleigh's hardships, but his mild demeanour suggests he bears punishment, deserved or undeserved, with patience. On the other hand, the narrator's description of the Coal River settlement as the 'Ultima Thule of the moral world', and his descriptions of the complicated horrors and suffering of the convict system, are overt social criticism. If necessary, however, Tucker could have denied that they were polemical, pointing instead to their historical, analytical or rhetorical intention.

Rashleigh's assimilation into the life of a tribe of coastal Aborigines is less difficult owing to the savagery he experiences as a convict, and he endures the initiation ceremony with comparative ease, 'Being indurated to torture' by the cats of the Coal River. He acquires three loyal Aboriginal wives, and treats them with more respect and dignity than, in the narrator's view, they are accorded by the tribal system, women's position there being interpreted by the narrator as 'no better than slaves'. In transforming Rashleigh into an Aborigine, Tucker allows him a rebirth into innocence and establishes his new and honourable character in white society through his rescue and preservation of Mrs Marby and her son and sister.

Rashleigh's life and the novel end suddenly when, as a station manager, he is speared while pursuing Aborigines who have killed a shepherd on a neighbouring property. His death is supposed to occur in 1844, the year Tucker apparently began writing, and the narrator aligns himself with the critics of government attempts to protect the Aborigines. The narrative avoids attributing Rashleigh's death directly to the convict system, but does indirectly attribute it to the government's protective policy towards Aborigines which forbade shepherds—most of whom were assignees or ex-convicts—to carry arms. The last sentence speaks of the expiation of Rashleigh's early errors, but if *Ralph Rashleigh* is Tucker's act of expiation, it also, from the first chapter to the last, offers a critique of the authorities in Britain and Australia charged with the administration of law and the punishment of crime.

Charles Rowcroft, who spent only four years in Van Diemen's Land gathering material for *Tales of the Colonies; or, the Adventures of an Emigrant* (1843), *The Bushranger of Van Diemen's Land* (1846) and *An Emigrant in Search of a Colony* (1851), engages some of his characters in debate about the colonial dilemma. Essentially he uses the new arena as a setting for typical adventures in which the action itself raises colonial issues, as in *Tales of the Colonies* where an Aboriginal villain, Musqueeto, abducts a white child. Rowcroft's style is racy even at its most formal. In *The Bushranger of Van Diemen's Land* the wit and melodrama verge on parody of the colonial bushranging genre, although the introduction claims that those who think 'the noblest study of mankind is man', will be deeply interested in 'the curious psychological phenomena developed by the peculiar condition of solitude to which the modern Cain, of which this history treats, was exposed'. As a bushranger tragedy it is less psychologically convincing than the plays of Burn and Harpur, since the gothically named Mark Brandon declines abruptly from a sardonic adventurer into a human tiger, and his fatal plunge into a bushfire, from a precipice on which he has been slowly mutilated by a revengeful eagle, is a fantastic image from Greek and medieval mythology. In this colonial adventure, Mr Silliman, initially a clown who pratfalls into the perils of snakes, tarantulas, Tasmanian devils, wombats, deer, kangaroo and Aborigines, benefits from 'the transmogrifying qualities of the new country' and wins approval and respect. The bush inculcates in Major Horton and Ensign Trevor enlightened attitudes towards social manners, rank and Aboriginal people, and the tendency of the writing is egalitarian and humane.

Within a context of theories of primitive and developed cultures, the confrontation of white settlement and Aboriginal civilisation is consciously analysed in William Howitt's *A Boy's Adventure in the Wilds of Australia; or, Herbert's Note-Book* (1854). In depicting this and other colonial problems, Howitt achieves a nice balance between the eager observation and reception of youth and the prudent conclusions of experience. The narrator acknowledges all the virtues he can perceive in Aboriginal life and custom, but is baffled that on the fringes of white settlement he finds 'a picture of savage life which would not, I think, enchant even a Rousseau'. Bushranging, fire, gold-mining, death in the bush and other stock incidents are treated with such depth that colonial experience becomes a genuine process of enlightenment. Two extreme responses of the European migrant are summed up in the comically resourceful boy Jonas and his timid cousin Phineas. Jones is exhilarated by the variety and strangeness of the flora and fauna. The solitude and boundlessness of the forests and wildernesses into which he rides excite him with the most delightful solemnity and awe. Phineas, however, is terrified by the wildness and remoteness of the landscape, and the 'deep, resounding glens, stretching ever onward and inward, he knew not whither' appal him. Although today these may be seen as the extrovert and introvert response to a landscape which is also an image of the beholder's psyche, the interpretation made by Howitt's contemporaries may have been that Phineas, unlike Jonas, was not a true Australian colonist. After stumbling upon a lode of gold, Phineas returns to England.

The fiction of this period uses the didactic possibilities of writing to offer both general moral instruction and specific information and advice about colonial life. Catherine Helen Spence, writing in

Adelaide, introduces also an early feminist critique of the expanding scope and values of a women's life in colonial society. *Clara Morison: A Tale of South Australia during the Gold Fever* (1854), is the first colonial work that may fairly be compared with that of George Eliot or Elizabeth Gaskell. *Clara Morison*, with some wit and satire to lighten its earnestness, looks at the ethos of Adelaide society from the intellectual and religious perspective of an industrious middle-class family, in which colonial opportunities give sensibilities as fine as those possessed by the best of Jane Austen's characters, scope for the intelligent use of their lives. Spence, whose *An Agnostic's Progress from the Known to the Unknown* (1884) ascribes her later maturity and enlightenment to the strength of Unitarian thinking, is an important figure in the history of the literary influence of Unitarianism, not only in colonial Australia but also in America and Victorian England.

Mary Vidal shares none of Spence's social and religious liberalism. Although she appreciates the weight that pioneering conditions add to female social, domestic and moral responsibilities, her *Tales for the Bush* (1845) and *The Cabramatta Store* (1850) advocate duty rather than encourage aspirations for personal development. Even the well-observed colonial setting effects no transformation in submissive attitudes to rank and authority. Vidal, the wife of a clergyman, spent only four years in New South Wales, and her works are essentially cautionary tales for working-class women and their mistresses. Women's role as God's police in the colony brings them such rebukes as Grace receives from her husband in *The Cabramatta Store*, when her scruples argue against his involvement in a tricky venture: 'Your old-fashioned nonsense has ruined us: we have come to this country to get rich; and now we are here, you want to keep my hand in my pockets, and do nothing.'

The same efforts to achieve neo-classical balance and comprehensiveness, together with a romantic emphasis on exploring the detail of the individual, the personal, the strange and the unique, are found in the work of colonial essayists. Here, too, there is a conscious attempt to transform traditional themes by writing them into the colonial environment, but the essayists are perhaps even more hopeful than the fiction writers that their work will leaven the materialism of colonial culture. Henry Savery's essays in *The Hermit in Van Diemen's Land* (1829-30) dignify public incidents with reflection, and present portraits of leading Hobart citizens in the eighteenth-century manner of Addison and Steele. Formality also characterises James Martin's *The Australian Sketch Book* (1838), in which the eighteen-year-old schoolboy acknowledges his debt to Washington Irving. Yet Martin's enthusiasm is obvious in his adaptation of colonial material to conventional themes like 'The Sublime in Nature', 'A Visit to the Scenes of Youth', 'A Church-Yard Reverie' and 'Christmas in Australia'. In the same year, William Woolls published his *Miscellanies in Prose and Verse*, which shows the interaction of his classical erudition and scientific interest with his new homeland. A more romantic mood characterises *Peter Possum's Portfolio* (1858) by Richard Rowe, which includes sketches in the manner of Lamb and De Quincey, among them 'A Trip Up the Hunter' which opens with a Dantesque sketch of Sydney at night, and is uncompromising in its nostalgic preference for English scenery. The most original colonial essayist of this period is Daniel Deniehy, but the only prose to appear outside journals in his lifetime was the prose satire *How I Became Attorney-General of New Barataria: An Experiment in Treating Facts in the Form of Fiction* (1860), which ridicules the pretensions to status and power of colonial politicians.

Poetry, with its heightened response to all stimuli and its sensitivity to form, displays the most complex interaction of neo-classical and romantic attitudes and styles, used by writers conscious of acting on and being acted upon by their environment, and conscious of old restrictions and new freedoms. Barron Field, a judge of the Supreme Court, recalled on the charge that his work was unsatisfactory, could only rhyme 'Australia' with 'failure' in his poem 'The Kangaroo'. His *First Fruits of Australian Poetry* (1819) shows his wry appreciation, in a gentle parody of late Augustan verse, of the colony's 'desart forests' and 'barren plains'. As a poet, he was reluctant to leave the flora and fauna to the 'nick-naming' of botanists, 'many, and good cheap', when poetry might effect a better transformation. An even earlier minor poet, the convict Michael Massey Robinson, wrote of exile in his first published ode in the *Sydney Gazette* in June 1810, but one of his last pieces, a drinking song for the Anniversary Dinner in February 1826, ends with a bold attempt to rhyme 'Australia' with 'gala' and with a recognition of the new homeland.

A much more substantial work, *Australasia* (1823), a poem in heroic couplets by William Charles Wentworth, won second prize in the chancellor's poetry competition at Cambridge. Wentworth makes a natural colonial transformation when the opening lines present England as the place of exile: 'Land of my birth! tho' now, alas! no more / Musing I wander on thy sea-girt shore.' But the theme is imperial, not republican, proclaiming a splendid future for this 'new Britannia' which, following the lead set by Macquarie's regime, will devote itself not to martial aggression but to the arts and sciences. *Australasia* is a good example of the conjunction of neo-classical form and visionary sentiment, and it attempts to transform colonial realities, like the crossing of the Blue Mountains and the first tracing of gold, into images of the future.

Wild Notes from the Lyre of a Native Minstrel (1826), by Charles Tompson, is a complex and in some ways moving product of a talented nineteen-year-old poet who believed that his experience, and the dignity of the literature of the new country, required a careful adherence to classical and eighteenth-century English models. The colonial dilemma facing those who love the country and respect the native inhabitants on whom they intrude, and who are conscious of their violation, is resolved morally and philosophically by a belief in the 'sweets of social life', and the 'schools of learning and the paths of truth' that Tompson offers the Aborigines in his poem on the deserted 'Black Town'. The violation of nature by art, however, presents another irony in Tompson's 'Retrospect; or, A Review of my Scholastic Days', when he revisits the site of the Reverend Henry Fulton's school in the Nepean Valley. In careful heroic couplets and neo-classical diction and imagery, Tompson complains that 'the spoiling axe' has lopped the native forests, and that the 'civilizing reign' of Art leaves the landscape shining 'beneath a borrowed hue'. The young poet seems unaware that he himself has borrowed from a convention of Art cultivated by a generation earlier than his schoolmaster's. In 1827, as a would-be pastoralist, Tompson expressed his feelings about the denial of land grants to native-born settlers more spontaneously, in vigorous and imaginative prose:

> We have horned cattle—sheep—horses, etc. etc. *we* (of all others) are compelled to *depasture them on sufferance*; is it just to reduce us to what the Helots were in Ancient Rome? Slaves, doomed never to possess one inch of Territory?

H. M. Green's observation that the strongest of earlier colonial talents were absorbed in action or in literature that was a by-product of action, is relevant in explaining the difference between Tompson's confined meditative verse and his urgent, strenuous prose: when obviously practical action was required, new conditions compelled colonists to evolve new voices.

The first colonial poet to demand serious attention was Charles Harpur who wrote that 'Words *are* deeds' and gave to his vocation of poet the same dedicated energy other colonists gave to their agricultural, pastoral and commercial pursuits. Harpur's poetry was first inspired by his idyllic childhood in the beautiful Hawkesbury valley and Wordsworthian romanticism was natural to him. He expanded the sound elementary education given by his emancipist father, schoolmaster at Windsor from 1811 to 1825, to use creatively the work of Homer, Virgil, Dante, Goethe and Schiller, as well as that of the English poets from Chaucer to Byron.

His first published poems from 1833, the exuberant 'An Australian Song', and 'The Glen of the Whiteman's Grave', an elegy at the grave of a bushranger's victim, have ease, control, and spontaneity of response to real emotion and event that no earlier colonial poetry had shown. In the visionary 'The Dream by the Fountain', which resembles Goethe's 'Zueignung' (1784), the virgin country is transformed into a venerated 'old Hawksbury'. The Australian Muse recognises that, in such poems as 'The Creek of the Four Graves', 'The Bushfire' and 'A Storm in the Mountains', Harpur is already recording the countryside. The Muse notes that even as a boy the 'fire-robe of thought had enwound' him and, apart from a few trivial verses, all Harpur's poetry, including nature lyrics, is indeed tempered by his ardent debate and speculation. Longer poems like 'The Word and the Soul' and the Monodies on the death of his father and his son, are dramatic evidence of Harpur's struggle with evolutionary theory and the mysteries of time, space and death. Inspired by W. E. Channing and Ralph Waldo Emerson, Harpur's moral faith in self-reliance and integrity underlies his enormous opus of patriotic and political verse. This intellectual content often transforms the parochial interest of Harpur's political criticism.

Religious mysticism and high seriousness are important characteristics of Harpur's work, and its sensuousness recalls the seventeenth century rather than the nineteenth. His most radical transformations coalesce forms and common topics from different literary periods, as in meditative lyrics like 'A Mid-Summer Noon in the Australian Forest', 'A Basket of Summer Fruit', and the many love sonnets and poems exploring concepts of beauty and ideality.

'The Creek of the Four Graves' (1845), a vivid narrative of an Aboriginal attack on the settler Egremont and four of his 'most trusty and adventurous men', involves the colonial dilemma in which the intruders are also victims, and the Aboriginal defenders are also aggressors. Harpur's attitude to the patriarchal Egremont, who also appears in 'The Bush Fire', is ambivalent. Although Egremont looks for new streams and pastures for his fast augmenting flocks, the description of the landscape, one of the attractions of the poem, is coloured by the settler's consciousness of it. If he is a greedy intruder he is also an appreciative and awed spectator who is just beginning to feel a little at home in the forest. The 'murderous crew' of Aborigines is described as 'Beings as fell' as 'Hell's worst fiends' when they come in vengeance, and the narrator's sympathy seems to be with the murdered men and the hunted Egremont, whose wife and children pray for him at home. Although 'The Creek of the Four Graves' only unconsciously engages with the colonial dilemma, the poem becomes marvellously complex because of its presence. Harpur's conclusion is wholly concerned with the indifference of the harmonious universe to 'Man's wild violence'. Here, as elsewhere in his work, the tragic clash of good and evil is subsumed by a belief in the inevitable progress of the universe towards an ultimate perfection. Even the earliest version of the poem alleges the incident occurred in 'the old times', as though such events were no longer possible in 1845.

Harpur's verse and prose not only form a dialogue with the cultural past, his political present and a visionary future, but are also alive with debate, and with the presence of historical and contemporary figures, not all of whom he respected. His writing frequently urges and instructs, and rarely persuades or allows the subject to state itself. His ideas are often expressed in lively images, but when the images are found by a conscious appeal to art the reader is sometimes too aware of the intellectual effort involved. Yet Harpur's poetry almost always has dignity and enthusiasm and it can be imaginatively exciting. These are the qualities of his best work, including long and very different narratives and visions like 'The Tower of the Dream', 'The Slave's Story' and 'The Witch of Hebron'.

Harpur's literary criticism in verse and prose, his copious notes, and the *Discourse on Poetry*, part of which was printed in the *Empire* on 3 October 1859, are an intelligent blend of neo-classic and romantic principles arguing that poetry is a high and sacred, yet practical pursuit, which could teach, delight, idealise and prophesy. Although in his lifetime he published only *Thoughts: A Series of Sonnets* (1845), *The Bushrangers, A Play in Five Acts, and Other Poems* (1853), and three pamphlets of verse, his belief in poetry as an integral function of society, and the great amount of serious work he

published in journals, helped to transform a British settlement into a colony with the beginnings of its own culture.

The dilemma of invasion and expansion, and the tension between order and freedom which characterise this period of Australian literature, are epitomised in colonial drama with its mixture of neo-classical tragedy, romantic idealism, preoccupation with tyranny, liberty, law and conscience, ambivalent depiction of Aborigines, and its defence of individual liberty in a corrupt society. Melodrama, and gothic tragedy and romance, dominated early-nineteenth-century theatre in Europe. Penal settlement and the exile experience offered a natural setting for the psychology of passion, crime, retribution and spiritual desolation that underlies melodrama and gothic tragedy. The European outlaw or bushranger genre, with its element of tragic melodrama, was peculiarly appropriate to the Australian colonial experience.

The earliest bushranging plays include David Burn's *The Bush-Rangers* (1829, 1971) in which the Tasmanian bushranger Matthew Brady and his companion McCabe are noble outlaws, preferring death to the undeserved tyranny of the penal settlement. Sympathetic caricatures of the working-class settlers and unsympathetic caricatures of the Aborigines provide more local colour. Burn, a free settler, later added scenes trenchantly lampooning Lieutenant-Governor Sir George Arthur as a self-serving autocrat. A different attitude to Aborigines is seen in Henry Melville's 'The Bushrangers: or, Norwood Vale' (1834), a fictional melodrama in which a bushranger attack is defeated with the help of an Aborigine loyal to the white settlers.

All the typical ingredients, except the Aborigines, are found in the five-act verse drama by Charles Harpur. In 1835 the *Sydney Monitor* published excerpts from Harpur's 'The Tragedy of Donohoe', based on the life of the bushranger John Donohoe. Harpur rewrote the play for publication in *The Bushrangers, A Play in Five Acts, and Other Poems* (1853), but its final version, *Stalwart the Bushranger* (1867), was not published until 1987. The *Monitor*'s editor, Edward Smith Hall, correctly assessed 'The Tragedy of Donohoe' as at least equal to the melodrama performed at Barnett Levey's newly opened Sydney Theatre Royal. *Stalwart the Bushranger* is a complex verse tragedy, in which Harpur dramatises in the gothic mode themes of tyranny, passion, retribution and remorse, setting them in the metaphysical context of the struggle between good and evil.

Caricatures of Sydney authorities and bullies in office, and other local detail, allow the play to be seen as a myth of its time, but excess of poetic imagery, although useful to the themes, weakens the dramatic impact of the dialogue. Stalwart is a memorable Byronic hero whose remorse for his destruction of the girl who loves him, and of the idealised lovers, Abel and Linda, drives him to madness in which he welcomes death, proclaiming his guilt in defiance of human law and as an appeal to divine mercy. Harpur also completed some 1200 lines of a closet drama, 'King Saul', in which the Biblical story gives ample scope to his republican hatred of kingly tyrants and his belief in the divine power of poetry.

Other historical themes, treated in tragedies imitating the neo-classicism of Addison's *Cato* rather than Shakespeare, were taken up by colonial playwrights like Burn, Samuel Prout Hill ãnd Tucker. In the colonial context, the strong assertions of liberty, such as found in Prout Hill's *Tarquin the Proud, or The Downfall of Tyranny* (1843), may be read as even more significant than such lines usually are in plays of this kind.

Transformation of English models is seen also in the farces, musicals and lighter plays of the period. James Tucker's *Jemmy Green in Australia* (1955), written about 1845, is an excellent example of colonial adaptation of those perennial stories in which an apparent simpleton defeats the tricksters trying to enrich themselves through his innocence. The colony abounded in Jemmy Greens, of whom Harris' Lieutenant Bracton is a superior example, and Tucker's play substitutes dishonest agents and stockmen, factitious land developments, bushrangers and false arrest by reward-hungry bush constables for the London cheats and fraudulent business ventures usually found in these stories. Farcical as most situations and characters are, in transforming their traditional situations, these lighter plays contain clearly recognisable elements of the colonial dilemma.

Notes

Additional writing before 1855 includes: [Mrs G. R. Porter], *Alfred Dudley; or, The Australian Settlers* (1830); Thomas McCombie, *Arabin; or the Adventures of a Colonist in New South Wales* (1845); W. H. Leigh, *The Emigrant: A Tale of Australia* (1847); Ellen Clacy, *Lights and Shadows of Australian Life* (1854); George Henry Haydon,

The Australian Emigrant: a rambling story containing as much Fact as Fiction (1854); and John Lang, *The Forger's Wife* (1855). Colonial journals and newspapers print many examples of verse; see also Elizabeth Webby, *Early Australian Poetry* (1982). 'The Importance of a Rhyme. A Story of the Old Dock-Yard', the only extant short story by Charles Harpur, appeared in *The Weekly Register*, 30 August 1845, and is reprinted in *Australian Literary Studies*, 7 (1976).

Historical, biographical, critical and interpretative material includes: G. B. Barton, *Literature in New South Wales*, and *The Poets and Prose Writers of New South Wales* (1866); Miles Franklin, *Laughter, Not For a Cage* (1956); Grant Carr-Harris (ed.), *The Secrets of Alexander Harris* (1961); Tom Inglis Moore, *Social Patterns in Australian Literature* (1971); James Normington-Rawling, *Charles Harpur, An Australian (1962), Judith Wright, Preoccupations in Australian Poetry* (1965); Coral Lansbury, *Arcady in Australia* (1970); Barry Argyle, *An Introduction to the Australian Novel, 1830-1930* (1983); Laurie Hergenhan, *Unnatural Lives* (1972); Leslie Rees, *Towards an Australian Drama* (1953), and *A History of Australian Drama* (1987); Anne Summers, *Damned Whores and God's Police* (1975); Paul Depasquale, *A Critical History of South Australian Literature, 1836-1930* (1978); Ann-Mari Jordens, *The Stenhouse Circle* (1979); Margaret Williams, *Australia on the Popular Stage, 1829-1929* (1983); Susan Magarey, *Unbridling the Tongues of Women* (1985), a study of Catherine Helen Spence; P. R. Eaden and F. H. Mares (eds), *Mapped but Not Known: The Australian Landscape of the Imagination* (1986); Elizabeth Perkins (ed.), *Charles Harpur: Stalwart the Bushranger with the Tragedy of Donohue (1987).*

Collections and anthologies include: Ian Turner, The Australian Dream (1968); Charles Tompson, *Wild Notes, from the Lyre of a Native Minstrel*, G. A. Wilkes and G. A. Turnbull (eds) (1973); Adrian Mitchell (ed.), *Charles Harpur* (1973); G. A. Wilkes, (ed.), *The Colonial Poets* (1974); Harold Love, (ed.), *The Australian Stage, A Documentary History* (1984); Elizabeth Perkins (ed.), *The Poetical Works of Charles Harpur* (1984); Michael Ackland (ed.), *Charles Harpur: Selected Poetry and Prose* (1986); Helen Thomson (ed.), *Catherine Helen Spence* (1987).

PART III

Chapter 10

PERCEPTIONS OF AUSTRALIA, 1855-1915

SHIRLEY WALKER

A central focus of all perceptions of Australia during the period 1855 to 1915, whether of visitors, emigrants or Australian-born, was the land itself. The fact that much of Australian nature was so alien and inhospitable and the cause of so much hardship through drought, bushfire, flood and sheer hard work, probably accounts for the many disturbed and ambiguous responses to it. The perspective was almost invariably Eurocentric, that is Australian nature was measured against the green and pleasant landscape of the northern hemisphere. Even the most euphoric reactions to Australian nature, those that rely for their energy on strangeness and wonder, such as the often repeated catalogue of antipodean reversals ('a land where the birds cannot sing nor flowers give perfume') reveal an underlying disturbance, a need always to relate the unknown to the known in a denigrating manner.

Expressions of wonder were countered by expressions of distaste for the landscape, the main criticism being its killing monotony. Observers such as Marcus Clarke who, in 1876, saw the dominant note of Australian scenery to be that of 'Weird Melancholy', read it in terms of their own psychic disposition. Antoine Fauchery, in his *Lettres d'un Mineur en Australie* (1857) reveals his own cynicism. Australia's 'virgin forests' were to Fauchery but 'stunted old virgins which, through a whole eternity of sunshine, would not make the slightest move away from the ground to hide their ugly faces behind some fresher shoots', and its animals, though of 'inoffensive habits', had 'execrable flesh'. Meanwhile the disaffected Englishman Richard Rowe, in *Peter Possum's Portfolio* (1858) expressed his distaste for the bush in images of disease and death:

the same ragged gum-trees, reminding you of men with dirty, tattered shirts ... the same charred, prostrate trunks like blackfellows knocked down in a drunken squabble ... the same black, jagged stumps, like foul decaying teeth ... the same not grass, but graminaceous scurf, as if the earth had got ringworm.

It seems that most perceptions of Australian nature were defensive attempts to assert some sort of order and control over the vastness and sameness of the landscape, the very featurelessness of which suggested chaos to the European mind. There is an iconography of order and control, one which asserts that the Englishman is able to impose his own civilised values upon this nihilistic chaos. Some images of this iconography are equestrian man, the kangaroo and emu hunt and the picnic, a feature of both colonial literature and photography. The picnic, for instance, takes the indoors outdoors to assert the ordering role of civilised manners and social ritual in a wide variety of settings, many of them uncomfortable and inhospitable. Even the great set pieces of colonial literature, such as the bushfire and the flood, exploit awe and wonder but ultimately assert control. The ability of an artist or writer to capture them in paint or words implies some sort of victory over the power of nature.

Another way of asserting control was through botanical categorisation, an expression of the Victorian passion for science. The new continent, its flora and fauna, from the tropic north to the sub-arctic, had to be pinned down, classified and absorbed into the European consciousness as an act of possession. A number of those engaged in this work were women, either gifted amateurs such as Georgiana Molloy in Western Australia in the 1830s and Louisa Atkinson in the eastern states, or professionals such as Konkordie Amalie Dietrich who, working virtually alone in the Queensland bush from 1863 to 1870, amassed a superb collection of specimens for the Godeffroy Museum of Natural History in Hamburg. Her comment, 'It is just as if Herr Godeffroy [her employer] had made me a present of this vast continent', is illuminating. A parallel to this systematic classifying and naming of nature can be found in the great journeys of exploration which implied that, by crossing the continent, for instance, and by naming its features, one appropriated it and owned it. It is significant that both John McDowell Stuart and Augustus Gregory were accompanied on their journeys by prominent Australian botanists George Waterhouse and Ferdinand von Mueller respectively. Both Mueller and Gerard Krefft challenged the dominance of the British hegemony in botany, although each did contribute to the *Flora Australiensis* (1863-78), edited in London by George Bentham. By the Centennial in 1888 Australian and European botanists were on equal terms and the task of classifying Australian nature was virtually complete.

Alongside these assertions of control there is clear evidence of psychic disturbance. The iconography of this response is that of the madman or woman in the bush (the best-known literary example is in Lawson's 'The Bush Undertaker') and the lost child. The mythic meaning of the repetition of these motifs throughout the literature and art of the period is that of the fear of the vast and unknown bush. The old-world myth of the lost child, for instance in *Hansel and Gretel*, was concerned with the metaphysical, the cosmic battle between innocence and active evil. Innocence triumphed; the children were saved. In the new-world myth a disobedient child, who has ignored all warnings about nature, confronts a natural reality which is either treacherous or totally indifferent to human suffering, and the price is death. Each of the major literary versions, in Henry Kingsley's *The Recollections of Geoffry Hamlyn* (1859), Marcus Clarke's 'Pretty Dick' (1869), Ethel Pedley's *Dot and the Kangaroo* (1899), Henry Lawson's 'The Babies in the Bush' (1901), Joseph Furphy's *Such is Life* (1903), as well as the McCubbin painting *Lost* (1880), reveals a variation of the truth about Australian nature and national identity. For instance, if Mary Halloran in Furphy's *Such is Life* is the symbol of an energetic, independent nationalism (and this is what the text suggests), then her death in the uncaring bush is both a personal and a national tragedy. Meanwhile both McCubbin's *Lost* and Ethel Pedley's *Dot and the Kangaroo* suggest an integration with nature. In *Lost* the bush is no longer threatening. The child, framed in the tonal greys of the eucalypts, is part of nature, while Dot, in *Dot and the Kangaroo,* is preserved by the bush creatures (a benign nature) and returned to her parents. This is a significant advance in the perceived relationship between human beings and nature.

Two antithetical ways of perceiving Australian nature were to emerge during this period: towards a celebration in art, literature and popular sentiment of the Australian scene for its own sake, and a contrary impulse to read a transcendental meaning into it. John Docker has seen this as an opposition between a 'radical nationalist' tradition and the 'metaphysical ascendancy'. A favourite comparison in the metaphysical tradition was that of Australia with a new Eden. For instance the exclamation in Henry Kingsley's *The Recollections of*

Geoffry Hamlyn (1859) which begins: 'A new heaven and a new earth! . . . All creation is new and strange . . . We are in Australia!' has euphoric possibilities: man can either rebuild his lost paradise or repeat, all over again, the old crimes. A far more dangerous comparison, from a social and political point of view, is the Old Testament one which Kingsley and others make between the squatters and the 'patriarchs moving into the desert with all their wealth, to find a new pasture ground . . . the first and simplest act of colonisation'. These references suggest that the squatter is the chosen of God and the land is another Promised Land, destined for him by Divine right. This then justifies the seizure of the land and the 'dispersal' of the Aborigines. A strain of metaphysical inflation is apparent, too, in the work of those poets of the period, as distinct from the bush balladists, who saw the possibilities of the new landscape for philosophical speculation, or appropriated it for romanticism. Charles Harpur, for instance, although he aspires to become the true poetic voice of Australia, is consciously writing in a European tradition which exploits the sublimity and violence of nature to demonstrate, in a colonial situation, the redemptive possibilities for man. Henry Kendall too, in poems which choose to celebrate those aspects of Australian nature (the mountains, the cool and mossy dells) which best suit the transcendental dream, turns away from many aspects of Australian nature which resist it. John Shaw Neilson translates the landscape into cosmic images of good and evil, ignoring much of the particular for the vision, while for Christopher Brennan the landscape is almost completely universalised; the drama almost completely psychic.

However, at the same time, another more indigenous tradition in verse, and indeed in all forms of art, was evolving; one which celebrated the land and its people as the proper material for art. This was part of a generalised movement towards nationalism and identity which found a primary focus in the Centennial celebrations of 1888. From at least the 1850s there had been two clearly opposing perceptions of Australia: an optimistic and euphoric view as against a more realist, subversive one. This opposition is clear in the 1850s, the period of the great goldrushes, where the wave of euphoria which swept thousands of emigrants to Victoria was challenged by most, if not all, of those who came, saw and reported. On the one hand Australia was hailed by Samuel Sidney, the writer of *Sidney's Australian Handbook: How to Settle and Succeed in Australia* (1848) as 'El Dorado and Arcadia combined', and by an effusive clergyman in the

London *Times* (17 April 1852) as 'a glorious country, fertile, uninhabited; a Promised Land . . . a realized El Dorado, paved with gold', while popular melodramas on the London stage such as Charles Reade's *Gold!* (1853) helped to whip up the enthusiasm. A contrary view was that of William Howitt, a seasoned traveller and serious social observer. In his *Land, Labour and Gold, or Two Years in Victoria* (1855), Howitt warns that 'hundreds upon hundreds rush back again, cursing the false, flattering and interested statements which lured them out'. He deplores the hardship, accidents and sickness, the heat, flies, mud and slush and the 'rude, blackguard state of the lower society in this suddenly thrown-together colony'. His bitterest comments, however, are reserved for the land question (the failure of the government to release land for settlement) and for the corruption of the licensing system on the goldfields which was to lead to the Eureka uprising in 1854. Perhaps the most amusing comment is that of the Frenchman Antoine Fauchery in his *Lettres d'un Mineur en Australie.* His cynical dismissal of Australia with its 'monotonous forests, its sealing-wax gentlemen, its sterile mine-shafts, its convicts drunk on gin and its eternal potatoes in their jackets' suggests a colony which, though booming, is raw and brash to the cosmopolitan eye.

Even so, the 1850s was probably the period of greatest social change in colonial history. There was a vast increase in population, a disturbance of class and status barriers, and a movement towards cosmopolitanism and egalitarianism. Moreover the influx of great wealth into cities like Melbourne, and to a lesser extent Sydney, provided the basis for the establishment of cultural foundations, universities, libraries, art galleries and museums, which in turn were to alter the perception of Australia as a cultural backwater. Drama in particular was given an impetus at this time which it did not lose throughout the second half of the nineteenth century. Not only were serious dramas performed from the 1850s onward, but popular melodramas with Australian themes, drawing on stock dramatic characters such as bushrangers, convicts and miners, helped in the 1870s and 1880s to form a stereotyped and romantic view of the recent past and to create a sense of identity in Australian audiences.

The celebration of the Centennial (1888) gave a greater impetus to the self-determining process. One expression of this was the series of self-congratulatory publications which marked the event. The most fulsome of these were undoubtedly the massive histories, for instance Alexander Sutherland's *Victoria and its Metropolis* (1888) and W. F. Morrison's *Aldine Centennial History of New South Wales* (1888), magnificently produced catalogues of progress in city, mining and pastoral enterprise, with potted biographies of hundreds of leading citizens who had made good in each area. These were accompanied by the *Picturesque Atlas of Australasia* (1883-9), which employed many local and imported graphic artists to celebrate the progress and unique quality of Australian life.

The image of Australia which resulted from this self-determining process was an indigenous one, centred upon the bush. By the 1880s and 1890s the bush had become a label for both the landscape and a social reality characterised by egalitarianism, collectivism and 'mateship'. Central to this perception of the bush was the dignity of rural work, the elevation of the bush worker as hero, and the celebration of radical nationalist values which were presumably to be found in their purest form in the bush among bush workers. The focus of this celebration was the Sydney *Bulletin,* established in 1880 and seen by its presiding genius, J. F. Archibald, as an instrument for the expression of the national ethos. Its snappy paragraphs, verses and ballads, anecdotes and short stories, all of great vigour and authenticity, helped to mould a group myth about the nature of Australians and their society.

The most striking aspect of this myth is its favouring of rural over urban images. Despite overwhelming evidence to the contrary (for instance in 1891 over two-thirds of Australians lived in cities or large towns) the perception of Australia as rural with its typical inhabitant the bush worker has always caught the Australian imagination. Michael Roe sums it up in his comment that 'whereas the appeal of the bush has been the great myth of Australian history, the appeal of the city has been the great fact'. It is arguable whether this image of the bush was one gradually evolved in folk consciousness in frontier conditions which then permeated urban thinking under the influence of the *Bulletin* and the 'new unionism' (Russel Ward's hypothesis in *The Australian Legend,* 1958), or whether it was one created by writers and artists, themselves predominantly city dwellers, disillusioned by urban poverty and squalor. The painters of the Heidelberg school and their Sydney contemporaries, for instance, were city dwellers enthused by European concepts of proper subject matter (the dignity of work and the realistic presentation of nature) and the means by which to express it *(en plein air).* But this urbanism and cosmopolitanism were not all; they were, as well, heirs to a populist tradition which included the graphic arts and photography—illustrations of picturesque Australian scenes and colonial 'types' in periodicals such as the *Australasian Sketcher* and the *Illustrated Australian News* and the works of such excellent photographers as Antoine Fauchery in the 1850s and J. W. Lindt and Nicholas Caire in the 1870s an 1880s. These stereotyped images of colonial scenes and 'types' were given a further focus in the massive volumes of graphic art and photography which marked the Centennial, such as *The Picturesque Atlas of Australasia* and *Cassell's Picturesque Australia* (1887-9). The painters—Roberts, Streeton, McCubbin, Conder and others—took up these populist images and raised them to a heroic level. Paintings such as Arthur Streeton's *Golden Summer, Eaglemont* (1889) both captured the uniqueness of Australian light and atmosphere and cultivated the taste for it. Meanwhile the preoccupation of the European Naturalists with the subject of men at work was deliberately Australianised in such great canvases as Roberts' *Shearing the Rams* (1890) and Streeton's *Fire's On* (1891). The notion of the pioneer as hero was also fostered in the paintings of Frederick McCubbin, from *A Bush Burial* (1890) and *The North Wind* (1891) to *The Pioneer* (1904), an almost religious celebration (in triptych form) of the conquest of the land. These perceptions of Australia, so powerfully presented, helped both to create and to focus the nationalistic surge of the 1880s and the 1890s.

The principal writers of the *Bulletin* school were also heirs to both a populist tradition (the bush ballad, the bush yarn) and a cosmopolitan one. As Graeme Davison has pointed out, many of them were urban dwellers, closely associated with radical movements such as secularism, republicanism and land reform which would have promoted the same egalitarian ethos which Russel Ward maintains was derived from the conditions of early settlement. Moreover they were significantly influenced by literary models—for example Dickens' London and Blake's apocalyptic city—which would have sharpened their perception of the squalor of their own cities and encouraged their yearning for rural life. There is ample evidence too of the poverty and degradation of nineteenth-century Australian cities. While many visitors to Sydney commented upon the beauty of the harbour, Frank Fowler (1859) describes a city where:

> Serpent-like gutters, choked with filth, trail before the tottering tenements, and a decayed water-butt, filled with greasy-looking rain-catchings—across which indecent slime-bred flies dart and dazzle in the sun—stands and rots at the end of each court. Brazen women, hulking bullies and grimy children, loll about the doorways . . .

Francis Adams (1893) too speaks of the 'brutality' of officialdom and the 'hopeless criminality' of the inhabitants of Woolloomooloo, while William Lane's *The Workingman's Paradise* (1892) gives a vivid impression of the cruelty of city life for the poor. In *Australia for the Australians* (1888) 'Banjo' Paterson records his revulsion from the poverty, 'vice and sins' of the city, and his longing for the 'vision splendid of the sunlit plains extended' probably owes as much to this recoil as to his happy childhood memories of station life. Lawson's case is more complex. His perception of the city, as shown in his verses and short stories, would certainly have been a factor in his elevation of the bush and bush society to a mythic level. On the other hand, after his famous trip to Hungerford in 1892-3, 'his sole experience of the outback' according to A. G. Stephens, Lawson determined never to face the bush again. The power of his vision is probably a matter of balance: the stark realism of his perception of the bush and, at the same time, his elevation of the human qualities of its inhabitants. In any case Davison's view of the mythology of the bush as largely the creation of disaffected urban radicals is too simplistic; it fails to take account of the part played in its evolution by the *Bulletin's* many bush readers whose contributions fostered a group myth about the unique qualities of their society.

The popular perception of the pioneer as hero was probably also ambivalent. J. B. Hirst has traced the evolution of this, analysing the literature and art which eulogises the pioneer and the ideology which it serves. According to Hirst the image is a distorted one in that it fails to distinguish between the squatter like Kingsley's Geoffry Hamlyn, who rode around on a splendid horse while underlings cleared his land, and battlers like Steele Rudd's Dad *(On Our Selection,* 1899). Furphy summed it up in *Such is Life*:

> The successful pioneer is the man who never spared others; the forgotten pioneer is the man who never spared himself, but being a fool, built houses for wise men to live in, and omitted to gather moss. The former is the early bird, the latter is the early worm.

Despite the celebration of the pioneering life in, for instance, Paterson's 'Song of the Future', Lawson's 'How the Land Was Won' and McCubbin's *The Pioneer*, the notion of his well-being was contradicted by much contemporary evidence. The Selection acts of 1861 and 1862 were a failure; the land available was, according to Francis Adams (1893) 'droughtland', where it was impossible to earn a decent living; and the rural recession of 1892-5 caused intolerable hardship. A disturbing account of the hardship and squalor of the pioneering life (admittedly in the comic mode) is that of the M'Swat family in Miles Franklin's *My Brilliant Career* (1901).

Much of this ambivalence is carried over to the popular perception of the typical Australian. Throughout the century there had been a preoccupation with the evolution of a national 'type'. Few observers were as pessimistic as Henry Kingsley's Frank Maberly (*Geoffry Hamlyn*, 1859) who condemned native-born Australian males as 'lanky, lean, pasty-faced, blaspheming blackguards, drinking rum before breakfast, and living by cheating one another out of horses'. Speculations about the national character were more likely to be optimistic and, by the 1880s and 1890s, the typical Australian was seen, in literature, art and folklore, as the idealised bush worker, possessed of the stock male virtues of the bush: independence, fairness, resourcefulness, resentment of authority and loyalty to his mates. There were, however, suggestions of a darker side to this image; one which involved violence, drinking, boasting, and either the mistreatment of women (and horses) or a strange sexlessness. It is interesting that there is little suggestion of love or passion in the male poetry of the period. Moreover the stock perception of the typical Australian required a reassessment of the past: the rehabilitation of the convict and the bushranger to bring them into an historical relationship with the popular image. Russel Ward proposes this historical relationship when he suggests that the values of 'mateship' originated in the close bonds between fellow convicts, and Mary Gilmore rewrites the past and brings it into line when she suggests in 'Old Botany Bay' that the convicts were the first pioneers:

I was the conscript
　Sent to hell
To make in the desert
　The living well;

I split the rock;
　I felled the tree:
The nation was—
　Because of me.

In the convict novel the guilt shifts from the convict, no longer the villainous Vandemonian of the 1850s, to the system itself (imposed on the colonies by the British). In Marcus Clarke's *His Natural Life* (1874), at least, the suffering of the convict is justified in metaphysical terms—

he becomes a Christ-like figure who gives his life for another. Meanwhile bushrangers, earlier seen as brutal and rapacious, are romanticised in folklore and in popular novels such as Boldrewood's *Robbery Under Arms* (1888); while in Tom Roberts' *Bailed up* (1895) the bushrangers are seen to to be behaving in a relaxed and almost benign manner. Shortly before, Ned Kelly had become a national hero, a victim, in popular opinion, of the oppression of small selectors by the squatters and the law, not least because of his Irish ancestry. Kelly himself (in his Jerilderie letter of 10 February 1879) clearly draws the parallel between his own case and that of Irish peasants ground down by 'the Saxon', forgetting that over 80 per cent of *his* oppressors, the Victorian police, were Irish-born. Clearly the past was being rewritten at this time in order to romanticise the short span of Australian history and to rationalise its more violent aspects.

Another feature of the national image was its xenophobia. Most Australians in this period wished to exclude other races, who were almost always seen in derisive terms. Australia's white Anglo-Saxon or Anglo-Celtic (to include the Irish) make-up was always emphasised; racial purity was a national obsession and violence to minorities such as Aborigines was endemic. Perhaps the Major Mills in Rosa Praed's *My Australian Girlhood* (1904) who called the blacks 'big game' and shot them from the trees, having first ordered them down three times in the name of Queen Victoria, is an exception. However the massacre and 'dispersal' of the Aborigines is well documented. It was sanctioned, in both spirit and terminology, by a popular misreading of Darwinian notions of the survival of the fittest. The attitude of Anthony Trollope, in his *Australia and New Zealand* (1873), that the Aborigines were doomed to extinction, and the sooner the better—'That he should perish without unnecessary suffering should be the aim of all who are concerned in the matter'—was a common one. Certainly, despite the careful work of anthropologists such as A. W. Howitt and L. Fison in their *Kamilaroi and Kurnai* (1880) and Howitt in his *Native Tribes of South-East Australia* (1904), as the century progressed the Aborigine was seen more and more in popular perception as a figure of fun or vilification. This was particularly apparent in cartoons in the popular press and in light verse. Thus Brunton Stephens was capable of a poem such as 'To a Black Gin':

> . . . thou some lover hast, I bet a guinea,
> Some partner in thy fetid ignominy,
> The raison d'être of this piccaninny.

and Kendall, who is his better moments wrote a moving lament for 'The Last of his Tribe', could also in his own words 'out blackfellow' Stephens to pen such derisive verse as 'Jack the Blackfellow' and 'Black Lizzie'. The horrific violence resulting from these contemptuous attitudes is probably best exemplified in Francis Adams' short story 'Long Forster' from his *Australian Life* (1892). Long Forster is a gentle giant, kind to children, 'about the softest-hearted cuss ever lived'; in fact he is the 'typical' Australian male, the precursor of Lawson's admirable Mitchell. Yet in the most appalling act of vengeance (a group of emaciated Aborigines has killed his mate) he kills thirteen blacks, men and women whom he has trapped in a cave, with a tomahawk:

> . . . I reached in and got hold of another. It was a gin, and I gripped her by the leg and pulled her out, and 'bout broke her head off with a crack on the back of the neck. Then I laid hold on another one and smashed his skull in like the first one. And all the while I was reachin' in and pullin' 'em out they never made a sound, but kept up that sorter wimperin' like pups when the mother's gone. I killed the whole lot. There was thirteen of 'um. I counted.

Hatred of the Chinese and violence towards them also contradicted the popular self-image of benign decency. It is debatable how much of this was due to the perceived threat of being swamped by sinister yellow hordes, and how much to a covert fear of white women being seduced by wily orientals (very few female Chinese emigrated). Anti-Chinese riots broke out at Buckland River in 1857 and Lambing Flat in 1861 and examples of the attitudes towards and treatment of individual Chinese emerge in the short stories of Cecil Hadgraft's collection, *The Australian Short Story Before Lawson* (1986). These include the crushing to death of a Chinese cook in a wool-press by a drunken gang of shearers ('The Premier's Secret' by Campbell McKellar), the massacre of Chinese who are about to stake out a new gold-find, under the guise of protecting a white woman ('Chinese Ginnie' by A. G. Hales) and the characterisation of Mrs Sin Fat, whore to the Chinese and recruiter of innocent white girls for the doss house and Chinese brothel ('Mr and Mrs Sin Fat', by Edward Dyson). In these stories, chosen by Hadgraft as 'the best of this period' (from 1830 to 1893) and as those which 'illustrate contemporary concerns', the extent of violence towards the Chinese is obvious, as is its economic and sexual basis.

The nationalist self-image of the 1880s and 1890s was also

exclusively masculine. 'Mateship', an expression of male solidarity, rigorously excluded the woman, delegating to her the passive virtues of stoicism and endurance. These virtues were then eulogised in such works as the frequently anthologised 'The Women of the West' by George Essex Evans. Such idealisation of colonial women cloaks a disturbing reality which clearly emerges in documentary collections such as Beverley Kingston's *The World Moves Slowly* (1977), Ruth Teale's *Colonial Eve* (1978) and Kay Daniels' and Mary Murnane's *Uphill All the Way* (1980). The last documents the hardships suffered by women in domestic life, childbearing and sweated labour; the invidious double standards of colonial society and, most disturbing of all, the prostitution of convict and Aboriginal women and the removal (for their own good, of course) of children conceived by them. Feminist histories such as Anne Summers' *Damned Whores and God's Police* (1975) and Miriam Dixson's *The Real Matilda* (1976) challenge the idealised images of women. Dixson sees the distinguishing feature of Australian society to be its contempt for women, and traces this to our 'formative decades' with their violence and brutality towards women and widespread prostitution of women.

The literature also suggests the reality underlying the stereotypes. Lawson, for instance, spoke of the courage of women in the 'land where gaunt and haggard women live alone and work like men', and his women certainly embody the standard virtues of endurance and passivity as they stoically await, like the drover's wife, the return of their nomadic males. What is more, the women suffer vicariously from the criminal or irresponsible behaviour of husbands or sons until they are, like Mrs Spicer in 'Water them Geraniums', 'past carin''. In Furphy's *Such is Life* women are treated derisively by the narrator (who claims that the distinguishing mark of an 'Australienne' is her moustache), and in both Lawson and Furphy women are blamed for male suffering. Mitchell, Steelman and the Oracle have all been let down by women, while the standard enquiry of a suffering male in *Such is Life* is 'Who is she?'; in short, which woman (and it must have been a woman) is to blame for this male trauma?

This distrust of women is a characteristic of colonial literature. Not only are women seen to slide all too easily into drink, deceit and whoring, but the authors, whether male or female, are all too eager to punish the victim. Though a good woman such as Gracie Storefield in *Robbery Under Arms* can redeem a man, there is no rehabilitation for the female sinner, either in short stories such as Henry Kingsley's 'My Landladies' (1872), or in novels such as Caroline Leakey's *The Broad*

Arrow (1859) or Elizabeth Murray's *Ella Norman* (1864). In fact three novels written by women during the 1850s and the 1860s—Catherine Spence's *Clara Morison* (1854), *The Broad Arrow,* and *Ella Norman,* set respectively in South Australia, Tasmania and Victoria—are frank about the dangers for unattached women in the colonies. Ellen Clacy in *A Lady's Visit to the Gold Diggings of Victoria in 1852-53* (1853), 'written on the spot', had maintained that 'the worst risk you run' in coming to the colonies 'is getting married; and finding yourself treated with twenty times the respect you may meet with in England'. This view was obviously shared by committees such as the Female Middle-Class Emigration Society of 1862 which worked assiduously to export virtuous young women to the colonies to hunt for husbands. The reality which these novels (all written from first-hand experience) expose is that of the shortage of compatible males, the desperate search for appropriate work, and the sweated labour and ignominy which the position of governess often entailed. Each is concerned with the fate of the genteel woman, forced into prostitution through either naivety or hunger, her destination the streets, the degraded shanties on the goldfields or, in the case of *The Broad Arrow,* a convict prison and assigned labour.

Although these early novels by women writers have been criticised on the grounds of melodramatic plot or moralistic purpose, nevertheless each displays its author's clear-eyed perception of social and political injustice and concern for moral regeneration in colonial society. Later women writers—'Tasma' (Jessie Couvreur), Ada Cambridge and Rosa Praed—have been accused of writing escapist fiction which deals in colonial stereotypes (for instance heroes who are lost heirs to English fortunes) and have been seen as irrelevant to the Australian male literary tradition with its concern for national identity. Susan Sheridan has argued against this, placing these writers in an Australian female literary tradition concerned with an alternate reality, that of domestic life, and concerned also with social satire. The biographical material relating to these women gives a far more disturbing perception of female life. Ada Cambridge's poems *Unspoken Thoughts* (1887) reveal her revulsion from married life, much of which is seen as legalised prostitution, the woman being 'Wife by the law, but prostitute in deed' ('Fallen'). The poems also reveal Cambridge's strong attraction towards other women. Rosa Praed rejected marriage to live with another woman, Nancy Harward, whom she believed to be the reincarnation of a priestess of Isis.

The most challenging perceptions of female life in the bush are to be found in the works of two women writers at the turn of the century: Miles Franklin's *My Brilliant Career* and Barbara Baynton's *Bush Studies* (1902). In its bounciness, colloquial language and its love of the bush, *My Brilliant Career* is in the male tradition of the 1890s, but in spirit it rejects the clichés of that tradition. In the bush society the woman is seen as little better than a drudge, worn out like Sybylla's mother by constant childbearing and hard work. Women are disposed of as property either in marriage or in arrangements like that in which Sybylla is traded off as a governess to the ignorant and foul M'Swats to pay off her drunken father's interest bill. There is no place in this society for Sybylla as a writer. That is why Harold Beecham, a 'typical' Australian male, is firmly rejected, together with all the stultifying aspects of life in the bush. In Baynton's short stories the bush is grotesque and actively malevolent, inhabited by sinister and predatory creatures both male and female. The victims, mostly women, are raped or murdered or left, broken-backed, to die when their usefulness is over. The bush society is far from the egalitarian, caring community of Lawson's dreams 'where people toil and bake and suffer and are kind'. Its most grotesque female manifestation is the wretched old hag begging for money for drink at the roadside shanty in 'Billie Skywonkie':

> she pointed to her toothless mouth (the mission of which seemed to be, to fill its cavernous depths with the age-loosened skin about and below). A blue bag under each eye aggressively ticked like the gills of the fowls . . . Alternately she pointed to her mouth, or laid her knotted fingers on the blue bags in pretence of wiping tears. Entrenched behind the absorbed skin-terraces, a stump of purple tongue made efforts at speech. When she held out her claw, the woman understood and felt for her purse . . .

Images such as this should be set against the sentimental versions of pioneer womanhood which reinforced the narrow male tradition.

It is clear then that there were two opposing perceptions of Australia during the second half of the nineteenth century: one the 'boosting' or over-optimistic, the other the challenging or subversive view. The over-optimistic had been obvious from at least the 1850s onward, when Australia was seen not only as El Dorado (for a brief period), but also as an Arcadia where the poor from the mother country could establish prosperous lives on smallholdings, and where surplus spinsters could find rich and grateful husbands. This then merged, in the last two decades of the century, into the indigenous myth of the bush; of an idyllic community peopled by idealised shearers and drovers. Just as all of these affirmative perceptions were over-stated and to a certain extent on the defensive, so too were the egalitarian and nationalistic sentiments which went with them. Although the shearers' strikes of the 1890s and the formation of parliamentary Labour parties reaffirmed the democratic principles of Eureka, Australia was, at the end of this period, far from being an egalitarian society. David Denholm in *The Colonial Australians* (1979) suggests that, as late as the 1940s, power structures in Australia were still in the hands of the descendants of founding families, and class differences were still obvious in, for instance, the perceived social distance between the grazier on his property and the 'cocky' on his farm. Even the notion of the coming of age, at Federation, of a proud but loyal colonial society still assiduously fostered the notion of dependence. For all the assertion of the occasion, Australia at Federation was still perceived as a national identity within and part of a greater imperialistic whole. This was demonstrated not only by the terms of Federation (many powers were still in imperial hands) but also by the fervour with which young Australian males (16,000 of them) hastened to Britain's aid in the Boer War, forgetting the many similarities between the maligned Boers and the much vaunted Australian bushmen. While the *Bulletin* was one of the few voices raised in opposition to the war, ranting against British imperialism, featuring vindictive anti-Kitchener cartoons, and branding returning soldiers as 'farmburners', its anti-imperialism did not survive the outbreak of the Great War, when even writers who had opposed the Boer War, such as Christopher Brennan, joined in the patriotic frenzy. Indeed this event found a nation, with its romantic perception of the value of self-reliance and of individual courage and endurance, pitifully ill-prepared for what was to come: the mass and indiscriminate slaughter at Gallipoli and the Somme.

Notes

For the legend of the 1890s see Vance Palmer, *The Legend of the Nineties* (1954); A. A. Phillips, *The Australian Tradition* (1958) and Russel Ward, *The Australian Legend* (1958). Bernard Smith's *Place, Taste and Tradition* (1954) and *European Vision and the South Pacific* (1960) survey the history of ideas in relation to art. Geoffrey Serle's *From Deserts the Prophets Come* (1973) surveys the period in detail, while Coral Lansbury's *Arcady in Australia* (1970) suggests the influence of English literature, in particular the writings of Samuel Sidney, Charles Dickens and Charles Reade, in the development of hyperbolic images of Australia. Since the 1970s a number of important works have challenged the whole notion of the nationalistic, egalitarian 1890s and the aspects of 'mateship', nature and culture which go with it. These are (in chronological order): Michael Roe, 'The Australian Legend', *Meanjin*, 21 (1962) (contains an answer by Russel Ward); Humphrey McQueen, *A New Britannia* (1970); Graeme Davison, 'Sydney and the Bush: an Urban Context for the Australian Legend', *Historical Studies)*, 18 (1978), (Russel Ward's rejoinder to this is 'The Australian Legend Re-Visited', in the same issue of *Historical Studies); J. B. Hirst, 'The Pioneer Legend', *Historical Studies*, 18 (1978); G. A. Wilkes, *The Stockyard and the Croquet Lawn* (1981); Ross Gibson, *The Diminishing Paradise: Changing Literary Perceptions of Australia* (1984) and Leigh Astbury, *City Bushmen: The Heidelberg School and the Rural Mythology* (1985). Richard White, in his *Inventing Australia: Images and Identity, 1688-1980* (1981) suggests that cultural images are invented in order to suit the demands of social and political ideology and need not necessarily have any realistic basis, while Graeme Turner, in his *National Fictions: Literature, Film and the Construction of Australian Narrative* (1986) brings the notion of cultural construction to bear on selected Australian literature and films. For an overall discussion of this argument, see Alan Frost, 'On Finding "Australia": Mirages, Mythic Images, Historical Circumstances', *Australian Literary Studies*, 12 (1986).

For reactions to the landscape see Brian Elliott, *The Landscape of Australian Poetry* (1967). The quotation from Marcus Clarke is from his preface to a new edition of Adam Lindsay Gordon's *Sea Spray and Smoke Drift* (1876); Ann Moyal in her *A Bright and Savage Land: Scientists in Colonial Australia* (1986) gives an account of the botanical classification of Australian flora and fauna.

For further reading on the goldrush period see G. Serle, *The Golden Age* (1963) and *The Rush to be Rich* (1971); Ellen Clacy, *A Lady's Visit to the Gold Diggings of Victoria, 1852-53* (1853); S. T. Gill, *Sketches of the Victorian Goldfields* (1852); John Sherer, *The Gold-Finder of Australia: How He Went, How He Fared, and How He Made His Fortune* (1853). Margaret Williams, in her *Australia on the Popular Stage, 1829-1929* (1983) gives an account of popular drama in the period under discussion.

For the racial make-up of the Victoria Police Force, see Patrick

O'Farrell, *The Irish in Australia* (1986). Judith Wright's *The Cry for the Dead* (1981) and Geoffrey Blomfield's *Baal Balbora* (1981) are concerned with the massacre and 'dispersal' (the two were often synonymous) of Aboriginal tribes. Francis Adams' story 'Long Forster' is reprinted in Cecil Hadgraft's selection, *The Australian Short Story Before Lawson* (1986). Francis Adams was one of the number of distinguished literary visitors to Australia in the period under discussion. Other were R. H. 'Orion' Horne (1852-69); Anthony Trollope (in Australia 1871-2 and 1875); H. Havelock Ellis (1875-9); Joseph Conrad (1879 and 1893) and J. A. Froude (1885). For a more complete account of literary visitors see Kay Harman (ed.), *Australia Brought to Book* (1985).

Susan Sheridan's essay 'Ada Cambridge and the Female Literary Tradition' is to be found in *Nellie Melba, Ginger Meggs and Friends* (1982), edited by Susan Dermody, John Docker and Drusilla Modjeska. For a typical account of Cambridge, Praed and 'Tasma' see John Barnes, 'Australian Fiction to 1920' in Geoffrey Dutton (ed.), *The Literature of Australia* (1964). For further biographical and autobiographical material on women writers see Susan Magarey, *Unbridling the Tongues of Women* (1985), a biography of Catherine Helen Spence; Ada Cambridge's autobiography *Thirty Years in Australia* (1903) and her *The Retrospect* (1912) and Rosa Praed's autobiographical *My Australian Girlhood* (1902) and *Australian Life: Black and White* (1885).

Chapter 11

JOURNALISM AND THE WORLD OF THE WRITER: THE PRODUCTION OF AUSTRALIAN LITERATURE, 1855-1915

KEN STEWART

During the first ten or a dozen years immediately succeeding the discovery of gold in Victoria, its magnetic influence attracted hither . . . a certain number of men of letters and artists, whose habits, occupations and professional training were certainly not such as to qualify them for the hard work at the diggings, and who could scarcely expect to find any demand for the productions of pen and pencil in a community so unsettled and so absorbed in the acquisition of gold and gain as that which was then encamped, rather than settled, in this hive of restless and adventurous human beings.

Thus in 1907 James Smith, octogenarian critic, essayist, journalist, playwright, novelist, lecturer, literary editor, veteran colonial 'man of letters', reminisced on 'talent in exile' during his first years in the colonies. The 'talent' of the 1850s was diverse, scattered, transient. Some visitors, like the pre-Raphaelite poet and sculptor Thomas Woolner, and Dickens' collaborator William Howitt, were men of established reputation. Others, like Caroline Leakey, Ellen Clacy and Henry Kingsley, began modest literary careers by drawing on the experience and settings of their Australian sojourn to write fiction and less romanticised prose commentary. Charles Whitehead and 'Orion' Horne, versatile and long-established but fading English authors, would not gain a firm literary footing in the colonies. Whitehead published important, now neglected, work in fiction, drama and poetry, but died alcoholic, and in poverty. Horne stayed until 1869, a dauntless but toothless literary lion who enjoyed more prestige than authority.

The most influential of the new literati in a mainly expatriate and immigrant community were journalists, professional men and academics who gravitated in the later 1850s and 1860s to the metropolitan centres, and introduced a new professional expertise and confidence to literary operations. In Melbourne in particular they supplanted the more dilettantish authority of longer resident quasi-aristocratic cultural guardians, such as Redmond Barry and Chief Justice Sir William à Beckett, a great-grandfather of the novelist Martin Boyd. À Beckett, whose family are the fictional Langtons in *A Cardboard Crown* (1952), wrote a pamphlet titled 'Does the discovery of gold in Victoria, viewed in relation to the moral and social effects as hitherto developed, deserve to be considered as a national blessing or a national curse?' (1852), and pronounced the latter. More generally, however, the goldrush immigrants joined with politically liberal resident literati of the professional classes, and with native-born writers like Daniel Deniehy and Henry Kendall, to establish or extend those networks of communication, exchange and support which gave writers and readers their literary bearings. They thought of their literary community as provincial and growing, no longer tiny and isolated.

The external manifestations, sometimes pompous displays, of colonial cultural awareness provided a focus for those colonists determined to reassure themselves that even in misbegotten, money-bound Australia 'the intellect [should] be regarded as a certain commodity, equally worthy of purchase with hides, wool, cedar and fat'. Newspapers of quality such as the Melbourne *Argus*, established in 1846, and sturdy enough in 1883 to be vaunted by the English visitor R. E. N. Twopeny as 'the best daily paper published out of England', and its rival the *Age* (1854), provided greater scope for professional and serious literary journalism than before the goldrushes. Standards of criticism improved, and the spread of cultural institutions such as universities, libraries, galleries, schools of art, mechanics' institutes, intellectual and literary societies, theatres and country newspapers was taken for granted. A number of immigrants had befriended or collaborated with English literary figures, in particular with Dickens, G. H. Lewes, J. S. Mill, Douglas Jerrold and Thackeray, and these connections confirmed, even (or especially) for the native-born, imperial and cosmopolitan cultural links. Whereas before the goldrushes the major European literary influences were frequently from earlier periods, especially from eighteenth-century neo-classicism and the romanticism of the early Wordsworth or Sir Walter Scott, serious poets, critics and journalists turned increasingly to contemporary overseas models: the journalists tried to re-create the literary London of Jerrold and Dickens; Kendall supplemented Wordsworthian themes by following the metrical experiments and narrative genre pieces of Tennyson and Arnold, and indeed anticipated Swinburnian rhythms; the experienced James Neild introduced the very modern criterion of a strictly representational poetic stage realism to dramatic criticism.

The extent of involvement in literary pursuits has often been underestimated, owing to popular misconceptions about 'colonial' society. The colonial literati themselves, conscious of the cultural magnetism and centrality of London and Europe, and of the dearth in a small population of symbolically 'great' writers, helped to create a legend of the neglected artist in a practical, sports-minded community. The prominence given to practical and rural pioneering myths and stereotypes, and to dreams for the future of cultivated democracy, has distracted attention from the opportunities of writers and readers in a highly literate community which enjoyed more free time, and could afford to buy more books *per capita*, than those of most other countries. By the 1880s Melbourne boasted both the largest Shakespeare Society and the best-attended horse race in the world. Some elements of colonialism should not be mistaken for its aggregate, especially within a reading community in which distinctions between 'popular' and 'high' culture may be more difficult to define than in the twentieth century.

For the cultural missionaries, 'men of letters' whose voluminous journalism and commentary confirmed a literary presence by continually expressing the fear of its absence, culture was to be the elixir of national maturation. 'By providing for the nurture and sustenance of the arts, we shall assist to promote the happiness, refine the tastes, increase the enjoyments, elevate the morality and extend the reputation of our people,' announced James Smith in 1856, comprehensively but typically. Although popular literature was by no means invariably lofty, and the literati enjoyed, often wrote, popular fiction, farce and melodrama, in this milieu the responsible colonial writer was officially expected to keep Mammon and vulgarity at bay. For Harpur, Kendall and Catherine Spence in the 1850s and 1860s, as for O'Dowd, Sydney Jephcott, A. G. Stephens and sometimes Lawson in the 1880s and 1890s, the writer's purpose was, at least in part, to explore ethical and spiritual realities and ideals on behalf of the emerging and potentially wayward nation. At its most serious, this critical nationalism was neither mere chauvinism nor a self-conscious revelling in the locally familiar; the literati believed art and seriousness themselves confirmed the growth towards national 'maturity'.

In each of the major cities there were important coteries and literary groups, some more bibulous than bibliolatrous. Adelaide, 'incubated by philosophers and nursed through a rather fractious infancy by doctrinaires', had a literary association which met in London before its pioneer settlers had actually founded the city; Catherine Spence thought the colony from the beginning to be 'culturally richer' than she anticipated. Hobart's 'Macquarie Debating Society' (1855-80) was more an eclectic discussion group of literary friends than an arena for gladiatorial eloquence. Literary networks formed more slowly in Brisbane, owing to its slower early growth and to greater decentralisation in Queensland, but in 1879 its new 'Johnsonian Club' was admonished by Brunton Stephens to ensure that its 'virtues' be 'in this order reckoned / Fellowship first, Decorum a bad second'. Like the initially bohemian Yorick Club, founded by Marcus Clarke in Melbourne in 1867, the Johnsonians became a respectable gentleman's club; more serious literary assemblies were left to radicals and socialists like William Lane and his followers.

Preconceptions concerning the deprivations of literary life and opportunity in the country might also be challenged. The squatters often possessed imposing libraries, and some organised their own recitations and informal or public discussions. Rolf Boldrewood records a typical visit to his friend James Irvine in the Victorian Western District:

> I went over to Dunmore and spent a pleasant evening every now and then, rubbing up my classics and having a little 'good talk'. I had a few books which I had brought up with me in the dray—Byron, Scott, Shakespeare . . . with half a score of other authors, in whom there was *pabulum mentis* for a year or two. I had, besides, the run of the Dunmore library—no mean collection. So I had work, recreation, companionship, and intellectual occupation provided for me in abundant and wholesome proportion.

The squatters William Forster, Thomas McCombie, E. M. Curr and Cuthbert Fetherstonhaugh wrote literature worthy of preservation, in various genres. Although the billiard tables and cheap fiction of local mechanics' institutes became notoriously popular, their collections of books of 'higher learning' and of current periodicals were, as accounts of auto-didacts like Furphy, Neilson and O'Dowd confirm, regularly used by the fit audience. Rural workers and itinerant shearers were often provided by employers with periodicals and books, or shared their own purchases. In the towns displaced journalists ran some country newspapers which attained a 'literary-ness' and quality unimaginable today, providing access for country dwellers, if not to an intellectual cosmopolis, at least to some similar influences to those available to the literary minded city dweller: the dichotomy of 'city versus country' is apt to obscure shared traditions. From the 1860s onwards the literary weeklies, companions to the metropolitan dailies, were sent by coach and rail to thousands of country readers, some of whom in turn contributed to these journals. A high proportion of the most influential city journalists of the 1880s and thereafter, including J. F. Archibald, John Farrell, W. H. Traill, William Lane, A. G. Stephens, and Thomas Heney (the first Australian-born editor of the *Sydney Morning Herald*, but earlier a poet, novelist and critic in Wilcannia), were previously editors or associates of country newspapers. This emphasis is not intended to idealise either the literary culture of rural areas, or the onerous, deprived and isolated conditions of many country dwellers, especially those (relatively few) who were distant from towns. It may, however, help to explain the fact that the overwhelming majority of recognised colonial authors and journalists between 1860 and 1900 either were brought up in rural areas or spent a significant part of their writing careers there; and to place in a wider perspective the arguments of recent commentators who stress the extent to which images of the bush were created by city journalists in urban publications for suburban readers. Neither urban nor country press created any single image of the bush and, whatever the diverse effects of the press in shaping styles and attitudes may have been, in most cases these necessarily interacted with experience.

After the first goldrushes, Melbourne remained the largest colonial bookselling and publishing centre, and until the emergence of the *Bulletin* in 1880 was usually slightly ahead of Sydney in the quality and quantity of its literary journalism and criticism. During the 1850s, however, talent and circumstances in Sydney allowed the achievement of that rare colonial phenomenon, a challenging, somewhat cosmopolitan climate, conducive to the operations of a small, homogeneous but probing literary intelligentsia. The milieu was essential to the development of Henry Kendall, since the contacts he made provided mentors, contemporary models, books, ideas, financial assistance, and publishing opportunities; but the interaction assisted as well other younger journalists—critics, essayists, satirists—including Daniel Deniehy, editor of the *Southern Cross* (1859-60), and the visitors Richard Rowe and Frank Fowler, editor in 1856-7 of the *Month*. The older, mentor figures were primarily Nicol Drysdale Stenhouse, an immigrant Scottish lawyer, who employed Deniehy as articled clerk, and made his home, library, financial help, intellect and general patronage available to the coterie; John Woolley, Professor of Classics at Sydney University; the squatter poet and satirist William Forster; J. Sheridan Moore, who saw Kendall's first volume through the press; and James Lionel Michael, a Sydney lawyer and brilliant conversationalist, who employed Kendall in Sydney and later in Grafton. Although Fowler's efforts to formalise 'the Stenhouse circle' into a Literary Association of New South Wales were unsuccessful, the close-knit group met often amongst themselves, at dinner parties, soirées and in smaller gatherings, to probe scholarly and theoretical issues from the classics to Kant and Tennyson, and to explore such issues as a 'national literature' and standards in colonial criticism. 'In the local journalism of that time there was a purely literary element which has since almost, if not altogether, disappeared', commented Kendall in 1870, referring particularly to the interest displayed in theoretical, critical, and scholarly issues.

Throughout the century journalism remained in many respects the mainstay of colonial literary production. To publish a book in the colonies was risky and expensive, owing to high production costs (of labour, paper and distribution), a small market, and the appeal of established British authors and of 'home' as subject matter. Journals and newspapers provided outlets for publication and often financial remuneration. Frequently, as in Britain, novelists, poets and playwrights sought from journalism their basic source of income. In the colonies, however, the difficulties of book publishing, the indigenous nature of journalistic ventures, and the conspicuous lack of self-supporting doyens like Dickens and Carlyle, encouraged journalists to think of themselves as champions of the cause of colonial literature. 'The Caxton Fund', a benevolent fund for needy Australian writers modelled loosely on the Royal Literary Fund in Britain, was set up in Melbourne in 1871, but with a widened scope, so that journalists and pressmen were to be eligible for benefits. Although small colonial magazines were continually failing (the obstacles to success were similar to those of book publication), the contributing author did not have to bear the financial brunt; despite apparently dismal prospects, there was sufficient enthusiasm, or recklessness, amongst proprietors to maintain a steady succession of little magazines. Moreover, larger newspapers and weekly journals provided reliable outlets for fiction, poetry and professional journalism. 'This is essentially the land of newspapers', remarked Richard Twopeny in 1882, referring to the fact that wealth and literacy resulted in Australia in a *per capita* purchase of newspapers far in excess (Twopeny claimed five times) of that in Britain.

As a consequence, literary Australia was largely journalists' Australia. The advantage was at best the versatility and ebullience of journalism itself, both as a vehicle for new writing, and as the detailed reporting of literary events, lectures, and meetings of literary societies. The journalists' sketches, commentaries and satires, notably those of Marcus Clarke and John Stanley James ('The Vagabond'), offered an urban subject matter frequently neglected in fiction and verse. The limitation of the journalists' world was the exclusiveness of its influence, which in the 1890s prompted the crisp strictures of the Scottish visitor Francis Adams:

> Literary Society is the synonym for the company of journalists, and has superseded the old Bohemianism.
>
> A second rate and third-rate pseudo-intellectualism reigns in it, and only too often it becomes a pseudo-intellectualism of no rate at all. . . .
>
> The *Bulletin* is the only really talented and original outcome of the Australian press, but its literary criticism is that of clever, sixth-form schoolboys and imperfectly-educated pressmen, and all it knows about culture is to perpetually spell it 'culshaw'.

Despite the many sorrowful legends of colonial Grub Street, from the 1860s onwards recognised, talented and popular literary journalists could make at least a reasonably comfortable living from salary and commissions. The field was competitive; but stories of failure amongst the talented are usually associated with impractical ventures in proprietorship (like Marcus Clarke's), intemperance, or with an inability or unwillingness to supplement 'legitimate' writing with commercial literary copy. In the 1880s Melbourne's senior literary journalist, James Smith, received an annual retaining fee of £500 from the *Argus*, which he could liberally supplement. Marcus Clarke was paid £300 as theatrical critic for the *Argus* in 1867, but soon after was making £750 from freelance criticism, commentary and leader writing. Nevertheless, without the prop of journalism or some form of supplementary income, to earn a livelihood from literature was inevitably difficult. The privations of the poet Victor Daley's widow influenced Alfred Deakin, himself a poet and literary journalist, to institute, as prime minister in 1908, the Commonwealth Literary Fund, a cautious formal beginning to state assistance to writers.

The bibliography of Miller and Macartney lists about 830 individual titles of volumes of poetry published between 1850 and Federation. Of these 85 per cent were published in the colonies, whereas in the same period only 34 per cent of fiction titles had Australian publishers. Poetry constituted about 44 per cent of the aggregate of verse and fiction titles, but most of the poetry volumes were slim, feeble as literature, privately sponsored. Many were either prettified exercises in gum-tree romanticism or debasements of celebratory neo-classicism, written for the openings of exhibitions, town halls and so forth.

The poets sought Australian publishers mainly because the larger London houses, which would guarantee the costs from suitable fiction writers, perceived slender talents and small markets, and were understandably not interested. Australian publishers as we think of them today evolved from bookselling and printing businesses, when proprietors established separate publishing departments as a secondary line. The first was bookseller George Robertson, in Melbourne in 1859; in the 1860s printers Clarson and Massina followed suit. There were three ways to print and distribute: the most common was for poets to cover costs from their own pockets, or by subscription; another was to come to an arrangement with a 'publisher' which might relieve the author of a portion of the costs; the third, rarely manageable with poetry before A. B. Paterson, was to contract with a publisher who would guarantee production costs in return for a proportion of the profits on sales or the purchase of copying rights. In these circumstances, to publish a book of verse one needed not so much talent or popular appeal as money or backing; especially before the 1880s 'book' poetry was mainly the preserve of the bookishly wealthy or exceptionally determined, and the quality and subject matter reflect those preconditions. It would be exaggerated but not totally misleading to conclude, given the spirited longevity of anonymous colonial folk balladry, that before A. B. Paterson the most popular verse was unpublished, and the most unpopular was published.

Poets of some talent such as Kendall and Gordon made little or
nothing from their books. The publishing processes they chose
demonstrate some of the options available. To launch Kendall's first
volume, for example, his mentor J. Sheridan Moore placed this
advertisement in the *Empire* and the *Sydney Morning Herald*, in
January 1861;

THE MUSE OF AUSTRALIA—in preparation for Publication (by
subscription), THE POEMS AND SONGS OF HENRY KENDALL, the boy-poet
of Australia. At the request of several literary and influential gentleman,
and after a severe critical examination of the work, MR SHERIDAN MOORE
has consented to superintend the publication. So convinced is he of the
merit that he has no fear of commending it to the taste and patriotism of
the country. Subscription Lists lie at several book and music dealers, in
town and country.

In publishing Kendall's second volume, *Leaves from Australian
Forests* (1869), George Robertson agreed to pay production costs, on
the condition that all receipts from the first 700 of the 1500 copies
printed should go to the publisher: Robertson lost £90. A. L. Gordon
mounted his own production costs, with Clarson, Massina and with
Robertson respectively; he lost on each venture. In 1880 Kendall,
with a more populous colonial market and perhaps a more popular
verse style, made £100 from *Songs from the Mountains* (1880), his
profits apparently based on sales after he covered his own costs.

'Poets' abounded. If the legend of the Australian male as a
practical man suspicious of literary pursuits is founded in historical
fact, the 'suspicion' may have derived as much from exposure to local
versifiers as from ignorance of verse. 'Original poetry' was published
as a matter of course in many newspapers and periodicals; but
generally was paid for only in the larger journals, at fairly low rates.
Some was sent overseas.

By nearly every mail comes an appeal from the neglect which genius
finds in the colonies to the more liberal and impartial literary courts of
the mother country, justified by parcels of manuscript verse and
newspaper clippings.

Thus commented the London *Athenaeum* in 1862, adding that few
aspirants showed talent. A prominent theme of colonial verse,
especially Kendall's, is the neglect of the sensitive poet in a practical

community; but the sales and popularity of Tennyson, Shelley, Browning and Burns, for example, were probably at least equal *per capita* to those in Britain, and these poets were widely read and discussed in suburban literary societies.

Miller and Macartney list over 1000 individual titles of books of fiction published between 1849 and 1901. Of these, 54 per cent were published in the eleven years before Federation, during which period 422 titles were published in London, as against 143 in Australia. Measured exclusively in terms of productivity, the 1890s was fiction's decade of boom; but the quantity published in Britain, proportionally higher even than in each of the four preceding decades, complicates assessment of a nationalistic nineties legend. On the other hand the fiction which *was* published in Australia, notably by the new and growing Sydney house of Angus & Robertson and by the Bulletin Publishing Company, was frequently dissimilar in character and quality to that preferred by British publishers. Thus, despite the substantial increase in the volume of domestic and adventure romance and light colonial exotica which English publishers (not inflexibly) preferred, new opportunities and lines of direction were established in the 1890s, especially in Sydney, and outlets were made available for the various anti-romantic styles and genres of such writers as Henry Lawson, Steele Rudd, Albert Dorrington and Joseph Furphy.

The question of how and whether the English and Australian markets and outlets conditioned the choice of genre, style and subject of writers is nevertheless complex. Colonial and English tastes overlapped substantially before the 1880s. Although the English publishers' estimation of the popular tastes of the home market clearly enough influenced their selections and financial terms, the preferences of editors and proprietors of colonial journals also affected the range of writers' offerings. The most significant colonial development in the production of Australian fiction as a popular and commercial enterprise was the establishment in the late 1850s and 1860s of popular weeklies, adjuncts to metropolitan daily newspapers widely circulated in both city and country areas, which contained substantial literary sections and published short stories and fiction in serial form. The *Sydney Mail* (companion of the *Sydney Morning Herald*), the *Australasian* (of the *Argus*), the *Leader* (of the *Age*), the *Observer* (of the *South Australian Register*), the *South Australian Chronicle* (of the Adelaide *Advertiser*), the *Queenslander* (of the *Brisbane Courier*), and in 1870 the *Australian Town and Country*

Journal (of the Sydney *Evening News*) attracted talented novelists, including Ada Cambridge, 'Tasma' and Rolf Boldrewood, who were paid enough to make a bare living, had they chosen, solely from their writing.

The range of fiction in these journals has not to date been fully indexed or defined (as recently as 1986, for example, several generally unknown works by Ada Cambridge came to light), but there is some evidence to suggest that editors may have considered anti-romantic genres and vernacular styles to be unpopular or unsuitable. It is probably significant that in 1882 both the *Town and Country Journal* and the *Australasian* rejected Boldrewood's *Robbery Under Arms* on the basis of a reading of the first two chapters. Presumably, the older, English-born, and traditionalist editors considered Dick Marston's assertive vernacular undesirable; perhaps, too, the currency of the Kelly gang's reputation made the book's values, in these early chapters, seem dubious or threatening. Samuel Bennett's *Town and Country Journal* had previously serialised seven of Boldwood's more 'Anglo-Australian' novels; but the new serial's immediate success in the *Sydney Mail*, edited by the younger New Zealander F. W. Ward, seems to confirm the popularity of the vernacular. Certainly, some of the most influential journalists and editors, including James Smith of the *Argus* (editor of the *Australasian* in the 1860s and 1870s) and Thomas Heney of the *Sydney Morning Herald*, were later suspicious and critical of 'the *Bulletin* School'. Smith, one of the most traditionalist and socially elitist, required that literary values be 'ennobling' and forms 'harmonious', in ways that would preclude his appreciation of Lawson and Baynton. In 1889 he advised J. C. Williamson that the ending of Ibsen's *A Doll's House* (1879) should be romantically altered for colonial performances; and he vigorously condemned the 'impressionist' techniques and values, as he saw them, of the *plein air* school of colonial painters. Whether editorial influences and lack of outlets seriously retarded anti-romantic, vernacular, and apparently 'untailored' forms of expression would be difficult to establish with certainty, but the reaction to J. F. Archibald's opening of literary floodgates when he became sole editor of the *Bulletin* in 1886 suggests that pressure for such outlets had been building up for some years.

No writer of fiction made a fortune in Australia; and although publication overseas by authors living in Australia could provide a healthy supplement to the payments for Australian serial rights, this was by no means necessarily more lucrative in its own right than colonial serial publication. Catherine Spence, who initially hoped to make her living from fiction, gave up working 'for a coolie's wage', and turned to journalism exclusively, which she found both more profitable and socially influential. She received £30 from her English publisher for *Clara Morison* (1854), £20 for *Tender and True* (1856) and £35 for *Mr Hogarth's Will* (1865). Both Marcus Clarke, who made £100 including a £50 advance, 'sight unseen', for the colonial serial rights to *His Natural Life* (1870-2), and Ada Cambridge, who wrote cordially of her 'little boom' before the syndication of serial fiction to Australia in the 1890s, appear to have gained more from Australian serial rights than from English publication; but the reverse is true of Rolf Boldrewood, who could command excellent terms from Macmillan after *Robbery Under Arms*. Although in ' "Pursuing Literature" in Australia', Henry Lawson wrote bitterly of his small earnings, in other contexts he acknowledged the fair treatment of his publishers and the difficulties of the Australian market. From a purely financial point of view, Lawson was right to advocate that any recognised writer should 'go steerage, stow away, swim and seek London', though he might wisely have added that the expatriate's talent should be directed towards romance, not *Bulletin* vernacular realism. By the turn of the century the resounding precedents of lucrative and popular Australian romance written in Britain had been established by, amongst others, Nat Gould, B. L. Farjeon, who wrote over fifty novels to 1903, Guy Boothby, who published fifty between 1894 and 1907, and the more serious 'domestic' romancier, Rosa Praed, who wrote forty. Some *Bulletin* writers who left Australia, notably Albert Dorrington and J. F. Dwyer, found great prosperity overseas, Dwyer becoming the first Australian-born 'bestseller' millionaire; but there is no doubt that in exchanging the styles and techniques they had adopted in the *Bulletin* for those of internationally popular adventure romance (albeit with Australian settings) these writers sacrificed literary quality for popular success.

In the field of drama the lot of the colonial writer was still more frustrating. The aspiring playwright could witness, between 1850 and 1880, the spectacular transformation of colonial theatre from the clumsy operations of a distant outpost into a socially pervasive, grandly successful institution, surpassed in the Empire only in London; but circumstances conspired to deprive him of any major or well-paid participation in this otherwise lucrative carnival. Until the 1870s, the stars of British and American stage shone brightly over the antipodes, and returned with colonial gold: G. B. Brooke, Charles and Ellen Kean, Barry Sullivan, Madame Ristori, Thomas Jefferson, Walter Montgomery and so on, in regular succession. Australian actors, managers, audiences and critics were gratified, but playwrights remained victims of the tragedians' preference for Shakespeare, the managers' and audiences' taste for Boucicault and English melodrama, the virtually non-existent copyright procedures, the required repertoires of many mediocre visiting actors, and the scant remuneration paid by entrepreneurs. James Neild of Melbourne, considered by theatre historian Harold Love to have been the most accomplished and arresting dramatic critic in the Empire, launched in the 1850s his thirty-year campaign on the playwrights' behalf against 'coloniophobia':

> There is a settled conviction in the minds of Victorian managers that nothing good in the shape of a play can be written in Victoria, and it is still more convenient to urge this belief when they can buy English plays for a shilling a piece. Some of these days we may get something in the shape of an international copyright, and as this is a kind of protection which extends in two directions, it is not unlikely that anybody but the managers will object to it.

Neild argued in 1888 that the attitudes of managers were so unsympathetic to playwrights that talented authors amongst his friends refused to write drama.

Though managers would not be seduced into a full-scale, financially expensive patriotism, nevertheless they sprinkled the repertoire with local writing. The most successful colonial works before the 1880s were the adult pantomimes and burlesques—social, political and satirical—of W. M. Akhurst, Marcus Clarke and Garnet Walch. But markets and lack of copyright favoured the managers more than the playwrights, and from the 1880s onwards some of the most successful actor-managers wrote their own Australian material. George Darrell, Alfred Dampier and Bert Bailey gave their audiences the opportunity to celebrate Australian myths and the social environment in their original melodramas or in adaptations of fiction, notably *His Natural Life* (1887), *Robbery Under Arms* (1890), and *On Our Selection* (1912). Darrell, who in the 1890s made over £500 per week, wrote with all the popular flair and theatricality of a seasoned, witty professional of the theatre; but the well-deserved success of the experienced actor-managers, who proved Neild correct and J. C. Williamson wrong concerning the viability of local subject matter, shows the hold of commercial formulas over the colonial drama. The circumstances governing production required in Australia, as elsewhere before Ibsen, that plays be written either for grand, three-tiered popular theatre, or for the closet; and for nothing in between.

The segregation of masculine and feminine cultures, together with a patronising subordination of women when the two overlapped, was normal practice. 'Here,' wrote 'New Chum' on the subject of the Sydney Public Library in the 1880s, 'as in many similar buildings throughout the colonies, the fairer sex has a room set apart from the unfair, where in maiden meditation fancy free, they may study all and everything, from Shakespeare to Ouida, apart from the manly throng.' Women were excluded from or exceptional within many of the clubs and more influential coteries. Although they outnumbered men in town and suburban literary societies, their roles required them to sing, to recite, and to provide refreshments; males usually held office and presented papers. Wives were often unsung literary partners, providing an intellectual companionship basic to the husband's success: the literatteurs David Blair, H. G. Turner and James Smith penned tributes to that effect. Others were the victims of their literary spouses' bohemian or intemperate lifestyles, as Henry Kendall acknowledged in several poems.

A high proportion of colonial women who gained literary recognition avoided, modified or abandoned the colonial Victorian wife-mother role, and demonstrated a discipline and will that was socially extraordinary, or behaviour that was unconventional. In diverse ways this was true of Rosa Praed, Ada Cambridge, Mary Gilmore, Miles Franklin, Jessie Couvreur ('Tasma'), Barbara Baynton and Zora Cross. Catherine Spence, a feminist campaigner throughout the second half of the century, claimed that she 'kept a watch over [her] affections', since marriage would interfere impossibly with her cultural mission. Awareness and experience of the complexities, dilemmas and personal politics relating to women's roles are reflected in much of the fiction of these novelists, despite its romantic conventions.

The inquest into the tragic death of Marie St Denis in 1876 was a *cause célèbre* of mid-Victorian colonial feminism. An atheist, she wrote unpublished plays, essays, fiction, and a treatise on 'The Position and Duties of Women', and was one of the most talented actresses in Melbourne. Her aim was to achieve the independence and recognition due, she felt, to a self-made, unconventional woman who feared the lot of the Victorian wife. The cause of her first suicide attempt was the humiliation arising from her inability to pay a heavy hotel bill. Her second attempt, an overdose of laudanum motivated by her passion for an unattainable married man, resulted in her death. The *Argus* voiced society's response of awe and reproof:

> she was a very extraordinary woman, fired with strong passions, quivering with sensitiveness, possessing great talents and knowing it, vain to a superlative degree, ambitious, despising conventionalities, and with a vivid imagination, all culminating in an intense desire to shine in life with the blazing brilliancy of a comet rather than the calm radiance of a fixed star.

In rare instances before Louisa Lawson established the *Dawn* (1888-1905), literary journals had been owned and edited by women (the *Spectator*, 1858-9, edited by Cora Weekes, was the first), and some women's literary societies operated in the 1880s (Ada Cambridge was for a time president of a Victorian group). But it was not until Rose Scott organised her campaigns for suffrage and women's education that colonial feminism and support for women writers gained a broad and forceful collective momentum. 'Her drawing room,' observed Miles Franklin, 'was the only real salon that Sydney knew.' In the 1890s Scott brought together factory women, unknown literary aspirants from the suburbs and the country, eminent visiting authors, politicians, and the Sydney literati, bohemian and respectable. Letters indicate that she was the catalyst of several literary careers and numerous literary friendships, and that she organised the beginnings of a support system amongst literary women who had felt its absence with 'sorehearted antagonism'. Her influence, with that of her collaborator Lousia Lawson, was a counter to the masculinism of pervasive *Bulletin* coteries in ways that benefited both females and males.

Radical papers and magazines such as Lane's *Boomerang* (1887-92) and Bernard O'Dowd's *Tocsin* (founded 1897) created a new kind of reader and writer and an alternative literature. Lane founded a Bellamy Society, and in 1890 serialised the American journalist's popular novel *Looking Backward* (1887) in the Queensland *Worker*. Though Henry George, Bellamy and Marx were the chief objects of study in radical discussion societies, popular ballad forms, Dickensian styles and literary techniques as diverse as Shakespeare's, Byron's and Whitman's became vehicles of radical didacticism or disputation. The discussion of ideas in Joseph Furphy's *Such is Life* (1903) and *Rigby's*

Romance (1905-6), the slogan ballads of Henry Lawson, and the prophetic rather fustian rhetoric of Bernard O'Dowd's poetry are well known; the neglected verse of John Farrell wittily exploits Byron's *ottava rima* techniques, and provides some of the most stinging satire of the colonial period.

In January 1880 the first issue of a weekly newspaper brashly informed its public that it aimed 'to establish a journal which cannot be beaten—excellent in the illustrations which embellish its pages and unsurpassed in the vigor, freshness and geniality of its literary contributions'. A key to the popularity of the *Bulletin*, which quickly flourished where other radical liberal and nationalist literary journals were to fail, was the acumen of its editors in judging and packaging writing which combined seriousness and quality with popular appeal. 'Eschewing antiquated models and superannuated methods', as an editorial put it, hiring excellent cartoonists and competent literary staff, W. H. Traill and, in particular, J. F. Archibald divined and developed a house style of complex vernacular intimacy and comic splash. Whatever their politics, Australian readers knew the intricate games of wryness, toughness, pith, grim understatement and insouciant irreverence that the *Bulletin*'s commentators, writers and illustrators were playing. Circulation increased from 10,000 in 1880, to 18,000 in 1887, to an alleged peak in the 1890s of 80,000. With a captive audience, Archibald and A. G. Stephens, his literary editor from 1894 to 1906, could afford to publish discussions of literary topics (Shakespeare, Nietzsche, George Eliot, 'realism', the French Symbolists, for example) which ordinarily would not sell in a comic newspaper; the context and style of forum commentary provided an outlet for critical discussion, and helped to popularise intellectual issues.

To aspiring writers the welcoming familiarity created the sense of a national literary club. You might be told in print that your work was ridiculous, but at least you felt recognised. Advertisements cajoled:

> Every man can write at least one good book; every man with brains has at least one good story to tell; every man, with or without brains, moves in a different circle and knows things unknown to any other man . . . Mail your work to the *Bulletin*, which pays for accepted matter.

Literally hundreds of men and women did, every week. (One reader, James Dwyer, commenced his lucrative literary career by smuggling a poem out of Goulburn goal.) Archibald and Stephens wrote in person to promising contributors, and invited them to call at the *Bulletin* office, which they flooded. In such a familiar, club-like atmosphere, contributors wrote to one another; in the cities, especially Sydney, they met in homes, pubs and literary clubs, and added to their network of acquaintance. 'In evening went to Louie's at Neutral Bay. I enjoyed the evening very much, all very literary, and artistic! I talked to Mr Chris Brennan, said to be a genius but slightly mad. Splendid to talk to though', Ethel Turner informed her diary in 1893.

Archibald's promise of recognition and payment of *individual* talent was honoured. Although a more or less official editorial line put forward in leaders and the literary Red Page advocated the values and styles for which the paper became legendary, in practice scores of contributors were encouraged to explore a range of aesthetics and *métiers*. The official line sanctioned or preferred terse, economical prose ('Boil it down!'), bush subject matter, democratic and nationalistic sentiment, an aesthetic of realism, egalitarianism, and social utility, and the racism of 'Australia for the white man'. Certainly, the production of much Australian literature was conditioned and shaped by these preferences: consciously or otherwise, many writers either learnt the 'rules', or now found a paying outlet for their natural literary inclinations. Nevertheless, few set attitudes were *required*. Stephens and Archibald promoted Shaw Neilson's almost Blakean lyrics, Brennan's esoteric symbolist poetry and theoretical criticism, the arcane verbophilia of Furphy's fiction, the ornately wordy and melodramatic stories of Price Warung, the pre-Raphaelite romanticism of Victor Daley; and they tolerated much bathetic verse and prose melodrama.

Archibald and Stephens were at once populist and cultural missionaries. They accepted and enjoyed the *Bulletin*'s populist nationalism, and at the same time employed it strategically, to undermine the cultural influence of mid-Victorian and English traditionalists and sentimentalists, and to encourage a new writing which by assimilating and subordinating local influences might also transcend them; but they were sanguine enough not to exaggerate either the achievement of the 'universality' of Australian writing. Stephens, in particular, placed a post-Arnoldian stress on the ethical and metaphysical potentials of literature. The *Bulletin* had developed, through its irony and satire, and through the checks and balances within the diversity of its projections of 'Australia' (which ranged from the nihilistic to the heavily idealised), a kind of built-in critique of Australianism in literature. But after a quarter of a century in which it had become institutionalised, and with the departures of Archibald and Stephens, it was becoming trapped within its own traditions, conventions and games. Editorial successors, with the exception perhaps of literary editor David McKee Wright, were more exclusively commercialist and populist. Increased reliance on permanent staff, the literary decline of certain established writers (like Lawson), the expatriation of others, and lack of originality and definite talent amongst new contributors, tightened the hold of formulas and stereotypes over Australian literature written at home. A belated recognition of the importance of urban subject matter produced mainly comic entertainment, journalistically competent but limited. Some writers and critics, while maintaining nationalist emphases, began to feel swamped by bush stories and ballads and by the exaggerated assertiveness of the literary ethos. Moreover, the twentieth century's gradual widening of a gap in literary consciousness between 'popular' (downgraded to 'mass') and 'minority' cultures led to the formation of small coteries with a more narrow and ideological base. Earlier hopes for some kind of general fusion of the popular, 'Australian' and 'legitimate' elements of literature were undermined. Before the 1920s these splintered coteries lacked sufficient momentum and certainty of direction to be influential. It is perhaps in part because Australian writers between 1900 and 1920 had difficulty in establishing their literary bearings that the period is often considered relatively undistinguished, and that some of its most recognised figures either wrote as expatriates, compelled like Henry Handel Richardson to define an 'Australian' literary perspective in relation exclusively to European and British referents and models; or felt, like Christopher Brennan, culturally disoriented and alienated within their local surroundings.

Notes

Some of the most helpful sources of information on literary production and livelihoods of writers are biographical studies. These include: Clive Turnbull, 'Mulberry Leaves' in his *Australian Lives* (1965), on Whitehead; Ann Blainey, *The Farthing Poet* (1968) and Cyril Pearl, *Always Morning* (1960), both on R. H. Horne; J. Normington Rawling, *Charles Harpur, an Australian* (1962); W. H. Wilde, *Henry Kendall* (1976); Brian Elliott, *Marcus Clarke* (1958); Hugh Anderson,

Bernard O'Dowd (1968); 'Denton Prout',*Henry Lawson: The Grey Dreamer* (1963); Eric Irvin, *Gentleman George* (1980), on Darrell; Susan Magarey, *Unbridling the Tongues of Women: A Biography of Catherine Helen Spence* (1985); and Brian Matthews, *Louisa* (1987) on Louisa Lawson.

James Smith's reminiscences on literary life during the goldrushes are quoted from 'Recollections of an Octogenarian, No. 7, Talent in Exile', *Leader* (Melbourne), 10 August 1907. His remarks on nurture of the arts are from *Argus*, 16 December 1856; his comment on *A Doll's House* is discussed in a letter to him from J. C. Williamson, now in the James Smith papers, Mitchell Library, Sydney; he writes on the 'impressionists' in *Argus*, 17 August 1889. Lurline Stuart's unpublished doctoral thesis, 'James Smith: His Influence on the Development of Literary Culture in Colonial Melbourne' (Monash Unversity, 1983), investigates Smith's literary career and provides a compendious checklist of his voluminous writings. Excellent insights into journalistic, literary and theatrical life in Melbourne are provided in Harold Love's forthcoming biography of J. E. Neild. Kendall discusses the Stenhouse Circle in his unsigned sketch 'About some Members of a Colonial Dinner Party', *Australasian*, 2 April 1870.

Little research has been published on metropolitan literary milieux other than Sydney and Melbourne. The reference to Adelaide's cultural beginnings is from H. G. Turner, 'Our Sister Cities', *Melbourne Review*, (1884). See also Paul Depasquale, *A Critical History of South Australian Literature, 1836-1930* (1978); Ronald Lawson, *Brisbane in the 1890s* (1973); and Peter Bolger, *Hobart Town* (1973).

Lurline Stuart's *Nineteenth Century Australian Periodicals* (1979) is a comprehensive annotated bibliography. R. E. N. Twopeny's comments on journalism are from *Town Life In Australia* (1883), Francis Adams' from *The Australians* (1893). Further information on patronage, coteries and journalism may be found in Ann-Mari Jordens, *The Stenhouse Circle* (1979); B. Bennett (ed.), *Cross Currents* (1982); V. Burgmann, *In Our Time* (1985); in chapters by Susan Sheridan, Ken Stewart and Deborah Campbell respectively in *Nellie Melba, Ginger Meggs and Friends*, ed. S. Dermody, J. Docker and D. Modjeska, (1982); and in Ken Stewart, 'The Support of Literature in Colonial Australia', *Australian Literary Studies*, 9 (1980). The Yorick coterie is sketched in Hugh McCrae, *Story-Book Only* (1948).

The figures concerning quantity and places of publication of colonial poetry and fiction in book form are based on a count of the entries in E. Morris Miller and F. T. McCartney, *Australian Literature*

(1956). Catherine Spence discusses her novel writing, journalism and feminism in her *Autobiography* (1910), from which the quotations in this chapter are taken. Ada Cambridge refers briefly to literary earnings and the literary scene in *Thirty Years in Australia* (1903). Henry Lawson's ' "Pursuing Literature" in Australia', published 1899 and quoted in this chapter, is reprinted together with contemporary documentary material on literary production by A. G. Stephens, Joseph Furphy and Vance Palmer, in John Barnes (ed.), *The Writer in Australia* (1969). Boldrewood's account of his visit to 'Dunmore' is quoted in T. Inglis Moore, *Rolf Boldrewood* (1968); Alan Brissenden's *Rolf Boldrewood* (1972) provides financial and other relevant detail.

Further information on dramatic and theatrical production, especially of pantomime and melodrama, can be found in H. Love (ed.), *The Australian Stage: A Documentary History* (1984); Margaret Williams, *Australia on the Popular Stage* (1983); and Eric Irvin, *Australian Melodrama* (1981). The letters of Charles and Ellen Kean from Australia, published as *Emigrant in Motley*, edited by J. M. D. Hardwick (1954) are contemporary responses of touring tragedians.

'New Chum' is Percy Clarke; his remarks are extracted from his *The 'New Chum' in Australia* (1886). William Lane's literary affiliations are traced by Michael Wilding in his introduction to *The Workingman's Paradise* (1980, facsimile of the 1892 edition). Miles Franklin's remarks on Rose Scott and her salon are from her essay on Scott in *The Peaceful Army*, edited by Flora S. Eldershaw (1938). Of much primary and secondary material available on Archibald, Stephens and the *Bulletin*, the most comprehensive book studies are Sylvia Lawson, *The Archibald Paradox* (1983) and Patricia Rolfe, *The Journalistic Javelin* (1979); figures concerning the *Bulletin*'s circulation in 1887 were uncovered from audited records in the New South Wales State Archives by Barry Andrews. The reference to Brennan is from Philippa Poole (comp.), *The Diaries of Ethel Turner* (1979), entry for 23 November 1894.

Chapter 12

THE BALLADS: EIGHTEENTH CENTURY TO THE PRESENT

CLIFF HANNA

Let me have the making of a nation's ballads, and I care little who makes its laws.

Montaigne

Australia's history in ballads differs from that of older countries: its beginnings lie not in the traditional form, or 'folk ballad', which endures through oral transmission, but in broadside, or street song. One gains its energy and its charm through continuous change, the other is fixed in print. The older form was rural in origin, the younger a product of advanced technology and growing urbanisation. The settlement of Australia occurred at a crucial point in the evolution of the British ballad. Initially, broadsides were the province of the upper, literate class; the publishing activity that commenced at the end of the eighteenth century was aimed at the lower, urban class, which produced much of our early population.

Clearly, those broadside ballads concerned with Australia are not, in a strict sense, indigenous. Should we regard them as a part of our literature? Many came in their original form and would have been sung by the convicts. It is a vexed question since some of these songs are already included in our ballad canon. Major anthologies such as Stewart and Keesing's *Old Bush Songs* (1957), Russel Ward's *The Penguin History of Australian Ballads* (1964), and Hugh Anderson's *The Story of Australian Folksong* (1970), include the broadsides 'Botany Bay', 'Botany Bay, A New Song', 'Van Diemen's Land' and 'The Black Velvet Band', among others. In addition, there is 'Botany Bay', or 'Farewell to Old England', which was pieced together from old convict broadsides for an 1885 London burlesque called

Little Jack Sheppard. The ditty has been so commercialised that the 'too-ral li-oor-al li-ad-dity' refrain alone has become synonymous with Australia's convict heritage. Having enshrined the song in our culture, should we exclude the broadsides that make up its parts? And what of their companions, which number well into the hundreds? This is no idle quibble: they can fill a crucial gap in the ballad history of this country. Of the few indigenous convict songs that survive, none derives from the first forty years of the colony. Perhaps, as is commonly suggested, the first native ballads were suppressed as treason songs. This might explain, for example, why a bushranger song like 'Johnny Troy', composed at the time of the Donahue songs, disappeared from Australia. The British ballads go some way towards filling the hiatus, for in professing to speak for the convicts they offer contemporary impressions of the initial colonial feelings. They also provide pre-settlement responses to the colony.

It is fitting, given Australia's rich pub folklore, that the earliest known balladist of Botany Bay was a Birmingham publican. John Freeth, or 'Poet' Freeth, was an outspoken Liberal and keen political commentator. A true balladeer, he versified topical issues and sang them to his patrons. The widespread interest in Botany Bay towards the end of 1786 inspired, among others, an idealistic adieu to the First Fleet, called 'The Convict's Departure':

> What if the parting day is at hand,
>   Never at fate be railing,
> Though from a rich and plentiful land,
>   We must be quickly sailing;
> Let not our bosoms fear display,
>   Future events concerning,
> Though we are going to Botany Bay,
>   Never from thence returning . . .

In contrast, the Anacreontic Society, founded in honour of a Greek poet who was also fond of the convivial glass, expressed a cynical, post-lapsarian attitude. Legend has it that 'Botany Bay Song' (1788) was sung to Sir Joseph Banks at a Society meeting:

> You have read of Captain Cook our late worthy commander,
> The great Sir Joseph Banks, and Doctor Solander,
> They sailed round the world, were perplexed and teiz'd too,
> To find out a place where the King might send the thieves to.

Another society or club piece, 'Botany Bay, A New Song' (1790), goes further by suggesting that if dishonesty was the criterion then most of England should be packed off.

These songs are not ballads in the strict sense of the term. A traditional ballad like 'Tam Lin' is a narrative to music, or a song that tells a story. Since the sixteenth century, however, the term has embraced popular song. A general rule is that traditional ballads work from a narrative and popular ballads, like the ones above, express a sentiment.

'Broadside' and 'broadsheet' are also flexible terms including ballads, verse, and prose narratives. A common form was the 'execution sheet', a forerunner of the tabloid, which was a lurid account of a murder or hanging illustrated with a gory cartoon and verses supposedly penned by the miscreant. Speed was essential, competition was fierce. In the case of Henry Savery, later the author of Australia's first novel, *Quintus Servinton* (1830-1), a Bristol printer named H. Shepherd 'jumped the gun'. His first broadsheet details Savery's arrest for forgery: the second, 'The Sorrowful Lamentation of H. SAVERY, ESQ.', mourns his death sentence. The third, entitled 'The Last Awful Moments of H. SAVERY, ESQ.', is adorned with a woodcut of a hooded body dangling on a scaffold:

> On Friday, a few minutes after 12 o'clock, the malefactor appeared . . . perfectly resigned to his fate . . . and after a few minutes devotional exercise . . . the fatal signal was given, and he was launched into a boundless eternity. —The concourse of spectators was almost beyond conception.

Unfortunately for Mr Shepherd, the day before the execution another Bristol printer published the 'RESPITE of H. SAVERY, ESQ.'

Street literature, or 'illiterature', is a vast, largely unexplored area. Between 1800 and 1820 thousands of ballads reached the streets of Britain. The greatest street publishers were Johnny Pitts and Jemmy Catnach: Pitts commenced in 1802, and Catnach in 1813. Through their convict broadsides they effectively publicised the colony. There are a flock of street songs called 'Botany Bay' but only two models, and both probably started with Pitts. The earliest derives from an earlier society or club piece, 'A New Song Made upon the Lads sent to Botany Bay'. Like his contemporaries, Pitts was not above stealing and modifying ballads, then passing them off as his own. The first stanza retains the jovial conviviality of the parent song:

Come all you young fellows,
Who ever that you be
Who delight in a song,
Join chorus with me.
I will sing to you a song,
Which was made the other day,
Concerning some poor lads,
Who were sent to Botany Bay.

Also known as 'The Transport', the second 'Botany Bay' is one of the most famous convict songs and is still sung by British folk singers, while lines have found their way into American prison songs. A typical 'Come all ye', it is a cautionary tale which owes much of its reformist flavour and consequent success to the moral climate. Near the end of the eighteenth century a flood of religiously oriented broadsides and chapbooks, or Cheap Repository Tracts, were written to divert the popular mind from the French Revolution, prostitution and the heresies of Tom Paine. The opening verse is steeped in missionary zeal:

Come all young men of learning,
  And a warning take by me,
I'd have you quit night walking,
  And shun bad company;
I'd have you quite night walking,
  Or else you'll rue the day,
When you are transported,
  And going to Botany Bay

According to English folk historians, the Poaching Act of 1828 provoked many songs. The most famous, 'Van Diemen's Land' or 'The Gallant Poachers' (1829-30), became one of the best-known ballads in nineteenth-century Britain. Anger at the act stimulated initial interest in the song; the popularity of poaching, particularly in hard times, and the threat of transportation for those who were caught, assured its continued success. Poaching was also a courageous way for the poor to thumb their noses at the gentry:

Come all you gallant poachers, that ramble void of care,
That walk out on moonlight night with your dog gun and snare

The lofty hare and pheasants you have at your command,
Not thinking of your last career upon Van Dieman's Land.

The song's message of alienation must have sounded a deep chord in the Victorian mind; the image of lower-class people driven from their homeland to endure a life of hardship far from their dear ones applied to both the emigrant and the convict.

The heyday of the British broadside (1800-40) coincided with the years of convictism, and a multitude of convict pieces were written. Invariably, the colony is a fallen world and a popular theme is the fall from grace through a false love. The best-known, 'The Black Velvet Band', traversed the British Isles and the nineteenth century, evolving through at least three broadside versions before arriving in Australia and America, both in its final printed form and as a sea shanty. Another broadside type, the convict 'narrative' or 'history', ranged in length from a broadsheet to a chapbook and established a style of published convict experiences that culminated in works such as Henry Savery's *Quintus Servinton*, and Marcus Clarke's *His Natural Life* (1870-2).

The Irish convict songs are refreshingly free of the self-pitying morality characteristic of the English variety. Like some twentieth-century counterparts, the nineteenth-century Irish convicts saw themselves as political prisoners. In 'The Connerys', the singer's self-righteous rage brings to mind twentieth-century Belfast:

Accursed Cuimin, I pray for distress and the hatred of God for you,
And the gang that is bound fast to your side.
It was you who swore by the books, invoking them in the lie
That sent the Connerys over the sea to the New South Wales.

Many songs venerate transported Irish patriots such as John Mitchel, Thomas Meagher and Thomas Burke, and pour scorn on perfidious England.

Of the indigenous ballads, only 'Jim Jones at Botany Bay' purports to predate Jack Donahue's death in 1830. Opinions vary about the song's origin: whether it is an oral version of an English broadside, or was penned by the convict balladist Francis MacNamara, better known as 'Frank the Poet'. Transported in 1832, MacNamara is acknowledged as the author of one of the Donahue songs. The singer's antagonism towards the authorities and cry of rebellion seem more Irish than English. The fact that there is just one version of 'Jim

Jones', published in Charles MacAlister's *Old Pioneering Days in the Sunny South* (1907), does not imply a wide currency. MacAlister includes the name of an air—'Irish Molly, Oh!'—but 'Jim Jones' reads more like a literary ballad than a song. The uneven stanza pattern— ten lines in the first and twelve in the second—is suspiciously like those in MacAlister's own ballads. Did he write it himself?

If 'Jim Jones at Botany Bay' is mainly MacAlister's work, then together with MacNamara's ballads the Donahue and Troy pieces are among our earliest extant indigenous songs. The seemingly endless versions of Donahue songs in the British Isles, America and Canada, confirm the importance of the rebel to the oppressed. Frank the Poet's work indicates the direction the indigenous utterance will take, for while his songs are derived from the English broadside tradition they are Irish in opposing its submissive moralising, and in preaching a hatred of authority. His defiant 'coat of arms'

> My name is Frank MacNamara,
> A native of Cashell, County Tipperary,
> Sworn to be a tyrant's foe
> And while I've life I'll crow.

probably derives from two lines in a Johnny Pitts publication called 'While we live we'll crow': 'My name's Dick Dash, a high up blade / My motto is—That while I live I'll crow.' Renowned as the author of 'A Convict's Tour to Hell', modelled on Swift's satires, Frank would have been at home writing for Pitts or Catnach; certainly his work reflects a knowledge of contemporary broadside ballads. One stanza of his haunting ballad 'Moreton Bay' begins in a hackneyed broadside fashion with the singer wandering by a river and meeting someone in distress, another commences with an allegiance to 'the land of Erin', a stock opening in Irish ballads.

Like MacNamara, new settlers continued the broadside tradition by publishing songs in colonial newspapers and magazines. These Australian 'broadsides' range from 'farewell lines' much like the standard Pitts or Catnach tear-jerker, to 'Australianised' versions of popular ballads. To name but five: 'Song' ('The Girl I Left Behind Me'), 'The Exile of Erin on the Plains of Emu' ('The Exile of Erin'), 'Billy Barlow in Australia' ('Billy Barlow'), 'Sam Holt' ('Ben Bolt'), and 'Australian Courtship', or 'Botany Bay Courtship', written with an eye on a broadside called 'The Newry Transport', itself a version of 'Justices and Old Baileys', the song later plagiarised by the author of 'Farewell to Old England'.

Emigrant songs have aroused little notice, yet they are a natural bridge between the songs of the convicts and those of the goldrush. Through broadsides, newspapers and magazines, drawing-room songs and music-hall ditties, not to mention oral pieces, they are the most numerous of all types of nineteenth-century song relating to Australia. There is one noteworthy change: Polly, the symbol for the convict's loss of love and home, becomes Mary: 'Farewell my love, my Mary true, / Adieu! my native land, adieu!'. The representative English broadside in this genre is 'God Speed the Good Ship', subtitled 'The English Emigrant':

> God speed the keel of the trusty ship
>   That bears you from our shore,
> There is little chance that you'll ever glance
>   On our chalky sea-beach more:
> You are right to seek a far off earth,
>   You are right to boldly strive,
> Where labour does not pine in death,
>   And the honest poor man thrive.

Many songs display a dissatisfaction with their native situation, but there is a marked difference between the English and Irish writers. 'God Speed the Good Ship' exhibits only fleetingly the liberalism in England in the mid-nineteenth century, preferring to dwell in arcadian memory. Generally more emotional and imaginative, the Irish writers continue the sense of injustice that characterised their convict songs. 'The Exile's Lament, or Lay Me', for instance, attacks harsh eviction laws:

> Beneath a far Australian sky, an Irish exile lay;
> The sand from out his glass of life was passing fast away . . .
> Eviction, foul and cruel, sent him far across the foam,
> From that sweet spot which Irishmen, where'er they be, call home.

Goldrush broadsides from all over the British Isles competed with local ditties by Charles Thatcher and William Coxon. The dominant feature is exuberance: never before had so many come by choice. Australia is a desirable destination, if only to plunder. The writer of 'Australia Our Home' certainly thought so:

> Here's off, here's off to the diggings of gold,
> Australia's our home where wealth is untold;
> Up, up, with your picks, take your shovel in hand,
> Here's off, here's off to a happier land.

Some songs deride the emigrant guidebooks by showing the disasters awaiting the green new chum. In 'Emigration', the prospective Swan River settler ends up

> Depriv'd of house, of bed and bedding,
> Without a home to put your head in;
> You 'gin to grieve that you're a rover,
> And curse the ship that brought you over.
> As 'neath the trees that form your vistas,
> Sand flies cover you with blisters . . .

The concern is with freedom, since the colony is home. In keeping with the new attitude, 'Botany Bay' gives way to 'Australia'.

The most popular bard of the goldfields was undeniably Charles Thatcher, 'the diggers' poet', a prolific young English songwriter who arrived in 1852 and immortalised Ballarat and Bendigo through numerous ditties in the music-hall style. While Thatcher effectively continued the broadside, or printed form of the ballad through newspapers, the occasional sheet and his various songsters, he and others helped to revolutionise the street song by taking their compositions into the goldfields theatres and giving them dramatic settings. Some of his songs, such as 'Look Out Below' and 'Where's Your Licence?', quickly passed into the oral tradition. In its humorous caricature of the hardships of goldfield life and criticism of the establishment ('The New-Chum Swell', 'Captain Bumble's Letter'), Thatcher's work reflects the waning of the British broadside ballad into the communal, mock-serious melodramatic world of the music hall and vaudeville.

Given the widespread popularity of felon songs like the Donahue ballads, it is puzzling that none of the numerous transportation broadsides received lasting oral currency. After nearly one hundred and twenty years, in collecting his *Old Bush Songs* (1905), Banjo Paterson could find only a fragment of a convict ballad. Doubtless, after the system was dismantled people simply wanted to forget. Then there is the vast difference in attitude between the British broadside and the indigenous song. The convict street songs represent an English moralistic attitude that condones felonry and seeks to retain the subservient colonial mentality. They may well have been ignored by most of the convict community. On the other hand, the Donahue ballads are Irish in feeling, with a hatred of the authorities so intense that the convict is willing to die rather than submit. The bushranger offered a mythical haven for the frustrated imagination. To a submissive population uncertain of its identity and starved of heroic myths, the idea of courageous rebellion would have been essential. Donahue is our first mythological figure, and the ballads about him laid the groundwork for our greatest mythical character, Ned Kelly. The old bushranger songs did not die with convictism; in fact one of the Donahue versions quickly evolved into 'The Wild Colonial Boy' and grew in mythic stature. Consequently, the bushranger ballad is the true link between the convict period and the later bush song since it evinces the convict's anti-authoritarianism and determination to be free, as in 'Moreton Bay', and the bushman's identification with the environment as well as foreshadowing the anti-city feeling synonymous with the bush tradition.

There is an enduring if contradictory bond between Australia and its bushrangers. Other countries worshipped outlaws and law officers alike; Australia elevated its thieves and murderers into legends and reviled those who sought to capture them. One can appreciate an oppressed convict population idealising Jack Donahue, Johnny Troy and Martin Cash in the first half of the nineteenth century; more enigmatic is the veneration of a proven murderer, Ned Kelly, by the respectable, law-abiding, urbanised population in the 1880s, particularly when the Kelly myth celebrates what to them must have seemed a contemptuous disregard for the forces of law and order. His rebellion fuelled nearly a century of fears, guilts and hatreds; the use of 'Moreton Bay' in the Jerilderie Letter suggests that he saw himself in convict terms. Kelly, who reputedly sang 'Farewell to Greta' shortly before his execution, would have agreed with Montaigne's words, used as epigraph to this chapter.

Many of the early bush ballads develop the master-servant relationship of the convict system into the antagonism between the itinerant bush worker or swagman and the squatter. The eternal victim, the bushman is often a naive, good-natured dupe much like Billy Barlow. Interestingly enough, the down-at-heels swaggie, the woebegone character bemoaning his luck, as in 'The Old Bark Hut', closely resembles the gullible new chum since initially both were figures of fun. Hatred of authority was a predictable convict legacy.

In early bush ballads like 'The Overlanders' and 'The Eumerella Shore' the Australian character is not unlike a bushranger in his determination to exploit the English authority figure, the squatter. The same mentality governs the social principle: in 'The Eumerella Shore' we are invited to an ideal existence based on theft.

The sea shanty exerted no little influence on the bush song. Typical bush favourites like 'All for Me Grog', 'Brisbane Ladies', and 'The Wild Rover' were fashioned from English and Irish songs on the emigrant ships and wool clippers. Oral versions of convict songs like 'Maggie May', 'Ten Thousand Miles', 'Botany Bay', 'Van Diemen's Land', 'The Black Velvet Band' and many more moved out from the ports and were accepted into British, American and Canadian folksong. The shanty endowed Australian balladry with some of its most rollicking pieces. For example, 'South Australia' derives from an old 'outward bound' shanty called 'Heave Away'. There would have been as many interpretations as there were ships. The sailors simply changed the point of departure and the destination, as in this American version called 'The Codfish Shanty':

> Glos'-ter girls they have no combs,
> Heave away, heave away!
> They comb their hair with codfish bones,
> We're bound for South Australia.

The heyday of the shanty encompassed the goldrushes, the land acts of the 1860s and much of the era of pastoral expansion, and helped to develop the adventurous, good-natured enthusiasm characteristic of the bush ethic.

Literary ballads and poems existed as early as the colonial newspapers, developed through goldfield versifiers, and poets such as Adam Lindsay Gordon ('The Sick Stockrider', 'From the Wreck', 'Wolf and Hound'), Henry Kendall ('Jim the Splitter'), 'Ironbark' Gibson ('Sam Holt'), Barcroft Boake ('Where the Dead Men Lie') to anthologies like Douglas Sladen's *Australian Ballads and Rhymes* (1888). Of these, the most important is undeniably Gordon, who significantly influenced the pre-*Bulletin* poetic environment. In his famous preface to *Sea Spray and Smoke Drift* (1867), Marcus Clarke perceived in Gordon's work 'the beginnings of a national school of Australian poetry'. Gordon was not an innovative poet: his dependence on Byron, Scott, Swinburne and particularly Browning has been well documented. His daredevil riding and untimely death were as important to his poetic fame as the quality of the verse, but in 'The Sick Stockrider' (1870) he wrote with a genuine affection and an ease of expression which present the bush in a warm and vivid way; 'The Sick Stockrider' and 'How We Beat the Favourite' (1870) gladdened many rural firesides. Shaw Neilson could say many years later: 'My poor verses will be forgotten when 'The Sick Stockrider' is remembered.' Not until Paterson and Lawson, however, was the literary ballad embedded in the bush ethos and given a national relevance.

Banjo Paterson's *Old Bush Songs* is the bridge between the bush song and the literary ballad, not the least because Paterson was clearly influenced by the former and was the finest exponent of the latter: there are few better traditional Australian ballads than 'Travelling Down the Castlereagh' and 'Waltzing Matilda', while in some respects 'The Man from Snowy River' is a descendant of 'The Wild Colonial Boy'. An uneven mixture of broadsides, oral songs and recitations, Paterson's anthology offers some guide to the image of the bush and its characters around the time of Federation. More than one-third of the songs deal with the fool who becomes both victim and figure of fun. Half of these are new chums, the rest swagmen; in some cases the characters are interchangeable. The largest, most exalted group belongs to the horseman. One of the earliest bush songs, 'The Overlander', depicts him as a law unto himself; 'The Dying Stockman' shows how venerated he eventually became: unlike ordinary mortals, he was interred reverently with the symbols of his profession.

The dichotomy between hero and victim is exemplified in the difference between Paterson and Henry Lawson. As Paterson explains it: 'I had done my prospecting on horseback with my meals cooked for me, while Lawson had done his prospecting on foot and had to cook for himself.' By the 1890s, the horseman was an elitist figure combining the heroism of the drover and bushranger with the aristocratic image portrayed in the verse of Adam Lindsay Gordon and the colonial novels of Henry Kingsley and Rolf Boldrewood, and epitomised by *Bulletin* writers like Paterson and Harry 'Breaker' Morant. The monopoly was such that writers derided the *Bulletin* school for its 'horsey poets'. Judging by ballad popularity, the backbone of the bush ethos was not the egalitarian pastoral worker but Clancy the elitist stockman. The Australian mystique, then, centres on the worship of an English-style authority figure.

Selectors, shearers, swagmen, down-and-outs, the victims of bush life—'the poor and honest bushman'—were the province of Henry Lawson. In 'The City Bushman' and 'The Men Who Made Australia', Lawson displays an antagonism towards authority identifiable with the Irish broadside sentiment and the ballads of 'Frank the Poet'. Indeed, his sympathetic response to the victims of society, and opposition to the authority that created them, recall the ballads of John Freeth. Yet Lawson's ballads manifest an ambiguous response to authority. On the one hand he voices a rebellious egalitarian sentiment, symbolised in the term 'mateship', that reaches back through the bush worker, gold digger and emigrant, to the bushranger and the antagonism of the Irish convict ballads. On the other, utterances like 'The New John Bull' and 'England Yet' reveal a colonial subservience. Truly, one could rephrase Manning Clark and say that the Australian ballad is Lawson 'writ large'.

In their famous 1890s 'debate', Lawson and Paterson accused each other of falsifying the bush situation, yet in one sense the validity of either view is irrelevant: Lawson's emotionalised, idealised studies of mateship through the eyes of the underdog and Paterson's heroic equestrians were politicised for Federation, and canonised at Gallipoli and Beersheba. After them, the 'fair dinkum' subject for the ballad, and indeed Australian literature, was the bush.

The most influential modern interpreter of the bush ethos is Russel Ward. In the foreword to *The Australian Legend* (1958), he argues 'that a specifically Australian outlook grew up first and most clearly among the bush workers in the Australian pastoral industry'. His idealistic belief in the nineteenth-century shearing industry as an egalitarian, 'collectivist' force that became the backbone of the bush ethos, and went on to achieve a national mystique through the political and literary turmoils of the 1890s is not supported by the shearing ballads:

> The truth is in my song so clear
> Without a word of gammon:
> The swagmen travel all the year
> Waiting for the lambin'.

Far from a staunch, collective independence, they mainly depict isolation, loneliness, and, like 'The Ryebuck Shearer', a penchant for bragging. Witness 'The Murrumbidgee Shearer', who has been everywhere and done most things, usually 'on the cross', and, like the singers in 'The Overlander' and 'The Eumerella Shore', prefers to live like a bushranger. Springtime certainly brought on the shearing, but after that brief time the representative image is that of the lonely swagman reliving real or imagined glories: 'It is then you will see the flash shearers / Making johnny-cakes round in the bend.' From a ballad viewpoint, Ward's theory has much of Lawson's 'The Men Who Made Australia' about it, placing little relevance on the conflicting legendary qualities represented by the stockman and the bush worker. An 1890s sentiment, it is a victim of the 'Legend' it seeks to define.

'Bush ballad' is an elastic term in the hands of the *Bulletin* rhymers. Lawson and Paterson wrote of the city as well, while Edward Dyson's *Rhymes from the Mines* (1896), and E. J. Brady's *The Ways of Many Waters* (1899), for instance, focus elsewhere. Yet they have much in common apart from a love of jog-trotting metres: an egalitarian sentiment, call it mateship or fellow-feeling, a good-natured, nationalistic idealism and a wry humour. The finest *Bulletin* ballads come from the 1890s. Most of the major writers published later verse, but none recapture the sparkle of their original work. It is significant that their last disciple was C. J. Dennis; his *The Songs of a Sentimental Bloke* (1915) voiced bush values from the back streets of Melbourne. Although 'John O'Brien' (Patrick Hartigan) achieved fame through his poems of Irish Catholic life in *Around the Boree Log* (1921), especially 'Said Hanrahan', the bush ballad as a nationally popular form ended with Dennis. There is no single reason for the decline of the *Bulletin* style of ballad after the Great War; undoubtedly it was too closely identified with a single period, but equally the lyric became a more popular poetic form than the narrative. As well, the poetry espoused by the 'Vision' poets preferred mythical Greece and an interpretation of Nietzsche.

The history of the Australian ballad in the twentieth century is that of an escapist rural ethos enshrined in an urban race, just as its suppressed colonial ancestors imagined the bush into an escapist myth of freedom. Kenneth Slessor taps the sentiment in 'Country Towns' where, after painting a traditional rural world, he yearns to dwell there: 'Till, charged with ale and unconcern, / I'll think, it's noon at half-past four!' The dualism of the bush ethos is evident in modern writers searching for cultural security. David Campbell's 'The Stockman' (1949), brings to mind Paterson's horsemen, while a Lawsonian nostalgia for the bush and its myths inhabits Les Murray's 'Noonday Axeman' (1965). In its resignation to the conflict between the legendary past and the metropolitan present, Murray's poem gently evokes the traditional conflict between the city and the bush in a modern way.

Of the modern balladists, John Manifold comes closest to the nineteenth-century bush feeling through a sophisticated blend of Irish rebelliousness and Lawsonian idealism. His ballads on Ned Kelly are particularly striking. In a splendid elegy, 'The Tomb of Lt. John Learmonth A.I.F.' (1945), Manifold quietly rejoices in a bush ballad tradition that has instilled what amounts to a mythic resolve in the modern Australian personality:

> I heard the air though not the undersong,
> The fierceness and resolve; but all the same
> They're the tradition, and tradition's strong.
>
> Swagman and bushranger die hard, die game,
> Die fighting, like that wild colonial boy-
> Jack Dowling, says the ballad, was his name.

Looking back over the history of the ballad in this country, the most striking feature is the neglect of the traditional form. The Australian ballad originated from the fixed, printed style and was sustained by it. Apart from a few bushranger pieces and versions of the MacNamara songs, the convict ballad legacy is almost totally the province of the broadside. Similarly, the emigrant and goldrush songs did not issue from 'the folk' but from newspaper poets, broadside ballad writers, and goldfields singers like Thatcher and Coxon. Nineteenth-century oral transmission is apparent in songs like 'Wallabi Joe', 'The Overlander', 'The Eumerella Shore', some goldrush ditties and the later bushranger pieces, but the list is relatively small. And some of our most popular bush ballads, for example 'The Dying Stockman' and 'The Banks of the Condamine', originated overseas. Admittedly, much has been irretrievably lost; however, there is little evidence in the ballads to support the romantic image of 'the folk' gathered around their campfires collectively composing new songs. The sea shanty is important here, for songs did leave Australia and travel to other cultures, while others arrived renewed through oral transmission. From the 1890s until the 1930s, only the various editions of *Old Bush Songs* and the 'Bill Bowyang' *Recitations* (1932-40), sought to preserve our oral culture, and it is worth remembering that Paterson's anthologies contained broadsides. Compared to the painstaking labour undertaken in other countries,

Australia's attempts to preserve its oral culture were lamentable. Our reasonably respectable canon is quite a recent effort; the fertile memories of Sally Sloane, 'Hoop-Iron' Jack Lee, Joe Cashmere and 'Duke' Tritton are a guide to what was available to the folk collector in the first thirty years of this century. Despite common belief, while the oral form was always popular in the bush, it seems to have had only a limited influence on the major balladists. Gordon and many of the *Bulletin* writers would have heard songs sung, but only in Paterson is there any deep influence. Although many of the *Bulletin* ballads have passed into oral currency, the form itself is really a separate species.

According to Ron Edwards, Vance Palmer's *Old Australian Bush Ballads* (1951) 'really sparked off the folksong revival in Australia'. The resurgence has produced a profitable market, and while field work continues the ballad is now largely the province of singers who tend to remain within existing boundaries. However, Freeth and Lawson would have smiled upon Eric Bogle, while the rebellious strains of contemporary band Redgum are reminiscent of the anger of the nineteenth-century Irish ballad.

Notes

John Freeth's ballads are in *The Political Songster* (1790). The Henry Savery broadsides can be found in the Bristol Library. For an interpretation of street literature see Leslie Shephard, *The History of Street Literature* (1973).

For Francis MacNamara see *Frank the Poet* (1979), by John Meredith and Rex Whalan. The largest collection of Jack Donahue ballads is *The Wild Colonial Boy* (1982), by John Meredith. A version of 'Johnny Troy' is included in Russel Ward, *The Penguin Book of Australian Ballads* (1964). For poems and ballads in Australian colonial newspapers see *Early Australian Poetry* (1982), by Elizabeth Webby.

There are numerous collections of sea shanties; the most influential are Joanna Colcord, *Songs of American Sailormen* (1938); William Doerflinger, *Shantymen and Shantyboys* (1951); and Stan Hugill, *Shanties from the Seven Seas* (1961).

For nineteenth-century collections of bush songs see *Queenslanders' New Colonial Camp Fire Song Book* (1865), which contains 'The Overlander' and 'Wallabi Joe'; J. Small, *The Colonial Songster*

(1884); *Tibb's Popular Australian Songs and Poems* (1888); *Native Companion Songster* (1889).

A collection of Charles Thatcher's songs is in *Gold-diggers' Songbook* (1980), by Hugh Anderson. For William Coxon, see *Coxon's Comic Songster* (1858-9).

The standard text for the Australian bush ballad is *Old Bush Songs* (1957), edited by Douglas Stewart and Nancy Keesing. A companion, covering the literary ballad, is *Australian Bush Ballads* (1955), by the same editors. An influential collection is Vance Palmer, *Old Australian Bush Ballads* (1951).

Palmer's *The Legend of the Nineties* (1954), explains the traditional idea of mateship; *The Australian Legend* is re-examined in depth in *Historical Studies,* 18 (1978). Russel Ward has written three articles on Australian ballads: 'Australian Folk Ballads and Singers', *Meanjin,* 13 (1954); 'Collectivist Notions of a Nomad Tribe', *Historical Studies,* 6 (1955); and 'Felons and Folksongs', *Meanjin,* 15 (1956). John Manifold replied in 'The Sung Ballad', *Meanjin,* 14 (1955). See also Richard White, *Inventing Australia, Images and Identity: 1688-1980* (1981).

The best traditional ballad collections are Hugh Anderson, *Colonial Ballads* (1955), and *Farewell to Old England* (1964); J. S. Manifold, *Who Wrote the Ballads?* (1964); John Meredith and Hugh Anderson, *Folksongs of Australia and the Men and Women Who Sang Them* (1967). For bush music instruments see John Manifold, *The Violin, the Banjo and the Bones* (1957).

The largest modern collection of songs is Ron Edwards, *The Big Book of Australian Folk Song* (1976). Included is the most comprehensive index of Australian songs to date. Edwards has published two volumes which include previously unknown broadsides: *The Convict Maid* (1985) and *The Transport's Lament* (1986). An interesting adaptation of the traditional song is *Builders' Labourers' Songbook* (1975).

Warren Fahey's Folkways shop in Paddington, Sydney, has a comprehensive collection of recorded and printed ballads. For information on the modern folk scene, see the journals *Gumsucker's Gazette, National Folk, Singabout* and *Australian Tradition.*

Chapter 13

MELODRAMA AND THE MELODRAMATIC IMAGINATION

ELIZABETH WEBBY

Melodrama, a word literally meaning 'a play with music', has for most of the twentieth century been used as a term of abuse. Particularly in its adjectival form 'melodramatic', it has come to imply an event, action or person that is excessive, out of control, over-emotional. The noun originally described a type of theatrical performance which, beginning in France towards the end of the eighteenth century, came into its own as a people's theatre during the French Revolution. It was rapidly transported across the Channel and hence eventually to the new English colonies in Australia.

Melodramas, together with pantomimes, are the most characteristic forms of nineteenth-century English theatre. Both, originating in various ways from dumbshows, are distinguished by an emphasis on spectacle, music and movement rather than dialogue. Both make a stronger appeal to an audience's senses and emotions than to its intellect. As other types of popular entertainment—films, radio and television—have been created in the course of this century, they have progressively taken over melodrama's forms, themes and audiences. While few people now regularly visit the theatre or even the cinema, millions watch episodes of such television melodramas as the American serial *Dallas* or the Australian mini-series *Return to Eden*. So melodrama and the melodramatic remain important modes of the modern imagination.

The continuing appeal and the critical condemnation of melodrama both appear to derive from its particular presentation of reality. While its central characters must remain sufficiently human to enable some audience identification, they speak and behave in ways which are often far removed from the everyday. The world of melodrama has sometimes been compared with the world of a dream: it draws on 'real life' but shapes this material according to conventions of its own. Its audience becomes involved in the action but is, at the same time, aware of these conventions and their fictionalising effects. So, as Ien Ang has observed, melodrama aims at emotional rather than empirical realism.

Something similar could be said of romance which, like melodrama and mostly for the same reasons, has been a highly popular but critically damned form. Besides a certain disdain for romance and melodrama just because of their popularity, the moral and didactic bias of most literary criticism has tended to favour intellectual empiricism over emotional fictionality. Romance may be distinguished from melodrama by its greater emphasis on the emotions of love and desire rather than those of hatred and fear. While romance often features a quest or journey of successful discovery, melodrama centres on themes of loss or threatened loss, with imprisonment as a frequent motif.

The first play to be performed in Australia, in 1789, was an eighteenth-century comedy, George Farquhar's *The Recruiting Officer* (1706), but professional theatre began with one of the most popular nineteenth-century melodramas, Douglas Jerrold's *Black-Ey'd Susan* (1829). This play, which opened Barnett Levey's Sydney Theatre Royal in 1832, shows most of the characteristics of early English melodrama, both formally and thematically. Major characters enter and exit to appropriate music, which also underlines the high points of the drama; there are several interspersed songs. Each act is broken into a number of scenes, with swift changes made possible by alternating simpler scenes played near the front of the stage and more elaborate ones played further back. Characters are easily recognisable stereotypes. The minute a character appears on stage his or her moral worth is usually signalled, not only by the accompanying music, but by costume, make-up, physique and voice. The democratic origins of melodrama are still apparent in *Black Ey'd Susan*, where the villain is a ship's captain, the hero an ordinary seaman. Other typical features include an innocent heroine subject to sexual pressure from the villain, a hero imprisoned and on the point of death, a last-minute reprieve and a happy ending.

As the century progressed, the simple verities of early melodrama became more complicated. In Britain, working-class audiences turned away to the new music halls; theatre became increasingly the preserve of the middle classes, who demanded more sophisticated entertainment. Perhaps because of the smaller population, Australian audiences seem to have remained more mixed in character. This, at least, is what one may infer from Australian melodramas which, at their peak in the 1880s and 1890s, were very old-fashioned by contemporary British standards. Plays had been written in Australia from at least the 1820s, though with an initial emphasis on farce, pantomime and romantic tragedy rather than melodrama. An exception was Henry Melville's *The Bushrangers; or, Norwood Vale* (1834) with its virtuous heroine, Marian Norwood, and evil escaped convicts, Bill Fellows, Harry Fawkes, and Charley Hoodwick. (In early melodrama, characters' names signal their moral worth just as clearly as their costumes and make-up.) Melville's melodrama was performed in Hobart and Launceston, but more restrictive licensing laws meant that similar plays could not be produced in Sydney, the theatrical centre until the goldrushes.

The popularity of farces and pantomimes with local settings showed that Australian audiences were keen to see themselves up on the stage. From the 1850s censorship relaxed sufficiently to allow the development, belatedly, of Australian melodramas. Two of the most successful were adaptations of popular novels, a frequent practice in English melodrama. Since the dramatist was one of the most poorly paid members of the theatrical team, there was no time for much originality nor, indeed, would it have proved welcome to contemporary audiences. All that was required was to fit the familiar melodramatic grid, of stock characters and spectacular action, across the characters and episodes of the original novel and trim, add or adjust where necessary.

Alfred Dampier, one of the leading Australian actor-managers of the second half of the century, is supposed to have planned an adaptation of Marcus Clarke's *His Natural Life* (1870-2; 1874) before the latter's death in 1881. It was laid aside because Clarke did not wish his tragic ending to be altered to the traditional happy one of melodrama. By 1886, however, two different dramatisations of the novel had been produced in Australia; there were also versions playing in England and America. These adaptations continued to draw audiences in Australia till the end of the century and have been succeeded by numerous others for film and television. In 1986 *For the Term of His Natural Life*, a title used only after 1882, became the first Australian novel turned into a Classic Comic.

The other continuing success was an adaptation of Rolf Boldrewood's *Robbery Under Arms* (1882-3; 1888). Here the adaptor's task was more difficult. Clarke's novel had provided ready-made melodramatic staples such as the innocent but persecuted hero and the villain of blackest dye. There was even, in the Rev. Mr Meekin, a character easily adaptable to the comic new chum, already a stereotype of Australian drama.

Robbery Under Arms, a romance rather than a melodrama, had bushranging heroes who persecuted others and, apart from the bad bushranger Moran, no really evil character. Dampier and his collaborator Garnet Walch solved this problem by making one of the policemen, Inspector Goring, 'a modern Jonathan Wild', to quote from the playbill for the first production. On his first appearance in Act I, Goring makes his villainy plain by offering to connive at the escape of Aileen Marston's father if she will marry him. So, according to the morality of melodrama, the Marstons are now the persecuted heroes. In the stage version of *Robbery Under Arms* (1890; 1985) the police also provided the equally necessary comic new chums in the persons of two Irish troopers, Maginnis and O'Hara. Further comic relief came from another comic stereotype, the old maid. None of these comic characters, of course, appeared in the original novel. That the hallmark of nineteenth-century popular theatre was novelty rather than originality is demonstrated by the reappearance of comic scenes and characters almost identical to those of *Robbery Under Arms* in Arnold Denham's 'The Kelly Gang' (1899). No matter whether a play owed its inspiration to real life or fiction, audiences expected to laugh as well as cry.

To say, then, that another leading actor-manager of this period, George Darrell, wrote original rather than adapted Australian melodramas invites the question of what 'original' means in relation to a form so dependent on stereotypes and conventions. Darrell's playwriting career did, in fact, begin with adaptations of English novels. He wrote or adapted at least twenty-three plays but only one appears to have survived. *The Sunny South* (1883; 1975) was first performed in Melbourne but has survived in the version submitted for licensing before the 1884 London production. Reading any dramatic text requires a great deal of imaginative participation. This is particularly true of melodramas which depend so much on non-verbal effects and even truer of *The Sunny South*, a text which, never intended for publication, lacks musical cues and often has 'Business' as its only stage direction. A careful reading, however, shows how skilfully Darrell constructed the play to manipulate, satisfy and, at times, even surprise his audience.

Like all forms of popular entertainment, melodrama offers much variety within carefully regulated parameters. *The Sunny South* includes some topical satire in the earlier scenes set in England (perhaps added especially for the English production), broad comedy among the servant characters and comedy of cross-purposes among those of higher rank. There is also a good deal of verbal humour, particularly at the expense of a new chum unfamiliar with Australian slang. There are, of course, plenty of thrills and chills, pathos and sentiment and love interest. Darrell makes an interesting play with theatrical conventions here. Melodramas frequently had a second pair of lovers, played by the light comedy man and the soubrette. In *The Sunny South* the soubrette plays Bubs Berkley, 'Bred in the Bush', and in love with the play's hero, Matt Morley. She, and the audience, expect Matt to marry the play's English heroine, Clarice Chester. Darrell, however, breaks the traditional coupling of leading man and leading lady to allow Bubs to marry her 'dear old pal'.

Early in the twentieth century, life in the bush began to replace convicts and bushrangers as the staple subject of Australian melodrama. There was a particular vogue for plays with bush heroines, the most successful being a play by 'Albert Edmunds', *The Squatter's Daughter* (1907) which established a record for an Australian play of seventy-two consecutive performances, only six fewer than the then record for an English play in Australia. The same authors, Bert Bailey and Edmund Duggan, were responsible for the adaptation of Steele Rudd's popular story sequence *On Our Selection* (1899). The stage version of *On Our Selection* (1912; 1984) won instant recognition for its 'Australianness' and was an overwhelming success. That Rudd's 'Dad and Dave' are two of the few characters from Australian literature to have passed into folklore is largely a result of the many successful stage, screen and radio versions of his stories.

Adapting *On Our Selection* for the stage inevitably resulted in some distortion of the conventions of melodrama as well as considerable changes to Rudd's stories. Whereas Boldrewood's adaptors had to find a villain and invent comic characters, Rudd's had an ample supply of comic characters but had to find a plot. The one they found was classic melodrama: a wealthy squatter, John Carey, is after Dad Rudd's farm; his son, Jim, after the virginity of Dad's daughter Kate. Jim is murdered and Sandy, Kate's beloved, wrongly accused, but, of course, all comes right in the end. *On Our Selection*, however, functions less as a confirmation of conventional moral values than as a celebration of Australian ones. As Margaret Williams has observed, in *On Our Selection* the Australian characters have finally moved from minor roles to centre stage. So *On Our Selection* can be seen as the culmination of the popular theatrical tradition in Australia, and not only because the cinema was just about to take over.

The adaptations of both *On Our Selection* and *Robbery Under Arms* showed that successful plays could be made out of works which had few intrinsic melodramatic features. *On Our Selection*, like so many other works of Australian literature, celebrates survival against the odds. When, as here, the villain is the land and the climate, melodrama becomes difficult if not impossible. Though it has more melodramatic elements, Boldrewood's *Robbery Under Arms* is best described as a romance. As already noted, there is little attempt to represent evil beyond the minor notes of hooting owls, Dan Moran and Terrible Hollow. The ambiguity of Terrible Hollow, which is both prison and refuge, hell and paradise, is a pointer to the essentially non-melodramatic nature of *Robbery Under Arms*, since melodrama abhors ambiguity. *Robbery Under Arms* can, perhaps, best be read as a masculine romance, a celebration of freedom not only from authority, but from women, respectability and the need to earn a living. Its continued popularity and potency in a predominantly male culture, which has always idealised the lone hand or the true mate over the respectable family man, needs little explaining.

Most Australian novels written between 1855 and 1915 would, for a wide variety of reasons, also be classed as romance rather than melodrama. Some exceptions can be found in the as yet little-studied area of Australian detective fiction. Like melodrama, detective fiction first developed in nineteenth-century France and initially had much in common with the older genre. The murderer provided an obvious villain; a wrongly accused innocent, the hero. In earlier stories, as with Dickens' Inspector Bucket in *Bleak House* (1852-3), the detective approximates to the helpful, often comic, servant or friend who frequently comes to the rescue of the hero in melodrama. This is true of one of the earliest Australian detective novels, John Lang's *The Forger's Wife* (1855), and also of one of the best-known, Fergus Hume's *The Mystery of a Hansom Cab* (1886), which became an international best-seller. Hume had initially hoped to become a dramatist, and some of his later novels have theatrical settings as do Francis Adams' *Madeline Brown's Murderer* (1887) and Guy Boothby's *Connie Burt* (1903), among others. With the detective's assumptions of the central role of hero, there was a move away from melodrama towards romance. Though this development is particularly associated with Conan Doyle's Sherlock Holmes, there were many earlier examples. In Australia, for instance, the still mysterious 'W.W.' was publishing stories, many featuring the detective Mark Sinclair, in the *Australian Journal* from its commencement in 1865. She appears to have been Australia's, and possibly the world's, first woman writer of detective stories.

Though 'W.W.' has had many successors in other countries, particularly England, the most successful twentieth-century writers of Australian detective fiction have been Arthur Upfield and Peter Corris. Between 1928 and his death in 1965, Upfield published over thirty works in this genre but is probably best remembered for his creation of 'Bony', otherwise the part-Aboriginal Detective-Inspector Napoleon Bonaparte. Corris, drawing more on the American private-eye than the Sherlock Holmes tradition, has since 1980 won a considerable following for his works featuring Cliff Hardy, a tough Sydney individualist. The shift from English to American influences, and from Upfield's outback to Corris' inner-city, reflects the broader changes within Australian literature from the 1920s to the 1980s.

The *Australian Journal* also serialised the original version of Marcus Clarke's *His Natural Life*, the nineteenth-century Australian novel which comes closest to being a work of the melodramatic imagination in the sense in which that term has been used by the critic Peter Brooks. Brooks argues that tragedy was only possible in a world with a stable society and authority figures: gods and kings. Once these figures were toppled, melodrama arose, becoming, in the words of an 1835 French critic, 'the only popular tragedy befitting our age'. Through melodrama's dramatisation of the conflict between innocent but seemingly powerless virtue and seemingly all-powerful but eventually defeated evil, the moral principles essential to society's survival, but no longer sanctioned by the paternal authority of Church and Monarch, were reaffirmed.

As we see from Clarke's other works, particularly his article 'Civilization Without Delusion' (1880), he was a humanist who believed that mankind, and civilisation, could survive without God. In *His Natural Life* he tested this faith by subjecting an innocent man, Richard Devine, to the torments of a literal hell on earth, life in the convict settlements of Macquarie Harbour, Port Arthur and Norfolk Island. Devine, in his new identity as Rufus Dawes, survives, or at least he did in the first, serialised, version of the novel. Clarke's radical faith in humanity was clearly too much for the burghers of

Victorian Melbourne who felt that an ex-convict, however innocent, could never again rejoin respectable society. He was persuaded of the need for a more 'tragic' ending, with Dawes dying in the arms of his beloved during a shipwreck, instead of saving her daughter and, by raising her as his own, slowly being restored to humanity.

The deletion of the original ending, where Dawes' rehabilitation is played out against the background of the fight for freedom at Eureka Stockade in contrast to the penal colonies of the earlier sections, also required a new beginning for the novel. Interestingly, Clarke resorted to the stage, for which he also wrote, opening with a scene from 'a domestic tragedy' (a synonym for melodrama) whose messages would have been very familiar to a contemporary audience. This tableau immediately establishes Richard Devine as the wronged hero, protecting a suffering woman from an aggressive male authority figure. The revised opening has generally been preferred to the original for reasons which include its improved motivation, critics believing it more credible for Devine to sacrifice himself to protect a guilty mother than an innocent wife. The new opening certainly has greater figurative power. Clarke, with hindsight, is now able to shadow forth the central relationship between Devine/Dawes, the aggressive authority figure Maurice Frere and Frere's suffering wife Sylvia. Yet, as Brian Elliott has observed, Clarke's revisions, though often improvements when considered in isolation, were achieved at the expense of the original design. The revised *His Natural Life* is no longer 'a moral allegory in the shape of a historical melodrama'.

Elliott remains puzzled as to why the black-haired Richard Devine should be called, in his convict guise, Rufus Dawes. Both names are part of the moral allegory, which forces a right-hearted, and so divine, man through the red gates of pain and torment. The alchemical associations of 'red gates' are at one with the emphasis on alchemy in the original opening and closing episodes of the novel. Originally, Richard Devine went through four changes or states of identity: from Richard Devine to Rufus Dawes, then to Tom Crosbie, the Victorian shepherd, and finally back to Richard Devine. So, at exactly parallel stages, did the corrupt convict, John Rex, who begins as Lionel Crofton, becomes Rex during the convict episodes, impersonates Richard Devine while Devine himself is living as Crosbie, but ends as his true self, 'a mere animal, lacking the intellect he had in his selfish wickedness abused'. So as well as the 'rising and falling' pattern noted by Elliott, *His Natural Life* originally had parallel plots, one centred on Dawes, one on Rex, linked by the corrupt authority figure of Maurice Frere.

What was being tested was the power of circumstances. Was man merely a creature of his environment? In the original version of *His Natural Life* the answer was a resounding 'No!'. Dawes, thanks to his unselfishness and the power of human love, is able to survive. Living as a convict may corrode but cannot totally consume his innate goodness. Equally, Rex may impersonate Richard Devine but living as a gentleman cannot transform his innate 'selfish wickedness'. He ends as a 'mere animal'; Dawes once more becomes Devine. Though Clarke rearranged the text of *His Natural Life* in order to retain the story of Rex's impersonation, in the revised version his allegorical significance as a reversed parallel to Dawes has largely been lost.

As well as destroying the balance of the original plot structure, Clarke's revisions also reversed the basic direction of the novel. Instead of ending with an Oedipal murder—Dick Purfoy's of his father, Maurice Frere—it now begins with one: John Rex's of his father, Lord Bellasis. Instead of looking forward to the future, to a free society, the solution of the original mystery and Dawes restored to Devine through the love of a child, it looks back to the past and Devine condemned through the sins of a parent. Evil, both generally in the form of the convict system and specifically in the person of Frere, is not defeated. As Northrop Frye has observed, 'In melodrama two themes are important: the triumph of moral virtue over villainy, and the consequent idealizing of the moral views assumed to be held by the audience.' The revised *His Natural Life* retains many of the formal features of melodrama but loses its ultimate meaning and consolation.

The continued popularity of the convict era with Australian writers may in part be attributed to its ready-made images of evil, which appear to have been in short supply elsewhere in nineteenth-century Australia. Aboriginals are seen as evil figures in some early works but as victims in others. Their standard role in stage melodrama soon became one equivalent to the comic servant. So the half-caste Warrigal, who is an ambiguous figure in Boldrewood's *Robbery Under Arms*, loses all his menace in the stage version. Bushrangers were ambiguous figures from the start, supplying the necessary villains in some early novels and plays but being treated sympathetically in others. The convict era, however, provided two sources of the absolute evil needed for melodrama, as well as many of the attendant topoi such as mistaken identities, sudden revelations, escape and imprisonment. Evil could be seen as residing in the convicts themselves, in their gaolers or, as in *His Natural Life*, in both. While convict authors tended to put the blame on their fellow prisoners rather than the system, most later writers have taken the opposite stance. The popular, anti-authoritarian origins of melodrama assisted in this exposure of corrupt authority. Price Warung's *Tales of the Convict System* (1892), and later collections, originally appeared in the *Bulletin* where their attack on the system formed part of that paper's then strongly anti-British stance. The deliberate structure and heightened language of Warung's stories may seem at odds with common perceptions of the *Bulletin* as the home of understated bush realism. But,of course, there were many *Bulletin*s.

Elaboration and excess are, as Peter Brooks suggests, part of the melodramatic imagination. Stage melodrama can manage with a minimum of dialogue since its larger-than-life effects are conveyed mainly though music, gesture and scenic spectacle. Writers of fiction and poetry have to try to achieve the same emotional impact through their work's structure and language alone. Disdain for melodrama, together with a tendency in past Australian criticism to favour realism over other literary modes, has led to an underestimation of writers such as William Gosse Hay. His first novel, *Stifled Laughter* (1901), is actually subtitled 'A Melodrama' and divided into a prologue and two acts. Like his five later works, of which *The Escape of the Notorious Sir William Heans* (1919) is considered the best, it is set in the convict period and written in a heightened or 'poetic' style which many critics have found disturbing. (Melodrama, indeed, aims to disturb before it affirms.)

Like Hay, Hal Porter deliberately used melodramatic modes, particularly in his novel *The Tilted Cross* (1961) and his play *The Tower* (1964; 1963), both of which are set in early Hobart. Thomas Keneally has also written novels and a play set during the convict period: *Bring Larks and Heroes* (1967), which won the Miles Franklin Award and first attracted critical attention to his fiction, and its stage adaptation *Halloran's Little Boat* (1966; 1975) and *The Playmaker* (1987). The fluctuations in Keneally's critical reputation (though his sales have continued to grow) may perhaps be partly attributed to his fondness for portraying characters in extreme situations, often involving what has been seen as excessive blood and violence. Another writer frequently criticised for her excess, Christina Stead, has in *The Man Who Loved Children* (1941) produced a major work of the melodramatic imagination, though one which, like many of Keneally's, questions the conventional binary oppositions of melodrama.

At the end of *The Man Who Loved Children*, its heroine Louie Pollit walks away from her enclosed familial world of good and evil. While she is not looking for anything in particular, she is now looking freely, 'without prejudice'. Her situation is similar to that of the protagonist at the end of Christopher Brennan's *Poems [1913]* (1914). Brennan, who has left a few other traces in Stead's novels, must be considered as a major figure in any study of the melodramatic imagination in Australia. While Clarke and Stead were convinced humanists, Brennan was brought up as a Catholic and suffered the loss of faith in absolute authority which Peter Brooks sees as the originating impulse of melodrama. As his biographer, Axel Clark, has observed, Brennan then 'turned to poetry to satisfy a truly religious need'. Accordingly, *Poems [1913]* has usually been seen as a dramatisation of Brennan's quest for a new Absolute. It is important to recognise, however, that it is a quest whose failure is implicit from the very beginning of the poem.

Poems [1913] differs from most other Australian long poems in rejecting linear narrative in favour of a discontinous dramatisation. Terry Sturm offers a summary of its structure in terms which strongly recall many of the effects of melodrama: 'a cyclic pattern, relying on effects of dramatic statement and counter-statement and on a "musical" interweaving of motifs, images and symbols'. Like a traditional melodrama, *Poems [1913]* is divided into five parts or acts, the first three of which have many internal divisions. Brennan's original text also employed many of the visual signals so important in melodrama, with poems printed in different typefaces and sometimes separated by blank pages.

The swift changes of mood characteristic of melodrama are equally characteristic of *Poems [1913]*. Its first section, 'Towards the Source', opens with an invocation of youthful innocence, beauty and romance, using traditional symbols of the dawn, spring and nature. The counter-statement of experience, passion and suffering, with its symbols of night, winter and the void, is, however, present from the very first stanza:

> Sweet days of breaking light,
> or yet the shadowy might
> and blaze of starry strife
> possess'd my life;

These same rapid mood changes, particularly from elation to despair, from awe to disgust, are found in Section II, 'The Forest of Night'. So, though the quest here takes an opposite direction towards darkness and the subconscious, it is equally full of contradictions and equally foredoomed to failure. Finally, at the end of Section III, 'The Wanderer', the protagonist comes to realise that it is the quest itself, rather than the goal, that is important. This realisation is tested and confirmed in the last two, much shorter, sections. Though *Poems [1913]* ends with an affirmation, the promise of 'fidelity to old delight', this is clearly as contingent as the positive endings of melodrama. The protagonist has, however, achieved the 'clear-sightedness and authenticity' which Brooks sees as melodrama's lesson: 'Virtue has become the capacity to face the abyss even if its content may be nothingness, and to assume the burden of consciousness that results from this confrontation.'

It has been easy for critics to take one of Brennan's poems out of its dramatic context in *Poems [1913]* and pull it to pieces. It is equally easy to do the same with many passages from *His Natural Life*. And it is hard to find anything more banal than the printed text of a nineteeth-century melodrama. Melodramas and works of the melodramatic imagination achieve their emotional power through an accumulation, a piling-up of effects and images which individually may be unremarkable. In this sense, also, they can be seen as democratic. Strange company, one may think, for Brennan the intellectual. Yet at the end of *Poems [1913]* the protagonist identifies with the passing crowd, seeing their 'unwitting need' as

> one with my own, however dark,
> and questing towards one mother-ark.

Perhaps it is not entirely coincidental that one of the most popular Australian television melodramas of the 1980s was called *Return to Eden*.

Notes

Good introductions to stage melodrama are provided by James L. Smith, *Melodrama* (1973) and Eric Bentley, *The Life of the Drama* (1964). Developments in England and America are traced in Michael Booth, *English Melodrama* (1965) and David Grimstead, *Melodrama Unveiled: American Theatre and Culture, 1800-1850* (1968). A preliminary attempt to outline some of the semiotics of melodrama may be found in Gilbert B. Cross, *Next Week—East Lynne: Domestic Drama in Performance, 1820-1874* (1977). Australian melodramas are discussed in Margaret Williams, *Australia on the Popular Stage, 1829-1929* (1983) and Eric Irvin, *Australian Melodrama* (1981) and *Gentleman George, King of Melodrama* (1980).

The term 'melodramatic imagination' comes from a provocative study by Peter Brooks, *The Melodramatic Imagination: Balzac, Henry James, Melodrama and the Mode of Excess* (1986). Some of Brooks' points had been anticipated by Wylie Sypher, 'Aesthetic of Revolution: the Marxist Melodrama', *Kenyon Review*, 10 (1948). See also John Docker, 'In defence of melodrama: towards a libertarian aesthetic', *Australasian Drama Studies*, 9, 1986 and 'Antipodean Literature: A World Upside Down?', *Overland*, 103, 1986. Some contemporary developments are discussed in Ien Ang, *Watching Dallas: Soap Opera and the Melodramatic Imagination* (1985) and Jon Stratton, 'Watching the detectives: television melodrama and its genres', *Australasian Drama Studies*, 10, 1987.

A pioneering study of melodrama in Marcus Clarke's work is John Burrows, '*His Natural Life* and the Capacities of Melodrama', *Southerly*, 34 (1974). Brian Elliott discusses the two versions of *His Natural Life* in his introduction to the Angus & Robertson classics edition (1975). For an opposing view of the significance of the revisions see Joan Poole, 'Maurice Frere's Wife: Marcus Clarke's Revision of *His Natural Life*', *Australian Literary Studies*, 4 (1970). See also Laurie Hergenhan, 'The Redemptive Theme in *His Natural Life*', *Australian Literary Studies*, 2 (1965) and Michael Wilding, *Marcus Clarke* (1977). For a full discussion of Australian convict novels see Laurie Hergenhan, *Unnatural Lives* (1983).

From the extensive array of Brennan criticism, this chapter draws particularly on G. A. Wilkes, *New Perspectives on Brennan's Poetry* (1953) and 'Interpreting Brennan's Poetry; or "The I of My Verses is not Necessarily ME"', *Southerly*, 37 (1977); Axel Clark, *Christopher Brennan: A Critical Biography* (1980) and Terry Sturm's introduction to his edition of *Christopher Brennan* (1984). For counter views of *Poems [1913]* see A. L. French, 'The Verse of C. J. Brennan', *Southerly*, 24 (1964), and Annette Stewart, 'Christopher Brennan: The Disunity of *Poems [1913]*', *Meanjin*, 29 (1970).

Chapter 14

ROMANCE: AN EMBARRASSING SUBJECT

FIONA GILES

Introducing his study of nineteenth-century romantic fiction, R. Keily felt it necessary to begin with an apology: 'The English romantic novel is, in some ways, an embarrassing subject . . . They are not all bad', he then admitted; 'indeed some are very good'. But they have a calamitous aspect, as 'for most . . . confrontation and breakdown are not merely fictional themes but structural and stylistic problems.'

Criticism of Australian romance has been similarly perplexed. Why has a form which has always been popular, and which, in its contemporary formulation, comprises the largest-selling section of the publishing industry, been presented so often in a spirit of defence or apology, or simply ignored?

Not all of the late nineteenth and early twentieth century romance literature has been subject to this attitude. The ballad romances of Banjo Paterson and many of the stories of Henry Lawson (which some say are more romantic than we have previously allowed), have retained their broad popularity since they were published in the 1890s. Paterson's and Lawson's complete works, published in 1984, sold in very large numbers. The posthumous career of the English-born poet Adam Lindsay Gordon has been less smooth, but he too retains his identity as a writer who was acclaimed for helping to create a nationally distinctive poetic voice.

The ballad romances of Paterson, Lawson and Gordon celebrated the bush life of itinerant workers, usually male, in the settlements and the outback, where their trials in a less than generous environment led to the development of close relations within shifting male communities. Briefly put, Lawson celebrated unionism and nationalism as an extension of this principle, while Paterson and Gordon celebrated the prowess of the horseman and adventurer in the bush in a fictional world closer to that of the bush heroes found in the novels and stories. Linked to the oral tradition, the ballads were a narrative verse form which was often used for recitation; 'Reciters', or books designed for home entertainment, were popular up to the early decades of this century.

Other poets—Henry Kendall, 'Australie' (Emily Manning), Susan Nugent Wood and John Shaw Neilson, to name a few—tended to be romantic in their attention to the relationship between the poetic voice and Australian nature. Kendall and 'Australie' in particular, transformed this attention into a typically romantic quest for literary possession of nature through poetic description. In Kendall's 'After Many Years' (1869) and 'The Weatherboard Fall' (1877) by 'Australie', for example, the sense of a failure to achieve this possession amounts to a salutation to the landscape and a motive for turning to the life of the spirit.

Adam Lindsay Gordon is an important figure for illustrating the dual nature of the romance genre and the way in which this has contributed to critical ambivalence. As Leonie Kramer has shown, Gordon wrote both popular and 'serious' verse. Yet romance itself has always been divided between what one critic calls popular and aristocratic traditions. According to Gillian Beer's definition in *The Romance* (1970) the genre derives from the epic, one of the oldest literary forms, and it has always displayed this dual character. In the nineteenth century, with the development of the realist novel on the one hand, and the romantic movement on the other, a post-romantic popular romance became more common.

The essential feature of both types of romance is that the narrative is organised around the quest of a hero or heroine for an ideal, where the heroic figure must overcome both internal and external obstacles in its pursuit. In its aristocratic form, the quest is on a large scale and interweaves a number of different narrative strands, often converging around the interests of one family or community. During the nineteenth century it was aligned with the family saga, but earlier with the religious allegorical romance such as *The Faerie Queen* and *The Holy Grail*. In its popular guise, romance is closer to the ballad, which has a single narrative interest, often that of an individual hero in pursuit of romantic love or political conquest. Additionally, romance presents the hero's quest for spiritual values, and while both forms have incorporated the supernatural to represent or thwart those values, the former has tended to employ allegory to do this, while popular romance tells of its ideal through the psychology of the individual subject. While the two strains could sometimes be combined in the one piece, in the nineteenth century the differences became polarised, as Gordon's case shows; and it is important, in any reading of romance from this period, to take these two sides of the genre into account.

Australian romance was principally written in novel form, often in the three volumes made popular by the English publisher Richard Bentley, and distributed through the circulating libraries of Britain. But some shorter fiction and stories also belong to the genre. The literature of this period, whether in the form of poetry, novels, or shorter fiction, is perhaps best regarded as Anglo-Australian, since much of it was published in London and distributed in England, as well as in Australia and other colonies. This term is also useful to acknowledge the way in which the genre relates to the dynamics of colonial relations. As a narrative in which a heroic protagonist pursues his or her quest for an ideal, the literature is distinguished by its attention to the journey as a means for accommodating the literal journey from England to the colonies, and sometimes back again. This may be in part a materialist justification, as it is for the pastoral quest of Henry Kingsley's *The Recollections of Geoffry Hamlyn* (1859). Or the transition between countries may be dealt with through a choice of suitors which many of the heroines are required to make before their acceptance of, and by, a domestic order in Australia. These two examples again display the polarity in the genre: the former is closer to the aristocratic strain, and has received more critical attention; the latter, being popular romance, is less respectable.

The reading of this fiction has thus been variable and, for popular romance in particular, critical resistance has been most evident. In Australia this resistance can be seen to be compounded by a number of nationally distinctive conditions.

In the second half of the nineteenth century, there was, as in Europe, an Australian reaction by realist writers and critics against romance. This is now identified with the *Bulletin* writing of the 1890s and later, but in fact a realist opposition to romance can be traced to the picaresque satire of James Tucker's *Ralph Rashleigh* (written 1845, published 1952) and the fiction of the social reformer Catherine Helen Spence, who claimed that her first novel, *Clara Morison* (1854), was 'more domestic than exciting'.

What made the Australian critical debate different from that in

Britain, Europe and America was that the realist writing of the 1880s
and 1890s, in part linked to the *Bulletin* editorial formula for
simplicity and directness, became allied to the cause of political
independence from Britain. Concerned to describe what was unique
about living in Australia, and being an Australian, the fiction of
Lawson, 'Price Warung' (William Astley), Barbara Baynton and
Joseph Furphy found little use for the expansive description of a
pastoral ideal so central to the romantic sagas in an Australia which
Henry Kingsley had described in 1859, to an audience intrigued by
the possibility of emigration, as 'heaven on earth'. After Federation
the romance literature which the realist writers claimed to dislike has
continued to be regarded as un-Australian or culturally deficient.

The second and related reason for the problematic attitude to this
literature was the political division of periods created by Federation
in 1901. Unless secure in the nationalist, and therefore formative
Australian tradition, literature written before this date is necessarily
colonial and culturally inadequate. As Honoria Longleat complains in
Rosa Praed's *Policy and Passion* (1881) the term 'colonial' could not
be a 'worse compliment'. 'To be *colonial* is to talk Australian slang;
to be badly dressed, vulgar, everything that is abominable.'
Particularly for the romance fiction, cultural home is Britain, or
London, regardless of the travels of its characters. But it is also a
feature of the romance form that it appealed to the values of a past
which its characters come to terms with in their fictional present, and
inevitably these were English values.

A small number of writers—including Rosa Praed, Ernest Favenc
and G. Firth Scott—sought to construct a romantic history based on
the myth of Lemuria, an Australasian equivalent to a lost Atlantis.
But the majority of romantic writing was addressed to the cultural
primacy of Europe and Britain. Much of the romantic poetry, for
example, is based on a sense of the difficulty of revealing eternal
verities through its portrayal of what was, for the white culture, an
historically blank landscape.

There are, of course, other reasons for the defensive attitude of
criticism to this literature, which relate in part to the anti-Victorian
stance of the modern and post-modern periods and to changing
fashions in critical reading. This chapter will look speculatively at
two other reasons for critical resistance, while also describing briefly
the nature of the existing criticism. It will then return to look at those
reasons for critical embarrassment, and attempt to show that these
indicate aspects of the genre which, while contributing to the sense of

embarrassment, also draw attention to embarrassment as itself an important feature, or stage, within the operations of the romance quest.

The first of these reasons is that the apparently 'narrow' domestic and social world of some of the women's writing has resisted incorporation into a literary tradition seen as essentially representing a culture which is outdoors and informal. This problem applies especially to what has been called feminine romance, which traces the heroine's quest for domestic fulfilment, love and a sense of self-determination. It is arguable that these heroines have represented a cause for embarrassment as foregrounded female subjects within a culture that has been presented as predominantly masculine.

A second feature of the genre which is potentially disconcerting is its preoccupation with the discovery of origin and the ways that a sense of origin can be integrated into the present. The trials and adventures encountered by the hero during the quest are understood to represent obstacles to a culturally sanctioned sense of existential purpose which enables self-understanding. The heroic quest leads backwards, or inwards, and further progress, or concluding stability, is based on this sense of arrival at an incontestable and determining explanation of beginnings. In white Australian culture this explanation is largely inherited from Anglo-Celtic mythology, but necessarily also incorporates the early history of Australia, including convictism, misogyny and maltreatment of Aboriginals.

Criticism of the romance appears to fall, generally speaking, into two categories. The first questions the opposition between definitions of realist and romantic literature; and writers in the second argue for a continuity in Australian romantic preoccupations, particularly in relation to the development of national character. In Australian romance criticism the second category is exemplified by two studies: G. A. Wilkes' *The Stockyard and the Croquet Lawn* (1981) and B. Argyle's *An Introduction to the Australian Novel* (1972). Both argue that the romantic strain has been continuous in Australian literature, undeterred by its realist opposition and in some ways incorporated into it. They usefully question the divisions which were thought to have been established in the 1890s and were reaffirmed in the 1950s by Russel Ward's *The Australian Legend* (1958) and Vance Palmer's *The Legend of the Nineties* (1954).

Desmond Byrne's *Australian Writers* (1896) belongs to the first category of criticism, possibly being the first and last full-length account of a colonial romantic tradition, and including chapters on the major prose writers, as well as the poetry of Adam Lindsay Gordon. Byrne's contribution is to break down the model which sees the romantic as unpatriotic and the realist as nationalist. His work is of particular interest because it shows how the romance fiction of the period does not necessarily amount to a neglect of Australian aspirations to a distinctive national writing; it was not simply a matter of romance appealing to an escapist English audience and realism to what Furphy called the offensively Australian. His book is also significant for the amount of space it grants to a consideration of progress within what was being rejected as imperialist literature, and he compares this progress with the American experience while also accounting for some of the material features of publishing and reading relations between England and the colonies in the late nineteenth century.

While the romantic-colonial and realist-nationalist categories have been constructed as opposites by criticism, and by early realist writers, the literature itself, as Byrne shows, does not always conform to this pattern. As Jean Radford notes in *The Progress of Romance* (1986), nineteenth-century romance fiction continued to adopt realist strategies from the novel, revealing 'that far from being always antithetical, romance and realism could become close and compatible literary bedfellows'. This is also borne out by Frederick Sinnett's comment in 1856, in his *Fiction Fields of Australia*, that many of the novels acted as guidebooks for prospective immigrants and thus included profuse material detail, however implausible the plot. Additionally, it is within some of the romance fiction that evolving relationships between an emergent culture and its characters in the 'Young' world, as Rosa Praed saw it, is discussed. Byrne argues that the novelists have achieved a kind of balance between the militantly everyday and the idealisations of romance. He introduces Tasma in the following terms:

> Between the writers who profess not to see anything individual in the life of Australia and those others who confine themselves to describing a few of its principal characters, Tasma holds a middle and independent place . . . Her materials are chosen for some quality of picturesqueness rather than for the purpose of illustrating any phase of life at the Antipodes or elsewhere.

Byrne thus points to the sense in which romance offers an appearance of freedom from the details of place and time to enable the workings-out of the interior life of its characters, placing an emphasis on their personal and familial, rather than social, history. The forces of romantic love, rights of property inheritance, and the family itself are usually established as absolute values originating in an ideal realm of the past which offers a precedent for the future. Much attention in Tasma's fiction is given to the genealogy of her characters: many of her heroines are in search of their parents, such as Pauline in *In Her Earliest Youth* (1890). Ada Cambridge's *The Three Miss Kings* (1891) depicts three sisters attempting to enter 'Society' only to find that they will simultaneously recover their family; and Ellen Clacy's much earlier short story, 'Lillian', from *Lights and Shadows of Australian Life* (1854) reveals that this quest for family intrigued Australian writers throughout the period. In Rolf Boldrewood's *Robbery Under Arms* Dick Marston will break any laws except those protecting the safety of his family and childhood love.

In general these are bourgeois values which enable the forming of the hero or heroine as an individualist subject. But the fiction also describes the conditions of the present in which the characters live. Praed believed that people are essentially the same everywhere but are influenced by their natural environment. She sees the bush, in particular, as an ideal site for the revelation and intensification of passion, as her short story 'The Finding of The Waterhole' (1902) dramatically shows.

Many romance novels also consider the importance of distance between the two cultures and the difficulty of the choice between them which their characters were often required to make. In *The Recollections of Geoffry Hamlyn* the Thornton and Buckley families have migrated to Victoria where they establish themselves as the new landed gentry. But their purpose is to renew a fortune which will enable them to resume their position in English society. For the ambitious and misguided heroine, Mary Thornton, Australia represents a site of moral renewal as well, and after ridding herself of an undesirable husband in the appropriate setting of a penal colony, she is free to marry the stalwart English countryman Troubridge, a figure who links the best of provincial England with the best of colonial pastoralism.

Travel is also a feature of Rolf Boldrewood's *Robbery Under Arms*: Starlight has arrived from England in the indeterminate past, and has continued to travel between Australia and New Zealand, and within Australia, both by sea and land. For Starlight, the effort to escape from an unhappy past precludes the option of return, but he is essentially a 'swell', an outsider from both Australian and European worlds.

The travels of the female hero are slightly different. Caroline Leakey's convict heroine in *The Broad Arrow* (1859) dies in Van Diemen's Land in a state of isolated defeat and tragic loss of worldly fulfilment similar to that of Rufus Dawes in *His Natural Life*, which novel is said to have been influenced by Leakey's work. But Praed's *An Australian Heroine* (1880) has the young Esther Haggart, daughter of a convict, transported back to England from an island off Queensland to serve a sentence of reinsertion into English provincial society. By the time of Tasma's third novel, *The Penance of Portia James* (1891), the heroine refuses the option of remaining in England by choosing to be faithful to her past in Australia, whatever its deficiencies. She returns with her less than worthy Australian husband after an alluring dalliance in London and Paris bohemia. This is similar to Gertie's decision in Kingsley's slightly later novel, *The Hillyars and the Burtons* (1865).

Finally, to provide a sense of the range of treatments of this theme, Praed's *Lady Bridget in the Never-Never Land* (1915) has the Irish aristocrat heroine confronted with a similar choice. After runnning away from her squatter husband in 'Leichardt's Land' (Praed's fictional Queensland), she returns, revitalised by a timely inheritance, to the shelter of his own version of 'bush chivalry'. In contrast to the pattern in *Geoffry Hamlyn*, (although not to *The Hillyars*) Lady Bridget's rejection of English society along with her English suitor, Mr Willoughby Maule, is actually facilitated by opportune adjustments in the family fortune in England. Whereas Kingsley used colonial pastoral development to renew his characters' English property and maintain their social status, Praed shows that material and spiritual interests can be reconciled within the new world. And Bridget's love develops in a rough nuptial tent, in the bush.

These examples indicate the danger of isolating any of the novels as exemplary. Well over 200 novels and story collections were published in this period, in addition to the many stories and serials appearing in the periodicals and annuals. The fiction varies from the heavily didactic temperance novels of 'Maud Jeanne Franc' (Matilda Jane Evans), to the Lemurian adventures of Ernest Favenc, G. Firth Scott, John Boyle O'Reilly and John David Hennessey, to tales which include documentary accounts and anecdotes from life, in addition to far-fetched happy endings, such as the stories of Ellen Clacy in the

1850s. Similarly, there is a range of narrative forms and tone within the romance structure—from the satiric comedy of manners in Tasma's *Uncle Piper of Piper's Hill* (1889) to the first-person confessional of Rosa Praed's *Sister Sorrow* (1916).

The novels of Catherine Helen Spence and Henry Handel Richardson should also be mentioned as works which have been taken more seriously, although Spence received much less recognition until the 1970s. While their novels, Richardson's *The Getting of Wisdom* (1910) in particular, are presented as realist texts, the quest of the heroine, not for romantic love but for self-definition and a sense of purpose, suggests that generally they should be regarded as romances. Spence's last novel, *Handfasted,* which remained unpublished until 1984, but was written in 1879, is a utopian romance in which a politically progressive heroine strives for ideal feminist conditions of marriage. Miles Franklin's *My Brilliant Career* (1901) provides an example of a work which professes to distance itself from romance fiction, as did Spence's and Praed's for that matter, but traces the quest of a heroine who, while rejecting the conventional romantic option of love and marriage, proposes her own romantic future as the splendidly isolated literary outsider.

An important aspect of Australian nineteenth-century romance which is yet to be addressed is the contribution to the formation of national heroic models provided by this wide range of heroines in the women's writing. And not only the heroines are missing from nineteenth-century literary history; the heroes those heroines desired have also been left unattended. Athough Barry Argyle has noted the absence of the heroine, he attributes the gap to the literature rather than the criticism. 'There has never been an Australian heroine,' he wrote:

> Generalising, it can be said that nineteenth-century fiction is the record of woman's disappearance. What became of her is undoubtedly one of the major problems for any present-day critic of Australian literature.

Recent feminist readings of romance fiction have argued that the polarisation of the two romance strands in the eighteenth and nineteenth centuries was accompanied by a division of the genre into masculine and feminine forms. The popular romance was regarded as feminine literature, and as it became increasingly favoured by women readers, the genre fell in status, while masculine romance (some of which was written by women) gained critical ground, if marginally, as did detective fiction. Many of the feminine romances continued to be didactic and religious, as is the fiction of Ada Cambridge, 'Maud Jeanne Franc', Ellen August Chads, and Mrs A. Blitz. But by now, such didacticism was being applied to the domestic dramas of the middle class, and found itself in yet another category somewhere beneath the 'high arts'. Perhaps this explains, in part, the apparent absence of the heroine in nineteenth-century Australian fiction.

Yet Rosa Praed's first novel, published under her family name of R. Murray Prior in 1880, is actually called *An Australian Heroine*. It traces the fortunes of Esther Haggart who is described in some detail as a daughter of the bush with a special spiritual quality, but one who has also inherited the dramatic looks and impetuosity of her dead mother. She travels to England to live with her father's relatives, and this enables her to pursue an unscrupulous English suitor. To survive in England she must make a series of compromises with her dreamy temperament—as well as learning table manners—but it is clear that her outstanding moral integrity and stamina is fortified by her Australian origins.

That Praed was intent on contributing to the formation of national heroic types, both male and female, is even more evident from her second novel, *Policy and Passion* (1881). Here an Englishman courts Honoria Longleat, daughter of the Premier of Leichhardt's Land. Honoria is powerful but isolated and inexperienced; she is also motherless, and alienated from her father. Hardress Barrington, who like many of Praed's English heroes, is morally suspect, though clever, makes the following declaration:

> 'These lotus lilies,' he said, 'remind me of a type of womanhood which I know—passionate yet pure—combining the frankness of innocence with the strongest susceptibility to the influence of love ... Such a creature could only have had a birth in a wild free atmosphere. She belongs to the woods and streams [being a new chum his vocabulary is slightly inappropriate]; she is the classic nymph—the essence of womanliness. You are the ideal Australia.'

In 1889 Tasma's first novel, *Uncle Piper of Piper's Hill*, offered a similarly formidable Australian heroine in Laura Lydiat who is a 'new woman' of the period, but who, like Honoria (and Esther), is without motherly guidance and defies her father, mainly because she—like her own subsequent critics—finds him embarrassing.

The cultural allegory implicit in this pattern is clear. They, along with many other heroines, are faced with the difficult task of accepting the right husband, having to choose between the refined but unsuitable Englishman and the less sophisticated, naturally virtuous, Australian—often a squatter. In the process of choice, the women come to terms with the inadequacies of their parents (often their mother has been negligent to the point of dying), and enact the uncertainties created by their unprecedented significance as important agents in an emerging culture—in another sense motherless.

Australian women writers also spent some time describing their male heroes, many of whom bear little resemblance to their realist counterpart, the mate, or to the rogues and heroes in Kingsley, Boldrewood and Clarke. Well-intentioned but initially awkward in the company of women, they have often endured hardships in the bush, but will inevitably win the heroine by means of the same perseverance and faith that saw them through the droughts, floods and banking crises. They are often self-educated 'gentlemen of nature' who benefit from further social and moral refinement after falling in love.

Praed's 'The Bushman's Love-Story' (1909) contains a fine description of the Australian heroic couple, reunited in London, on the basis of their commitment to Australia as well as each other. The heroine, Theodora, is a powerful agent in resolving the narrative, since she has saved her lover's property by buying it back from the bank to which it was lost in the Great Drought. Carr, another visiting Australian, but a city man, describes Theodora as a 'woman with big thoughts and fine ideals':

> there's nothing she can't do—ride as well as any stockman, sit a buckjumper and cut out a scrubber on a cattle camp. And she can cook a dinner that you'd enjoy eating, and make her frocks—and look stunning in them too. And as for brains. Why, she's taken her M.A. degree in Sydney University, and now she's training herself to deal with the Woman Question— . . .

The narrator, an older woman friend of both lovers who enables their meeting in her flat, describes the hero, Jim Beamish, as 'a long lean brown creature with the physiognomy of a Greek god who had been keeping house with Pan and was somewhat weather-beaten in consequence'. Despite 'all his little Australian roughnesses', 'good blood cannot lie . . . the chivalrous gentleman showed forth'.

This story is particularly interesting for its overt equating of romantic love with national loyalty. In addition to financial good fortune, the emotional resolution of the romance is also favoured by an Australian future. Whereas Lady Bridget's commitment was assisted by her Irish family's wealth, here the hero has fled from his Australian past only to be returned to it through the capable assistance of an ideal 'Australian girl'.

As these examples suggest, an important feature of romance is its concern with origins, whether they are national, familial or metaphysical. If the quest of the male or female hero is to have any credence, it must be based, as noted earlier, on a retrieval of the best from the past. But the quest must also contend with the past's less acceptable features. This was Spenser's message in relation to the pervasiveness of evil in *The Faerie Queene*, as much as it is Praed's and Tasma's when they use their heroine's ultimate compromises and readjustments to illustrate that absolute escape from inherited difficulty is simply not possible.

The concern of romance with origins also accounts for some of the features of the fiction, particularly its unfashionable narrative techniques, which contribute to critical embarrassment. Coincidence for the purpose of narrative progression, and repetition of plot from novel to novel, are examples of such conventions, which although evident in the very early Greek romances of the first centuries A.D., can also be seen to speak to many of the ontological concerns of the Victorian era.

As Marcus Clarke records in *Civilization Without Delusion* (1880), the later Victorian period was a time of profound doubt concerning origins, the meaning of existence and the life of the soul and—as Darwin's important treatise of 1859 was called—the origin of the species. The explanations of Genesis were no longer convincing, and other answers, made all the more urgent by a colonial relationship which portended the formation of a separate national identity, were being sought. Ada Cambridge's novel *The Three Miss Kings* (1882) discussed the problem of religious orthodoxy in relation to the needs of its characters who are doubly 'outsiders' because an English familial breakdown has left them with a colonial identity. Their reintegration can only be effected through the discovery of an Englishman who is lover, cousin, social reformer and unorthodox Christian.

Clarke's story 'Human Repetends' (1872) provides an example of an alternative account of the question of origin. In this partly autobiographical piece, Pontifex is commanded by Marston to tell the story of his 'embodied ghost', a murder mystery based on the recurrence of a women's image, first in art, then in the streets of Melbourne. He discovers that all the characters in the mystery had previous incarnations and were destined to re-enact the misfortunes they had inherited from earlier souls. In conclusion, Marston asks Pontifex: 'You do not think that men's souls return to earth and enact again the crimes which stained them?' and the narrator replies:

'I know not. But there are in decimal arithmetic repeated "coincidences" called *repetends.* Continue the generation of numbers through all time, you have these repetends for ever recurring. Can you explain this mystery of numbers? No. Neither can I explain the mystery of my life. Good night.'

The importance of memory, the past, and repetition is more gravely affirmed in Praed's last novel, *Sister Sorrow* (1916), and further explicated in her record of a past life, *Soul of Nyria* (1931). In confirmation of this transcription of Nancy Harward's memories of a previous existence, she asserts that 'Nothing which has once existed can be lost' but becomes a form of 'picture gallery provided for us in space, accessible to those who possess its key'. Similarly, the Australian writers who sought a Lemurian origin for their romances revealed a desire for a sense of historical place within a wider determining order. The theory that Australia formed part of a lost continent provided a fictional history to resolve mysteries confronted in Australia since European settlement—its gold, and Aboriginal culture in particular.

In his study 'Narrative Time' (1980), Paul Ricoeur offers another explanation of the purpose of repetition in romance, by reference to its particular model of time. He argues that the use of 'return'—of sideways journeys and backward glances—within the plot (and, by implication, between plots) interrupts the linear progression of the hero on the quest. He explains that 'The kind of repetition involved in this travel is rather primitive, even regressive, in the psychoanalytic sense' but is finally 'superseded by an act of rupture' towards the end of the narrative, and prior to its resolution. The sense of repetition, he argues, provides a 'metatemporal' narrative structure which allows the coexistence of linear and circular temporal patterns and is not, then, ahistorical. This narrative form enables the development of an historical consciousness 'in stories whose function it is to provide an identity to the doer'.

Thus the heroic subject achieves understanding, not through rejection of the past, but through its reappraisal. The value of overcoming critical embarrassment is endorsed, then, by the structure of the fiction itself, which aims for historical reformation by following the course of the journey. Perhaps critical readings of nineteenth-century Australian romance have fled from their prehistory in the same inevitably unsatisfactory way as Pontifex fled from his crimes, Honoria from her father, and countless blushing heroines from speaking their desire.

Jean Radford suggests that

> romance fictions may certainly refer us back to (psychologically) primitive ways of seeing the world, but whether this 'regressive' experience is a positive or a negative one is ... determined not by the romance itself but by the interaction of text and context.

As this history of Australian romance shows, understanding this interaction can help account for the selective use of the literature in public statements of national identity with its masculine bias, as well as revealing the more private, psychological journeys of its heroines and heroes.

Notes

There are still many gaps in the study of nineteenth-century Australian romance which can best be filled by reading the many novels, short-story collections and periodicals. A selection of romance fiction by women is now being reprinted by the Virago and Pandora presses in England and Penguin in Australia. Scholarly editions are also being published by the University of New South Wales Press. For a collection of short romance fiction by nineteenth-century Australian women, see *From the Verandah* (1987), an anthology edited by Fiona Giles.

Periodicals which carried literature, for example, the *Australasian* and the *Australian Journal,* and the better-known *Bulletin*, which published some romance stories, are a source of literature and reviews as well as information on the cultural background. Lurline Stuart's *Nineteenth Century Australian Periodicals: An Annotated Bibliography* (1979), is valuable for tracing them.

Colin Roderick's anthology *Henry Lawson Criticism, 1894-1971*

(1972) also includes a useful bibliography. For an account of the posthumous reputation of Adam Lindsay Gordon, see Leonie Kramer's article 'The Literary Reputation of Adam Lindsay Gordon' in *Australian Literary Studies,* 1 (1963), and for a general introduction, C. F. MacRae, *Adam Lindsay Gordon* (1968). For a biographical and critical study of Banjo Paterson, see Clement Semmler's *The Banjo of the Bush: The Work, Life and Times of A. B. Paterson* (1974).

Recent feminist criticism of nineteenth-century Australian women's romance can be found in Susan Sheridan, 'Temper Democratic, Bias Offensively Feminine: Australian Literary Writers and Literary Nationalism', *Kunapipi,* 7, 2/3, (1983., 1985) and 'Ada Cambridge and the Female Literary Tradition' in S. Dermody, J. Docker, and D. Modjeska (eds), *Nellie Melba, Ginger Meggs and Friends* (1982). More specialised studies of popular romance are provided by Tania Modleski, *Loving With a Vengeance* (1982), and the two chapters on 'Gender and Genre' in J. Batsleer, T. Davies, *et al., Rewriting English* (1985). For a brief introduction to the best-known women romance writers, see R. Beilby and C. Hadgraft, *Ada Cambridge, Tasma and Rosa Praed* (1978).

Chapter 15

REALISM AND DOCUMENTARY: LOWERING ONE'S SIGHTS

PATRICK MORGAN

In 1871 Anthony Trollope described an outing on his son's property near Grenfell in New South Wales:

> One seems to ride forever and to come to nothing, and to relinquish at last the very idea of an object. Nevertheless, it was very pleasant. Of all places that I was ever in this place seemed to be the fittest for contemplation.

Trollope here records two contrasting impressions of the Australian bush. The openness of the country encouraged rumination and giving free rein to fancies, yet it provided so few points to fix upon that a certain lack of coherence became overwhelming. Australia was beguiling but elusive. The imaginative urge could lead to extravagant hopes, the documentary urge to despondency. The country induced you to let go, then trapped you when you did. Imagination could get in the road. The fertile romantic mind was often employed in Australia not to intensify reality, but to impose fantasies on a perceived vacuum. Only after time did writers learn to defer to the country's otherness, and to let that be the basis of their inspiration. Henry Lawson was born in the Grenfell area four years before Trollope's ride. A quarter of a century later he too noticed that you could travel for miles 'without being able to fix a point in your mind'.

Lawson benefited from the movement towards realism which developed during the second half of the nineteenth century. There was a new focus on the everyday actions of ordinary people, rather than on those of aristocrats or the specially endowed. The writer aimed to present an objective account of specific events, and refused to saturate his material with his own emotional fancies. Realism was seen as allowing writing to be open to new experiences, to record a situation as clearly as possible, and to let it produce its own resonances. The documentary urge was uppermost, and the imagination in its control. In this way Lawson was able successfully to reconcile the contrary tendencies which had so perplexed Trollope.

Up till Lawson the progressive unfolding of the Australian landscape—coast, mountains, plains—had not fitted in neatly with the ideas and literary modes of the day. The opening up of the outback plains occurred at a time when the literary imagination was engrossed in adventure stories in picturesque mountain surroundings. The Industrial Revolution had provoked in England a desire to return to earlier forms of rural life, but frustrated this in reality. The vast, open lands of Australia, it was imagined, could accommodate a leisured life where squires were supported by loyal yeoman retainers. But this eighteenth-century arcadian ideal was, by the 1850s, at odds with the current focus in Australia on the range areas. This disparity led early writers incongruously to set extensive sheep stations in the wooded hills of Australia, rather than on the broad, open plains.

We see this uneasy amalgam in the novels of two talented Englishmen who spent some years in gold-rush Victoria in the 1850s: Henry Kingsley's *The Recollections of Geoffry Hamyln* (1859) and William Howitt's *Tallangetta, The Squatter's Home* (1857). The stations in both novels are similar: vast cleared expanses protectively surrounded by forests and mountains, with a fine house situated, eighteenth-century style, on a knoll in the middle distance. The novels are unrealistic about economic factors; the stations arise in perfect condition without any pioneering struggle. The main characters do little work (that is left to the overseer and retainers imported from England) and enjoy a comfortable social life visiting neighbours, chatting on the veranda, or smoking after the evening meal.

These novels have a number of strands which have not been woven into a whole. There is a documentary layer expressing the journalist's wide-eyed wonder at the strange new world opening up before him. The main party in *Tallangetta* traces a journey north-east from Melbourne, passing diggers on the goldfields and shepherds in huts. Kingsley's novel describes places in the western district and the north-east of Victoria, and includes extensive botanical and geo-logical observations. This carefully observed background material, interesting to us today as environmental and social history, is not closely related to the plot. Discrete episodes are interpolated into the main structure, like the 'Bogong Jack' legend in *Geoffry Hamlyn* and the 'Black Thursday', 'Melbourne Merchant' and 'Old and New Squatter' segments in *Tallangetta*. As well there are set-piece scenes (an outdoor picnic, a child lost in the bush, a rescue in a flood) designed to thrill English audiences with the unexpected delights and terrors of the Australian bush. Such lightly fictionalised insertions are tenuously, if at all, linked to the novels' main lines of development.

The story in both books concerns dispossessed English gentry who come to Australia to regain their lost status. The authors discard the plot for large sections of the novel. A villain, in both cases a convict, highwayman and forger, is exposed and defeated at the end, and the family is restored to its rightful ancestral place in England. The families succeed by overcoming human perfidy rather than by triumphing over Australian rural conditions. The novelists' desire for a neat conclusion leads to Victorian formula fiction—dramatic climaxes, the death of a loved one, improbable adventure stories and contrived resolutions which strain credulity. Gothic melodrama feels out of place in sunny open Australia. As a result the plots move towards fantasy and remain at odds with the documentary material in the books. The plots may be sketchy, but the myths underlying them are crucial. The novels share the assumption that a better life could be lived in Australia—whether land, labour or gold was the way to riches was the point at issue.

Another important novel of the 1850s, *Clara Morison* (1854) by Catherine Spence, does not share this confidence. This is an urban novel, written by a woman, mainly about women, where things go wrong, improvement is not automatic, and hopes for the new country not so extravagant. Clara considers herself a gentlewoman, but sinks to the level of domestic servant; after many onerous jobs in service and as a governess, she finally regains her lost status and marries a squatter, Charles Reginald. As in the Kingsley and Howitt novels, the eighteenth-century notion of status in society is the main preoccupation of the characters. Australia is depicted as a loose and fluid society with rapid changes of fortune. Clara yearns for (and herself becomes) a haven of stability in this turbulent world. Like Clara, the infant colony of South Australia itself has status anxieties: it does not want to fall behind the other colonies, but it also does not want to fall prey to those free and easy ways later summarised as the Australian legend. There are three images of Australian life from which the narrator and Adelaide society recoil: life on squatting runs, where men degenerate because of the lack of civilisation, life on the Victorian goldfields, which is a free-for-all, and life in brash and vulgar boom-town Melbourne, awash with goldfields money. *Clara Morison* inaugurates the line of middle-class novels of society developed later by Rosa Praed, 'Tasma', Henry Handel Richardson and Norman Lindsay.

Catherine Spence's novel depicts the ups and downs of life in Australia. The original title of Rolf Boldrewood's first novel, *The Squatter's Dream*, was *Ups and Downs* (1878). The novel, which for the first two-thirds closely follows Boldrewood's own life, is a flawed attempt at perpetuating the arcadian idyll. After leaving Marshmead (based on Boldrewood's Squattlesea Mere) in south-western Victoria, the hero, Jack Redgrave, moves to a northern Riverina station, just as Boldrewood moved to a sheep station near Narrandera in 1864. Jack Redgrave tries to set up the Kingsleyan ideal of the perfect run ('the romance of a freehold') where a gentleman may live in comfort and independence. Jack does not work much (overseer Sandy McNab manages the run), he visits his Melbourne club as well as his sociable neighbours, the Stangroves, and their daughter Maud. The station, with its efficient manager, humorous Chinese gardener-cook, childlike Aborigines and unreliable itinerant workers, becomes a stock picture in later Australian fiction, such as Mary Grant Bruce's. As the first title *Ups and Downs* indicates the idyll turns sour. Jack Redgrave is defeated not by English villains but by Australian conditions—drought, fire, floods, and poor prices ('want of rain and want of credit')—just as Boldrewood was driven off his Narrandera property by drought in 1869.

But Boldrewood's heart was not in depicting failure. He tried in literature to realise the squatter's dream which had eluded him in life. In *Old Melbourne Memories* (1884) he recalls the early squatting days as a golden age. The last part of *The Squatter's Dream* suddenly reverts to the Kingsleyan pattern to compensate for failure. Jack Redgrave moves to the far outback on the edge of the desert and finds a magnificent wilderness property with rivers and lakes. After a series of unlikely adventures in which he is tricked out of the title by a crooked land speculator, everything finally comes right, he makes money, marries Maud Stangrove and rebuys Marshmead, thus regaining his patrimony. The contrived events and the sudden quickening of pace make the last part of the novel unconvincing. Interestingly, in his next novel, *Robbery Under Arms* (1882-3, 1888) Boldrewood succeeded by mythologising the squatter's natural enemies, the cattleduffers and bushrangers, and by retreating from the outback plains to the range country as a suitable locality for their adventures. Here everything suited his romantic imagination. This may explain the dearth of good novels on squatting—an imagination nourished on writers like Scott found it hard to depict the unvariegated life of squatters on the open plains. Factual accounts like Anthony Trollope's *Australia and New Zealand* (1873) give a more realistic picture of squatting than many novels.

Trollope's Australian Christmas tale *Harry Heathcote of Gangoil* (1874) is based partly on his son's experience on a station near Grenfell, though the novel is set in the Maryborough district of Queensland. Unlike Jack Redgrave, Harry Heathcote works day and night, and like a selector, is so obsessed by success in his venture that he has little time for socialising. His greatest hindrance is not economic or climatic factors, but the threat posed by malevolent employees and neighbours who threaten to burn his fences and property. The ending is typically Victorian, with dramatic fire scenes, melodramatic love scenes and clear-cut villainy. Harry Heathcote eventually comes out on top, whereas in real life Trollope's son Frederic relinquished his property, costing Trollope senior a considerable sum of money. This novel is a half-way house between squatting and selector fiction.

Completely outside the mainstream is Havelock Ellis' half-recollection, half-reverie *Kanga Creek*, based on his year as a schoolteacher in the Liverpool ranges near Scone in 1878, and published in 1922. The location is an enclosed valley with the narrator cut off from all normal human relationships. It is an idyll, but of a quite different type from that attempted in squatting literature. The narrator is a visitor, not a settler, without the constant worry of making a go of things on the land. Against the current of the time, he does not try to assert his mastery over nature; instead he gradually merges back into the scenery. The narrator is not attempting to build a new world but exulting in Australia as a domain of innocence, where 'the mystery of the early world is still alive', and where one is released from the repressions of civilisation. In this, Ellis foreshadows D. H. Lawrence's attitude to Australia. The narrator briefly notices the struggling selectors of the valley, whose children attend the school. In their run-down condition we have a small glimpse of things to come—the ranges, up till now an arena of picturesque adventure, are soon to witness the tragedy of the collapsing small farmers.

At the start and finish of *Kanga Creek* Ellis describes the fictional town of Ayr. Australia was not just Sydney or the bush: goldrushes and selection had increased the importance of country towns. The best early account of them is found in Marcus Clarke's 'Bullocktown' tales of the 1870s, based on Glenorchy in the Ararat region, where Clarke worked on stations from 1865 to 1867. Clarke's quicksilver temperament provided varied responses to the bush, sometimes conventionally mawkish as in 'Pretty Dick' and 'Poor Joe', but stories like 'An Upcountry Township' (or 'Bullocktown') introduced an important new style which prefigures the breakthrough of the 1890s. The town is already down on its heels, the exalted names given to local features contrasting with the depressing reality. Bullocktown's characters (like the former gentleman and the skite) are already living on their past. The townspeople attend a temperance meeting and sign the pledge for something to do. But grog soon triumphs over religion, blotting everything out. Such pointless activity reminds one strongly of Lawson's 'The Union Buries its Dead'. Clarke adopts the short story mode, which suits a situation where existence itself, rather than dramatic incidents, is the real focus. These brilliantly sharp sketches of people striving against the odds to preserve some semblances of civilisation are the literary equivalent of an S. T. Gill sketch.

The long boom from the 1860s to the 1880s produced a prosperous Australian middle class for the first time. The Adelaide writer Richard Twopeny published his book on these developments, *Town Life in Australia,* in 1883. Like Spence, Twopeny realised that Australia, being recent, was a fragile society where rapid rises and declines in fortunes were common. Boldrewood found similar ups and downs in the bush. Twopeny, again like Spence, saw Australia as a respectable middle-class British society transported here. He looked down on nationalism, being appalled by larrikinism and the infant Sydney *Bulletin* which, though 'very clever and exceedingly readable', was 'vulgar' and 'coarse to a degree'. Two novels which give the flavour of the times are Rosa Praed's *Policy and Passion* (1881) and Tasma's *Uncle Piper of Piper's Hill* (1889). These two women authors left Australia in their mid-twenties and wrote in Europe. Both novels focus on powerful self-made men of humble origin who wish to control the lives of their offspring. In both, the young heroines have to choose between personal inclination and adaptation to the fathers' circumstances. Rosa Praed's novel describes a Premier of Leichhardt's Land (Queensland) who superintends a broad web of personal and political intrigue in city and country. *Uncle Piper* becomes a significant social document by concentrating on the life of a *nouveau riche* merchant, with impressive scenes of Melbourne boom-mansions and races at Flemington.

The focus of attention was now turning to Melbourne. 'It is here,' writes Twopeny, 'the visitor must come who wishes to see the fullest development of Australian civilization.' Melbourne was then considered a bustling and progressive, even slightly brash, city compared with a Sydney more set in its ways. On the Melbourne middle classes we have, as well as Tasma's *Uncle Piper of Piper's Hill*, Marcus Clarke's 1874 journalistic piece 'Nasturtium Villas', a brilliantly detailed satirical portrait of a St Kilda Rd softgoods merchant who displays 'money without taste'. Clarke and Twopeny both noticed a significant social change taking place at this time. In *Clara Morison* in the 1850s the heroine worked in service. Now later in the century young girls preferred factory work to domestic occupations. Though pay and status were lower, they liked the shorter hours, increased leisure and independence that such jobs gave. They now admitted their working-class position and exulted in vernacular modes of behaviour, such as the larrikinism of their male counterparts. This is the group we meet later in the writings of Dyson, Stone and C. J. Dennis.

The clearest picture of the working class emerges from Marcus Clarke's journalism on Melbourne low life. For the first half of this century Australia was a sedate and settled country peopled mainly from the British Isles. But last century Melbourne had a colourful cosmopolitan population: people arrived from all over the world seeking gold, many being left stranded when it ran out. It was a polyglot population of deserting sailors, ex-convicts, vagabonds and gentlemen down on their luck. We got the flotsam and jetsam of the world as well as the most energetic. Following the English social reformer Henry Mayhew and French romances such as Eugène Sue, journalists like Clarke and 'The Vagabond' (John Stanley James) did not write about the respectable working class who settled down in employment. They focused on the Dickensian underclass of oddballs who frequented bars, Chinese gambling dens and pawn shops. These fringe-dwellers lived in the desperate lodgings and doss-houses of lower bohemia or slept under bridges. Though in cities, Clarke likened them to men in the wilderness, stripped of all refinement and scrounging like animals to survive.

Marcus Clarke was himself attracted to upper bohemia, the life of theatres, literary societies and the demi-monde, as distinct from involuntary or lower bohemia from which one could not escape. Both Clarke and The Vagabond wrote in the Mayhew tradition of crusading journalism, forcing comfortable public opinion to face the destitution which was the other side of the coin of their prosperity. The Vagabond, though interesting as a recorder, was himself too imbued with middle-class morality to be disturbing. Clarke provides better detail, and like his subjects, he is sharp, zany and eccentric. His main aim was not so much reforming society as gathering material which engaged his own original imaginative talents. He had nothing in common with the colonial establishment or with incipient suburbia. He was a natural cosmopolitan attracted to continental European culture (like Archibald and Esson after him) rather than to England. Clarke was drawn to the odd, the exotic and the dramatic because nothing in Melbourne stretched his talents. He had its measure, which made him such a good satirist. He had to turn to the extreme abnormality of the convict hell to find a subject to fully satisfy his compulsions. The best-known novels of the period, Clarke's *His Natural Life* (1874) and Rolf Boldrewood's *Robbery Under Arms* (1888), represent romance's last fling in Australia; both focus on past eras (convicts and bushranging) in the mountain range area. They turn away from the developing social currents of the time, which in the 1890s were centred on the coastal cities and the outback plains. But the two novels should not be seen as inferior forerunners of the literature of the 1890s; they stand as major works of Victorian fiction in their own right.

The fabled decade of the nineties, associated with Henry Lawson, the *Bulletin* and bush mateship nationalism, came to have a special status in Australian culture. Writers had earlier given their imaginations free rein and imposed an English idyll in Australia; now they imposed an indigenous one, A sudden awareness of identity presaged, it was believed, a new start. Australia was for the first time revealing itself in all its splendour; the Australian story was one of inevitable progress. Though there was some truth in this view, it was more optimistic than the facts allowed. As at other times there were ups and downs. The year 1888 itself provided a stark contrast: it was the centenary of Australia's foundation, which gave rise to great hopes, but it was also the year of the land-boom crash, which caused severe economic depression throughout the 'great days' of the nineties. This led to a literature of harshness, loss and disillusionment, to which readers have only recently given due weight. Earlier generations selected the more optimistic material, but commentators like Leon Cantrell have emphasised the themes of destruction and alienation, and so restored the balance. In the 1890s the ups and downs previously evident existed simultaneously, and each was more intense—this is what made the decade unique, and a mixture of both is needed to convey the true picture. Some writers expressed utopian longings as a comforter against the depressing conditions; as Lawson wrote, 'the more the drought bakes them, the more inspired they seem to become'. Others swung between the two views, depending on their mood. In a famous debate staged in the *Bulletin* in 1892, Lawson argued for the superiority of the city and Paterson for the bush. Writers at the time emphasised the contrast between the two, but today we notice the similarities—much of the literature shows how badly off both city and country were.

Life on the open plains did not suit the intricate and exotic Victorian imagination, which could no longer take shelter in the wooded valleys of the ranges. Nor had the arcadian ideal worked. Large stations, struggling selectors and the nomadic life of outback workers fitted in with neither. The real problem was neither human villainy (as in Kingsley) nor natural disasters like flood, fire and drought (as in the squatting novels) but something more elusive. People came to Australia and to the bush full of high hopes and excitement, but purpose and meaning quickly drained away. Human life and human society seemed not to have taken root here. Boredom and montony are the keynotes of many Lawson stories: the drover's wife can find nothing to relieve the sameness as she walks along a track. This is a condition which the high action, conventional obstacles and neat conclusions of Victorian fiction could not accommodate.

The timing of the movement towards realism was especially fortunate for Australia, where the stark life of the open plains was being revealed. Writers in Australia had to abandon all preconceptions if they were to succeed in capturing the unique feeling of life lived here without discernible goals or progress. For this the short story was a suitable vehicle. It had little plot and could focus on endlessly repeated daily routines rather than, like the novel, on a sequence of incidents moving towards some resolution. This suited Australian writers who were creating psychological profiles of ordinary people struggling to survive in difficult conditions. The 1890s sensed that it was witnessing some important development, but was too close to define it accurately. For the first time the progressive unfolding of the Australian landscape was accompanied by a literary mode perfectly adapted to capturing it.

We see an example of this in Lawson's 'The Union Buries its Dead'. The people in the story have little to do, and use the union man's funeral to break the monotony. They have to attend the funeral for companionship, but they also have to suppress its meaning. They have no aims, and attempts to set up anything positive are immediately undercut, the main device by which the story works. Death was a key romantic scene, but here its importance is undermined. Emotions are non-existent. Lawson explicitly destroys the sentimental romantic ending—there was no wattle, no tears, no mate, no sunset. The expected chronology and movement of the story are broken up. What remains is the pleasurable vacancy which the characters inhabit.

The main short story collections dealing with selection and its vicissitudes are Lawson's *While the Billy Boils* (1896) and *Joe Wilson and his Mates* (1901), Steele Rudd's *On Our Selection* (1899) and Barbara Baynton's *Bush Studies* (1902). The three authors were influenced by their parents' struggle and their own briefer experiences in the bush. In many of the stories the males are anxious and obsessive about the success of their farms, and find it hard to accept their lot. The women and children form what human community there is in the unpromising environment, organising local gatherings (birthday parties, meals for visitors, church outings) as a relief from the cheerless prospects which lie around and ahead of them.

The three writers have different ways of coping with failure. Everything goes so wrong for the Rudd family that they just sit down and laugh at it all. They recognise their helplessness when kangaroos eat the grass, a horse is no good or fire burns out a paddock, and such incidents become memorable tales to be recalled and laughed about in the future. In this way the family passes into the traditions of folklore. But by the second book, *Our New Selection* (1903), the family has moved to a better block at Saddletop and is on the way to moderate success. At the other end of the spectrum are Barbara Baynton's stories of unrelieved gloom and psychological desolation. All civilised restraints have gone, hell is let loose, and women, potential carriers of human decency, bear the brunt of it all. Lawson's early stories avoid the extremes of blandness and despair. They brilliantly combine horror and humour, each keeping the other in check. The *Bulletin* achieved its balance and its greatness by being generously eclectic: it included all groups—city, country towns and bush, the wealthier and poorer classes—and many modes of expression—anecdotes, cartoons, editorials, sketches, agricultural information, analysis, criticism, documentary description, short stories, advertising and odd bits of information. The magazine had a unique rapport with its clientele, who were encouraged to be contributors as well as readers. It became part of the living social fabric. As Sylvia Lawson shows in *The Archibald Paradox* (1983), the whole enterprise was skilfully orchestrated as a public variety show with Archibald as circus master.

Joseph Furphy devised his own method of exploring the intractable problems presented by the Australian bush in *Such is Life* (1903). The book reverses the attitude of earlier squatting novels, siding with itinerant bullockies against squatters impeding their access to grass and water. Furphy's often-quoted send-up of Kingsley's 'slender-witted, virgin-souled, overgrown schoolboys' gives the misleading impression that his main objection to the earlier genre was a native dislike of the English new chum. Furphy's far more radical objection was to the absurdly fanciful pattern of plot in the Victorian novel; this caused him to improvise a new novel shape more suited to Australian life. Furphy's characters wander over the immense Riverina plain, occasionally coming across other groups. Their lives are without anchor or focus. To capture this inconclusiveness Furphy chose not the short story, but endlessness, which is another way of depicting life apparently without shape. But is there some faint pattern, some limit to utter randomness in these strange solitary circumstances? Like Trollope, Furphy finds these plains 'to be the fittest [place] for contemplation', and he ruminates on how chance meetings and actions may have meaning in the wider scheme of things. Furphy infiltrates this subtle thread of causation into the apparently seamless garment of his narrative so that the phrase 'such is life' becomes in the end something more than a meaningless shrug.

Australian society was changing imperceptibly in the decades around the turn of the century. The collapse of gold and the selections drove people back to the coastal cities, and the depression of the 1890s kept them there. Settling down, perhaps disconsolately, in the burgeoning suburbs was the second stage in the nation's history. The first stage, pioneering with great hopes for the new south land, reached its apogee in the 1890s and then declined. Australians now had to adjust themselves to these changed circumstances. In response to this a new group of influential writers came to the fore. In the first fifteen years of this century the following prose writers published their first books: Henry Handel Richardson, Norman Lindsay, Katharine Susannah Prichard, Vance Palmer, C. E. W. Bean, E. J. Banfield, Mary Grant Bruce, Louis Stone, Miles Franklin, Mrs Aeneas Gunn and the playwright Louis Esson.

The old rural tradition was continued, but in a modified form, in three minor masterpieces of Australian letters: Banfield's *Confessions of a Beachcomber* (1908), Mrs Gunn's *We of the Never Never* (1908), and Bean's *On the Wool Track* (1910). These books break the habit of generalising about the whole continent by evoking the atmosphere of a specific place. Each goes beyond the central plains of New South Wales and Queensland to a region on the fringe of settlement still occupied by its first settlers. All are documentary accounts, not fanciful adventure stories. Bean reported as a young journalist on all aspects of the wool trade (stations, bullock teams, shearers, river boats, transport, selling) on the Darling River basin, a factual version of Furphy whom Bean had not read at the time. Banfield went with his wife to Dunk Island on the northern Barrier Reef to live a life of seclusion. He gradually felt at home among the exotic fish, Aboriginal customs and strange blooms of the island. Mrs Gunn's book is based on pioneering Elsey station in the Northern Territory in 1902-3. The book's humour derives from her description of a woman's tentative acceptance in a male community, as well as from the collapse of all human schemes in the tropics. As in the Dad and Dave stories, the characters' way of coping is to laugh helplessly when everything goes wrong.

All three books insist that we must be sensitive to the particular environment of a region. Bean has a wonderful chapter on how the desert encroaches when fragile native grasses are destroyed by close-eating sheep. These books are written by inexperienced city people, who enjoy going back to basics and improvising a simple life in contrast to the overprotectiveness of modern civilisation. All three identify the 'essential Australia' as still existing in their area. Such remote and exotic places became images of vicarious perfection to increasingly settled Australians, a vein reworked by Ion Idriess and Frank Clune.

A new view of working-class life appears in literature after 1900. Much 1890s urban writing is external, visual and stereotyped: the bohemian writer notices the marks of weakness and marks of woe on the faces in the street, the ragged urchin children in foetid alleyways, the men in shoddy overcoats and the sad sisterhood of painted prostitutes. These writers remained by and large in the Mayhew tradition, describing isolated down-and-outs rather than ordinary people living at home with their families and working in shops and factories. But the characters of Louis Stone, Edward Dyson and C. J. Dennis are convincing because they depict mainstream patterns of urban life still familiar to us. In contrast to the earlier tone of social reform, the post-Federation writers sentimentally admire their lively and resilient working-class figures. Cardigan Street culture in Stone's *Jonah* (1911) is one of warm, communal gaiety, in spite of the struggle to get ahead. In Dyson's *Fact'ry Hands* (1906) and *Benno and Some of the Push* (1911), the factory girls ('the Beauties') are gently mocked for putting on middle-class airs and graces. The knockabout humour and badinage of the packers, pasters and pieceworkers in the clothing factory comes more from the cartoon world of Norman Lindsay than from the spirit of the nationalist school.

The main characters in these works—Jonah and Ada, Chook and Pinkey, Doreen and the Bloke, and the fact'ry hands—have two ambitions: money and marriage. The women aspire to a more genteel way of life. The males regress into restless larrikinism unless reluctantly dragged away from the boys and inducted into domesticity and middle-class ways. Settling down is felt as an affront to their masculinity. This is the price you pay for 'getting on in the world'. An equally important, but much less visible theme, is 'going down in the world'. We have seen this with Clara Morison, with Clarke's lower bohemia of the 1870s, with Boldrewood's ruined squatter and with unsuccessful selector families. The great crash of 1888-92 and its long aftermath added to these failures. The families of Henry Handel Richardson and Mary Grant Bruce were in financial decline. Twopeny understood how fragile prosperity was here. Louis Stone was particularly interested in this theme, and in *Jonah* he shows Mrs Partridge, the Grimes family and Mrs Perkins sinking on the social scale.

For half a century writers had been worried by the new relationship between imagination and reality in Australia. Lawson had instinctively found a balance between them in his stories. In *The Getting of Wisdom* (1910) Henry Handel Richardson confronted the problem explicitly. In the first half of the novel Laura tests her strength against the regimen of the school, but this is an unequal battle and in the second half Richardson is preoccupied with her portrait of Laura as a growing artist. Laura tries her hand at every type of fiction, from romantic novels to the realism of Ibsen, in order to get the balance right. She finally achieves success in an imagined story based on the countryside she was familiar with in northern Victoria. Laura concludes 'not a word of narration was true, but every word of it might have been true'. Richardson wrote *The Getting of Wisdom* to overcome these problems so she would be free to write her major work, *The Fortunes of Richard Mahony*.

Last century many writers had treated Australia as though it were a blank page, on which any image they desired could be imposed. But inhabiting Australia, and writing about it, were not as easy as that. The unique nature of the continent gradually asserted itself, as Trollope sensed on his visit. Idealised conceptions of Australia, especially of the bush, were largely put to rest by Henry Lawson in his 1893 *Bulletin* article 'Some Popular Australian Mistakes'. Released from the more self-indulgent habits of the past, fiction was in better shape to record the Australian people of this century unromantically settling down in the cities. But the dominance of realism was to grow and to prove difficult to challenge.

Notes

Most of the works of fiction mentioned in this chapter have been reprinted over the last twenty years; details can be found in the 'Select List of Reprints and New Editions' at the end of volume 2 of Dorothy Green's revised edition of H. M. Green *A History of Australian Literature* (1984-5). More than a dozen documentary narratives of Australian life were reprinted in the Penguin Colonial Facsimile series of 1973-4. For accounts of the arcadian dream in Australia, see Coral Lansbury, *Arcady in Australia* (1970) and F. G. Clarke, *The Land of Contrarieties* (1977). The factual basis of Howitt's novel can be found in his travel book *Land, Labour and Gold* (1855; reprinted 1972), of Kingsley's novel in J. S. D. Mellick's biography *The Passing Guest* (1983), and of Spence's novel in S. Magarey's biography *Unbridling the Tongues of Women* (1985). From these and other recent biographical studies, we know that many nineteenth-century novels had a closer base in actual experience than previously thought.

An appendix on 'Trollope's Australian Novels' is included in the 1967 reprint of Trollope's *Australia*, edited by P. D. Edwards and R. B. Joyce (1967). The short story in the nineteenth century is covered in Cecil Hadgraft's anthology, *The Australian Short Story Before Lawson* (1986). Michael Wilding has edited a selection of Clarke's short fiction in *Stories* (1983). Marcus Clarke's journalism on Melbourne from the late 1860s onwards has been selected by Laurie Hergenhan as *A Colonial City: High and Low Life* (1972), and writings on similar topics a decade later by 'The Vagabond' (John Stanley James) have been published by Michael Cannon as *The Vagabond Papers* (1969).

The Lawson-Paterson exchange in the *Bulletin* is included in Leon Cantrell's Portable Australian Authors anthology, *The 1980s: Stories, Verse and Essays* (1977). Steele Rudd's story is told by his son Eric Drayton Davis in *The Life and Times of Steele Rudd* (1976). The story of the *Bulletin* is retold in Patricia Rolfe's illustrated history, *The Journalistic Javelin* (1979), and of its editor J. F. Archibald in Sylvia Lawson's biography, *The Archibald Paradox* (1983).

For a recent study of E. J. Banfield see Michael Noonan, *A Different Drummer* (1983). Edward Dyson's factory tales are now usually found in a selection of his stories called *The Golden Shanty* (1963). Dorothy Green's study of Henry Handel Richardson, *Ulysses Bound* (1973), was issued in a revised edition as *Henry Handel Richardson and her Fiction* (1986). David Walker's *Dream and Disillusion* (1976) covers movements in Australian culture in the first decades of this century.

Chapter 16

DREAMS, VISIONS, UTOPIAS

VAN IKIN

The notion of the 'Great Australian Emptiness' preoccupied many writers in the nineteenth century; they sensed that Australia lacked history and distinct identity, and were conscious of Australia as a land of absences. According to William Woolls, an early settler,

> this colony is not only devoid of any venerable remains of antiquity, but . . . it also is deficient in those interesting scenes which contribute so much to enliven and dignify the histories of other countries . . . [Australians] have no plains of Marathon, no pass of Thermopylae, on which we may feed an honest pride; nor are our towns decorated with the trophies of ancient victories, and the headless busts of heroes long forgotten.

Nearly two decades later, in 1856, the critic Frederick Sinnett made the same point more humorously, noting that

> No Australian author can hope to extricate his hero or heroine, however pressing the emergency may be, by means of a spring panel and a subterranean passage, or such like relics of feudal barons.

As if in response to these comments, the 1890s spawned a series of adventure novels set in the physical emptiness of remote parts of Australia. Influenced by the work of Rider Haggard (especially *King Solomon's Mines,* 1885), these works typically feature a band of hearty heroes (sometimes with heroine in tow) who mount an expedition to the interior in response to some Lasseter-like rumour of vast gold deposits. The heroes' journey inevitably leads to sensationalised encounters with blacks, bushfires, floods, cannibals, dingoes, or crocodiles, and nearly always ends with the discovery of a 'lost tribe' of natives who are guardians of the gold. As Frederick Sinnett predicted, the heroes cannnot be saved from danger by a spring panel or subterranean passage, but there is usually a volcano conveniently primed to erupt just as the adventure reaches its climax. (The spectacular eruption of Krakatoa in August 1883 may account for the volcanic upheavals in Fergus Hume's *The Expedition of Captain Flick*, 1896, G. Firth Scott's *The Last Lemurian*, 1898, and Rosa Praed's *Fugitive Anne*, 1903).

Such romances fill the emptiness by defining the emerging nation through its distinctive geography. Marcus Clarke claimed that 'the dominant note of Australian scenery . . . [is] Weird Melancholy', and the romances confirm his view that 'The Australian mountain forests are funereal, secret, stern.' In *The Golden Lake* (1890), by W. Carlton Dawe, the hero speaks of 'the weird and mystic charm' of the bush and the 'magnificent desolation' and 'weird and terrific beauty' of the deserts. More significantly, the romances create a mythical history for Australia: their worshipful respect for Leichhardt and other explorers provides a source for the 'honest pride' sought by Woolls, and the mythology of lost tribes (with their ancient rites, their arcane lore, and their secret store of gold) fills the historical vacuum with delicious hints of an exotic hidden pre-history.

It was common for adventure writers to forge explicit links between Australia and the lore of history. The discovery of a 'lost race' or a 'hidden Kingdom' often prompted a speculation that this might be one of the lost tribes of Israel (thereby making Australia's emptiness the key to solving one of the riddles of history), and the anonymous author of 'Oo-a-deen: or, the Mysteries of the Interior Unveiled' (1847) goes so far as to link the story's lost civilisation of Mahanacumans with the Tower of Babel, portraying Australia as the final home of a mighty race which, after dispersion, founded the Hindu lands, China, and Malaya. The most ingenious link of all was forged by the speculation that Australia was the remnant of the mythical 'lost continent' of Lemuria. As late as 1902, Rosa Praed was able to assert that the uncanny 'primeval' quality of the Australian landscape—'the land in its hoariness, and the convulsions that have torn it, . . . and the gum trees of such weird conformation unlike all other trees'—could be explained by the notion that Australia was really ancient Lemuria. This idea is given fictional form in Praed's *Fugitive Anne* (1903) and G. Firth Scott's *The Last*

Lemurian: A Westralian Romance (1898), in which an old Aboriginal's tale of a mountain of gold in 'the Westralian Never Never' inspires the heroes to venture into the desert, encountering a lost race of yellow-skinned pygmies ruled by the giantess Tor Ymmothe, Queen of Lemuria, and protected by a splendidly ferocious Bunyip.

The romances define the emerging nation by its geography and landscape, and—above all—by its putative *past*. They probably convey the spirit of the age of exploration, but they give no sense of the future to which such exploration might lead. The heroes find their mountains or lakes of gold, but the wealth is inevitably consumed by the ubiquitous volcano. In the words of a character from Fergus Hume's *The Island of Fantasy* (c.1912), '"You can't trust volcanoes, sir. They are treacherous monsters, and when least expected break out in full fury."'

Other writers, more boldly, defined the emerging nation by its future. Bernard O'Dowd's long poem *The Bush* (1912) shows the transition from the backward-looking vision of the romances to the forward-looking utopian speculations of the nationalist-radical movement. One of the few intellectual poems of its time, *The Bush* envisions a utopian future Australia which has become a temple to 'Freedom, Truth and Joy'. Like the earlier adventure writers, O'Dowd links this splendid future to past world history, arguing that 'Great Australia' is 'a prophecy to be fulfilled':

All that we love in olden lands and lore
  Was signal of her coming long ago!
Bacon foresaw her, Campanella, More
  And Plato's eyes were with her star aglow!

Australia is claimed to be 'the Eldorado of old dreamers'; 'She is Eutopia, she is Hy-Brasil'; Australia 'is the whole world's legatee'. This may not be so very different from asserting that Australia is lost Lemuria, but it does at least link the 'discovery' of an Australian past with a distinctively Australian future. Furthermore, O'Dowd is able to work the mundane *present* into his schema, satisfying William Woolls' demand for heroes by predicting that 'the farmer grubbing box-trees on the flat' and 'the miner cradling washdirt by the creek' will be the subjects of future true-blue Homeric epics eulogising the founders of this utopia. In the words of A. R. Chisholm, *The Bush*:

lifts us out of the immediate and thus makes up for our (comparative) lack of history. It brings out the fact that Australian culture is rooted in a very ancient past, and moving on towards a very long future, thus transcending the brief awkwardness of colonialism, and putting itself into the long perspective of anthropological time.

O'Dowd never suggests that Australia can expect to glide into an inevitable, predestined future. *The Bush* stresses that the new nation 'shall be as we, the Potter, mould: / Altar or tomb, as we aspire [or] despair', and this message is emphasised in O'Dowd's earlier, more celebrated poem, 'Australia' (1903). Beginning with yet another image of Australia-in-history ('Last sea-thing dredged by sailor Time from Space'), the poem stresses that Australians must make a choice about the direction their fledgling nation will take. Australia can replicate the social ills and injustices of Britain and Europe, failing to learn from their mistakes and becoming nothing more than 'a new demesne for Mammon to infest'—or it can take the path towards a better world and establish itself as the 'Delos of a coming Sun-God's race'.

Numerous Australian writers shared this lofty vision; in fact, O'Dowd was largely giving eloquent expression to attitudes and ideas which were already current and established. Summarising the similarities between these works, A. A. Phillips states:

> In all these writers there is the same belief in the importance of the Common Man, the same ability to present him without condescension of awkwardness, the same square-jawed 'dinkum' determination to do without the fripperies, the modes—and sometimes the graces—of aesthetic practice, the same unembarrassed preference for revealing the simple verities rather than the sophistications of human nature.

Seizing upon these superficial similarities, commentators such as Vance Palmer and Vincent Buckley have presented these writers as part of 'the legend of the nineties', grouping them together as 'utopians', or, like A. A. Phillips, gathering them under 'the democratic theme'. Unfortunately, whilst such accounts may have been immensely useful in their day, they share a number of serious deficiencies. They completely ignore a significant body of utopian fictions; they do not perceive the need to pay attention to the *differences* between utopian works (including those differences which underlie their apparent similarities); and they fail to concede the difficulties involved in the use of words such as 'utopian' or 'democratic'.

'The Monster Mine' (1845), a brief prose sketch by P.G.M., shows that the utopian impulse pre-dates the legendary 1890s by nearly half a century. Supposedly writing in the year 1945, using a device called the electrophonotypographical chair, the narrator extols the material prosperity bestowed by a century of wealth derived from a monster-sized copper mine in South Australia; for him, social progress is measured in bricks-and-mortar, and Australia's identity is to be located in its future potential, not in its past. (One wonders, though, if O'Dowd—with his worries about Mammon—would use the word 'utopian' to describe social improvement achieved through a mere fattening of wallets?) A materialistic 'progress ethic' also underlies Barcroft Boake's poem 'A Vision Out West' (1897), which traces the history of the Australian outback from the 'dim, long-forgotten age' when the dead heart was an inland sea through to the splendid day when 'vast colonies of men' travel inland from 'the sea-coast hills' to enliven the interior with 'a goodly city' of 'proud homes' and a network of 'spacious' roads for electric cars. Despite the continued focus upon tangible material achievement, Boake's utopianism is very different from that of P.G.M. Where P.G.M. sees wealth as the key to progress, Boake looks to technology (particularly the use of electrical energy) and offers no comment on the need for wealth to develop technology. And whilst 'The Monster Mine' seems concerned only with mundane 'creature comforts' (conveying the idea that It Would Be Very Nice to Live in a Prosperous Society), 'A Vision Out West' is also concerned with the stature and morale of the human spirit (the idea that It Would Be a Splendid Achievement for Man to Bring Civilisation to the Wilderness).

Robert Dixon has argued in *The Course of Empire* (1986) that the founding of a 'goodly city' was an emblem of civilisation's triumph over nature, and Boake's 'Vision Out West' certainly upholds this mystique. But if some saw the city as cornerstone to a brighter future, others recorded the flaws in that vision. A. B. Paterson's 'Song of the Future' (1923) retraces the path of Boake's 'Vision', picturing the development of the outback from the days when it was a land 'all unknown' to the triumphal moment when 'great busy cities' stand in the place where once 'the wild man's boomerang was thrown'. Paterson acknowledges the mystique of city-building, boastfully claiming that:

> nothing in the ages old,
> In song or story written yet
> On Grecian urn or Roman arch, . . .
> Could braver histories unfold
> Than this bush story.

But he also concedes the failure of the grand venture, admitting that 'Within our streets men cry for bread', and that

> Our willing workmen, strong and skilled,
> Within our cities idle stand,
> And cry aloud for leave to toil . . .
> [While] The stunted children come and go
> In squalid lanes and alleys black.

The ironic title of William Lane's novel *The Workingman's Paradise* (1892) heralds not only an attack upon the mystique of the city but also a kind of utopianism based upon radically different assumptions. Lane's account of city life in Sydney makes it clear that the 'goodly city' has not yet been built—and, moreover, will not be built whilst ever man persists in treating nature as his plaything, rather than as his model. Rejecting the bricks-and-mortar outlook completely, Lane asserts that 'civilisation has failed' and proposes a metaphysical socialist vision to revive it.

Ned Hawkins, a bushman, has come to Sydney to visit his childhood sweetheart, Nellie Lawton, who turns out to be a committed socialist. Their reunion occurs in 1888-9, as events are building towards the 1890 maritime strike, and the action of Part I of the novel concerns Nellie's determined effort to transform Ned's unthinking unionism into committed socialism. As a first step towards this political education, Nellie takes Ned to see 'a little bit of real Sydney', and there follows what Michael Wilding describes as 'a relentless proletarian realism . . . a remorseless encounter with the over-crowded slums, sweated labour in the garment industry, the long hours of shop assistants and waitresses'. Ned is introduced to a circle of bourgeois socialists who hold that their ideology is 'the total force, the imperishable breath, of the universe', and in Part II he emerges as an active and committed unionist, helping to organise the notorious Queensland shearers' strike of 1891.

Lane's socialist utopianism is mixed with a strand of metaphysical thinking. In lines of verse specially written for *The Workingman's Paradise* by F. J. Broomfield, it is asserted that

> . . . the harmony of heaven and the music of the spheres,
> And the ceaseless throb of Nature and the flux and flow of years,
> Are rudely punctuated with the drip of human tears.

Social injustice, in short, is seen as an affront to the good order of the universe. Such a notion of natural cosmic harmony is central to Lane's thinking, and all ills can be measured against it. Sweated labour is thus wrong because it robs human beings of their god-given energy and denies them access to the sun and fresh air; excessive wealth in the hands of one person is wrong, *not* because that person may not have earned the wealth, but because the imbalance is an affront to cosmic harmony.

A significant feature of *The Workingman's Paradise* is its attempt to reverse certain prevailing social stereotypes and turn them in the direction of utopianism. Socialists are not the shifty, conspiratorial plotters of social stereotype; they are shown to be urbane, civilised folk who live in nice (but not extravagant) homes and talk eloquently about culture while they sip their wine. Nor is the bushman allowed to remain the easy-going, shallow-thinking figure of stereotype. At the beginning of his political education, Ned is inclined to take refuge in the hypothetical opposition between town and country living, carelessly allowing himself to believe that the problems of the city are different from those of the bush. But he is eventually forced to realise that the socialist movement represents the interests of *all* labour.

The verse of Henry Lawson is also uneasy with prevailing stereotypes, though in Lawson's case the uneasiness seems to derive from a fear that the stereotypes might be accurate. This possibility can be seen by relating the image of the average Australian in 'Andy's Gone with Cattle' and 'Middleton's Rouseabout' (1896) to the revolutionary politics of 'Freedom on the Wallaby', 'The Star of Australasia', and 'Faces in the Street' (all 1896). Andy the drover is not exactly a passionate utopian advocate. More like Lane's Ned Hawkins, he just wears a 'cheerful face' in times when 'things are slackest', he merely whistles happily at his chores when 'Fortune frowns her blackest', and his main achievement seems to lie in keeping the cattle-station gates in good repair. Andy is a stoical survivor, a man too wise to set his sights too high, and as such he is similar to Middleton's rouseabout (also named Andy) who is content to live for the sake of a 'Pound a week and his Keep' and who 'Hasn't any opinions, / Hasn't any "idears"'. It is worth noting that this image of the common man as crass conservative is also found in Louis Esson's play *The Time is Not Yet Ripe* (1912) and Randolph Bedford's novel *The Snare of Strength* (1905). Despite this picture of the complacent common man, Lawson's more stridently political verse not only insists that Australians have opinions and ideas, it also calls upon them to back those ideas with anger and action:

> Once I cried: 'Oh, God Almighty! if Thy might doth still
> endure,
> 'Now show me in a vision for the wrongs of Earth a cure.'
> And, lo! with shops all shuttered I beheld a city's street,
> And in the warning distance heard the tramp of many feet, . . .
> And soon I saw the army that was marching down the street.
>
> ('Faces in the Street')

> There comes a point that we will not yield, no matter if
> right or wrong,
> And man will fight on the battle-field while passion and
> pride are strong . . .
>
> ('The Star of Australasia')

In one of the most rousing statements of revolutionary fervour, Lawson's 'Freedom on the Wallaby' concludes with the threat-cum-promise that

> We'll make the tyrants feel the sting
> Of those that they would throttle;
> They needn't say the fault is ours
> If blood should stain the wattle.

Given Lawson's account of the complacency of the two Andy characters, these lines carry the implication that it *will* be 'our fault' if (through sheer gormlessness and gutlessness) injustice is accepted and blood does *not* stain the wattle . . .

Lawson's first publication, 'A Song of the Republic' (1887), shows that his utopian notions are similar to those of Lane and O'Dowd. In a call-to-arms which O'Dowd was later to echo, 'A Song of the Republic' urges all Australians to 'Banish from under your bonny skies / Those old-world errors and wrongs and lies'. Then, in reasoning reminiscent of Lane's ideas, it points out that such errors are 'Making a hell in a Paradise / That belongs to your sons and you'. Yet there are also ways in which Lawson's vision differs from that of Lane and O'Dowd, and these departures are just as important. In O'Dowd's verse the greatest enemy of utopia seems to be lethargy or apathy—the inertia which would prevent Australians from seizing and moulding the 'Eldorado' which is within their reach. Lawson, like Lane, sees the enemy differently, in terms of social class and individual elements of the society: 'toffs' and 'tyrants' are the foe in 'Freedom on the Wallaby', and it is 'the apathy of wealthy men' which causes the anger on the 'Faces in the Street'. Lane sneers at Ned Hawkins for being content to accept 'what's fair' and settling for reasonable pay and 'rations at a fair figure'; Lane shows such a moderate stance to be naive, pointlessly self-sacrificing, and both tactically and ideologically unsound. But whilst Lawson acknowledges the debilitating effect of a readiness to accept a 'Pound a week and his keep', Lawson is greatly attracted by the concept of 'what's fair' and is prepared to value human judgements (particularly in the areas of 'fair play' and mateship) over the dictates of ideology. Thus, whilst Lawson, Lane, and O'Dowd may all be talking about a utopian vision, they are by no means talking about the *same* vision.

Joseph Furphy's *Such is Life* (1903) extends the range even further, introducing an alert, ironic awareness of the problems involved in utopian speculation. On the publication of *My Brilliant Career* in 1901, Furphy wrote to the young Miles Franklin, urging her to acquire 'a patient faith in the Scheme of the Universe—that is to say, a rational appraisement of the value of life, and a definite theory of its purpose'. The narrator of *Such is Life,* the pompous and dim-witted (but likeable) Tom Collins, devotes his narrative to a similar project, outlining 'a fair picture of Life, as that engaging problem has presented itself to me'. In pursuit of this aim Collins reiterates most of the familiar utopian arguments, exhorting his reader to 'think how measurably higher are the possibilities of a Future than the memories of any Past since history began'. He describes Australia as a 'recordless land' which is 'committed to no usages of petrified injustice . . . clogged by no fealty to shadowy idols, . . . cursed by no memories of fanaticism and persecution'. Lauding 'the Coming Australian', he asserts that 'we're going to have a race of people in these provinces such as the world has never seen before'. Tom Collins, then, is a staunchly nationalist advocate for a utopian future—but Furphy has designed the narrative in such a way that it qualifies (and sometimes even undercuts) this argument.

A specific example of this involves the notions of mateship and fair play, each of which is crucial to the development of a utopian future. Whilst observing that bushmen seem genuinely to *believe* in these values, Furphy is quick to show that their behaviour does not match their ideals. Teamsters gathered round a camp-fire criticise their mates as ` soon as backs are turned, Tom Collins feels no compassionate mateship for the luckless Andy Glover, and ideals of fairness are jeopardised by a general acceptance of pilfering and sharp dealing. These observations, of course, are not new (for Lawson's stories are alert to the absurdities and breaches of the mateship code), but in Furphy's work they herald a set of deeper, more serious reservations.

Sketching 'A Day on a Selection', Lawson satirised the gap between ideals and reality by means of an amusing dialogue in which the male selector's pompous discourse on utopian ideas is constantly interrupted (and undercut) by the intrusion of stray chooks and misbehaving children. The structure and concerns of *Such is Life* allow Furphy to present this theme in more sober terms, raising a stimulating question-mark over the whole enterprise of utopian speculation. This is done by creating a series of disparities. On top of the differences between behaviour and ideals, the novel emphasises the disparity between the garrulous, pseudo-learned Collins and the average bushmen who are his exemplars. It also stresses the disparity between Collins' theory about life and the reality upon which that theory is based (for Collins often fails to notice what is happening before his very eyes), and—on top of *that*—it reveals the disparity between Collins' theory and that of others (such as Stewart). The reader is thus encouraged to nurture a healthy mistrust of grandiose theoretical pronouncements, weighing them carefully against the pluralist diversity of human types and the fundamental fallibility of the human character and intellect. Furphy is not *opposed* to utopian enthusiasms, but he is wholesomely sceptical about their practicality.

Furphy's misgivings seem justified. It is clear that even the body of recognised utopian writers could not agree amongst themselves about matters of aim and emphasis, and the situation becomes even more dire if one considers the utopians whose works have been ignored.

The neglected works are those which draw upon elements of science fiction or fantasy (though the reasons for neglect would probably have as much to do with judgements about prose style and the plausibility of the ideas expressed as with the abandonment of realism). *The Coming Terror: A Romance of the Twentieth Century* (1894), by S. A. Rosa, pictures a popular revolution which leads to price-fixing, equal pay for female workers, and legislation to set maximum daily work hours and a minimum weekly wage. However, in contrast to the ideals of the time, Rosa's utopia will have nothing of democracy, preferring the rule of a benevolent dictator:

> for centuries the people had been swindled, plundered, and oppressed by corrupt ruling gangs called Parliaments. They would now see what could be done by the rule of one good, wise, and capable man.

Conversely, Joseph Fraser's *Melbourne and Mars: My Mysterious Life On Two Planets* (1889) suggests that it is the education system, not parliament, which is the doorway to utopia. Fraser's central character—an ageing Melburnian who leads a bizarre double life as a child in the utopian society of Mars—is able to see that the rigid Australian educational system holds back the nation's material progress and scars the psyche of its citizens, whilst the Martian method brings utopia within reach. *Melbourne and Mars* is a notable work because it combines a materialistic admiration for the 'goodly city' (and its electric flying cars) with a genuine concern for the spiritual and psychological aspects of utopia.

Miles Franklin used the pages of *My Brilliant Career* to sound a warning against the excessively masculine orientation of the nationalist and utopian movements, and other writers shared her alarm. Though not published until 1984, Catherine Helen Spence's *Handfasted* (1879) offers a divergent agenda for utopian reform, with an emphasis upon change to marriage customs. Isolated from the rest of the world, the utopian Commonwealth of Columba has evolved a system of trial marriage called 'handfasting'. An Australian traveller falls in love with a Columban and takes her back to his own society, triggering a series of conflicts which test the utopian system. Unlike other utopian writers (who tend to exhibit their reformist proposals without considering the practical problems of implementation), Spence provides an unflinching account of the difficulties faced by the couple when they try to practise handfasting in Victorian England. Unflinching, too, is Mary Ann Moore-Bentley's *A Woman of Mars: or, Australia's Enfranchised Woman* (1901), in which a Martian girl is sent to Earth to see to 'the emancipation of Woman and the regeneration of the [human] race'. In the Martian view, these two goals are inextricably linked, for the question of 'the Woman's Right' is 'the bedrock foundation upon which a statesman [*sic*!] must seek to establish a happy, progressive social State'. This is nothing less than a smart slap-in-the-face to the ideas and assumptions of the better-known utopians.

William Lane stands apart from this rebuke, for *The Workingman's Paradise* shows genuine concern for 'the Woman's Right'. But there is another charge that Lane must face. Virtually all the utopian writers had no place in their vaunted scheme for Aborigines or the Chinese; the concepts of democracy, equality, and a fair go did not extend to those denied a white skin. William Lane can fairly be called a racist, for his attacks upon the Chinese are abusive, vitriolic, and tinged with loathing for the colour, appearance, and smell of the race. Most other writers, though, should be judged somewhat less harshly, for in some cases theirs were sins of omission (a failure to mention coloured people in cases where their interests were clearly involved), and in others their racial prejudice was motivated by an apparently genuine fear that Australian culture (and its utopian hopes) faced inundation under Asiatic hordes. War with Asiatic invaders has been the theme of numerous works, including William Lane's *White or Yellow? A Story of the Race War of A.D. 1908* (serialised in the *Boomerang* in 1888), *The Coloured Conquest* (1904) by 'Rata' (Thomas Roydhouse), *The Australian Crisis* (1909) by C. H. Kirmess, and more recently *The Invasion* by John Hay (1968). Utopianism and racism come together in Erle Cox's *Out of the Silence* (1925), in which the sole survivor of a prehistoric Earthly civilisation proposes to turn the present world into a utopia by wiping out every last member of the 'coloured races'. Cox's protagonist, a typical average Aussie named Alan Dundas, overcomes some initial reservations to conclude that this is a pretty good idea.

One other figure stands alone in the utopian ranks. Though Christopher Brennan looked to European attitudes and influences at the same time as fellow writers were wrapt in a nationalistic fervour, his *Poems [1913]* nevertheless reflects a 'paradisal instinct'. But Brennan's utopia is reached through the psyche, and has nothing to do with society, politics, or reformist schemes. Revolted by the material world of 'heartless homes' and 'unending pavement', Brennan turns from 'the inhuman town' to seek an Eden of spiritual self-sufficiency, a state of 'natural ecstasy'.

Strangely enough, it is Brennan's utopianism which seems to hold sway in the late 1980s. M. Barnard Eldershaw's novel *Tomorrow and*

Tomorrow and Tomorrow (1983; first published in slightly abridged form as *Tomorrow and Tomorrow* in 1947), demonstrated convincingly that utopia is an elusive grail with a different meaning in every age, and contemporary writers of speculative fiction have produced no enthusiastic utopian visions, preferring to examine the dangers and pitfalls of utopian fervour. The most notable of these works are *Beloved Son* (1978) and *Vaneglory* (1981) by George Turner, and *Valencies* (1983) by Rory Barnes and Damien Broderick. Judging by critical acclaim, the utopianism of the present is best conveyed by David Ireland's *A Woman of the Future* (1979) and Peter Carey's *Bliss* (1981), both of which, like Brennan's poems, seek an Eden of the spirit.

Notes

The 'Great Australian Emptiness' is a phrase used by Patrick White in his essay 'The Prodigal Son', *Australian Letters,* I, 3 (1958). The other quotations in the first paragraph are from William Woolls, *Miscellanies in Prose and Verse* (1838), and Frederick Sinnett, 'The Fiction Fields of Australia', *Journal of Australasia,* I (1856).

The standard accounts of Australia's literary utopians are provided by (in chronological order): Vance Palmer, *The Legend of the Nineties* (1954), A. A. Phillips, *The Australian Tradition: Studies in a Colonial Culture* (1958), Vincent Buckley, 'Utopianism and Vitalism', *Quadrant,* 3, 2 (1958-9). Russel Ward, *The Australian Legend* (1958), provides a detailed account of the general nature and development of the bush ethos. In general, these works seek to elucidate and promote the myth of the 1890s.

A more questioning view is taken by G. A. Wilkes, 'The Eighteen Nineties', *Arts,* I (1958), but the limitations and shortcomings of the myth of the 1890s are discussed most fully in G. A. Wilkes, *The Stockyard and the Croquet Lawn: Literary Evidence for Australia's Cultural Development* (1981).

The above works by Palmer and Phillips, together with those by Wilkes, provide the main accounts of Lawson and Furphy as utopian writers; more recent critical studies tend to concentrate upon aspects of form. Bernard O'Dowd's utopianism is discussed in Hugh Anderson, *The Poet Militant: Bernard O'Dowd* (1969), and W. H. Wilde, *Three Radicals* (1969). *The Workingman's Paradise* is discussed in Michael Wilding, 'William Lane's *The Workingman's Paradise:*

Pioneering Socialist Realism', *Words and Worlds: Studies in the Social Role of Verbal Culture*, edited by S. Knight and S. N. Mukherjee (1983), and Van Ikin, 'Political Persuasions: *The Workingman's Paradise', Westerly*, 28, 1 (1983). The ideas and work of Louis Esson are discussed in David Walker's *Dream and Disillusion: A Search for Australian Cultural Identity* (1976).

Lemurian speculation and the early romances are canvassed in J. J. Healy, 'The Lemurian Nineties', *Australian Literary Studies*, 8 (1978).

The work of Catherine Helen Spence is set in a biographical context in Susan Magarey, *Unbridling the Tongues of Women* (1985). The 'neglected' utopian writers are discussed in Nan Bowman Albinski, 'A Survey of Australian Utopian and Dystopian Fiction', *Australian Literary Studies*, 13 (1987), and in the introduction to Van Ikin (ed.), *Australian Science Fiction* (1982)—a book which also contains brief excerpts from some of these out-of-print works.

PART IV

Chapter 17

PERCEPTIONS OF AUSTRALIA, 1915-1965

BRIAN KIERNAN

Writing *A Short History of Australia* (1916) during the early years of the Great War, the Professor of History at the University of Melbourne, Ernest Scott, could boast that although the story he told began with a blank space on mariners' charts, it ended with the inscription of a new name on the map of the world, that of Anzac. More clearly than any other historic event—the founding of the colony, the goldrushes and Eureka, or Federation—Gallipoli focused Australians' perceptions of themselves and how they wanted others to see them. It signified the fulfilment of long-standing expectations that a new strain of the British race and culture would eventually evolve in response to the new country's different soil and climate. In his prewar accounts of his travels down the Darling, C. E. W. Bean had joined the generations before him who had found in the bush the true Australian character and, by extension, the distinctive characteristics of the new nation. The first volume of his *Official History of Australia in the War of 1914-1918* (1921) celebrated these.

According to Bean, the expected evolution had advanced more rapidly in Australia than in any other British dominion. Climate and an active outdoor life had already differentiated a new type in this embryonic great nation, 'the body wiry and the face clean, easily lined, thin-lipped'. The new type spoke with a distinctive accent and subscribed to a creed inherited from the gold miner and the bushman, 'of which the chief article was that a man should at all times, and at any cost, stand by his mates'. Bean's Anzac marked what Russel Ward, towards the end of the period here under survey, called 'the apotheosis of the nomad tribe': he was the embodiment of those traits that the historical and literary imagination had perceived in the experience of convicts and settlers, gold-diggers and shearers. Even though Bean knew that, statistically, his digger was just as likely to come from the cities as the bush, he still saw him as having deeply implanted in his consciousness memories of that 'mysterious half-desert country where men have to live the lives of strong men,' memories which he himself had as a result of his travels along the Darling.

The war consolidated a growing sense of nationhood, though still nationhood within the Empire; patriotism and imperial loyalty were comfortably compatible. Until well after World War II, probably most Australians, and they were overwhelmingly of British descent, saw themselves as W. K. Hancock described them to an English readership in 1930, as 'independent Australian Britons'. His *Australia*, in a series on Empire nations, discerned the beginnings of a national literary tradition in the poetry of Henry Kendall and Bernard O'Dowd, and the prose of Lawson, Furphy and other *Bulletin* writers. To him, the challenge for the postwar generation was to build on this tradition inherited from the previous century. While the literary tradition, like that of painting, was still at a descriptive stage emphasising local colour, the novelists Henry Handel Richardson, Martin Boyd and Barnard Eldershaw had discerned the significance of Australian history as 'the sending down of roots in a new soil'.

Other contemporary writers Hancock mentions are 'Furnley Maurice' (Frank Wilmot), Vance Palmer, Katharine Susannah Prichard and Louis Esson, who with others formed the Pioneer Players, an attempt to found a national theatre that would express 'the spirit of the country'. Although the Players enjoyed little success with their seasons in Melbourne between 1922-6, they formed a concentration of talents useful for considering the perceptions of Australia which nationalistic writers projected after the Great War. At the same time it needs to be acknowledged that other writers were reacting against nationalism and aspiring towards modernist sophistication or cosmopolitan traditionalism; for example, the younger writers associated with the Sydney journal *Vision* (1922-4), Jack Lindsay, Kenneth Slessor and R. D. FitzGerald, who scorned 'verse about shearers and horses'.

As models for an Australian theatre that would be popular yet serious, Louis Esson had in mind innovative contemporary European and American companies. The character types, situations and settings employed by the Pioneer playwrights, however, were broadly continuous with those found in prewar writing. Esson and Palmer were deliberately attempting to build on the tradition of Lawson and Furphy. For Palmer, Lawson 'had opened up a new world for us in our youth', and he gained Lawson's permission to adapt the short story 'Telling Mrs Baker' for the stage. Palmer was also attempting to win wider recognition for Furphy. Esson agreed that Lawson's shearers and other bushmen represented the 'real Australians', and his own most admired play, the one-act *The Drovers* (1919), expresses a stoicism reminiscent of Lawson's short stories from the early 1890s. For Prichard, Lawson provided a point to depart from: she felt his vision of Australia was 'grey and distressing', and she wanted to give her writing a colour that would express the contrasting 'beauty and vigour of our lives'.

The plays Esson wrote after the war have much in common with those he had written earlier. *Digger's Rest* (or 'The Battler'), written in 1921, was the Players' first production; set up-country, its mode was that of already dated Abbey Theatre 'country comedy'. The three-act *Mother and Son*, written the same year and also set up-country, bears similarities to his bleak one-act *Dead Timber*, first produced in 1910. The full-length, urban low-life melodrama *The Bride of Gospel Place*, produced in 1926, has a class setting reminiscent of the larrikins and doxies in his one-act *The Woman Tamer*, also first produced in 1910. As well as presenting contemporary urban sub-cultures, or more conventionally 'typical' slices of up-country or outback life, the playwright seeking to capture 'the spirit of the country' could also set his scenes in the past and reveal the historical roots of the national character. Esson's last complete works were his Eureka play *The Southern Cross* (posthumously published in 1946), partly inspired by *Australia Felix* (1917), the first volume of Henry Handel Richardson's trilogy *The Fortunes of Richard Mahony* (1930), and 'The Quest', about the visionary voyager De Quiros. Stewart Macky, one of the company's founding members, based two plays of convict life on tales that Price Warung had written in the 1890s. Prichard dramatised an incident involving convicts from her prize-winning novel of 1915, *The Pioneers* (which was first adapted for the screen in 1916). Her first full-length play, *Brumby Innes*, written in conjunction with the novel *Coonardoo* (1929), shared its theme of brutal white exploitation of the Aborigines, especially the women. Esson's one-act *Andeganora*, produced in the 1930s, had a similar outback setting and social concern.

In 1927, after the players had disbanded, *Brumby Innes* won a prize offered by the Sydney magazine *Triad*. Writing to Palmer,

Esson hoped that the production promised for the winning submission would provide the first professional performance to date of any 'decent' Australian play. (In fact, *Brumby Innes* was not to be produced until the 1970s, in Melbourne's 'alternative' theatre.) Esson added that '*On Our Selection* and *The Sentimental Bloke* have done a lot of harm'. These adaptations for the stage of Steele Rudd's comic tales of selection life and C. J. Dennis's larrikin-dialect verses were among the most successful examples of popular indigenous theatre. First produced in 1912, *On Our Selection* ran repeatedly on stage through the 1920s, was filmed by Raymond Longford in 1920 (sequels followed in the 1930s) and, as 'Dad and Dave', it was adapted for decades of radio serialisation, and eventually became a television series. Longford filmed *The Bloke* in 1919 and *Ginger Mick* the next year; both were praised, here and overseas, for the realism of their types. He also filmed *The Pioneers* in 1926. Frank Beaumont Smith, the entrepreneur behind Bailey's long-running stage adaptation of Lawson's *While the Billy Boils*, held the film rights to Lawson's and Paterson's work. In 1920 he filmed *The Man From Snowy River*, and *While the Billy Boils* the year after. As Margaret Williams' study of the popular stage and John Tulloch's of early cinema show, the stock of theatrical styles, situations and settings (with the constant contrasting of country and city values) passed into the cinema. The Pioneer playwrights, although they attempted to be critical realists and to distance themselves from such base entertainments, drew on the same stereotypes.

The Pioneer playwrights sought 'the spirit of the country' on remote selections, in isolated country towns, on outback stations or in the Never Never. The spirit they found was defiant in the face of fire, flood or drought, and the repressive social systems met by convicts, selectors, gold-diggers at Eureka and striking shearers. After 1915, another generation of diggers, stoically confronting the ultimate enemy, could be assimilated into the historical legend of the formation of the Australian character in adversity. *Smith's Weekly*, founded in 1919 as 'the defender of the Digger', typified him as 'a white-collar city worker with a larrikin streak'. The past thirty years have seen much critical analysis, and debunking, of the self-images that post-World War I Australia inherited from the nineteenth century, as though legends were verifiable by, or vulnerable to, statistics. Since the 1970s, commentators have been less interested in debunking and more in discerning how such national myths are produced and propagated, and how they function. In the face of the economic and political crises of the 1920s and 1930s, and the social divisiveness they revealed, popular entertainments of that time could be seen as sentimentally resolving, or evading, these by inviting audiences, overwhelmingly urban, to share vicariously in a common pioneering past.

It had been observed as a paradox, from at least the end of last century, that, while Australia was among the most urbanised of nations, its cultural images and literary settings were drawn preponderantly from beyond the life familiar to the majority of its inhabitants. Almost invariably, the explanation given was that provided by T. Inglis Moore when introducing *Best Australian One-Act Plays* in 1937: 'in the country, in the life of the bush . . . the Australian character has been most fully developed and the tone of the national atmosphere set.' Between the wars, film and radio, especially ABC drama, propagated aspects of the bush legend to vastly larger audiences than the Pioneer Players had even contemplated. When a popular and serious theatre emerged after World War II, with Sumner Locke Elliot's *Rusty Bugles* (1948) and Ray Lawler's *Summer of the Seventeenth Doll* (1957), it played both with and within the received stereotypes of the national character.

But by the end of the 1920s, as Vance Palmer observed in *Louis Esson and the Australian Theatre* (1948), most literary activity was being directed away from poetry and drama towards the novel. At the end of the period this chapter considers, Harry Heseltine surveying fiction since the 1920s, and employing the metaphor of organic development, saw novelists between the wars as primarily responsible for the transformation of an earlier 'pugnacious nationalism' into 'a mature sense of nationhood'. Employing 'the saga, the picaresque and the documentary', they created 'an imaginative vision of the country's past and present'. As well as the historical novels of Richardson, Boyd and Barnard Eldershaw, there were also, notably, those of Miles Franklin under her own name and later those under her pseudonym Brent of Bin Bin, and Brian Penton's *Landtakers* (1934) and *Inheritors* (1936). And as well as imaginative historical exploration there was also geographical. Prichard's novels set in the fictional present explore a variety of locales and communal ways of life: the opal fields of far western New South Wales in *Black Opal* (1921), the karri forests of Western Australia in *Working Bullocks* (1926), station life in the outback of Western Australia in *Coonardoo* (1929), and so on through successive novels.

In a recent book reappraising the 'literary evidence for Australian cultural development', G. A. Wilkes remarks of the far-north outback setting of some of the most notable novels between the wars, including Xavier Herbert's *Capricornia* (1938), that it became 'a new "frontier"', and produced a literature in which 'the values of the 1890s are tested over again'. The country town or settled district furnished an even more common location for exploring varieties of distinctively Australian experience, as well as a variety of literary concerns and modes, as can be suggested by a spectrum of titles that range from realism in a traditional pastoral key to modernist preoccupations with alienated consciousness: Norman Lindsay's *Redheap* (1930), Kylie Tennant's *Tiburon* (1935), Leonard Mann's *Mountain Flat* (1939), Eleanor Dark's *Prelude to Christopher* (1934), and Patrick White's *Happy Valley* (1939). It could still be observed, though, that most fiction was set outside the cities in which the majority of the population lived, even if the bush depicted was on the cities' outskirts, in the Blue Mountains or the Dandenongs. Among obvious, outstanding exceptions to this were Christina Stead's *Seven Poor Men of Sydney* (1934) and Kylie Tennant's *Foveaux* (1939); but in general it was not until after the war that the contemporary city became a more familiar literary landscape, through such novels as Barnard Eldershaw's *Tomorrow and Tomorrow* (1947), Ruth Park's *The Harp in the South* (1948), and, perhaps most notoriously, Frank Hardy's *Power Without Glory* (1950).

As the Pioneer playwrights shared a stock of types and settings with film-makers and, later, radio dramatists, so novelists shared theirs with more popular writers. At all levels, there was interest in reading about the country's regions and history. *Walkabout* magazine began publishing in 1934, and travel books were extremely popular; one that has remained so is Francis Ratcliffe's *Flying Fox and Drifting Sand* (1938). Beginning with *Lasseter's Last Ride* in 1931, Ion Idriess wrote travel books, biographies of 'representative' Australians like Flynn of the Inland and Kidman the Cattle King, and novels of adventure set in remote areas. In the 1930s Frank Clune also began writing (or having ghosted for him, by P. R. Stephensen among others) books of travel, histories of bushrangers, and novels. Both he and Idriess averaged a book a year into the 1960s, books which were very successful commercially and which provided generations of readers with impressions of Australia's physical variety and colourful history.

Overseas visitors' impressions still, as in the previous century, stimulated local readers' perceptions of themselves and their country. D. H. Lawrence's visit in 1922 provided him with the experience for his quasi-autobiographical novel *Kangaroo* (1923); characteristically, his responses were intuitive, penetrating, and ambivalent. Somers, his protagonist, sees Sydney as a colonial imitation of London or New York, the bush as dismayingly empty and inhospitable. There seems to be no essential relationship between culture and nature; yet Somers comes to respond more positively to the easy-going egalitarianism of Australian society, even though he discovers in the returned diggers, secretly organised into a crypto-fascist militia, political forces similar to those that have driven him from Europe. This imaginative engagement with the Australian character, and the character of Australian society, by one of the most prominent, and controversial, of English writers stimulated writers here, as well as readers. More popular than fiction about Australia, though, were descriptive works intended for readers overseas, which aroused local curiosity in how others saw us.

An extraordinarily successful example of the travel book was *Cobbers* by the young Englishman Thomas Wood, which was reissued continuously after first appearing in 1934. Having completed a leisurely exploration of the geographical and historical variety of each state, Wood concluded that:

> to Australians as a whole, Australia is first and England close behind . . . they are as pro-British as they are pro-Australian. The intensely national feeling that was paraded in the '90s is not paraded now.

This persisting cultural alignment with England that Wood (like Hancock before him) had observed was noted also by C. Hartley Grattan, who had spent a couple of years here in the later 1930s researching a survey that would explain Australia to American readers. Like Wood's account from an English point of view, Grattan's *Introducing Australia* (1942) ran through a series of reissues and revisions until after the war, both in the United States and here, so that it also helped introduce Australia to the Australians.

In his introductory chapter 'As I See Australia', Grattan explained that he began his study by reading as widely as he could in Australian literature:

> The ideas about Australia and the Australians I got from reading Henry Lawson, Tom Collins [Furphy], Bernard O'Dowd, Shaw Neilson—even Marcus Clarke and Rolf Boldrewood—are still the foundations on which whatever understanding I have of Australia really rests.

Following his first visit in 1927, Grattan had published a pamphlet in the United States, *Australian Literature* (1929), with a preface by Nettie Palmer. Like Hancock, Grattan had contacts with the Palmers and others associated with the Pioneer Players, the first of these being Frank Wilmot. When Grattan edited the symposium *Australia* (1947) for the United Nations, Vance Palmer contributed the chapter on culture and H. M. Green, a fellow 'nationalist', that on literature. Grattan, sharing Palmer's enthusiasm for Furphy, was responsible for the 1948 American edition of 'the greatest book yet produced in Australia', *Such is Life*. The literary tradition that Palmer had seen imperilled after World War I, the literature of 'the common man', was, after World War II, being presented to the world as the dominant tradition. In *Introducing Australia*, Grattan had described it as 'a compound of sound learning, rebelliousness, ordered faith in the common man, and even more faith in the Australian future. What better tradition could any nation want?' Yet, sympathetic as Grattan was to what was still a minority literary culture—perhaps because it had more in common with the democratic American tradition than the English—he felt that 'utopian, republican, national democratic' values had been more alive in the previous century and were now being evoked nostalgically.

A note of nostalgia for a lost ethos can be detected in the major studies of the bush legend and the democratic or Lawson-Furphy tradition that appeared in newly affluent postwar Australia. Not even in the 1890s themselves, so consistently alluded to as the formative period in the nation's history, had there been such a concentrated concern with national identity as began in the 1950s. Issues of identity and tradition constituted a discourse in which historians, literary critics, art historians, and pundits of all persuasions engaged, at a time when Australian literature and history were beginning to be introduced into university and secondary school courses. Such courses were made possible by, and in turn stimulated, the publication of anthologies like C. B. Christesen's *Australian Heritage* (1949), collections of cultural essays like W. V. Aughterson's *Taking Stock* (1953), collections of records like C. M. H. Clark's *Select Documents in Australian History* (1950), and histories, both by imaginative writers, like Kylie Tennant's *Australia: Her Story* (1953), and professional historians. Tracing (or disputing) the emergence of national characteristics in the past these writers were conscious of living in a very different present; Crawford, for example, writing that Australia had still to forge 'an intellectual and artistic culture at least as responsive to its present industrial society as to its pastoral age'.

Vance Palmer's last book, *The Legend of the Nineties* (1954), both demonstrates his conviction that in the 1890s Australia 'acquired a character and a sense of community' and admits the doubt that 'in our search for a literary tradition we have made too much of one narrow period'. A similar doubt, that possibly 'our tradition is at once too dominating and too rigid', is entertained in Russel Ward's conclusion to *The Australian Legend* (1958), which traces the evolution of a national type through the historical phases so familiar from imaginative literature about convicts and settlers, squatters and selectors, diggers, shearers and Anzacs. The same year, A. A. Phillips' collection of essays on, among other topics, Lawson, Furphy, Douglas Stewart's verse play *Ned Kelly* (itself a remarkable articulation of contradictions inherent in the bush legend), and the 'cultural cringe' appeared under the combative title *The Australian Tradition* (1958). While clearly committed to winning wider recognition for a democratic literary heritage, Phillips was also apprehensive of its potentially stultifying influence on the present.

H. M. Green's *A History of Australian Literature* (1961) provided the most ambitious attempt to relate perceptions of a literary tradition to those of the evolution of a national character. In the 1890s, a fervent democratic and nationalistic spirit, best expressed by the doctrine of mateship, is seen as having pervaded social and political life. After his account of this period of 'Self-Conscious Nationalism', Green wavers in pursuing his announced intentions of relating social and literary developments, and of providing a concluding discussion of national types and characteristics. Perhaps he wavered because, as his introduction to the 'Modern Period' suggests, the democratic idealism of earlier times had become dissipated in cosmopolitanism and pessimism. Green, like Palmer and Ward, is conscious of writing at a time when the tradition he discerns is under attack.

Already in *Essays in Poetry: Mainly Australian* (1957), Vincent Buckley had cast a cold eye on 'the Australian Tradition' which 'the various outback schools have managed to foist on our editors'. In *Australian Accent* (1958), John Douglas Pringle described 'a counter revolution' in Australian poetry congruent with the 'Counter Revolution in Australian Historiography' postulated by Peter Coleman in the symposium he edited, *Australian Civilization* (1962). Pringle saw the satirical treatment of Australian subjects by A. D. Hope and James McAuley, and their attraction to traditional

European forms and themes, as a new development affecting other poets, among them Judith Wright. Her critical work, *Preoccupations in Australian Poetry* (1965), is an historical study of tensions between the native and European traditions. Impatience with the prevailing stereotypes of the distinctively Australian was not, however, confined to the academies and the still small but increasing number of literary journals. Richard White provides evidence of this from a popular (and perhaps unexpected) source—*Man* magazine's attack in 1945 on 'the traditional Lawson-Patterson *[sic]* jingle':

> it is half a century old ... Nobody says, 'We have cities as well as country, and even so, all our country is not red sand and broken fences and hopeless teeth-grinding women.'

The established stereotypes still proved durable on the screen (as they continue to). Undoubtedly the most popular entertainment medium before the arrival of television in the second half of the 1950s was film. Charles Chauvel, whose celebration of the Anzac legend *Forty Thousand Horsemen* (1941) was one of the few films produced in the country during the war years, made *Sons of Matthew* (1949), within the conventions of the saga of pioneering, and *Jedda* (1955) within those of Aboriginal-white relations in the outback. Such staples of the earlier cinema as the Eureka Stockade, the history of the Kelly gang, and *Robbery Under Arms* were remade, this time by overseas companies. In fact, most Australian feature films were made by English and American companies in the two decades following the war. In *The Overlanders* (1946), English director Harry Watt had Chips Rafferty and Daphne Campbell playing stock types from nineteenth-century melodrama—the lean laconic drover and the resourceful daughter of the bush—to responsive audiences around the world. Hollywood used Australian locations for free adaptations of *Summer of the Seventeenth Doll* and Neville Shute's novel *On the Beach* (both 1959). With these and other international films made here, an added interest for local audiences was the image of Australia they projected abroad.

Other images, or variations on traditional landscapes and legendary subjects, by the painters Nolan, Drysdale, Boyd and Tucker, were drawing the attention of a different kind of viewer in Britain and the United States during the same years. Bernard Smith's *Australian Painting* (1962) traced the history of its subject from first settlement through the emergence of a national school in the 1890s to contemporary antagonisms between internationalist and nativist groups.

A perception shared by both those who celebrated the bush tradition and those who were dismissive of it, at all levels of cultural expression, was that contemporary, industrialised Australia was not only a predominantly urban but essentially a *suburban* nation. The spiritual malaise of suburbanism, which Palmer and Esson had recoiled from after World War I, seemed to most commentators after World War II to have taken over the whole country, and it became the subject of a wide range of diagnoses. The plays seen as heralding a long-awaited theatrical renaissance were all set in suburbia and were critical of, or at least ambivalent about, aspects of the national legend: *Summer of the Seventeenth Doll*, Richard Beynon's dramatisation of cultural tensions between old and New Australians, *The Shifting Heart* (1960), and Alan Seymour's dramatisation of different generations' attitudes to Anzac Day, *The One Day of the Year* (1962). Ambivalence also characterises Patrick White's *The Season at Sarsaparilla* (1962), a play about life (and Life) in surburbia. White had become the most controversial of Australian novelists, and a focus for the debate over Australianness in literature, after receiving international acclaim for his novels *The Tree of Man* (1955) and *Voss* (1957): modernist variations on, in the first instance, the saga of pioneering; and, in the second, the heroic journey of exploration and the visionary quest. In his short stories and plays of the earlier 1960s, White caricatured life in Sarsaparilla and the suburbs surrounding it, which he modelled on the area of outer Sydney in which he was living. His next novel, *Riders in the Chariot* (1964), presents as its chief satiric targets the Sarsaparillan matrons Mrs Jolly, with her love of all things pink, and Mrs Flack, with her pastel-blue dressing-table set.

Proponents of a democratic national literary tradition, including Realist Writers' groups, were appalled by what they saw as the misanthropy and elitism of the country's internationally best-known writer, and his isolates' pursuit of 'the mysteries of life' rather than their endurance of shared adversities. Yet White's satiric caricatures shared many traits, as well as possessions, with the popular stage stereotypes created by Barry Humphries in the mid-1950s: Edna Everage, the brash, flighty Moonee Ponds housewife, and Sandy Stone, the ageing, bemused returned serviceman of Gallipoli Crescent, Glen Iris. Sandy particularly focused nostalgia for a way of life that was passing; as, in a younger generation, did Barry

McKenzie, Humphries' serge-suited Awful Ocker Abroad who first appeared in the English satirical weekly *Private Eye* in 1965. As well as Humphries' stage shows and long-playing records, there were satiric television programs like 'The Mavis Bramston Show' and, in the traditional medium of print, the enormously popular *They're a Weird Mob*, purportedly written by a recent Italian immigrant 'Nino Culotta' (John O'Grady). These works helped make Australians more conscious than ever before of their 'image' (a term that took on a new aptness with the arrival of television).

Also stimulating self-awareness was a spate of widely discussed products of the higher journalistic art of impressionistic sociology. For most of their authors, Sydney was the focus for what was seen as most typical in the Australian way of life. Richard White observes that increasingly through the 1950s photographs of Sydney's beaches and varied cityscape were challenging 'the familiar iconography of outback Australia—the homestead, the sheep, the lonely gum and the proud Aborigine' in such books. Even though it lacks photographs, this observation is borne out by Pringle's *Australian Accent*. Written primarily for a British audience by a Scot resident in Australia, it describes the culture, social, political, artistic, of 'the sub-urban civilization of the coastal fringe' instead of 'the Dead Heart or the Outback'. For Pringle, contrary to most earlier commentators, Australia is neither British nor American in character but uniquely itself. Yet, culturally distinctive as the country might be, the highest ambition of its average denizen was to secure a 'little' house in a lower-middle-class suburb and live there complacently.

In *The Australian Ugliness* (1960), architect Robin Boyd invited his readers into one such house, asking them to imagine the typical Australian, and 'successful featurist', driving home from the office in a two-tone Holden Special to have tea with his wife in the sun-room with its pastel-hued venetian blinds and its table 'groaning with all kinds of good food set in a plastic dream'. The good food and the plastic dream are metonymic of a conflict between nature and culture which Boyd elaborates historically, He contrasts the functionalism of the past (convict-built Georgian edifices, rude but handsomely honest pioneering buildings closely related to their purposes and environments) with the featurism of the present, which proclaims only the possessor's materialism and modishness.

Plastic, wall-to-wall burgundy Axminster carpet, reindeer-frosted glass doors, and flights of plaster ducks over converted fireplaces drew the aesthetes' scorn—and, often as not, audiences' guffaws of self-recognition. But there was also nostalgia for the values (and associated material trappings) of a more 'authentically' Australian working-class life which had been overtaken by events: the war, the steadily rising affluence during Menzies' unprecedently long reign, and the ambivalently resisted processes of Americanisation. There was conflict between the values of this older, more authentic Australia and the brashly new, between a guilty recall of the previous half century of war and depression, and the seductive opportunities and consumer satisfactions of postwar Australia. This conflict is dramatised in George Johnston's novel *My Brother Jack* (1964). Whereas Jack, the larrikin, grows up to become an unskilled worker who is driven to gold-fossicking during the Depression and then (like his father in 1914) is one of the first to enlist when war comes, his brother David Meredith escapes from the 'terrifying mediocrity' of the suburb full of 'Emoh Ruos' in which they were born, into a career as a journalist and, temporarily, into middle-class suburban respectability. After the war, David moves on towards expatriation (the course taken by many writers and artists), opportunistically yet guiltily abandoning Jack and the traditional Australia he represents.

Donald Horne's *The Lucky Country* (1964) was the best-selling of the commentaries on contemporary Australia. For Horne, Australia was among the first modern suburban societies, in which 'for several generations most of its men have been catching the 8.02, and messing around in their houses and gardens at the weekends'. His scorn was reserved for the various elites who disparaged or betrayed the values of middle Australia, including the writers, most of whom seemed unable to 'come to grips with their own people' as observable human beings. Instead they either caricatured them or idealised them impossibly, so that literature and the arts no longer expressed 'the moods and attitudes of the community'. Other writers could be seen as sharing Horne's perception that 'the profusion of life doesn't wither because people live in small brick houses with red tile roofs'. Whether with irony or not, poets like Bruce Dawe and Chris Wallace-Crabbe, older novelists like David Martin and Judah Waten (even Patrick White), and newer ones like Thea Astley and Thomas Keneally were locating Australian life in the suburbs. There was also a succession of autobiographical novels which evoked the golden age of childhood in cities or country towns: memorably, among novels, Christopher Koch's *The Boys in the Island* (1958) and Randolph Stow's *The Merry-Go-Round in the Sea* (1965), and among autobiographies, Hal Porter's *The Watcher on the Cast-Iron Balcony*

(1963) and Horne's own *The Education of Young Donald* (1967).

From the present vantage point, postwar Australia up to the mid-1960s seems to have gone through a self-reflexive phase during which a sense of independent national identity that necessitated appraisals of its nature, extent, and worth was more widespread than ever before, even than in the 1890s. By the end of this period, however, Australia was involved in another war, in South-East Asia. In the later 1960s Australians, particularly younger generations who had grown up during the decades of postwar affluence and expansion of educational opportunity, were exposed to a new range of cultural influences, including the predominantly American counter culture. These were to stimulate fresh critical and imaginative perceptions of their society and its traditions.

Notes

References in the text to the following five studies have been identified by their author's names: Harry Heseltine, 'Australian Fiction since 1920', in Geoffrey Dutton (ed.), *The Literature of Australia* (1964); John Tulloch, *Legends on the Screen* (1981); Margaret Williams, *Australia on the Popular Stage* (1983); G. A. Wilkes, *The Stockyard and the Croquet Lawn* (1981); and Richard White, *Inventing Australia* (1981), from which the quotations from *Smith's Weekly* and *Man* are drawn.

The quotations from Palmer and Esson are taken from Vance Palmer, *Louis Esson and the Australian Theatre* (1948). For detail on the Palmers and their circle see Vivian Smith, *Vance and Nettie Palmer* (1975), and David Walker, *Dream and Disillusion* (1976). Leslie Rees, *The History of Australian Drama* (1973; rev. 1978, 1987) is a comprehensive history which includes consideration of radio and television drama on the ABC. Harold Love (ed.), *The Australian Stage* (1984) is a documentary history with substantial information on this period. Andrew Pike and Ross Cooper, *Australian Film, 1900-1977* (1980), itemise all feature films made here. Studies with a social historical interest in the fiction of the period surveyed in this chapter include: D. R. Burns, *The Directions of Australian Fiction, 1920-1974* (1975), Ian Reid, *Fiction and the Great Depression* (1979), and Drusilla Modjeska, *Exiles at Home* (1981), on women writers in the 1930s.

Among historians and critics, social, literary and cultural, discourse on the national character reached its peak towards the end of this period, at a time of rapid expansion in local publishing. R. M. Crawford, in *An Australian Perspective* (1960), lectures delivered and originally published in the US, advanced the view that the nation's 'coming of age' had occurred not with Gallipoli but in the years immediately preceding World War II. Crawford's argument provided the common stimulus for contributors to Peter Coleman (ed.), *Australian Civilization* (1962), which countered 'the standard radical-leftist interpretation of Australian history' and criticised the 'legend' as 'radical, populist, nationalist, racialist'. In his contribution, social psychologist Ronald Taft substituted for the received stereotype of the typical Australian the increasingly popular figure of the suburban commuter on the 8.10 train.

The same year saw the publication of Douglas Pike, *Australia: The Quiet Continent* in the UK, and in Australia C. M. H. Clark's *A History of Australia*, volume 1, and Marjorie Barnard, *A History of Australia*. Australian history, now a popular interest as well as an academically respectable and independent subject, was marketed both here and overseas; and literary history was also being addressed in a revisionist, or 'counter-revolutionary' way, as in Grahame Johnston's anthology *Australian Literary Criticism* (1962). Histories published overseas include Kylie Tennant, *Australia: Her Story* (1953); A. G. L. Shaw, *The Story of Australia* (1955); Manning Clark, *A Short History of Australia* (1963); A. L. McLeod, *The Pattern of Australian Culture* (with contributions by Australians); and Russel Ward, *Australia* (1965), which notes the recent controversy over the 'Whig' interpretation of the country's past. The 1969 revised edition of Clark's *Short History* ruefully registers a shift in perception: 'It seemed as though from Darwin to Hobart and from Broome to Brisbane suburbia was to be the last fate of a country which in previous generations had produced . . . a W. C. Wentworth, a Ned Kelly, a Robert O'Hara Bourke.'

For specifically literary critical engagement with the issues in the period, especially in literary journals, see Brian Kiernan, *Criticism* (1974). Geoffrey Serle, *From Deserts the Prophets Come* (1973, rev. 1987) contains much detail on the period in a general cultural historical account.

Chapter 18

MARKETING THE LITERARY IMAGINATION: PRODUCTION OF AUSTRALIAN LITERATURE, 1915-1965

RICHARD NILE AND DAVID WALKER

In March 1915 George Robertson of Angus and Robertson received a letter from an obscure writer who wanted to publish a volume of verse. The writer was 'pretty confident' that he could persuade 300 subscribers to pay five shillings a volume, but he wondered if there might not be scope for a popular edition as well. Nine months and seventeen tons of paper later, C. J Dennis' *Songs of a Sentimental Bloke* had sold 50,000 copies. *The Moods of Ginger Mick* followed in October 1916 and sold 40,000 copies within six months. Down went another forest. Dennis' work was staged, filmed, broadcast on radio, recorded on gramophone, performed as a ballet and made into a musical in the early 1960s; a remarkable series of media and technologies.

The technology of publishing changed remarkably in the twentieth century. The growth of cities and suburbs, improved standards of literacy and education generally, the rise of an urban middle class, increased leisure time and wages for workers and the declining role of the *Bulletin* as the custodian of a peculiarly national consciousness have all been cited as contributing influences. Many surveys have stressed a connection between a new, twentieth-century, national consciousness and the emergence of a mature literature. But almost no detailed survey has traced the connections between the writing, publication and distribution of Australian literature—the marketing of the Australian literary imagination.

The role of the publisher in determining literary tastes should not be undervalued. In this period the production of Australian writing took place within the framework of old imperial connections. The commercialisation of mass culture intensified the struggle for control, radically reshaping the face of writing, publication and distribution.Yet the image of a hunched author with a stub pencil, a pale light suffusing the scene, persisted well into the century.

In the half century from 1915, it was commonly asserted that Australian writing was the poor relation of English literature, that writers were poorly rewarded and that many of the best of them were forced to publish overseas for the want of a reliable publishing industry in Australia. Some saw the need for writers to become more organised. In 1915, Vance Palmer, just turned thirty and the author of a slender volume of poetry, formed the Australian Writers' Guild. He was to remain near the centre of literary politics until his death in 1959. Palmer's guild made little headway in wartime Melbourne and the *Bulletin* was disdainful of what it regarded as an attempt to unionise writers. The conviction that writers would have to press their own claims led to the formation in Sydney in 1928 of what subsequently became a genuinely national and enduring literary organisation, the Fellowship of Australian Writers (FAW). Mary Gilmore and Roderick Quinn both claimed credit for the idea, but the FAW could not have succeeded without a general agreement among writers that they needed to be better organised. Among its vital tasks was the regeneration of the Commonwealth Literary Fund, which had begun in 1908 as one of Alfred Deakin's exciting initiatives. By the 1920s, the CLF, long starved of funds and enthusiastic support, doled out some meagre pensions to a very odd assortment of claimants.

Agitation by the FAW played an important role in the dramatic revival of the moribund CLF. With a fourfold increase in its 1939 budget, the fund broadened the range of its activities to include a system of annual fellowships, a program of university lectures on Australian literature, and assistance to magazines like *Meanjin*. From the 1950s *Overland* and *Quadrant*, among other journals, received funding. While assistance was welcome, a conviction remained in literary circles that literary consciousness was a guttering flame that needed encouragement and careful tending if it was ever to burn at all brightly in Modern Australia. It is hazardous to generalise about literary morale over half a century, but it was not high. Achievement needed to be balanced against failures and disappointments; against the accumulated damage that real or suspected neglect could inflict; against the the work that was abandoned, never attempted or hastily executed. While local difficulties were plentiful enough, this half century saw a world battered by wars, depression and some of the cruellest atrocities ever recorded. Did writing, Australian writing, have a point in such a world? Behind the bright lights and solid facts of what was published in our period lurks the shadowy world of what might have been published, written or achieved. And what literary losses did the nation suffer as a result of nearly one hundred thousand deaths in two world wars?

The clearest statistical patterns emerge from a consideration of the novel. In the period 1900-40, Londo was the centre of publication for Australian novels for all but two years, 1933 and 1934, when Sydney eased ahead. Geoffrey Hubble, *The Australian Novel: A Title Checklist* (1970), indexes 1218 London published novels or 54.4 per cent of all Australian titles listed for the forty years. For the same period, Sydney claimed 29.2 per cent of the total and Melbourne 15.5 per cent. Australian publishing was a tale of three cities, one of them half a world away. Figures from Miller and Macartney, *Australian Literature* (1956), are more striking still, with London publishers producing close to 66 per cent of Australian titles from 1920 to 1940. The largest London publishers of Australian titles were Hodder and Stoughton, Hutchinson and Ward Lock, though the fact that they accounted for only 18.4 per cent of all Australian titles shows how dispersed the London market was. In 1930 Angus and Robertson in Sydney took over from Hodder and Stoughton as the leading publisher of Australian titles and retained the lead throughout the period.

The novel was perceived in publishing circles as the literary medium of the twentieth century. From the early 1920s it dominated literary production, though magazines still published verse and short fiction. Fewer publishing companies were interested in collections of shorter works. In 1927, E. J. Brady, at the time a well-known literary figure, sent a volume of short stories to Angus and Robertson. They fired it back by return mail claiming they were unable to 'induce booksellers to stock volumes of short stories—not even if written by E. J. Brady'. Brady tried a volume of verse with the Endeavour Press and succeeded in having *Wardens of the Sea* published in 1933. Encouraged, he sent a further collection of verse to Angus and Robertson in the following year and a book of short stories to Bookstall. Both were turned down. Angus and Robertson had 'practically given up publishing verse for the time being' and added that 'short stories and sketches were not saleable either'. Bookstall replied in the same terms. They were not interested in short stories and sketches, but would be interested in Brady's proposed novel on 'the romance of the Australian gold discovery'. The novel did not materialise and Brady died in 1962 having published nothing in book form for thirty years. In the period 1920-40 Angus and Robertson published twice as many novels as volumes of verse. For Cornstalk the balance was much more even, but it only published forty titles in the entire period. When it came to the bigger runs of the Bookstall series, novels far outnumbered volumes of verse.

The success of the New South Wales Bookstall company was extraordinary. Guided by its managing director, A. C. Rowlandson, the company saw its sales rise from one million in the period 1900-10 to three million in the following decade. By 1920 the company had over one hundred authors on its lists. For a time during the Great War, Rowlandson's brightly covered paperbacks rose to 1s. 3d. a volume—compared to 6s. 6d. for a hardback novel—but for the most part it was a shilling series. Rowlandson was the only publisher to achieve a lasting success with the shilling novel. By the late 1920s the company had bought the printing rights for all of Steele Rudd's works. Bookstall's eight bookshops and fifty railway stalls were a factor in the success, but high circulation figures turned narrow margins into solid profits. In 1922 more than three thousand shops sold Bookstall novels. A. G. Stephens found 'their covers brightening the limited display of packed tea and candles' in a back-street grocery in Auckland. That New Zealand provided a crucial market for Bookstall paperbacks is a useful reminder of the close literary links established by the imperial connection. Of all the Bookstall authors, Steele Rudd was the most successful, but Ambrose Pratt, Arthur Wright, Edward Dyson, Beatrice Grimshaw, Norman Lindsay and Sumner Locke were all prominent and popular Bookstall contributors. Striking illustrations and bold covers were a feature of the series with the Lindsays—Norman, Percy, Lionel and Ruby— forming an essential part of a team of over thirty illustrators which also included David Low and Will Dyson. The Bookstall Company continued well after Rowlandson's death in 1922, but the company had passed its peak as a publisher of Australian titles.

The 1930s experienced a distinct shift in emphasis to Australian publishers, with Angus and Robertson providing the major challenge to overseas rivals. For many years, George Robertson presided over local bookselling and publishing. His legacy lived on long after his death in 1933. In 1923, Angus and Robertson moved its printing operations to Eagle Press, later renamed Halstead Press, and by doing so made considerable technological advances. Eagle Press claimed that it could typeset, print and bind four thousand copies of a 300-page book in a week and provide a coloured dust jacket as well. In December 1924 George Robertson wrote: 'Getting a book out of Penfold and Co (our former printers) used to be like drawing a refractory cork—the Eagle Press drops them into our backyard like bombs from an aeroplane.' In that year the Eagle Press produced over 350,000 volumes for Angus and Robertson. Thomas Bermingham, the proprietor of the Eagle Press, believed this to be 'a record for Australia, and that, with additional plant to be installed in the New Year, we have the most up-to-date book producing plant in Australia'.

The Eagle Press was certainly efficient, though Australian titles were by no means the firm's only concern. By 1926 total output of the half-crown Platypus series was 403,000 volumes. The largest sellers were *Anne of Green Gables* (23,000), *Anne of Avonlea* (17,000) and *The Man from Snowy River* (17,000). What a coup *Anne from Snowy River* might have been! There was also a Bellbird series, in which *Anne of Green Gables* was again the best-seller. In the same period Angus and Robertson produced a quite extraordinary print run of 47,000 copies of *The Life and Works of Henry Ford*, while the perishable *Sally in Rhodesia* sold 20,000 copies. Henry Ford's Australian triumph deserves more attention than it has received, though not for its contribution to Australian literature. It was a book the young Johannes Bjelke-Petersen claimed to have read many times. In 1930, a tariff commission asked Angus and Robertson how it was able to produce this book more cheaply than it was manufactured in the United States. There were worthier projects. From as early as 1912 George Robertson had wanted an Australian encyclopaedia. Fourteen years later, as the *Henry Fords* rolled off the press, so too did 10,000 sets of the two-volume *Australian Encyclopaedia*, selling at £5 a set.

While Angus and Robertson was the major publisher in the interwar period, negative exchange rates drew a number of smaller local companies into the publishing field, including P. R. Stephensen and Co. Though both companies floundered in the mid-1930s they were sufficiently productive to raise the false hope that Australian publishing was about to enter a newly independent phase. When a somewhat chastened Stephensen addressed the FAW Authors' Week in Sydney in August 1935, he complained that local production was strangled by the 'operations of a trade-ring of importing booksellers, [and] by unfair competition from overseas'. He also warned his audience that the recent 'lusty uprising of Australian authorship' was less a product of writing and publishing efforts than the 'economic fluke' of an exchange rate that suddenly favoured local production.

Even so, writers sometimes found it difficult to summon up appropriate enthusiasm for local publishers. George Robertson advised some Australian writers to try their luck in England, including Vance Palmer, Katharine Prichard, Marjorie Barnard and Flora Eldershaw and E. V. Timms. Stephensen insisted that because Angus and Robertson was principally a bookseller and not a publisher, the local scene suffered from a collective sense that anything Australian was second-rate. He believed that Australia needed a solid national publisher willing to produce local goods. Marjorie Barnard and Nettie Palmer shared his commitment though they were unconvinced that he was the person for the job. Barnard considered it an 'acid joke' that Stephensen and Angus and Robertson should be so scathing of the other's literary tastes: 'There is a lot to be said for local publication' she confided in Nettie Palmer, 'and a lot to be said against local publishers.'

Criticism of Angus and Robertson was widespread and sprang from the same sources as the persistent discontent with the *Bulletin*. Each dominated the small, insecure world of Australian literature, yet neither had convinced many Australian writers that their sights were trained on anything above commercial expediency. Craig Munro has written of Angus and Robertson:

> This canny old bookselling and publishing firm played safe not only financially but also in terms of subject matter. Descriptive and travel writing was safer and more lucrative than socially conscious fiction . . .

In 1929 Angus and Robertson rejected Katharine Prichard's *Coonardoo* (Cape, 1929) and M. Barnard Eldershaw's *A House is Built* (Harrap, 1929) joint winners of the *Bulletin* novel competition in 1928. Those who did not feel encouraged by Angus and Robertson in the interwar period, among them Leonard Mann, Xavier Herbert, Eleanor Dark and Miles Franklin, represent a who's who of Australian writing.

Vance Palmer was convinced that Australian writers faced an insoluble dilemma over the question of where they should publish their work. His experiences in England at the end of World War I convinced him that the Australian novel had to 'address itself primarily to a public overseas', but in doing so, what he called the 'genuine Australian novel that takes its native setting for granted', was at a disadvantage. He thought it unlikely that the people who patronised English circulating libraries would be much interested in the 'genuine' novel. Yet when Leslie Rees sought Palmer's opinion in the mid-1930s he was advised to publish in England 'where you have a natural public and could get those big headlines'. Palmer had earlier warned Rees that Angus and Robertson could not see much beyond Ion Idriess and 'the sentimental distortion of some genuine impressions of the jungle of North Queensland or the islands of the Torres Straits'. He was adamant that Angus and Robertson only wanted novels of the 'frothiest sort'. His disillusion resulted from his having two novels published in Sydney after being convinced by Frank Dalby Davison that new conditions for publishing existed in Australia.

Palmer's impressions of Angus and Robertson are borne out by their 1935 catalogue of new and used books where just over two thousand titles were grouped under fourteen sections emphasising adventure, romance and the Pacific Islands. In the following year, Angus and Robertson made its first venture into overseas publishing when it marketed thirteen Australian titles in Britain and America. Palmer's thirst for the genuine Australian novel had to be satisfied by the inclusion of Marcus Clarke's ever reliable *His Natural Life* (1874). Idriess was represented with *The Cattle King* (1936); the Pacific with *Adventuring on Coral Seas* (1936) and *Ocean Islands and Nauru* (1936) and the frothy with *Sky Pilot in Arnhem Land* (1936) and *Sky Pilot's Last Fight* (1936).

For those who saw themselves as serious novelists, self-publication may have seemed attractive; but it was an alternative that accounted for a very few titles. Verse and short fiction were much more suited to private publication or the subscription volume. Much of Frank Wilmot's poetry was published privately, while Christopher Brennan and Jack Lindsay distributed collections of their work in print runs of seventy-five—an impossible number for a novel—marketed as deluxe editions and sold by subscription only at three guineas. Of his four volumes of verse published by Sydney J. Endacott between 1917 and 1922, Frederick T. Macartney later wrote,

> I have never expected any sort of wide interest in them, so they were printed and more or less casually distributed among booksellers who in any circumstances would have regarded them as so much lumber.

It was a different world for novelists. Frank Dalby Davison published his first two novels privately, a tactic which Marjorie Barnard believed placed his literary reputation at risk: 'There is a story that Davison printed both books on a hand press in his back garden, but he denies it. They do look the work of an amateur.' Twenty years later Frank Hardy printed *Power Without Glory* (1950) privately and discovered that 'Fools rush in where printers refuse to tread'.

By the late 1930s a newly organised group of writers, centred on the FAW, had emerged. Its objective was to achieve professional status for writers. For the most part the FAW was dominated by novelists who saw themselves as modern, serious and socially conscious, whose Australian readership was likely to be small but, they hoped, discerning. This group was often frustrated in its attempts to foster a national literature. Shortly before her death in 1954 Miles Franklin complained that Australian readers were conditioned to accept a third-rate English novel ahead of a first-rate Australian one. In 1943 Katharine Prichard remembered she had once been told that 'You're better dead' than to be a writer in Australia. By 1962 Prichard had made more money from translations of her works than in the local market: 'in Russia one of my novels was issued in an edition of 140,000 and the goldfields trilogy went into second and third editions of almost the same size', she wrote to Beatrice Davis at Angus and Robertson. In private correspondence many writers worried that local publication might damage their literary reputation. Many protested against the need to publish overseas, but invariably they felt more comfortable with solid British firms.

The outbreak of World War II brought some striking improvements in conditions for local writers, though changes, as in the period 1933-4, owed much more to economic considerations than to agitation by writers themselves or, indeed, publishers. In evidence given to the 1946 tariff board report on the publishing industry, the acting national librarian, H. L. White, noted that by 1942 Australians were experiencing a 'general drought of books'. In the immediate prewar years, British publishers averaged 16,220 titles a year. By 1942 the figure had slumped to 7241 titles. Moreover, shipping books to Australia was poor use of wartime resources. There was a sudden demand for local books and an increase in publishing houses trying to meet the demand as best they could, despite manpower and paper shortages. In consequence the CLF in 1944 commissioned various Sydney and Melbourne publishing companies to print cheap editions of classic Australian works in runs of twenty-five thousand, a figure more normally associated with popularisers in the Idriess tradition. Though ten novels were published, Katharine Prichard and Leonard Mann both told the tariff board that they had been disappointed by what they considered a poorly publicised venture. Moreover, the cheap paper which was used in a time of shortage was unattractive once the war was over. Interest in the series soon dried up. Prichard's *Haxby's Circus* (1930) sold sixteen thousand copies to 1946 but huge backlogs cluttered the shelves of booksellers.

In the 1940s British publishers lost their dominance in the Australian market. According to figures derived from Hubble, in the decade to 1949, local publishers produced 596 titles to London's 119. It was a striking reversal of fortune. In the period 1954-65 there were 1028 locally published Australian novels as against 415 published in London. No less striking was the fact that 868 of the locally published titles were produced in Sydney. Though the margin was clear, the 1940s stand out as a high point for local publishing. The importance of the 1940s in local production is also borne out in figures derived from the *Annual Catalogue of Australian Publications*. A list of 1678 locally published titles covers fiction in the period 1936-60, with a peak of 237 in 1946. In the same period local publishers produced 854 volumes of verse and 106 plays.

While some crude, though instructive patterns emerge from the production of titles, the evidence is much more uncertain for print runs, sales and royalties. This is precisely the information needed to test contemporary efforts to comprehend changes in literary tastes. Did the changing pattern of publishing generate a greater confidence in Australian themes among writers and their public as Vance Palmer, among others, frequently suggested would happen? Or did it merely continue established practices in a new guise? If print runs, sales figures and royalties were available for the five thousand or so titles listed by Hubble, would a new clarity be at hand or a statistical nightmare? While the scope to produce meaningless figures is large, a refinement of publishing statistics would undoubtedly stimulate interest in the social history of the book and the nature of reading in our culture.

The fact that Australian books were published did not mean that they were easy to locate. The Palmers frequently had to lend their dog-eared edition of Furphy's *Such is Life* (1903) to other Australian writers because copies were almost impossible to acquire. Frank Wilmot, first director of the Melbourne University Press, complained that booksellers were reluctant to display Australian works. A request for an Australian book would have them rummaging into obscure corners for the requested title. On occasions the misguided reader would be encouraged to sample an enticing overseas title rather than waste time and money on the local product. When Hilda Esson went in search of Katharine Prichard's *Working Bullocks* (1926) she was enraged to hear a 'mere flapper' dismiss the novel as a weak Australian attempt to write a modern novel. Hilda snatched her copy of the novel from the flapper's hands, made what she hoped was a withering reply and returned home indignant.

It became a common complaint among writers that while Australia was known for its primary products, wool, mutton, beauty contestants and soldiers, it was regarded as an unlikely place to find writers with any claim to be taken seriously for their contribution to modern literature. One of the thorniest and most interesting questions bears upon the reputation of Australian books and the nature of writing itself. The collective testimony of writers suggests that what they were doing was often regarded with suspicion. Looking over a literary career spanning forty years, Hal Porter (1975) wrote that a serious writer might better be thought of along with 'cripples ... midgets, Fat Ladies, female impersonators, Siamese twins, and Jo Jo the dog-faced boy' all of whom displayed 'their special abnormalities for money'. Writing was considered a morally unhealthy pursuit, a personal disorder rather than a skilled occupation which deserved appropriate rewards. But who was to determine what was appropriate? This often turned into a rather more particular question about the special claims that could be made for the Australian book. Feeling ignored at home and abroad, writers could imagine their proper audience to be a more responsive posterity who would find qualities in their work that prejudiced contemporaries had been unable to discern. Perhaps they were right. It took over thirty years for Katharine Prichard's *Coonardoo* (1929) to be published in Australia. Its first Australian edition in 1960 quickly sold 20,000 copies.

In the half century to 1965 the restless search for the Great Australian Novel was at its most intense. It seemed that the appearance of just one unequivocal masterpiece would show the sceptics, once and for all, that Australian conditions did not inhibit the growth of an indigenous literature. For George Cowling, Professor of English at Melbourne University, Australian literature was permanently disabled by its lack of tradition and its distance from the centre of the civilised world, London. In his famous rejoinder to Cowling, P. R. Stephensen felt he had to demonstrate that an Australian literature already existed and would continue to develop. But the burden of proof remained. In 1940 Professor J. I. M. Stewart was invited by the CLF to lecture on Australian literature. He observed that since the fund had failed to provide any Australian literature he would lecture instead on D. H. Lawrence's *Kangaroo* (1922). Dorothy Green encountered an academic poet who wondered if 'Australian literature' was not a contradiction in terms.

Australian writing struggled for acceptance in schools and universities. Although occasional classes were offered, the field was left to the WEA, mechanics' institutes and literary societies. J. L. Tierney's simply titled Sydney University masters' thesis 'Australian Literature' (1922) was the first postgraduate work on the topic. A second thesis waited another fourteen years and a third was submitted in 1939. It was not until 1945, when J. K. Ewers' *Creative Writing in Australia* appeared, that a volume of criticism was made readily available to readers and students. Issued by Georgian House in Melbourne, the book went to four revised editions in twenty years. To 1965 Australian universities produced four doctorates (PhDs in 1948 and 1955 and DLitts in 1953 and 1955) and twenty-six masters' degrees in Australian literature, compared with the 152 theses on European literature. The first chair of Australian literature was established at Sydney University in 1963.

The monumental bibliographical labours of E. Morris Miller and H. M. Green made it plain that whatever might be said of its quality, Australian literature was much more voluminous than all but a handful of bibliophiles had suspected. In the same spirit, though on a smaller scale, P. R. Stephensen and Frederick T. Macartney were fond of listing Australian writers and their work. Posing as a national selector of a literary eleven, Stephensen challenged his critics to pick a team of contemporary English writers as good as his representative national team. On another occasion he listed fifty Australian novels that he considered as good as anything Cowling was able to produce.

If the uncertain status of Australian writers was a constant aggravation, poor returns for their efforts deepened the malaise. It was only in rare cases that writers were able to live by their writing. Louis Esson's income as a dramatist between 1910 and his death in 1943 was too small for him to put a figure on. Yet, the mechanics of making a living from journalism exerted a powerful fascination and he retained a guilty respect for those who were more disciplined, systematic and better paid: 'I never or hardly ever reach ten pounds in a week,' he wrote in January 1924, 'and often I don't manage half, which is only a minimum wage.' Esson became so preoccupied by rates of pay that he joked at not being able to consider verse on its merits any more: 'My comment is 10/6 or 12/-.' Getting the money was another matter. The *Sydney Mail* had accepted a short story in February 1924, but there was still no payment six months later. 'Our performance is very poor,' Esson wrote of Australian writers, 'but the conditions are almost impossible.'

Esson admired Vance Palmer for his systematic approach to publishing, though he wondered if too much system destroyed inspiration. From his period in Edwardian London Vance Palmer acquired a lasting memory 'of dreary hack work carried far into the night, the sound of rejected manuscripts dropping in through the downstairs door, and the depressing smell of cocoa boiled on a tiny tin petrol stove'. Palmer detailed some of his experiences for the *Bulletin* in 1915; the stories paid for at a guinea a thousand words around basic plots supplied by the agent or written around pictures which magazine editors had sent him. Palmer's agent is a rather shadowy figure whose role and effectiveness remain unclear, though it is apparent that he considered an agent vital in the precarious world of freelance writing. Palmer contributed to over one hundred papers and magazines and he wrote under such pressure that it is a wonder he found time for those cups of cocoa. At the end of his first nine months in London he had ground out ninety-one stories. Titles like 'A Seaside Philander: Mr Jupp and the Lady with the toy Pomeranian' suggest the forced humour and Cockney stereotyping required of him. In severe reaction, Palmer's humour became quiet to the point of inaudibility in what he regarded as his genuinely Australian work.

Palmer's output to 1925 was immense and most of it he disowned. His need for ready money prompted him to write for the Bookstall series under the pseudonym of Rann Daly. *The Shanty Keeper's Daughter* appeared in 1920 and *The Boss of Kilara* two years later. The rewards seemed so much less than the effort required. A cheque for £3 2s. 6d. from the *Bulletin* in November 1921 represented a Red Page article, a plain English article, a piece of verse and two paragraphs. 'We scrape along', Nettie wrote, conscious no doubt, of their two small children who needed care, time and attention, not to mention food, clothing and shelter. In the period 1924-5 to 1929-30 the Palmers averaged a joint income of £482 per annum when the average salary of an adult male in the Commonwealth Public Service was £320. The combined income takes no account of costs: paper, postage, pens, ink, typing, travel and books. Vance Palmer's tiny handwriting owes less to toilet training than to his need to conserve paper when he was struggling as a freelance. Katharine Prichard's experience with *Working Bullocks* (1926) highlighted the problem of costs. In 1926 she paid more to have the manuscript typed than she received in royalties for a book hailed in the period as a candidate for the Great Australian Novel. In 1935, after receiving a six-month royalty statement from Angus and Robertson covering four books, Frank Dalby Davison found that he was still in debt to his publishers. He had borrowed £78 10s. against the sales, but had only earnt £30 5s. from royalties.

Between 1935 and 1940 Eleanor Dark's average weekly income from four novels amounted to half that of a junior journalist. In 1940 Miles Franklin wrote wryly to W. G. Cousins that 'Australia as a subject must be too remote as they told me in New York'. When Franklin died in 1954 she bequeathed her £8922 estate for an annual prize to encourage excellence in Australian literature. In the same year Kenneth Mackenzie was in miserable poverty on a small property in the Blue Mountains. Tax returns for 1949-52 show an average income of only £247. He was unable to support his family and his marriage was crumbling. He died in 1954 at the age of forty, a few months after Colin Roderick had predicted that the best was yet to come from Kenneth Mackenzie. Angus and Robertson paid £78 9s. 6d. for the funeral expenses and since nobody wanted his ashes they were dispersed by the crematorium. In 1955 £5000 was offered for the film rights to Mackenzie's novel *The Refuge* (1954).

The decline of the freelance writer was a persistent theme. Edward Dyson felt driven to the paradoxical conclusion that improved conditions for the journalist were 'mainly responsible for the fading out of the unattached contributor'. Dyson was perhaps the best paid freelance writer in the country. He had developed an 'elaborate system of literary book-keeping'; helpful literary jottings went into notebooks and a ledger kept track of each publication and its earnings. Nothing was lost. By 1915 his earnings stood at around £800 a year, an awesome figure to younger writers. Though Dyson's system required enormous discipline, it also depended on a literary market that left rich pickings for the freelance. By 1920 it seemed clear that the scope had narrowed dramatically as salaried journalists got more of the work that once had fallen to the freelance. In 1925 Nettie Palmer noted that doors were continuing to close against the freelance and that after forty years Edward Dyson was 'feeling the pinch'.

The freelance fraternity of the 1890s had virtually disappeared by the end of the Great War. The key to this change was the formation of the Australian Journalists Association as an industrial union in 1910. The AJA favoured the employment of staffers in a full-time capacity working for award wages and hours. It sought professional status for journalism. By 1917 journalists worked a standard week of forty-six hours and secured minimum wage rates in cities of £8 per week for senior journalists, £7 per week for general reporters and £5 per week for juniors. Although men and women shared the same award, journalism was dominated by men. Perhaps the difficulties women faced in journalism produced unforeseen gains for our literature. 'More women than formerly are turning out major fiction,' noted Miles Franklin, 'yet how many women are in the editorial press? Even periodicals with feminine names are edited by men . . . Many jobs with big salaries are held by men, only occasionally by women.' By 1923 weekly rates were £10, £9, and £6 a week respectively for journalists. In 1927 Louis Esson called the journalist 'the aristocrat of the world of letters', whereas the writer was more than ever an outsider whose conditions were less protected than those of the junior reporter.

There were, of course, writers with impressive sales, but they were rarely esteemed for their contribution to the nation's literature. J. M. Walsh, Frederick Thwaites, Ion Idriess and Frank Clune were all immensely productive and their books sold well. Still in his mid-thirties in 1929, Walsh had written over forty novels published either in serial or book form. Thwaites' first novel, *The Broken Melody* (1930), went through over forty editions and by 1936 he had done well enough to form his own publishing company. By the 1950s dust jackets informed readers that combined sales stood at four million copies. That sounds like wishful thinking, though a military librarian was astounded by Thwaites' popularity among soldiers in the 1940s: '"Have you got a 'Thwaites?" was the usual question.' Idriess averaged a book a year between 1931 and 1964 and was so closely associated with Angus and Robertson that he wrote many of them on their premises. *Flynn of the Inland* (1932), perhaps his most popular work, sold around 120,000 copies in all editions. Frank Clune produced over sixty books between 1934 and 1971, many of them with assistance from P. R. Stephensen. Despite his sales, Clune claimed that his 'average royalties received up to 1942 have not amounted to a living wage'. If Clune fell short of the living wage, it is certain that the great majority of writers saw such a wage as an impossible dream.

For a time, Xavier Herbert thought that he had a basic wage within sight. He had contracted to write short stories for the *Australian Journal* at thirty shillings per thousand words. An 11,000-word story a month and another £4 for paragraphs and articles for the *Sunday Sun* made a monthly income of around £20 which 'in the hands of a superb manager like Sadie [his wife] for work that was to qualify me for a job that I knew somehow would make me famous was like a lovely dream.' The lovely dream ended six months later when the editor ordered Herbert to cut his monthly stories to 6000 words. Herbert tried to increase his contributions to the *Sunday Sun*, but staff journalists limited his scope. 'My hope of becoming an established writer . . . seems remote,' he wrote to Arthur Dibley in the mid-1930s; 'As I am living at present I am only a Bum.'

CLF fellowships promised some respite. But in 1938, the first year they were advertised, the ninety-one applicants learned that Frank Dalby Davison and Xavier Herbert were the only successful fellows, while Miles Franklin and Doris Kerr each received literary pensions for 1939. Of the women applicants, none described themselves solely as authors, journalists or freelance writers. With twelve written and nine published novels by 1938 and thirty years' work as a journalist in Europe, America and Australia, Miles Franklin was among those who nominated 'home duties' as her occupation. Virginia Woolf's ten pounds a week and a room of one's own was more generous than anything Miles Franklin had in mind: 'Ah, if only I could have one pound per week or even two for the last nine years,' she wrote to Nettie Palmer in 1931, 'my tale would have been different.' Like most of her contemporaries she felt pressured into innumerable unpaid jobs: 'I have done so many now that I am destitute, and have no one to push and encourage me as I have spent my life in doing for others.' Serious writing had become a form of martyrdom.

Though productive and critically acclaimed as one of the leading Australian novelists of her generation, Katharine Susannah Prichard's income from royalties fell well short of a wage. In the mid-1930s her royalties slumped to as little as £1 10s. for a six-month period. By the 1940s royalties had virtually dried up as she pushed on with the goldfields trilogy which occupied most of her time in the 1940s. In an application for a CLF fellowship she listed her income 'from all sources' using 1940 as an average year:

Military pension £2/2- per week
Writing: short stories and articles £24
Broadcasting: £32
Radio Plays: £32

Even with the military pension, which she received after her husband's suicide in 1933, her income was meagre, though it is interesting to note the role that broadcasting now played in providing a new source of income for writers. In 1941 Miles Franklin received £25 for a serialised reading of *All That Swagger* (1936).

For Vance Palmer, ABC broadcasting provided a new audience and a vital addition to his income. Between 1941 and 1959 he broadcast almost four hundred talks on contemporary literature in regular book programs. In addition his 'mellow Anglo-Australian voice' could be heard discussing a range of literary issues. In 1956, for example, alongside his twenty-two broadcasts in the Current Book series, he spoke on 'The Rise of Australian Nationalism 1890-1914', 'Travellers' Tales—The Finnish Sauna,' 'Fifty Years of Changing Literature', and 'English Life Today'. He was then seventy-one and still hard at work. Between 1937 and 1957 nine of his plays were broadcast by the ABC.

In 1936 Palmer's friend and mentor, Leslie Rees, joined the ABC with the intention of broadcasting Australian playwrights. He organised Australian Drama Weeks in 1937 and 1938 and from that time 70 per cent of plays broadcast on the ABC were by local authors. Within two years of Rees' appointment there was a sharp rise in hourly fees from a lowly guinea to fourteen guineas. Ken Inglis, the historian of the ABC, noted that only two dramatists, Max Afford and Edmund Barclay, made a living writing ABC dramas. Both worked on contracts and while Barclay's salary in 1936 was a handsome £18 per week, the pressure was enormous: 'Afford was grey-haired at thirty, and Barclay used to disappear for days on binges, returning just in time to write the next episode for waiting actors.' A list of some Australian plays produced by the ABC between 1935 and 1953 contained almost two hundred titles.

Rees' prayer that he would one day find the great Australian radio play was answered in 1941 when he read an extract from Douglas Stewart's *The Fire on the Snow* (published 1944). The broadcast play was critically acclaimed and the grateful author dedicated the published work to Leslie Rees and Frank Clewlow, who had produced the play for the ABC. *The Fire on the Snow* was presented many times and was described by the BBC's Tyrone Guthrie as 'one of the few important works which radio has so far produced'. Encouraged by his success, Stewart wrote *Ned Kelly* (pub. 1943) and *The Golden Lover* (pub. 1944), both of which won ABC prizes. His achievements enticed other writers into the field of verse drama. The radio serial also acquired legendary status from the 1940s. Gwen Meredith's *The Lawsons* (pub. 1948) began in February 1944; five years later *Blue Hills* (pub. 1950) went to air. It became, in Inglis' happy phrase, 'an Australian metaphor for longevity'. On 28 October 1972 between 250,000 and 400,000 listeners tuned to episode 5000.

The ABC had an enormous impact on literary production from the late 1930s, particularly in the area of radio drama. Indeed Rees wondered if audiences were too well satisfied to bother with live theatre. Certainly in the postwar households responsible for the baby boom, it was cheaper and easier to tune in to the radio than go to the theatre. Moreover, the high-minded character of the ABC ensured that literary news would be broadcast to an unprecedentedly large audience. 'Current Books Worth Reading' may not have rivalled 'Blue Hills', but it proved to be an impressively durable program.

All writers who had dealings with the ABC were made aware that their work was subject to censorship. Miles Franklin was delighted to learn that *All That Swagger* (1936) was to be broadcast and was so pleased at how well it sounded that she wrote to congratulate the reader. He warned her that there would be cuts in some of the last episodes: 'Some priest in NSW has written to say that the religious controversy between Danny and his wife is embarrassing to both churches. Lovely, ain't it?' Earlier, in the 1930s there was constant strife over political balance, with broadcasters on the left feeling under constant pressure to trim their wings. In 1934, the ABC offered prize money for local plays and sketches, but blasphemy, bad language, 'representation of sex problems, and controversial questions concerning politics and religion' were forbidden, along with characters who showed signs of insanity or bodily defects. To have submitted a play about Billy Hughes would have been unthinkable under these conditions. In the 1930s, over three hundred overseas books and thousands of political pamphlets, journals and periodicals were prohibited as illegal imports. Local writers were made aware of the censor's powers when Norman Lindsay's *Redheap* (1930) and *The Cautious Amorist* (1932) were banned, followed by J. M. Harcourt's *Upsurge* (1934), Australia's first communist novel. In the 1940s Robert Close had the distinction of being gaoled after his book

Love Me Sailor (1945) was published. In 1950 Frank Hardy achieved notoriety after *Power Without Glory* was published against the background of Menzies' attempts to have the Communist Party outlawed.

With deepening conservatism in the 1950s, a group of radical intellectuals with communist links, associations and entanglements formed the Australasian Book Society. At its peak in 1961 it had just over three thousand members. The society wanted only those works that reflected Australian 'life struggles and militant traditions'. When they were not rushed by spurned authors, the society began its series with Ralph de Boissiere's West Indian novel *Crown Jewel* (1952). By 1965 the ABS had published just under fifty titles and had issued a handful more, including Arthur Phillips' *The Australian Tradition* (1958), to members.

If the Left Book Club was a sign of the 1930s, the appearance in July 1935 of the first Penguin reprints priced at sixpence a volume was another. The experiment was an immediate success. In 1937 Penguin moved on to publish original titles, rather than reprints alone, with sales often reaching a quarter of a million copies. Former *Bulletin* cartoonist and Bookstall illustrator David Low published three books of wartime cartoons with Penguin, while W. K. Hancock's *Argument of Empire* appeared in the Pelican series in 1943. Four years later Penguin books established a subsidiary company in Melbourne and by 1956 Penguin's Australian sales stood at around 750,000 copies a year. By this time a new generation of Australian best-sellers had emerged. Eric Lambert's World War II novel *The Twenty Thousand Thieves* (1951) was reprinted seven times in Corgi paperbacks in the 1950s and sold around half a million copies. Jon Cleary's *The Sundowners*, published in 1954 and later filmed, sold about 750,000 copies in Fontana paperbacks.

The fifty years from 1915-65 witnessed profound changes in the technology of marketing Australian books. Yet it is uncertain that publishing practices themselves changed. In 1934 P. R. Stephensen charged that Australian literature was controlled by overseas publishers and importing booksellers such as Angus and Robertson. He argued that although Australians were avid readers they were served a diet of inferior books and durable English classics. In 1965 Angus and Robertson still dominated local publishing, though as the years passed they were periodically exposed to outside interests and the growth of specialist and regional publishing. The precise influences which commerical practices and attitudes had on writing in this period are difficult to determine, but Australian publishers were certainly reluctant to support literary experiment.

Notes

The *Australian Dictionary of Biography* and *The Oxford Companion to Australian Literature* (1985); H. M. Green, *A History of Australian Literature* (1961; rev. 1985); E. Morris Miller and Frederick T. Macartney, *Australian Literature* (1956); Geoffrey Hubble, *The Australian Novel: A Title Checklist* (1970); Australian National Library, *The Australian Catalogue of Publications* (1936-60); Stephen Torre, *The Australian Short Story: A Bibliography, 1940-1980* (1984); S. M. Apted, *Australian Plays in Manuscript* (1968); and Grahame Johnston, *The Annals of Australian Literature* (1969) are the major bibliographical sources consulted for the chapter. Periodicals include *All About Books* (1928-37) and the *Bulletin*.

Other information is scattered through various manuscript collections, publications and government reports: Tariff Board Reports into the importation of printed matter 1930 and 1946; at the Mitchell Library, Sydney, Angus and Robertson Papers, Fellowship of Australian Writers Papers, Marjorie Barnard Papers, Eleanor Dark Papers; at the Australian National Library, Canberra, Palmer Papers, H. E. Boote Papers, Louis Esson Papers, Frank Wilmot Papers, Xavier Herbert Papers, E. J. Brady Papers, Katharine Susannah Prichard Papers, Dymphna Cusack Papers, Phillip Whelan Papers; at the Australian National Archives, Canberra, Trades and Customs Department Files, Leslie Allen Papers, Attorney-General's Department Files, Commonwealth Literary Fund Files.

Secondary sources include David Walker, *Dream and Disillusion* (1976); Drusilla Modjeska, *Exiles at Home* (1981); Geoffrey Serle, *From Deserts the Prophets Come* (1972); K. S. Inglis, *This is the ABC* (1983); Craig Munro, *Wild Man of Letters* (1984); Richard Nile 'The Rise of the Australian Novel' (PhD, UNSW, 1987).

Chapter 19

LITERATURE AND CONFLICT

BRIAN MATTHEWS

Before he was approached for his opinion of the Ern Malley poems (published in the autumn 1944 number of *Angry Penguins*), Herbert Read had already heard about the hoax. Two young poets, James McAuley and Harold Stewart, with a series of pseudonymous letters and a concocted volume of poetry entitled *The Darkening Ecliptic*, had managed to convince *Angry Penguins* editor Max Harris and his colleagues that one Ern Malley, deceased, had been an unknown but considerable Australian poet who wrote in the manner of the so-called Apocalyptic School of Dylan Thomas, Henry Treece and others. As Read wrote to Harris not long after the hoax was exposed on 5 June 1944, 'the news was even splashed in our own papers, which only take notice of poetry and art when it is associated with a crime or sensation of some sort.' The situation was, of course, no different in Australia. The respectable burghers of Adelaide who insulted and reviled Max Harris in North Terrace and King William Street were speaking not from a considered ideological position on surrealism but from the obscure and uneasy conviction, exultantly peddled to them in the press, that arty people like Harris and his supporters were a threat to morals and stability and that the mysteries they practised—incomprehensible, non-rhyming poetry and unrecognisable 'art'—were unnatural and ought to be repressed. Like the French cab driver in Sartre's Paris who, having lost an argument about the fare, shouted after his departing client the vilest abuse he could come up with: 'Espèce d'Existentialiste!', uninvolved Adelaideans picked up the very terms and nomenclature of the argument and turned them into execration. Art was on the streets; the university, studios, coteries and tucked-away editorial offices of insignificant journals had suddenly disgorged their denizens and their mad conflicts into real life. The confrontation was volatile but essentially unproductive and misleading: on the one side an irruption of buried and scarcely thought-out fears prodded to life by a philistine press; on the other, seen almost as an irrelevance, a distraction from the real issues. Herbert Read's view of the Malley affair, elaborated in the letter to Max Harris already mentioned, proved to be a very interesting one and is often cited with admiration. 'I read the poems,' he says,

> in an objective spirit, and though I find them very uneven, often obscure and sometimes absurd, yet allowing as I would normally do for some adolescent crudity, the general effect is undoubtedly poetic, and poetic on an unusual level of achievement. There is not only an effective use of vivid metaphor, a subtle sense of rhythmic variation, but even a metaphysical unity which cannot be the result of unintelligent deception . . .
>
> It comes to this: if a man of sensibility, in a mood of despair or hatred, or even from a perverted sense of humour, sets out to fake works of imagination, then if he is to be convincing he must use the poetic faculties. If he uses these faculties to good effect, he ends by deceiving himself. So the faker of Ern Malley. He calls himself 'the black swan of trespass on alien waters,' and that is a fine poetic phrase. So is 'hawk at the wraith of remembered emotions' and many other tropes and images in these poems. Others are merely sophisticated or silly:
>
> The elephant motifs contorted on admonitory walls
>
> Move in a calm immortal frieze
> On the mausoleum of my incestuous
> And self-fructifying death.
>
> I have mistrusted your apodictic strength
>
> This kind of rhetoric is modern Ossian, but, like Ossian, can understandably deceive the best critics. So much for Ern Malley.

It was not at all surprising that Read should have been able to tender such an urbane, critically sensitive and, perhaps above all, confident response. He had already encountered the same critical issues in another similarly combative but much more intellectually flexible forum. The comparison is instructive.

In March 1942, Read received an invitation from George Orwell, who was then Talks Assistant with the BBC, to take part in a program on contemporary English poetry. 'I want you,' Orwell wrote,

> to deal with the new movement which has arisen in the last few years starting, I suppose, with Dylan Thomas and George Barker. There is quite a group of young writers centring round the Apocalyptic movement who I think would make material for an interesting talk. I had tentatively named your talk Surrealism but if you think that this term cannot strictly be applied to literature, we can easily change it.

Read accepted Orwell's commission and gave the talk more or less as suggested except that they agreed to change the name of the poetic school from Apocalyptic Movement to New Romantics. Out of this original program grew the idea for what Orwell called a radio magazine, entitled *Voice*. The first program of *Voice*, which went to air later that same year, was built around the new poetry. There was a poem by Herbert Read, three poems by Henry Treece, and Dylan Thomas' 'In Memory of Ann Jones'. After William Empson had read the latter, Orwell invited the panel (John Atkins, Mulk Raj Anand and Empson) to discuss it, leading off with:

> I suppose the obvious criticism is that it doesn't mean anything. But I also doubt whether it's meant to. After all, a bird's song doesn't mean anything except that the bird is happy.

Empson, with a kind of explosive, pinpointing testiness that seemed to be often his mode of address in these discussions, rounded on this judgement with great trenchancy, branding it as 'nonsense, and . . . very unfair to Dylan Thomas. That poem is full of exact meanings.' Orwell conceded that 'you grasp at once that this is a poem about an old woman' but insisted on its essential meaninglessness: 'just listen again to the last five lines,' he urged.

> These cloud-sopped, marble hands, this monumental
> Argument of the hewn voice, gesture and psalm
> Storm me forever over her grave until
> The stuffed lung of the fox twitch and cry Love
> And the strutting fern lay seed on the black sill.

'The last two lines in particular,' Orwell concluded, 'defy interpretation and even the syntax is a bit funny. But as sound, that seems to me very fine.' Empson's counter was quite crushing in its limpid straight-forwardness.

> I think he takes for granted that she had a fern in a pot and a stuffed fox in her cottage parlour. The comparisons of woods and seas and so on are of course meant to tell you about the breadth of her own nature and its strength and kindness. It may be obscure but it is obviously not meaningless.

When the panel turned its attention to Henry Treece, a poet who, in Atkins' view, 'consciously [controlled] his material more than Dylan', there was some talk of 'uneven effect', 'a sort of surrealism', an 'undisciplined manner . . . sometimes to the point of absurdity'; but the focus was soon very much on the romantic nature of the Apocalyptic School in reaction to the 'Auden-MacNeice School, which [was] classical by implication'. Atkins' lengthy discourse on this theme brings another eruption from Empson:

> These distinctions seem to me all nonsense. Treece is a perfectly good poet, and that means he is using the whole instrument, mind and passions and senses. These poems are no more all Romance than Dylan Thomas's poems are all Noise. Whether Treece has been irritated by a prose book by MacNeice is quite another thing; if he was, I daresay he was quite right. But his writing has plenty of intellectual toughness under it to carry it. And it's absurd for anybody to think that they're somehow pressing him by saying that he hasn't.

One does not necessarily have to accept the critical judgements being proffered in the *Voice* discussion in order to recognise perhaps its most outstanding feature: the relaxed pluralism that copes as easily with possible meaninglessness as with various other modes; the absence of ideological anxiety (though not, of course, of ideology); the assurance with which tendentious concepts like 'schools' are exploited or dispensed with according to their usefulness or otherwise at different points of the argument; the confident approach to questions of meaning and obscurity in poetry. In the public forum provided by *Voice,* Orwell could insist that Dylan Thomas had perpetrated meaninglessness without thereby wanting the poet suppressed, silenced or humiliated; and Empson could vigorously set aside certain literary distinctions and champion Treece without thereby being accused of insensitivity to absurdity and a penchant for back-slapping.

The achievements, oddities and excesses of the Apocalyptic poets were the subject of considerable controversy in Britain, but it was a discursive controversy: it opened the subject up, it did not seek to close it forever with an irresistible Sunday punch. The debate was much more cut-throat, more terminal so to speak, in Australia.

As Vivian Smith has rightly observed, 'for anyone to think now that poems add up to achieved artistic wholes is to lose all sense of standards and perspective'. The hoaxers' stated aim and justification tend to obscure the fact that a number of Australian poets quite unconnected with and even hostile to the Angry Penguin group were striking chords not dissimilar to Malley's in the legitimate pursuit of their entirely different poetic goals. How many pundits, for example, not already in the know, would pick the author of this poem?

> Dark cry, claim the dark-shored lake.
> Quicken your echoes round the hills. Dwell
> in, possessing, earth and sky. Take
> farewell . . .
>
> Engined with knowledge, as fast
> that very way the confident mind must push,
> cry of a winging wild duck cast
> to the insatiable hush of the bush.

Many might wrongly hazard Ern Malley rather than a 1940 poem by Rex Ingamells. Following this embarrassment, the battering testiness of an Empson might be summoned up to defend the Ingamells poem from the implied stigma of Malleyite incomprehensibility.

The Darkening Ecliptic is now less worth arguing about than the motives, so far as we know them, which produced it and the dynamics of the literary culture on which it burst, momentarily as a sensation, later as a revealed hoax. Though it may be true, as Smith rather starlingly suggests, that the hoaxers' concocted letters in the name of Ethel Malley are the most interesting aspect of the whole affair, their explanation following the exposing of the hoax remains fascinating despite its having been much pored over. Geoffrey Dutton remarks, accurately enough, that the 'story of the hoaxers, James McAuley and Harold Stewart, has always been accepted'. His clearly presaged disagreement, however, has to do with the question of premeditation and planning rather than with the explanation's actual content. Dutton claims that 'the hoax had been planned and discussed between Hope,

McAuley and Stewart for at least six months', but the letter of 22 June from Hope to C. B. Christesen which he cites in evidence does not really establish this. 'I've been sitting on the bank for the last six months watching Maxie played for a sucker', exults Hope in this letter. This means he had known about it in January 1944. In his limited edition of *Ern Malley's Poems*, Harris says he received the first letter from Ethel Malley 'early in 1944' so that all that is established by the correspondence so far is that Hope knew about the hoax once it had been set going. This does not prove that the hoax poems themselves had a long gestation. Later correspondence from Hope, quoted by Dutton, does nothing to alter this: Hope reveals that he had been planning his own hoax but concedes that the McAuley-Stewart version is superior; and he remarks that 'the whole of Ern's works were composed at a sitting'. That there was much communication between Hope and McAuley from roughly the time that Ethel Malley first wrote to Harris is placed beyond dispute by this correspondence. If the whole affair was the subject of plotting among the three of them at some time in 1943, however, this correspondence does not hint at it.

Dutton's insistence on this aspect of the letters has perhaps led him to be less attentive to the immoderate and often malicious exultation with which Hope viewed and contributed to the discomfiture of Harris and others. 'What a lot of hate there's going to be in Adelaide from now on', Hope remarks in the 22 June letter with obvious relish; he refers to the Malley affair as 'the super hoax' and, later, when it appears 'that Maxie is off on another wild goose-chase', he reveals, again with palpable anticipation, that, 'If he follows this up he will stick his neck out for the axe a second time.' Hope was an equally enthusiastic destroyer apart from the actual hoax itself. The alacrity with which he accepted Christesen's invitation to review Harris' novel, *The Vegetative Eye*, and the witty but devastating piece that resulted are probably too well known to detail. But Hope directed his brilliant satiric weaponry at many other targets. Turning his attention during his first year of serious reviewing (1941) to the Jindyworobaks, he labelled them memorably as 'the Boy Scout School of Poetry' and in subsequent reviews he set about Rex Ingamells and Ian Mudie in particular with gusto and deadly accuracy. Hope's objections to the Jindyworobaks put their point of view, he says, in a 'series of emotional outbursts masquerading as argument'; referring to Jindy-worobak views on Aboriginal culture, he argues that 'the poet who tries to write like a second-hand abo[rigine] is no more likely to produce sincere work than the poet who writes like a second-hand

Englishman'; of Mudie's *Poems, 1934-44,* he says, among other things: 'Mr Mudie has done nothing but rewrite the first poem in the first volume of verse he published'; the later poems, he says, reflect 'a stage of mass hysteria at which it is impossible to think at all' and he compares Mudie with 'the German poets of the Third Reich who sank to the level of loud-speakers blaring at a Youth Rally'. Likewise, 'Mr Mudie's verse sinks to that of the rejected entries for a patriotic song competition.'

The point is that Hope's fusillades during the period of his most intense reviewing activity (1941-8 for *Southerly, Meanjin* and *Poetry)* represent less a concerted, ideological attack on modernism—which is how Dutton sees his work at that time—than an exuberant, sometimes callous revelling in highly developed powers of satire and lampoon. This becomes even clearer if we notice Hope's treatment of much lesser lights than Harris or the Jindyworobaks, writers who could not remotely be construed as appropriate targets for an enemy of modernism. One of these targets was Joseph O'Dwyer, author of a collection called *The Turning Year,* and another unpretentious poet whose work suffered the Hopean scourge was Norma Davis. Hope reviewed her *Earth Cry* in *Poetry,* 15 (1945), and slaughtered it. Some samples:

> The gold medal (and bar) for exuberance this year goes not to Daisy III, the thousand gallon cow, but to Miss Davis's Cry from Tasmanian Earth.
>
> Her muse is a lush and exuberant adolescent female and Miss Davis's next tasks are to get her off an exclusive diet of honey dew and wild raspberries, to teach her to use a knife and fork and not to speak with her mouth full and, finally, to lead her gently but firmly to the corset counter. Miss Davis will find these tasks a little easier if she can manage to get the pixies out of her hair.

Seen in the context of such flailing, self-consciously brilliant and totally merciless attacks on all and sundry, high and low, Hope's gleeful response to the Malley hoax and even his enthusiastic destruction of *The Vegetative Eye* begin to look much less like ideological campaigning and more like the unrestrained effusions of someone intoxicated with his own wit, hypnotised by the flash of the scalpel in one hand and the rhythmic thud of the bludgeon in the other.

Two more features of Hope's reviewing career during this turbulent period are relevant. First: though his work for *Southerly, Meanjin* and *Poetry* more or less spanned the decade (1941-8), his fearsome reputation was based on a relatively small selection of his total review output—namely, on his treatment of the Jindyworobaks and his no-holds-barred attacks on Harris, O'Dwyer and Davis. Apart from these, his reviewing was sometimes acerbic, always stringent, but basically calm and scholarly. Second: during this period, Hope was curiously disjoined from the literary and cultural life of which, if one were to judge by his corrosive and fearless reviews, he seemed such an inured, rough-and-tumble member. Dutton quotes from a letter to Christesen which partly testifies to this species of chosen isolation:

> What am I prepared to do? The answer is nothing that will make in-roads on my private time, and apart from my time as a lecturer or at ABC — I would always rather write poetry than write about poetry and I don't give a damn for culture really . . . a certain time each year is devoted to Australian writers of whom I know so little and by whom for the most part I am profoundly bored or irritated.

But perhaps even more pointed because so ingenuous, is his admission in a letter to Flexmore Hudson that, despite the extremely abrasive nature of some of his reviews, it had never occurred to him that some of his victims might consider legal action:

> I must admit that the thought of legal action never occurred to me. It should have. But I live in such complete isolation from the world of writers and publishers that I am apt to write about books by living writers as I would about the writers of past ages—finding the cause of their faults in their characters as human beings—or like a surgeon I trace the symptom to its disease. It does not occur to me that the patient will resent the description of his disease enough to sue me for mentioning it.

The posture of dispassionate critical rectitude here (the surgeon's knife) is in itself interesting but that in turn is nurtured, along with an apparent vagueness about some of the world's ways, by isolation. That same isolation from the world into which his virulent sallies were tossed presumably blinded Hope to other possible consequences of his slashing attacks. He was awakened to these in the worst possible way and the effect upon him was decisive. Shortly after his dismantling of Norma Davis' *Earth Cry* in *Poetry* 15, she died (November 1945). *Poetry* 17 was dedicated to her memory. Writing in February 1946, after the appearance of the memorial issue, Hope is devastated. Just as it had not crossed his mind that his trenchancy might attract legal action, it is obvious from his letter to Hudson that he had simply not considered the extent to which real and personal, as against literary, 'surgical', wounding might result from his exultant tracing of the symptom to its disease. Blaming himself far too heavily, Hope cannot prevent himself from speculating on the possibility that Norma Davis might have read his corrosive review on her deathbed. The whole incident, he tells Hudson, 'finishes' him for 'the reviewing business'. He will 'take [his] big boots off' and henceforth do no more reviewing. Thereafter, though he did review again (including for *Poetry*), he never aspired to the scorched-earth panache that had earned him his reputation. He did not pursue the Jindyworobaks any further after about 1945. But in his *Native Companions* (1974), he retracts: 'Some amends are due, I think, to these Jindyworobaks . . . I made the mistake of supposing that if a case is badly argued, there is nothing in it at all.' Hope attacked the poetry of Eliot and Pound and there is plenty of evidence to establish that he was no friend to the modernist movement. Nevertheless, his response to the Ern Malley hoax and his review-articles in the three or four years before and after have neither the unity of focus nor the overtone of program that are among the identifying marks of a campaign. Hope wrote of Christesen that 'as an editor, he is the apple of my eye. His selection is not narrowed by quack theories.' Hope's targets at the height of his reviewing activities in the 1940s were not mainly modernism but quack theories and theorists and sloppy practitioners. If he was often scarifying as he cleared the ground to get at these targets and if his aim when he fired was deadly, it is also true that his essential humanity was undiminished. Hope blamed himself too readily for the *Earth Cry* review, but in any case, regardless of what happens in the heat of battle, only the compassionate and the humane hang up their boots forever after the fray and apologise. Likewise, Hope's attitude to the local literary product may have been, in those heady days, less than tolerant, but it would be a distortion to leave the matter there. A decade or so later, for example, C. B. Christesen, in a long letter to T. Inglis Moore (who was then a lecturer in English at Canberra University College), described his frustrations, his sense of being embattled, as editor of *Meanjin* in a hostile literary and political climate. One thing, however, for which he had cause to be grateful was that 'the attitude to *Meanjin*' of certain influential people 'had changed remarkably during the last six months'. He goes on to add his suspicion that:

> Alec Hope . . . had a lot to do with that—for one thing his support of the introduction of Australian Literature courses in the University, which . . . had [been] long opposed, and Alec's review of the Autumn issue [of *Meanjin*] this year.

Christesen was not the only one who, in the 1950s and after, had cause to be grateful for Hope's championship of the national literature in universities and elsewhere.

Hope's comparison of Mudie's poetic voice with Nazi street propaganda ('loud-speakers blaring at a Youth Rally') is devastating; but there is no suggestion that he wants to brand Mudie personally or seriously to associate him with the views or actions of the Third Reich. What he *does* want to do is to obliterate poetry which, in his opinion, has the automatism, the mindlessness and the absence of inspiration characteristic of blaring propaganda or the 'entries for a patriotic song competition'. It may all be too severe and exultant but there is no question that the poetry which has triggered it is particularly bad. On the other hand, it must be added in fairness that where Hope sees promise or achievement in Mudie's collection he salutes it just as unequivocally: in some later poems he notes 'the voice of the individual, the man with the deep love and tenderness for the shapes and colours . . . [who] begins to see the real pattern and detail of the world he lives in'. That Hope would, in due course, 'come to know Ian Mudie, to have his ungrudging friendship and to admire his poetry' is perhaps only another, if retrospective, indication of the humanity that lay at the heart of even his most virulent onslaughts.

In their explanation of the Malley hoax, McAuley and Stewart draw an analogy which is strikingly similar to Hope's reference to 'German poets of the Third Reich'. The 'cultism' of the New Apocalypse and Angry Penguins, they suggest,

> resembles on a small scale, the progress of certain European political parties. An efficient publicity apparatus is switched on to beat the big drum and drown opposition. Doubters are shamed to silence by the fear of appearing stupid (or worse) *reactionary*. If anyone raises his voice in protest he is mobbed with shrill invective. The faithful, meanwhile, to keep their spirits up, shout encouragements and slogans, and gather in groups so as to have no time to think.

There is a big difference: Mudie's poetry may not have deserved the extreme castigation that Hope visited upon it (perhaps nobody's does) but it patently merited a stringent criticism. The hoaxers' analogy, however, is an absurdly simplistic, even scurrilous view of a theory and practice which cannot with any intellectual integrity be so trivially dismissed. We do not need to have the slightest patience with the Angry Penguins, the New Apocalypse or surrealism generally in order nevertheless to recognise that trial by jibe and insulting analogy will not even begin to deal with their complexity, their besetting weaknesses and their undoubted strengths. Hence the seriousness of Orwell's *Voice* panel whose members, no matter what their differing positions on the overall phenomenon of surrealism, recognised it as a subject susceptible of serious attention and debate.

'It was, after all, fair enough,' insist the hoaxers in another part of their explanation in the Sydney tabloid *Fact*. 'If Mr Harris proved to have sufficient discrimination to reject the poems, then the tables would have been turned.' But to what extent *would* the tables have been turned? If Max Harris had rejected *The Darkening Ecliptic* for what McAuley regarded as the right reasons, can we credibly convince ourselves that McAuley and Stewart would then have owned up, revealed the failure of the hoax and begun a rethink of their views about the Surrealist or Apocalyptic School and its critics' sensitivity 'to absurdity' and their capacity for 'ordinary discrimination'? As Eliza Doolittle so memorably announced: 'Not bloody likely!' Further: suppose the hoax, having worked beautifully as history records, had not been exposed by *Fact* on 5 June 1944 or by anybody else at any other time. Are we to believe that the hoaxers would then have cherished their knowledge close to their hearts? What would be the point of 'a serious literary experiment', the result of which could not be disseminated among both the faithful and the enemy? In fact, of course, it would have been all through the literary world like a cancer, to Harris' and the Angry Penguins' great discomfort and shame. But Harris was on a hiding to nothing: if he *had* judged correctly, who would have known? To Harris it would have appeared as just another editorial rejection, while the hoaxers, veiled by anonymity, would have been under no pressure whatsoever to concede the failure of their hypothesis.

The poetic terrain above which the Angry Penguins edifice briefly and exotically towered and which the Jindyworobaks enlivened with their theories, disputes and occasionally good poetry, had been drab enough before these two contrasting groups emerged. They were reacting in their different ways to much the same situation. The

Australian novel may have been often stranded up-country throughout most of the 1930s and 1940s and thus not to everyone's taste, but it was at least alive and well (Frank Dalby Davison, *Man-Shy*, 1931; Brian Penton, *Landtakers*, 1934; Kylie Tennant, *Tiburon*, 1935; Eleanor Dark, *Return to Coolami*, 1936; Miles Franklin, *All That Swagger*, 1936; Xavier Herbert, *Capricornia*, 1938); Australian poetry in the same period spent a lot of time at the bottom of the garden—with the fairies—or in embarrassingly Hellenised bush settings, or in other inappropriate or grotesquely misconceived situations. The *Bulletin* Red Page throughout the 1930s is clear testimony to this, despite the occasional appearance of FitzGerald and Douglas Stewart (both of whom were absent from Australia for much of this period). Little magazines, which first began to appear in this decade, were often more adventurous but rarely reached much of an audience and rarely survived beyond a few issues (e.g. *Stream, Verse, So This is Adelaide, Foolscap, Pandemonium, Manuscripts, Yesterday and Most of Today*, and so on). And even though, as Grahame Johnston's *Annals of Australian Literature* shows, the number of published volumes of verse increased annually between 1930 and 1944 the quality was mediocre with only rare exceptions. In short: when Ingamells looked over the poetry scene from the standpoint of, say, 1937—in which year he delivered his address 'On Environmental Values' to the English Association in Adelaide—he saw very little poetry that satisfied his requirement of Australian inspiration, Australian content and imagery; and when Max Harris surveyed the same scene at the start of the new decade he saw the burgeoning Jindyworobaks and not much else—nothing that seemed to have much connection with or awareness of the cultural world beyond the antipodes. And, by and large, they were both right.

The Ern Malley affair (and the subsequent obscenity trial—which no one, least of all the hoaxers, had expected) discredited poets and poetry in the eyes of the general public but only for the very short time that it remained newsworthy. When the dust settled, it was to reveal: the Jindyworobaks faltering for reasons internal to themselves and to Rex Ingamells' insecure grasp of where *he* saw them going; Slessor fully established (*One Hundred Poems 1919-1939* published in the year of the hoax); FitzGerald powerfully emergent (*Moonlight Acre*, 1939, and *Heemskerck Shoals* on the way, 1949); Judith Wright on the horizon with emphatically modern (if not modernist) poems that would make up *The Moving Image;* and beyond them, as before, a vast mass of vaguely Anglophile or vaguely nationalist poets of the kind that Hope had briefly and enjoyably lambasted at his reviewing peak. Because the literary experiment was itself phoney—geared to produce only one kind of useable result and to bury the other options inherent in the hypothesis—it could have no really serious impact on the enormously complex mass of creative theory and practice for which *Angry Penguins* was the Australian outlet. (It was precisely the recognition of that challenge that moved Orwell to devote so much time and attention to the new movements in his own 'journal', *Voice*, while having himself great misgivings about much of what he encountered from modernist artists.) The bad publicity, of course, did not help poets or the standing of their craft and art. The caution with which the so-called 'university poets' (Vincent Buckley, Chris Wallace-Crabbe, Evan Jones, Philip Martin and, in some early poems, Bruce Dawe) went about the task of refurbishing the image of poetry and the poet in the early 1950s (note, for example, the number of poems about the art of writing poems) may be some evidence of a Malley hangover.

But forty years on, the Ern Malley hoax's greatest interest is perhaps its archetypal quality: the make-or-break nature of the debate; the application of a pseudo-scientific test which could produce an uncompromising answer from such imponderable material signalled the confrontationist, take-no-prisoners style that would distinguish so much Australian literary disputation in the years that followed. There had of course been premonitions before 1944—in what Michael Wilding calls the 'firmly anti-modernist' stance of the Vision School or rather in some enunciations of that stance; and in what Bernard Smith has seen as the 'conscious, willed and *creative* refusal of many dimensions of modernism' among pioneer Australian painters. But these scarcely exhibited the full-blown polarisation so thoroughly exposed by Ern Malley's poems and so evident, one way or another, in most subsequent literary and intellectual encounters. In the world at large, beyond the walls of the increasingly reviled academies, any tendency towards modernist, or worse, surrealist art activated general public, journalistic and some intellectual embargoes: William Dobell's portrait of Joshua Smith (Archibald Prize, 1944); the publication of Patrick White's *The Tree of Man* (1955) and *Voss* (1957); the furore over the purchase of Jackson Pollock's *Blue Poles* (1973). Not even naturalism—so favoured on the Australian stage until the 1970s—was safe if national myths were impugned; hence the stormy passage of *The One Day of the Year* into the more accommodating dramatic waters of the 1980s.

As for the academies themselves: the author of *The One Day of the Year*, Alan Seymour, bemoaned the condition of the intellectual in 1968.

> a note for the — please pardon the dirty word—intellectuals . . . Give up . . . Turn yourself to the approved bourgeois delights: experimental theatre, Hippy Happenings, LSD. Refuse all temptations to turn your attention outwards to the so-called problems of the world. Turn ever inwards in ever-smaller circles until you disappear up the only avenue left.

Less than a year later, Clement Semmler was cautiously optimistic:

> The only hope . . . is the intellectual and the writer (he [sic] may even be a writer-intellectual). The act of scholarship, of research, or creation is the best antidote to a power-complex. If he is a historian he will profit by what he reads of the follies and foibles of the power-mongers of the past; if his field is literature or art the glorious and elevating concern with things of the spirit and the imagination will triumph.

Seymour may well be excessively gloomy. On the other hand, there has been little in Australia's small literary-academic world to suggest that the glories of literature have much mitigated the notorious powermongering within the country's university literature departments. The seemingly endless controversy about the centrality or otherwise of Australian literature; the likewise recurrent issue of Australian versus foreign appointments in English; the bitter confrontations that divided the English departments of Sydney University and the University of Wollongong; the slanging match between Professor Colin Roderick and Professor Manning Clark over 'the real Henry Lawson' are only a few—and the more publicised—of the acrimonious, win-or-lose encounters undertaken in the name of the glories of English and the national literature. The academic art world has been no less tumultuous, the most recent (though amazingly muffled) argument being the use of the William Dobell Bequest to fund a chair for a specialist in European rather than Australian art. And so on . . .

All of these controversies share with the Ern Malley affair the following characteristics: opposed sides each of which is convinced not only that it has the answer but that the insistence on the ultimate victory of that answer is crucial to the well-being and balance of the broader cultural scene; the supplanting of debate, evidence, concession and consensus with power-plays, abuse, pseudo-scientific tests, numbers counting or the discovery of loopholes; the assumption that the encounter will be resolved by one side winning and the other being obliterated either by numbers or by public ignominy.

For anyone interested in what has been called the 'literary gang warfare' in this country, the Ern Malley hoax retains perhaps its most vital fascination as an archetype, even though at the time it appeared to protagonists as some sort of climax, a watershed. From the vantage point of the 1980s, its effect on the literary culture remains unprovable though speculatively interesting. Its other historical interest is as a gaudy stage for the play of personalities who remained dominant in Australia's cultural development and who all, in one way or another, tended to repudiate the affair in the end. Perhaps the very last words should be left to Dylan Thomas and Ern Malley as, in their feverish dredging of the volatile unconscious, they eerily echo each other's tone, each other's inchoate and unquenchable longing:

until

The stuffed lung of the fox twitch and cry Love
And the strutting fern lay seed on the black sill.

Among the water-lilies
A splash - white foam in the dark!
And you lay sobbing then
Upon my trembling intuitive arm.

Notes

Ern Malley's *The Darkening Ecliptic*, with an explanatory introduction by Max Harris, statements from the protagonists and an appendix covering the obscenity trial, are reprinted in Max Harris (ed.), *Ern Malley's Poems* (1961).

The material from *Voice* is included in W. J. West (ed.), *Orwell: The War Broadcasts*, London 1985. See also: Brian Matthews, 'Understanding George Orwell', *Quadrant*, 30, 1986.

Rex Ingamells' poem 'Dark Cry' appeared in his *Selected Poems* (1945).

Vivian Smith's reference to the Malley poems are in Leonie Kramer (ed.), *The Oxford History of Australian Literature* (1981).

Geoffrey Dutton's treatment of the Malley affair is in his *Snow on*

The Saltbush ((1985). Letters from Hope quoted in this chapter are taken from Dutton, except for the letter to Flexmore Hudson which is in the Menzies Library, Australian National University. One letter has been paraphrased because of its personal nature. Hope's reviewing in the 1940s is discussed in John Dally's unpublished PhD thesis, Flinders University, 'The Jindyworobak Movement, 1935-1945' (1978) and thanks are due to Dr Dally for permission to use this material.

Hope's reviews of O'Dwyer and Davis appeared in *Poetry*, 15 (1945). His commentary on the Jindyworobaks was published in *Southerly*, 2, (1941) and his review of Mudie's *Poems 1934-44* in *Poetry*, 17 (1945).

C. B. Christesen's letter to T. Inglis Moore, dated 6 October 1955, is in the H. V. Evatt Collection, Flinders University Library.

For a discussion of the Malley hoax in a larger cultural context, with special emphasis on its possible relevance for the 1950s 'University poets', see Brian Matthews, 'The Live Point: Should "Poetry . . . speak when spoken to?"' in Peter Quartermaine (ed.), *Readings in Australian Arts* (1978); and Peter Cowan, 'Angry Penguins and Ern Malley's Journal' in Bruce Bennett (ed.), *Cross Currents: Magazines and Newspapers in Australian Literature* (1981).

Michael Wilding's comment is made in his introduction to Jack Lindsay, *Life Rarely Tells* (1982), and Bernard Smith's is quoted in Peter Fuller, *The Australian Scapegoat: Towards An Antipodean Aesthetic* (1986).

Alan Seymour's comment appears in *Meanjin*, 2 (1968), and Clement Semmler's in *Meanjin*, 1 (1969).

Concerning the Dobell bequest, see George Petelin, 'Cultural Cringe Creeps up on Dobell', *Australian*, 23 March 1987.

Chapter 20

WOMEN WRITERS

SUSAN SHERIDAN

Women have been significant contributors to Australian writing since at least the middle of the nineteenth century, yet it is appropriate to discuss some of their work separately here because in the middle of the period 1915-65, women writers achieved such prominence. As Drusilla Modjeska says:

> The 1930s were remarkable years in Australian cultural history. Women were producing the best fiction of the period and they were, for the first and indeed only time, a dominant influence in Australian literature.

That historical phenomenon alleviates but does not solve the problem of how to set up a category of 'women writers' without reinforcing the idea of women as outsiders whose activities and achievements must be on the margins of a notional mainstream. While recognising this as a danger to be avoided, feminist critics have pointed to the necessity of considering the specific position of women in relation to a male-dominated culture (which is a relationship of power, material and intellectual), and of investigating the kinds of writing and the kinds of audiences that have been available to women in different historical periods.

This chapter investigates some of the ways in which women writers during the 1930s and 1940s engaged with issues concerning the construction of a national cultural identity, issues which achieved prominence during commemorations of the beginning of white colonisation and again during World War II and its Cold War aftermath. Without assuming that women writers would inevitably take a critical stance on these issues, we might expect to find evidence in their work of an ambiguous, if not overtly conflicting, relationship to patriarchal cultural institutions and discourses. The later part of the chapter examines evidence for white women writers considering analogies (partial though these might be) between their oblique relationship to discursive power, and the silence of Aboriginal people.

Given such aims, this chapter will not attempt the alternative tasks it might have set itself: a history of women writers from the beginning of white settlement to the present, a survey of women writers in the period 1915-65, an attempt to fill in gaps left by other chapters, or an explicit theoretical challenge to male-dominated traditions of literary history and criticism. It aims to convey a sense of the ambiguity of all celebrations of nationalism past and present, reinforced by a feminist perspective on the complex relationship of this group of women writers to the production of a discourse on national identity.

'Who's on whose margins?' was the subtitle of a recent essay on migrant women's writing in Australia by Sneja Gunew. The question succinctly exposes the very notion of margins and centres as a matter of perspective and of power: of positioning. Most of the women writers to be considered here were favourably situated in terms of class and ethnic background. They could define themselves as occupying central rather than marginal positions in the debate on cultural nationalism during this highly politicised period. Yet they were working within and against a deeply patriarchal tradition. Moreover, they had no explicitly feminist position available to them from which to question the tradition's exclusion of women and its denigration of matters feminine.

The difficulties of this situation for women intellectuals can be discerned in their contributions to a cluster of anthologies produced by groups of women in several States to mark the centenary (in Victoria and South Australia) and the sesquicentenary (in New South Wales) of white colonisation. How did they perceive their relation to each other, to other women past and present, and to the society then celebrating its strife-torn origins? While few explicit feminist statements about the struggles of women as a group can be found in them, the commemorative volumes can be read as collective statements as much by what they omit as by what they affirm.

Affirmative they certainly were. The Victorian *Centenary Gift Book* (1934) initiated the theme of women as pioneers, the first item in its list of contents being 'The Women Who Made Us' by Mary Grant Bruce. The book features a refreshing mixture of the famous and the unknown, and touches on a range of activities from the arts and professions to domestic and other physical labour. As Frances Fraser, co-editor with Nettie Palmer, modestly puts it in the foreword:

> Pioneering ... still goes on. Woman has gradually made a place for herself in almost all walks of life ... Not usurping man's place, she has been his mate in higher things as she was in the more humble.

Yet the emphasis on pioneers brings with it a limited notion of history as the celebration of past achievements and, despite the signatures of women well-known for their activism and creativity, there is little sense of the current challenges facing women or of work in progress. For instance, most of the literary contributions, notably those from Katharine Prichard and Henry Handel Richardson, are reprints.

A similarly limited conception of pioneering as history, and a comparable silence about current issues, is even more noticeable in the sesquicentenary volume *The Peaceful Army* (1938). Not only was it merely a year away from the outbreak of war, but most contributors had been active during the 1930s in the liberal and socialist left. Yet the main articles all concern the lives of individuals in the past: Elizabeth Macarthur (by M. Barnard Eldershaw), Mary Reibey (by Dymphna Cusack), Caroline Chisholm (by Eleanor Dark), Rose Scott (by Miles Franklin), 'Some Pioneer Women Writers' (by Winifred Birkett) and 'Some Pioneer Women Artists' (by Margaret Preston). The final essay, Kylie Tennant's 'Pioneering Still Goes On', repeats the sentiment of Frances Fraser that pioneering still goes on in the present, and is 'a matter of character and opportunity'; she adds, though, that it is a matter of city life now, and of cooperative rather than individual effort. This emphasis on social welfare is shared by the other contributors, of course; but it is only in the poems that one can hear clearly a note of fear for the future. Mary Gilmore's 'Memorial Ode' ends with a prayer:

> If ever in the dark embrace
> Of fear it is our lot to stand,
> Vouchsafe, O God, to us this grace:
> That we may be as those who stood,
> Lone on the threshold of this land,
> In their enduring womanhood.

And Helen Simpson sends from London a wry comment on the

miracles of communication technology, 'Australia is so modern', and 'Sesquicentenary: London, Sydney' which casts doubt, from a classic feminine posture, on speed of progress, of

> growth . . .
> Not to be checked, carrying something of terror—
> Pang of a woman who halts, her hand at her bosom.

The vice-regal presence in this book, in two separate forewords, is striking. Lady Gowrie writes with great aplomb of the pioneers having conquered 'this beautiful land' and 'bequeathed it to us'. She also introduces the South Australian women's centenary volume, *A Book of South Australia* (1936), this time in the company of Lady Dugan. Indeed, the South Australian collection contains several other Ladies among its contributors, and is distinguished by its attention to that State's worthies, past and present, from 'Our Viceregal Ladies', by Lucy Webb, to 'Our Pioneer Women and Our Natives' by Daisy Bates CBE. It is ironic, however, that although there are tributes to Catherine Spence and Mary McKillop and articles on women's work in welfare and the professions, the only contribution to make reference to women's struggle to achieve equality as an ongoing effort, is 'Reminiscences' by Marie Carola Galway, whose husband was State governor from 1914 to 1919. She notes with concern that

> under certain regimes a halt to the new-born equality has been called. More than that, the first and easiest way of making an impression on the problem of unemployment has been to remove as many women as possible from the labour market.

While there is much to criticise about these celebratory volumes, their eagerness to present in such an official context information about and creative work by women has to be appreciated in an historical perspective. They are virtually the only collective statements about women's history and experience that are now available to us from that time. It is little wonder that they lack critical and historical analysis, appearing as they did at the end of a period of backlash against feminist assertions of solidarity among women and of pride in female achievements. For instance, one would have been hard-pressed to find, in the mid-1930s, any easily accessible account of the lives of women like Caroline Chisholm, far less ex-convict Mary Reibey. Alice Henry's 'Marching Towards Citizenship' tells of the suffrage struggle in Victoria in considerable detail, as if she could not take it for granted that her readers would know about it, 'although the winning of the vote seems such an old story now'. Opportunities to survey and reflect upon the achievements of women writers, artists and reformers outside the columns of 'women's magazines' were rare. Ways of praising women were generally limited to the class-defined stereotypes of the lady philanthropist or the saintly bush mother (referred to by Kylie Tennant, who gently blames Henry Lawson for its predominance).

Women's fiction, dominant as it was during this period, seldom provided challenges and alternatives to these stereotypes. Female characters were rarely central or, when they were, it was often as the object of harsh criticism: for instance, several of Dymphna Cusack's early works dealt with communities of women (*Jungfrau*, 1936; the play *Morning Sacrifice*, 1942; *Come In Spinner*, 1951), but the strength of individuals within them is defined through irreconcilable conflicts stemming from differences of class, age, and sexual morality, and woman's inhumanity to woman is a repeated theme.

The general backlash against feminism as divisive and old-fashioned, and the isolation of women intellectuals from other women (despite their progressive politics), may explain why their interest in women tends to be critical or merely marginal. Claiming a group identity as women was not on their agenda, whereas claiming a part in the revived struggle for national identity was. The major fictions of Prichard, Franklin, Barnard Eldershaw, Devanny, Dark and Tennant during the 1930s and the war period employed the genres of pioneering family sagas, historical reconstructions, tales of communities defined by geographical location and forms of labour. In constructing these epic forms, they claimed to speak for all Australians to all Australians, in ways which may be questioned sharply from current political and theoretical perspectives. They tended (and they intended) to universalise or to totalise, exactly as Lubacs maintained was the role of the novelist and of the historical novelist in particular. The effect was to homogenise an Anglo-Celtic 'Australianness' in which people of other races and cultures were silent presences, if they were there at all. They tended to appeal to an Australian essence which resided in the landscape. Their realist narratives, however rich in psychological and social conflicts, always strove to present these conflicts in ideologically and aesthetically resolvable forms. Having inherited a deeply masculinist national culture and having outlived the earlier strong feminist challenge to it, the women writers, if they were going to get into the act at all, had to set aside feminine experiences, interests, desires. It seems to have proved, as Drusilla Modjeska concludes in her study of their work, 'impossible to unite their concerns with the situation of women and with politics'.

Henry Handel Richardson and Christina Stead, because of their location in Europe and their long fascination with European literatures, approached the issues of Australianness rather differently from their contemporaries, although they also confidently used epic and other genres not conventionally feminine. Richardson's major work, *The Fortunes of Richard Mahony*, was published in three volumes: *Australia Felix* (1917), *The Way Home* (1925) and *Ultima Thule* (1929). It has been justly described by her foremost critic and biographer, Dorothy Green, as 'the archetypal novel of white settlement' in which 'all the main issues that define the direction of white Australian society and its values from the 1850s onwards can be discerned either in embryo or fully developed'. The architecture of the trilogy makes space for the execution of such large-scale exploration, yet in the texture of the writing there is no straining after significance but a slow and deliberate movement back and forth between absorption in the detail of the moment and its metaphorical extension. Here is an extract from the proem to *Australia Felix*, a description of the Ballarat goldfields in the 1850s:

> This dream it was, of vast wealth got without exertion, which had decoyed the strange, motley crowd, in which peers and churchmen rubbed shoulders with the scum of Norfolk Island, to exile in this outlandish region. And the intention of all alike had been: to snatch a golden fortune from the earth and then, hey, presto! for the old world again. But they were reckoning without their host: only too many of those who entered the country went out no more. They became prisoners to the soil . . .
>
> A passion for the gold itself awoke in them an almost sensual craving to touch and possess; and the glitter of a few specks at the bottom of pan or cradle came, in time, to mean more to them than 'home,' or wife, or child.
>
> Such were the fates of those who succumbed to the 'unholy hunger.' It was like a form of revenge taken on them, for their loveless schemes of robbing and fleeing; a revenge contrived by the ancient, barbaric country they had so lightly invaded. Now, she held them captive—without chains; ensorcelled—without witchcraft; and, lying stretched like some primeval monster in the sun, her breasts freely bared, she watched, with a malignant eye, the efforts made by these puny mortals to tear their lips away.

A comparable vision of human compulsion and the resistant power of impersonal forces, both historical and natural, informs Christina Stead's first novel, *Seven Poor Men of Sydney* (1934). In the lyrical extravaganzas that punctuate the narrative there *is* a sense of strain, but also a rhythmic excitement and semiotic play which spill over the boundaries of realist prose. The following passage is a kind of incantatory history of Australia: it begins with an account of the origins of the water continent in the Ice Age, 'south without land to the pole, in the rough swilling sullen sudden surly southern ocean, last post of the land world'; it ends with a succinct 'history' of white colonisation:

> Catholic Spain, proud Portugal, sent their sailors steering for Solomon's Isles, the Moluccas with fruits and china bells, and the jewels of the unconquered uncatholic uncommerced new world. Captains from Holland and the North Sea unwound their wakes upon the waters of the world. Fires were lighted, murder done, ships cast away, cargoes plundered, robbers clothed in silk, rafts seaswept, women lost, sacrosancts profaned, mutinies smothered, hostages taken, chartings made, shore-lines plumbed, reefs struck, wreckers enriched, the Chinese rolled from port to port, the Kanakas perished in the cane, mountain bluffs were climbed, the blackfellow destroyed, the plains bore flocks, the desert of spinifex spouted gold, the new world began. And after all this notable pioneer tale . . . in the overpopulated metropolis . . . the despair of the heirs of yellow heavy-headed acres. What a history is that; What an enigma is that?

Stead's notion of Australia as the water continent, or 'the island continent in the water hemisphere', is recalled in the prologue to her novel *For Love Alone* (1944). Entitled 'Sea People', it omits the reference to the dispossession of the Aborigines and celebrates Australia as a 'great Ithaca', a breeding ground of Homeric wanderers. This serves as a neat contradiction to both the emigrant melancholia that characterises Richard Mahony's relation to the country and the level-headed settler character of his wife, Mary. Seascape rather than landscape, willing wanderers rather than settlers or exiles, a place on world trade routes rather than an outcast outpost of the British Empire: Stead's emphases all fall differently from those of her contemporaries whether at home or abroad.

Another extraordinary meditation on Australianness, another wanderer's tale, is Eve Langley's 1942 novel, *The Pea Pickers*. In this female picaresque the narrator, Steve, and her sister, disguised as boys, travel about the country following seasonal picking work. Their main object is Gippsland, their mother's country, 'patria mia' (as Steve calls it; and they call their mother Mia). They have been dispossessed, but believe they can only reclaim their land as men, or through men. Steve tries (often with comic effect) to persuade Macca, her boyfriend, to return her passion because 'You are Gippsland; you are Patria Mia: and you must love me'; but, although comely, Macca is a slow fellow and distrustful of passion, especially the literary kinds. Among the many paradoxes encountered in this portrait of the artist in drag is the passionate desire to belong to the land and to the line of bushman heroes, to claim the inheritance denied to her mother because she was 'only a woman'. Another puzzle is the presence of the Italians, fellow itinerant workers: to Steve they are variously figures of fun, ungrateful migrants, 'poetic Fascisti, black-shirted and brilliant', and the noble descendants of Michelangelo and Raphael, Dante, Tasso and Petrarch; at times Italian culture seems to offer an alternative object of devotion for which she would 'give up my dreams of being a great Australian, a pioneer in racial purity and a passionate single-hearted lover of my country', an ingenuously racist sentiment that appears inseparable from passionate patriotism.

This frustrated desire to belong to the land, sharpened by the knowledge that the land can never belong to her because, as a woman, she cannot inherit, recalls the adolescent Sybylla of Miles Franklin's *My Brilliant Career* (1901), with her final words: 'I am only an unnecessary, little, bush commoner, I am only a—woman!' In her novel *All That Swagger* (1936), Franklin perhaps at last made good her claim to inherit. Certainly by the time it was published she was a prominent writer, welcomed home after years living in the United States and Britain and leaving behind her the 'Brent of Bin Bin' pseudonym. *All That Swagger* is, as Marjorie Barnard has noted, a 'saga, a family chronicle, a chapter of national development'. Yet its major character is the pioneer patriarch, Danny Delacy, despite Franklin's sympathy for the hardships which women pioneers underwent *and* despite her mockery of the hypocrisy and pretensions that accompanied the pioneer fever of the 1930s (which fuelled her satirical collaboration with Dymphna Cusack, *Pioneers on Parade*, 1939). Franklin repeats the pattern of gender attributes which Richardson had put into play with Richard and Mary Mahony, of male dreamer and female materialist, when she has the main actor at the end of the book (also a male Delacy) ponder on his inheritance: from the women 'that alloy of ruthlessness—horse-sense—to armour him amid the wreckers and pluckers' and from the Delacy men, the Irish dreamers, those qualities which his grandmother called weaknesses (but which any reader of such novels knows to be strengths), 'blathering poetry and ranting like red-raggers against moneybags . . . or else giving away all they had'.

Given the ambiguous position of those women who claimed the right to speak publicly of and to the national identity, it should come as no surprise to find them, as Franklin does here, taking up a narrative position which attempts gender neutrality but which, especially when dealing with elements of national identity, inevitably shows up the masculine bias of the apparently neutral or universal. Two other novels of the period illustrate some of the gains and losses for the woman writer of a 'universal' narrative stance: Eleanor Dark's *The Timeless Land* (1941) and M. Barnard Eldershaw's *Tomorrow and Tomorrow* (1947).

Tomorrow and Tomorrow has a male protagonist, a writer called Knarf, and one important side effect of this choice, noticeable on the very first page of the text, is that the natural world is metaphorically seen as female. An autumn night is described as having 'a feeling of transience, of breaking ripeness, of doomed fertility, like a woman who does not show her age but whose beauty will crumble under the first grief or hardship'. This metaphor is just as 'natural' to anyone using the dominant conventions of literary discourse as the use of the generic masculine in generalisations about humankind, or Australians. Along with the masculine narrative stance goes an absence of female characters. While Barnard Eldershaw set out to generalise in a serious and critical manner about 'progress' by looking back over contemporary Australia from a hypothetical future, their long view is still largely devoid of women.

Eleanor Dark's trilogy of the history of white colonisation, of which *The Timeless Land* is the first volume, is another attempt during the war period to reflect on issues of national identity and political crisis. Since she follows the conventions of historical narrative and the contours of the available source material, the major actors are inevitably male and the major actions are those 'epoch-making events' which, as Anne Summers pointed out in her 1975 study of women in Australia, have been foregrounded by the way in which Australian history has been written. Although Dark does attempt to write what social historians have called 'history from below', when she makes Aboriginal characters central to the action of *The Timeless Land*, the role of women as historical agents on either side of the invasion is nevertheless minimal. Thus even her attempt to reconstruct the Aborigines' social and psychological environment at the moment of 1788 focuses on Bennelong and other male characters: because of the nature of historical records and the institutions which shape them it is they who are 'historical figures', as Dark notes in her preface, while the female characters are imaginary.

How did women writers, most of them engaged at some level with the struggle to define a national culture, write of 'other women', of Aboriginal women in particular? The discursive process by which dominant images of identity, whether national or female, are constructed involves the naming of others against which the subject is defined. A feminist analysis of this process must question it, as Gaytri Spivak has noted, asking not merely Who am I? but Who is the other woman? How am I naming her? How does she name me? Were the white women writers of the period, engaged in the effort to define a national culture, self-conscious about ways in which Aboriginal women were named? For instance, when Miles Franklin wrote that one of the gravest literary themes demanding treatment at the end of the 1920s was '"black velvet", the Aboriginal skeleton in the colonization cupboard', what were (and are) the implications of this naming for patriarchal definitions of white women and their sexuality? How did the writers imagine circumstances in which Aboriginal women would be in a position to name *them*, and to be heard?

Cultural representations of any social group not in a position to speak for themselves and be heard are bound to be limited in range and complexity. This is not to suggest, however, that when members of such a group do become producers of signs in the dominant culture, they can speak of themselves directly and authentically. Rather, they must of necessity engage with those dominant representations and discourses. The work of women writers, whether they are conscious feminists or not, demonstrates the continuing need not only to kill off the Angel in the House (Virginia Woolf's image of the self-censoring good-woman aspect of femininity) but equally to summon up her opposite, and to use these two sets of cultural images to explore the conflicts and ambiguities of their situation as women.

So it is no surprise to find that Aboriginal women are principally represented in the writing of white women, whatever their political allegiances, as objects or as symbols; as the 'other woman', indeed. For instance, the Aboriginal woman herself does not appear in a work like Henrietta Drake-Brockman's play *Men Without Wives* (1955) although she is referred to as part of the (white) problem indicated by the title; but again, the central position of Coonardoo in Katharine Prichard's novel of that name does not prevent her from functioning as a symbol of spiritual connection with the land and as a vessel of natural sexuality, a symbol signifying a distinctively white desire.

Men Without Wives is initially of interest here because it won a sesquicentenary drama competition in 1938 and was published in the *Sydney Mail*, which would suggest that it was considered to have a significant statement to make nationally, and one suitable for the celebration of white settlement. Despite the title, the play actually focuses on the white women, not the men: Ma Bates and her two daughters and Kit, a 'flash tart from the South', who has been brought to a remote station in the north-west of the continent as a bride. The play concerns her initiation as a bush woman. The debate is about the women's duty to stay there for the sake of the men who, if left 'without wives', are bound to take up with the 'gins'; but whether this duty is to protect the Aboriginal women from exploitation, or to preserve the morals of the white men or to maintain inter-racial harmony, is not clear. The diffuseness of purpose undermines the play's treatment of the 'social problem', turning it in the direction of a morality play in which sexuality (a quality of white men and Aboriginal women) is presented as a danger which can only be controlled by the white women's presence as God's police. A similar moral instruction for white women can be read in Prichard's play, *Brumby Innes* (first performed 1975, but written in the 1920s), with its portrayal of a weak and frivolous southern girl and a sexually potent Aboriginal woman; but they are hardly in a position of competition for Brumby, whose brutal clarity about the uses of a white wife puts paid to the notion of any policing role for her: 'I want youngsters,' he declares, 'and I want'm thoroughbred'. Marriage has granted him ownership rights and if his wife will not enjoy his 'natural lust' then he has the women of the camp at his disposal, and others whom he can 'buy' for a rifle and a couple of blankets.

It is striking how these fictions involving sexual relations between black and white all deny to the white women characters any active desire. In both *Coonardoo* (1929) and Mary Durack's *Keep Him My Country* (1955), the younger white women are shallow and prudish, like Kit, and the older ones, the mothers of the heroes, characterised as 'masculine' in their strength, like Ma Bates. In both the novels, the Aboriginal woman is the object of the hero's true desire and also the vessel of sexuality itself. In this sense, all desire is displaced onto her.

Coonardoo in Prichard's novel and Dalgarie in Durack's, in their central relation to the hero, are the freely desiring agents, while the men are sexually inhibited and guilt-ridden. In each case, their love is explicitly distinguished from the brutal sexual exploitation practised by other white men, as well as from the sexlessness of the white women. These relationships could be read as displacements of the white woman's fantasy of reciprocal desire fulfilled or even of the superior power of female sexuality in its 'natural' state. In this respect, what we seem to be dealing with is a justificatory myth of the kind Nadine Gordimer wrote about among white liberal writers in South Africa in the 1960s. In that case it was an 'apocryphal black-white brotherhood', a friendship between a young black and young white man which she described as 'the literary wish-fulfilment of what South African society could be, would be, if only the facts of the power struggle could conveniently be ignored'.

There is a further dimension to this justificatory myth, however. In each case the relation between the black woman and the white man is portrayed as a deep spiritual bond, ultimately a bond with the land itself. In *Coonardoo* the single moment of their sexual union principally signifies Hugh's giving himself not so much to Coonardoo (who is 'like his own soul' and so at this level indistinguishable) but to 'the spirit which drew him . . . to the common source' of their lives, which is the land. Finally, without her presence ('the well in the shadows'), Hugh's station fails to prosper and she, driven away by his sexual jealousy, returns there only to die. Similarly in *Keep Him My Country* the Aboriginal women (Dalgarie and, before that, his father's mistress) are represented as binding Stan to the land by their magic. The title comes from a woman's love song which goes

> I talk to my country for she is woman
> The water and the soil of life, . . .
> I cry to my country—
> 'Keep him that he may come to my side . . .
> I wait for my lover.'

The love story, woman-centred and Aboriginal-centred as it is, can nevertheless be read as a justificatory myth in defence of white colonisation because it appears to be at the instigation of the Aboriginal women in his life that Stan forms a properly spiritual attachment to the land; but he does not stop being its owner, in white terms, and the boss. There is a false notion of reciprocity invoked here.

So, too, in *Coonardoo* the notion of love as mutual need suggests a complementarity of man—woman, white—black, human—natural which obscures the crucial historical relationship of colonial exploitation and violence.

Another way of considering literary representations of suppressed peoples is to look for instances where such figures are made central not as symbols or as objects of observation but as conscious agents, as narrative points of view. Nene Gare's novel *The Fringe Dwellers* (1960) does this. Published only five years after Mary Durack's, it addresses a situation far removed geographically and socially from that of the Aboriginals portrayed in *Keep Him My Country*. All the characters are Aboriginal people and they represent a range of attitudes to their position on the margins between the white society from which some of their fathers came and the tribal lands of their Aboriginal ancestors. The major conflict is between those like Mrs Comeaway, who are satisfied to remain 'fringe dwellers' in the camps and missions, and her daughters, who want access to white society. But the girls differ from one another in this: Noonah takes up nursing training but is able to maintain primary ties with her family, while Trilby, the rebel, wants to leave all of that behind. All three women are treated sympathetically and their values respected, but these differences are presented ultimately as differences of temperament, with the implication that all could be accommodated by a more generous liberalism on the part of whites, to make integration policies work. This Aboriginal community is portrayed as being held together by ties of affection, but without collective agency or culture.

In fictional representations of Aboriginal people in the period before 1967 there is a near-total silence about the history of colonisation. Xavier Herbert's *Capricornia* (1938) is of course a notable exception; so too, is Jean Devanny's *Cindie: A Chronicle of the Canefields* (1949), which is set in the 1890s and takes up the case against the White Australia policy of the Labor Party. Generally, however, the history of Aboriginal resistance is neglected. During the 1930s, for instance, there were activist groups in the eastern states working against many aspects of the government's assimilationist policies, and protests against the sesquicentenary celebrations were organised—events which are not represented in the history and fiction of the period.

The tendency to represent Aboriginal cultures as if they were timeless, eventless, is reinforced by two kinds of writing about them which were popular during the period: anthropological studies (which attempt to reconstruct traditional tribal societies) and books for children (a category encompassing both tales of outback life and bowdlerised translations of Dreamtime stories). A strange example is *All-About: The Story of A Black Community on Argyle Station, Kimberley* (1935) by Mary and Elizabeth Durack. Although H. M. Green classifies it with children's stories ('a direct descendant of Mrs Gunn's *Little Black Princess*'), it is awkwardly poised between the genres of children's fiction and racist adult humour. Although dedicated to its subjects, it is not addressed to them, for 'You will never read this, for to learning you have no pretensions'; however the preface by the then lieutenant-governor of Western Australia can state unabashedly: 'This tale of station life will appeal to all real Australians.' The caricature-style illustrations, offensive though they are, might suggest an intended audience of white children; however the text is more explicit about sexual matters than is usual in children's fiction, although this may be simply a consequence of constructing Aboriginal people *as* children.

Anthropological studies like Daisy Bates' *The Passing of the Aboriginals* (1938) and Phyllis Kaberry's *Aboriginal Woman: Sacred and Profane* (1939) were widely read. However the anthropologist A. P. Elkin, in his introduction to *Aboriginal Woman*, makes no mention of amateurs like Bates and Ernestine Hill in his impressive list of Kaberry's professional forerunners (all of them men). Her book offered a materialist analysis of women's economic and ceremonial life in the far north-west of Australia and this seems to have caused Professor Elkin some hesitation over the assumed naturalness of sexual segregation: 'Some may prefer to argue [against her] that both the dichotomy manifested in economic life and also in ritual life may arise from the physiological differences between men and women.' Kaberry's books also offered, for the first time, a woman-centred perspective, a challenge to anthropology that has recently been taken up again by Diane Bell in *Daughters of the Dreaming* (1984). It undoubtedly influenced many of her contemporaries who were writers; for instance, Dymphna Cusack mentions its importance to her, and Mary Durack dedicated *Keep Him My Country* to Kaberry.

Many of those who wrote about Aboriginal people also acknowledged their debts to Mary Gilmore. Most of her poetry on Aboriginal themes was not widely known until published in book form in the early 1930s (*Under the Wilgas*, 1932); this feature of her work was prominent, too, in the two books of reminiscences she published then: *Old Days: Old Ways* (1934) and *More Recollections* (1935). Most of this material had been written before 1924 'but no journal would use it', she claimed. From her father she had heard stories of the hardships endured by the early settlers but also of their acts of genocide in hunting down Aborigines with dogs and guns. These stories and her own childhood experiences of staying with members of the Waradgery tribe near Wagga in the 1870s inform such poems as 'The Hunter of the Black' ('All the methods of his calling learned from the men he stalked' who 'Shot, for him who stole the country, him who killed a sheep'). There are laments such as 'The Aboriginals', 'Australia' and 'The Waradgery Tribe', which ends with the lines:

> O, the lost tribes! . . .
> There came a ghost
> Where once there walked a host.
> O, the lost tribes!

These brief lyrics of Gilmore's remind us that the people were hunted off their lands, that they did not simply disappear with the passage of time, as the dominant ideology would have it.

'Those perennial poems on the last of his tribe, the Australian contribution to the *ubi sunt* tradition', as J. J. Healy puts it, had no space for the recognition of the survivors, even when they politicised the tradition to the extent that Gilmore did. Judith Wright's early poems on Aboriginal themes are also laments, but they gain urgency from the sharp influx of guilt experienced by whites who, 'like my grandfather, / must quiet a heart accused by its own fear' ('At Cooloola', from *The Gateway*, 1953). Perhaps the best-known of her earliest poems in *The Moving Image* (1946) is 'Bora Ring'. It rehearses the lament that Gilmore and others had sung:

> The song is gone; the dance
> is secret with the dancers in the earth
> the ritual useless, and the tribal story
> lost in an alien tale . . .

but it ends with an evocaton of 'the ancient curse, / the fear as old as Cain'. Decades later, Judith Wright returns to this theme, but now in words addressed to the survivors, to her friend Kath Walker, in particular:

> You brought me to you some of the way
> and came the rest to meet me,

> over the desert of red sand
> came from your lost country
> to where I stand with all my fathers,
> their guilt and righteousness.

This poem, 'Two Dreamtimes' from *Alive: Poems 1971-72*, claims some shared interests, shared griefs:

> our grief for a lost country,
> the place we dreamed in long ago,
> poisoned now and crumbling . . .
> sad tales of women
> (black or white at a different price) . . .

Yet it does not flinch from the political realities of their different griefs:

> The knife's between us. I turn it around
> the handle to your side,
> the weapon made from your country's bones.
> I have no right to take it.

Kath Walker's book of poems *We Are Going* (1964) was the first book to be published by an Aboriginal woman. Thus the period ends, appropriately, with the advent of a new group of women writers speaking for themselves. Their literary discourse, like Wright's image of the knife offered, is implicated in the traditions of white writing as well as Aboriginal culture. But the difference lies, initially at least, in the expression of a political will. The dedication of Kath Walker's first book to the Federal Council of Aboriginal and Torres Strait Islanders Advancement sets up a historical and political context for her poems. While some of the rhymed lyrics recall the powerful simplicity of Gilmore's verse, the political context transforms the statements of feeling into something like a knife. So, too, the songs of lament produce a social meaning that is radically different from the laments written by poets like Gilmore and Wright. The title poem, for instance:

> They came here to the place of their old bora ground
> Where now the many white men hurry about like ants . . .
> They sit and are confused, they cannot say their thoughts . . .

But the poet invents a voice for them, in which to affirm the continuity of their presence at the moment when the passing of their old ways, laws and legends is mourned;

> We are the shadow-ghosts creeping back as the
> camp fires burn low.
> We are nature and the past, all the old ways
> Gone now and scattered . . .
> And we are going.

But this is perhaps the last of such laments, and much of Kath Walker's work in the years since she published *We Are Going* has been dedicated to the reclaiming of those old ways and places, and to encouraging younger writers. The survivors are no longer a silent presence.

In the years since 1964 the field of Australian writing has become diversified, with work published in English by Aborigines and by migrants as well. There is more regional writing and publishing, too. In such a situation of diversity, there will perhaps never again emerge an identifiable group of women writers like those of the 1930s and 1940s. Yet it is still possible and indeed necessary to speak of women writers as a group, to consider their work in relation to one another and to the cultural and political issues of their time. This is not to construct a unity of 'women writers' or a feminine aesthetic, but to look at the various ways in which they deal with the marginal position assigned to women and to see what differences and what connections emerge. When this is done, the extent of women's reconstructions of the dominant culture become visible. As the editors of *The Penguin Book of Australian Women Poets* (1986) put it: 'The power of the margins is exactly in the reconstruction. There is a way of understanding the centre from the margins.'

Notes

My major debt in this chapter is to Drusilla Modjeska's *Exiles at Home: Australian Women Writers, 1925-45* (1981). It is a group biography of the major women writers of this period, with an historically informed analysis of their writing and their politics, feminist and socialist. There is no general history of women writers in Australia, but studies of individual writers are slowly increasing. The only such studies referred to in this chapter are Dorothy Green, *Ulysses Bound: Henry Handel Richardson and Her Fiction* (1973 rptd 1986) (but the actual remark quoted comes from a biographical sketch of Richardson in Marilyn Lake and Farley Kelly (eds), *Double Time: Women in Victoria—150 Years*, 1985); Marjorie Barnard, *Miles Franklin* (1967); Dymphna Cusack, T. Inglis Moore and Barrie Ovenden (eds), *Mary Gilmore: A Tribute* (1965); Norman Freehill, *Dymphna Cusack* (1975).

Much detailed work on the history of women in Australia has been produced in recent years as part of the revived feminist movement, but general discussions of women's cultural production are relatively few. Anne Summers' first chapter, 'A Sexist Culture', in *Damned Whores and God's Police: The Colonisation of Women in Australia* (1975) raises some crucial issues. Much of the debate and research findings have been published in Australian feminist journals, *Hecate, Refractory Girl, Scarlet Woman* (all of which date from the early 1970s) and, more recently, *Australian Feminist Studies. Meanjin* published two special issues on women and feminism (34, no. 4, 1975 and 38, no. 3, 1979). A sample of the wide variety of feminist approaches being employed in criticism can be found in Carole Ferrier (ed.), *Gender, Politics and Fiction: Twentieth-Century Australian Women's Novels* (1985). Sneja Gunew's essay in this collection, 'Migrant Women Writers: Who's on Whose Margins?' raises important questions about differences amongst women writers; the specific questions I have quoted as a challenge to the ethnocentrism of feminist theory ('who is the other woman?') come from Gayatri Chakravorty Spivak, 'French Feminism in an International Frame', *Yale French Studies*, 62 (1981). Two approaches to analysing white representations of colonised peoples which I have drawn upon are: Nadine Gordimer, 'Literature and Politics in South Africa', *Southern Review*, 7, (1974), and Stephen Muecke, 'Available Discourses on Aborigines' in Peter Botsman (ed.), *Theoretical Strategies* (1982). A useful study of the representation of Aboriginal people in Australian writing is J. J. Healy, *Literature and the Aborigine in Australia, 1770-1975* (1978).

Chapter 21

WAR LITERATURE, 1890-1980

ROBIN GERSTER

For many years following World War I the New South Wales returned servicemen's journal *Reveille* campaigned vigorously against the 'nauseating muck' spread by foreign writers, whose anti-war poems, novels and memoirs were then flooding the international literary market. The British writer Robert Graves was a prime target for attack, because in *Goodbye to All That* (1929) he had had the temerity to record admitted Australian atrocities committed against German prisoners. *Reveille* reported that such 'slanders' had prompted the federal executive of the Returned Services League to canvass the government with the object of censoring authors 'who defame Australian soldiers'. Though too dmuch notice should not be taken of the voice of a veterans' organisation understandably determined to defend the good name of its members, the obsessional concern of *Reveille* for the reputation of the Australian Imperial Force can tell us much about the parochial, conformist and exceptionally heroic character of Australian war literature since World War I.

The war of 1914-18—the 'Great War'—was a literary as well as historical watershed. The carnage along the Western Front in Flanders and France quickly convinced most European writers that the long tradition of heroic battle literature, stretching back almost three thousand years to Homer's epic of war and masculine virtue, the *Iliad*, was no longer valid. Twentieth-century warfare seemed, even then, such an impersonal enterprise: technological advances in weaponry had made the martial hero obsolete. Heavy artillery mocked pretensions to prowess, and luck, not skill, decided the warrior's fate. Even an Achilles would have stood no more chance against the force of a long-range, high-explosive shell than the most craven weakling. Consequently, in the important poetry produced by the war (such as that of the Englishmen Wilfred Owen and Isaac Rosenberg), the old epic assertiveness, inflated rhetoric and grandeur of perspective were transformed into a subjective lyric mode which registered war's impact on the private, usually despairing and disenchanted, sensibility. The international cry of protest replaced the chauvinistic boast. In fiction, in such major French, German, American and English war novels as Henri Barbusse's *Under Fire* (1916), Erich Maria Remarque's *All Quiet on the Western Front* (1929), Ernest Hemingway's *A Farewell to Arms* (1929) and Richard Aldington's *Death of a Hero* (1929), the protagonists are victims rather than heroes, passive sufferers rather than champions of racial valour. The almost unanimous contention of World War I fiction that battle degrades, not ennobles, that it produces shuddering horror, not exaltation, has been immensely influential in shaping modern fictional responses to war: in Joseph Heller's *Catch-22* (1961) and Timothy Findley's *The Wars* (1977), for example, the antiheroic motifs and myths of 1914-18 are evident.

The majority of Australian writers ignored this revolution in war literature. At the time heroic man was fast disappearing from war writing abroad, Australians were celebrating the birth of a latter-day Achilles, a warrior who was bigger, braver and better than the poor excuses for soldiers who comprised rival armies. The storming of a small beach on the Gallipoli peninsula on 25 April 1915 inspired a sustained burst of literary activity which soon elevated the Anzac to a supreme place in the pantheon of national heroes, his very name ensured against debasement by the 1921 parliamentary statute 'Protection of the Word Anzac'. This ideal figure was perceived to be recognisably and uniquely Australian, while also embodying the qualities of the Homeric heroes who trod the battlefield at Troy, so tantalisingly close to Gallipoli itself. The anachronistic nature of his promotion is exemplified by William Baylebridge's uninhibited use of archaic imagery in *An Anzac Muster* (1921), especially his focus on the Australian liking for the bayonet. Those who wrote of the achievements of the AIF in the less primitive, more mechanised military conditions in France were scarcely more restrained. To C. E. W. Bean, who as the official Australian war correspondent and later as official historian was the godfather of the national 'baptism of fire' myth, the Western Front was a forcing-house for classical Australian talents. In his account of the disastrous Battle of Fromelles of July 1916, Bean juxtaposed the ineffectual efforts of the Germans, who timorously tossed stick-bombs from the comparative safety of their trenches, with the daredevilry of the Australians, who, 'up on the parapet, flung their missiles like cricketers throwing at a wicket'.

Nevertheless, it is perhaps too easy to dismiss the raw chauvinism of the Australian response to World War I. After all, the burgeoning heroic myth did grow from a seed of historical truth. The fighting skills of the AIF were recognised by several foreign observers, particularly the English war correspondent Ellis Ashmead-Bartlett, whose Gallipoli reportage extolling a 'race of athletes' did much to establish the Anzac legend. Moreover, an emergent nation like Australia needed its home-grown heroes. (Battle-weary Europeans had a surfeit of them: they could afford to be cynical.) The Great War was an epiphany of the Australian national identity: C. E. W. Bean claimed that the country came to 'know itself' during the conflict. Success in such a crucial test of strength went some way to ridding Australia of its colonial sense of inferiority, replacing it with what one AIF memoirist, G. D. Mitchell, called a 'superiority complex'. The cocky tone of the Australian literary response stemmed from the assurance that, as another soldier-writer put it, 'the adolescent nation of the South Seas' had proved its 'fitness for manhood' in an adventure 'upon which were focussed the eyes of all nations'.

The war writers catered to a public which, as Bean observed, 'only tolerates flattery and that in its cheapest form'. Australians were impatient to hear of the nation's youth making it in the martial Big Time—it had had previous peripheral roles in the Maori Wars during the 1860s, in the Sudan in 1885, in the Boxer Rebellion of 1900, and in the Boer War of 1899-1902, but these were sideshows compared with the spectacular international drama of 1914-18. Probably the most-read war book by an Australian prior to World War I was W. H. Fitchett's *Deeds That Won the Empire* (1897), a collection of tales celebrating specifically English heroism (a contradiction in terms according to many in the AIF), which was in its twenty-ninth impression by 1914. Starved of the genuine article, Australians took passionately to a work like *The Moods of Ginger Mick* (1916), C. J. Dennis' colloquial verse-narrative about a Melbourne larrikin who is improbably transformed into a raging patriot and Gallipoli war hero. Its success, along with that of the even more popular *The Anzac Book* (1916), the archetypal digger's book selectively edited by C. E. W. Bean from contributions by the original Anzacs themselves, indicates a shift in literary tastes from the meekly colonial to the stridently patriotic. From April 1915 on, Australians gloried in what Ginger Mick calls 'Pride o' Race', agreeing with this former cynic that 'it's grand to be Australian, an' to say it good an' loud'.

The Boer War, despite its comparative insignificance as either a military or literary event, was an essential dress rehearsal for the later conflict. Indeed, it could be argued that the myth born on Gallipoli in 1915 was conceived around the turn of the century, on the *veldt* of southern Africa. Certainly, it produced the Anzac's immediate precursor. The reaction to the Boer War was mixed, a reflection of the controversy surrounding Australia's involvement in what many considered to be an iniquitous British adventure. The pro-war propaganda of the jingoes was counterbalanced by those who advocated the cause of the oppressed Boers. Poets from the *Bulletin* stable, among them Henry Lawson and Randolph Bedford, were in the vanguard of the anti-war movement. Unable to tolerate the idea that an increasingly self-assertive Australia should still be at the beck and call of Britain, their motivation was anti-imperial rather than pacifist. (Lawson's Great War poetry is as bellicose—and, incidentally, pro-British—as that of the most simple-minded militarist: a measure of that conflict's galvanising effect.) The outstanding Australian figure of the Boer War, the bushman and *Bulletin* balladeer H. H. 'Breaker' Morant, owes his heroic status to the view that the men of the colonial contingents were 'scapegoats of the Empire'. Morant's court-martial and execution for the shooting of Boer prisoners became a literary *cause célèbre*, the mainly romantic tone of which turned a disagreeable rogue into a victim of British vindictiveness. The great irony of this making of an Australian martyr is that Morant, like a significant number of men of the First AIF praised by Bean for being exemplary Australians, was English by birth, only arriving in Australia in his late teens.

Anti-imperialism was nothing new to Australian war writing. In his poem 'El Mahdi to the Australian troops', published in the *Bulletin* in early 1885, A. B. 'Banjo' Paterson implied that 'fair Australia' had been tainted by its participation in the 'unholy' British intervention in the Sudan, and expressed his contempt for the 'degenerate' English generals who enforced imperial policy. But perhaps this poem, Paterson's first published work, was an aberration, as his despatches from the Boer War, which he witnessed as a correspondent for the *Sydney Morning Herald* and the *Argus,* could hardly be more obsequiously supportive of the Australian role in assisting Mother England. Conversely, Paterson's Boer War journalism evinces a

proud nationalism which, when compared with the reactive parochialism of the anti-war writers, was more important for the future
development of a distinctive Australian war literature. Paterson was
among the first to link the established local hero, the bushman, with
conventional conceptions of martial prowess. Given that the battlefield seemed to offer an outlet similar to the bush for a manifestation
of the bushman's idiosyncratic virtues, it was not surprising that he
was transported from his harsh natural environment to the testing
fields of armed struggle. The mythical properties which were
ascribed the bushman by the literary nationalists clustered around the
Bulletin in the last years of the nineteenth century reappear in
Paterson's portrait of a soldier who combined resourcefulness, stoicism and independence with skilled equestrianism—qualities which
made him a fitting opponent for the hardy, unorthodox Boer.

As Paterson himself inadvertently reveals in his book of war
reminiscences, *Happy Dispatches* (1934), in which he remembers
biasing his reportage so that the Australians got 'fine advertisements'
out of them, his accounts of the South African fighting prefigured the
partisan distortions of the literature of 1914-18. The fighters themselves were very aware of their glamorous cultural associations and
willing to capitalise on them in their memoirs of battle. In *Tommy
Cornstalk* (1902), by J. H. M. Abbott, a Boer War veteran who was to
become a prolific historical writer and *Bulletin* contributor, the wiry,
egalitarian and irreverent Australians are firmly in the mould fixed
by Lawson and other promoters of a peculiarly Australian 'type'. But
Abbott introduces a new, and prophetic, note. The Australian soldier,
he observes, exhibits a 'flash' self-confidence that borders on arro-
gance, having a 'hardly veiled excellent opinion of himself'.

The heroic prototype developed in works about the Boer War was
consolidated by World War I writers, particularly by those whose
interest was that military repository for rural Australians, the Light
Horse. The soldier glorified by the Light Horseman and wartime
propagandist Oliver Hogue ('Trooper Bluegum'), and even by Ion
Idriess in his otherwise balanced memoir *The Desert Column* (1932),
not only survives the ordeal of fire, he positively revels in it,
chuckling as he makes another kill. The book that salvages the Light
Horseman from a mire of cheap publicity is Frank Dalby Davison's
novella on a famous charge of Australian mounted infantry in
Palestine in 1917, *The Wells of Beersheba* (1933). Though his narrative runs to less than ten thousand words, Davison lends the

military exploit an epic grandeur through the disciplined use of ceremonial rhetoric which cleverly intersperses Australian with classical imagery and motifs.

But of all the writers engaged in this process of cultural definition none was more important than C. E. W. Bean, whose six volumes of the gargantuan *Official History of Australia in the War of 1914-18* (published from 1921 to 1942) can collectively be seen as an 'Australian *Iliad*'. While he fulfilled the historian's duty to disclose the past faithfully, Bean exploited the mythology of the bush with the visionary fervour of the epic poet. Using the Homeric narrative technique of concentrating on small-scale (often man-to-man) infantry skirmishes, Bean drew on all the familiar attributes of the legendary bushman to evoke a warrior whose virtues and foibles (virtues, mostly) are further illustrated in an enormous catalogue of anecdotes contributed by the soldiers themselves.

The digger according to Bean is more a 'noble savage' than, as some less prone to hero-worship might argue, a somewhat graceless, rough-and-tumble colonial larrikin. Bean dubs him a 'child of nature', which is itself suggestive of the mystique attached to the bushman by the urban intellectuals of the 1890s. Not surprisingly, Bean objected strongly to a counter legend propagated by writers like Harley Matthews in his collection of stories *Saints and Soldiers* (1918). Matthews answered the sanitised, official portrait of the Australian soldier with a renegade character whose roots were more city than country, an uncouth, hard-drinking ancestor of the ocker with none of the martial virtues except the capacity to survive. Both these caricatures of the digger find expression in Baylebridge's *An Anzac Muster*. The hero here is part Nietzschean superman, part bronzed bushman, and part dissolute opportunist, especially in his dealings with women. Sexual lust mingles with bloodlust in this baroque and often bizarre collection of tales: as Miles Franklin noted, the book exposes 'the ravages of the fiery crutch as well as of the Fiery Cross'. Baylebridge's bayonet-thrusting, womanising Anzacs anticipate the swaggering, Errol Flynnish heroes of the popular fiction and film of World War II.

Self-congratulation was the norm rather than the exception in Australian literature of the Great War; there were, however, a few writers independent enough to question the heroic creed. As in Britain, the first dissenters came from the ranks of the poets. The prevailing belligerence of the poetic response to the war, most dismally exemplified by Christopher Brennan's racist *A Chant of*

Doom (1918), was repudiated in John Le Gay Brereton's volume *The Burning Marl*, published in 1919. Brereton's attack on mindless chauvinism in 'The Patriot' echoes, in a more strident register, Frank Wilmot's quietistic appeal for world peace, *To God: From the Weary Nations* (1916). That it was chiefly left to non-combatant intellectuals like Brereton and Wilmot (who wrote as 'Furnley Maurice') to condemn the glamorisation of warfare confirms the feeling that most Australian soldier-writers were primarily intent on self-vindication. While a few AIF poets, notably Leon Gellert in *Songs of a Campaign* (1917), expressed a perplexed disillusionment with the soldier's lot, there was never the concerted literary insurrection from the Australian trenches that there was from the British.

Two novelists influenced by the foreign 'horror school' of war fiction were Leonard Mann (*Flesh in Armour*, 1932) and J. P. McKinney (*Crucible*, 1935), both veterans of the Western Front. *Flesh in Armour*, though perhaps the finest of First AIF fictions, epitomises the tensions inherent in Australian war literature generally. Quite simply, Mann is unable to resolve the conflicting responsibilities of the serious artist and the committed publicist. The protagonist of *Flesh in Armour*, Frank Jeffreys, is an atypical figure, neither bushman nor larrikin, but an introverted school teacher with socialist sympathies. But Mann's most devastating heresy is to have made his hero a self-confessed coward who simply cannot fight. Isolated by his inability to meet the Anzac ideal, Jeffreys snaps under the strain of battle and eventually commits suicide. Yet Mann tries to combine his sympathetic portrayal of this individual's crack-up amid the mud, bloated rats and 'splattered red mincemeat' of the Western Front with intrusive assertions of Australian martial brilliance. Along with Vance Palmer and others of his literary generation, Mann saw himself as heir to the prewar *Bulletin* tradition, and was preoccupied with identifying the 'distinctive nationality' of Australians. And it is nationalistic hubris which finally destroys the coherence of *Flesh in Armour*. A couple of pages after the pathos of his hero's self-destruction, Mann unbelievably resorts to the use of statistics to stress yet again the pre-eminence of the AIF.

Just how difficult it was for Australian writers to resist the hegemony of the heroic myth can be gauged by the degree to which the iconoclastic literary territory was taken up either by women unimpressed by male histrionics, such as Angela Thirkell in her 1934 satire of the digger, *Trooper to the Southern Cross* (she was both female *and* English: a double-barrelled critical weapon), or by expatriates dissociated temperamentally, artistically and geographically from the mainstream culture, of whom Martin Boyd is the classical example. Boyd's memoir of his time in the British Army, *A Single Flame* (1939), uncompromisingly debunks idealism, while the gulf between military illusion and actuality is also a key theme of his later, partly autobiographical, war novel *When Blackbirds Sing* (1964).

A detached cultural perspective works to reverse effect in Frederic Manning's novel about a group of English Tommies on the Somme in 1916, *Her Privates We* (1930). Manning was an expatriate Australian who, having left his native country for England in his early youth, fought in the British Army and scarcely saw 'home' again. Yet, while there is little elsewhere in his writing (he was also a war poet of note) to suggest that Australia exercised an imaginative hold on him, a residual Australianness clearly informs *Her Privates We*. The native influence, principally invested in the enigmatic central character Private Bourne, colours a picture of war which allows equally for self-assertion and even nobility as well as the more familiar (in an English war novel) passivity and degeneration. Manning sees war, which he accurately if shockingly calls a 'peculiarly human activity', as an inevitable part of man's destiny, as a test of character to be faced with as much fatalistic grace as possible. His avoidance of anti-war polemic, his egalitarian focus on the dour courage of the common soldier, and his enthusiastic endorsement of comradeship all point to his Australian origins. *Her Privates We* was greeted with relief by English critics when it first appeared, in its original, unexpurgated form as *The Middle Parts of Fortune*, in 1929. As the historian Cyril Falls wrote at the time, 'Other books cause one to be astonished that we won the War; this helps one to understand that we could not have lost it.'

What a leading World War II novelist, Eric Lambert, called 'the legends of the terrible, laughing men in the slouch hats' were revived and revised by the events of 1939-45. The ironic allusions to 'big, bronzed Anzacs' that abound in World War II novels, as for example in Lambert's *The Veterans* (1954) and T. A. G. Hungerford's *The Ridge and the River* (1952), signify the pressures felt by the new generation in living up to the standards set by the original force. As the hero of Lawson Glassop's *We Were the Rats* (1944) laments, 'All our lives we've read about the Diggers being the best troops in the world.' Many novelists compensated for the futility of promoting the Second AIF as militarily the match of its famous forerunner by revamping the legend to satisfy the more sophisticated tastes and tolerances of the time. The easing of censorship restrictions meant that some formerly taboo traits of the Australian soldier, notably his prolific use of indelicate slang and his equally prodigal sexual propensities, could be treated more naturalistically than before. This, though, was a gradual process. Whereas the war fiction of the 1960s and 1970s is peppered with four-letter words (and acts), the mildly colloquial language of Sumner Locke Elliott's play set in an army camp, *Rusty Bugles* (1948), led to its being banned when first performed; two years earlier, in 1946, *We Were the Rats* had been prosecuted by the New South Wales Vice Squad, which complained that a few pages (in which the word 'bloody' featured prominently) were 'offensive to delicacy and chastity'.

The popular war novel as perfected by Eric Lambert and Jon Cleary (*The Climate of Courage*, 1954) appealed to an audience which had shed some of its inhibitions, and which liked its wars fought by strong men with passions to match. The 'Son of Anzac' is less naive and patriotic than his father, more sceptical and selfish, though often given to radical social and political views. Commonly he is an embittered product of the Depression for whom the army offers the prospect of well-paid, 'secure' employment with such fringe benefits as foreign travel and available women. He is also vastly more flamboyant than his father in showing off his sexual machismo. The degeneration of Eric Lambert as a war writer after his powerful first novel, *The Twenty Thousand Thieves* (1951), suggests that the aesthetic consequences of catering to the expanding postwar market exploited by aggressive publishers could be ruinous.

Martial prowess was by no means ignored by the World War II writers, though they were not as obsessed with it as their pre-decessors. *The Twenty Thousand Thieves* and *We Were the Rats,* both of which deal with the North African desert battlefields of Tobruk and El Alamein, contain many battle scenes designed to illustrate Australian military panache. Lambert's left-wing politics emerge in a composite portrait of a digger who is brave, bold, and anti-authoritarian: a Ned Kelly in khaki, armoured by his steely anti-fascist resolve. *The Twenty Thousand Thieves,* however, suffers from the particular contradiction that mars *Flesh in Armour,* being indulgent in its applause for the AIF's lethal combat capability while trenchantly proclaiming an anti-war philosophy. The novels set in the Pacific theatre offer different generic characteristics. The tortuous tropical terrain of the jungles of New Guinea and the Solomons was inimical to conventional warfare, and offered little scope for an epic literary treatment. The Australians in novels such as *The Ridge and the River* and *The Last Blue Sea* (1959), by 'David Forrest' (David Denholm), strive merely to keep body and soul together. Patience, cunning and endurance were needed just to survive the twin terrors of the Japanese enemy and the claustrophobic jungle itself. 'A man had no illusions among the leaves,' writes Forrest. Typically, the thematic interest is more psychological than socio-military, the sweeping vista of clashing armies contracting to a concentration on the 'private war' inside the isolated consciousness of the individual soldier. One New Guinea novel, George Turner's *A Young Man of Talent* (1959), is not really a war novel at all in the conventional sense, the military conflict serving only as an ironical backdrop to vicious internecine warfare among army personnel.

In the poetry of the Pacific campaign, as in the fiction, the dominating vegetable force of the jungle steals the limelight usually reserved for the diggers. David Campbell's fine ballad 'Men in Green' (1943) suggests man's vulnerability in such a hostile environment: 'Nature had met them in the night / And stalked them in the day.' Australian poets of World War II such as Campbell, Kenneth Slessor, Francis Webb, John Manifold and others rejected the old rhetorical polarities of chauvinistic celebration and pacifist polemic for a depth, breadth and complexity of poetic response. The exemplary poem is Slessor's elegy to the war dead of *all* countries, 'Beach Burial', while his hatchet job on the vainglorious General Blamey in 'An Inscription for Dog River' may be compared with John Manifold's unsentimental recognition of the charismatic appeal of 'the old heroic virtues' in 'The Tomb of Lt. John Learmonth, A.I.F'.

Diversity, indeed, is the great strength of Australian literature of World War II. Air warfare (perhaps the particular theatre for which the overall conflict will be historically remembered) provided a fruitful source of novels and memoirs, including Don Charlwood's account of his time flying with Bomber Command, *No Moon Tonight* (1956) and Geoffrey Dutton's comic novel *Andy* (1968). War journalism, an area in which Australians have consistently shone, reached its highest level of excellence during 1939-45. Australian correspondents such as Alan Moorehead, Chester Wilmot, Kenneth Slessor and Osmar White were responsible for some of the war's finest factual writing, Moorehead's *African Trilogy* (1944) and White's *Green Armour* (1945) being notably praised accounts of the desert and jungle wars respectively. World War II, a more palpable, everyday reality to Australian civilians than its predecessor, also produced several important novels which treat the home front. Xavier Herbert's *Soldiers' Women* (1961) and Dymphna Cusack and Florence James' *Come in Spinner* (1951) both dramatise the impact of the 'Yank invasion' on wartime Sydney. Like Herbert, Cusack and James deal with the opportunism of Australian women in their relations with the American GI, but with rather more compassion than Herbert, who in company with many of the soldier-writers (Eric Lambert in *The Veterans* is one) portrays the girls the diggers 'left behind' as hedonistic traitors. Another novel of the home front, Kenneth 'Seaforth' Mackenzie's *Dead Men Rising* (1951), is based on the breakout of Japanese POWs from the camp at Cowra, New South Wales, in 1944. Mackenzie's interest is not so much in the prisoners themselves, but in their partners in 'futile bondage', the Australian guards, and the emotional damage caused by their ignominious role.

But perhaps World War II's most valuable gift to the national war literature was the prisoner-of-war memoir, which has become a leading branch of the genre. Over 30,000 Australians were taken prisoner during the war, the majority by the Japanese. Their sufferings were by no means confined to the physical, though those were appalling enough. A self-image shattered by a long period spent in abject servitude, the belief that capture entailed the surrender of manhood, and a gnawing hatred of the captor all combined to magnify their ordeal. And it was an ordeal which did not necessarily end with their liberation, as the portrayal of the enduring POW trauma in Randolph Stow's novel *The Merry-Go-Round in the Sea* (1965) and John Romeril's play *The Floating World* (1975) both reveal. But whereas the POW may once have preferred not to advertise the fact, the literary output of these men since 1945 has been prodigious, and the reaction to their testimony one of fascination and sympathy. The mutual readiness of the prisoners and the general public to share the kind of inglorious experience movingly and honestly described in such books as Russell Braddon's *The Naked Island* (1952) and Ray Parkin's *Into the Smother* (1963) suggests that the old cultural ties to the heroic ethos have begun to unravel. The most popular Australian soldier-books of recent times— the POW memoirs of Stan Arneil and 'Weary' Dunlop, and A. B. Facey's spectacularly successful *A Fortunate Life* (1981), in which Gallipoli is dismissed as 'the worst four months' of the author's eighty-odd years—are either implicitly or overtly antiheroic. It has become possible for Australians to write about war without indulging in the boasts that once seemed mandatory, and without having to parade a forced jauntiness about the martial life.

The rise of the POW memoir is just one sign of the belated maturation of Australian war literature. Another is the refusal of writers of recent fictional reconstructions of the Great War to bow meekly before the Anzac deity. The demystification of the digger in Roger McDonald's *1915* (1979), David Malouf's *Fly Away Peter* (1982) and, more tangentially, in Les Murray's verse novel *The Boys Who Stole the Funeral* (1980), extends from a view of warfare which is not restricted to the battlefield itself. 'Modern' war writers like McDonald have enlarged the limited terrain of Australian war writing by tackling the metaphorical, as well as merely physical, aspects and connotations of war. Instead of exploiting ancient battles for their vestigial glamour, they relate the historical military experience to domestic violence and internal disharmony among individuals. Contemporary poets writing about the Great War have shown a similar unwillingness to trot out the standard heroic line. In 'The Photograph', from Geoff Page's anthology *Shadows From Wire* (1983), Rae Desmond Jones goes so far as to demand that a fading snapshot of a digger be 'burnt' as 'sentimental junk'. Such a poem represents the fallout from Alan Seymour's *The One Day of the Year* (1962), the controversial play which was crucial in undermining literary dependence on the paraphernalia of the Anzac story. Seymour's 'anti-Anzac', the university student Hughie, sabotaged some of the sustaining clichés of the myth: 'All that old eyewash about national character's a thing of the past. Australians are this, Australians are that, Australians make the greatest soldiers, the best fighters, it's all rubbish.'

The influence of *The One Day of the Year* in creating the current climate of revisionism was minimal, however, compared with the impact of the Vietnam War on attitudes to military endeavour. The repercussions of Australia's political decision to enlist in the American crusade against South-East Asian communism from 1962 to 1972, albeit in a subsidiary capacity, turned Vietnam into a divisive and destructive, rather than unifying and uplifting, national experience. The defeated conscription referenda of 1916 and 1917 had created deep scars in Australian society, but the kudos won by the AIF helped heal differences. Vietnam afforded no such military panacea. A cultural consequence of the widespread friction caused by the enforced conscription of young men into a messy, morally ambiguous and unwinnable conflict was a lapse in Australia's characteristic reverence for its fighting men. Even the 'protest poetry' of the non-combatants who opposed the war, for instance, tended to ignore the Australian 'lackey', while pouring vitriol on the ogre of US imperialism. (The anti-Americanism that is endemic in Australian literature of the Vietnam War, and which also surfaces in Thomas Keneally's picture of US involvement in national affairs during World War II in his 1980 novel *The Cut-Rate Kingdom*, derives from the same colonial defiance that prompted the outrage against Britain during the Boer conflict.) In the fiction, John Rowe's *Count Your Dead* (1968) similarly limits its focus to an exposure of the perceived immorality of the American execution of the war, while Kenneth Cook's *The Wine of God's Anger* (1968) and John Carroll's *Token Soldiers* (1983) debunk the digger with a cavalier ruthlessness.

Significantly, two soldier-novelists, William Nagle and 'David Alexander' (Lex McAulay)—both former Regular Army men—do their best to keep Vietnam within the hallowed heroic tradition. In *The Odd Angry Shot* (1975) Nagle scathingly denigrates the effete, 'long-haired bastards' of the anti-war movement and praises the 'gutsy' combatants, while in *When the Buffalo Fight* (1980) Alexander's fundamental defensiveness leads him to applaud Australian military skills, which he compares favourably with those of the Americans—just as the Great War writers used to praise the diggers and decry the English Tommies. Alexander's gung-ho boast that 'the Australian is superior to the man of every other nation' sounds absurdly anachronistic. Fittingly, the last word on the demythologising effect of Vietnam comes from a conscript, Michael Frazer. At the end of his novel *Nasho* (1984), a group of veterans gathered together on Anzac Day agree that 'embarrassed' is the term which best describes their feelings about their time in Vietnam. That Australian soldiers should describe their war service in this way indicates that future writers who try to rescue Vietnam from controversy and condemnation may well be fighting a losing battle.

Vietnam tarnished the tradition, but it did not destroy it. While the nuclear age has sharpened revulsion against warlike practices, the Anzac story still manages to captivate Australian writers and (increasingly) film-makers: so much energy continues to go into its recounting. And for every iconoclast there are those, like Peter Weir, director of the 1981 film *Gallipoli* (which he co-scripted with David

Williamson), who show an almost naive admiration for the men of the AIF. Even McDonald's *1915*, for all its probing beneath the surface of the myth, nurtures a nostalgia for a time when patriotism could propel men into an enterprise 'larger than oneself'. The most famous of all fictionalisations of the Anzac legacy, George Johnston's *My Brother Jack* (1964), illustrates a similar ambivalence. Johnston's alter ego, David Meredith, is attracted by the myth but repelled by the complacency of the culture that bred it. He deliberately divorces himself from his heritage, but this brings him a sense of treachery and personal inadequacy. Deference to the heroic ideal wins the moral case over cynicism and nonconformity. With 'enemies' like Meredith, *Reveille* need never have worried about the digger's reputation. 'The legends of the terrible, laughing men in the slouch hats' retain their power to move Australians, and to inspire them in their writings.

Notes:

Much of the primary source quotation in this chapter is taken from Robin Gerster, *Big-noting* (1987). This work's analysis of the promotion of an heroic theme in Australian war writing forms a contrast with Bernard Bergonzi's study of the parallel breakdown of the epic tradition in Britain, *Heroes' Twilight* (1965). The central critical study of twentieth-century war literature, however, is Paul Fussell's *The Great War and Modern Memory* (1975).

The literature of the Boer War is discussed in Shirley Walker's article 'The Boer War: Paterson, Abbott, Brennan, Miles Franklin and Morant', in *Australian Literary Studies*, 12 (1985). The historical account *The Forgotten War* (1979), by L. M. Field, is also worth reading. For a first-hand account of the Morant 'affair' see George Witton, *Scapegoats of the Empire* (1907).

Historical writing about World War I is prolific; literary criticism less so. J. T. Laird has surveyed the literature in two articles for *Australian Literary Studies:* the poetry in 4 (1970), and the prose in 5 (1971). Humphrey McQueen, 'Emu into Ostrich', *Meanjin*, 35 (1976) analyses the literary response to the war from a political angle. H. M. Green's descriptive account of the writing of both world wars in *A History of Australian Literature* (1961) is still valuable. Bean, Ellis Ashmead-Bartlett, and George Johnston—three of the major propagators of the Anzac legend—are individually discussed in:

David Kent, 'The Anzac Book and the Anzac Legend: C. E. W. Bean as Editor and Image-Maker', *Historical Studies,* 21 (1985): Kevin Fewster, 'Ellis Ashmead Bartlett and the Making of the Anzac Legend', *Journal of Australian Studies,* no. 10 (June 1982); and Barry Smith, 'George Johnston's Anzac', *Quadrant,* 22 (1977). In the historiographical field, Bill Gammage, *The Broken Years* (1974) examines the diaries and letters of the frontline soldiers; a very readable work of popular history is *The Anzacs* (1978), by Patsy Adam-Smith. The assimilation of the bushman myth by the war writers is touched on by Russel Ward in *The Australian Legend* (1958). Other studies of the combined matter of war and Australian nationalism include: K. S. Inglis, 'The Anzac Tradition', *Meanjin,* 24 (1965), which focuses on the cultural influence of C. E. W. Bean and C. J. Dennis; Geoffrey Serle, 'The Digger Tradition and Australian Nationalism', *Meanjin,* 24 (1965); and Lloyd Robson, 'Images of the Warrior', *Journal of the Australian War Memorial,* 1 (1982).

The exploitation of the Anzac image in the fiction of World War II is discussed by David Walker in 'The Getting of Manhood', a chapter in *Australian Popular Culture* (1979), edited by Walker and Peter Spearritt. Rick Hosking, 'The Usable Past: Australian War Fiction of the 1950s', *Australian Literary Studies,* 12 (1985) examines World War II novelists such as Eric Lambert; Nigel Krauth's article on the New Guinea war novel in *New Literature Review,* no. 12 (1983) is illuminating.

The poetry and fiction produced by the Vietnam War is surveyed by Peter Pierce in *Meanjin,* 39 (1980); the poetry by Graham Rowlands in *Island Magazine,* 6 (1981).

Aspects of the contemporary preoccupation with Australia's participation in past wars are discussed in Roger McDonald, 'Who Owns the Great War?', a review of *Shadows From Wire* in the *Age Monthly Review,* 3, 9 (1983). The most complete survey of this sub-genre is Laurie Hergenhan, 'War in Post-1960s Fiction', *Australian Literary Studies,* 12 (1985). This article appears in a special issue on Australian war literature, which in addition to the aforementioned articles by Shirley Walker and Rick Hosking, contains discussions of historical works, poetry, women's responses to war, journalism, perceptions of 'the enemy' in Australian war literature, and extensive bibliographies.

Among anthologies, J. T. Laird, *Other Banners: An Anthology of Australian Literature of the First World War* (1971) contains some useful critical comment; and *Clubbing of the Gunfire: 101 Australian*

War Poems (1984), edited by Chris Wallace-Crabbe and Peter Pierce, has an excellent introduction. A less specialised anthology, Carl Harrison-Ford, *Fighting Words* (1986), is an accessible mix of 'classic' Australian war writing with much that is unfamiliar.

Chapter 22

THE PASTORAL POETS

IVOR INDYK

If we define pastoral as the poetry of fulfilment and ease, in which the world of nature acknowledges and celebrates the desires of man, then we should have to admit that there are not many genuine examples of Australian pastoral. Australian nature or landscape poetry on the other hand, which we might otherwise call pastoral, is by comparison a tortured affair, with estrangement, isolation, and the fear of passing time among its most compelling features.

Hugh McCrae habitually sings of desire and fulfilment in poems which are clearly pastoral in the narrow sense defined above.

> I love to lie under the lemon
>   That grows by the fountain;
> To see the stars flutter and open
>   Along the blue mountain.
>
> To hear the last wonderful piping
>   That rises to heaven,—
> Six quavers to sum up delight in,
>   And sorrow in seven—
>
> To dream that the mythic wood-women,
>   Each brown as the honey
> The bees took their toll of from Hybla,
>   On days that were sunny,
>
> Come parting the hedge of my garden
>   To dance a light measure

With soft little feet on the greensward,
   Peak-pointed for pleasure.

While Pan, on a leopard reclining,
   And birds on his shoulder,
Gives breath to a flute's wanton sighing
   Until their eyes smoulder.

But while this is pastoral, the landscape could hardly be called Australian. The poem, aptly called 'Fantasy', appeared in Norman Lindsay's *Vision* anthology *Poetry in Australia 1923*, alongside other similar expressions of sensual abandonment and vitality, cast in the pastoral form but eschewing an Australian setting. While they clearly answer to Lindsay's demand for a poetry which would create 'the passionate image of desire, born in the blood, and moulded by the dynamic energies of the mind', they also testify to a reluctance to see the Australian landscape as suitable for the celebration of desire.

This is evident in the poems by Kenneth Slessor published in Lindsay's 1923 anthology. In 'Pan at Lane Cove' a stone faun, refugee from the world of classical pastoral, stands lonely and forsaken in a primeval Australian landscape, under godless skies until, with a wave of his wand, the poet transforms the recalcitrant setting into a momentary Arcadia. One marvels at the poetic prestidigitation, but the indifference of the landscape is clearly meant to be felt as a formidable obstacle. There is a similar setting in 'Mangroves' where, in a travesty of the conventional pastoral attitude, the poet sings of grief and loss from a submarine perspective under the crusted boughs of a mangrove. The poem reveals Slessor's habitual way with pastoral, which is simultaneously to invoke and negate its characteristic features:

O silent ones that drink these timeless pools,
   Eternal brothers, bending so deeply over,
Your branches tremble above my tears again . . .
   And even my songs are stolen from some old lover
Who cried beneath your leaves like other fools,
   While still they whisper 'in vain . . . in vain . . . in vain . . .'

The same use of the Australian landscape as an expression of negated desire is to be found in Slessor's later poems—'Music', 'Elegy in a Botanic Gardens', 'Crow Country', 'Talbingo', 'North Country'. It is also obvious in 'South Country', where the macabre animation of the landscape—

As if, rebellious, buried, pitiful,
Something below pushed up a knob of skull,
Feeling its way to air.

—firmly places Slessor in the line of Harpur, Gordon, Lawson and Brennan, for whom the Australian landscape's most compelling signification is death, 'defeated glory', and despair.

Like McCrae, Slessor sets his worlds of desire elsewhere, in erotic fantasy and the exotic realms of romance, both factitious and highly literary in nature. The same may be said of Shaw Neilson, though his literariness is of a more homely order. Neilson was represented in the 1923 anthology by 'You, and Yellow Air':

I dream of an old kissing-time
And the flowered follies there;
In the dim place of cherry-trees,
Of you, and yellow air.

It was an age of babbling,
When the players would play
Mad with the wine and miracles
Of a charmed holiday.

Bewildered was the warm earth
With whistling and sighs,
And a young foal spoke all his heart
With diamonds for eyes.

The dream is of desire and community, but the perspective is that of old age. Like Slessor, Neilson is haunted by death, so that it not only lurks in the background, unsettling his pastoral affirmations, but enters actively into his conception of desire: 'Grave as the urge within the honeybuds, / It wounds us as we sing.' Paradoxically, in Neilson the very urge to life and love impels the lover to a heightened sense of vulnerability and mortality. The image of the young boy which haunts the adult interrogator in 'The Orange Tree'—

Was he, I said, borne to the blue
  In a mad escapade of Spring
Ere he could make a fond adieu
  To his love in the blossoming?

—is but one in a series of such images in Neilson's poetry, of youth consumed by spring, or burnt up by the 'cynical' heat of the Australian summer.

—Does he, I said, so fear the Spring
  Ere the white sap too far can climb?
See in the full gold evening
  All happenings of the olden time?

If desire opens out into the reaches of time, it is not to the future as one might expect, but far into a past shorn of all specificity and historical substance, a past 'as old as the naked beginning of Time'. In 'The Bard and the Lizard' the lizard who proclaims triumphantly 'the folly of Spring' is an anachronistic survivor from primeval times: 'His eyes are too old to be merry, / He knows where the lovers have been.' Similarly in 'The Magpie in the Moonlight':

Old is the love in his music, and cool to the ear:
His joy is the width of a sorrow, the weight of a tear.

He fails not: the many loud singers he will out-shine:
Death he will take into Love in his song without wine.

Neilson's landscapes of desire may be as factitious as those of McCrae and Slessor, but the perspective from which they are viewed qualifies the pastoral vision in ways which can be thought of as characteristically Australian. It is significant that Neilson should choose the lizard and the magpie as emblematic creatures which, while inhabiting the vast stretches of time, continue to affirm the value of desire, for this is the perspective from which the poet himself sings, vulnerable, isolated, yet seeking in desire communion with the lovers of all time. It is perhaps the sense of isolation which is uppermost—it often seems as if death were Neilson's only intimate acquaintance: 'Oh, the Unseen—I like not / The long talk with him.' The sense of vulnerability follows from this—the presence of death is so powerful, so pervasive, that not only is life seen to be a fragile and

delicate matter, but in a way it has to be so if it is to cheat death of
its prey.

> Let your song be delicate.
>   Sing no loud hymn:
> Death is abroad. . . . Oh, the black season!
>   The deep—the dim!

This perspective, life poised and delicately flickering against a cold,
black backdrop, is one which Neilson shares with the later pastoral
poets Judith Wright and Douglas Stewart.

And there is another feature of this perspective which Neilson
shares with David Campbell. In 'The Orange Tree' the young girl
counters the adult's tragic conception of desire by immersing herself
in the natural world, by in effect becoming one with the orange tree.
As an antidote to vulnerability and isolation the human takes its
place in nature, obedient to the spirit which animates the whole. This
vision of unity achieves its most powerful expression in the figure of
the crane in 'The Crane Is My Neighbour',

> The bird is my neighbour, he leaves not a claim for a sigh,
> He moves as the guest of the sunlight—he roams in the sky.
>
> The bird is a noble, he turns to the sky for a theme,
> And the ripples are thoughts coming out to the edge of a dream.

The poem is a good example of what we might call mystic
pastoral—rather then using the landscape to express a mood or
emotion, the poet stresses instead the interrelatedness of its parts,
affirming the unity of nature which, by implication or direct assertion,
includes the poet himself in its large embrace. But if the intention is
to assert unity, nevertheless the perspective is one which implies
isolation. It the bird is claimed as a neighbour it is because the
natural world provides a sense of fellowship and belonging which is
evidently not available in human social terms.

This social dimension is more likely to be found in the novel than
in lyric poetry. Only a few years after the appearance of Lindsay's
anthology, Katharine Susannah Prichard published *Coonardoo*
(1929) in which the dry cattle country of the far north-west of the
continent provides the setting for a pastoral idyll—or at least, for
what shapes up as a pastoral idyll until destroyed by the inhibitions of

a puritanical Anglo-Saxon morality. In this and other novels, particularly *Working Bullocks* (1926), *Haxby's Circus* (1930), and *Intimate Strangers* (1937), Prichard employs a range of Australian landscapes (the forest, the cultivated countryside, the sea) to explore the complexities of desire in sexual, social and political terms. It is hard to think of another Australian writer who uses pastoral in such a wide-ranging and sophisticated fashion (despite the critical claim that Prichard is a primitivist at heart), although she is not alone among the socialist realist writers in setting her characters in communities which draw their vitality from the natural landscape. Similar uses of pastoral are to be found in Vance Palmer, Xavier Herbert, Eleanor Dark, Eve Langley, Frank Dalby Davison, Kylie Tennant, in some cases with an ironical application, in others with a strong sense of the energies abiding deep within Australian soil.

But when the poets associated with the Jindyworobak movement seek to discover a social and historical dimension for Australian pastoral in the late 1930s and 1940s they overlooked the fact that the novelists have been there before them. Moreover, the experience of the pioneering communities is not regarded as suitable subject matter—not at least until later. The golden age of Australian pastoral must be sought much further back, in the landscape of the Aboriginal Dreaming. Even so, the vision of an arcadian Aboriginal existence, lived in harmony with the land, is haunted and usually overwhelmed by the spectres of death and dispossession.

Mary Gilmore provided a precedent for the Jindyworobaks with her two collections *The Wild Swan* (1930) and *Under the Wilgas* (1932). Gilmore's Aboriginal pastorals portray a people whose identification with the landscape is complete but doomed, as in 'O Race the Forest Knew':

> The brolga called you brother, and the swan
> Declared your name on high;
> The lizard wrote your shadow on
> The rock at noon; and when the night came, wan,
> Your starry symbol lit the sky.
>
> Now there is no one left to name the stars
> Whose constellations spake
> For you the way your fathers trod . . .

Typically, these pastorals take the form of a lament or a dirge. Often it is the moon, or the wind, which stirs the imagination to recall the golden past which it cannot claim as its own. In 'The Lament of the Lubra' Gilmore employs a motif which recurs in later poems of this type, the Aboriginal mother mourning the death of her child, as the land mourns the death of its children, 'Now must the wilgas weep, / Where thou, alone, must sleep!' Though their setting is more obviously Australian, more originally Australian, these poems share the same elegiac perspective as those of Neilson; the empty landscapes and godless skies left by the destruction of Aboriginal life have much in common with Slessor's Australian settings; and their leading characteristics are those of the earliest stages of the Australian pastoral tradition, the sense of guilt and melancholy so pervasive in the landscape of Harpur and Gordon, Clarke and Lawson.

Indeed the more 'Aboriginal' the poem, the more clearly this melancholic strain is heard. Rex Ingamells' 'Moorawathimeering' may aspire to a genuinely Australian perspective in its use of Aboriginal language and myth, but the mood is unmistakably one which has been present in white Australian landscape poetry from the beginning.

> Far in moorawathimeering,
> safe from wallan darenderong,
> tallabilla waitjurk, wander
> silently the whole day long.
>
> Go with only lilliri
> to walk along beside you there,
> while douran-douran voices wail
> and Karaworo beats the air.

Through the annexation of Aboriginal mythology, the Jindyworobaks sought to enter into possession of a country 'instinct and occult with living spirit' (as Ingamells was to put it in *The Great South Land*), but in reality their poetry is most convincing when they mourn its absence or acknowledge their perception of it as discordant and strange. Ingamells' landscapes are aflame with energy, but they are also uninhabited, save for the ghostly remnants of Aboriginal tribes, and more frequently, the cockatoos and parakeets whose bright colours and raucous cries express both the power and the alien character of the spirit of the land. There is little that is really social or cultural about this use of an Aboriginal perspective, and no real sense of history. Often it seems as if the main use of the Aboriginal is in providing an opening to the primeval and the prehistoric—again, by no means a new feature in the poetry of the Australian landscape.

Of the poets most closely identified with the Jindyworobaks, Roland Robinson offers the most sustained, and certainly the most intense poetic achievement, precisely because he declares his perspective to be that of the alienated outsider, and uses his Australian settings to dramatise and celebrate this condition. In the poetic sequence *Deep Well* (1962) the poet as wanderer passes through an enchanted landscape charged with strange energies, a limitless country of exile, and of grace also, 'where I have lived and suffered, sometimes known / strange peace, strange harmony invading me.' 'The Brolgas' is a good example of just how strange Australian pastoral can be, when measured against the arcadian ideal:

Because I came at dawn and stood
outside those ruins on the plain
where spilt among the stones like blood,
the desert-pea spread out its stain,

and saw, out of the pale dark sky
where solitary stars were dying,
those five oncoming brolgas fly
with *'quoak'* and *'quoak-quoak'* of their crying,

to pass, with outstretched necks and fringed
beating wings above my head,
towards the fire of day that tinged
eroded ranges parrot-red,

I stood immortal there. I burned
in ageless youth and, from its mood,
renounced the world again, and spurned
all but that fierce proud solitude.

We may call this Gothic pastoral—among Robinson's novelist contemporaries the same visionary intensification of the sense of alienation is to be found in Patrick White's *Voss* (1957) and Randolph Stow's *To the Islands* (1958).

It is in the poetry of Judith Wright, most notably in her first volumes, *The Moving Image* (1946) and *Woman to Man* (1949), that we first feel the consciousness of history working to affirm a close pastoral identification with the Australian landscape. There were precedents: Gilmore, again, in such poems as 'Malebo' and 'The Harvesters', presented poetic landscapes imbued with the memory of her own family history and with a sense of community. Wright's pioneering pastorals celebrate the primary act of imaginative possession, the legendary figures of Australia's white past investing the land with their visions and love. These poems may be overlaid with Biblical associations; they are clearly intended to have the force of myth, as if they were inaugurating a white Dreaming. Moreover, as Wright may without artifice claim the pioneers as her own ancestors, so she stands within the process of history, heir to their investments. In 'For New England', in a characteristic movement, the focus shifts from the winter landscape to the memory of an old cottage set within the landscape, to an ancestral figure within the cottage, and forward again to the poet, the bearer of these memories. There is no mistaking the triumphant note of affirmation which this movement produces:

> Many roads meet here
> in me, the traveller and the ways I travel.
> All the hills gathered waters feed my seas
> who am the swimmer and the mountain river;
> and the long slopes' concurrence is my flesh
> who am the gazer and the land I stare on;
> and dogwood blooms within my winter blood,
> and orchards fruit in me and need no season.
> But sullenly the jealous bones recall
> what other earth is shaped and hoarded in them.

Yet even here the identification is troubled by a sense of division, between the poet's English and Australian inheritances. And there are other, deeper divisions troubling Wright's sense of history. In 'Bora Ring', one of a number of Aboriginal pastorals, Wright recalls 'the ancient curse', the killing of brother by brother, which prevents the 'alien tale' of white history in Australia from drawing on 'the tribal story' of its vanished Aboriginal inhabitants; in 'At Cooloola' the contemplation of a blue crane, 'the certain heir of lake and evening' only serves to remind the poet of her own estranged condition, and of her grandfather at the same place ninety years before, accused by the ghost of an Aboriginal warrior. For Neilson the crane had been a vision of mystical unity—Wright, however, is oppressed by feelings of 'arrogant guilt'. Guilt, as the burden of white history, is felt again in the division between the settlers and the land itself, despoiled by greed and incomprehension.

> These hills my father's father stripped;
> and, beggars to the winter wind,
> they crouch like shoulders naked and whipped—
> humble, abandoned, out of mind.

The final stanza to this poem ('Eroded Hills') has the bare hills regenerated by the poet's own thoughts standing like trees, the poetic imagination providing recompense for the depredations of history. But since, in Wright, the imagination draws its strength from history, so it must be affected by these divisions. The dominant mood of Wright's poetry, despite its affirmations, is elegaic. 'What drives us is the dead, their thorned desire': at times it appears as if death itself were the motive force of history.

Perhaps because of this, Wright also seeks a more primitive kind of affirmation, outside or before history, at a source 'deeper than the shadows of trees and tribes . . . the spring that issues in death and birth'. This prehistoric tendency is apparent in the Jindyworobaks; it is even more marked in the poetry of Douglas Stewart. Wright has a number of feminine pastorals which celebrate the organic relationship of women to nature (in contrast to the assertiveness displayed by Wright's masculine forebears). In the most biological of these the pregnant woman, discovering in herself the world of nature, becomes one with the source of life, 'I am the earth, I am the root, / I am the stem that fed the fruit'. History has no part to play in these biological identifications, just as it is absent from Wright's other kind of primitive pastoral, in which the ancient features of the landscape open out (in a manner similar to Lawrence's in *Kangaroo*) into the vast reaches of time, and back to the primeval origins of life.

This kind of primitive pastoral (exemplified by Wright's poem 'The Cycads') dominates Douglas Stewart's volumes *Sun Orchids* (1952), *The Birdsville Track* (1955), and to a lesser extent *Rutherford* (1962). Stewart handles the form with great delicacy and with an almost microscopic intensification of focus, which discovers the vital spirit of the natural world in its smallest or most ephemeral features—the trigger-flower, the flannel-flower, firetail finches, the bush robin and most poignantly, in the many species of native orchid. The delicacy of effect achieved in these poems is evident in 'The Snow-Gum', where the tree's perfection of form is seen as a reflection, the play of light and shadow upon the snow.

> Out of the granite's eternity,
> Out of the winters' long enmity,
> Something is done on the snow;
> And the silver light like ecstasy
> Flows where the green tree perfectly
> Curves to its perfect shadow.

The effect is reminiscent of Neilson, as is the juxtaposition of life against the vast perspectives of time. But in Stewart the contrast is heightened by his magnification of the ephemeral detail—as the tiny bird or flower is held up to one's attention, so too is one's sense of its fragility and the magnitude of its surroundings increased. Again and again the background threatens to overwhelm the focus, as in 'Frogs', where the sound of tiny frogs 'under the dark leafy hills' prompts the thought

> It might be that frail cry that first
> Crept out of time's enormous waste
> When bright as dew some bubble broke
> And life awoke, and stared, and spoke.

'Time's enormous waste', 'time's great dark'—life, so fragile and evanescent, is constantly portrayed flickering against the backdrop of eternity, as if there were nothing substantial between, no social context certainly, no sense of history as a meaningful process. This long and empty perspective is an invitation to mysticism—as in 'Sun Orchids' where Stewart hints at 'some secret knowledge' in the blue of the orchid's cup—for while it bestows great significance on the microscopic landscape, it allows no ground other than eternity upon which this significance might be determined. Here the primitive nature of this kind of pastoral becomes most apparent, for in relation to eternity there can be only one source of significance, and that is the source of life itself, the fundamental ground of existence. For Stewart this is the point at which life decays and rots and becomes life again—it is of the earth, vegetative, indifferent of course to the special claims of humanity. In 'Helmet Orchid' the flower listens 'intent and secret' to the voice of nature

> Out of the depth of the world
> Dark and rainy and wild
> Sounding through all eternity . . .

Stewart has a repertoire of emblematic creatures whose home is in the depths of the world: the frog, the centipede, the wombat, the snake, the giant moth, the fungus. As they dwell in the earth, at the source of existence, so they embody in an undifferentiated form the oppositions—life and death, good and evil, grace and abomination— regarded as fundamental to the definition of existence. The landscape of Stewart's chthonic pastorals is perhaps best observed in 'The Fungus':

> And under those crimson tentacles, down that throat,
> Secret and black still gurgles the oldest ocean
> Where, evil and beautiful, sluggish and blind and dumb,
> Life breathes again, stretches its flesh and moves
> Now like a deep-sea octopus, now like a flower,
> And does not know itself which to become.

Stewart's own chosen emblem was the spiny anteater, 'hugging so close to earth and the roots of the rocks', and this is apt. David Campbell's favourite emblem is the hovering hawk,

> the mind
> That rides at peace in hurrying air . . .
> And all of time in his still stare.

The two perspectives are contrasting, and yet complementary. There are differences of course, but both poets view the landscape under the aspect of eternity (in Campbell's case from the standpoint of the timeless moment). Like Stewart, Campbell's pastoral perspective is essentially ahistorical: his use of white pioneering figures ('Harry Pearce', 'The Stockman') and Aboriginal references ('Ku-ring-gai Rock Carvings', 'Enigmas in Cave and Stone') is transcendental rather than historical; they function as elements in a timeless vision. Campbell, again like Stewart, does not generally present humanised landscapes, invested with emotion. The perspective of the hawk implies emotional detachment, a mind at peace, contemplating at a distance the order and pattern of the natural world. It is a visionary, mystical perspective, very different to Stewart's primitivism, yet sharing its timeless aspect, and its subordination of the human to the world of nature.

And the two poets have another point in common, for as their landscapes are not generally invested with historical or social values, or with the emotions of the observer, so there is a question as to what kind of significance the elements in these landscapes might have. Where Stewart goes back to the source, Campbell habitually determines the significance of one natural element by relating it to another:

Such early hills, the snow-gum tree
Sucks its spare blossom from the stone,
From stone the everlasting daisy
Looks back in silence at the moon . . .

in a process which ultimately allows significance to reside in the whole order of nature. This process of relatedness is usually accompanied by a second process of magnification, whereby the whole of nature is absorbed into one of its parts, as with the old ram in 'Ariel':

His tracks run green up the mountainside
Where he throws a shadow like a storm-cloud's hide;
He has tossed the sun in a fire of thorns,
And a little bird whistles between his horns.

But while these processes work to affirm the unity of the natural world, they do not account for the position of the human observer in that world. Consequently there is in Campbell's poetry a third process of introjection, whereby the observer is magnified, taking the landscape into his mind or his embrace in an act of identification similar to that performed by Wright in her maternal pastorals.

Bird, tree and hill with scattered coins
Of flowers are in my embrace
When I hold you and through our loins
The river leaps, while in your face
Thrown back as if to take the sun
Shines the first wonder of the dawn.

This poem, 'Such Early Hills', is one of Campbell's finest, precisely because it does fuse the human and the natural worlds in its celebration of desire. James McAuley noted that the distinguishing feature of Campbell's best work was 'its yes to life', and this is certainly true. Of all the poets we have considered he comes closest to the arcadian ideal in his apprehension of the harmonies which order the natural world. On the other hand, the detachment which underlies this affirmation also works to restrict the poet's involvement in the very landscape whose unity he affirms. In the visionary poems ('Ephemerons', 'Hear the Bird of Day', 'Lizard and Stone'), with their extraordinary clarity and intensity of focus, the observer is almost completely effaced, his gaze absorbing him into the mystical consonances of nature. At other times, the processes of magnification and introjection draw the landscape into the observing mind, asserting unity, but leaving the observer largely undefined. The restrictions imposed by Campbell's detachment and self-effacement are perhaps most clearly felt in his dependence on a single role—that of the lover—to define his relationship to the landscape. Campbell's rewriting of Renaissance court pastorals with Australian settings may appear overly decorous, but in the best of the love poems ('Night Sowing', 'Summer Comes with Colour', 'Hairbell', 'Such Early Hills') the landscape answers to the poet's projections, so that its elements are bound, not by mystical consonances, but by the unity of mood or emotion. Campbell's attempts to increase the emotional range of his projections may be observed in the two pastoral sequences 'Cocky's Calendar' (particularly 'On Frosty Days' and 'Pallid Cuckoo') and 'Works and Days', where the poet's working relationship with the land allows the expression of a variety of moods not otherwise available to the lover, or the timeless stare of the hawk.

One of the achievements of Australian pastoral poetry is to have offered over time a full range of Australian landscapes—but the question that needs to be put finally is whether these landscapes have been invested with a full range of emotions. The question applies not only to the poets we have considered, but to others as well: to William Hart-Smith, for example, whose clarity of perception is as fine as Campbell's, but whose emotional detachment is even more pronounced; and to John Blight, whose seascapes offer an inexhaustible supply of analogies, which often languish because their emotional burden permits of only limited elaboration or development. There is also James McAuley, whose search for a 'land of similes' produces in his last volumes some of the most moving and expressive pastoral poetry in Australian writing.

For McAuley, saying yes to life was a complex matter, a constant struggle with despair, dread, and an intrusive sense of the emptiness at the heart of things which lurks even in the poet's most committed acts of affirmation. So strong is the undercurrent of negation, 'the emptiness that seems an active power / Assimilating life', that McAuley is often led to seek greater consolation in the natural world than it can offer convincingly. The early poem 'Terra Australis' is a case in point: the poet requires of the Australian landscape not only that it should be hospitable, the heart's home—sufficient in itself, one would have thought, given McAuley's feelings of dispossession and belatedness—but that it should also offer prophetic truth, and spiritual ecstasy. In *A Vision of Ceremony* (1956) and *Captain Quiros* (1964) the demands McAuley makes on the plenitude of the natural world grow more insistent. The need to affirm the power of poetic vision and religious faith, and the yearning for revelation, mean that the landscape is made to carry a symbolic burden which is often overwhelming.

In *Surprises of the Sun* (1969) this heroic conception of the poetic act gives way to a more personal view which allows the poet's doubts and fears to become the proper subject of the poem. The result is apparent in the final section of *Collected Poems 1936-1970* (1971), and *Music Late at Night* (1976), where nearly all the poems are in the pastoral mode. Paradoxically, now that the fear of emptiness is freely admitted, the poet immediately and almost effortlessly it seems, strikes a responsive chord from nature.

McAuley's pastorals are economical and understated (again in contrast to his heroic poems), usually no more than a catalogue of natural details with a concluding sentiment to make their mood explicit, as in the opening stanza of 'The Garden':

> Afternoon light shines like blood
> In the dark-red prunus tree,
> Blackbirds stab the lawn for food,
> Madame Hardy lures the bee,
> Flagstone cracks are seamed with thyme;
> Lateness is my fear, my crime.

It is as if McAuley has at last found his land of similes—the focus is unerring, each detail evocative of a particular aspect of the poet's feeling. The feeling may be one of fulfilment, and the land replete with 'sense and use', as in 'At Rushy Lagoon'. At other times, the details jar unnaturally, become strange and menacing in chilling evocations of dread. In the most powerful poems the two kinds of emotion are set side by side, with a compression which suggests the urgent need for resolution, as in the couplet from 'St John's Park':

> A dark-green gum bursts out in crimson flowers.
> Old people slowly rot along the wall.

—or as in 'Nocturne' where the first stanza runs through a range of emotions, from the anticipation of death through sorrow and then anger to the consolation offered by the recurring rhythms of nature:

> A gull flies low across the darkening bay.
> Along the shore the casuarinas sigh.
> Resentful plovers give their ratcheting cry
> From the mown field scattered with bales of hay.
>
> The world sinks out of sight. The moon congealed
> In cloud seems motionless. The air is still.
> A cry goes out from the exhausted will.
> Nightmares and angels roam the empty field.

In these late poems, humble in their way and heroic in their confrontation with death, McAuley is able to convey complexity of emotion in a form of exceeding simplicity. They are his finest achievement, and an important contribution to the development of Australian pastoral.

Notes

Two works which deal with 'the landscape obsession' in Australian poetry are Brian Elliott, *The Landscape of Australian Poetry* (1967) and Judith Wright, *Preoccupations in Australian Poetry* (1965)—the phrase is Elliott's. The issue is also examined in two essays by Chris Wallace-Crabbe, 'The Spells of Landscape' in his *Melbourne or the Bush* (1974), and 'Squatter Pastoral' in Harry Heseltine (ed.), *A Tribute to David Campbell* (1987). Scholars of pastoral tend to fall into two groups: the purists, who regard ease or fulfilment as the proper mood of pastoral to the exclusion of all other concerns, and the Virgilians, who are forever using pastoral to speak about those other concerns. For the first view (particularly appropriate to David Campbell) see T. G. Rosenmeyer, *The Green Cabinet: Theocritus and the European Pastoral Lyric* (1969), and for the second, Virgil's *Eclogues* and William Empson, *Some Versions of Pastoral* (1935). Most of the poets I have dealt with can be read in selected and collected editions of their work, but for the Jindyworobaks see Brian Elliott's anthology *The Jindyworobaks*, published in the University of Queensland Press Portable Australian Authors series (1979).

Chapter 23

DOCUMENTING AND CRITICISING SOCIETY

DAVID CARTER

'Facts are the new literature.' This bold assertion comes from *Strife*, edited by Judah Waten in 1930. It expresses a radical impulse towards documentary writing, a break with all prior literary traditions, and a sense of the present as a moment of crisis:

> 'STRIFE' is another force added to the world-wide movement to uproot the existing social and economic order of chaotic and tragic individualism! ... The proletarian writer will break with the sickly plots, ... sex triangles, and individual heroisms of the past. He will work with facts.

The stand of the avant-garde *Strife* is extreme, but its linking of an artistic break from bourgeois fiction with a compelling sense of social crisis is shared by a wide range of fiction and commentary from the early 1930s to the early 1950s. The sense of social crisis was a distinctive response to the Depression, international fascism, and then war. Fascism particularly affected writers, being perceived as the very antithesis of culture. These successive movements of history are linked in numerous writings as symptoms of the one disease, capitalism. From M. Barnard Eldershaw's *Tomorrow and Tomorrow* (1947):

> The whole world was sick. The war was not an accident but the expression of a deep and terrible distemper, erupting from within ... [W]ithin society the cracks widened and competition hardened and increased, competitive living, competitive loving, competitive suffering and death.

For many writers the historical sequence of depression, fascism and war meant a profound disturbance in their sense of social relations. Society becomes not just an arena for the play of individual motives but of momentous historical forces, of class divisions and 'mass villains, mass victims . . . an awakened mass consciousness' (*Tomorrow and Tomorrow*). Contemporary social upheavals are represented not just as local disorders but, in the words of *Australian New Writing*, as an apocalyptic 'crisis in the history of civilisation . . . a clash of two irreconcilable ideologies: fascist against democratic, barbaric against civilised, hysterical brutality against reason'.

This notion of crisis was itself symptomatic of a crisis in liberal humanism, whose traditional terms seemed inadequate to comprehend such massive social change. Mass social forms and ideologies seemed to threaten human nature as a source of value and continuity. For a number of writers this ideological crisis produced a serious involvement with communism—if not the Communist Party—or with socialist and populist ideas, often in nationalism. Frank Dalby Davison wrote in 1942: 'national unity, to which we are now trusting so much, is the stronger for having been confirmed in . . . our nascent literature'. For all the writers considered here, the period meant heightened debate over cultural meanings: a reformulation of the relations between fiction and society, individuals and society, and not least intellectuals and society.

In order to engage with this new social reality—at once individual and historical—works of fiction are forced into formal experiment. Conventional plots and characterisation are transformed as texts are opened up to 'facts', political rhetoric, and utopian images. Such expanded forms of fiction in Australia include novels of large scope like *Tomorrow and Tomorrow*, Dark's *The Little Company* (1945) and Frank Hardy's *Power Without Glory* (1950). The claim by *Strife* to a 'new form based on facts' suggests that more 'modest' kinds of documentary fiction should also be included.

The forms of documentary developed in the 1930s were not simply modes of recording contemporary experience. Style and subject-matter were politically motivated as writers attempted to represent forcefully, in literary discourse, facts and attitudes which they believed literature had conventionally excluded or falsified:

London, 25 November—The late Mr Harry Bellingham Howard Smith, shipping director, who died in Australia, left estate in England and the Commonwealth valued at £1,077,012—*News item.*

From the bowels of the tourist ships the firemen can sometimes hear the laughter of the passengers and the slip, slip of their feet dancing on the deck above them.

Each passenger pays £35 for a trip round the islands. The firemen are paid £2 per week.

For four hours at a time they stand half naked before roaring furnaces shovelling in the coal that drives the mighty engines. The sweat that's wrung from out their blackened bodies leaves streaks of cleanness on their hides.

From where they work the firemen can sometimes hear the laughter of the passengers and the slip, slip of their dancing on the deck above them.

Texts such as this by Alan Marshall need to be seen as contesting the claims of well-made fiction to reflect reality. Marshall's sketch, typically, challenges any clear-cut distinction between the aesthetic and the documentary. By forgoing certain aesthetic effects while emphasising others, the text assures that it is read neither as 'mere' fiction nor 'mere' documentary. This ambivalent status is characteristic of documentary and socially critical fiction, which both claims and disclaims art in order to establish its own truth.

In the 1930s and 1940s Marshall and John Morrison published sketches of proletarian life in left-wing journals. It is arguable that links extended back to the sketches of Lawson and the *Bulletin*, but any similarities are due more to a common marginal position in relation to the cultural establishment than to a continuous Australian literary tradition. The significant influences were contemporary and international: Hemingway, Dos Passos, Sherwood Anderson, *New Masses*, and writers' and artists' organisations. In Australia, Workers' Art Clubs began in 1931; a Writers' League was established in 1935, amalgamating in 1938 with the Fellowship of Australian Writers; and by the mid-1930s New Theatre groups were operating. The prose sketches can be compared to the graphic art and theatre of the period (Betty Roland published scripts in *Communist Review*, 1937-8, such as 'The Miners Speak' and 'Workers, Beware!'). In the three areas, documentary and didactic modes overlap in highly stylised work.

The prose sketches show a range of techniques for creating efforts of immediacy: short sentences, a compressed time-span, present-tense and second-person narration (in contrast to the yarning narrators of Marshall and Morrison's better-known stories). Morrison repeatedly begins his waterfront sketches with an abrupt statement of time and place: 'The Compound. Mid-winter. Eight o'clock Friday morning' ('Tons of Work', 1947). Similar bold effects are present in descriptions of the new subject of work in Kylie Tennant's *The Battlers* (1941) and Jean Devanny's *Sugar Heaven* (1936):

> Each man took his place at the head of a row of cane; the left hand grasped the thick stick; the broad-bladed short-handled knife was wielded to sever the stalk on a level with the ground. No time for waste motion. Another stroke with the knife severed the top; two downward motions cleaned the trash from the stalk. The fifth motion heaped the sticks . . .
>
> Cut low! Cut lower! Cut right into the ground! It's every last vestige of sugar content harvested or the 'sack' . . . Big Boss Ratoon needs a clean stump to spring from! And Big Boss Sugar Baron hears the sweet chink of gold emanate from the clean fields!

The effect of rapid notation, the unfinished quality of the sketches, their very fragmentation and plotlessness operate to signal the writing's 'authenticity'. The formal disruptions and excesses of style—of overstatement and understatement—are ways radical documentary has of marking its difference from bourgeois fiction. Such a difference is doubly marked in Marshall's *How Beautiful Are Thy Feet* (1949) by a division in the text between italicised passages and the main narrative. The former are the site of a shifting didactic, 'camera eye', or collective voice:

> *The Factory snarls as it eats . . . it rears its head above the damp of narrow streets . . . above the swamp of houses . . . it is a dinosaur . . . it is Tyrannosaurus Rex . . . it is destruction . . . its talons are steel . . . its entrails are machines . . . its mouth is a door . . .*

The bulk of the narrative is more conventional except that again the narrative focus is highly mobile. The text is a collage of short scenes or sketches. One effect of this is to alter the presence of character, to register an altered sense of the relation between social forces and subjectivity. As Humphrey McQueen states, 'Marshall challenged all the canons of Australian literature and bourgeois individualism by making a boot factory the protagonist of a novel.' The characters are only voices or gestures; but rather than a reduction of individuals to types, the novel produces a *multiplication* of types. Characters no longer represent subjectivity, but are sites where social forces and ideologies play out their effects.

In incorporating a range of characters the novel is not merely being faithful to reality. Its sheer abundance of voices and plots opens up the narrative to contemporary social 'facts' conventionally excluded from fiction. First, work itself becomes a primary subject. Second, the novel's multiple voices generate an excess of erotic energy, spilling over the bounds of sentimental romance, and juxtaposed with the sheer facts of work. The conventional marriage plot is displaced by multiple plots; and like many novels of the period *How Beautiful Are Thy Feet* includes the story of an abortion, representing the contemporary crisis in social relations. Third, in dialogues throughout the text, the novel incorporates political discourses beyond liberalism: communism, fascism, social credit, even eugenics. Here too there is a kind of excess beyond the needs of documentary or plot, expanding the fiction towards history.

In reclaiming this writing we can underline not the naturalness of its discourse, but its modernity. Though less intellectually wrought, Marshall's novel bears comparison with, say, Christina Stead's *Seven Poor Men of Sydney* (1934) or Dark's *The Little Company*. Major novels of the 1930s and 1940s can be productively read, not as reflections of life nor as organic unities, but as narratives which mediate between the explanatory, evocative, or persuasive powers of different literary and non-literary languages: documentary, traditional realism, political theory, utopianism, even romance. The tension between these competing claims, as each novel situates itself in relation to other fiction, other fact, and other propaganda, generates the distinctive and diverse forms of the period. Their diversity argues against the view of social realist writing expressed in Patrick White's historically momentous phrase describing Australian fiction as 'dun-coloured . . . journalistic realism' (1958). To stress diversity is also to resist a pressure towards homogeneity inherent in national literary histories especially when focused on prose fiction, seen by H. M. Green, for example, as 'that part of [literature] which most clearly reflects the national life'.

The tensions within realism are extreme in works with a positive revolutionary message which forces the text to engage directly with political rhetoric. Both Devanny's *Sugar Heaven* and J. M. Harcourt's *Upsurge* (1934) have a documentary base: the former records a cane-cutters' strike, the latter conditions for relief workers during the

Depression. The documentary, though, is part of a larger political design revealed through communist characters and stories of politicisation. However, the politics of each text lie beyond plot, in the relationships between political and erotic themes, and the different rhetorical models which each narrative incorporates. This entails thinking of propaganda, not as the bits of political rhetoric insufficiently made over into art, but as an available narrative strategy.

Both novels signal their break with 'mere' fiction. The language of sentiment is displaced *in* the narrative by the language of politics. In *Upsurge*, magistrate Riddle's disquiet at the disintegration of 'modesty' is reinterpreted by his communist friend Graham. In the exchange, the narrative anticipates, as it must, the charge of propaganda:

> 'The morality of a civilization,' said Graham, 'is an ethical reflection of the economic organisation of that civilization . . .'
>
> The magistrate shook his head irritably . . . 'You attempt to solve every problem you encounter by reference to Karl Marx. His theories dominate your whole outlook.'
>
> 'Marx made the obvious discovery that the first task of the human species is earning a living,' Graham observed, 'and that that task is sufficiently important to colour all our other activities, our art, morality, philosophy, religion . . .'

The significance of Graham's language is not that it announces a correct political line but that it provides an alternative rhetorical mode, another way of understanding, beyond the immediate and the ethical. From this point on the two narrative scales are read off against each other.

Graham, a chemist, embodies the scientific appeal of Marxism (though, given the text's frequent images of explosives, perhaps his profession has a dual significance). By contrast, Theodora Luddon is politicised through industrial experience. The story of betrayal by conventional union leaders, presented here, is a recurrent theme in radical fiction—from Katharine Susannah Prichard's *Working Bullocks* (1926) to Dorothy Hewett's *Bobbin Up* (1959)—indicating the narrative's own break with convention. Another character, Peter Groom, is moved from despair to political enthusiasm by the power of agitational rhetoric. Groom's 'reckless elation' is thus combined with Graham's logic and Theodora's experience. Through Groom and Theodora the novel enacts the shift from individual to mass consciousness—at a demonstration they are together 'borne along by the irresistible current of the crowd'. Finally there is the working-class communist Steve Riley who embodies communism as the force of history, revolutionary 'upsurge', itself. His extreme character is a means of representing the violent disruptions to the bourgeois order of a 'new ideology . . . a new consciousness'. This new consciousness is shown also to be a characteristic of certain *illegal* texts:

> Between novels by Henri Barbusse, Romain Rolland, John Dos Passos, Jack London, Upton Sinclair, were sandwiched such works as the 'Capital' of Karl Marx, the 'Socialism' of Engels, the 'State and Revolution' of Lenin, the 'Communist Programme' of Bucharin. The mantel was loaded with the literature of class-war and revolution!

The list, even the sandwiching of revolutionary doctrine between fiction, provides models against which *Upsurge* itself can be read. Part of the novel's challenge to the bourgeois order is challenge to the order of its fiction. The novel provides frequent models—allusions to other texts, narrative styles, or ways of reading—in order to proclaim its own status as a *new* kind of fiction. For example, Riddle views a didactic, highly stylised political play. It is 'weird and unreal', but disturbing precisely because of its unreality: 'Was that extraordinary play a true representation of the facts? . . . His mind was still troubled by the bizarre fantasy he had witnessed.' The play 'justifies' the novel's departures from illusionism. The stylisations of propaganda and theory in the text's own 'bizarre fantasy' of revolutionary upsurge are a true representation of 'facts' that could not otherwise be represented. A contemporary comment on *Upsurge* might be truer than it intends, describing the novel as 'quite in the modern vein of realism at any price'.

In *Sugar Heaven* characters are also associated, beyond personality, with alternative narrative genres and political options. Hefty represents physical vitality, like 'the blood in the stalks' of the cane; but he is 'only a militant'. Bill is able to talk theoretically, but is less 'clean' (a key figure in the novel). Eileen is 'militant and clever', but 'fluent, without discipline or restraint', embodying the erotic and political desires, distributed elsewhere throughout the text, whose organisation would have revolutionary potential. The communists provide figures of discipline and restraint. Hendry, the communist leader, is one of the novel's many figures of transformation: once 'rough' now 'clear and . . . philosophical'.

The central story is Dulcie's transformation from self-consciousness to class-consciousness. Like *Upsurge*, the text figuratively links erotic and political desire in enacting this transformation. Dulcie's conventional morality entails an 'instinctual allegiance to conventional political forms'; these are linked in turn to conventional literary forms. Dulcie 'had fed voraciously on paper-backed editions of the early Victorians' until, significantly, 'crisis conditions had . . . dried up the fount of her literary digest'. In response to the 'exotic infringements' of canefields physical vitality and politics, Dulcie's 'self-sufficiency' is transformed:

> Here was drama! Here was colour! The great Painter, Life, was at work upon the hitherto dull canvas of her existence. The colours were impure, the brushstrokes heavy, but like a Goya canvas they projected intense and mordant life.

Dulcie had kept herself 'clean' in conventional terms—through repression; 'hate and desire' intermingle in her subsequent violent transformation: 'She felt herself changing, not subtly nor delicately, but violently, in leaps; a development in keeping with the lush tropical growth.' Ultimately, both sexual and political passion are cleansed and cleansing. Dulcie reflects: 'The strike has washed all sorts of impurities out of me.'

The reference to Goya is also significant, for the images describe one of the novel's own styles, a vitalist mode that links natural beauty, sexual desire, and even industrial militancy. The intense, subversive emotions of this mode are juxtaposed with the reasoned discourse of communism. Out of the 'impure' rhetorical styles of desire and 'revolutionary hysteria' the narrative attempts its own transformations, at times neither 'subtly nor delicately'. Its documentary modes, though shading into the register of propaganda, are anti-utopian. Nonetheless the novel rises to (in Devanny's term) an 'epic' pitch, characteristic of attempts to express 'the spirit of the war of the classes . . . its immensity, its dramatic force, its terrific fervor'. At these moments the novel does not 'lapse' into propaganda, in Modjeska's phrase, so much as launch into it. Dulcie's first apprehension of class consciousness is a moment of 'sublime reason' born out of 'emotional tumult'; and the utopian moments are in visionary and *sensuous* language: envisioning 'expanded joys and vibrant life'. The mode here is that of 'revolutionary romanticism'.

Katharine Susannah Prichard claimed *Upsurge* as 'Australia's first truly proletarian novel'. Jean Devanny wrote of *Sugar Heaven* as 'the first really proletarian novel in Australia'. Both claims are made in the context of the doctrine of socialist realism. In the words of Zhdanov, at the 1934 First All-Union Congress of Soviet Writers:

> The truthfulness and historical exactitude of the artistic image must be linked with the task of ideological transformation . . .
> Romanticism is not alien to our literature, a literature standing firmly on a materialist basis, but ours is a romanticism of a new type, revolutionary romanticism.

Both *Upsurge* and *Sugar Heaven* can be understood as revolutionary romanticism. However they represent arguments towards, rather than applications of, socialist realism. In the attempt to construct a narrative that shows historical veracity, artistic conviction, and revolutionary optimism, the novels are relentlessly self-reflexive, '(that is, they have an inbuilt self-consciousness as literary and verbal constructions)'.

The history of socialist realism in Australia is complex, as the diversity of novels by Prichard, Devanny, Harcourt, Waten, Hewett, and Hardy suggests. First, until the late 1940s socialist realism was only one option—or an array of options within itself—for radical artists. The possible models for a socially committed realism were diverse: from Lawson to Gorky, from Dickens to *New Masses*. Only in the Cold War years did the Communist Party of Australia give socialist realism a full policy weighting. Second, whatever its policy functions, socialist realism did offer a coherent theory of the relations between fiction, fact, and political doctrine (and between intellectuals and society). If it is crude perhaps this is only aesthetics. Third, the history of socialist realism cannot be separated from those of literary nationalism and populism.

What did occur, in the 1940s and 1950s, in the interaction between Communist Party policy, socialist realist theory, and nationalism was the favouring of more orthodox modes of literary realism. Writers positioned themselves less on the radical margins than at the centre of a tradition. *Bobbin Up*, which resembles the novels already discussed more than its own contemporaries, was criticised in the communist press for its 'naturalism' and 'concentration on the unusual or sensational . . . pre-occupation with anatomical description of woman [sic], an overstressing of physical relations'. Over the same period the New Theatre turned towards more classic and illusionist drama, and to nationalist and popular themes.

Prichard's career is instructive. *Working Bullocks* and *Intimate Strangers* (1937) share thematic and structural qualities with *Upsurge* and *Sugar Heaven*: the displacement of romance by desire, the transformation of self-consciousness into class-consciousness, and mixed rhetorical strategies for incorporating a revolutionary perspective into a faithful picture of a non-revolutionary society. Pat Buckridge has recently demonstrated the juxtaposition in *Working Bullocks* of three narrative options for political fiction: romance, a folk tradition, and a propagandist mode (Mark Smith's language is alternately factual, theoretical, and agitational). Each has its own powers of representation and transformation yet none is sufficient, and the novel proceeds by a juxtaposition of rhetorical styles and the values each represents. There are also parallels with *Upsurge* and *Sugar Heaven* in the way that political purpose is 'disseminated through the entire text as a form of *desire*'. Mark Smith's rhetoric is represented simultaneously as common sense and fantasy, fact and art, inspiration and seduction. But despite its authority, his is an alien discourse ('such talk had never been heard'). This sense of foreignness is characteristic of Prichard's fiction. Not only political discourse, but also passion (in certain novels), is represented as alien, powerful and exotic, able to transform common sense. It is often represented by foreigners or wanderers, characters who are both insiders and outsiders, like Tony Maretti in *Intimate Strangers* and Nadya Owen in *Golden Miles* (1948). Jack Lindsay has remarked of *Intimate Strangers*: 'we feel the socialist viewpoint as something strange, almost foreign and exotic, set over against normal Australian life'. However this is not simply an ideological problem; it is also a narrative problem and its solution.

Prichard's writings reveal a commitment not only to political purpose but to a liberal humanist tradition, stressing organic form, which held that great art was beyond propagandist rhetoric. The message, in other words, must be both concealed and revealed. *Intimate Strangers*, from its title on, produces a pattern of associated images of strangeness or foreignness, with Tony, his mother, Guido, Jerome, Prospero, even Elodie ('Elodie had her roots in mixed blood, Slav instincts'). These characters, and associated images, provide the novel's critique of bourgeois institutions, acting to defamiliarise them. The foreign characters also provide the novel's intellectual framework—and it is a novel of ideas, a political novel, in its treatment of romance (not a domestic drama with a factitious political ending). The narrative does not simply contrast false romance with the realities of sexual and economic exploitation. Like *Working Bullocks* the predominant mode of the novel itself is romantic: its task, then, is to split romance, to separate sentiment from sensuousness, false utopias from true, the false promises of art from its true transformative capacities. In Elodie Prichard mediates between the familiar and the foreign, and her music provides the narrative's self-reflexive models. Only Beethoven is adequate to her 'passion and despair'. This music, contrasted to 'blithe, sentimental ditties' elsewhere, recalls Mark Smith's rhetoric:

> Chords . . . crashed with a proud violence. The lyric at its core, rising triumphantly, soared and dominated with its wild sweet song. The dark turbulent floods of destiny might carry it away . . . but defiant in defeat, it could still sing on, inviolate, immortal.

It also prefigures Tony's political speech, where Elodie and the working-class audience are transformed by a 'dazzling vision'. The text appropriates the very imagery of romance that would seem to belong to Jerome: the 'struggle of the working people' is transformed from a 'pitiful, hopeless resistance' to a 'magnificent adventure, as magnificent . . . as the adventure of Columbus embarking to discover a new world'.

In the goldfields trilogy—*The Roaring Nineties* (1946), *Golden Miles* (1948), and *Winged Seeds* (1950)—the prominent foreigners, who are also women, again introduce a radical intellectual framework and history; plus, as Sneja Gunew has argued, a sexual politics which is pushed to the fringes by the more explicit critique of capitalism. There is a different ordering of genres and discourses in the later novels which shows the influence of socialist realism. Further, whereas *Intimate Strangers* is Prichard's novel of the 1930s 'crisis of modernity', these are Cold War novels. They are without the sense of crisis which characterises much 1930s and 1940s fiction. Instead they provide a long historical perspective, less apocalyptic than evolutionary.

The form of the trilogy might be described as the yarn expanded into saga, or documentary expanded into social history. Its governing rhetorical mode is matter-of-factness in sober speech, common sense, and facts; the novels *are* prepared to risk their organic form for the sake of the inclusion of documentary material. Through the central figure of Sally Gough the texts seek to turn political rhetoric into experience: to merge nature, common sense and doctrine. One of the novels' triumphs is the linking of Sally and Kalgoorla, for the Aboriginal woman represents the most alien but also the most immediate political experience. Sally's function, and Dinny's, indicate the novels' populist vision and in particular the manner in which such populism precludes, for the most part, writing about 'the nexus between sexuality, the unconscious and nature', as Modjeska puts it. As this populist, matter-of-fact mode is itself inadequate to produce either a narrative or political resolution, the foreign characters and discourses (Chris Crowe's utopian mumblings, Pat and Pam's exotic modernism) act as supplements in the text, meeting a lack in its dominant genre. In this respect the trilogy's formal inventiveness, as well as its realist orthodoxy, needs to be emphasised.

In Australian criticism since the 1940s, the term 'social realism' has overlapped with 'socialist realism'. But while the latter is derived from an explicit theory, the former is rather the result of a *lack* of theory. The difficulty is that the term appears to be self-evident, concealing assumptions about the ways in which art 'reflects' life. It becomes a way of not talking about language and politics, for it conceals the variety of realist solutions to the problem of relating artistic form and political purpose.

The ambiguous status of Kylie Tennant's work in the Australian canon is symptomatic of ambiguities in the notion of social realism. Her novels have been described as examples of 'social realism' (Inglis Moore) and 'the sociological novel' (Hadgraft). Perhaps they do resemble sociology in concentrating on a group of characters primarily in their social relations. However the novels' 'social realism' is not self-evident. Documentary and popular low-life modes— multiple characters and episodes, comic types, picaresque structure— are reclaimed for a 'new' kind of popular narrative.

We can see this process in *Tiburon* (1935), in the description of the play 'The Mackoniculls of Kilmuckie'. This episode has been used as an example of Tennant's lack of 'art'—though praised for its humour, the scene is criticised for its irrelevance. The play itself is a terrible mishmash of music hall and melodrama. Yet it is a success, and not merely because of the vulgarity of its audience. The reader joins in the carnival, as the play's sentimental conventions are constantly subverted by breaches of artistic decorum which make a low comedy out of what would otherwise have been high melodrama. This play can be compared with another—'the heroine . . . had done nothing but lie on a green satin couch uttering aphoristic and charming words while the players fell in love with her'—which contrasts unfavourably with the sheer excess of 'The Mackoniculls of Kilmuckie'. We can read *Tiburon* itself through this contrast, as redeeming the artifice of certain popular forms by its own comedy and excess, and subverting the artifice of other sentimental and highbrow forms.

Subversive qualities are found in the most unlikely places: in one character's stubbornness or vulgarity or in another's sentimental verse. But the comic perspective of the narrator allows vulgarity to express originality, sentimentality a desire for beauty, both in opposition to the power of convention and class. What have been seen as Tennant's strong working-class sympathies might be seen more broadly as a principle of resistance to institutionalised power, which finds its figures in the dispossessed and the misfits (not simply the proletariat). Again there is a sense of fiction being opened up to what it had previously excluded, as the novel breaks down distinctions between the documentary and the aesthetic. *Tiburon* shifts the conventions of the realist novel to allow its so-called sub-plots to crowd onto centre-stage.

Brian Matthews has analysed the documentary aspects of *The Battlers* and shown how the novel's descriptions can be 'intensely ideological'. A strong protest is implied throughout Tennant's fiction against a social and ethical system which produces a dispossessed class and then blames it for being dispossessed. This protest is also expressed in a satirical mode aimed at utopian or idealist systems of thought—from institutionalised charity to eugenics—exposed as self-perpetuating systems of power. Communists, clergymen, and capitalists all become targets, while in the economy of the novels 'the battlers' can become figures of rebellion or independence, less because of their virtues than their outcast status (linked in *The Battlers* with the 'real Australia'). All utopian and institutionalised systems are comically subverted, including those of art itself.

Tennant's 'social realism' cannot be seen simply, in Adrian Mitchell's terms, as 'in the unruly manner of documentary' or as reproducing 'the false realism, the factitiousness, of the popular fiction of the period'. In these criticisms, her work is caught between the demand for an art that is true to life and the demand for organic form. Tennant's fiction is calculated to violate expectations of organic form. On one hand it is structured so as to create the artistic *illusion* of 'the unruly manner of documentary'. On the other, like Furphy's *Such is Life*, the move beyond conventional plot means that the narratives comically exploit their own unavoidable 'factitiousness'—their mediations between different formal (and ideological) options.

For many novels of the period we could take the epigraph to *Intimate Strangers*: 'The international chaos, the social chaos, the ethical and spiritual chaos, are aspects of one and the same disorder.' This understanding motivates Eleanor Dark's *Waterway* (1938) and *The Little Company*, and M. Barnard Eldershaw's *Tomorrow and Tomorrow*. The dynamic of these novels, however, is less the struggle between capitalist and working-class than an ideological struggle between optimism and despair—a crisis of faith in human nature. For Gilbert Massey in *The Little Company*: 'This, finally, was the issue which split the world in two, split nations, split parties, split friendships and families—do you believe in human beings, or don't you?'

The interior monologue, the primary mode of Dark's novels, provides a means of linking the 'international chaos' and the 'ethical chaos': registering the pressure of social upheaval on the individual psyche, and showing character itself as a complex of ethical, political and spiritual discourses. The novels expand 'inwardly' as each character's memories and reflections are unfolded; and characters are shown to be 'living in history', as Marty puts it in *The Little Company*, as history is compressed into critical moments in individual lives. The effect of compression and expansion in *Tomorrow and Tomorrow* is even more remarkable: on a single day in the twenty-fourth century Knarf reads out his vast historical novel of Australia. The novel's futuristic fiction is its means of comprehending an apocalyptic present. It is dated 1940-2, and the crisis it expresses, of civilisation collapsing from within, is close to that expressed in *The Little Company*, set in 1941-2; close also to Vance Palmer's 'Battle', in the 'Crisis' issue of *Meanjin* (1942).

Waterway is also apocalyptic, in its double climax. A march of unemployed gets entangled with a society wedding, with violent consequences, which arise less from political consciousness than from a 'return of the repressed' in the organism of society. Then a ferry carrying many of the novel's main characters is sunk in a collision. This is a disturbing scene, because although it cannot be turned into any simple allegory it nevertheless fully dramatises the novel's sense of social and ethical chaos: 'a happening so monstrous and cataclysmic and yet so utterly formless'. This phrase expresses what

Dark shares with the more explicitly political writers, but also what distinguishes her liberal humanist view.

The source of the novel's power, as with *The Little Company*, is its ability to signify disorder simultaneously on different levels—in the psyche, in society, and in nature. The novel's framing character, Oliver Denning, provides the underlying structural and thematic figures of the narrative:

> it seemed a very fair slice of time, this barely recordable blink in humanity's existence! And, crossing your own life, it held many other lives, touching, running parallel for a little while, closely woven, breaking away, so that you could never . . . study a life solely your own, but always a life thrumming and alive with contacts, reacting to them in harmony and discord like the strings of a violin.

The figures of harmony and discord link relations between conscious and unconscious in the human organism; relations between individuals and between classes in the social organism; and finally the relations between civilisation and nature. A sense of Australian history as the story of civilisation in discord and harmony with its environment—the subject of Dark's *The Timeless Land* (1941)—provides *Waterway* with its final resolution. The discord of 'turbulent human life' is displaced by the image of harmony between the 'eternal' and 'its people'.

The Little Company engages more directly than *Waterway* with contemporary history and political, specifically communist, doctrine. It is also more intensely self-reflexive, one aspect of what Modjeska describes as its 'dialogic' structure. Rather than a single, authoritative viewpoint the novel provides a series of dialogues between different ideologies, different ways of seeing (from communism to moralism). The novel positions itself in the midst of crisis, between the old order and the new, a moment represented by the writer's block which both the central characters, novelists Gilbert and Marty, suffer. The harmonies possible in Gilbert's early novels are fractured by a new historical awareness, beyond 'mere' fiction: 'Characters . . . which he would once have regarded as mere fictional material could no longer be regarded as such when they had become manifestations of a social disorder.' For both, a new kind of fiction is projected, linking an individual story with mass historical change; for Gilbert, optimistically, 'the old but always new story of the dynamic of humanity . . . expressed in terms of one obscure life'.

In *Tomorrow and Tomorrow* social crisis is comprehended in similar terms: 'The microcosm of the individual reflected the macrocosm of society.' Like *The Little Company*, its politics lie in reflections on its own status as historical fiction. Two notions of history are contrasted in Knarf and Ord, an archaeologist, contrasting a humanist and a materialist ideology—the very crisis for liberal intellectuals in the 1930s and 1940s. Knarf and his son swing the debate towards humanism and 'liberty', but the narrative's own historical excursions suggest that liberal humanism 'needs' the explanatory power of a materialist system. The novel leaves a question as to which mode is the utopian one. Like Dark's novels, *Tomorrow and Tomorrow* finally looks beyond politics to the land itself to maintain faith in human nature, concluding: 'The earth remains.'

In the postwar period, a diverse range of realist fiction appeared from such writers as Vance Palmer, Leonard Mann, Donald Stuart, Gavin Casey, and F. B. Vickers. Some of the most striking novels of the period, however, are identifiably communist novels: Prichard's trilogy, Frank Hardy's *Power Without Glory*, Ralph de Boissiere's *Crown Jewel* (1952), Judah Waten's *The Unbending* (1954) and Dorothy Hewett's *Bobbin Up*. In these we see a continuation of themes and structural effects already noted: the desire to expand the scale of fiction to invoke vast historical movements; the foregrounding of conventionally excluded subjects; and the juxtaposition of documentary, 'novelistic', and political discourses.

Both *Power Without Glory* and *The Unbending* reveal divisions between a documentary mode which tends towards chronicle and historical specificity; and a self-consciously literary mode which tends towards plot and universal significance. Critics have frequently rescued *Power Without Glory* from itself, as it were, by reading it as a study of power—universalising its story against the grain of the novel's historical specificity and class analysis. The narrative frequently turns to a 'history voice', directed at a contemporary audience, and breaking down the effect of aesthetic autonomy. It can be contrasted in this respect with Dal Stivens' *Jimmy Brockett* (1951), a fable of corruption that yet makes no claim to a specific history, one that the reader *shares*. However, *Power Without Glory* also shares the aspirations of its critics towards the traditionally perceived universal qualities of literature, especially in the ethical language of its characterisation of John West. The novel cannot fuse its two modes, but their juxtaposition has its own narrative and political force in a tension between moral and historical perspectives.

The Unbending draws together documentary and a more classic realist form. On one level the novel's realism is characterised by its scepticism towards rhetoric: its prose is unadorned, in characters reticence is preferred to fluency, story-telling itself is shown to be dangerously seductive and utopian. At the same time, the novel includes the rhetoric of radical propaganda (in speeches and quotations from documents); again less to lay down a correct political line than to include perspectives that realist novelistic discourse could not otherwise include. The novel juxtaposes utopian images (including of revolution) with alternative perspectives and a long historical view. Throughout, foreigners are figuratively linked with the working-class, especially with the radical organisation International Workers of the World (known as the Wobblies). We see both Hannah Kochansky and George Feathers gaining *speech* in opposition to dominant religious and patriotic languages. In concentrating on these marginal groups the novel offers an alternative history of class conflict: the Wobblies, not the Anzacs, provide the initiating moment of a modern national history. The novel desires classic realist form, but also to go beyond 'bourgeois' realism. It remains divided, but its effectiveness is due in part to the way it is forced to highlight divisions between different rhetorical styles.

Bobbin Up, by contrast, recalls earlier radical fiction because of its narrative focus on 'myriad lives woven and interwoven' and collage-like juxtaposition of scenes. The novel's formal inventiveness is again an aspect of foregrounding conventionally excluded subjects: the everyday lives and dreams of an inner-city working class, politics, and above all, desire. The novel is rich in different voices, sensuous and rhythmic, contrasting with the neutral prose of other realist writers:

> 'My heart was achin' that night at Harry's . . . plentya booze and the jazz, the jazz . . .' hot and sweet and restless, dust and sweat and sand and sea, shuffling feet and moths sizzling against the fairy lights . . . 'Another day older and deeper in debt'.

The novel targets romance, linked here with consumer society. Against which, as Veronica Brady has suggested, there is 'a letting loose of desire in general and in particular of the desires of young women—normally taboo in patriarchal society'. It could be argued that most of the male 'social realist' writers cut themselves off from this most powerful fictional language for representing social crisis and *political* desire. The erotic and the unconscious are marginalised as inessential to the political, as 'merely subjective'. *Bobbin Up*, as Brady suggests, is able to show 'lively, defiant, sensuous young men and women fighting to take possession of themselves, their bodies, their desires, their hopes in a world intent on alienating them'.

All the novels mentioned can be placed in a broad category of realism. This discussion has argued for their diversity and, indeed, their modernity. In the face of successive social crises which appear to redefine history and reality itself, the forms of realist representation are constantly reinvented. A desire to expand, and even violate, the limits of fiction distinguishes each of these texts— few of which until very recently have received sustained critical attention.

Notes

The most useful works for this period are Drusilla Modjeska, *Exiles at Home: Australian Women Writers, 1925-45* (1981); Ian Reid, *Fiction and the Great Depression: Australia and New Zealand, 1930-50* (1979); and Tim Rowse, *Australian Liberalism and National Character* (1978).

For details on *Strife*, other magazines, and writers' organisations see Charles Merewether 'Social Realism: The Formative Years', *Arena*, 46 (1977) and *Art and Social Commitment: An End to the City of Dreams* (1984); also Julie Wells, 'The Writers' League: A Study in Literary and Working Class Politics,' *Meanjin*, 4 (1987). *Australian New Writing*, edited by George Farwell, Katharine Susannah Prichard and Bernard Smith, appeared 1943-6 (I have quoted from the foreword to the first issue). For further remarks on the magazine, and cultural debates of the 1940s, see Smith's 'Reds and Other Colors', *Age Monthly Review* (October 1981).

Alan Marshall's sketch comes from 'Australian Picture-Book II' in *Battlers* (1983), first published in *Left Review* (December 1937). His novel, originally titled *Factory*, was completed by 1937 (Harry Marks, *I Can Jump Oceans: The World of Alan Marshall*, 1976); the passage quoted appeared first in *Communist Review* (February 1938). Humphrey McQueen's comment on the novel comes from his stimulating book *The Black Swan of Trespass: the Emergence of*

Modernist Painting in Australia to 1944 (1979). John Morrison's waterfront pieces have been collected as *Stories of the Waterfront* (1984); 'Tons of Work' originally appeared in *Sailors Belong Ships* (1947).

H. M. Green's remark on prose fiction is from the introduction to volume 2 of his *A History of Australian Literature, Pure and Applied* (1961), while Patrick White's oft-repeated phrase concerning 'dun-coloured . . . journalistic realism' comes from 'The Prodigal Son', *Australian Letters*, 1, no. 3 (1958). From the important collection *Australian Writers Speak* (1942) come Frank Dalby Davison's comment on 'national unity', in his essay 'What is Literature?' and Jean Devanny's description of *Sugar Heaven*, in her essay 'The Worker's Contribution to Australian Literature'. The quotation on 'the spirit of the war of the classes' is from a review of *Sugar Heaven* by L. Harry Gould, *Worker's Weekly*, 19 June 1936.

For further comments on socialist realism see Carole Ferrier's 'Jean Devanny, Katharine Susannah Prichard, and the "Really Proletarian Novel"' in the collection she edited, *Gender, Politics and Fiction: Twentieth-Century Australian Women's Novels* (1985); this book also contains Pat Buckridge's essay, 'Katharine Susannah Prichard and the Literary Dynamics of Political Commitment'. Prichard's comment on *Upsurge* is cited in Richard A. Nile's introduction to the 1986 edition of the novel, and the contemporary criticism is from a newspaper review reproduced on the front cover of this edition. On Prichard's fiction I have also referred to Jack Lindsay, 'The Novels of Katharine Susannah Prichard', in his *Decay and Renewal: Critical Essays on Twentieth-Century Writing* (1976); Sneja Gunew, 'Katharine Prichard's Political Writings and the Politics of Her Writing', in John Hay and Brenda Walker (eds), *Katharine Susannah Prichard: Centenary Essays* (1984); and Modjeska's introductions to the recent Virago editions of Prichard's goldfields trilogy.

The descriptions of Kylie Tennant's fiction are from T. Inglis Moore, *Social Patterns in Australian Literature* (1971); C. Hadgraft, *Australian Literature: A Critical Account to 1955* (1960); and Adrian Mitchell, 'Fiction', *The Oxford History of Australian Literature*. Brian Matthews writes on Tennant in '"A Kind of Semi-Sociological Literary Criticism": George Orwell, Kylie Tennant and Others', *Westerly* (June 1981).

Crown Jewel, *The Unbending* and *Bobbin Up* were all first published by the Australasian Book Society. See Jack Beasley, *Red*

Letter Days: Notes from Inside an Era (1979). The communist critique of *Bobbin Up* which I have quoted is from Jack Beasley, 'Questions of Australian Literature', *Communist Review* (January 1960). Veronica Brady's comments are in a review of the Virago reprint (1985): 'Rites of Passage', *Australian Society* (February 1986). Frank Hardy's work has been reassessed in John Frow, *Marxism and Literary History* (1986), and Peter Williams, 'Interventions and Obsessions: The Work of Frank Hardy', *Southern Review*, 14 (1981). On the New Theatre see Ken Harper, 'The Useful Theatre: The New Theatre Movement in Sydney and Melbourne, 1935-83', *Meanjin*, 4 (1984), and Angela Hillel, *Against the Stream: Melbourne New Theatre, 1936-86* (1986).

Chapter 24

QUESTS

ANTHONY J. HASSALL

This chapter is concerned with three interrelated quests which have haunted the imaginations of European Australians, and which have found continuing expression in the history, poetry, drama and fiction that seek to define Australia and the experience of being Australian. The quests are: the voyage in search of Australia; the quest for 'home' in Europe; and the journey into the centre of the country. The basis of these quests in historical fact has been the subject of some dispute, but during the period with which we are concerned, 1915 to 1965, they achieved the status of a national mythology.

The year 1915, the year of Gallipoli, is a crucial date in the formation of that mythology. There are many fictionalised accounts of the Australian return to Europe, but Gallipoli is the one which has captured the twentieth-century Australian imagination. The story of Anzac was mythologised for a grateful nation by C. E. W. Bean, wartime correspondent and later official historian of World War I. Bean's volumes on the war, of which *The Story of Anzac* (1921-4) was the centrepiece, were very widely read for such a monumental, official history; and the religion of Anzac developed rituals which spread throughout the land, touching the imaginations of all Australians. Gallipoli is located close to Troy, the Homeric battleground which stands at the very beginning of European literary and mythic history, as Sidney Nolan, in particular, has recognised and exploited in his Gallipoli series of paintings. The Anzac soldiers who fought there were thus initiated into European manhood on the Homeric soil where such stories began some 2500 years before; and the myth of national 'maturity' was fashioned out of their 'blooding', or 'lad-testing' as Xavier Herbert calls it in *Soldiers' Women* (1961).

Quests celebrated in European literature include those for the Golden Fleece and the Holy Grail, the recovery of Eden, the re-founding of Troy in Rome and, after the replacement of the epic by the novel, the quests for a new and just society, and for personal maturity and sexual identity. In more recent colonial and post-colonial literatures, quests of discovery into the interior, and quests in search of the cultural 'home' have recurred. The quests in Australian literature draw upon these earlier quests, while also taking on individual qualities in a country that was itself mythologised as the object of questing before its discovery by Europeans. Literature which aspires to mythologise such experience reinterprets and reinforces the nation's inchoate self-image. It turns to the half-realised beliefs buried in the nation's folklore and collective unconscious, and seeks to draw those beliefs into conscious prominence, to work them into shapely narrative, and to privilege them with the status of art.

The quest for the Great South Land, the myth with which European Australia began, attracted, in the period with which we are concerned, a number of Australian poets. They were seeking a mythic structure to embody their perceptions of a contemporary, and newly Australian cultural awareness. In 1960 Douglas Stewart anthologised six *Voyager Poems,* dating back to 1931, which he saw as 'narratives "moving towards the epic"', and which celebrated the emerging myths for which he believed the country was searching:

> [T]here seems to come a time in the history of nations when whatever it is that moves the production of poetry—some spirit moving in the nation and the time—demands that the poets should sing the nation itself into shape.

The poems—by Kenneth Slessor, R. D. FitzGerald, William Hart-Smith, Francis Webb and Stewart himself—used epic journeys like those of Cook, Tasman, Shackleton, Eyre and Leichhardt to explore the ambitions and achievements of those Europeans who imagined, sought, discovered, and explored Australia. The country of which they expected so much, about which they fantasised so luxuriantly, finally eluded Quirós, Tasman and Bougainville. Cook, who reached and explored the east coast of Australia, was the most accomplished of the voyagers, but he has never caught the public imagination in Australia in the same way as gallant failures like Scott or Ned Kelly. The legend of failure and disappointment is deeply ingrained in the

Australian imagination, and in seeking to establish an Australian mythology, the Voyager poets generally reinforce it, portraying what Stewart calls 'the great ancestors of the tribe' experiencing failure rather than success.

In his 'Five Visions of Captain Cook' (1931), Slessor celebrated Cook's 'courage, nerve, imagination, shrewdness and self-confidence', qualities displayed in his decision to turn west towards the Australia he was to discover, instead of north towards safety, like Tasman and Bougainville: 'So Cook made choice, so Cook sailed westabout, / So men write poems in Australia.' By contrast Shackleton, whose epic of endurance is celebrated in Stewart's own 'Worsley Enchanted' (1952), demonstrated an astonishing capacity for survival against the odds, but the only new territory he gained was for the human spirit. And even Cook was eventually humbled by Slessor's old enemy time, dying on a barren Pacific strand:

> There he had dropped, and the old floundering sea,
> The old, fumbling, witless lover-enemy,
> Had taken his breath, last office of salt water.

Cook did not suffer the metaphysical torments of the Leichhardt portrayed in Francis Webb's 'Leichhardt in Theatre' (1952) or indeed in Patrick White's *Voss* (1957). He sought the geographical Australia, not its metaphysical meaning or his own psychic nemesis, and if he left his bones in the Pacific, as Leichhardt and Burke and Wills were to leave theirs in the centre of Australia, his great work was successfully completed before he died. He is the most successful, the least complicated, and therefore the least typical of Australia's voyager heroes.

R. D. FitzGerald's ancestor Martin Mason, imaginatively recreated in 'The Wind at Your Door' (1958), is morally more ambiguous, compromised by the brutality of the convict system of which he is inescapably a part. And the poet, his twentieth-century descendant, cannot escape his own complicity in the system. 'Heemskerck Shoals' (1949) is also concerned with lost opportunity—Tasman's decision to follow orders rather than to sail to the east coast of New Holland. FitzGerald's long philosophical poems 'The Hidden Bole' (1934) and 'Essay on Memory' (1937) follow Christopher Brennan in their romantic pursuit of 'the quest of our imaginings', while affirming the ultimate value of everyday human endeavour. FitzGerald's characteristic combination of opulent imagination and sober pragmatism is evident in Tasman's musing:

. . . It was unthrift
of the faculties to dazzle them on a glitter
of wishes that dulled the mind; men would do better
to ask of the southern land in sober terms
what could be made of it . . .

The South Land, with its 'futile heart within a fair periphery' as James McAuley described it, was to elude many of its early seekers, and to disappoint many of its would-be exploiters; so much so that the expectation of disappointment entered into the national mythology, to be laughed at by Joseph Furphy, made tragic by Henry Handel Richardson, and mournfully celebrated by Henry Lawson.

'A Drum for Ben Boyd' (1946), Francis Webb's first major poem, explores from a series of viewpoints of a variety of contemporary observers, the complex character of the visionary founder of 'a young town grown from myths at the world's end / Where the South is a swaggering fantasy, not yet sober'. Like so many Australian heroes, Boyd was ultimately defeated by a combination of the country, a timid establishment and his own ambition. He left his bones somewhere in the Pacific, and the expedition which went in search of him in 1854 returned, like the Leichhardt expeditions of the 1850s and 1860s, empty-handed, save for the legend. But if Boyd was ultimately a failure, he did for a time at least fulfil the dream of so many of the early questers: 'Here, between the beach and the mystic Centre / I shaped a forming foothold and the future.' Webb returned to the enigma of such figures in his later 'Eyre All Alone' (1961), which charts the inner isolation of the explorers who ventured into the mystic centre.

The bleak continent of Antarctica is another image of difficult, challenging terrain which recurs in Australian literature. Like the unexplored heart of Australia, Antarctica inspired epic journeys of courage and endurance, not against heat and thirst, but cold and starvation, and it provided stories of heroic endurance and survival (Shackleton in 'Worsley Enchanted'), visionary romanticism (the Captain in Rosemary Dobson's 'The Ship of Ice', 1946), moral compromise (Thomas Keneally's *The Survivor,* 1969), and tragic defeat ennobled by uncompromising courage (Scott in Stewart's radio verse play *The Fire on the Snow,* 1939).

Captain Robert Scott's expedition fitted the Australian myth of exploration so precisely that Stewart made a number of attempts to write the story of his unsuccessful race against Amundsen for the

South Pole as a narrative poem, before eventually reworking it as a radio play. Stewart portrays Scott not as a scientific explorer like Cook, nor as a great leader like Shackleton, but as a voyager into the void like Voss, a psychic adventurer who pits himself against huge odds for the sake of 'one man's dream', and who is satisfied with a simple, if splended heroism as justification for his attempt and failure. Scott chose his own fate deliberately, seeing in his death on the snow a clean and simple version, as his companion Wilson suggests, of the tragedy and triumph of every human life:

> We dreamed, we so nearly triumphed, we were defeated
> As every man in some great or humble way
> Dreams, and nearly triumphs, and is always defeated,
> And then, as we did, triumphs again in endurance.

The Fire on the Snow is a powerful, haunting tragedy, Greek in its poetic simplicity, and very Australian in its mythic pattern.

Stewart's stage play *Ned Kelly* (1940) is less successful, though the story of the Kelly gang, which epitomises the Australian myth of courageous, defiant failure against overwhelming odds, has haunted the Australian consciousness as the Irish have haunted Australian history. Joe Byrne, the poet of the gang, has his own version of the European quest for Australia:

> . . . he still came out from prison.
> From the black rains of the slums, perhaps, to the sunlight;
> From the fenced fields, the fenced streams, the fenced
> Rabbits, to a place where a man could shoot a rabbit,
> And the streams belonged to the ducks instead of the squire,
> And a man could cross an open paddock in the sun
> On his horse—not crawling on his belly.

Like Sidney Nolan, who also recognised the potential of the Kelly story, Stewart was not so much creating a myth, as rendering artistically visible one already firmly implanted in Australian folklore.

James McAuley's *Captain Quiros* (1964), published four years after Stewart's *Voyager Poems,* explores similar themes, though it is more substantial (the length of a brief epic) and more ambitious. The poem also has close affinities with R. D. FitzGerald's *Between Two Tides* (1952) and Rex Ingamells' *The Great South Land* (1951); and the Quiros story that attracted McAuley forms the subject of an unpublished play, 'The Quest' (1928) by Louis Esson, and of a television opera by Peter Sculthorpe (1982). Like Dobson's Captain in 'The Ship of Ice', McAuley's Quirós represents the idealistic impulse which sought a new and uncorrupted world in the South Pacific, and his experience represents the inevitable disillusionment of a Christian idealist with the squalor of the actual colonies. The more recent squalor that accompanies those same colonies' quest for political independence is searchingly portrayed in Thea Astley's *Beachmasters* (1985), which is partly set on Quirós Bay of the Two Saints. That idealistic dreams died hard in Australia is evident in the socialist expedition led by William Lane in 1893 to set up a utopian New Australia in Paraguay, an endeavour that ended, like Quirós' settlements at Graciosa Bay and on Espiritu Santo, in failure and disillusionment. It has recently been fictionalised by Michael Wilding in *The Paraguayan Experiment* (1984).

As epics, the voyager poems are fragmentary, internalised, searching rather than celebratory. The European Renaissance epics ranged from voyager poems like Camões' *Os Lusiadas,* through military epics like Tasso's *Gerusalemme Liberata,* to essentially religious poems like Dante's *Divina Commedia* and Milton's *Paradise Lost.* Australia was born at the end of the great age of European exploration and discovery, when such epics were going out of fashion, and twentieth-century poets have not found it easy to recuperate the form. Even in prose, Patrick White could make of *Voss* only a strangely modern version of epic. It is therefore hardly surprising that Australia has not produced an *Aeneid* to celebrate its origins and consolidate its emerging myths, but rather a series of epic fragments. As in other parts of the modern world, the epic impulse that animated literary myth-making was to find its fullest expression not in verse or drama, but in the novel.

If Australian writers found the novel more congenial than the epic, they still had to contend with an unfamiliar landscape, and a history that did not accord with received mythic patterns. Perhaps because it seemed at first so alien to European eyes, the landscape has loomed larger in Australian writing—and in Australian painting—than it has in North America, where a fertile country welcomed refugees from a decaying and repressive Europe. That myth of the new world was not easily applied to Australia, though novelists like Henry Kingsley and painters like John Glover sought to portray the landscape as a pastoral Eden. In pioneer sagas like Brian Penton's *Landtakers* (1934) and *Inheritors* (1936), Miles Franklin's *All That Swagger* (1936),

Eleanor Dark's *The Timeless Land* trilogy (1941-53), and Judith Wright's *The Generations of Men* (1959), the authors saw the landscape as less than Edenic but still challenging and full of promise. More pessimistic were Marcus Clarke and D. H. Lawrence, who sensed an alien challenge in the bush, and Henry Lawson and Barbara Baynton who wrote with despairing passion of its destructive effect on those who struggled to domesticate it. The more urban Christina Stead also has Kol Blount bitterly lament 'the malign and bitter genius of this waste land' in *Seven Poor Men of Sydney* (1934). Judith Wright, who has celebrated Australia's landscape and history in poems of haunting, passionate insight, crystallised both these hostile feelings towards the landscape, and the Quirós-like dreams of a brave new world, in 'Australia's Double Aspect', the classic essay which introduces her *Preoccupations in Australian Poetry* (1965).

Europe was not alone in offering its novelists a landscape and a history that fitted traditional forms. In addition to their fertile northern-hemisphere landscape, the Americans had a history to draw on that Australian novelists like George Johnston in *Clean Straw For Nothing* (1969) could only envy:

> The Yanks . . . proved it to themselves long ago . . . Revolution, civil war, frontiers to subjugate, mountains to climb, rivers to ford, plains to cross, the Redman as the perfect adversary, the right sort of issues like slavery or liberty . . . they can dream up their own mythologies out of what they've done . . . They're *intact*, you see, they've got a shape.

The mythologies that Australian novelists embraced to structure their very different history were less sanguine, reflecting the Australian experience of stoic endurance and courage in defeat. As Barron Field discovered, and as Les A. Murray restated in a recent poem, 'failure / was the first rhyme for Australia'. The novelists' response to the landscape was more extreme: either they turned back from Australia to the landscape of 'home' in Europe, or plunged into its arid interior in the hope of solving their alienation by immersion.

Henry Handel Richardson made the dilemma of these contradictory loyalties central to her trilogy *The Fortunes of Richard Mahony* (1917-30), which is also a classic statement of the Australian myth of heroic failure in the pursuit of self-realisation and an abiding home in the new continent. As Mikhail Bakhtin has pointed out, 'the life course of one seeking true knowledge' is one of the oldest of European fictional forms. Richardson has relocated this form in a new country, recognising that Australia in the nineteenth century attracted a disproportionate number of those restless seekers who were unhappy in Europe, and who were unlikely to find in a raw new country the peace of mind that had eluded them in the settled lands of their birth. Whether they fretted under constriction, like Mahony, or plunged into the wilderness like Voss, they lacked the steadiness and attachment to place of a Mary Mahony, and could not easily come to rest in any part of the world. Their presence in Australia contributed to the construction of one of the myths described in this chapter: the restless, heroic, unsuccessful pursuit of some ultimate metaphysical goal, which found its most tangible image in the centre of Australia.

The Fortunes of Richard Mahony thus exemplifies both the quest for a home in Australia and the quest for 'home' in Europe. Fretting in what he sees as the provincial backwater of Ballarat, Mahony decides to return to the metropolitan culture of Europe. His return is not successful, however, partly because he is chilled by the narrow provincialism he finds in England—and in particular by the petty-minded snobbery with which his wife Mary is treated—and partly because his restlessness is a pathological condition inflamed by a prolonged stay in any place, whether European or Australian.

Unlike Stow and White, Richardson is not preoccupied with landscape, but she uses it as they do at crucial times in the narrative to reflect the inner geography of character. *The Fortunes of Richard Mahony* opens with a miner buried alive on the Ballarat goldfields, which the greed of the Ballarat miners has transformed from a lovely grassland adorned with the 'brief delirious yellow passion' of the native wattle into the 'feverishly disembowelled' Gravel Pits. It ends more peacefully than it began with Mahony's burial within sound of the sea near Gymgurra. There the bare, undulating country that claims his body—though it cannot contain his 'wayward, vagrant spirit'—is scarcely disturbed by man. In the climactic scene at Barambogie, in which Mahony contemplates suicide as an escape from his coming madness, he sprawls 'at full length on the wet and slimy ground' as he wrestles with his own soul and the earth that would receive him. Barambogie epitomises in its ugliness, its ignorance and meanness, its failing economy, its false promise, and its tormenting mill whistle, all that Mahony has come to hate about Australia. But Richardson makes it clear that Mahony is projecting on to the country his own tormented failure to find a self to which he can accommodate his restless ambitions. The search for a self proves as exhausting and as unsuccessful as the search for gold. But if Mahony's quest ends in failure, it is an heroic failure, fought out, essentially, against the Australian landscape that finally claims his remains.

The psychic divisions and divided allegiances that exacerbate Mahony's restlessness reappear in Martin Boyd's Montfort and Langton families, whose repeated journeyings between Australia, England and Southern Europe are chronicled in *The Montforts* (1928) and the Langton tetralogy, *The Cardboard Crown* (1952), *A Difficult Young Man* (1955), *Outbreak of Love* (1957) and *When Blackbirds Sing* (1962). The continuing restlessness of the next generation of Australians lies at the heart of George Johnston's trilogy, *My Brother Jack* (1964), *Clean Straw for Nothing* (1969) and *A Cartload of Clay* (1971). In addition to these urban and Europe-oriented conflicts, there are the frontier conflicts of part-Aboriginal Australians—like Trilby Comeaway and her family in Nene Gare's *The Fringe Dwellers* (1961) and Norman Shillingsworth and his family in Xavier Herbert's *Capricornia* (1938)—who are divided by their mixed inheritance. Like Thomas Keneally in *The Chant of Jimmie Blacksmith* (1972), Herbert recognised that the violence practised by European Australians on the Aborigines invited a similarly violent response. But *Capricornia* ends more enigmatically than *Jimmie Blacksmith*, poised somewhere between the tragedy of Tocky's death, the sometimes wild comedy that precedes it, and Norman's confrontation with his halfcaste identity in a racist society that marginalises yeller fellers along with full-blood Aborigines.

Norman's quest for a name, a father, and a social identity—a place and a space in which to live—is paralleled in *Capricornia* by Herbert's quest for an Australia he can celebrate. Despite the savagery of Herbert's satire, *Capricornia* is imbued with the author's 'measureless spiritual love for the living land that bore me'. Herbert shared the desire of Stewart and Nolan, and of the 1890s nationalists, to give voice to the distinctive culture that had evolved in Australia. He followed Lawson and Furphy in finding the real Australia in the outback, where the frontier collision between imported European habits of thought and behaviour and an antipathetic climate and landscape is most violent, and most productive of distinctively Australian cultural adjustments. The brothers Oscar and Mark Shillingsworth represent the extremes of those adjustments to the tropics. Oscar dresses formally, remains respectable, and marries into the local squattocracy, while Mark goes combo and on the grog, ending up as a criminal and a refugee from what passes for society in Port Zodiac. Mark fathers and then deserts Norman, who is later adopted by Oscar. Norman's quest develops from these irregularities in his genetic and family inheritance.

Herbert's passionate concern with the Australian character, which he documents as obsessively as Joyce documents the Irish, is evident in the nationalistic monologues of Andy McRandy of Gunamiah. McRandy lauds his fellow countrymen: 'We're a great people, we Australians. There's nuthen to touch us in the World.' He has less conventional praise for Aboriginal Australians: 'People accuse 'em of bein' too stupid to practise husbandry. Quite the contrary. They practise it in the most amazin'ly clever fashion.' Norman's particular destiny is to inherit the potential of both these races, and Herbert has expressed in *Poor Fellow My Country* (1975) his disappointment that Australia did not produce a 'creole' race combining the best qualities of black and white Australians. Katharine Susannah Prichard is more despairing about the outcome of sexual relations between black and white in *Coonardoo* (1929). Coonardoo's fate is tragic, and both she and Hugh are destroyed by his failure to accept their love and their common humanity. Herbert was well aware of the sexual exploitation, the brutal dispossession, and the crude, unremitting racism that disfigure the European treatment of the Aborigines, and also of the ecological, and indeed spiritual superiority of Aboriginal culture, which most Europeans despise. There is little hope at the end of *Capricornia* that any of the quests it depicts will be successful, but Norman is not destroyed as Richard Mahony is destroyed.

The Australian quest for 'home' is given classic expression in Martin Boyd's *Lucinda Brayford* (1946). Like *Capricornia, Lucinda Brayford* was written in England, and they thus share the status of home thoughts from abroad. But the homes they recall are very different, and one wonders what the urbane Boyd, whose Melbourne characters regard the Riverina as primitive beyond endurance, would have made of the Northern Territory. Boyd and Herbert do, however, share a concern with sexual and marital relations between different racial and tribal groups. Boyd portrays the ultimately destructive effect of intermarriage between Melbourne 'society' and the English aristocracy. Like *Coonardoo* and *Richard Mahony, Lucinda Brayford* is a tragedy, a record of the failure of a life that had seemed to promise much, and that had known success of a kind. While Mahony's tragedy results from conflicts within his own character, Lucinda, like Coonardoo, is a victim—of her mother, her husband, her lover Pat, and her son Stephen, as well as of the larger forces destroying the civilised world she has come to love.

Though primarily concerned with Lucinda's journey 'home,' Boyd's novel includes a journey into the centre of the country, which parallels Teresa Hawkins' journey to Harper's Ferry in Christina Stead's *For Love Alone* (1945). The first part of *Lucinda Brayford* ends with a picnic in the Christmas Hills near Eltham on the outskirts of Melbourne, and it is Lucinda's last, passionate contact with her native land:

> Lucinda lay back and closed her eyes against the sun, white and blinding in the mid-heaven. Hugo began to make love to her. At first she tried to restrain him, because of the time and place. But then the time and place, the high and piercing sun, the stark earth, seemed to fuse her body in a wild desire.

Her son Stephen is conceived on the Australian earth which he is never to see, and which she is never to see again. Boyd's choice of this landscape to typify what is old and new, eternal and procreative about Australia is in striking contrast to the images he chooses to represent the culture of England. On her first night in England Lucinda goes to see Nijinsky's *Scheherazade* at Covent Garden. At the climax of the ballet she has 'an involuntary bewildered vision of the hill-top where she had picnicked with Hugo, on the day before they left Melbourne'; but her overwhelming impression of the ballet, Hugo's family, and the society to which they belong, is of a richer and more passionate world than the one in which she has lived her previous life.

Boyd's other major images of the aristocratic tradition of European civilisation are Crittenden, the Brayfords' country home, and King's College Chapel, with its unequalled choir. Both the book as a whole, and the fourth part which is devoted to Stephen, begin and end at Cambridge. And on his last night as an undergraduate, Stephen reflects on the qualities that make the University his spiritual home:

> In this city of palaces, built not for the aggrandisement of individuals but as centres of learning, the pervading spirit was more sympathetic to him than that of any place he knew, even more than that of Crittenden . . . it seemed to him as if this eternally renewed flow of youth, all these bright spirits passing unceasingly through courts and halls and chapels, had left in them the echo of their hopes, so that they were not like places sacred because the dead were buried, but sacred because there the spirit lived.

The spirit is under great threat in *Lucinda Brayford* from men like the Australian newspaper baron Straker, who buys the title of Lord Fitzauncell, and helps to plunge Europe into the war which destroys Stephen, and with him the Crittenden line, and the aristocratic culture that Boyd admires. England is a graveyard at the end of the book, and Lucinda's quest for a richer, fuller, more civilised life in Europe has failed—as similar quests fail in *Richard Mahony* and in Patrick White's *The Aunt's Story* (1948)—though Lucinda is left with some hope that the human spirit will survive the war. Boyd's Europe is a cultural museum, full of gorgeous buildings, but in the process of losing its cultural wealth and acquiring the corrupted values of Straker and Lord Wendale.

Theodora Goodman in *The Aunt's Story* also finds Europe—in the form of the *Hôtel du Midi*—destroying itself about her, and she fails to complete her journey back to Australia. Theodora's quest, though ostensibly directed towards Europe, and the original Meroë after which her childhood home was named, becomes an inner quest for self-realisation. She eventually finds a sanity in the madhouse of prewar Europe, and a paradoxical madness in the 'sane' United States. Her ending is characteristically ambiguous, both a defeat and a triumph.

Like Theodora, Teresa Hawkins in Christina Stead's *For Love Alone* flees at the first opportunity from the inexorable demands of an insensitive and exploitative family. Marriage, the routine 'escape' for women, seems worse than the predicament to Teresa, who is appalled by the ritual sacrifice of the 'golden youth' of her favourite cousin Malfi March to a 'hole-in-a-corner' marriage in the suburbs. Teresa, haunted by Malfi's departing plea ('Don't think too badly of me'), is passionately determined to escape a similar fate, despite her recognition of the terrible risk involved:

> There was a glass pane in the breast of each girl; there every other girl could see the rat gnawing at her, the fear of being on the shelf. Beside the solitary girl, three hooded madmen walk, desire, fear, ridicule. 'I won't suffer,' she said aloud, turning to the room to witness. 'They won't put it upon me.'

Teresa dreams instead of travelling to the great universities of Europe, and attaches herself to Jonathan Crow, a clever boy from the slums, who has won a 'travelling scholarship to a European university', and who preaches a free love he is unable to practise.

Crow absorbs Teresa's passionate idealism and intellectual curiosity without responding to her emotional and sexual hunger, offering instead only his desiccated and self-pitying careerism. In choosing Crow as her vehicle for escape from a fate like Malfi's, Teresa is ironically imprisoning herself in an illusion no less stultifying than a suburban marriage.

After Crow's departure for England, Teresa embarks on a four-year course of overwork—which turns into a severe bout of anorexia—during which she accumulates her fare to Europe. Her passionate belief that she must leave Australia to realise her 'secret desires' is not shared by Shannon Hicks in Kylie Tennant's *Ride On Stranger* (1943). Shannon's determination to escape the paralysing constrictions of her family, and her personal quest for professional commitment and love, parallel Teresa's but they are enacted within Australia. It is, however, within urban Australia, since women are excluded from exploring the mystic centre: '"I wish, oh, I wish, I was a man!"' laments Fanny Hyde in M. Barnard Eldershaw's *A House is Built* (1929). '"I'd go exploring" . . . She thought of Mr Eyre pushing out toward nothing, something, the unknown.' Teresa blinds herself to Australia, and eventually reaches England, where her sufferings are rewarded, not with the university education of her dreams, nor with the cultural richness that Lucinda Brayford discovers, but with self-realisation. *For Love Alone* thus follows the traditional pattern of the *Bildungsroman*, rather than the model of Henry James and Martin Boyd in which apparent success is followed by bitter disillusionment. Unlike Boyd, James and Tennant, Stead does not follow Teresa beyond her personal and sexual liberation. Teresa's last thoughts are not for her own release, however, but for the continuing imprisonment of others less fortunate than she: 'It's dreadful to think that it will go on being repeated for ever, he—and me! What's there to stop it?' She herself, however, does escape from what she sees as her imprisonment in Australia, and from her debilitating personal subjection to Jonathan Crow. Her 'buffoon Odyssey', her quest for her personal 'Cytherea', is a real, if qualified success.

David Meredith's quest for his Greek island is less successful, and more in accordance with the Australian myth of courageous failure, which is also muted success. It is not exactly a quest for 'home', though it begins as a quest for Europe. In *My Brother Jack* David is restless at home because of his family's heavy legacy of service in the already legendary Great War, and his brother's conformity to the Australian stereotype that the war had reinforced, and from which he believes himself to be distressingly aberrant. Marriage and suburban conformity increase a restlessness that is only partly relieved by his travels as a war correspondent in World War II. His real quest begins at the end of *My Brother Jack* when, like Teresa, he exchanges a dead relationship for a vital one, with Cressida Morley. This relationship is explored in the second volume of the trilogy, *Clean Straw for Nothing* (1969), when he and Cressida move to Sydney, to London, and to the Greek island of Hydra. Unlike *For Love Alone,* the second and third volumes of the Meredith trilogy follow the new relationship through to its end in bitterness, betrayal and death. They show that the fantasised quest for an idyllic island retreat, where David can pursue his supposedly true vocation as a writer, is in fact a self-indulgent illusion masking a reality that is frequently squalid. Ironically, however, David's realisation that his quest has failed enables him to begin the trilogy that establishes his reputation as a writer. After the long years of expatriate questing he finds his true subject in the Australian life from which he has fled.

David Meredith typified the postwar generation of artists and intellectuals who deserted what they saw as an impoverished cultural climate in Australia for the richer culture of 'home'. But the traffic was not all one way, and 1948 saw the return to Australia of Martin Boyd and Patrick White, both of whom had lived in Europe before and during the war. Boyd was to stay only three years, while White remained to write a series of major novels that won him, and Australian literature, an unprecedented international reputation. Unable to settle for the 'dun-coloured realism' of life in the littoral suburbs, and wanting to attempt the infinite in one form or another, some of the more restless and adventurous Australians of recent decades have sought self-realisation not back 'home' in Europe, but in the central deserts of the prophets and explorers. It is not to Lawson's bush that they turn—though Patrick White has written his version of that Australian myth in *The Tree of Man* (1956)—but to the deserts of the interior. And while generations of Australian tourists have made the pilgrimage to Europe in search of their cultural roots, 'the *fons et origo* of Western Man' as A. D. Hope describes it in 'A Letter From Rome' (1958), they have also journeyed to Ayers Rock, searching for the heart of Australia.

Like David Meredith, Rick Maplestead in Randolph Stow's *The Merry-Go-Round in the Sea* (1965) is unsettled by his wartime experiences. Unable to conform to the stereotype of the 'smug wild-boyos in the bars', and the conventional expectations of his family,

Rick allows his relationship with Jane Wexford to founder, and he deserts Rob Coram and the family to go to Europe. C. J. Koch's *Across the Sea Wall* (1965) also begins as a conventional quest for Europe but ends as a passage to India, thereby anticipating later fictional quests into Asia by Koch himself, *The Year of Living Dangerously* (1978), Blanche d'Alpuget, *Monkeys in the Dark* (1980) and *Turtle Beach* (1981), and Robert Drewe, *A Cry in the Jungle Bar* (1979). *The Merry-Go-Round in the Sea* and *My Brother Jack* are searching novels, but neither is strictly speaking the story of a quest, as *Clean Straw for Nothing* and *To the Islands* (1958) are. Stow's *Tourmaline* (1963) is also the story of a quest though, like White's *Riders in the Chariot* (1961), the quest is physically localised rather than peripatetic.

In *To the Islands,* Stow appropriates an Aboriginal quest, the search for the islands of the dead, and attaches it to a European quest for the centre, for a meaning, an explanation for the 'strange country' of his soul. The landscape through which Heriot travels in the company of his Aboriginal guide Justin images the inner, psychic landscape that he is also driven to explore. Like *Capricornia, To the Islands* is set in the harsh physical landscapes of the north, where the clash between black and white Australians is most clearly visible; and if *Capricornia* depicts the brutal, dehumanising racism of secular white Australia, then *To the Islands* depicts the more principled, guilt-ridden response of the southern churches to 'the Aboriginal problem'. The confrontation between the two cultures, which Heriot personally re-enacts in his conflict with Rex, prompts him to question the value of the European culture with which he and his mission are endeavouring to colonise the Aborigines, and which sits as uneasily upon them as his scraps of European poetry sit upon the alien landscape. He abandons the mission and in the course of his journey in search of the Aboriginal islands of death learns humility—as Voss does—and is reconciled with Rex. If his end is ultimately tragic, it is not without hope.

Teresa and Lucinda are in search of love. Heriot and Voss have experienced love, and are now in search of death, perhaps because, like Alistair Cawdor in Stow's *Visitants* (1979), they see death as the ultimate opportunity for an enlightenment about the meaning of life. Certainly many of White's protagonists experience enlightenment of a kind in the hours preceding death. Stow is less certain that enlightenment will come, however passionately it is sought, and Heriot's end is hedged about with uncertainty. It is not clear whether he sees the islands, or whether, if he does, they are an illusion. But he searches for an experience that can give meaning to his life.

If Martin Boyd represents the Henry James phase of Australian cultural history—the obsession with a Europe that is perceived to be corrupt, but which remains so fascinating that it cannot be relinquished—then Patrick White represents the coming home of Australian culture. *Voss* (1957) is the book for which he is most widely known, and while it does not yet enjoy the status of the Anzac myth, with which this account began—and it is certainly less widely understood—its significance for Australian literary history would be difficult to exaggerate.

Both *Voss* and Anzac are stories of failure, of idealism and courage recklessly spent on quests that were in objective terms of little value, though of profound subjective value to those involved. Australian explorers occupy a special place in the popular consciousness. Like the Anzacs, like Phar Lap and Les Darcy, they are ungrudgingly admired for taking on overwhelming odds, battling courageously, and, if they failed, showing courage and determination to the end. In *Voss*, White has sought to elevate the explorer legend he drew on, using the journals of Eyre and Leichhardt, into the most literate form of popular mythology, the novel. *Voss* explores the meaning of journeys of exploration like those of Eyre and Leichhardt for mid-twentieth-century Australians, who are 'troubled' by the legends—the tales of the tribe—they have inherited. He seeks to domesticate those legends for suburban Australians, who sense the interior of the continent as a reservoir of meaning about the essential Australian experience, and so to make the myths available, and to facilitate, as Stewart and the Voyager poets did, the development of an indigenous mythology.

White portrays Voss as a Nietzschean madman, fiercely determined to impose the 'royal instrument' of his will on the unexplored and unyielding continent of Australia. As such, he is an extreme type of the European invader, careless of the true nature of the country, patronisingly contemptuous of the indigenous culture and wisdom of the Aboriginal inhabitants ('my people'), unconcerned about the welfare of those who share his endeavours, and ignorant even of his own human needs and weaknesses. Voss is defeated, and his will eventually fails; but in the process he learns something of the country and its people, something of love and humility, and his spirit haunts the land as his story will haunt his countrymen.

In the proem to *For Love Alone* Christina Stead suggests that 'there is nothing in the interior' of Australia. For White and Stow, however, it is the very seeming emptiness of the interior, which mirrors the spiritual emptiness ascribed to Australians, that challenges exploration and discovery. At Belle Radclyffe's party on the evening of the memorial service for Voss, the musician Topp laments 'our mediocrity as a people', prompting the painter Willy Pringle to reflect:

> I am confident that mediocrity of which he speaks is not a final and irrevocable state; rather it is a creative source of endless variety and subtlety . . . common forms are continually breaking into brilliant shapes. If we will explore them.

Laura Trevelyan suggests that the quest she shared with Voss was for 'true knowledge', which 'comes of death by torture in the country of the mind'. It was a quest for love as well as knowledge, though a very different kind of love from that depicted by Boyd or Stead. Teresa starved in Sydney and dreamed of England; Lucinda was carried off by the style and cultural richness of Europe; but for White, Europe was a disintegrating *jardin exotique*, and the empty deserts of Australia drew him back in search of a meaning that Europe did not offer.

Voss is a book of breathtaking ambition. Not only does it chronicle the exploration of Australia, it is itself an exploration of what Australian history can be made to mean to contemporary Australians. It is an exercise in the construction of a mythology that is indigenous, though related to Europe: a mythology that would release the variety and subtlety of the country, and break its apparent drabness and mediocrity into brilliant shapes.

Riders in the Chariot (1961) is an equally ambitious attempt to seek out and construct a mythology of postwar Australian suburbia, a mythology derived from the major religions of Europe, Judaism and Christianity, but so domesticated in the Sydney suburbs as to be unmistakably indigenous to the white tribes of the area.

The four riders in the chariot are outsiders, separated from the culture in which they find themselves, but united by the spiritual quest they share, which White sees as an 'unprofessed factor' in the secular life which surrounds and rejects them. After surviving the European holocaust, Mordecai Himmelfarb, one of the zaddikim of his time, leaves the Israel to which he has been sent and journeys in quest of Australia. He is crucified on a mutilated jacaranda tree in the yard of the Brighta Bicycle Lamps factory at Barranugli, but his failure, like Christ's, is a spiritual triumph. White's audacity in thus transposing the central event of Christianity from its comfortable distance in history and ritual, and reconstructing it in a very recognisable contemporary suburban locale, is matched by the naturalistic density that he gives to the life story of Himmelfarb, both in Germany and in Australia.

Surrounding Himmelfarb when he is taken down from his cross are his fellow visionaries. Mary Hare enjoys a mystical, almost Aboriginal sympathy for and indentification with the flora, the fauna and the country which encroach on Xanadu, her lovely, crumbling, European mansion. Xanadu and its grounds—imported garden and native bush—are destroyed by the bulldozers of suburban development, but Miss Hare lives on as a spiritual presence, a local daemon, to trouble the residents in the fibro houses. Ruth Godbold also troubles the conventional, and her employer, Mrs Chalmers-Robinson, regards her as 'a kind of saint'. The only one of the four to remain alive at the end of the book, she continues to spread her goodness through her daughters, her 'six arrows at the face of darkness'. The halfcaste Alf Dubbo is marginalised by white society, like Norman Shillingsworth: 'Officially, of course, he was not a man, but a blackfellow.' He feels unable to intervene in the crucifixion of his friend Himmelfarb. But like Willy Pringle in *Voss*, and Hurtle Duffield in *The Vivisector* (1970), Alf Dubbo is an artist, who turns Himmelfarb's crucifixion into a painting which, like *Riders in the Chariot* itself, locates the Christian story inescapably in contemporary Australia.

It is in Dubbo's paintings of 'The Deposition' and of 'The Four Living Creatures in the Chariot'—which he completes, like Duffield's god paintings, in the days before he dies—that White's ambitions in the book are most clearly stated. The paintings may be lost, but White's book is not, and with it a giant stride has been taken in the quest to construct an Australian mythology which draws on the complex heritage of Australians, both European and Aboriginal. Richard Mahony's vagrant spirit may never have been claimed by his adopted country, and the Vane-Chapman heritage of Lucinda Brayford may have petered out in postwar England, but Patrick White's visionaries live and die in Australia, and their spirits continue to trouble those of us who live here.

So many of the protagonists of Australian literature, and so many of the authors who created them, were restless, driven, and ultimately defeated. Poets like Barcroft Boake and Adam Lindsay Gordon killed themselves; Lawson drowned his talent in alcohol; and not a few of the more gifted later writers have sought refuge from the strains of living and writing in Australia in exile or alcohol or suicide. The heap of bones in the desert is their haunting image, the suggestion not necessarily of suicide exactly but of a partly self-destructive unconcern with mere survival. The taint of defeat is, however, ennobled by the manner in which it is met, in accordance with the myth that both Anzac and *Voss* in their different ways express. That myth lies at the very heart of the Australian self-image, as reflected and enacted in its literature, especially its literature of quests.

Notes

In addition to the standard histories of Australian literature by H. M. Green, revised by Dorothy Green (1984), G. A. Wilkes (1969), Leonie Kramer (ed.) (1981), and Ken Goodwin (1986), together with Leslie Rees, *A History of Australian Drama* vol. 1 (1978), and the indispensable William H. Wilde, Joy Hooton and Barry Andrews, *The Oxford Companion to Australian Literature* (1985), I have drawn on Northrop Frye, *Anatomy of Criticism* (1957); Roland Barthes, *Mythologies* (1972); Thomas Shapcott, 'Developments in the Voyager Tradition of Australian Verse' in *South Pacific Images*, edited by Chris Tiffin (1978); Helen Tiffin 'Towards Place and Placelessness: Two Journey Patterns in Commonwealth Literature' in *Awakened Conscience*, edited by C. D. Narasimhaiah (1978); Drusilla Modjeska, *Exiles at Home* (1981); Judith Wright, *Preoccupations in Australian Poetry* (1965); and Dorothy Green, *The Music of Love* (1984).

Among many studies of individual works and authors I am particularly indebted to: Dudley McCarthy, *Gallipoli to the Somme: The Story of C. E. W. Bean* (1983); Dorothy Green, *Henry Handel Richardson and Her Fiction* (1986); Joan Lidoff, *Christina Stead* (1982); Dorothy Green, '"The Fragrance of Souls": A Study of *Lucinda Brayford*', *Southerly*, 28 (1968); H. P. Heseltine, *Xavier Herbert* (1973); Garry Kinnane, *George Johnston: A Biography* (1986); Anthony J. Hassall, *Strange Country: A Study of Randolph Stow* (1986); Brian Kiernan, *Patrick White* (1980); and G. A. Wilkes (ed.), *Ten Essays on Patrick White* (1970).

Chapter 25

RESPONSES TO MODERNISM, 1915-1965

JULIAN CROFT

Many of the more illuminating remarks on modernism in Australian literature have occurred in connection with discussions on modernism in Australian art—Humphrey McQueen's *The Black Swan of Trespass* (1979), Richard Haese's *Rebels and Precursors* (1981), and Geoffrey Dutton's *The Innovators* (1986). All point out that responses to European modernism were quickly seen in the visual arts, but that reaction against modernism was deep-seated and long-lasting. The same was true of literary modernism. Whether modernist innovations came from Melbourne (Haese) or Sydney (Dutton), seems of interest in terms only of the debate about the traditions of those two cities. What is apparent is that by the end of the 1930s significant modernist poems were written in both Melbourne and Sydney, while discernible effects of the revolution in English prosody were apparent in most of the State capitals. By the end of the same decade, at least five major Australian novels had been written using new styles in whole or in part (Chester Cobb's two novels, Henry Handel Richardson's final volume of the Mahony trilogy, Dark's *Prelude to Christopher* and White's *Happy Valley)*, but although each had an Australian setting, all were published abroad. On the stage and in film the response was not so obvious, but the great florescence of serious writing for radio in the 1930s and 1940s shows distinct modernist qualities. There is now enough evidence to suggest that Australian writers were promptly aware of what was going on in Europe from 1910 onwards, but they were slow to respond (World War I might have been one reason); nevertheless they did so in the second and third decade of the century in quite significant and distinct ways.

Modernism is a peculiarly slippery term because its contemporary meaning often depended on just when a culture became aware of changes in the sensibilities and preoccupations of its artists and was moved to use the word to describe them. Modernity, like time, was relative after 1915. In Brazil, a good comparative example for Australia because of its physical isolation from European culture and its provincialism in the late nineteenth century, the coming of modernism was apparent, self-conscious, and easily dated.

The Brazilian cultural model at the time was France, and in the manner of French writers of making manifestos and publicly proclaiming the arrival of the new, Brazilian *modernismo* was inaugurated in a 'Week of Modern Art' in São Paolo in February 1922. As with the innovators in France, this modernism was an attack on the authority of the previous age. It was nationalist, committed to the future, and full of references to contemporary artistic movements (surrealism, jazz) and to intellectual movements (the changes in physical sciences and in psychology), and of course the stylistic experiments of French writers such as Apollinaire and Cendrars.

The public proclamation of artistic movements was not unknown in Australia. In 1923 the magazine *Vision* was started in Sydney and ran for four issues with a platform of a renaissance in Australian art based on the vision of the great writers of classical antiquity, of the Renaissance itself, and of the romantic movement, but only those writers who best exemplified the creative passion of nineteenth-century vitalism. It was anti-nationalist and anti-modernist, and like Wesley's devil it had some of the best tunes in the form of the most promising young poets—Slessor and FitzGerald, as well as the young Jack Lindsay who was one of its editors. The modern movement in art according to the Lindsays (Jack's father Norman was a major supporter of the magazine) was a retreat to decadence, to the uncivilised, a celebration of the primitive and the childish, and a direct assault by charlatans and Jews on the finest traditions of Western art. Nevertheless, even those in the Lindsay circle could feel the strength of the siren song of the unconscious, the allusive austerities of *The Waste Land* and its solipsistic pessimism, and even be excited by the terrible uncertainty produced by the anti-Newtonian Physics of the 1920s. These ideas circulated throughout Australia, and although style took some time to respond, the ideas themselves took vigorous root. In contrast to developments in Brazil, the modernist movement was not immediately apparent in stylistic experiments. However, its temperament—concentration on interior states, the depiction of alienated consciousnesses, a concern with the limitations of language, and the total uncertainty in an agnostic age—was clearly seen in novels and poems in the 1920s and the 1930s. As well, there was no need for Australian writers to feel embarrassed about using those ideas because until well into the 1960s the term 'modernism' was not widely used in Australia to describe them. Thus in Brazil we have a self-conscious use of the term and a celebration of modernism; in Australia there was little sense of modernity being an issue other than on the grounds of stylistic decadence or ugliness.

Modernism is a blanket term under which snuggle many comfortable and uncomfortable bedfellows of various 'isms', all of which can be seen in the literature of the period under discussion. Futurism with its positive regard for machinery, the car and modern technology, can be seen in much of the minor poetry of the 1930s and in the celebration of the powerful six- and eight-cylinder cars in Eleanor Dark's novels, which give her tormented characters the freedom to commute between a traditional polarity of Australian life—the town and the bush. Surrealism arrives a little late but coincides with its appearance in British poetry in the mid-1930s, and in the 1940s it flowers unexpectedly and quite strikingly in the hoax-poems of Harold Stewart and James McAuley, masquerading as the working-class poet Ern Malley. Expressionism does not make its greatest impact on the stage until the 1960s, but it is apparent in the radio drama of the 1930s and the 1940s where in its milder forms it is the most natural way of developing the intricacies of complex characters. Imagism was taken up and developed almost as soon as it was promulgated in London before World War I; its main proselytiser, surprisingly, was Norman Lindsay, and it is Lindsay whom both Slessor and FitzGerald thank for what they saw as the basis of their styles—the use of the concrete image and the avoidance of abstraction. The more extreme forms of anti-rational art as developed in Switzerland during World War I—Dada, for example— did not make much impression until the early 1960s when works by Tzara and Schwitters were performed in Sydney (notably Schwitters' sneeze poem), as were, at the same time, works by Jarry and Artaud. The interest in the originals of the Theatre of the Absurd followed the growing interest in Brecht and Beckett during the late 1950s and 1960s, though the historian of that period in explaining the apparent lack of influence of those two playwrights on what was being written at that time speculated that it might have been because Australian playwrights traditionally put more emphasis on matter rather than manner. The same is true of the film. Much of the early attraction of film was its capacity to represent coherently a recognisable world. This was especially prized by Australian audiences, and most films of the silent era self-consciously used Australian settings, both urban and rural. The expressionist techniques incorporated into German films after World War I and the use of film for surrealist ends by the French and Spanish made little impression on Australian production until the 1960s.

Not only was modernism a substantial part of Australian literary culture by the 1930s, but its form in Australia was different from that found elsewhere. Modernism in Europe was a response to the authoritarian and materialist beliefs of the nineteenth century, but in Australia it was also a reaction against the widespread acceptance of vitalism and deterministic Darwinism. This view underpinned much of the intellectual debate in the first two decades of the twentieth century and can be seen in particular in Norman Lindsay's idea of an organic life-force which produced beauty according to pre-existing laws, beautifully summed up in Lionel Lindsay's 'Modernism in art is a freak, not a natural evolutionary growth'. Lindsayan vitalism was the aesthetic and biological equivalent of Newtonian classical mechanics. The new physics and psychology of the twentieth century brought about an erosion of belief in such predictable systems and universal standards, and an element of despair entered the work of poets and novelists who did not have a belief-system, such as Marxism, to replace them. But it was only an element, for one of the remarkable features of Australian modernism is that, contrary to a 'gloom' thesis that alienation and loss were the principal concerns used to explain the writers of the previous generation, much of the response to the uncertainty of the early twentieth century was a celebration of a meaning beyond mere deterministic explanation. Journeys to the interior might confront a vacuum and death, but insight resulted; twentieth-century families, rather than the nineteenth-century bush, might be 'the nurse[s] and tutor[s] of eccentric minds' but their baleful influence could be broken away from; and the God who had died and whose fertility rites had been forgotten could be invoked and brought to life again by an ordinary farmer (*The Tree of Man*), a German explorer (*Voss*), or a gifted painter (*The Vivisector*). The suicides, nervous breakdowns and the early deaths of the later generation of modernist writers in England

and America in the 1950s and 1960s, for example Dylan Thomas, John Berryman, and Robert Lowell, did not reach epidemic proportions in Australia. Perhaps that was because Australian modernism offered some hope, whereas in other cultures a sterile constructivism, a destructive apocalyptic romanticism, irony, and a pervasive anomie had become the order of the day.

But to return to the beginning of modernism. If modernism's subject matter is a depiction of the inner state of the alienated psyche, and, as Edmund Wilson has argued, modernism is also an extension of symbolism, then Brennan's poetry of the late 1890s and the early years of the twentieth century is quintessentially modern. His style is not. If we look for the stylistic features of modernist poetry, specifically free verse, then we do in fact find that the impact of modernism is delayed until the late 1920s. With the novel, we can say that the modernist text is one which again represents an alienated consciousness through narrative techniques in which consciousness is represented directly through first-person narrative or through an omniscient stream of consciousness. By these criteria Furphy's *Such is Life* could be argued to be (pre-)modernist, and certainly all those techniques were apparent in Chester Cobb's novels in the mid-1920s. In the drama the change to the new style was not so obvious. The plays Louis Esson wrote before he went overseas in 1915 were realist in temper, but those written after his visit to the Abbey Theatre in Dublin and his correspondence with Yeats, could be classified as 'poetic naturalism', a style which can be seen as having modernist affiliations. With the ground at least partly prepared for the seeds of the new European sensibility, how aware were Australia's writers of what had happened after that month, October 1910, in which Virginia Woolf sensed that human nature, religion, politics and literature had changed for good?

In the summer holidays after the Armistice in 1918, the seventeen-year-old Kenneth Slessor, who had just left Sydney's Shore school, read some of Edith Sitwell's *Wheels* anthologies and became aware of the great changes which had taken place in poetry during the war. Fifteen years later he had read (or knew of) the 'Haveth Childers Everywhere' section of what was to become Joyce's *Finnegans Wake*. In Melbourne in 1922, Frank Wilmot ('Furnley Maurice') was vigorously defending Carl Sandburg's use of free verse and noting the 'adventuresomeness' of the young Oxford poets while asking wryly of conservative Australian writers and readers, 'Had Sassoon and not Gellert been our war poet, how would we explain him away?' The

American example of the new prosody of free verse was something which Wilmot felt could be useful in Australia; something which would break the influence of the dead hand of the kind of editor who 'sits ticking off verse accents on his fingers to decide whether a contribution is poetry or prose'.

Neither Slessor nor Wilmot responded to the new directions of poetry at that time. Wilmot kept to traditional forms to express his vision of urban dislocation while Slessor, under the influence of the Lindsays and his reading of the Parnassian poets of nineteenth-century France, cultivated the style of Gautier's *Emaux et Camées* and the sonorities of Tennyson. Nevertheless even in his early poems the spiritual depression of the postwar world could be seen in the midst of all the Lindsayan vitalism. The death's head came along with him to every party—as much a part of him as the bottles of beer in his briefcase, or the beer bottles in Joe Lynch's overcoat. The stylistic change to a richly decorated free verse was a movement as significant for him as the shift of the French poets of the late nineteenth century away from the alexandrines of Héredia and Leconte de Lisle. Slessor's 'Captain Dobbin' (1927) marks the emergence of the modern in Australian poetry, as does the Eliotian anthropology of 'The Old Play' (1932), drawn from Slessor's reading of that most necessary of texts for the 1920s, Jessie Weston's *From Ritual to Romance*. The way was then prepared for the great achievements of the 1930s: R. D. FitzGerald's wonderful meditative poem 'The Hidden Bole' in 1935 and Slessor's 'Five Bells', his great elegy for his drowned friend Joe Lynch, but also for the modern world, which was about to change utterly when the poem was published in 1939. Both Slessor and FitzGerald attempted to ally their nineteenth-century vitalist inheritance (which stressed the determined structure of the world) with the relativity and uncertainty of the modern world. Slessor admits failure in 'Five Bells'; FitzGerald in his tightly structured 'The Hidden Bole' and in the 'Essay on Memory' struggled to accommodate them both, and then in 1944 gave full voice to mid-twentieth-century despair in 'The Face of the Waters', which, unlike most of his work, was written in free verse.

When looking at this early Australian response to modernism it is worth bearing in mind a simple distinction: that between modernist themes and preoccupations, and modernist styles. In the poetry of the 1920s and the 1930s it is quite possible to see a prompt and profound response to the changing intellectual milieu in Europe: relativity, time, despair, hopelessnesss—all the sights and sounds of

The Waste Land, but without the stylistic features which conveyed that awful vision. We should remember, too, that poetry in England in the 1930s did not persist with the stylistic changes which Eliot introduced. The powerful influence of Norman Lindsay over the young Sydney poets and nationalist feeling in Melbourne worked against the adoption of the new internationalist style of free verse in English. Thus the poets turned their attention to the subjects of modernism but the forms and language they used were derived from the traditions of the previous age. Most of them were unable to give up the sensual drug of beauty for the cold water of the bare line devoid of music and rhyme.

One who did, and who possibly was able to because of his absences from Australia and direct contact (as distinct from textual contact) with what was going on in Europe, was Bertram Higgins, the Melbourne poet who published Australia's first modernist poem, which was also one of its finest: *'Mordecaius' Overture* (1933). In style and scope it is the equal of early Eliot and later Pound, and in its modernist treatment of the apocalypse and the search for sense in the midst of ruin, it was the perfect poem for Australia at the height of a depression. As with all prophets in their own country and more so in Australia with its oversupply of deserts, few read it; notable exceptions were H. M. Green who treated it at some length in his history, and A. R. Chisholm who praised it as being superior to Eliot's poems of the time. Despite this, the poem remained in relative obscurity until its republication in 1980.

More neglected, in that they have never been republished, are the novels of Chester Cobb, *Mr Moffatt* (1925) and *Days of Disillusion* (1926). Both were published in London, but like Joyce in exile writing in obsessive detail of the minute reality of Dublin, Cobb writes about the eastern suburbs of Sydney. The novels are remarkable for their unaffected use of the stream-of-consciousness technique and their marvellous evocation of a great Australian theme—the ennui of suburban life. In doing so, Cobb used Joyce's method of showing accurately and objectively the material reality of a city, and of counterpointing it with a convincing portrayal of a consciousness (male and lower-middle-class) responding to that city. Unlike Joyce, Cobb did not see the necessity for a prefigured metaphor such as that of the *Odyssey* to give shape and substance to his work. Cobb's novels have the lack of closure of modernist fictions, but they use symbolism to convey a sense of ending; consequently an explanatory metaphor in the title is not necessary. As with the few Australian modernist novels before World War II, the material and the real were foregrounded—not the mythic level, nor the metaphysical. They were still the province of poetry.

In London a couple of years later, a newly-arrived Christina Stead wrote her tribute to Sydney of the 1920s and its people in *Seven Poor Men of Sydney* (started 1928, published 1934). Her compassion and commonsense saved her from the worst excesses of D. H. Lawrence, and her program of ideas was more coherent and mainstream, being Marxian and Fabian in orientation. Stead's narrative voice runs through the various tones of sympathy, irony, playfulness, and rhapsodic description, while the story-line is let out several notches to accommodate a characterisation which has the genius of what Les Murray was later to celebrate as 'sprawl'.

Also completed in 1929 was *Ultima Thule*, the final volume of Henry Handel Richardson's trilogy *The Fortunes of Richard Mahony* (1930), which, although it has much of the nineteenth-century tone of the previous novels, has some modernist features, features which have a profound effect on a reading of the whole three-volume work. The trilogy is a study of alienation based on two different paradigms. One paradigm is deterministic—that Mahony's personal flaws and final death are the product of a long-developing disease (probably syphilis); the other is less materialist and more spiritual—that Mahony's restlessness and personality disorder are the product of a spiritual antipathy to an age of materialism. The final volume of the trilogy stresses the personal and interior nature of Mahony's agony by using dream, reverie and hallucination. By doing so it gives the conclusion of the trilogy the nature of a coda, for on one hand the story demands a deterministic interpretation (Mahony's madness was the slow unfolding of a disease of the body), but on the other, the last volume with its modernist bias suggests that the disorder is as spiritual as it is physical and thus makes the reader re-interpret the whole of the three-volume work. The famous final paragraph of the work stresses the division between body and spirit and also suggests that while European materialism (the body) can be absorbed into Australia, the spirit, if it is still an alienated European consciousness, cannot.

These were some of the positive responses by Australian writers to modernism in the 1920s and 1930s; and one must note that the majority of them were from expatriates. At home the negative response was virulent and as full of the claims of tradition and nation as the violent attack on the cosmopolitan Jew, Leopold Bloom, by the one-eyed Cyclopean Irish citizen in *Ulysses*. Norman and Lionel Lindsay, R. G. Menzies, State libraries and art galleries, and a horde of newspaper columnists and editors all attacked modern art and literature on the grounds of ugliness or obscenity. The various State police forces took on the guise of moral censors (as they were later to be State censors in the early war years) and their efforts are graphically described in Eleanor Dark's *The Little Company* (1945) and M. Barnard Eldershaw's *Tomorrow and Tomorrow* (1947). Adrian Lawlor's blast at Menzies and the art establishment in his polemical essays *Arquebus* (1937) and *Eliminations* (1939) and later in his self-indulgent *Horned Capon* (finished 1944, published 1949) give some impression of the widespread resistance to bohemianism, nonconformity, and modern art in Australia. Much of the common complaint about modernism in the 1930s was that it was not realistic, and if it were, it concentrated only on the negative and seamy side of life; that the styles adopted by writers like Stein, e. e. cummings, and Joyce (the usual demons cited) were incoherent and an attack on the very basis of language, or worse, obscene and perverted affronts to the fundamental values of Australian society. Similar responses could be heard from the *petite bourgeoisie* in Europe and America, but the majority of the population in Australia was very insular. The range of periodicals read by the working and lower-middle classes in the 1920s was narrower than in the 1880s and 1890s. This insularity combined with the power of the press to induce hysteria in governments which led to a degree of censorship (based mainly on alleged obscenity) which was rivalled only by the Irish Republic, and which was to last until well into the 1960s.

The other line of resistance was aesthetic. The notion of craft and beauty in true works of art was defended strongly by the traditionalists who felt that the barbarians were moving in on the Royal Academy and the Louvre (Athens, Rome, and Alexandria having succumbed generations before) and that righteous Melbourne (or even sun-blessed Sydney) was to be the last bastion of all that was best in Western art, in the face of a cosmopolitan degeneration brought on by black culture (jazz and cubism) and Jewish wealth and taste. Even P. R. Stephensen, who had had considerable contact with major British modernist writers in the 1920s and early 1930s, could still rage in 1941 against modernism as decadent Jewish mysticism. Combine both the puritanical and aesthetic reactions against modernism and the way was prepared for the conception and the reception of the poetry of Ern Malley.

Yet another antagonist of modernism was the powerful influence of Soviet realism in the 1930s and 1940s. The realist novel had a strong tradition in Australia from the nineteenth century and was encouraged by the nationalist movement and by the widespread influence of socialist aesthetics during the period under consideration. There were exceptions. A realist and socialist writer such as Katharine Susannah Prichard could suffuse her realism with a poetic colour often taken from the Lawrentian palette. *Coonardoo* (1929), more than her other novels, has a metaphoric depth to its landscapes and human relationships which can be seen as one of the influences of modernism on a strongly resistant ideological aesthetic. The power of the Communist Party of Australia to discipline and censor its writers varied from individual to individual, but it was often exercised, and became more oppressive in the 1940s and the 1950s. The formulations of Marxist literary aesthetic adopted in the 1940s and 1950s (Zhdanovism) did much to keep left-wing writers from experimenting with the forms of later modernism in the 1940s. For example, it was not until after her separation from the party in 1968 that Dorothy Hewett took up the styles of non-naturalistic drama.

Realism as an issue was not confined to the Communist Party of Australia. John Anderson in Sydney in the 1930s had praised Joyce for his realism, which Anderson argued was a form of classicism, romanticism being its opposite in that it was a rejection of the real and a flight into illusion and fantasy. The feeling that modernism might in fact be a new form of classicism had been put forward in Melbourne in 1933 when Cyril Pearl, writing about Bertram Higgins' poetry and A. R. Chisholm's praise of it, argued that Higgins, like Eliot, was a classicist: 'the classicist strives after order and precision, "harmony, clarity and integrity," the romanticist smothers his thought in a tangle of extraneous imagery.' The same reliance on Joyce's formulation of Thomistic aesthetics in *A Portrait* can be seen in A. D. Hope's writing on aesthetics during the early 1940s. Following Anderson's writing on Joyce, Hope wrote at length on the aesthetics of James Joyce in the *Australasian Journal of Psychology and Philosophy*. It was in part a reply to Anderson and it shows Hope's breaking with the Andersonian empiricist position that a thing is only beautiful for its own sake (which was Anderson's version of realism), to a position that beauty exists outside the perceiver and the artist. In this version of scholastic aesthetics (a period of philosophy which Anderson detested) can be seen the intellectual basis for the neoplatonic tendency of Hope's poetry in the late 1950s and 1960s.

But in the 1940s Hope's and Anderson's distrust of romanticism and their interest in and use of (but in Hope's case, an increasing repugnance towards) psychoanalytic theories show that the response to modernism was not as polarised as the Ern Malley hoax would seem to indicate. Hope in particular showed some sympathy for the ideas present in modernism in his writings in the 1930s, but like Anderson he responded more to the classical temper of the time than to the subterranean surrealism present in some poetry and art. Again one cannot be too prescriptive, for much of the imagery of Hope's earlier poetry owes a lot to surrealism and Freudianism, despite his dislike for these traditions expressed in his writings in the 1950s. There are, however, indications in poems such as 'Soledades of the Sun and the Moon' (1957) that Hope could see merit in poetry which was generated from the irrational, or as he calls it 'the raving sybil'. It was not so much the content of such poetry which antagonised Hope, but the manner in which it was written. It was style which was the issue with Ern Malley, and in Hope's aesthetic writings in the 1940s and 1950s it was form and harmony which were seen to be the main attributes of an art which could fill the spiritual vacuum of modern life.

The major reaction against modernism apart from the Lindsays' in the 1920s was the Ern Malley hoax of 1944, though the modernism which the perpetrators of the hoax, Harold Stewart and James McAuley, were attempting to ridicule was not the same beast which had slouched towards Australia two decades before. The hoax was directed against *Angry Penguins*, a journal edited by Max Harris, who had filled it with cosmopolitan and avant-garde material cheek by jowl with the work of local artists and writers. Harris and the *Angry Penguins* artists and writers formed a group who actively promoted a style of modernism which was psychologically oriented, based on individual experience, and anarchist in temperament. It was opposed to both academic traditionalism and Marxist determinism. Harris' surrealist novel *The Vegetative Eye* (1943), which was savaged in a famous review by A. D. Hope, shows both the strengths of innovation and the failures of incoherence.

Stewart and McAuley set out to show that craft and art were not present in the kind of poetry published by Harris. To do so they constructed poems supposedly by chance (using surrealist methods and anticipating John Cage by some decades), picking lines at random from whatever books were to hand and then combining them into nonsensical poems. That was the intention, but as commentators have pointed out since, many of the poems make coherent sense, depending, of course, on what reading strategies are used. For Stewart and McAuley, and for the public at large when the hoax was exposed in a Sydney newspaper, Ern Malley's poetry made as much sense as the ravings of a madman; that a madman's ravings do make sense if you know their code was an issue close to the heart of the *Angry Penguins* group. The public exposure of the ease with which modern poetry could be written, and the subsequent prosecution of Harris for publishing obscenities (one poem describes events which take place in a park at night), did much to strengthen the anti-modernist forces in Australia.

There was little non-naturalistic drama written for the Australian stage before the 1960s. I have already suggested that radio drama in the 1930s and the 1940s was far more receptive to this style of writing than the stage. An exception can be made of Sydney Tomholt's plays which were collected in 1936. Some of his work is in the naturalistic mode but its psychological intensity and its austere method of presentation ally it with some of the modernist European plays of the early twentieth century. Other shorter plays deal with hallucination and the prophetic (*The Crucified*), and characters at the edge of mental catastrophe (*Life and the Idiot*) or involved in allegorical conflict (*The Woman Mary*). Tomholt's work is interesting on the page, but it might lack the compelling force in performance which a later generation of playwrights working in this mode—for example Stephen Sewell and Louis Nowra—were to achieve.

Dulcie Deamer's plays of the 1930s show some interesting experimental aspects. In *The Heart of a Woman* the set of an oriental inn is used to represent a woman's heart, while beneath it is the crypt of the subconscious. But most of her work draws on traditional styles, such as the morality play, or else it has naturalistic dialogue and sets even when the play (*That by Which Men Live*) is a fable set twenty years in the future in an Australia where religion has been supplanted by reason.

The major outlet for the poetic imagination in dramatic form during the 1930s and 1940s was radio. Musette Morell's poetic evocation of the world of animals addressed serious issues through fantastic dialogue, but the greatest triumph of the metaphoric transformation of reality—of which radio is uniquely capable—was the wave of verse drama for radio in the 1940s. Verse dramas on stage in the 1930s and 1940s had been quite popular overseas (Anderson, Auden, Eliot, Fry, Isherwood), but their example did not stir Australian poets until Douglas Stewart's *The Fire on the Snow* was produced for the ABC in 1941. Because radio was not constrained by the naturalistic demands of the early twentieth-century stage, it could directly represent consciousness. As well, language could be elevated without alienating the audience; time too could be easily juggled, and fantasy and hallucination accommodated. Combine these features and many of the techniques of the experimental stage (based on German expressionism) can be seen in Stewart's radio play. Elements are also present in his verse dramas for the stage—for example the final scene of *Ned Kelly*. We should not be surprised that Douglas Stewart, writer of traditional verse, close associate of Norman Lindsay, and apostle of conservatism to the class of '68, could be seen as responding positively to some of the currents of modernism. By the 1940s what was considered modernist was not what caused blood pressure to rise in the 1920s; then it had been free verse and ugliness, now it was the resurgence of a mild form of surrealism and the high-powered, but formal rhetoric of the apocalyptic romantics such as Dylan Thomas—whose wider reputation was also made through radio.

The most obvious examples of the effect of expressionist techniques used on the Australian stage were the series of Patrick White's plays produced in the 1960s. Of these, the earliest (1947, produced 1961) and most impressive is *The Ham Funeral*; it echoes in its combination of realistic set, working-class dialogue, poetic reverie and surreal horror Joyce's technique of combining dream and reality in the 'Circe' episode of *Ulysses*.

White's novels were written in reaction to what he saw as the 'dreary, dun-coloured offspring of journalistic realism' and in the face of a deterministic agnosticism, and are the most significant and extensive body of modernist writing in Australian literature, but his sole volume of poems, *The Ploughman* (1935), is thoroughly Georgian, though with 1930s *Angst*. His first novel, *Happy Valley* (1939), is far more adventurous in form and method than his poetry; in it he uses atmospheric exteriors to parallel internal states, invokes the dreams and reveries of the people of Happy Valley, and uses stream of consciousness. The subject matter of adultery and sexual games counterpointed with the eternal rhythms of rural life and human reproduction is a common one for the period, but White's ability to portray the inner life of a wide range of characters is impressive and shows the evident influence of modernist fiction from the early years of the twentieth century.

Although *Happy Valley*'s subject matter is Australian, the novel, unlike his volume of poems, was published abroad, and it could be argued that like Chester Cobb's novels of the previous decade it should not be used to suggest that modernist influences were so advanced within Australia itself. However, the novels of Eleanor Dark which appeared during the 1930s and 1940s show clearly the acclimatisation of this mode in Australia. *Prelude to Christopher* (1934) is one of the major novels written in Australia during the decade. It is a combination of romance—the dark, crippled satanic wife and the blonde well-made nurse fighting for the soul and genes of the tortured Byronic hero-doctor—and an acute observation of the psychological and sociological confusion of Australia after World War I. The latter is a product of the collapse of idealism, and of the horror of a deterministic and inescapable historical process which is allegorised in the wife, a biologist, who believes she has an inheritable insanity. Far more than *Happy Valley* this novel evokes unforgettably the tragedy of Australian life and its usually thwarted struggle to break free from a determined process (themes dealt with by the poets Slessor, FitzGerald, and Wright). The power of the novel comes from the author's reading in abnormal psychology (an interest Dark shared with Christina Stead) and an eerie mixture of realism and romance which perfectly captures the feeling of the subterranean horror which flows silently under everyday life. White was to accomplish similar things in the 1950s and 1960s, and in those later novels to go beyond the scope of Dark's work, but nevertheless Eleanor Dark in this novel and *The Little Company* (1945) showed that the modernist tradition in the novel was as much at home in Katoomba where she lived as in Ebury Street.

Christina Stead's masterpiece, *The Man Who Loved Children*, published in America in 1940, drew heavily on her Australian childhood in Sydney although the setting was changed to the eastern United States. Plot and the economical development of a story-line were not part of her strategy; and in this respect her novels were part of the modernist tradition of serious (as distinct from recreational) fiction. As in Dark's fiction the underlying theme is the escape from a deterministic process—the vitalist biology which Stead's naturalist father had passed on to her—exemplified in the transmission of not only genes, but of a dysfunctional family culture from the father, Sam, the man who loved children. Louie, the adolescent female child, rebels at the end of the novel, and breaks the family bond and frees herself by being instrumental in the death of her stepmother.

Likewise Teresa Hawkins in Stead's Australian novel *For Love Alone* (1944) escapes first from the constriction of her family and then from an emotionally parasitic lover to find freedom. In this novel Stead celebrates the notion of a rite of passage—to somewhere out of parental (or more specifically, paternal) Australia—and like Eleanor Dark conveys both the social oppression and natural freedom of the Australian environment: both the reality of Teresa's daily life and the deeper levels of her aspirations, dreams, and reveries.

Another major fiction writer of the late 1930s and early 1940s whose work shows modernist tendencies was Marjorie Barnard. The title story of her *The Persimmon Tree and Other Stories* (1943) has much of the spare realistic detail but symbolic weight of the early stories in Joyce's *Dubliners*, and her style shows the same simplicity and neutral narrative tone of early modernist short stories. In collaboration with Flora Eldershaw, Barnard wrote a series of novels in this period which also have innovative features. In *Tomorrow and Tomorrow* (1947) self-reflexive narrative is used in a highly imaginative way and anticipates post-modernist complex literary structures and fabulism. (The latter offers a consciously constructed verbally orientated 'fabulous' version of reality rather than purporting to 'represent' reality.) It can be read as an ironic comment on the 'realist history' novel in which M. Barnard Eldershaw had made their name in 1929 with *A House is Built*, and which was a popular form in the late 1930s and 1940s.

For all the experimentation and restlessness in Australian literature in the 1940s, much of it brought about by the need to express complex political feeling, the following decade saw a retreat from foreground political issues to a concern with spiritual matters. The revival of liberal conservatism and the lessening of state control and planning led to a return of individualism and introspection. As the physical and the real, sharpened by the stimulation of the war, dulled in focus, their complementary tradition, the metaphysical and pastoral, returned but with differences produced by the relativism and uncertainty of language and identity. Underneath the materialist stupor of the new suburbs of the 1950s ran the dark rivers of white Australia's doubt: what was that land outside the safety of fibro and brick veneer? who were the people within?

Judith Wright addressed both questions, but her answers were not what people wanted to hear. Her poetry, the first volume of which appeared in 1946, can be seen in the metaphysical tradition of Brennan in its search for the lost unity of perception and creation and an unwillingness to accept social or biological determinism. The store of ideas in her poetry is modernist in orientation and expresses the crises in Western culture in the mid-twentieth century: the failure of language; the dislocation of subject and object which leads to a despiritualised utilitarian world, and ultimately to the atom bomb; and the provenance of love and poetry is such a world. The poems of this period which express these themes are within the traditions of formal prosody and the metaphysical mode of extracting a universal from a point of a particular observation—the style favoured by Douglas Stewart who published Wright's early poems in the *Bulletin*. During the 1960s Wright's style concentrated more on close observation and description of the natural world (*Birds*, 1962) over which metaphor could be cast to make a general point. Unlike Stewart's romanticism, Wright's modernism can be seen in her themes that language cannot be trusted, and that although things resist naming, the net of the poet's art can be used to capture at least an ethical abstraction if not the metaphysical essence of the particular.

The neo-classicist manner of Australian poetry which John Douglas Pringle remarked on in 1958 was a product of the power of such editors and polemicists as Douglas Stewart, James McAuley, and A. D. Hope. McAuley's *The End of Modernity* (1959) and Hope's *The Cave and the Spring* (1965) argued for the need for the styles of traditional art in the face of a decline in faith: in McAuley's case in Christ, in Hope's in art. Such appeals to tradition did not inhibit the development of poets who wanted to concentrate on the subjective experience of religion and art, and whose styles were idiosyncratic and personal. In fact many of them were encouraged by Stewart in the *Bulletin* in the late 1940s. The most important of them was Francis Webb.

Webb, more than any other Australian poet in this period, confronted the problems of identity in a Cold War world of conflicting and destructive belief systems. Webb's early poems show a resistance to the older modernism of the 1920s: 'They were no "hollow men"' and 'This is why/(In an era of free-verse, poor company)/I pin my faith on slipping images . . .'.

His poetry is full of the rich surrealist-influenced imagery of the 1940s. His major work from this time, *A Drum for Ben Boyd* (1946) is structurally inventive in its use of multiple voices and a self-conscious narrative form. Webb developed and refined the tradition of radio verse-drama started by Stewart in 1941, and utilised the narrative techniques pioneered by Slessor in 'Five Visions of Captain Cook' in 1932. In 'Leichhardt in Theatre' (1947) and 'Eyre All Alone' (1961) Webb concentrates on the internal states of the explorers and projects them outward onto an expressionistic landscape which could have been painted by Sidney Nolan. The same technique is used by Patrick White in his retelling of the Leichhardt story, *Voss* (1957). Webb's poetry also treats the disturbances and triumphs of the internal life. During the 1950s he wrote a series of poems about St Francis of Assisi using multiple viewpoints as in the explorer poems to express a sense of hope and healing in the world. This series probably had a personal dimension derived from Webb's long struggle with schizophrenia. Those poems which deal with his sickness and recovery and relapse in the 1950s and 1960s are as powerful as any written by Lowell in the same period, though unlike the American poet's, Webb's confessions use a public rhetoric and seem richer and more moving for it. Webb's later poems still have many of the features of the style Australian poets developed for radio verse-drama: active and energetic visual imagery and the high pressure and urgent tone of the speaker who must convince through rhetorical flourishes.

As Patrick White's novels developed more and more into expressionist parables—*Riders in the Chariot* (1961), *The Solid Mandala* (1966), and *The Vivisector* (1970)—other novelists kept a more equal balance between the recognisable world and its metaphoric other, while still maintaining a modernist temper in their work. Elizabeth Harrower's four novels of the late 1950s and 1960s have the same dimension of psychological intensity as Christina Stead's, but her dialogue is sparer and her observation of character and setting is in a lower key. In her best novel, *The Long Prospect* (1958), an Australian novelist again depicts the family as a deterministic system from which the female child must escape or be condemned to repeat the awful examples of her grandmother and mother in her own adult life. The slow evolution of Emily through the years of her early adolescence to an informed rejection of her grandmother's and mother's values is wonderfully shown through a restrained but ironic narrative voice capable of relating subtle transactional analysis and crude family bickering, while at the same time placing the child in a carefully described set of domestic interiors which are as fine an allegory of the family's disorder as the symbolic landscapes of Gothic romances.

The other major modernist novelist (and poet) of the late 1950s and 1960s is Randolph Stow. He published five novels in the period under review, two of which, *To the Islands* (1958) and *Tourmaline* (1963), use the poetic devices of older modernist fiction to explore the isolation of the individual and the testing nature of the Australian landscape. Stow's *The Merry-Go-Round in the Sea* (1965) is another Australian novel of childhood (this time male). Again it develops the image of the family as a deterministic structure, a containing circularity—though in this case benign rather than destructive and symbolised by the merry-go-round. What had been positive celebratory actions for Stead's Louie and Harrower's Emily—the first purposeful steps in a straight line out of the family circle—are for Rob Coram hard and difficult, and produce a bitter realisation of the loneliness and dislocation of adult life.

The effects of the break from parental Australia and the dispersal of many of its young writers in the postwar period can be seen in Peter Porter's poetry which can be contrasted with that which Stow wrote while he was still in Australia. Here, Stow combined his childhood love of romantic poetry and ballads with the Western Australian landscape to produce poems which dealt with visions expressed in a poised but neutral style. Porter's style developed in England and is classical and bitter and contains much of the sense of moral indignation found in imperial Roman poetry. Stow writes from a centre which is a vacuum, 'out where the dead men lie', and he hears the 'glum Victorian strain' of the suicidal romantic Australian poets who found no religious vision in the centre of their continent. Porter writes from the centre of a civilisation full of significance and traditions, but he is also aware that in such an excess of culture 'the trivial is immortal'. Porter's persona in the poems written up to 1965 is a mid-century Prufrock, an outsider aware of his social gaucheries, but also aware of his importance as a poet who has to make sense of the European disasters of the twentieth century—the Somme, Auschwitz, possible nuclear war—and to come to terms with the masters of the past, the composers and poets, whose insights need translation to the present. More than any other Australian poet, Porter combines with ease and fluency both the traditions of early modernism and the directions taken by English poetry in the 1930s and 1940s. His debt to W. H. Auden is evident, as is his debt to the anti-romantic social commentary of the Movement, but in his combination of a sceptical distrust of any system and a sense of the individual's powerlessness he is an Australian modernist poet, as he is in his belief that there is a redeeming force in human affairs—and for Porter, that force is art.

The struggle of modernism was against the nineteenth century's deterministic systems of Darwinism and Marxism. Similarly, it was opposed to Newtonian predictability and order and embraced the new physics of Einstein, Heisenberg, and Schrödinger and the ultimate notion that nothing is as it seems. The Australian version of it picked up an old theme in Australian literature: the inability of the individual to do much to change his or her situation—a thwarted idealism which leads to a sense of failure and a consequent desire for self-destruction. Australian poems and novels written between 1915 and 1965 often show this struggle with determinism and a desire to break free and assert an heroic individuality, either through a humanist program or a reliance on a greater metaphysical order (Hurtle Duffield's indi-ggoddd, or A. D. Hope's neoplatonic great harmonies). This essential belief in *something* (sometimes as vague and as undefined as the visionary light in Kendall's poems) distinguished Australian modernism from that of Europe. Whether Molly and Leopold Bloom overcome their difficulties, Lily Briscoe's painting is ever seen, or K. finds out what he was charged with we will never know—but in Patrick White, in Randolph Stow, in Eleanor Dark's *Prelude to Christopher*, in Christina Stead's Louie Pollit and Teresa Hawkins, in R. D. FitzGerald's Hidden Bole, even in Kenneth Slessor's beach at El Alamein we are given a future and a possibility. That there was little faith in a purposeful world in the Australian imagination of this period there is no doubt, but despite that, at the core of the major works even in the desperate years of the 1930s and the 1940s, there remained a certainty that one had to press on even in the face of modernist despair; a certainty that there was always someone to water the geraniums, someone to write in indelible pencil on the face of the sea, and enough spit to be found to mark the dust of even the greatest drought.

Notes

The three book-length studies of modernism in Australian art are: Humphrey McQueen, *The Black Swan of Trespass* (1979), which set the boundaries of the debate on modernism; Richard Haese, *Rebels and Precursors* (1981), a meticulously researched account of the modernist movement in Melbourne and Adelaide (it has the best and the most extensive treatment of the political and aesthetic background to the *Angry Penguins* group); and Geoffrey Dutton, *The Innovators* (1986) which is written in reply to Haese and analyses in detail the intellectual movements in art and literature in Sydney from the 1930s to the end of the 1960s in order to assert the equal importance of Sydney in the revolution in taste and practice during those decades. Edmund Wilson in *Axel's Castle* (1959) charts the movement from symbolism to modernism in the early twentieth century.

The resistance to modernism and the nineteenth-century underpinnings of the reactionary movement may be seen in Norman Lindsay, *Creative Effort* (1920) and Lionel Lindsay, *Addled Art* (1942).

The historian of drama alluded to is Leslie Rees, for his *Australian Drama* (1973; 1978). Dennis Douglas has written on the influence of Expressionism on Patrick White's drama in Leon Cantrell (ed.), *Bards, Bohemians, and Bookmen* (1976).

I learned of Kenneth Slessor's reading in his late teens from a conversation with him in the Journalists' Club in Sydney in 1965; he alludes to *Finnegans Wake* in an address at the Sydney University Union in 1931 (*The Union Recorder*, 1 October 1931). Frank Wilmot's *Romance* (1922) is one of the best and earliest accounts of an Australian poet's response to the new movements in poetry in Europe and America. The neglect of Chester Cobb's novels extends only to reprinting; Colin Roderick wrote on him in *20 Australian Novelists* (1947) and Stan Tick in *Southerly*, 4 (1961).

Drusilla Modjeska's *Exiles at Home* (1981) has done more than any other work to rescue the reputations of many fine novels by women in the 1930s.

Hope's writing during the 1930s and 1940s is listed in Joy Hooton's bibliography *A. D. Hope* (1979). His major article, 'The Esthetic Theory of James Joyce', may be found in the *Australasian Journal of Psychology and Philosophy*, 21 (1943). John Anderson's aesthetic writings have been collected in Janet Anderson, Graham Cullum, and Kimon Lycos (eds), *Art and Reality* (1982).

John Douglas Pringle's *Australian Accent* (1958), chapter 7 entitled 'Poetry: the Counter-revolution' describes the anti-nationalist, anti-modernist poetry and polemic of Hope, McAuley, and Harold Stewart.

Some of the best accounts of the fortunes of modernism can be found in autobiographies of those who were in the thick of intellectual movements of the time: Donald Horne's *The Education of Young Donald* (1967) describes the intellectual temper of Sydney University under the influence of Anderson in the late 1930s and 1940s, and of the pronouncements of Hope and McAuley at this time; the final section of Bernard Smith's *The Boy Adeodatus* (1984) describes his exposure to trends in modern art in Sydney in the late 1930s. Vincent Buckley in *Cutting Green Hay* (1983) gives one of the best personal accounts of the intellectual milieu of the 1950s, in particular the conflict between Roman Catholicism and communism; it includes a sympathetic portrait of Francis Webb. Patrick White's autobiography *Flaws in the Glass* (1981) does not deal in theories but reflects the evolution of the modernist temperament in his own outlook between 1912 and 1970.

Geoffrey Dutton's *Snow on the Saltbush* (1984) analyses the tension between British attitudes and indigenous literary culture. His chapter 'Enemies of Modernity' is an excellent discussion of the reaction to the second phase of modernism (1940 to the 1970s). A lot has been written on the Ern Malley hoax, but Dutton's account in this chapter is a good introduction.

Recently literature and literary criticism of the 1950s have been explained by using a model of Cold War stasis. John Docker's *In a Critical Condition* (1984) does this and also reviews the influence of modernism on literary critical practices. Docker's previous book, *Australian Cultural Elites* (1974) surveys the 1950s as well, but has a stirring treatment of Norman Lindsay's aesthetic and its effect on Kenneth Slessor and an account of John Anderson's impact on Sydney's literary life. Jack Beasley's *Red Letter Days* (1979) gives an informative and personal account of socialist realism and the literary politics of the Communist Party of Australia during the 1940s and 1950s.

PART V

Chapter 26

PERCEPTIONS OF AUSTRALIA, 1965-1988

BRUCE BENNETT

In the present age, 'literature' has attained a broad definition, similar in some respects to that which preceded the intervention of Anglo-American New Criticism in the universities in the 1940s and 1950s—a definition which includes essays, journalism, autobiography and historical writings as well as the traditional literary genres of novels, poems and plays. Such a broad coalition of literary interests would have been accepted quite readily by interwar literary critics and scholars such as Walter Murdoch or H. M. Green, but they could hardly have foreseen the rapid technological changes of our time which have altered the whole notion of 'text'. In the timespan 1965 to 1988, purveyors of the word have had to take increasing account of visual images, while television (from 1956), a resurgence of Australian feature films (in the 1970s), satellite communications and the growth of the computer industry have transformed the reading and viewing habits of Australians. Literary genres are now considered as relatively open, provisional categories; high and low culture are no longer so distinguishable. In this new mix of cultural discourse, Australians have been learning afresh how to 'read' the country they inhabit in the welter of texts at their disposal. This chapter suggests something of the range and significance of these new texts and contends that they should not be perceived as static documentary 'pictures' but as evidence of a dynamic interrelationship of authors and readers with their place and time.

The relationship between writers and readers developed in problematical ways during this period, due partly to increasing numbers of students continuing their education in universities and colleges, where Australian literature had become a subject of study.

Specialist audiences thus developed and the 'common reader' became an ever more elusive creature. An ironic manner is recognisable in Australian literature (especially poetry) from the early 1960s, along with an increasing sophistication and self-consciousness. Modernist and post-modernist experiments were less common in literature than in the visual arts. However, the prose fiction of Murray Bail and the verse of John Tranter and John Forbes in the 1970s and 1980s indicates the preference of a literary avant garde for the 'cool' (and ironic) rendering of experience as an intellectual or perceptual puzzle. In this literature, an enhanced role is assumed for the reader. Michael Wilding's collection of stories *Reading the Signs* (1984) indicates this trend, placing its emphasis on the reader's role in constructing meaning. A fascination with the reader, and the process of reading, has not however led to the 'death of the author' in Australia. On the contrary, the success of recent collections of inter-views with Australian authors, such as Candida Baker's *Yacker* (1986) and *Yacker 2* (1987), and Jennifer Ellison's *Rooms of Their Own* (1986) indicates a continuing interest in writers' experience and its relation to their work. Yet a spirit of scepticism about definit-iveness remains—a sense, induced by the scale and rapidity of change in these times, of the impossibility of final readings (or writings) of texts.

In this climate of critical uncertainty and scepticism it is difficult to draw clear lines of literary and cultural development since 1965. The metaphor of linearity itself seems out of tune with its times; and the metaphor of organic growth seems even more difficult to sustain. However, in the publication explosion which has characterised this period, and the consequent jostling for public attention of a multi-plicity of texts, another metaphor, of centres and peripheries, may offer more scope. Writers and social groups previously considered marginal in Australian culture have pushed themselves closer to the centre of attention, calling into question the notion of a central tradition. Feminist texts and writing by Aborigines and recent immigrants have challenged previous conceptions of Australia and presented contentious images of landscape and people. Conceptions of Australia as a symbolic emptiness, which were prevalent in the 1950s, gave way to more precisely located fictions and a growth of regional awareness. Above all, the new technologies of travel and communications, together with relatively higher levels of affluence in the Australian population, led to a reorientation of relations with the wider world, and hence of Australians' conceptions of themselves.

These changes signify a remaking of Australian cultural history, in which professional historians and social scientists as well as fiction writers, film-makers and others have played their part. Geoffrey Blainey's *The Tyranny of Distance* (1966), for instance, tackled the difficult question 'Where is here?'. In that book, Blainey argues that Australia has been defined largely by its distance from other countries as well as its internal distances. The *idea* of distance had been as important as its physical manifestations; its 'enemy' is efficient transport. Blainey's argument is ironic insofar as it celebrates distance, as well as man's ingenuity in overcoming it. This irony is compounded in the book's concluding image of the Antipodes 'adrift', Australia's dependence on Britain having slackened in spite of the diminished distances. There are rumblings here of Blainey's later discontent, expressed in *All for Australia* (1986), over Australia's new alignment with the geographically closer countries of the Asia-Pacific region, and consequently increased levels of Asian migration to Australia in the 1980s.

C. M. H. (Manning) Clark has a more tragic than ironic conception of the present age. In the revised version of *A Short History of Australia* (1963; 1986), prolegomenon to his *A History of Australia* (5 vols, 1962-81), Clark pictures Australia in the years immediately after World War II as 'between two worlds' before it plunges during the 1970s and 1980s into the present, Mammon-led 'age of ruins'. The only signs of resurrection were a renewed Aboriginal concern for redressing their 'ancient wrong', and the idealism and energy of environmentalists who showed a practical concern for 'this ancient continent'. Clark's *A Short History of Australia* presents the author as a modern-day prophet crying in the wilderness for the return of civilised, humane and democratic values. The society in which he finds himself is twice flawed—once by British philistinism and now, since the late 1960s, by American and Japanese materialism. A more independent Australia is desired, but no modern writer could match the ideals of Henry Lawson. Clark's iconography of recent times presents an Australian prime minister, Gough Whitlam, as a larger-than-life heroic figure whose demise, though different from Lawson's, nevertheless dramatises that tragic fall which seems a consequence of greatness in Australia. Clark describes Whitlam's period as prime minister from 1972 to 1975 as 'a moment of hope and promise in the brief history of European civilization in the ancient, uncouth continent'. Elsewhere, the early 1970s have been described as a 'cultural renaissance' in Australia, signifying an enhanced role for writers, artists and film-makers in shaping perceptions of the country and its people.

The title of Donald Horne's book *The Lucky Country* (1964), one of the most popular non-fiction books of its decade, sounds more optimistic than Clark: but a curious fact of its reception is that the irony of the title went unrecognised by many readers, especially outside Australia. Horne's mildly reformist nationalism did not include xenophobia. He argued that more access to, and interchange with other cultures should stimulate greater cultural activity in Australia; for instance, 'a greater concentration on Asia might liberate Australian intellectual life from its narrowness and frust-ration'. The chief obstacle was Australia's ruling elites in education, politics and business, who were still, in general, alienated from the culture of the country which they inhabited. A belief in the value of counter-cultural mythmakers, expressed forcibly in *The Public Culture* (1986), connects Horne with the idealists and protestors of the late 1960s and 1970s, who vigorously contested the stance of an assumed 'middle Australia', on issues ranging from the war in Vietnam to sexual behaviour and the rights of minority groups. Horne's preferences read like an agenda for much literary activity of the period, which expressed a sense of independence, and difference, from the dominant, often British-derived conventions of Australian life. Such a stance rejects reliance upon any new form of imperialism, but it is an irony of this period that American counter-culture provided the chief models for Australian protest movements, as some of Frank Moorhouse's stories show.

Relations with the 'mother' country have been a major topic, and sometimes an obsessive concern in Australian literature since 1788, but the 1960s mark the first decisive shift from this tendency. In public life, the chief signs are the end of the 'age of Menzies' in 1966, British Prime Minister Macmillan's 'winds of change' speech in 1963, and Britain's protracted entry into the European Economic Community. The close cultural links with Britain, which have persisted beyond economic and political ruptures, have often been treated unsympathetically by writers and critics, as if they threaten Australia's identity. C. J. Koch is one writer who registers sympathet-ically the changing relations with Britain, and also the opening up of new worlds for Australian writers. He recalls the emotionally compelling 'blood ties' with England felt by a pre-World War II Australian child:

No English man or woman will ever be able to experience what a colonial Australian or New Zealander of British descent felt about England . . . We were subjects of no mortal country. Hidden in our unconscious was a Kingdom of Faery: a Britain that could never exist outside the pages of Kenneth Grahame, Dickens and Beatrix Potter.

The long, slow sundering of this umbilical cord is shown in Koch's work. His second novel, *Across the Sea Wall* (1965; rev. 1982), shows a rupture of the childhood idyll. In this novel, Koch relates the shipboard love affair of a young Australian, Robert O'Brien, escaping the tedium of suburban expectations in the 1950s, with a refugee showgirl from Latvia, Ilsa Kalnins. The relationship signifies the wider social convulsion of Anglo-Celtic Australia's difficult and often clumsy accommodation to a post-war influx of European immigrants—known as 'displaced persons' or 'reffos'. O'Brien's journey to London is never completed. In one of the first Australian novels set in Asia, Koch's protagonist leaves the ship and travels through India with his lover, discovering other cultures and learning the pain of unfulfilment. The novel is a parable of a baffled and as yet unawakened Australia faltering towards new relationships with other countries. Koch developed this theme further in his third novel, *The Year of Living Dangerously* (1978), in which his Australian journalist hero is injured, though not fatally, in the events surrounding Indonesian 'Confrontation' in 1965. His year of living dangerously reflects both the geographical proximity and psychological distance between Australians and Asia.

An increasing desire among Australians to understand their role on the international stage has had significant literary consequences. Most important, perhaps—though often omitted from national literary histories—are those images of Australia published by Australian expatriates or travellers abroad, observing or recalling the country they left behind through a screen of other cultural values and assumptions. Because national confidence was still tinged with insecurity, readers and critics have resisted these often original and critical responses to Australia, just as other outsiders *within* the country have been held at the margins. The bifocal vision which characterises talented expatriate writers such as Peter Porter, Barry Humphries, Clive James, Germaine Greer and Randolph Stow (in England), Glenda Adams, Sumner Locke Elliott, Shirley Hazzard and Robert Hughes (in the United States) or Janette Turner Hospital (Canada) gives them a special, if often unrecognised value to

Australians. As this list suggests, Australian expatriates have most often chosen to project themselves and their work from England, particularly from London, but artists Donald Friend (South-East Asia) and Jeffrey Smart (Italy), poet Harold Stewart (Japan) and film directors Peter Weir and Fred Schepisi (United States) indicate a more diverse pattern.

The London-based writers have provided trenchant and memorable expatriate images of Australia. Peter Porter, for instance, who left Brisbane for London in 1951, and has lived there ever since, with regular return visits to Australia since 1974, alludes often in his poetry to his Australian origins and subsequent impressions of this country. Ironic, erudite and seriously comical, Porter's observations defy simplification into easy banners of belief. In the personal allegory of his writings, his mother's death when he was nine marks the point at which he is 'locked out of paradise'; only much later is he able to return and face the ghosts of his past. An early poem is *Once Bitten, Twice Bitten* (1961), 'Mr Roberts', ridicules the continuance of the English public school in Australia; but in 'Reading MND in Form 4B' the poet lyrically suggests a linking of northern and southern hemispheres through the language of Shakespeare. 'Phar Lap in the Melbourne Museum' presents an ironic view of Australian sports lovers:

> It is Australian innocence to love
> The naturally excessive and be proud
> Of a thoroughbred bay gelding who ran fast.

Whereas Bruce Dawe would identify more closely with the sports lovers, and Patrick White would be scathingly satiric, Porter's tone is complicatedly ironic, tinged even with admiration. 'I am fond of the overdone', he laments, self-mockingly, in a later poem, 'I'll never learn simplicity . . . I was never young'. Emblems of the Australian past recur in Porter's poetry and literary criticism. 'Sydney Cove, 1788', for instance, recalls the horror and violence of Australia's beginnings as a convict prison; it concludes, however, with a lyrical celebration of lovers triumphing against the odds, hinting that victory achieves most significance when it is snatched from defeat. For Porter, Australia's desperate beginnings paradoxically offer more hope than America's, which were characterised by high idealism and faith. Porter characteristically refuses utopian panaceas, including nationalism. His vision is cosmopolitan, based on an image of 'The permanently upright city where / Speech is nature and plants conceive in pots' ('On First Looking into Chapman's Hesiod', 1975). This city is an ideal too, fuelled by a poetic imagination which responds to words, ideas, music and painting more than to sense impressions of the natural world. These qualities make Porter an ideal jousting partner for Les Murray (and a vigorous one), as we shall see, in the latter's desire to claim agrarian Boeotia rather then urban Athens as the matrix of Australian cultural values.

The images of Australia which Barry Humphries and Clive James have projected, chiefly from London, have been less disturbingly complex, hence more popularly acclaimed than Porter's. Each has relied, to some extent, on English-derived stereotypes of the comically naive and uncouth Australian, which complemented their own observations before they moved to England, Humphries in 1959 and James in 1962. Both have the intelligence and verbal facility to turn their satiric comedy upon both British and Australian audiences, as is apparent in James' books of television criticism and two volumes of autobiography, *Unreliable Memoirs* (1980) and *Falling Towards England* (1985). The most famous of Humphries' stage creations, Edna Everage, first appeared in a Melbourne revue in 1955, but it was 1962 before she joined Sandy Stone in 'A Nice Night's Entertainment', the first of Humphries' one-man shows. Edna and Sandy were satiric caricatures of middle-aged suburbanites of the 1950s, when the suburbs seemed ripe for ridicule. Robin Boyd's *Australia's Home* (1952) and *The Australian Ugliness* (1960) had criticised the 'featurism' of Australian suburban architecture: Humphries moved inside these houses to exaggerate and ridicule their contents and their owners, in a theatrical tour de force unequalled in Australia for audience involvement, or self flagellation. In the 1970s, the suburbs would be resuscitated from the stings of Humphries' inspired satire by serious critical attention from Bernard Smith, Hugh Stretton, Donald Horne, Craig McGregor and others. Edna also marched on, transcending her lowly origins to become a Dame of the British Empire. When she appeared in 'The Last Night of the Poms' in the Albert Hall, London, in 1982, her performance culminated in a 'Loud Audience Singalong':

Let our voices swell with pride,
We are extremely satisfied:
Australia you're the land for me.

Such sentimental nationalism was a frequent target of Humphries' criticism, as of other Australians who chose to live and work abroad, though they could succumb to versions of it themselves. Humphries' satiric presentation of another Australian type in Barry ('Bazza') McKenzie is two-edged. McKenzie is the crude Australian male— beer swilling, 'chundering', 'pointing Percy at the porcelain', failing to 'get his oats'—an Australian picaro among the Poms. Barry McKenzie first appeared in a cartoon strip in *Private Eye* in 1965 (with drawings by Nicholas Garland) and subsequently in two films (1972, 1974), played by Australian actor Barry Crocker. As a popular portrait of the Australian innocent abroad, McKenzie appears to have been superseded by Paul Hogan's Crocodile Dundee in the film of that name in 1986, which may signal a change from entertaining popular British prejudices about Australian males to more genial (and ignorant?) American expectations of the laconic bushman hero. There is an irrelevance to contemporary reality which some critics noted in Barry Humphries' latest satiric caricature, Sir Les Patterson, Cultural Attaché to the Court of St James, in *Les Patterson's Australia* (1978) and the film *Les Patterson Saves the World* (1987), and this indicates the passing of an era when London seemed the sole base for talented Australian writers and performers to project themselves internationally. The danger is that one mode of comic cultural subservience will be replaced by other forms which are less intelligent and less flexible.

When Christina Stead returned to Sydney in 1969, after forty-one years in England, Europe and America, she wrote of a reactivated childhood sense of the 'wide waters and skies' in a country where a person is 'nearer to the planets'. By contrast, Germaine Greer's fleeting returns since her departure in 1964 have reinforced her sense of the boredom, anti-intellectualism and anti-feminism of Australian society. Shirley Hazzard, who left Australia in 1947 and now lives mainly in New York, recreated in *The Transit of Venus* (1980) a 1930s, English-dominated education for girls which placed Australia 'in perpetual, flagrant violation of reality'. Her 1984 Boyer lectures for the ABC show her preference for a modern Australia which is increasingly involved in the international community of nations.

Immigrant writers in Australia have traditionally been considered even more peripheral to the development of literary traditions than expatriates. Yet one in five Australians in the 1986 census was born overseas and their contribution to changing concepts of Australia has been considerable. 'Assimilation', which had been government policy for migrants in the 1950s, gave way to 'integration' in the 1960s and 'multiculturalism' in the Whitlam era of the early 1970s. By the late 1980s a reassertion of national goals rather than separate development of migrant groups seemed imminent (in a proposed National Language Policy, for instance). An assimilationist ethic underlies the popular comic novel by 'Nino Culotta' (John O'Grady), *They're a Weird Mob* (1957), filmed in 1966. Richard Beynon's play *The Shifting Heart* (1960) dramatises a darker, more violent side to Australian prejudice against Italian immigrants in inner-city Melbourne, revealing a need for more compassion among 'old' Australians as well as for the migrant to 'accept'. Although neither O'Grady nor Beynon was Italian-born, their assimilationist ideas were accepted by many immigrants.

An Italian-Australian cultural seminar, held in Melbourne in 1968, outlined three broad stages in a migrant's life: first, nostalgic reflection on an idealised past; second, a coming-to-terms with the new environment, still from the original country's point of view; third, identifying oneself with the environment, achieving a sense of harmony, and speaking and writing in English. This 'three stages' model of assimilation is too simplistic to account for the actual variety of migrant writing in the 1970s and 1980s, as is shown in anthologies such as Sneja Gunew's *Displacement, Migrant Story Tellers* (1982) and Peter Skrzynecki's *Joseph's Coat: An Anthology of Multicultural Writing* (1985). A selective listing of writers who have come to prominence since the 1960s, with their countries of birth, indicates a great diversity of talent and experience among first generation immigrant authors: Walter Adamson (Germany), Sylvana Gardner (Dalmatia), Lolo Houbein (Holland), Don'o Kim (Korea), Manfred Jurgensen (Germany-Denmark), Vasso Kalamaris (Greece), Stephen Kelen (Hungary), Rudi Krausmann (Austria), Serge Liberman (Russia), Cornelis Vleeskens (Holland), Ania Walwicz (Poland). These authors all write from the perceived 'edges' of Australian culture. But publication has placed them in a wider community of letters, where their frequent images of dislocation may reach an Australian population of readers which is recognising its changing composition and mobility.

Three writers *not* in the list above may indicate the diverse forces of the migrant experience in shaping literary perceptions of Australia: Rosa Cappiello, Dimitris Tsaloumas, and Ee Tiang Hong. Rosa Cappiello's *Paesa Fortunata* (1981 in Milan, published in English in 1985 as *O Lucky Country)* recalls the horrific encounters of a young woman migrant in Sydney in the early 1970s with Australian authorities and institutions. In a style sometimes reminiscent of Christina Stead, Cappiello observes the common misery of her fellow prisoners in the 'prefabricated hell' of the migrant hostel. Her sense of alienation is temporarily relieved by a lesbian relationship which leaves her suicidal when it ends. But she survives, a latter-day Lazarus, realising, however tentatively, that her 'never-ending tunnel of woe' is a fate shared by many. Dimitris Tsaloumas' literary strategy is quite different: a calm authority pervades his poetry, which his remained firmly rooted in his Greek language, history and customs, though he left his native Leros for Melbourne in 1952. In the first bilingual Greek-English selection of his poems, *The Observatory* (1983)—which followed seven volumes in Greek editions, published mainly in Athens—Tsaloumas' translator, Philip Grundy, suggests that his poetry embodies a 'stubborn persistence of Hellenism' in its intensity, its sense of remoteness from the present environment and its underlying nostalgia for the 'distant remembered country'. Few poems deal directly with Australia. In one, a verse letter to a friend in Greece who has inquired about sending his son to 'foreign parts' for an education, Tsaloumas recalls the symbology of the desert in A. D. Hope's 'Australia' and Patrick White's *Voss*: 'No camels here, no comforts. / Only you, alone'. In another poem, his voice is that of a Greek prophet delivering a message through a 'courier of souls' to his dead mother from Green Cape, New South Wales:

> . . . Tell her that her son came down to the spray-misted
> headlands of the South and saw the onslaught of waves
> huge as island hills and cried out The sea! The sea!

Ee Tiang Hong's poetic voice is quieter, more oblique and ironic than Tsaloumas' or Cappiello's. Ee is a political exile from Malaysia, which he left to migrate to Perth in 1975. Much of his writing has explored the contemporary relevance of that complex internationalism of Portuguese, Dutch, British Chinese and Malay which characterises the history of his home town of Malacca. In his epilogue to *Mythe for a Wilderness* (1976), Ee pictures himself at 'the crossroads of civilization'. A decade later, his poem 'Coming To' registers Australia as a place of near drowning, regaining consciousness, finding land, 'new faces, fellow Australian'. The predominant images of these migrant writers then, are of prison, desert and sanctuary; all are traditional images, but contemporary migrant experience lends them peculiar force.

Elizabeth Jolley's short fiction and novels, which have received an enthusiastic reception in Australia and overseas in the 1980s, indicate the ways in which an 'outsider' (in Jolley's case, a migrant, a woman, a Western Australian) may assume a central myth-making function in contemporary Australia. Born in Birmingham, England in 1923 Jolley moved to Western Australia in 1959. From her first book of stories, *Five Acre Virgin* (1976) to the novel *Sugar Mother* (1988), Jolley has been concerned with the 'migrant spirit'—how people move from one country, or location to another in the spirit of hopes and dreams. Working often with material from her childhood in the 1930s when her Quaker parents, an Austrian mother and English father, sheltered refugees from prewar Europe, Jolley's displaced persons are at the centre of her art. In *Milk and Honey* (1984), a poetic prelude to the novel describes the 'whirlwinds' of Europe which picked up and blew 'cones' of this soil to Australia, which settle 'on the fragments of other cones ... in order to preserve themselves and remain unchanged for as long as possible'. In this way, the Heimbachs transport their hothouse prison of isolation with them, with violent and destructive consequences—a theme which Thomas Keneally also exploits in *A Family Madness* (1985). But like the author herself, a number of Jolley's characters seek solace and a sense of purpose in their new country by obtaining a small piece of land beyond the city, and working it. Here, the rural rituals of planting, pruning and burning off provide an often lyrical accompaniment to the sense of suffering and loss which are inherent in the migrant spirit.

The argument so far has contended that outsiders such as expatriates and immigrants have projected images of themselves and Australia which give them a place in the national consciousness; a consequence of this is the complication and possible negation of the notion of a central Australian tradition of consensual, democratic and nationalist masculine values, such as those proposed in A. A. Phillips' *The Australian Tradition* (1958). Books, plays and films by Aborigines and by women, especially feminists, since 1965 have complicated and enriched the sense of a plural inheritance. These developments raise the question of whether there exists, or can exist, a still centre to the turning world of Australian culture, a set of core values to which most Australians might consent. Such a question invites consideration of the work of Les A. Murray.

The poetry and prose of Les Murray place him as the major claimant to the middle ground of Australian culture in the late 1980s. His prophetic, bardic stance links him with Australia's first poet of substance, Charles Harpur. Murray, like Harpur, has proposed an Australian republic based on Christian values and egalitarian, democratic principles, but more than a century of European settlement between them has enabled the development of a vernacular language which locates Murray's poetry more firmly in its Australian environment. Yet in the poem 'Noonday Axeman' in his first volume, *The Ilex Tree* (1965), Murray says, 'It will be centuries / before men are truly at home in this country.' An agenda is, nevertheless, set. For Les Murray, making Australians 'at home' involves the development of local awareness and an appreciation of continuities in culture and society. Murray locates his search for a useable past in the rural poor, in whose language and ways of living he finds the 'folk ways' of the country most evident. The territory from which Murray begins, imaginatively, is the farming and forest country of the New South Wales mid-north coast, around Bunyah, where he lived on his father's dairy farm as a child and to which he has returned regularly from Sydney. The search in Murray's work for rituals and shrines of remembrance for Australians goes beyond sectarian differences to encompass, most significantly, Aboriginal experience. Like the Jindyworobaks, but more successfully, Murray has striven to incorporate Aboriginal rhythms and perceptions in his work—most notably in poems such as 'The Ballad of Jimmy Governor', 'Cycling in the Lake Country', 'The Bulahdelah-Taree Holiday Song-Cycle' and the verse novel *The Boys Who Stole the Funeral* (1982). His work, like much Aboriginal storytelling, calls up the spirit of place. Murray's vision of Australia has been called provincial, but this is inaccurate: his concern for named places in an environment localised by use and memory is enriched by allusions beyond those mentioned above to non-metropolitan outlooks from other countries and times, such as those of the Hindus, the Celts and the Boeotians.

Les Murray's vision of Australia had achieved widespread recognition in his country by 1988. With his stamp set upon named places in all corners of Australia, he seemed to embody in the ample girth of his poetic ego, the vast continent. The vision is of a humanely Christian society raised on the agrarian virtues (but not excluding the killing of animals, blood rituals and the use of machinery). It is characterised by equanimity rather than intensity of feeling:

illumination is not a blinding light but the finding of meaning in everyday events and people. Murray's ability to incorporate the spoken language of ordinary Australians into a wide variety of verse forms gives his poetry a populist quality, which does not match Bruce Dawe's poems of suburban Australia for accessibility, but outdoes them in verbal pyrotechnics, ranging from laconics to what has been described as a 'rural baroque' style. Yet what gives pressure to Murray's vision is a sense of the imminent loss of rural Australia to the cities and industry. Hence the importance of the public debate in poems and articles in the late 1970s between Murray and Peter Porter, the former eloquent in his defence of country values (provincial, pastoral, home-based, religious and celebratory), symbolised in Hesiod's rural Boeotia in ancient Greece, and the latter defending Athenian city values (cosmopolitan, sophisticated, migratory and sceptical). Both are idealised, conflicting models of civilisation; both have their adherents (with varying degrees of adhesion) in contemporary Australian poetry. Among the Boeotians of this time might be counted David Campbell, Robert Gray, Geoffrey Lehmann, Rhyll McMaster, Geoff Page, Mark O'Connor and Judith Wright; the Athenians are a more disparate group, including (in parts of their work at least) A. D. Hope, Vincent Buckley, Chris Wallace-Crabbe, John Forbes, John Tranter, Vicki Viidikas and Fay Zwicky. Murray claims that Boeotia always loses to Athens, but the imaginative outcome is far from certain in Australia, where the most sustaining myths have grown from failure and apparent defeat.

Awareness of regional characteristics and differences increased during the 1970s and 1980s. The image of Australia as a vast untamed Outback had been propounded in popular fiction from the 1930s to the 1950s by authors such as Ion Idriess, Arthur Upfield and Neville Shute, who kept alive a myth that a frontier existed, which would be pushed back by brave individualists with enterprise and engineering skills. An alternative vision was proposed in the literature of the 1950s in Patrick White's *Voss* (1957) and Randolph Stow's *To the Islands* (1958), in which the real test was not of ingenuity and engineering skills (which both Voss and Heriot would fail) but their capacity for spiritual growth. For these authors, Australia provided 'raw material' for what Randolph Stow described in 1961 as 'an enormous symbol: a symbol for the whole earth, at all times, both before and during the history of man'. Figures against this landscape would be seen as if with the eyes of 'the newborn'. The audacity of this Australia of visions and visionaries is evident in the paintings of Nolan and Boyd. But a more sobering irony was also in the air, exemplified in Chris Wallace-Crabbe's poem 'A Wintry Manifesto' (1959), in which limits were recognised as necessary to the imagination, and even accepted as valuable: 'Our greatest joy to mark an outline truly / And know the piece of earth on which we stand.' This is the spirit of regionalism: an acceptance of limits, of seeking meaning within the microcosm.

Regionalism has many faces and may be restrictive or liberating, a closure or an opening. Most local histories of the past two decades have been little more than commemorative catalogues of names, places and events. But Weston Bate's history of Ballarat, *The Lucky City* (1978), W. K. Hancock's *Discovering Monaro* (1972), Graeme Davison's *The Rise and Fall of Marvellous Melbourne* (1978) and C. T. Stannage's *The People of Perth* (1979) show some imaginative possibilities of this genre. Other non-fiction texts have revealed vistas of thought, feeling and reflection. Eric Rolls' *A Million Wild Acres* (1981) is a history of the Pilliga forest of north-west New South Wales by a farmer of the region: its narrative voice is alive with the personal discovery of plants, birds, insects, animals and soil and is informed by a belief in the possibility for white settlers in Australia of a sensitive, imaginative attachment to the land, akin to that of the Aborigines. A briefer volume by Rolls, *Celebration of the Senses* (1984) extends the poetic dimension of the previous book to explore the operation of the five senses—sight, taste, hearing, touch and smell—in interaction with a localised environment of humans, animals and landscape. Whether recalling sexual lovemaking, drinking wine or killing and hanging a lamb, Rolls' prose is abundant with sensuous knowledge which lends force to his maxims: 'The soil keeps a man in perspective. It gives him as much as he can wonder at. He gives it as much as he can learn.' A similar spirit informs the prose of a less recognised regional writer, Barbara York Main, whose books *Between Wodjil and Tor* (1967) and *Twice Trodden Ground* (1971) are loving re-creations of the wheatbelt district of Western Australia around Kellerberrin. As in Rolls' work, local colour is evident, but is subsumed in the presentation (in Main's case, as a trained zoologist) of a closely observed microcosm of rural Australia. Her brief meditative sketches show a landscape first trodden by the nomadic Aborigines, then settled by Europeans who changed the landscape according to the values of their Western civilisation and farming needs. Such attempts to trace continuity and change across the years from Aboriginal to European settlement have been a continuing concern of Judith Wright, whose poem 'Bora Ring' in her first volume, *The Moving Image* (1946) finds its counterpart in her later prose work about the impact of European settlers on Aborigines, *The Cry for the Dead* (1981). In *We Call for a Treaty* (1985) Wright urges support for the Aborigines' human and political rights.

There were signs in the 1980s that some white Australians were taking notice of Aboriginal perceptions of the land. In *Reading the Country* (1984), by Krim Benterrack, Stephen Muecke and Paddy Roe, the Roebuck Plains area east of Broome, Western Australia, is 'read' in a variety of ways by the three authors—Benterrack a painter, Muecke a linguist and Roe an Aboriginal native to the region. The book is a reorientation of ways in which place and region might be understood in Australia. Words, paintings, diagrams, photographs and interviews form a collage of impressions under a general concept of 'nomadology', which challenges European notions of settlement. While the book's French-derived post-structuralist ideas (via Barthes, Bachelard, Derrida) combine oddly with Paddy Roe's perceptions, a dialectic may nevertheless occur, calling for new ways of 'reading' different localities in Australia. A more accessible revision of attitudes is provided in an interview with Aboriginal poet Kath Walker at her Stradbroke Island home in 1986, when she spoke of the island threatened by mining as of a female person:

> That sort of destruction has been happening all the time on the island, so the island is suffering horribly. Though I'm amazed at [her] strength . . . she is still fighting back. She is trying to hold onto her greenery, to hold onto herself.

Resistance to urban industrial imperatives has also come from self-declared regional writers such as Peter Cowan, Hal Porter and Thea Astley. Cowan, for instance, has deplored the imitation of Sydney and Melbourne styles elsewhere in Australia. He sees in the Australian suburbs an attempt to erase differences and is attracted to the open spaces of the Western Australian interior. Yet even here the mining interests follow, with their instant towns and suburbs, attempting to shut out the 'quite pitiless but utterly attractive landscape' where 'outside [the] air conditioning and supermarts one can die in a couple of days, left alone'. The keynote in Cowan's selected stories, *A Window in Mrs X's Place* (1986) is silence, and an associated sense of space. As in American western literature, these qualities resist and reproach urban civilisation and industry. Albert Facey's popular autobiographical work *A Fortunate Life* (1981) graphically records a working man's experience of 'knocking about' in the Western Australian goldfields and wheatbelts, followed by action at Gallipoli. It appeals to Australians' sense of the bush as shaping the traditional Australian male—an idea going back at least to C. E. W. Bean and reinforced by Peter Weir's film *Gallipoli* (1981). T. A. G. Hungerford's first two autobiographical collections, *Stories from Suburban Road* (1983) and *A Knockabout with a Slouch Hat* (1985) connect this myth to World War II. Sally Morgan's *My Place* (1987) explores her Aboriginal inheritance in the north-west of Australia and an attempted obliteration of this past by suburban 'civilised' pressures. Young Western Australian male authors have found strong material for their fictions in the figure of the drifter. Tim Winton, Archie Weller and Colin Johnson find a capacity for truthfulness in the perceptions of the dropout from society, as does Robert Drewe in the novel *Fortune* (1986); this is a pattern which recurs in Tasmanian James McQueen's novel *Hook's Mountain* (1982), with its defiant individualism and conservationist ethic.

In spite of such resistance, a strong tendency in Australian literary self-definition in the 1970s and 1980s was towards the city centre. The pattern was set by Nobel prize-winning novelist Patrick White, whose part-mimetic, part-invented outer suburban setting of Sarsaparilla in novels, stories and plays of the 1960s was replaced by the city of Sydney in *The Vivisector* (1970) and *The Eye of the Storm* (1973), coinciding with White's own move from suburban Castle Hill to Centennial Park near the centre of Sydney. White knew he would set *The Eye of the Storm* in Sydney because, as he wrote in his self-portrait, *Flaws in the Glass* (1981), 'Sydney is what I have in my blood.' In his lifetime White had seen the city developing from 'a sunlit village into this present-day parvenu bastard, compound of San Francisco and Chicago'—a created environment of contending beauty and ugliness, ripe for irony, satire, and occasional epiphany. In Kate Grenville's first novel, *Lilian's Story* (1985), too, an eccentric protagonist has 'mad' visions of great imaginative vivacity against a background of Sydney streets and parks.

In Frank Moorhouse's writings, Sydney is a place of liberation for the drifters and disaffiliates of the counter culture, whose mythology is summed up in the title of Moorhouse's memorial to the 1970s, *Days of Wine and Rage* (1980). Moorhouse's fictional narratives simulate in their discontinuities, 'accidental' collocations and apparent inconsequences the tempo and mood of this mode of urban living, with its experiments in sex and drugs, its simultaneous drive for anonymity and commitment to causes. A myth of the new was in the air. Moorhouse's sometime friend Michael Wilding wrote in *The Short Story Embassy* (1975) that the coming of the contraceptive pill provided 'a whole different anthropology' for the writer: both he and Moorhouse became anthropologists. Communes, anti-Vietnam marches, underground newspapers, film-making and parties were perceived through the fresh (but not naive) eyes of an English immigrant (Wilding) and a refugee from an Australian country town (Moorhouse). A recurrent concern in Moorhouse's more than Wilding's work is the influence of America: in *The Americans, Baby* (1972) and *The Electrical Experience* (1974) especially, Moorhouse shows how American institutions such as Rotary, *Time* magazine and Coca-Cola had permeated Australian styles and habits of thought; in 'The American Poet's Visit' (1972) he comically exposes a new cultural cringe. David Ireland's Sydney novels, *The Unknown Industrial Prisoner* (1971), *The Glass Canoe* (1976) and *City of Women* (1981), like Moorhouse's fiction, use a collage technique to establish discontinuity as a primary feature of contemporary urban existence. While it commences with close observation, Ireland's work pushes towards violent fantasy and satire; his urban dystopias grow from nightmare. The city of Sydney becomes principally a vehicle for irony and satire. Yet Sydney has been a place of hope, too. Western Australian playwright and poet Dorothy Hewett located Sydney in her personal and literary mythology as the liberating City in opposition to the Garden of Western Australia, where Eden had been characterised by a brutal innocence. For Hewett, Sydney offered theatres and a poetic avant-garde in the work of writers such as Robert Adamson, Bruce Beaver and John Tranter, whose 'open form' verse based on American antecedents could mix autobiography and urban concerns.

In the mythology of Australian cities, Sydney has not been allowed to stand alone without its counterpart and competitor, Melbourne. A seminar in Melbourne to mark *Meanjin's* fortieth anniversary in 1980 was entitled 'St Petersburg or Tinsel Town? Sydney and Melbourne: Their Different Styles and Changing Relation'. From this seminar grew *The Sydney-Melbourne Book* (1986), edited by Jim Davidson. David Williamson entertained a number of these ideas and slogans of difference in his fourteenth play, *Emerald City* (1987), in which his protagonist, Colin, follows his creator in making the perilous journey from the 'puritan south' to the 'hedonistic north, the Emerald City of Oz'. Like Moorhouse, Williamson in Sydney, but a distinctively Melbourne-raised conscience speaks up in Colin's assertion of a non-chauvinistic nationalism, 'the residual integrity . . . [of] some deep-rooted sense of patriotism'. A more steadily Melbourne-based allegiance to democratic nationalist values is expressed in Jack Hibberd's plays, with draw on a ribald vernacular and music-hall traditions in their attempted revival of an Australian populist theatre. (By the mid-1980s, disillusioned with an apparent decline of interest among Australians in things Australian, Hibberd had stopped writing plays and returned to the practice of medicine.) Also firmly based in Melbourne are Helen Garner's *Monkey Grip* (1977), *Honour and Other People's Children* (1980) and *The Children's Back* (1984). In these works, quieter and less ebullient than Hibberd's, a finely etched map of inner-suburban Melbourne (mainly Fitzroy and Carlton) gives shape to the shifting relationships of a generation for whom liberation finally becomes a search for 'home'. Vincent Buckley's poetic sequence *The Golden Builders* (1976) covers similar terrain to Garner but in a more heightened, imaginistic way. In Buckley's poem, the hammers and drills of demolition are simulated in a poem of fragments, dislocations and changes of tempo. In the terrible magic of Buckley's city, which is both Melbourne and Jerusalem, images of fragmentation recur and the need for spiritual regeneration is shown. While other Australian cities have not yet been reimagined with the intensity evoked by Sydney and Melbourne, there have been some notable renditions of Australian urban and suburban experience, such as Robert Drewe's Perth in *The Savage Crows* (1976) and *Fortune* (1986), David Malouf's Brisbane in *Johnno* (1975) and *12 Edmonstone Street* (1985), Sara Dowse's Canberra in *West Block* (1983) and David Foster's in *Plumbum* (1983), and Barbara Hanrahan's Adelaide in *The Frangipani Gardens* (1980) and *Kewpie Doll* (1984).

'History is not the past, but the present made flesh,' writes Kate Grenville's protagonist in *Lilian's Story* (1985). The period since the 1960s has been characterised by such transformations. Epic journey of explorers provided less favoured subject matter in the 1970s and 1980s than international conflicts and the convict experience. For this was a period in which writers and film-makers felt liberated to examine the recent and more distant scars of Australia's past.

Vietnam was perhaps too recent. Although occasional works such as Bruce Dawe's poem 'Homecoming' could combine irony with feeling, the most successful works were as yet journalistic reports, such as Hugh Lunn's *Vietnam: a Reporter's War* (1985). William Nagle's book *The Odd Angry Shot* (1975) and the film (1979) exhibit a sardonic understatement which recalls C. E. W. Bean's Anzacs and contrasts radically with the hysterical, nightmare images of American Michael Herr's *Dispatches* or Francis Ford Coppola's film *Apocalypse Now*. The films *Breaker Morant* (1980) and *Gallipoli* (1981) signify a resurgence of anti-British, post-colonial nationalism. But new ground was broken in the small sub-genre of works which show Australians encountering Asia, including John Romeril's play *The Floating World* (first performed 1974), Robert Drewe's novel *A Cry in the Jungle Bar* (1979), Blanche d'Alpuget's novels *Monkeys in the Dark* (1980) and *Turtle Beach* (1981) and Christopher Koch's *The Year of Living Dangerously*. The film *Far East* (1982) confirmed the appeal of excitement in exotic places and the dramatic capital to be gained from a confrontation of Australian prejudice with Asian realities. Of all these works, it would be fair to say that they are explorations of Australians abroad as much as of the countries they visit: as such, they confirm Frank Moorhouse's observation in his collection of contemporary Australian short stories *The State of the Art* (1983) that travel writing is a vigorous genre, characterised by experiment with styles and encounters with one's nationality. Murray Bail's witty and inventive novel *Homesickness* (1980) is a stylistic tour de force, deriving much imaginative energy from the prospect of Australians abroad.

The Australian character is excavated differently in those works which re-examine Australia's convict origins. Whereas nineteenth-century convict novels such as Caroline Leakey's *The Broad Arrow* (1859), Marcus Clarke's *His Natural Life* (1870-2) and John Boyle O'Reilly's *Moondyne Joe* (1879) present innocent victims, late-twentieth-century reversions to this theme such as Thomas Keneally's *Bring Larks and Heroes* (1967), Jessica Anderson's *The Commandant* (1975), Patrick White's *A Fringe of Leaves* (1976) and Barbara Hanrahan's *The Albatross Muff* (1977) show the spread of duplicity and guilt to all who are implicated. Robert Hughes' rewriting of Australia's convict past in *The Fatal Shore* (1987) extends the significance of his parable beyond Australia's shores when he describes the convict system as a prefiguring of the twentieth-century Gulag. David Ireland translates convictism into the modern industrial state in *The Unknown Industrial Prisoner* (1971). By contrast, a break for freedom is dramatised in Michael Wilding's *The Paraguayan Experiment* (1984), which abounds with the hopes and ironies of William Lane's attempt in 1893 to found a new utopian society of Australians in Paraguay—an attempt which Wilding cleverly links with counter-cultural utopianism of the 1970s and early 1980s.

Where are we? Who are we? Where are we going? The questions raised by historians and sociologists at the beginning of this chapter have not been answered conclusively by writers, artists and film-makers of the past three decades; indeed the search for a core sample which would testify to a bedrock Australia seems less urgent than in the 1950s. A consensus on Australianness seems unlikely from the literary evidence, and an increasing diversity of images has given readers a sense of the heterogeneity of Australia and its imaginative possibilities. Ethnic and regional interests have been particularly evident in this period, and writing by women has been increasingly prominent. The more savage aspects of Australia's past have been reformulated as 'parables for the present'. Pastoral, nationalist and democratic traditions have been recalled, and reformulated. Momentous changes in international relations have led to a sense of decolonisation and the inclusion of America and Asia in literary and other cultural products. In this atmosphere of change, cultural myth-makers have complicated and enriched Australians' sense of themselves, projecting some of these images to an international audience which seemed increasingly ready to listen.

Notes

The following publications contain general discussions of literary developments since the 1960s: *Australian Literary Studies* ('New Writing in Australia' issue) 8 (October 1977); John Carroll (ed.), *Intruders in the Bush* (1982); Geoffrey Dutton, *Snow on the Saltbush: The Australian Literary Experience* (1984); Stephen Graubard (ed.), *Australia: The Daedalus Symposium* (1985); Ken Goodwin, *A History of Australian Literature* (1986); Richard White, *Inventing Australia: Images and Identity, 1688-1980* (1981); and G. A. Wilkes, *The Stockyard and the Croquet Lawn* (1981).

The quote from Christopher Koch is taken from his article 'Maybe It's Because I'm a Londoner' in *Kunapipi* (1986).

General discussions of Australian film may be found in: John Tulloch, *Australian Cinema: Industry, Narrative and Meaning* (1982) and Graeme Turner, *National Fictions: Literature, Film and the Construction of Australian Narrative* (1986). A selection of articles and reviews is contained in *An Australian Film Reader* (1985), edited by Albert Moran and Tom O'Regan.

The 'Boeotia' versus 'Athens' debate commenced with Peter Porter's poem 'On First Looking into Chapman's Hesiod' in *Living in a Calm Country* (1975). It was followed by Les Murray's essay on this poem in *Australian Poems in Perspective* (1978), edited by P. K. Elkin. Peter Porter's responses are contained in 'Country Poetry and Town Poetry: A Debate with Les Murray' in *Australian Literary Studies*, 9 (1979).

Contemporary writing by immigrants to Australia, especially those for whom Australian English is a second language, is discussed in: Sneja Gunew, 'Constructing Australian Subjects: Critics, Writers, Multicultural Writers' in *Diversity Itself* (1986), edited by Peter Quartermaine; the 'Immigration and Culture' issue of *Meanjin*, 42 (1983); Gaetano Rando, 'Italo-Australian Fiction', *Meanjin* 43 (1984), and the journal *Outrider*, edited by Manfred Jurgensen. The Italian-Australian cultural seminar referred to in this chapter is mentioned in Anna Fochi, 'Giovanni Andreoni: An Italian Writer in Australia', *Westerly* 28 (1983).

Further reading on women writers and the literature of Aborigines may be found at the end of Chapters 20 and 2 respectively.

Regionalism is discussed by Bruce Bennett in *Place, Region and Community* (1985) and in *Regionalism and National Identity* (1985), edited by Reginald Berry and James Acheson. The quote from Peter Cowan is from the 'Regionalism in Contemporary Australia' issue of *Westerly* 23 (1978). See also Susan McKernan, 'Crossing the Border: Regional Writing in Australia', *Meanjin*, 45 (1986). A major reference work of literary geography is *The Oxford Literary Guide to Australia* (1987), edited by Peter Pierce.

The comment by Kath Walker and some other perceptions of Australian writers are from Candida Baker's two collections of interviews, *Yacker* (1986) and *Yacker 2* (1987).

Chapter 27

PUBLISHING, CENSORSHIP AND WRITERS' INCOMES, 1965-1988

JUDITH BRETT

The beginning of the seventies coincided with my decision to become a full time fiction writer and with my turning thirty.
(Frank Moorhouse, *Days of Wine and Rage*, 1980)

Decades seem to take their shape from the new. Judah Waten, John Morrison, Peter Cowan, Vincent Buckley and Judith Wright were all writing in the early 1970s, yet the stories of their work would more likely be told in a chapter discussing the 1940s or 1950s than in one on the late 1960s and 1970s. That period seems more associated with writers like Frank Moorhouse, Michael Wilding, Peter Carey, John Forbes, John Tranter, Robert Adamson, and the playwrights of La Mama and the Australian Performing Group (APG) like Jack Hibberd and David Williamson. Such imaginative association of names with dates reflects the ways in which the younger writers saw and produced writing differently from their predecessors, and the ways in which they dissociated themselves from what had gone before.

Nancy Keesing has commented that the biggest change to affect writing in her time was the virtual disappearance of censorship. In 1969 the following books were banned in Australia: Gore Vidal's *Myra Breckinridge*, Stephen Vizenczey's *In Praise of Older Women*, Philip Roth's *Portnoy's Complaint*, Stephen Marcus' *The Other Victorians* (a scholarly study of sexuality and pornography in nineteenth-century England), Barry Humphries' *The Wonderful World of Barry McKenzie*, and more. These books could not be imported into the country, by either a publisher or a private person; they could not be bought and sold in the bookshops, and they could not be printed here. Although there was a widespread feeling that the law was ridiculous and that Australia was making an idiot of itself before the sophisticated eyes of Europe and North America, publishers were reluctant to challenge the law in the courts.

A student newspaper changed all this—*Tharunka*, later *Thorunka* and then *Thor*. In 1970 *Tharunka*, the newspaper of the University of New South Wales, gained a new group of editors with strong libertarian sympathies. They were not interested in simply editing a newspaper for students, but in reaching a broad intellectual readership. And they ignored the censorship laws. Frank Moorhouse, who was invited to write for them, says: 'It was my first experience of illegal or underground journalism, and it was the first time in our lives we had written for, or had available, an uncensored public outlet for our writing.' The consequences of their independence were widespread. The university authorities panicked; there were court cases; Wendy Bacon, one of the editors, went to jail. But the censorship laws were found to have little bite.

The law is part of the context in which writers choose their subject and their style. The apparent preoccupation of young writers in the 1970s with sex was partly a response to new possibilities. Open writing about sex of most sorts was now possible, hence relationships could be explored in writing in new ways. Helen Garner's *Monkey Grip* (1977) would not have been published a decade earlier and probably would not have been written; the subtle mechanisms of self-censorship are generally sufficient to enact society's strictures.

Censorship laws may no longer unduly inhibit writers' work, but defamation laws still do. The Australian States do not yet have uniform defamation laws and some are more severe than others. Fear of prosecution for defamation severely limits the publication of writing on contemporary life. Frank journals, diaries or letters are unlikely to be published while potential litigants are still alive. Fear of defamation may also limit the publication of fiction dealing with contemporary events. Amanda Lohrey had great difficulty finding a publisher for her novel *The Morality of Gentlemen* (1984), which was based on a bitter court case involving the Tasmanian Waterside Workers Union during the Labor Party split of the 1950s. The risk of defamation was the main reason given by several publishers for rejecting the manuscript; in the end the book was published by APCOL (Alternative Publishing Company), a left-wing press. As it turned out, the book did not even attract a solicitor's letter. Margaret McClusky's satirical novel of Sydney social life, *Wedlock* (1987), was originally titled 'Entertaining Susan Sangster'. The title was changed out of fear of defamation.

The challenge to censorship by the underground press was made possible by changes in printing technology. Printers had refused to publish anything that might leave them open to prosecution under the censorship laws, but with offset printing the traditional hot-metal printers could be bypassed.

The availability of offset printing led to an explosion of publications—little magazines, newsletters, poetry and story collections. These were usually funded by a group of enthusiasts, sold by footwork and friends, and often lasted only a few issues. More publishing is also more writing. Some of the established magazines like *Meanjin*, *Overland* and *Southerly* had been less than responsive to many of the younger writers and their editorial gate-keepers could now be avoided. In 1972 Frank Moorhouse, Michael Wilding, Brian Kiernan and Carmel Kelly established *Tabloid Story*, a short-story magazine for freer, more experimental writing.

Small poetry presses and magazines sprang up. John Tranter estimates that between 1968 and 1978 these young writers published 20,000 pages of creative and critical writing, including 100 volumes of verse. As with the fiction writers, the younger poets saw themselves as challenging the forms and assumptions of the established literary culture. John Tranter writes in his introduction to *The New Australian Poetry* that 'the experiments of the late 1960s and the early 1970s were not so much beginners' exercises as determined and serious attempts to revitalise a moribund poetic culture'. He clarifies the implied generational challenge by calling the young writers who first came to prominence in the closing years of the 1970s 'the generation of '68'.

The young writers of the late 1960s were mostly men. While their writing challenged many of the literary assumptions of an older generation, they also shared with that generation many assumptions about becoming a writer. The special issues of *Australian Literary Studies* on the short story (1981) included a section of authors' statements. T. A. G. Hungerford, the sort of writer these young men writers most definitely were not, wrote: 'I believe that the writer who has not evolved his own recognisable style by the time he is thirty should take up something else.' John Morrison said: 'The sooner a young writer gets into print the better for his resolution.' To an older generation, as to 'the generation of '68', writers became writers when

young adults and were assumed to be men. It was like choosing a
profession, what some boys did when they grew up.

If some of the women writers of the period had listened to such
advice they would never have published. Judith Rodriguez has
commented that whereas most men poets publish their first book
before they are thirty, most women poets' first books are published in
their forties. And there have been some spectacular late starters
amongst recent women fiction writers. Olga Masters and Elizabeth
Jolley both published their first books in their late fifties. The Oedipal
generational challenge which is such a feature of young men's
writing in the period has little relevance to these women.

In 1972 Australian fiction writing was not strong; only eighteen
novels were published. In 1973 the Literature Board was established
by the Whitlam Labor Government as part of the newly formed
Australia Council. It introduced programs of support for both writers
and publishers. The initial impact was dramatic and by 1974 it had
subsidised ninety-two titles, including thirty-six fiction and thirty-six
poetry. Without the subsidies most of these works would not have
been published. By 1985, after twelve years of funding, over 1000
writers had received grants or fellowships and over 1000 books had
been subsidised. From the low point of eighteen books in 1973, prose
fiction has emerged as the strongest form in current Australian
writing. David Malouf has commented that by the early 1980s the
excitement in Australian writing had shifted from poetry in the late
1960s and early 1970s to fiction. The interest in the short story is
part of that shift, and by the late 1980s it was far easier to get a book
of short stories published than a book of poems, the reverse of the
1950s.

State support for literature was not new in 1973; the Literature
Board took over from the Commonwealth Literary Fund which was
established in 1908. What was new, however, was the extent of that
support and its incorporation into a broad Federal program of
support for the arts. This led to inevitable comparisons between the
amounts of money given to literature and to other art forms. It also
led, as did the whole program of arts funding, to heated public debate
about the effect of State patronage on the production of culture.
There have been predictable philistine attacks on pampered artists,
pronouncements on the benefits of poverty for sharpening the wits,
and professions of belief in the wisdom of the market; but there have

also been more considered reservations. Addressing the 1983 annual general meeting of the Australian Society of Authors, the broadcaster and writer Allan Ashbolt said he worried about the psychology inherent in the hand-out system. Every two to three years writers must subject themselves to an authority which decides whether they and their project deserve support. This process is not without elements of self-abasement, as the continuing grumblings about the fairness of the system testify. Those who, through financial pressure, submit themselves to be judged need ways of recovering from rejection.

Financial pressures will always cause writers to look over their shoulders, be it to the market or a funding body, and just how these backward glances affect their writing is hard to know. But Peter Carey, one of the few Australian writers who has both a secure income and enough time to write, testifies to the freedom of not having to worry about money. 'When I write a book like *Illywhacker* . . . I don't have to worry about whether it's going to sell. If I want to throw it out at the end of two years I can afford to.'

Most writers, however, do have to worry about money, and complaints about authors' incomes were regularly heard throughout the period. In 1970 the *Australian Author* carried a report of writers' incomes. Of the 293 writers who responded, only seven earned more than $7000 per annum, nine between $5000 and $7000, eighteen between $2500 and $5000, and the rest less than $2500. These were gross earnings, before costs like typing and travel had been deducted. (The average male income for 1970 was $3848.)

A similar survey carried out in 1985 found that thirty full-time writers had earned more than $15,000 p.a. from writing over the previous five years. This was based on tax returns and so included money from fellowships, grants and prizes, as well as from royalties and the sale of rights. (The average male income for 1985 was $20,654.)

Since 1970 there have been some significant changes in the sources of authors' incomes. In 1987 the Literature Board provided twenty-nine fellowships worth $25,000, and forty-four worth $17,000 as well as twenty-one writers' assistance grants of $8000. Most published writers could expect to get some support from the Literature Board during their writing life. Usually such income was irregular, although between 1973 and 1984, twelve writers were supported for seven or more years (Dorothy Hewett, Rodney Hall, Les Murray, Murray Bail, David Ireland, Robert Adamson, Frank

Moorhouse, Barbara Jefferies, Hal Porter, Richard Beilby and Morris Lurie).

During the period the literary prize emerged as another form of state patronage to writers. Between them the premiers of New South Wales and Victoria dispensed about $100,000 worth of prizes annually and State rivalries will probably keep the amount high. South Australia has awards to coincide with the biennial Adelaide Festival, and in 1988 the Steele Rudd prize for a collection of short stories and a prize for biography were inaugurated in Queensland. There are also the National Book Council Awards, the Western Australia Week Literary Awards, the *Age* Book of the Year, the Vogel prize for an unpublished manuscript by a young writer, and a host of smaller prizes and awards.

Since 1974 the Public Lending Right scheme has also supplemented authors' incomes. This is a payment to authors in proportion to the borrowings of their books from public libraries. The Australian Society of Authors lobbied long and hard for PLR, and for some compensation for the income lost through photocopying. The Copyright Act of 1980 recognised the authors' and publishers' case for some form of compensation for this lost income and obliged educational institutions and government departments to keep records of multiple copies they made. According to these records, $5 million was owed in mid-1987, but the mechanism established for collecting this money was administratively cumbersome and met resistance from organisations which resented having to pay for something they had regarded as free. Little of this money had been collected and none had been dispersed to authors or publishers by mid-1987, but the principle of compensation for photocopying had been legally recognised.

The sale of rights, particularly film and television rights, was an increasingly important source of income for some writers. A successful film or television series based on a book also boosted the sale of the book—sometimes enormously. Colin Thiele's *Storm Boy* (1963) has sold 550,000 copies and Joan Lindsay's *Picnic at Hanging Rock* (1967) 300,000. Albert Facey's *A Fortunate Life* (1981) sold an extra 80,000 copies during and immediately after the television mini-series.

Some books are now being written with an eye to the film or television series to follow, or are seen from the beginning as part of a multi-media package. A biography of Sidney Nolan published in 1987 was issued with a video; four short books were issued to coincide with the Special Broadcasting Service mini-series on young people, *Winners* (1987). Writers were involved in all stages of these multi-media packages, but the book may no longer be the primary text. Of course, such developments will benefit only some writers and some forms of writing. The book of poetry, the book of reflective critical essays, or the modernist novel do not lend themselves to audio-visual interpretation.

The most common explanation for the low incomes of Australian writers is the smallness of the Australian market for books and its openness to books from both Britain and America. This keeps the print runs low, with consequent low royalty payments for authors and little profit for publishers. The *Australian Bookseller and Publisher* gives figures for 1983 showing that the average print run of a new hardback fiction title was 3000, of poetry and drama 1000, of new non-fiction 4000. Not all the books printed will sell; even if they do royalties calculated at 10 per cent of the retail price do not add up to a very big return to the writer. Nor does the publisher reap huge profits. The price of a book sold for $10.00 over the counter breaks down this way: bookshop/retailer $4.25; author $1.00; printer $2.00; distributor/wholesaler $2.00; publisher $0.75.

Until very recently, Australian publishers have not been able to look overseas to boost their print runs. Now, in the wake of the overseas interest, particularly in the United States, in Australian films there is more interest in Australian writers, particularly of fiction.

The current success of Australian fiction has added a new twist to the continuing tension between Australian and overseas in Australian publishing. Some Australian writers publish with overseas publishing houses, mostly based in London. David Malouf is published by Chatto and Windus, Patrick White publishes with Jonathan Cape. Peter Carey's *Illywhacker* (1985) was published by Faber in London and the University of Queensland Press bought the Australasian rights. This last example caused a bitter debate at the 1986 Adelaide Writers' Festival, Laurie Muller of University of Queensland Press accusing overseas publishers of luring successful Australian writers away from the Australian publishers who gave them their start. UQP had published Carey's three previous books.

At stake here is not just the pique of the spurned local mentor but the prestige of Australian publishing, the experience Australian editors gain from working with the best Australian writers, and the suspicion that the best Australian writing will happen when writers share an idiom and rhythm of experience with their primary audience. From the author's point of view the access to overseas markets and hence the likelihood of bigger print runs is argument enough for choosing an overseas publisher.

Local Australian publishers have always felt embattled in the face of powerful overseas publishing houses, but have fortified themselves with their nationalist commitment. In the period under consideration the balance between overseas titles and Australian ones 'shifted in interesting ways. The proportion of Australian books sold increased dramatically.

	Australian originated %	Imported %
early 1970s	10	90
early 1980s	44	56
1986	50	50

A big shift in the educational market was partly responsible for this. In 1986, 60 per cent of the educational market was Australian, to 40 per cent imported; less than four years earlier the ratio was reversed.

While books which had originated in Australia increased their share of the market, these books were less likely to be produced by an independent Australian publisher than they would have been twenty years earlier. Publishers vary greatly in size, and any list of independent Australian publishers will include many very small enterprises. But since 1965, once independently owned Australian publishers like Rigby, Jacaranda, Cheshire, Lansdowne, Sun Books, Ure Smith and Lloyd O'Neil have been acquired by overseas or non-publishing interests. In 1983 McPhee Gribble, begun in 1975 by two Melbourne women, entered into a marketing and distribution arrangement with Penguin. Sally Milner's Greenhouse Publications was acquired by Kerry Packer's Consolidated Press in mid-1987.

The university presses, particularly Melbourne (MUP) and Queensland (UQP) are now perhaps the most substantial Australian publishers with fully independent ownership. Significantly, each of these is attached to a larger organisation which gives support and protection. University of Queensland Press has been particularly important in the publication of fiction and poetry. Fremantle Arts Centre Press in Western Australia also benefits from being part of a larger institution.

Fremantle Arts Centre Press started publishing in 1976 with the aim of giving wider publication to the work of Western Australian writers, and has published books by Fay Zwicky, Elizabeth Jolley, Nicholas Hasluck, and T. A. G. Hungerford. It was also the first publisher of *A Fortunate Life* (1981) by A. B. Facey. The manuscript was brought to the Press by Facey's daughters who wanted 100 copies printed for family members. Editors Wendy Jenkins and Ray Coffey thought the work could interest a wider readership and worked on the manuscript with Facey. The book was an instant success and Fremantle licensed the paperback and subsequently volume rights to Penguin. It has gone on to be Penguin's best-selling Australian title and by mid-1987 had sold over half a million copies in its various editions. Facey's *A Fortunate Life* is a telling reminder that not all important books are written by people who see themselves as writers. It has given confidence to many other people to write the stories of their lives. Sally Morgan's *My Place* (1987), an autobiographical account of a young woman's search for her Aboriginal origins, was also published by Fremantle Arts Centre Press and has received widespread acclaim. While only a few such manuscripts will achieve commercial publication, they may be printed in more modest forms and circulated among friends and family or in a local area. The success of a regional press like Fremantle shows a contrary trend to the centralisation discussed in this chapter.

In the early 1970s there was much concern about the effect which increased foreign ownership would have on Australian publishing. The assumption was that foreign-owned companies would not encourage local books because they would compete with the parent company's books being marketed here. These fears did not seem to be borne out. Local editors were generally appointed to manage the local lists, and their identification with Australian literature and culture was generally as strong as their identification with their parent companies. In the period under discussion the publication of Australian titles increased rather than diminished. The expansion of the Penguin list (under Brian Johns and Jackie Yowell) was the most dramatic example of an overseas-owned company's commitment to local writing. Penguin took risks with new writers and republished important out-of-print works like the two novels of Criena Rohan, *Down by the Dockside* (1962) and *The Delinquents* (1963).

International publishing changed rapidly in the 1980s and Australian publishing was affected by these changes. The concentration of ownership and the disappearance of independent houses was a worldwide phenomenon and so cannot be understood only in terms of the particular characteristics of the Australian economy. Independent British and American houses were also disappearing. Rupert Murdoch's News Group, already the owner of Angus and Robertson and Bay Books in Australia and 41.7 per cent of the British house William Collins, bought the prestigious American house Harper and Row in 1987. Penguin acquired Hamish Hamilton, Sphere, Michael Joseph and Viking in the mid-1980s and in 1987 expanded its American base with the acquisition of New American Library. Peter Mayer, Penguin's chief executive, wrote a memo to Penguin staff on the acquisition of New American Library in which the key words were 'integration' and 'centralisation'.

Exactly what effect these developments will have on the quality and range of books published world-wide is hard to tell, as is its effect on Australian publishing. In the short term the increased concentration of ownership in Australia did not seem to reduce the number of good Australian books. But the sense of unease continued. When things get tough, will the boards of the overseas-owned companies pull back from their commitment to Australian publishing and see Australia once again primarily as a market? In 1985 Laurie Muller of University of Queensland Press, in a widely discussed paper, again stressed the fragile health of the publishing of Australian creative writing—a theme which recurs again and again in discussions of Australian publishing. It parallels the other recurring theme—the smallness and insecurity of creative writers' incomes.

While real conditions such as the size and vulnerablity of the market are a partial explanation for these continuing themes, there is something else to be heard in the prophecies of doom and the continued complaints about lack of recognition and adequate reward. Books are commodities, bought and sold in the market place; authors are workers trying to earn a living. But books are also bearers of culture, writers are also artists and thinkers. Novelists, poets, short-story writers, critics, biographers, historians, and the books they write also participate in a system of exchange quite other than that of the market: the swapping of images, narratives, ideas and interpretations; the conversations which knit us together, which excite and enliven us, which feed our inner worlds and show us new worlds, which give us meanings to try out on an ever shifting and elusive reality, and comfort us when that reality comes too starkly into focus. Books are commodities and yet not commodities, and the tension between these two competing ways of assessing value underlies most discussions about the production of literature. Writers, editors and publishers all feel their endeavours are contributing to culture as well as the economy; there is something perennially shocking in the recurring intruder from the world of commerce asserting that books can be sold just like soap.

This tension is embodied in publishing houses in the division between the sales and marketing department and the editorial department, and is seen again in the different self-images of the mass-market houses and quality publishers. Most of the larger Australian publishers have wide-ranging lists (fiction and biography as well as how-to-do-it books) and the money-spinners are frequently justified because they make it possible to take risks with less commercial but worthwhile books. There are two points here: many people who work feel compelled to put forward justifications for their less serious publications; and people still do take risks.

The tension over the commodity status of culture expresses itself somewhat differently in the debate over authors' incomes. The Australia Council has given a lot of attention to ways of improving artists' incomes and working conditions, and in doing so has employed the language of organised labour. Artists are seen as workers in the arts industry, or professionals with skills and long training. There is much point in this rhetorical strategy, but it is not the whole story, at least not for writers. Writers are self-appointed, risking their talents through their own choice. And they are engaged in work which is deeply satisfying, done in their own time. It must be remembered, too, that not all writers want to write full time. Some, like Bert Facey, are amateurs, one-book authors. Amateur writers are often scorned by professional writers who see their eagerness to get their name into print as undermining solidarity and keeping the royalty payments low. Amateur writers, like amateur painters and musicians, sit uneasily alongside the idea of the artist as workers. But amateur writers and one-book authors are not always driven by egoism or print fever. They also want to participate in the conversation of culture, and some of them write books of enduring value.

An Australian writer, though, may become very well known, almost a household word, and yet still have only a very modest and insecure income. The praise and public acclaim one may receive, and the consequent sense that one's work *is* of cultural value, contradict the small monetary return; this is galling in a society where money is the automatic gauge of worth. One *knows* that one is doing something that matters, one *knows* that many people think so, yet this knowledge has no external representation in the bank account.

Reading about and attending discussions on authors' incomes and Australian publishing during this period I was struck by the repetitiveness of the complaints and the continuing apprehension about the future. Changes are generally seen as being for the worst, and hopeful new developments are generally expected to be shortlived. Such continuing complaints and expressions of fear, like many repeated refrains, have ritual functions. An uncomprehending and unappreciative, or even actively hostile, opponent is generally projected—the marketing and advertising people, an ignorant public, philistine politicians; when writers get together, venal publishers. Thus those present are able to affirm the value and importance of what they do. These collective affirmations are particularly important for a group whose primary activity, while involving buying and selling, can only partly be understood in terms of profit and loss.

Notes

Days of Wine and Rage (1980), Frank Moorhouse's collection of various writings from the 1970s (poems, newspaper and magazine articles, letters), gives a good feel for the milieu in which many younger, particularly Sydney, writers worked in this period. In it will be found Moorhouse's own account of *Tharunka's* challenging of the censorship laws and Michael Wilding's account of the founding of *Tabloid Story*.

Interviews with writers are a good place to look for discussion of the ways in which economic considerations have impinged on their writing. For this period there are a number of collections of interviews with Australian authors: Jim Davidson's *Sideways from the Page* (1983); Candida Baker's *Yacker* (1986) and *Yacker 2* (1987); and Jennifer Ellison's *Rooms of Their Own* (1986). The interview with Peter Carey which is quoted is in *Yacker*. The statements by T. A. G. Hungerford and John Morrison are from the special issue, 10 (1981), of *Australian Literary Studies* on the short story.

The Australian Author, the quarterly journal of the Australian Society of Authors, began in 1969. In it will be found reports on the struggles to establish Public Lending Right and payment for photocopying, reports on surveys of authors' incomes, discussion of authors' relations with publishers, the possibilities of self publishing, the law of defamation, the Literature Board's policies, and much else. Barry Andrews' article, 'The Federal Government as Literary Patron' in *Meanjin*, 41 (1982), looks at the history of the CLF and the establishment of the Literature Board. The Literature Board publishes regular reports of its activities which can be obtained from the Board.

Geoffrey Dutton's *Snow on the Saltbush* (1984) has a chapter on publishing. Michael Wilding argues the dangers of foreign ownership in Australian publishing in 'A Random House: The Parlous State of Australian Publishing', *Meanjin*, 34 (1975). Dutton discusses the conclusions of a thesis by Valerie Hayes on the impact of foreign ownership on Australian publishing during the period, but unfortunately this was not available to the public at the time this chapter was being prepared.

The *Australian Bookseller and Publisher* is the journal of the Australian book trade. It publishes information on and discussion of Australian book publishing and selling, including reports of the statistics collected by the Australian Book Publishers' Association. Laurie Muller's paper on Australian publishing was given at a seminar on the economy and the arts in October 1985 and published in the *Australian Bookseller and Publisher*, December 1985-January 1986.

Chapter 28

CRITICAL ISSUES

VERONICA BRADY

The period since 1965 has been a lively time for criticism. The best place to begin perhaps is with the outrageous, with the claim which Humphrey McQueen made in his introduction to John Docker's *In a Critical Condition: Reading Australian Literature* (1984). McQueen says that this book, 'explaining why most criticism is worthless', was necessary 'because literary criticism has earned its low reputation'. Certainly Docker tried to show that this was so. His main point was political: that criticism was dominated by academics in general, and by professors in particular, who imposed their own kind of criticism on students, appointed those who agreed with them, and—by means of their influence on syllabus committees for schools as well as their own institutions—effectively controlled the canon, the list of books which mattered. But his objection to 'their' kind of criticism was also ideological. They were either New Critics, which meant that they saw the text as something which existed in its own right, set apart from culture and society, or followers of F. R. Leavis, for whom criticism is a matter of ethical, even metaphysical judgements, for which they relied on their own 'cultured' discriminations. Docker saw this as a kind of treason. For him literature mattered for the light it threw on social issues, and nothing else would do.

This is good knockabout stuff, with a touch of the melodrama which is never far from the scene in our culture, and it represents perhaps the final fling of the 'Days of Wine and Rage', the late 1960s and 1970s. But the issues Docker raised were and remain important; his attack on privilege and his concern for social issues echoes the Lawson-Furphy tradition with its 'temper democratic: bias, offensively Australian'. This was another count against his enemies, the academics, was that they were either English or English-educated. But Docker also pointed to the connection between knowledge and power, which Michel Foucault had explored in his work on the treatment of mental illness, the penal system and sexuality and which Roland Barthes discussed in his studies of fashion and advertising in particular and popular culture in general.

Docker, however, in old-fashioned Australian patriotic fashion, scorns their sophistication—the epilogue, subtitled 'the author faces death at a seminar on Roland Barthes', tells it all. For him, new theory of this kind is only the old New Criticism in disguise, a 'new formalism'. He is content to judge texts by their social content, whether or not they are on the 'progressive' side, critical of social injustices. So the canon he constructs of social realist writers as an alternative to one largely made up of 'metaphysical' writers, like White and Stow, Brennan and Webb, merely sets up a counter-orthodoxy. The notion of the canon itself remains unexamined, as do the distinction between 'high' and 'low' literature, and the nature of the relationships, if any, between literature and life.

But these issues were being examined elsewhere. The arrival of the electronic age posed urgent questions to those who identified culture with the reading of books. Indeed it challenged the very definition of culture. It was no longer a matter of taste, something inherited or acquired, learned from books, and the property of the educated, the enlightened and the elegant, but a way of seeing, of making sense of the world which belonged to everyone. So the distinction between 'high' and 'low' culture disappeared. It became necessary to study television, film and popular music, as well as magazines, newspapers and best-sellers; all these were as important as, perhaps more important than literature—if one were concerned with the connections between literature and power.

Geoffrey Serle's pioneering work *From Deserts the Prophets Come* (1973) had in a sense pointed in this direction, setting cultural history in the context of a general social history. Docker's earlier work, *Australian Cultural Elites* (1974), too, had argued that the difference in the literature produced in Sydney and Melbourne was a function of the differences between their social, political and economic histories. But the first significant work to focus on popular culture as such was the collection of essays, *Australian Popular Culture* (1979), edited by Peter Spearritt and David Walker. The theoretical issues involved, however, were canvassed more fully in the introduction to a later book, edited by Susan Dermody, John Docker and Drusilla

Modjeska, *Nellie Melba, Ginger Meggs and Friends: Essays in Australian Cultural History* (1982). Significantly, they acknowledge the influence of theories developed elsewhere, notably the work of the so-called Frankfurt School, in particular of Louis Althusser, and of the Birmingham University Centre for Contemporary Cultural Studies in England. Conventional literary criticism, in their view, had got it all wrong; it was not merely elitist but mistaken. Literary texts mattered not because they were concerned with questions of value or even because they were manifestations of individual consciousness but because they offered access to culture, which they defined as a way of life, as 'people's lived experience, lived through historically shaped cultural forms'. In this view the artistic impulse is not a force from elsewhere. It is the product of social experience, and this, not anything else, ought to be the critic's focus. It was not consciousness but the ways in which consciousness was produced and structured that mattered. The notion of an autonomous world of the individual imagination was nonsense, as were the ideas that people shaped their own lives and think their own thoughts.

Evidently this view owed a great deal to Marxist and neo-Marxist thought, to Stuart Hall of the Birmingham Centre, to Terry Eagleton and to Louis Althusser and Theodor Adorno. But Althusser also owed a debt to the formalist and structuralist tradition that draws on the work of the French semiotician, Ferdinand de Saussure, at the beginning of the century. Saussure's great insight had been into the social nature of language. Meaning, he saw, was not something given but something made. Words have meanings because they belong to communities which receive and recognise a network of codes, networks of signification. Meaning is thus related to the systems of power which prevail in a given society. More importantly, power is bound up with systems of meaning or ideology, in Althusser's definition, a system of meaning which 'installs everybody in imaginary relations to the real relations in which they live'.

While some critics moved to examine more closely the language and forms of popular culture from this base, others moved out in the direction of anthropology. Structuralist critics were inspired by the work of Roland Barthes and to a lesser extent Jean Baudrillard, who visited Australia in 1984, and the Englishman Dick Hebdige's *Sub Culture: The Meaning of Style* (1979). They brought their literary interest in style to bear on the politics of popular culture. Any such approach put paid to claims 'high' literature might make to special attention, of course. For the structuralist the study of *Ginger Meggs* mattered as much as, perhaps more than, the study of *King Lear*.

More conventional literary studies, however, also drew on these insights and offered ways of moving from the study of specific literary texts to the study of society. As Graeme Turner and Delys Bird argued in an important paper given at the Conference of the Association for the Study of Australian Literature in Adelaide in 1982 and published, somewhat exhausted, in *Westerly* the same year, Australian literature had long suffered from a lack of theory. The stock argument of its opponents was that Australian writing was not of 'world standard'; this could not really be answered unless some connection was made between literary texts and larger social and cultural contexts. Then, evidently, the standards applied would not be the same as those applied, say to the study of Shakespeare or Jane Austen, but different, of their own kind. Critical theory from elsewhere thus contributed to the task of creating 'Australian self-knowledge and self-definition and awareness of our own history and destiny', which P. R. Stephensen had called for so urgently in the 1930s.

Australian literary critics in this way became a part of mainstream social scholarship. The study of language in general and of symbol in particular has something to contribute to other disciplines like anthropology, history, sociology, psychology and even—a contribution to be discussed later—theology. So literary criticism took a place in new interdisciplinary studies, like Australian studies or women's studies. The growing dominance of the media and information technologies, of the study of symbols and symbolic formations became crucial.

Perhaps the best example of these new developments is to be found in the relations between Australian literary criticism and the study of Australian films. Titles tell their story here: John Tulloch's *Legends on the Screen* (1981) and *Australian Cinema: Industry, Narrative and Meaning* (1982), Brian McFarlane's *Words and Images: Australian Novels Into Film* (1983) and Graeme Turner's *National Fictions: Literature, Film and the Construction of Australian Narrative* (1986). Turner's book seems most conscious of the theoretical issues. Pointing out that Australian film criticism has been largely technical, he argues that the theory of narrative, developed by literary critics, has an important contribution to make. Taking it as his premise that patterns which dominate the Australian literary tradition also shape film narrative, he directs attention to these patterns, to the 'kinds of meanings which are preferred [within our culture], the forms in which they are circulated, and their ideological function'. In this view, the stories which people enjoy reflect the meanings they live by.

This kind of approach was useful also in women's studies in unmasking the assumptions and determinations underlying sexism and in helping women define themselves and their goals. The essays in *Gender, Politics and Fiction: Twentieth Century Australian Women's Novels* (1985), edited by Carole Ferrier and the less theoretical work *Who is She? Images of Women in Australian Fiction* (1983), edited by Shirley Walker, set the study of literary texts in the context of the discursive formations which assign women their role and status—or lack of it. In *Reading the Country* (1986) Stephen Muecke similarly applies semiotic theory to the stories of his Aboriginal friend, Paddy Roe, highlighting the difference between Aboriginal and Euro-Australian ways of experiencing the country they live in.

All this made criticism potentially more interesting for the general reader. Literary magazines reached out to discuss a wider range of interests. *Meanjin*, with its record of interest in the social and political reference of literature, commissioned a series of issues on Australian States and New Zealand and published articles like Graham Little's studies of Malcolm Fraser and Bob Hawke, which drew on psychoanalytic as well as literary analysis. It also introduced its readers to the work of theoreticians like Derrida and Foucault. *Westerly* and the Tasmanian *Island Magazine*, appropriately enough, raised questions of literary geography, amongst other questions about the relations between literature and society such as the power of the media (*Island* devoted an issue to the ABC) or historical periods (*Westerly* ran a special issue on the 1930s). *Australian Literary Studies*, which had done so much to set Australian criticism on a solid scholarly basis, also reflected the changes; it offered structural and semiotic analyses of traditional texts, for instance, and a special issue on the newer writing which also canvassed the writers' own views. A new venture into 'high' journalism, The *Age Monthly Review*, appeared and set about discussing—often abstrusely—matters of theory. So too did the ABC's weekly radio program *Books and Writing*, and lesser-known journals like *Local Consumption* kept devotees in touch with the work of theoreticians like Derrida, Baudrillard, Deleuze, Guattari and the feminist, Irrigaray. Literary theory was becoming modish, though publications like the occasional supplement on Australian Literature edited by Geoffrey Dutton, first in the *Bulletin* and later in the *Australian*, helped to keep the balance.

But new theory could also lead to obscurity. In part this obscurity was a reaction against the older criticism's trust in the 'common reader' and 'plain talk'. In part it was a response to the need to meet other disciplines on their own ground and develop a reader methodology and an exact vocabulary of reading. But theory had something to do with it also. Deleuze and Guattari, for instance, pointed out that a language is not homogeneous but contains a range of dialects and special language, each with its special place in the system of power. So critics began to look to their own language as well as to the languages of literature and to develop their own jargon. Populists might protest. In the *Age Monthly Review*, for instance, John McDonald coined the term 'artspeak' and accused its practitioners not only of snobbery but also—a more deadly charge to those who claimed to be radicals—of conservatism, of being mere technocrats. But 'professionalism' of this kind is and remains seductive.

Most mandarin perhaps were the Deconstructionists, whose numbers began to grow with the arrival in the late 1970s of Howard Felperin at the University of Melbourne to take up the Chair of English recently vacated by S. L. Goldberg, often referred to as the arch-Leavisite. For the Deconstructionists it is the written word, the literary text, which is primary. Basing themselves on the work of Jacques Derrida, who challenges the very basis of Western philosophy since Plato—its interest in meaning—they deny the text's reference to anything outside itself, concentrating instead on the play of language within it, in its own world of 'differance' (a word Derrida coined for the special kind of reality he was talking about). In this view neither language nor human self-awareness has any reference to 'things as they are'. Words are not mirrors which establish an identity, but a reduplication which establishes a difference. Meaning is thus a pure movement, the self-effacement of language. At best it is a matter of the 'trace', evidence of something not present but conspicuous by its absence.

This was to complicate the debate between literature and life in a crucial way by trying to redefine 'life', pushing its limits beyond the merely empirical. Some people would see the influence of Freud's work on dreams and the unconscious at work but in some ways, with its focus on the text as a closed system and on the contextless intelligence of the reader, it also resembled New Criticism. Yet Deconstruction was much more radical. Unlike New Criticism it has no place for ethical, still less metaphysical concerns—at least of the traditional kind. For Derrida metaphysical speculation was fumbling after shadows; it was a fractious substitution for, or to use his word, a supplement to, the discourse about things which is in turn a supplement to discourse about language itself. But in another way Deconstruction pointed back to questions which had become eclipsed by Structuralism and neo-Marxist analysis in particular. Where they tended to see literature as a function of the social, economic and political, Derrida points to more fundamental issues, the nature of 'reality' itself, to what 'meaning' actually means. This made for intellectual liveliness, though it could also lead to the stylistic libertinism and self-conscious nihilism of some of its practitioners. At best, however, it revived the question with which we began, the question of values—a question often ignored by those who are interested in social issues for their own sake.

Some critics continued to insist, however, that we ignore values at our peril. Most notable of these perhaps is Dorothy Green, best known for her *Ulysses Bound* (1973), a study of Henry Handel Richardson which is also a study in the history of ideas. Asked to contribute the afterword to *Nellie Melba, Ginger Meggs and Friends*, for instance, she insists that the question of value is the central question in any discussion of culture or politics. 'Aware that to raise the question of the religious dimension . . . in intellectual circles is to invite titters', she nevertheless insists that the crucial lack in our society is a 'dimension of depth', of concern for the meaning of words like 'truth' 'justice' and 'beauty'. To concentrate on the merely functional, or on systems of meaning, is to miss the real point. Echoing Dr Johnson, that 'men are but temporary grammarians or geometers but perpetual moralists', she declared that what is at issue is not the existence or independence of Australian culture but 'the more foreboding question whether culture in any intellectual sense of the word is any longer possible in a world whose triumph is the neutron bomb'. Turning the Marxist position on its head, she sees modish concern with structural determination as the product of the very structures and systems they criticise. Against what is at best 'humanisticism', she invokes the notion of absolute value, the 'dimension of depth', of 'real seriousness' as a kind of Archimedean point not merely outside the self but outside all historical systems and the basis for a proper humanism.

This position is reinforced by the beginnings of interest in the links between literature and theology and literature and philosophy— evident in the work of James Tulip, David Tacey, Peter Beatson and of myself as well as of professional theologians. Apart from Americans like J. Hillis Miller, Paul Ricoeur is an important influence here. His work on the symbol, which begins, like Derrida, with questions about the referential value of language, concludes that the symbol provides access to what cannot otherwise be expressed, the dimension of the ethical, the intuitive and the religious. As the notion 'humanity' becomes increasingly problematic, these insights may become increasingly important.

In a sense we end where we began. The relationships between literature and life, between the social and the metaphysical, are still under debate. But that is entirely healthy and points to the centrality of that debate. Criticism has become increasingly conscious of itself in the 1970s and 1980s and of the contribution it has to make. Although, or perhaps because, it has drawn heavily on ideas from elsewhere, Australian criticism has more insistently questioned its purpose and its place in national life. Moreover, the nature of power has changed; due to the development of electronic technology it lies now with those who control the imagination. The work of understanding and assessing the significance of language and the symbol therefore lies at the heart of Australian culture.

Notes

Further discussion of some of the issues raised in this chapter can be found in: Greg Manning 'Conditioning Critics: John Docker's *In A Critical Condition*', *Meanjin*, 43 (1984); Jim Legasse and Veronica Brady, 'In a Critical Condition—Two Responses to John Docker', *Westerly*, 30, 2 (1985); Graeme Turner and Delys Bird, 'Australian Studies: Practice Without Theory' *Westerly*, 27, 3 (1982); David Saunders, 'What Semiotics Is', *Age Monthly Review*, 2, 12 (1983); Kevin Hart, 'Maps of Deconstruction', *Meanjin*, 45 (1986); Imre Salusinski, 'Deconstruction', *Age Monthly Review*, 4, 5 (1983); David Brooks, 'Poetry and Sexual Difference', *Meanjin* 44 (1985); Stephen Muecke, 'Towards An Aboriginal Aesthetic', *Age Monthly Review*, 5 (1985); and Veronica Brady, 'Reading Black Literature', *Age Monthly Review*, 6 (1986).

Craig McGregor's 'Pop Goes the Culture: Academic and Other Prognostications', *Meanjin*, 39 (1980) offers a lively introduction to the issues of popular culture in general.

The essays referred to by Graham Little are: 'Fraser and Fraserism', *Meanjin*, 41 (1982) and 'Hawke in Place: Evaluating Narcissism', *Meanjin*, 42 (1983).

Chapter 29

A: POETRY SINCE 1965

JAMES TULIP

An explosion of energy and talent in verse between 1967 and 1972 has largely determined the course of contemporary Australian poetry. These years saw striking changes in Australian writing generally, but in poetry it was especially so. It was as if an act of deferred modernism was suddenly happening, making up for the long period of conservatism after World War II. The change was felt most sharply among the young poets who became known as 'the generation of '68'. They turned their backs on what they saw as the provincial preoccupations of Australian verse, and set themselves to follow international styles, particularly American ones. But the change was not limited to them. There were, in fact, several 'generations of '68', and the full story of Australian poetry in the years 1965 to 1985 has to account for a general transformation of the poetry scene.

The context of change, as it happened, was political. These were the years of the Vietnam War, of social protest and student unrest. The long Menzies era in Australian politics had come to an end and an alternative force was emerging under Gough Whitlam which promised a new perspective for Australian culture and society. It was as if a myth was enacting itself at a deep level of the Australian tradition, a myth of transformation, of a coming-to-power. Energies were flowing which were new, young, independent, vernacular, and at times republican. Different centres around Australia were identifying themselves as having distinctive voices. Balmain (Sydney), Brisbane, Canberra, Carlton (Melbourne), Newcastle and the Friendly Street poets of Adelaide became communities of writers who had their roots in social action and their outreach in the

475

international scene of art and politics. These changes were taken up and formalised in poetry workshops, new journals, by writers-in-residence and in the widespread growth of Australian literary studies in universities, colleges and schools. The appearance of the Australia Council and the Literature Board in 1973 consolidated the process of change.

The political impulse to contemporary Australian poetry, however, faltered in the 1970s, possibly as early as 1972 when the myth of a coming-to-power-of-the-new fulfilled itself in the election of the Labor government and the ending of the Vietnam War. From this point onwards poets were left to their own individualities or small regional groupings. The sense of a national movement broke down and many rivalries emerged among the different centres around Australia. Equally, the powerful American influence had largely spent itself by the mid-1970s. When Thomas Shapcott published his anthology *Contemporary American and Australian Poetry* (1976), which had been meant to point to the achievement of Australian writers within an international and comparative setting, it met with an uncertain reception. Some found it not radical enough. But the truth was that a tide was already flowing in an opposite direction away from the international connection for contemporary Australian poetry. The traditional Australian loneliness or isolation of the poet was re-emerging, and only the strongest of talents persisted through and survived the change. It has been the women's movement, rising from within a political base in contemporary Australian society, which has most clearly established a general front within poetry for affirming the experience of the 1980s.

The scene of contemporary Australian poetry, looking back from a vantage point in the 1980s, is complex. Young poets have made the running, but it is quite possible that it is the work of the older poets which will survive. There are many figures whom fashion has eclipsed and who may be waiting to be rediscovered. John Blight, Roland Robinson, Nancy Keesing, Nan McDonald, John Cowper, David Rowbotham and John Manifold come to mind. In this context, an eminent figure such as A. D. Hope has a unique position. His work was mainly done before the late 1960s; and in certain respects he has now come to be seen as a conservative force in Australian poetry with his preference for formal verse, rhyme, Augustan rationality and the discursive mode. He seems, however, to have resisted modernism almost successfully, and may indeed be a figure waiting to be taken up in the future by post-modernism with its emphases on reason and discourse. The problems of change since the late 1960s, nevertheless, have meant that Hope has been denied the role of leader or father-figure to the several generations of poets who followed him after 1968.

It is ironic that Hope has come to be seen as conservative, since the shift towards a personal, even 'confessional', poetry among his peers was something which Hope had entertained as early as the 1930s and 1940s. 'Pygmalion (1938-1941)' signalled a rare gift among Australian writers, of locating an urgent psychological experience between the sexes (though from the male point of view) within a context that was at the same time mythical and modern. Hope's 'The Return from the Freudian Islands' (1942) partly withdrew from this earlier seriousness in personal explorations, but helped him to prepare for the role of sensuous satirist which marked the great breakthrough in Australian poetry of *The Wandering Islands* (1955), Hope's text of rock-like achievement. His later writing in this personal idiom has continued in the poems of 1973 and 1974, 'Hay Fever' and 'In Memoriam: Gertrud Kolmar 1943', which take up into their orderliness the sharply dramatised elements of the style associated with Robert Lowell's *Life Studies* (1959). Hope's rationalism has never prevented a romantic impulse pushing up from within to test the limits of the controlling and containing forms in which he writes. This is his strength.

It is interesting, therefore, to compare A. D. Hope's position with a more modern equivalent in intellectual terms as, say, in John Forbes' *Stalin's Holidays* (1980). They offer two focuses for the process of change and the transformation in Australian poetry over the past thirty years. Hope's wit is constructive, critical, elitist and European. Forbes' complex comic sense, on the other hand, is deconstructive, analytical, populist and American. Hope often strikes off from Biblical subjects into satire. Forbes takes the drug scene and parodies it against itself. The scholar-satirist is set off against the larrikin-metaphysical. Hope's rounded, rational pentameters are broken open into Forbes' leaping irregular phrasings; classical finiteness is displaced by a kinetic continuum of associations. Hope's sense of art belongs to a world outside itself, to traditional culture for all the subverting of its solidity. Forbes refuses all transcendences, holding instead to the internal 'writing' as its own end. Hope uses irony and paradox as instruments of reason. Forbes in *Stalin's Holidays* introduces ideology alongside apathy, accepting alienation as a style sufficient for the times. Hope as a humanist gives way to Forbes as the humorist. The work of both poets has a loneliness surrounding it, as if the imagination leads nowhere and has to make do with its own world of fiction. There is a disturbing sense that it is very difficult for poetry to make a real connection with Australian culture and society.

The present concern, however, is with the general trends and aspects of the past twenty years. Apart from 'the generation of '68' (which is considered separately by Martin Duwell in the second part of this chapter), there seem to be four distinct phases of contemporary Australian poetry to be considered. First, there is the commitment to Australian tradition which Les Murray and poets close to him have established. Second, there has been the resurgence in the 1970s of poets who had established their reputations before the changes of the late 1960s. Third, there has been the middle generation of writers such as David Malouf, Rodney Hall, Judith Rodriguez, Thomas Shapcott and Roger McDonald who have broadened the cultural base of poetry in relation to other media such as the novel, journalism, film and opera. And, fourth, there has been the recent emergence of women writers as a new force in Australian poetry. *The Penguin Book of Australian Women Poets* (1986) has brought this movement into focus.

Les Murray's story is a classic one of modern Australia. A country boy, born in 1938 into a farming community of mid-north coast New South Wales, Murray came to Sydney at the end of the 1950s to attend Sydney University. Leaving the country for the city gave him the first subject for his poetry, and it has remained (together with its opposite in leaving the city for the country) the major subject of his writing in the past twenty-five years. Why this matters is because Murray caught his subject at a point when it had a sharp relevance to Australian social history. City versus country has always been a point of tension in Australia, but what was happening in the early 1960s was a major change in Australia in favour of the city. The American cosmopolitanism of Sydney presented Murray with a challenge which has driven him back in thought and imagination to consider the basis of the Australian cultural tradition. Defensively and aggressively, Murray has worked his way through personal, social and religious experience; he has found his own voice and verse form with an originality that places him among the leading poets in the English-speaking world today. His selected poems were titled *The Vernacular Republic* (1982), suggesting both his preference for Australian life and his own brand of radicalism.

Murray's earliest poems, published jointly with Geoffrey

Lehmann's in *The Ilex Tree* (1965), have an elegiac edge to them as if he is recognising the loss of his country world. 'Passing through Sawmill Towns', 'Noonday Axeman', 'Spring Hail' and other poems possess a directness and intentness of statement as of someone who has no illusions or romanticisms to offer about the country world. His Scottish ancestors had pioneered the land. Now in the 1960s it could not support him. When Murray from time to time did return from the city to visit the farm, it was to provide him with a gauge of his own personal development within a wider Australian context and as a poet. His early sequence 'Evening Alone At Bunyah' has the 'innocent sly charm' which in the poem he attributes to his widower father. His use of the first-person pronoun, the 'I' figure, however, is awkward here. Later country poems reveal his growth as a poet when he penetrates, as in 'Walking to the Cattle Place', more seriously into the life of the land:

> Beasts, cattle, have words, neither minor nor many
> The most frightening comes with a sudden stilt jump: the blood-moan
> Straight out of earth's marrow, that *clameur*, huge mouthed
> Raised when they nose death at one of their own
>
> And only then. The whole milking herd at that cry
> Will come galloping, curveting, fish-leaping in furious play-stops
> On the thunderstruck paddock, horning one another. A hock dance.
> A puddle of blood will trigger it, even afterbirth.
>
> They make the shield-wall over it, the foreheads jam down
> On where death has stuck, as if to horn to death Death
> (Dumb rising numerous straw-trace). They pour out strength
> Enormously on the place, heap lungs' heat on the dead one.

Meditation on 'the cattle place' is a focus for many planes of reality in Murray. Cattle in their creatureliness and passivities stand over and against 'the Action' of the cities. Cattle also belong deep in cultural history: Hindu and Boeotian customs are set by Murray alongside Australian ones. Country folk seem to be an extension for him of the animal world. A kind of natural sacramentalism is felt in his poetry's absorption in country detail. Murray is at ease in this world, and at one with it. His later country poems such as 'The Craze Field' and 'Bent Water in the Tasmanian Highlands' in *The People's Otherworld* (1983) almost lose themselves in their subjects, as if

Murray is pressuring words as an action painter does his pigments to find a way of expressing what is there. His country poems as a whole reveal the curve of his maturity as a poet.

There is a curious blending of humour and seriousness throughout Murray's writing. A gratuitous kind of folksiness sets off, or acts as a foil to, his gift for contemplative and religious thought. Gradually, the serious interests in Murray have developed and stabilised themselves in the form of Catholic doctrines embedding themselves in Australian vernacular culture. His recent poem 'Equanimity', his editing the *Anthology of Australian Religious Poetry* (1986), his highly personal essay on 'Some Religious Stuff I Know About Australia', and his intimate detailing of Australian customs and seasons in *The Australian Year* (1985) point to his capacity to move easily between literature, religion and culture. He ignores the old shibboleth of Australia being the most secular society in the world.

Murray's equanimity in the 1980s has been hard won from battles—largely within himself—over a wide range of modern Australian experience. His verse novel *The Boys Who Stole the Funeral* (1980) brought forward much of the anger he felt at the changes in Australian society of the 1970s. Telling the story of two ocker youths who wished to give an old Anzac a decent country burial, Murray released his negative feelings against city life, cultural trendiness and feminism, placing against them a kind of salvation achieved through tragedy and a coming to terms with an Aboriginal understanding of the land. Ocker, Anzac and Aborigine point to the emergence of a new kind of hero in *The Boys Who Stole the Funeral.* Yet the real hero in this book is what he calls 'The Common Dish', the food of ordinary people. Murray's interest in Aboriginal culture and writing is another striking feature of this book. His 1977 essay 'The Human-Hair Thread' and his long sequence 'The Buladelah-Taree Holiday Song Cycle', based on an Arnhem Land song cycle, are important developments in an area which has concerned a number of modern Australian writers.

The Younger Australian Poets (1983) is an anthology edited by Geoffrey Lehmann and Robert Gray, two poets who are closely associated with Les Murray. Lehmann and Gray intended the anthology to include the best of their contemporaries, but their selection has pointed up a continuing tension in Australian writing between groups which could loosely be called traditionalists and internationalists, as well as an imbalance of male and female writers (only six of the twenty-nine poets are women). Lehmann and Gray

are themselves different in their individual concerns. Geoffrey
Lehmann is rational, light and learned. He has found in *Ross' Poems*
(1978) a human figure with a reflective and practical cast of mind
for the Australian pastoral world. In his *Nero's Poems* (1981)
Lehmann has reached out for a classical subject to project modern
anxieties and tendencies. Robert Gray has been more open to
American influence. Whitman, Williams and Charles Reznikoff are
among his models. He has explored Buddhist modes of awareness,
and has adapted Japanese ways of addressing his subjects. His lines
have a musical phrasing to them, and he turns hard-edged Australian
images into sensitive aspects of themselves.

> A kangaroo is standing up, and dwindling like a plant
> with a single bud.
> Fur combed into a crest
> along the inside length of its body,
> a bow-wave
> under slanted light, out in the harbour.
>
> And its fine unlined face is held on the cool air;
> a face in which you feel
> the small thrust forward teeth lying in the lower jaw,
> grass-stained and sharp.
>
> Standing beyond a wire fence, in weeds,
> against the bush that is like a wandering smoke.

The blunt foregrounding of the figure-emblem-image here is a style
more familiar in Australian painting than in poetry. Gray's
originality, however, is felt in the interpretive impulses which are
lightly and loosely allowed to speak as if from within the poet. A
compact of fact and feeling results. Gray's manner is representative
of a general stance in modern Australian poetry. It expresses a
traditionalism in its preference for realism, meaning, and reference.
Yet it is internationalist in freeing up the image from any mere
captivity to the object it is portraying. A balancing of the external
and the internal within a dominantly naturalistic way of seeing
defines this act of imagination as characteristically Australian. It is an
impression which a reading of the many poetry journals and
magazines of the past twenty years would confirm.

Poetry Australia, to cite one journal which for twenty-three years has clearly moved in a traditionalist-internationalist ambience, offers a focus for this central contemporary style. *Poetry Australia* from 1964 onwards—through its sustained publications, Macquarie University conferences, and special issues for overseas poetry—has opened up and advanced the central space of Australian verse. Grace Perry, the editor, has in her own books, especially in her Berrima writing, suffused a world of fact with dream-like consciousness. John Millett, now an influential presence in *Poetry Australia*, has straddled Australian chronicle and surrealism, moving through a critical reading of international styles to his current neo-narrational manner. Bruce Beaver, a former associate of Grace Perry and whose *Letters to Live Poets* (1969) signalled early on the contemporary impact of American writing, has brought together a nervously expressive self-consciousness with a response to Sydney, its harbour and its beaches. Margaret Diesendorf, in *Light* (1981), has caught in conversational phrasing the intellectual and aesthetic interests of a European mind examining its affinities and alienation with respect to the Australian environment. *Poetry Australia* has been the vital link between innovation and tradition. Its achievement, historically speaking, was in leading the resurgence in the late 1960s of traditionalist poets adapting themselves to the new Australia of the 1970s.

James McAuley's *Surprises of the Sun* (1969) did, in fact, surprise his readers with its shift into the American 'confessional' manner. His earlier writing had ranged from a delicate lyricism to impassioned intellectual and mythic interests which were supported by a strong commitment to ceremony and decorum; his move into Australian family and domestic experience came as something of a shock to the Australian public. McAuley pursued this interest further in prose as well as poetry. His study of *The Personal Element in Australian Poetry* (1970) was a search through a century or more of Australian verse for a voice of independent and personal feeling. The 1970s, however, showed that McAuley became disenchanted with the self-dramatising aspects of this tendency. His later poetry reflects a reserved view of personal expression, and is notable for its return to the lyricism of his beginnings, now maturely and sensuously caught in reverie. The Tasmanian poems of *Surprises of the Sun* gave McAuley a rich, deft and musical idiom which he developed with rare mastery until his death in 1976.

David Campbell's transformation as a poet was in many respects even more striking. His *Selected Poems 1942-1968* confirmed among discerning critics his reputation as being much more than Australia's finest modern pastoral lyricist. The volume had barely appeared when Campbell, in *The Branch of Dodona* (1969), took on the subject of male-female relationships through a retelling of the story of Jason and Medea. Influenced by Lowell and Berryman, Campbell, although disguising personal experience in quasi-dramatic mono-logues, released new and darker energies in his verse drawn from war and marriage. His dilemma, as a World War II hero, over how to deal with the Vietnam War surfaced in his writing. It flowed across into a reassessment of Australian society; and his several volumes of verse in the 1970s mark a most penetrating exploration of cultural change in modern Australian poetry. He stands alongside Patrick White in this regard; but his view is from a country perspective and he finds more affirmation in relating the new to the old.

Campbell's buoyant delight in nature, his camaraderie with fellow poets and rich comic sense made him a centre of Canberra's new writing in the 1970s, and a bridge between the generations. Some of the best reviews of his Dodona poems and of his Kuringai Rock Carving sequence on Aboriginal art were written by younger poets of 'the generation of '68'. *Deaths and Pretty Cousins* (1975) sums up for Campbell the Australian pastoral tradition both at ease and at odds with city tradition. His 1970s writing is rich with sophistication. International poetry and painting inform his consciousness. He was acting out the transformation in Australian society of the early 1970s and his closeness to Canberra's gradual emergence in cultural terms as the national capital has given his late work a special appeal and relevance.

Rosemary Dobson worked with Campbell in the 1970s on 'translations' of Russian poetry. It was an interest which, (with Natalie Staples and R. H. Morrison), they had inherited from A. D. Hope and James McAuley, and showed that the Australian sense of international writing extended beyond America. Mandelstam, Pasternak and Akhmatova became their main subjects, providing models of a poetry steeped in personal experience that could rise to an impersonality and detachment of vision. These qualities appear in Dobson's recent book *The Three Fates* (1983) which marks a climax in her career. Known since the 1940s for the classical and formal achievement of her writing, Rosemary Dobson was able to find in *The Three Fates* a conversational idiom which allowed her to range about her subjects with acute insight and feeling. The precise, light qualities of Chinese verse are the discovery of these poems, their fineness being counterpointed with a deep elegiac note. Campbell,

McAuley and Christina Stead are among the fellow writers she sadly and gratefully remembers. Yet the tone of *The Three Fates* is predominantly one of celebration.

> White water pours down the hillside
> On the rock two fish swim under the water.
>
> Flannel-flowers splash in a falling torrent
> Push aside boulders, spill over the ledges.
>
> Held still in the eye like a fish carved in sandstone
> They become a white cloud visiting the rock face.

The poise found by Dobson in these lines is shared—but more problematically—by other women writers of her generation.

Judith Wright in her later poetry has a mature reflectiveness in the 'Habitat' sequence of *Alive* (1972), a study of a house as a correlative of the body. Wright has, however, used her poetry of the 1960s and 1970s for active political and social argument, taking poetic risks in the cause of public commitments. Gwen Harwood has articulated the experiences of women since the early 1960s in ways that have anticipated the feminist movement of the 1970s. Irony, non-fulfillment and a barely suppressed anger project themselves in her work in rational and satirical argument. Harwood often speaks through the personas of Professor Eisenbart and Professor Kröte, two figures who invite a mixture of scorn and sympathy. Harwood has, however, found a fullness of voice best in her later poems such as 'Father and Child' and 'At Mornington'. Her *Selected Poems* (1975) and *The Lion's Bride* (1981) document a critical awareness growing into a troubled and at times tragic self-understanding.

To many poets of the pre-1968 generation the challenges of the 1970s brought problems. Bruce Dawe, Vincent Buckley, Chris Wallace-Crabbe, Evan Jones and Philip Martin had set Melbourne clearly in the forefront of the Australian literary consciousness early in the 1960s with a variety of concentrations on moral and political—and at times religious—questions. Their development, however, was checked by the radicalism of the social and cultural changes which in 1968 engulfed them. Bruce Dawe's gift for dramatic and colloquial ironies had established him by the mid-1960s as Australia's most popular public voice in poetry. Dawe brought a social awareness to the foreground of his poetry and a moralist's reading of history and society.

We grew up in a time
when Karkhov, Liev and Dnepropetrovsk
were black foot-prints in the snow
and the beast was Nazi.

The forthright and at times prophetic tone of Dawe's writing almost always carries a sardonic self-irony. His Vietnam elegy 'Homecoming' has a heightened clarity of statement to it, the irony in this instance being directed outwards in anger and anguish at the war. *Sometimes Gladness: Collected Poems 1954-1982* catches with epigrammatic force many an irreverent self-truth about Australia. But there is also a sense to it that Bruce Dawe has not been able to go beyond the proletarian and ocker revolution of which his own verse offered one of the first contemporary prototypes.

Vincent Buckley, former Professor of English at the University of Melbourne and a major Australian critic, had by the mid to late 1960s brought together a rare combination of imaginative, social and religious interests. He was an early interpreter of Robert Lowell and the American poets. In such poems as 'Stroke' and 'Parents' he was able to step inside personal experience of an intimate and painful kind and invest it with resonance and general meaning. But since the 1970s Buckley's work has undergone several changes. A kind of literalism and plainness of statement together with a late lyricism appeared in his poetry. In *Golden Builders* (1976), after beginning with a Blake-like exploration of Melbourne as a latter-day London, he moved back into an open-form set of observations on people and localities, intertwined with moving self-dramatisation in his 'Practising Not Dying' poems. His Irish-Australian roots have taken his poetry—as well as his prose memoirs in *Cutting Green Hay* (1983)—into an historical sense of identity, narrowing and deepening his understanding of Australian culture.

The rational strengths of 1950s British poetry were the point of departure for other Melbourne poets close to Buckley such as Chris Wallace-Crabbe, Evan Jones and Philip Martin. Wallace-Crabbe, under the challenge of his readings in American poetry and the Vietnam years, moved towards a centrist stance balancing interiorised dream states of consciousness with public concerns. A tone and an awareness of spiritual anomie contest his outward-oriented probings of human passions and power games. With Buckley, Wallace-Crabbe has contributed widely to the critical self-understanding of Australian literature and culture. Evan Jones on a more limited front has persisted with a clarity of surface in recording domestic distress within the lifestyles of Melbourne suburbia. Philip Martin has held to a more lyrical note, forcefully rational and propositional yet maintaining a depth of religious awareness through his cultural explorations.

R. A. Simpson, another Melbourne poet of the same generation, has relaxed the academic temper of this school of writers and located his lyricism in a style that is both conversational and hard-edged. There is a modesty or diffidence of tone in his writing which together with an instinct for public communication makes *Selected Poems* (1981) a well-judged and agreeable volume. Other writers around Australia with similar experience, either as journalists or as public figures on the literary scene, include Geoffrey Dutton, whose career spans four decades and whose written work and centrality to publishing make his papers a storehouse of Australian literary history. Dutton had recently moved from a poetic base in reason and realism to explore the subtleties of love poetry with increasing success. David Rowbotham, the Queensland poet and journalist, began his career with a pastoral vision, then changed under a stressful experience of university teaching, which had a creative impact on his work but led him to retreat from full development in the 1970s. Hal Colebatch, a younger Western Australian exponent of tough realist verse, has carried this line of clear verse surfaces to its extreme or limit in 'Crowhurst' dealing with the lonely round-the-world yachtsman who was lost at sea. These writers have had quiet and steady Australian careers in poetry.

A more internationalist impulse, though with a conservative sense of form, has appeared in other writers of this generation. Peter Porter, since the 1950s an expatriate in London, has crafted a compacted modern Augustan style in which he draws fearful images of apocalyptic living as well as detailing the domesticity of an urbane Englishman. In recent years he has opened up a dialogue with the Australia he was once glad to leave. Randoph Stow, who also lives in England, has drawn deeply on life in Australia in both his novels and his poetry, seeing his homeland in a wide symbolic and conceptual context and allowing a spare lyrical voice, containing a nervous insight, to illuminate it. Similar to Porter and Stow is Vivian Smith; he is committed to living in Australia and his imaginative concerns are polarised between Hobart and Sydney, but this has not prevented him from moving internationally in an intellectual and poetic sense.

He has found himself as much at home with French surrealists and symbolists as with the American Robert Lowell, on whom he has written the first Australian monograph.

Central to the achievement of Australian poetry between 1965 and 1985 has been the work of the former Queensland writers David Malouf, Rodney Hall, Judith Rodriguez, Thomas Shapcott and Roger McDonald. Their contributions in numerous volumes of verse, as anthologists, critics and editors, and more recently through excursions into the novel, have consolidated and professionalised the core of their generation's writing. Malouf's return from England in 1968 coincided with a wave of university writing in Sydney and led him on from there to introduce the University of Queensland Press Paperback Poet series, a key development in Australian contemporary poetry. Rodney Hall played an influential role as poetry editor of the *Australian* in the years from 1967 to 1978, as Judith Rodriguez presently does on the *Sydney Morning Herald.* Thomas Shapcott is the current director of the Literature Board, while Roger McDonald has met with public success for the television series of his novel *1915.*

As writers, they share in varying ways a dramatising manner and an ironic consciousness. Judith Rodriguez has a forthright way of enunciating wit and argument. Her several volumes of verse are discharges of intellectual and emotional energy. *Nu-Plastic Fanfare Red* (1973), *Water Life* (1976), *Shadow on Glass* (1978), *Mud Crab at Gambaro's* (1980) and *Witch Heart* (1982) sustain and develop a professionalism of address while beginning and ending as personal statement. As against her directness, what is most interesting in Malouf, Hall, Shapcott and McDonald is the pattern of dualities or twinship structures through which their imaginations have found it necessary to work. It is as if the interplay of author and personas, such a feature of the modern dramatic monologue tradition, is here being taken a step further. The mood and structure of drama is internalised as characters' relationships within their work.

Malouf quickly established himself after his return from England with *Bicycle and Other Poems* (1970). His early work is marked with tautness of structure and satirical temper, like that of Philip Larkin and Robert Lowell, but in the 1970s Malouf began to respond to the deeper subjectivities of American poets like Wallace Stevens. 'An Ordinary Evening at Hamilton' scales down a philosophical meditation into sensuous surreal images.

The Pacific
breaks at our table,
each grain

of salt a splinter of its light at midday, deserts
flare on the lizard's tongue. Familiar rooms
glow, rise through the dark — exotic islands; this house

a strange anatomy
of parts, so many neighbours in a thicket:
hair, eyetooth, thumb.

Rodney Hall's poetry, both more detached and dramatising than Malouf's, has been an experiment in form, breaking up the author's omniscience into parts of a whole, only to reconstitute it within legendary and mythic sequences in patterns of doubleness and balance. Verse such as *The Autobiography of a Gorgon* (1968), *Heaven in a Way* (1970), *Romulus and Remus* (1971) marked the central projective finesse of Hall's art. Thomas Shapcott's plainer style has let him record Australian life from the 1950s onwards in a more direct way, his variation of the dramatic monologue having less ego involvement than do Malouf and Hall. *A Taste of Salt Water* (1967) brought the tradition of Slessor and Douglas Stewart forward into contemporary usefulness. After this point Shapcott's critical self-consciousness and his response to the changes of late 1960s poetry plunged him into experimental efforts and experiences which it has taken his poetry a dozen years to fully absorb. Beginning, however, with *Shabbytown Calendar* (1975) and its love-hate relation to his home town of Ipswich in Queensland, and running through his more recent *Welcome* (1983) Shapcott's poetry has found for itself an honest, nervous voice of high intelligence through which he speaks for mainstream Australia.

Roger McDonald's years from 1969 to 1976 as an editor with University of Queensland Press are important for modern Australian literary history. McDonald supervised the Paperback Poets series and many other projects which in the early 1970s expressed the new dynamism of writing at that time. His practical sense has also had its bearing on his poetry and fiction. There is an undercurrent of darkish realism beneath the surface of his verse in *Citizens of Mist* (1968) and *Airship* (1975), an undercurrent which has steadily drawn him across into the world of prose and history.

The decade of the 1970s saw complex developments in Australian poetry. The radical formalism of 'the generation of '68' turned its back on humanisms of every kind—moral, religious and intellectual—and concentrated on poetry for poetry's sake, especially in Sydney where the magazine *New Poetry*, edited by Robert Adamson, attracted a lively following. Melbourne saw a more politicised grouping of young writers, who appeared in *Applestealers* (1974). Kris Hemensley provided a focus for activity and international alternative writing, particularly as poetry editor for *Meanjin* from 1976 to 1978. The movement into post-modernism, however, has been best expressed by the Sydney poet John Tranter, who collected 'the generation of '68' in *The New Australian Poetry* (1979). It is a movement which has been followed through by Martin Duwell's *A Possible Contemporary Poetry* (1982) containing interviews with the new writers. John Forbes, Alan Scott, Alan Wearne and Laurie Duggan have developed from this base. Melbourne journals such as *Scripsi, Meanjin* and the *Age Monthly Review* have consolidated this movement into post-modernism.

Other centres around Australia consciously resisted the tendencies of the 'generation of '68'. Canberra saw a grouping of young poets in the mid-1970s—Gary Catalano, Geoff Page, Kevin Hart, Mark O'Connor, Phillip Mead and Alan Gould—who worked at a transfer of Australian traditionalism into modernist terms. They have since developed independently, Kevin Hart becoming a poet of philosophical and religious stature. In Adelaide, there has also been a lively scene among the Friendly Street poets. Andrew Taylor throughout the 1970s harnessed the intellectual concerns of Americans such as Wallace Stevens and Galway Kinnell to his own kind of lyricism, while Richard Tipping experimented with multi-media uses for poetry. In Western Australia there have been—in Perth and at the Fremantle Arts Centre—figures such as Fay Zwicky, Nicholas Hasluck, David Brooks, Philip Salom and Dennis Haskell enlarging the critical awareness of new trends in poetry. An interplay of ethnic and Australian traditions in verse is also evident in writers such as Peter Skrzynecki and Antigone Kefala in Sydney; Dimitris Tsaloumas in Melbourne; and Sylvana Gardner in Brisbane.

The strongest movement of the past ten years has been among women poets in Australia. The feminist presence was first voiced in Kate Jennings' anthology *Mother I'm Rooted* (1975). The *Sisters Poets* series (1979-) followed, with selections from a dozen or more women writers. Recently, *The Penguin Book of Australian Women*

Poets (1986) has confirmed the depth and achievement of this movement. Susan Hampton and Kate Llewellyn, the editors of the Penguin anthology, have drawn three-quarters of their anthology from writings of the past thirty years, yet clearly demonstrate the continuity and sustained power of women's writing in the Australian tradition. The achievement of the anthology is that it offers a poetry of experience, the voice of the writers having a wholeness and sense of purpose within the poems. A unifying tone within the verse marks it off from the dramatising or formalistic tendencies of male verse. Poems seem to be actions or events.

The 1970s verse of Judith Wright comes into its own in this context. Her 'Eve to Her Daughters' leads on to Fay Zwicky's 'Ark Voices' and Sylvia Kantaris' 'News From The Front'. Myth and legend are absorbed into sardonic comedy at male expense. Kate Llewellyn and Susan Hampton themselves create an openness of feeling, not through formal devices but directly in the candour of their statements and explorations of personal experience. Irony never masters the writing; it is there as an instrument of the feelings, whether of anger or love or compassion.

New writers in the *Penguin Book of Australian Women Poets* such as Anna Couani, Jenny Boult, Chris Mansell, Gig Ryan and Judith Beveridge seem at ease in experimenting with form. It is a quality that comes from the way the 'I' figures and voices in the poetry belong to the worlds from within which they are speaking. Beveridge's 'My Name' demonstrates a freedom with form without sacrifice of the poem's responsibility to truth and imaginative experience:

Someone is prowling around the borders of my name. They have
been there for days. I can't see them or hear them because in
the house of my name is a room of silence and a huge window of fog.
But I know they are there. My name is certified in a gold frame
that hangs on the room's wall. Everytime they move, it shakes.

   At first I didn't worry. But now they have begun rubbing
their sleeve over my name's glass. They are rubbing in circles that
are gradually widening. I scream that they can't do this and
repeatedly show them the gold frame. They take no notice. They keep
on rubbing. They rub until the fog disappears and their face becomes
visible.

The drama of possessing one's own identity in these lines flows out of a generation of women's writing. It is the context from which Germaine Greer came in the 1960s, and it is the generation which has seen a remarkable range of poetry by women published elsewhere in Australia in the past twenty years. Dorothy Hewett's 'Legend of the Green Country' and Fay Zwicky's 'Kaddish' are among the strongest personal poems of family experience in modern writing, filled respectively with comic and tragic impulses.

In the Penguin book, Jennifer Strauss transforms her academic learning in 'Guenevere Dying' into a sensuously realised drama. Margaret Scott's 'Grandchild' creates a still point of awareness within the swirl of happenings and future possibilities attending the birth of a child. Rhyll McMaster's 'A festive poem' makes something ceremonious out of the unceremonious lifestyle of an Australian family at Christmas. J. S. Harry in 'the poem films itself' matches wits with the best, and writes her own mini-history of the subject we have been considering here. 'Australian poetry 1965-1985' is seen in the *Penguin Book of Australian Women Poets* as part of a larger whole. Change, radical change, has happened in the past twenty years. But this anthology, which includes forgotten nineteenth-century voices, ethnic and Aboriginal voices, absorbs the challenge of the new in a way that includes the old and the several alternative cultures which now make up Australia.

Notes

The two main poetry journals, *Poetry Australia* and until recently *New Poetry,* came into existence from the same source (though at different times) and for the same reason. They both broke from *Poetry Magazine,* the journal of the Poetry Society of Australia, over the question of how much non-Australian material to include in an issue. In 1964 it was a matter of publishing Australian poetry translated into French which led Grace Perry to found *Poetry Australia.* In 1971 Robert Adamson and Carl Harrison Ford set up *New Poetry* to match the style of Donald Allen's Grove Press anthology *The New American Poetry* (1960). *New Poetry* became in the 1970s the Sydney focus for young and experimental writers, while *Poetry Australia* developed an open and eclectic stance.

The history of Australian poetry from 1965-85 can be told through the anthologies published in that time. Rodney Hall and Thomas

Shapcott's *New Impulses in Australian Poetry* (1968) signalled a change but was overtaken by events to such effect that Shapcott's *Australian Poetry Now* (1970) included sixty or more poets, most of whom had not been heard of before by the reading public. Shapcott's later anthology *Contemporary American and Australian Poetry* (1976) found itself flanked on either side by *Applestealers* (1974), the Melbourne salute to 'the generation of '68', and later by John Tranter's *The New Australian Poetry* (1979). The divisions among Australian poets have not yet been resolved adequately to allow for a truly representative anthology of the period. Harry Heseltine's *The Penguin Book of Modern Australian Verse* (1981) and Robert Gray and Geoffrey Lehmann's *The Younger Australian Poets* (1983) go part of the way.

Francis Webb's *Collected Poems*—almost all of them written before the period being considered here—was published in 1969 and had a powerful impact on all levels of Australian poetry. Webb is a poet's poet. After his death in 1974 a commemorative seminar was held in recognition of his achievement, the papers from which were subsequently published as a special issue of *Poetry Australia* (no. 56).

David Campbell, like Webb in the way he bridged the generations, has also received similar recognition. *A Tribute to David Campbell: A Collection of Essays* (1987), edited by Harry Heseltine, arose from a seminar at Duntroon House in September, 1985.

Philip Roberts' career in Australia from 1967 to 1979 is a kind of nerve centre for the period. A Canadian, Oxford-educated, Roberts taught English at Sydney University during his stay. He wrote five volumes of poetry which he brought together in *Selected Poems* (1978). He founded Island Press, acted as poetry editor of the *Sydney Morning Herald* 1970-4, and published a yearly anthology, *Poet's Choice*. He produced the Aboriginal writer Kevin Gilbert's book of poems *End of Dreamtime* (1971). Roberts' handpress texts, along with those of Alec Bolton's Brindabella Press, are collectors' items.

For critical discussion of Australian poetry 1965-85 see Joan Kirkby (ed.), *The American Model* (1982); Christopher Pollnitz on Les Murray in *Southerly*, 40 and 41; Ken Goodwin *A History of Australian Literature* (1986); Vivian Smith in *The Oxford History of Australian Literature* (1981); and Andrew Taylor, *Reading Australian Poetry* (1987).

B: THE 'NEW AUSTRALIAN POETRY'

MARTIN DUWELL

The poets referred to as 'the new poets' or, in a rather more European way, 'the generation of '68' form a coherent group within the great upsurge of poetic activity in Australia in the 1960s, documented in the earlier part of this chapter. They form such a coherent group that for a literary history the temptation to isolate them from other strands of this activity and treat them separately, as here, is irresistible. This isolation would please many of the poets who felt that their poetry was such a radical departure it could not be adequately described in the context of any existing Australian poetry. It creates problems, however, since clearly future literary historians will need to examine the interaction between the poetry of this group and that of the other poets in this period.

The boundaries of this mainly male group are usually established as membership of John Tranter's anthology *The New Australian Poetry* (1979). This anthology should not be treated as final, however, fixing the canon of important authors and poems. It selects from a wide range of material and since it was published halfway between the origins of this group and the present day it is to be expected that time has altered perceptions of the work and stature of many of the poets. Some, such as John A. Scott, have appreciably higher reputations than when the anthology was compiled and in any future anthology might well be represented almost entirely by poems written since 1979. At the same time many poets excluded from the anthology, including Richard Tipping, Pi O., Eric Beach and J. S. Harry, should probably be seen as part of this group, as should a group of younger writers, including Ken Bolton, Stephen Kelen, Gig Ryan and Susan Hampton, whose poetic output has increased in size and substance since the anthology was published.

Although it is true that there is no longer agreement as to what a satisfactory description of the work of contemporary poets will actually look like, one central issue for any initial attempt at describing the work of this group is the question of what the poets have in common. We need to know, particularly, whether there is an aesthetic common denominator since this would enable us to

493

determine in what direction they are attempting to steer (or, perhaps, bulldoze) Australian poetry. Firstly it is clear that Tranter's anthology is that of an existing group with a literary-historical self-consciousness rather than a grouping together of disparate poets with similar aesthetic ideas. The case of Andrew Taylor is instructive here. Only slightly older than most of the poets included in *The New Australian Poetry* he had, by the time of his third book, *The Invention of Fire* (1976), arrived at a passionate personal surrealism that is aesthetically more radical than the work of many of the poets who are included. The same can be said of his formal experimentation in the group of prose poems *Parabolas* (1976). And yet he is omitted from the anthology. Secondly, existing attempts at finding aesthetic common denominators have proven quite inadequate. Many of these attempts were, of course, polemical and not intended as serious analyses. It is, however, alarming to find the distinguished Sydney poet, Robert Gray, describing them as having 'appropriated wholesale an established anthologised American style of writing—that of the New York School', a bizarre description that by any conservative estimation would have to allow eighteen to twenty exceptions in a total of twenty-four poets!

What can be said of the aesthetics of these poets? Other parts of this book have described the way in which the modernist movement of the European twentieth century impinged on Australian writing: initially by destroying the hegemony of pentameter verse and admitting into literature the pathological, and secondly by sponsoring a surrealism which favoured the activities of the unconscious mind over the conscious, craft elements of form. The new writers belong to a third phase of modernism, a phase which is not a development within modernism itself but a return to original modernist sources. The central imperative is Pound's 'make it new' although the very vagueness of this injunction enables the poetry of the new poets to be, to an outsider searching for guidance, bewilderingly varied. The acceptance of this variety is important, however, for otherwise literary critics will forever seek in some '-ism' a philosopher's stone which will magically render the poetry easy to understand—a futile and exhausting search for an illusory, lazy option.

Though it is possible to approach the work of these poets historically, that is to analyse the three phases in which the movement developed, this initial study is not historical but geographical. Despite Australia's mobility of population and despite the mobility involved in the counter-cultural lifestyles of poets such as Charles Buckmaster and Michael Dransfield, and despite the existence of exchangeable magazines, there is a place-centredness about the new poetry, especially in its early stages. This is particularly so in Melbourne where two groups existed and seem to have made little or no contact. The first was associated with the La Mama poetry workshops. They were conducted by Kris Hemensley and began in September 1967, after a series of poetry readings sponsored by Betty Burstall designed to air the work of local poets. The early readings featured members of the influential group of poets at the University of Melbourne, and Kris Hemensley and Ken Taylor were two who found themselves at odds with 'this generally polite scene'. Taylor had recently returned from two years in America on a Harkness Fellowship, a stay that included studying writing with the American poet A. R. Ammons at Cornell University. Hemensley was a recently arrived English immigrant. The list of poets associated in one way or another with the La Mama workshops is a long one (it includes, notably, Charles Buckmaster, Robert Kenny, Garrie Hutchinson, Walter Billeter and Clive Faust) but the poetry of Taylor and the poetry and editorial work of Hemensley form its foundation.

After World War II and long before his poetic career began, Ken Taylor left Australia to travel in Europe. He is one of those writers who require a long familiarisation with the foreign before they can discover the exotic in the home they have left. This home, in Taylor's case, has two sites: the Ballarat of the years before the war and his grandparents' home in the Victorian coastal town of Lorne. As with many writers the social, historical and psychological march hand in hand so that Taylor's personal experience continually suggests wider significances, and much of the character of the poetry derives from a sense of historical destiny that is unusually underplayed and buried within the poetry itself rather than being an expression of rampant egoism. Ballarat becomes of special and exotic significance:

> Ballarat was the end of the British Empire and everywhere there was evidence of the end of a great imperial maritime venture: half-finished cathedrals . . . The especial pain . . . was that Ballarat was living through the end of its own sense of self-confidence.

The grandparents' camp, 'Valentines', obviously a place of childhood psychological security, is not a symbol of timeless reassurance since it too is subject to the same processes of change as Ballarat. Thus the core of Taylor's work is elegiac, as is that of Charles Buckmaster whose poems are obsessed by the lost forests of his home, Gruyere. It is not, however, nostalgic since it deals squarely with the processes of change rather than the past itself—one early poem is significantly titled 'How It Happens'. Many of the victims of this change inhabit what Taylor calls 'A Secret Australia', a kind of unrhetoricised and unpolemical vernacular republic. And 'At Valentines' is an extended lament for this change. Like Taylor's earliest poems it was written in America in 1966 in its author's mid-thirties. With its extraordinary form—it runs to over 700 lines and has barely more than double that number of words—its remorseless reclaiming of the details of the past, its refusal to use language heightened by tropes or to allow itself to centre around an analysing authorial presence, it must have seemed incomprehensibly unpoetic in its period. Taylor's poetry was, in fact, so distinctive that it was possible for it to be ignored almost completely. Twenty years later this is hardly the case.

Taylor's emphasis on the integrity of particulars made his poetry sympathetic to Kris Hemensley who had already found in the theories and practice of the Black Mountain poets a valuable model. The full extent of this model (usually called projectivist) is impossible to cover here, but the idea of the self as ego, emphasising understanding above the discrete integrity of other items in the universe, is replaced by the idea of the human at home among particulars as part of a field. As a result the poet becomes a kind of *homo loquens*, replacing the merely mimetic by kinetic re-enactment. Although the ramifications of this can result in vastly different poets (no less among the Black Mountain poets themselves) Hemensley's major long poem *The Poem of the Clear Eye* (1975) is built upon this principle of perception. This is especially true of its dazzling first section which, in the manner of a Kurt Schwitters sculptural collage, laces together particulars ranging from pub-talk to meditation. Other poets such as Robert Kenny and Clive Faust have pursued the emphasis on the act of utterance, contained in Olson's essay on projective verse, farther than Hemensley, and early poems of Richard Tipping show a similar influence. Hemensley is also one of the major editors of the period, particularly of the crucial journal *The Ear in a Wheatfield*, which played host to a generously wide range of new poetics and at the same time established connections with English and American projectivist journals. In retrospect Hemensley seems not so much theorist as host and supporter and, as often occurs, his pre-eminence as an editor has probably led to an unjustified lowering of his status as poet.

A few miles and yet lightyears away from La Mama, Monash University played host to three poets, almost exact contemporaries, whose reputations have continued to grow. The connecting lines between the work of Alan Wearne, John A. Scott and Laurie Duggan are so clear, especially between the first two, that it is difficult not to treat them as a unit. The tone of Scott's poetry is, however, vastly different from Wearne's. To simplify the contrast between their varied poetic outputs, Scott's language leans towards the dark and metaphorically intense ('Only this low lead sky, notched in the horizon / like the lid of a cauldron', for example, deliberately invokes Baudelaire's 'Spleen') whereas Wearne, if anything, recalls the bluffer language and rough-hewn metrics of Browning's nineteenth-century dramatic monologues. What unites them is their drive towards narrative. Wearne's first book *Public Relations* (1972) included many poems that were vignettes and which inevitably suggested that larger canvases lay behind them. His second book contained his first long narrative, 'Out Here', a group of dramatic monologues by characters brought into focus by an incident at a local school. 'Out Here' is full of a novelist's sensitivity to individuals' lives seen from within and it maps suburban mores with unsurpassed subtlety. Despite the poem's achievement, however, it is inevitable that it will be seen as a prelude to *The Nightmarkets* (1986), a remarkable novel-length series of dramatic monologues in a bewildering variety of verse forms that, using the same, almost voyeuristic, sensitivity to how people live that is Wearne's trademark, tackles the wider area of political and personal lives among people reaching adulthood in the 1970s. Laurie Duggan shares something of Wearne's sensitivity, but his ability seems to be in observing and placing the signs that reveal the character both of individuals and the large historical processes of which they are part. This has led to the writing of cruelly accurate satires, and also to his *The Ash Range* (1987) a huge collage of printed and spoken voices that attempts to allow a locality, Gippsland, and a history, to speak for itself.

John A. Scott's first book, *The Barbarous Sideshow* (1976), contained mainly short poems but, on the poet's own admission, his work before this had centred around vast narratives involving characters in a kind of 'twentieth-century mythology'. If Wearne's early short poems are vignettes, Scott's are footnotes. The drive towards narrative expresses itself fully in later books beginning with *The Quarrel with Ourselves & Confession* (1984) and *St. Clair* (1986) and one feels that the aim in both Wearne and Scott is to reclaim, to make narrative possible in later twentieth-century poetry without returning to naive narrative verse. The strain is clearly felt in Scott's long poems (more so than in Wearne's) where the drive towards narrative coherence seems to induce a powerful, counterbalancing drive towards fragmentation. Scott's central technique is to make the narratives self-referential (so that narrative becomes one of the subjects of the poems) but this is not done in a tritely fashionable way. The structures of narrative as well as other structures that dominate our lives are brought to the surface either covertly, as allegory, or overtly: the extraordinary 'Preface', for example, is replete with letters, diary entries and translations.

If there is a vast gulf in aesthetics between the Monash and La Mama poets, the poets centred in Sydney merely extend the diversity. If one can make generalisations about such radically different poets, one can say that many of them demonstrate different ways of admitting an extreme life into poetry. A brief comparison between the poems of Michael Dransfield and Robert Adamson will make this point. Michael Dransfield, who died in 1973 at twenty-five, developed early a brilliant lyric gift and a precocious mastery of rhetorical schemes. When these were employed in writing poems about an extreme lifestyle (involving, notably, drugs) he produced poems such as 'Fix', 'That Which We Call a Rose', 'Bum's Rush' and 'Parnassus Mad Ward' that quickly established themselves as classics of our poetry and remain as such today. One suspects that they are revolutionary in content rather than form, however, and that they are unusually brilliant examples of a recognisable lyric mode. It is true that within Dransfield's work there are many aesthetically adventurous poems, but the chaotic state of his publishing history makes it difficult to establish whether these came late or early in his writing career.

Robert Adamson's first books contained poems which, Rimbaud-like, embraced the violent life of the underworld, not only of drugs but of conventional crime. These poems still retain their capacity to shock but they escape melodrama by their strong self-referential element. If Dransfield's early death is a kind of seal that prevents his poems ever being read as melodrama, the disquieting experience of reading Adamson's early work is to be confronted by extremes of behaviour matched by extremes of self-awareness. The poems do not sit comfortably between these extremes, they oscillate from one to the other. Not all of Adamson's poems, of course, deal with extreme life and resolve its problems this way. The early poem 'The Rumour' is a major attempt at a long, open poem and in almost all of his books there are poems built around alchemical imagery as a way of transmuting the sordid events of life. The recent book *Where I Come From* (1979) contains a sparse, personal poetry that hints at a kind of poetic purification, perhaps like that of Yeats' *Responsibilities.* It might, on the other hand, be simply another example of self-awareness. Other poets such as Nigel Roberts, Vicki Viidikas and Rae Desmond Jones can be seen in this light. Roberts has an uncanny eye for the style of inner suburban life that recalls Wearne's except that the poet is usually present within the poems and they are, as a result, less dispassionate than either those of Wearne or Duggan. In the case of Rae Desmond Jones an extreme life expresses itself, especially in his second book *The Mad Vibe* (1975), as brutal dramatic monologues, gruesome and fantastic scenarios and often as an intense and erotic mysticism.

John Tranter is the most significant of the Sydney poets and this is not only because his career is the longest (stretching back to the early 1960s) but because his poetry contains such an immense variety within itself. Much of it is concerned with allowing the fast life of youth, drugs, sex and cars into poetry to effect the same kind of revolution in content I have been describing. However he has also evolved in a long career a wide range of approaches to the nature of poetry. His early poems collected in *Parallax* (1970) are often best seen in the light of symbolist theory as evocations of distorted states which are not strictly referential. A group of fragments of such poems, put together so that they create a 'field' rather than a linear, coherent narrative, forms the basis of the long poem 'Red Movie' which was published as the title poem of Tranter's second book. A poem such as 'Rimbaud and the Pursuit of the Modernist Heresy' is a fairly 'straight' analysis of the French poet and his influence whereas the long poem *The Alphabet Murders* (1976) begins as a reasonably sober meditation on what a satisfactory contemporary poetry might look like (it is built around Baudelaire's image of the voyage) and ends, often riotously, as though the material being discussed had distorted the fabric of the poem. The verbal excitement and ferocity of the last part of this poem, together with elements of parody as the poem tries out various approaches, only to reject them, is a part, though not the whole, of Tranter's poetic manner:

> We could point to the poem and say 'that map',
> the heart's geography, and words enact

the muscly parable of exploration: . . . The land is cruel
with existentialists, though lyric poets
wander through like crippled birds . . . but this map
is false and crazy . . . So we slog on
to navigate the fading resonance of our capacities
and find the luminescent map of armies
burning on the plain.

Tranter's recent poetry seems, like that of Wearne and, especially, Scott, to attempt to reclaim narrative and referentiality, but to varying degrees this element has always been present in his work. What remains certain is that his intense dissatisfaction with the way successful experiment solidifies into a rhetoric will ensure that his poetry continues relentlessly to explore all possibilities.

Poets whose work is marked by radical conceptions as to the nature of poetry itself include John Forbes, Martin Johnston (especially in his long sequence 'To the Innate Island') and Philip Hammial. Although Forbes is a surrealist this term now covers so many meanings that one is hesitant to use it. He is, if anything, a conservative surrealist concerned to generate poetry not from the unconscious (surrealism historically seems to have been rapidly hijacked by Freudianism) but from language itself. Many of the poems are best likened to abstraction in art where a removal of content places emphasis on the communicating medium (poetry) itself. In Forbes' terms a poem which relies on its content to support it infringes its own autonomy. To write poetry according to this credo places immense strain on a poet's self-critical faculties and it is one of the achievements of Forbes' best poems (such as 'Stalin's Holidays' and 'The Sorrowful Mysteries') that they seem right. They seem, as someone said, always to have been there. Another technique in Forbes' work to undermine the reader's desire for paraphrasable meaning is to stress the logical and meditative links within a long poem but to make its content seem spurious, as though it were a parody of laborious scholarly discourse. This technique, reminiscent of some of the work of the American poet John Ashbery, forms the basis of poems such as 'Topothesia' and 'Love's Body'. Other poems operate quite differently again. Part of Forbes' surrealism lies in the belief that culturally produced identities can be stripped away by the avoidance of the discourse these identities produce. One is left with the body as the ground of identity and many of Forbes' poems are rhapsodic celebrations of the body. 'Ode/"Goodbye Memory"', for example, concludes:

> Hello the yellow beach & the beauty
> that closes a book. Hello the suntanned skin
> & underneath that skin, the body.
>   Goodbye Memory!

The new poets began by mounting a strong (perhaps melo-dramatic) assault on the poetry of their forebears, confident that they had security in their talent and solidarity. They have avoided the usual fate of young rebels—of being courted and eventually absorbed by a flexible and pragmatic establishment. They have, arguably, avoided the next most undesirable fate of being agents whereby established and successful older poets are forced to rethink their aesthetics (as Robert Lowell was confronted by the poetry of Ginsberg or Verdi by the music of Boito). They have even been numerous enough to escape the fate of being a disgruntled ginger group on the rear deck of the serene ship of Australian poetry. They have, however, to some extent paid the penalty of indifference. Since they are Australian poets their fate lies within Australian literary history (a concept many of them, in the early 1970s, found intolerable) and since they are poets of demonstrable stature and achievement, it is increasingly difficult to understand ignorance of the full scope of their activity.

Notes

John Tranter's anthology is *The New Australian Poetry* (1979) but there are two other relevant anthologies. Robert Kenny and C. Talbot (eds), *Applestealers* (1974) contains the work of this group and has useful introductions detailing the history of the La Mama group. Thomas W. Shapcott, *Australian Poetry Now* (1970) was an initial sampling from the great outburst in poetic activity at the end of the 1960s and includes early work by many poets outside the scope of this chapter. Comments from the poets used in this chapter come from interviews collected in Martin Duwell, *A Possible Contemporary Poetry* (1982).

Little critical material of value is available on these poets. A number of interviews have, however, been published and the following studies of authors discussed here may be of use: Robert Kenny, 'A Secret Australia', introduction to Ken Taylor, *A Secret Australia: Selected and New Poems* (1985); James Tulip, 'New Writings of Kris Hemensley', *Southerly*, 37 (1977); Colin McDowell, 'John A. Scott: The Covering Cherub', *Scripsi*, 2, nos 2 and 3 (1983); *Scripsi*, 4, no. 3, which contains a series of articles devoted to *The Nightmarkets*; Michael Wilding, '"My Name is Rickeybockey": The Poetry of Robert Adamson and the Spirit of Henry Kendall', *Southerly*, 46, (1986); Trevor Q. Irwin, 'The Drama of the Separate Self in *The Mad Vibe*', *Australian Literary Studies*, 9 (1979); Andrew Taylor, 'John Tranter: Absence in Flight', *Australian Literary Studies*, 12, (1986).

Chapter 30

THE NOVEL

KEN GELDER

Like Britain and the United States, Australia has produced a small number of best-selling novelists writing fiction for an international audience: for example, Morris West and Thomas Keneally. Keneally's book *Schindler's Ark* (1982) won the Booker McConnell Prize in Britain; it has been referred to by Keneally himself as 'faction', a journalistic type of fiction which draws heavily on facts, provides verifiable scenarios and generally covers an historical moment of crisis. Recently, a significant number of Australian novelists have produced a comparable kind of 'faction' situated closer to home but also with internationalist aspirations. C. J. Koch's *The Year of Living Dangerously* (1978), Robert Drewe's *A Cry in the Jungle Bar* (1979), Bruce Grant's *Cherry Bloom* (1980), Blanche d'Alpuget's *Monkeys in the Dark* (1980) and *Turtle Beach* (1981) and Tony Maniaty's *The Children Must Dance* (1984)—all set in South-East Asia—are novels that juxtapose a journalistic style and a journalist's method of representation with a fascination for the exotic mysteries of other cultures that cannot be reported. The protagonists are often journalists themselves, attempting to represent those other cultures to Australians at home in a post-colonial era. Koch's *The Year of Living Dangerously* and d'Alpuget's *Monkeys in the Dark* are set in Jakarta at and after the fall of Sukarno in 1965: this is their historical moment of crisis, their central 'fact'. Events overpower the protagonists: the post-colonialists are baffled by a culture they report to Australians but cannot hope to understand themselves. In effect, these novels probe the limits of 'faction', turning to the unreportable, the mystical, the obscured.

Robert Drewe has commented on these recent examinations in the novel of the Austral-Asian experience: 'By 1975 we had had nearly a decade—since the end of the Menzies era—of politicians telling us that we were no longer an extension of Britain, as Menzies would have it, but intrinsically part of Asia.' In the fiction, the Australian is both part of and apart from the culture s/he works in: this contradictory position is also explored in Randolph Stow's *Visitants* (1979), set in the Trobriand Islands off the east coast of Papua (the first of Stow's novels set outside Western Australia). Drawing on (and undermining) the tradition of the verifiable report, Stow's *Visitants* offers a number of testimonies by a range of characters, including natives, about a climactic series of events, another moment of crisis. The visitants are in one sense the Australians abroad, setting up their house (to draw on Stow's metaphor) and evicting the tenants. This kind of fiction necessarily embroils itself in cross-cultural politics. Other examples of this kind of cross-cultural novel include Trevor Shearston's *Sticks that Kill* (1983) and *White Lies* (1986)), set in Papua New Guinea, and fiction set in the South Pacific, such as Thea Astley's *Beachmasters* (1985). A slightly different kind of Australian abroad, the tourist, has been analysed in Murray Bail's *Homesickness* (1980), an intricate novel that explores cross-cultural politics through that image of post-colonial cultural representation, the museum.

Australianness is marginalised in this recent fiction by cultures which are themselves, internationally speaking, on the margins. The natives of Papua, Jakarta, Astley's Kristi/Vanuatu, and so on, are here given a voice (albeit filtered through the dominant literary form of mainstream Western cultures, the novel). Recent writing in Australia has presented the voices of other marginalised groups *within* Australia: the migrant voice, for example. Judah Waten looked at the lives of Russian Jewish emigrés in Melbourne in *Distant Land* (1965); in *So far no further* (1971) he explored the differences between parent and child in the unstable migrant household: the migrant voice is not necessarily a unified one. The Jewish father in Waten's novel is a successful property dealer; in Morris Lurie's early comic novel *Rappaport* (1966) and its late sequel *Rappaport's Revenge* (1973), the hyperactive Jewish anti-hero is also a deal-maker, again operating in Melbourne. Immigrant life in Australian fiction may not be so successful. Rosa R. Cappiello's *Oh Lucky Country* (1981; trans. 1984) descends into 'the migrant's inferno', examining the present-day lives of Italian women immigrants struggling to make a living, exploited on the factory floor and elsewhere. These characters are buoyed up only by their intense energy and exuberance, and their occasional ability to exploit their exploiters. Cappiello presents a female network, a subculture of immigrant women living in Sydney's sleazier suburbs, Redfern and the Cross. Yet even here the migrant voice is denied its unity: the narrator, a writer, is different from the rest: she is 'not part of the gang . . .'

Migrants, too, are 'not part of the gang': as the theorist in Antigone Kefala's *The Island* (1984) tells the dreamy narrator, migrants are 'the people in between', no longer linked to their own culture and denied the comforts of Australianness. This position, however, may be advantageous: the theorist goes on to say that 'in order to understand history, one needed a type of vision that only people placed at the crossroads could provide'.

The migrant may be a kind of exile, with an exile's 'vision'. The notion of exile is central to David Foster's *The Pure Land* (1974) and *Moonlite* (1981), Thomas Shapcott's *White Stag of Exile* (1984) and David Malouf's *An Imaginary Life* (1978), which takes the Latin poet Ovid as its main character, banished from Rome to the outer reaches of civilisation (with clear links to Australia's position in the world). Exile and expatriation are issues in Malouf's first novel *Johnno* (1975) where, in the 1960s, the narrator Dante follows his friend Johnno to Europe to escape a life that had become 'easy, undemanding'. In London, Dante is sensitive to the criticism of his friends back home:

> Their resentment found its object in certain habits that they thought of as non-Australian and therefore a betrayal. Like calling the pictures the 'cinema' and sandshoes 'plimsols'. Impossible to tell them that all this was quite fortuitous. That I hadn't chosen 'silence, exile, cunning', had never left Australia in more than fact.

Dante aspires to the Joycean image of exile more than he may care to admit, however: as a schoolboy, he writes his address in Stephen Dedalus fashion, spiralling out from his provincial centre: '*Arran Avenue, Hamilton, Brisbane, Queensland, Australia, the World* . . . where do I really stand?'

Dante's 'fortuitous' exile in the 1960s disguises a deep nostalgia for Europe and the European scene. This same 1960s nostalgia is explored in, for example, C. J. Koch's *The Doubleman* (1985). Here, the Catholic narrator's 'enslavement to the past' is such that, for him, the Tasmanian landscape is constantly recoloured European: local suburbs 'didn't look like part of Hobart at all, but like places in Europe: Italian hill towns, perhaps', and so on. Yet while the narrators in *Johnno* and *The Doubleman* have looked nostalgically back to Europe, Malouf and Koch have themselves gained some reputation as regional writers, representing in their fiction the characteristics of their birthplaces. Postwar Brisbane is described at some length in *Johnno*, 'with its wooden houses perched high on tar-black stilts, its corrugated-iron fences unpainted and rusting, its outdoor lavatories, chicken houses, blocks of uncleared land where the weeds in summer might be six feet tall': the place is seen as un-kempt, provincial. In *The Doubleman,*'small, mountainous Tasmania' is set apart from the mainland, 'and this makes it different'. This difference is partly celebrated, partly apologised for: the regionalist here is not just separated from Europe but from Australia itself. Regionalism, in these novels at least, means isolation: the regional writer, also 'not part of the gang', is exiled twice over.

Malouf's more recent novel *Harland's Half Acre* (1984) presents the artist as an exile, with the *naif* painter and 'misfit' Frank Harland choosing finally to live isolated and alone on an island, 'public bagman, poor bugger and self-created outcast'. Frank Harland is perhaps a more humane version of the protagonist of Patrick White's massive novel *The Vivisector* (1970). Like Harland, Duffield is also a 'misfit': the novel takes the artist as its central figure, while showing the extent of his alienation from centralised modes of thinking. Several other contemporary novelists have drawn on the somewhat conventional image of the artist-as-misfit: in Elizabeth Jolley's novels, however, this convention is better served because the artist is always a woman. In *Mr Scobie's Riddle* (1983), Miss Hailey is a writer, eccentric and institutionalised: her handwriting is inscribed into the novel itself, yet her own manuscript remains unread. In *Miss Peabody's Inheritance* (1983) an Australian novelist, Diana Hopewell, sends letters and snippets of her work-in-progress to a lonely Englishwoman, 'Dotty Peabody'. Hopewell's new novel presents the familiar trip back to Europe for the sake of 'culture', and is about sexual frustration, sexual constraints; yet to Miss Peabody her writing offers 'strange, erotic, nocturnal adventures' from an Australia that would seem to represent liberation. Miss Peabody decides to emigrate but finds, on arrival, that the liberated novelist had spent her days confined to a hospital bed undergoing 'prophylactic operations'. The novel shows that 'utter liberation' is impossible, even in Australia. Indeed, Jolley's novels are often centred around places of confinement, institutions, to reinforce her point: the hospital, the girls' school, the nursing home.

The last two decades have produced a significant number of novels set in or around institutions, focusing on 'misfits' and examining the nature of confinement and the social structures that make such confinement seem necessary. The central characters in Dal Stivens' *A Horse of Air* (1970) and Walter Adamson's *The Institution* (1974; trans. 1976) are put into mental hospitals: Stivens' protagonist Harry Craddock, ornithologist and explorer, writes his journals there, which the novelist 'edits'. In Laurie Clancy's *A Collapsible Man* (1975), Paul O'Donohue's Catholic education leads him, finally, into a sanatorium. In Peter Carey's *Bliss* (1981), Harry Joy finds himself in a mental hospital run by Nurse Alice Dalton in an episode that is surely influenced by the American Ken Kesey's *One Flew Over the Cuckoo's Nest*. The institution novel may accommodate the fantastic, a kind of writing that reflects the madness of the protagonist: Adamson's novel is an example. Another example is David Ireland's early novel *The Flesheaters* (1972), set in an asylum named after an actual Sydney suburb, Merry Lands, presided over by the patriarch and law-maker O'Grady. The inmates are not insane but unemployed; or rather, society gives its unemployed the status of the insane, allowing them only to watch the world pass by their windows, classifying them as 'misfits' and sending them (without a choice) to society's margins. It is possible to read Merry Lands as Australia itself, similarly pushed to the margins of 'culture'; and yet from another point of view it stands at the centre of the world: 'The house stood on a tongue of land where three roads met. A set of traffic lights controlled the flows one way towards Africa and the other way in the direction of China.'

Patrick White has always been interested in the misfit: his scathing critiques of the dominant middle class have been accompanied by an interest in those people that class excludes, the down-and-outs, the eccentrics, the Aborigine, and in later novels especially, the landed gentry. *The Eye of the Storm* (1973), published the year White won the Nobel Prize for Literature, is, like Jolley's *Mr Scobie's Riddle*, partly a study of senility, taking as its central figure the dying aristocratic Elizabeth Hunter, institutionalised in her home. Like Jolley's novel again, *The Eye of the Storm* explores the freedom of memory, wandering at random through the past. With this free structure, Hunter evades the gaze of her pragmatic children who, like Mr Scobie's offspring, believe in institutions: in these novels, the younger generation has shifted politically to the right. In White's more recent *Memoirs of Many in One, by Alex Xenophon Demirjian Gray* (1986) the examination of the aged-as-misfit is extended, with the random wanderings of a senile (but still exuberant) mind inscribed into the novel itself. Alex is another of White's misplaced Sydney elite. About to be institutionalised under the direction of the caricatured German Dr Falkenberg, Alex has no future: she escapes into the 'womb' of the imagination, remaining (to mix the metaphor, as White often does) 'stranded . . . on the shores of memory'. Although presenting himself as editor of and a character in Alex's journals, White, also an ageing writer, makes the links between himself and his heroine explicit: 'Nothing is honest that isn't explicit.' White's identification with the female is perhaps consistent with the fluidity of his writing. Just as Alex in her random memories takes on a variety of roles, so White is able to 'act' female in a novel which, if nothing else, celebrates difference for its own sake: 'we, the explorers, stop at nothing . . . My range is immense'.

White's earlier novels had certainly explored character *differences*, setting up somewhat conventional oppositions in the text: for example, the intellectual Waldo Brown and his intuitive brother Arthur in *The Solid Mandala* (1966). In his later novels, this sort of opposition between the intellect and intuition is, rightly or wrongly, correlated with *sexual* difference, the difference between male and female; and since White has always valued the intuitive over the intellectual, he has turned his attention to the female in particular. In *A Fringe of Leaves* (1976), Ellen and Austin Roxburgh are distinguished in this way: Ellen is 'irrational', sensual and sensitive, while Austin is academic, inhibited, emotionally retarded. Speared by Aborigine after a shipwreck, his last words to Ellen sharpen White's focus: 'Ellen, you are different . . .' Ellen is the female misfit or 'miscreant', to use a term taken up in the novel to describe those living on the 'fringe' of society. Yet she is also, like Alex, an 'explorer' who stops at nothing. The novel takes her, alone, into the Australian bush, beyond civilisation, stripping her down to her 'core of being' (a process familiar to readers of White's earlier fiction). Ellen finally re-enters civilisation only to be judged eccentric by the (male) doctors and lawyers who examine her: the novel's appeal lies in the power of its sympathy for the female position.

White's most inventive novel to date, *The Twyborn Affair* (1979), takes the exploration of sexual difference several steps further. Each of the novel's three parts presents the same character in a different role; finally, it merges male and female, past and present, in one sentence. Here, perhaps, is its problem. Exploring the nature of sexual difference on the one hand, White is also inclined to resolve those differences under the glib unity of the androgynous ('the woman in the man and the man in the woman'). Indeed, it is White's nostalgia for unity that tempers his otherwise fluid and 'eccentric' writing and (for all his interest in misfits and miscreants living on the 'fringe') ultimately sends his own explorations in one direction only: to the centre.

In the 1970s especially, fiction in Australia explored sexuality and sexual difference in often explicit detail: to recall the remark from White's *Memoirs of Many in One*, 'Nothing is honest that isn't explicit.' The shorter fiction of Frank Moorhouse and Michael Wilding looked into the nature of heterosexual and homosexual relations; in David Ireland's *The Flesheaters*, the differences between the two are not at all clear, with the narrator refusing to be explicit about his or her own sex in a world that demands one thing or the other. Lesbian love has been the subject of Elizabeth Riley's *All that False Instruction* (1975), Beverley Farmer's *Alone* (1980) and Elizabeth Jolley's *Palomino* (1980)—indeed, most of Jolley's novels explore the sexual attraction one woman (usually older, more possessive) has for another. Looking into the heady drug-culture of Melbourne's inner suburbs in the 1970s, Helen Garner's popular *Monkey Grip* (1977) presents the heterosexual woman as sexually liberated, explicit about her own sexuality as she 'fucks' the man. Yet, by documenting the narrator Nora's growing dependence on the addict Javo, *Monkey Grip* also analyses the nature of (female) confinement and the need for security, for someone 'steady and complete'. Here, sexuality involves the kind of contradiction voiced by Nora when she confesses, 'I would like to love, and yet not to love': for all her sexual freedom, Nora remains fixed at the centre (to take up one of the novel's metaphors) while Javo, the unsteady and incomplete male, spins 'rootlessly' around her.

In *Puberty Blues* (1979), by Gabrielle Carey and Kathy Lette, the focus is on adolescent female sexuality, exploited in the machismo surfing subculture of Sydney's beach suburbs. The uneasy realm of childhood and adolescent sexuality is examined in the novels of Barbara Hanrahan, with their voluptuous and Gothic representation of corruption in the not-so-innocent leafy suburbs of Adelaide, a 'pastel-pink city' as it is called in Hanrahan's *The Frangipani Gardens* (1980). Gerald Murnane's *Tamarisk Row* (1974) and *A Lifetime on Clouds* (1976) look at the Catholic boy growing up in Melbourne, prohibited and inhibited, sexually awkward. The tortuous Catholic approach to sex is also presented in Thea Astley's *A Boat Load of Home Folk* (1968), through Father Lake's repressed homosexuality. The Catholic protagonists in C. J. Koch's novels are, by contrast, heterosexual and quietly confident in that heterosexuality: they suffer instead from their surrender to an ideological representation of the woman as Madonna on the one hand, and a destroyer of men on the other. Several of Thomas Keneally's novels directly explore the world of Catholicism: *Three Cheers for the Paraclete* (1969) is set in a Catholic seminary, another kind of institution with its own prohibitions on (sexual) behaviour. In *A Dutiful Daughter* (1971), however, Keneally examines adolescent sexuality in a place far removed from the prohibitions of the civilised world, the marshy coastal town of Campbell's Reach. Here, rigid Catholic symbols are juxtaposed with a more fluid notion of sexuality that seems radically unCatholic: 'There was a family out on Campbell's Reach . . . They had a little boy . . . When he's four he gets sick and begins to change into a girl.'

A Dutiful Daughter is a family saga with a difference, claustrophobic and introverted, merging the real with the fantastic, breaking the laws. The family saga has, of course, provided traditional material for the novel, allowing events to be represented realistically and in a straightforward chronological order. Olga Masters' *A Long Time Dying* (1985), for example, looks into the lives, loves and deaths of characters in a number of families living in a small outback town ('Cobargo was a terribly dull place in 1935 . . .'): its dedication 'To my brothers and sisters' declares the novel's interest in the family network specifically and humanity in general. For better or worse, Australia's best-known family saga is Colleen McCullough's *The Thorn Birds* (1977). The novel, centred around a Catholic family in the outback, draws heavily on Australia's more positive stereotypes (the resourceful woman, the loyal soldier), tracing the fortunes of illicit love: indeed, the prohibitions it places on behaviour parallel the prohibitions the fiction places upon itself, with its traditionalist interests. McCullough's novel takes 1915 as its point of origin; David Malouf's family saga *Harland's Half Acre* links the establishment of the Harland family to the origins of Australia itself. The novel celebrates the 'magnificent' patriarch and founder Clem Harland, placing him at the source of a genealogy that is quickly mythologised, at the 'site of the family's real and imaginary beginnings'. Peter Carey's *Illywhacker* (1985) merges the family saga with the picaresque: here, the traditionalist realist mode is upset by a narrator, Herbert Badgery, who is hopelessly unreliable and amazingly inventive. Another inventive scenario is presented in Rodney Hall's *Just Relations* (1982); like Masters' novel, this is not so much a family saga as a saga about families—living in the goldmining town of Whitey's Fall, threatened by market forces, abandoned by their children. *Just Relations* offers an ecological vision that turns to the country community for a celebration of humanity and nature that the city, obviously, cannot provide. The outback may have been conventionally represented as mysterious, even threatening: this image was behind Joan Lindsay's *Picnic at Hanging Rock* (1967), for example, and popularised in Peter Weir's film of that novel. Here, a schoolteacher and three senior girls from Mrs Appleyard's College for Young Ladies disappear (one girl is later found) at Hanging Rock near Mount Macedon in Victoria on St Valentine's Day, 1900: the date links the mystery of the outback to the imminent mystery of romance and sex, to be experienced beyond the college grounds as the girls venture 'out of the known dependable present and into the unknown future'. The 'unknown' outback is explored further in Gerald Murnane's experimental allegory *The Plains* (1982). Here, the narrator goes into the outback to examine 'those cultural differences between the plainsmen and Australians generally': the plains (the outback) become a place of difference, 'a land beyond the known land'.

Ecological issues are faced beyond the city in another kind of allegory, Michael Wilding's *Pacific Highway* (1982), with the narrator agonising over what is 'natural' and what is polluted: the novel looks at the impossibility of living together naturally, even in the most untouched places. In James McQueen's *Hook's Mountain* (1982), the protagonist Hook becomes a kind of ecological terrorist, waging war against logging companies, perched upon one of the last untouched outposts in the Tasmanian wilderness. Peter Carey's *Bliss* is less pessimistic: in a kind of ecological fairytale, Harry Joy flees the polluted city for the bush, where trees, love and stories flourish. This joyous kind of liberation—the escape into the bush—is also presented at the end of David Ireland's *A Woman of the Future* (1979). Here, Ireland acts as the 'editor' of Alethea Hunt's diaries, written from birth. As Alethea grows ('a healthy girl plant growing in the sun'), Ireland develops her metaphorical links with Australia itself, innocent, unsure about its position in the world, desired, different. Indeed, the novel endorses this difference through Alethea's closing transformation into a leopard (rather than, say, a kangaroo), leaving her as she runs off into Australia's interior. Here, in the bush, 'utter liberation' *is* possible and Alethea's progress, as 'an explorer of the human condition', might recall Alex's remarks in Patrick White's *Memoirs of Many in One*: 'we, the explorers, stop at nothing' (the explorers in both novels being women). But the sequel to *A Woman of the Future* returns to the city: the jaundiced *City of Women* (1981) is by contrast about confinement ('I stepped back, away from the window, grabbing for a curtain to pull across'), and the 'utter liberation' in the first novel is here denied.

David Ireland has been one of Australia's more experimental and ambitious novelists, often overturning narrative conventions: the use of a dog to narrate *Archimedes and the Seagle* (1984) rivals in inventiveness the narrator of Thomas Keneally's *Passenger* (1979), a foetus in the womb. Like White, Ireland has taken on the female voice, while the narrator of *The Flesheaters* is of indeterminate sex, male *or* female. By contrast, *The Unknown Industrial Prisoner* (1971) and *The Glass Canoe* (1976) explore the sexually definite world of the Australian male. The narrator of *The Glass Canoe* is appropriately named Meat Man and the novel is set in the Southern Cross Hotel, a 'waterhole' for men and a place (reversing the scenario in *City of Women*) from which the female is excluded. *The Unknown Industrial Prisoner* is set in another all-male domain, the Puroil oil refinery. This massive and rigorous novel shows Ireland at his most political and pessimistic: here, the dire need for revolution by the working class is contradicted by the representation of that class as divided against itself. In this novel, form reflects content: the fragmented nature of the working class is written into the novel's structure, a series of tiny and often unrelated scenes 'split, divided, fragmented', as the elusive narrator says, 'as I am split up and divided between page and character, speech and event, intention and performance'. With its black humour and bleak vision, this novel is more explicit than the work of some other Australian writers about its American influences, incorporating, for example, several passages out of the absurdist American novel *Miss Lonelyhearts* by Nathanael West to describe one of its main characters, the Samurai. The novel, like others by Ireland, moves away from the still dominant realist mode in Australian fiction, presenting events in a way that comes close to what has been called 'magic realism'. Indeed, Ireland himself has listed one of magic realism's major practitioners, Gabriel Garcia Marquez, as another influence—an influence 'fabulists' such as Peter Carey have also admitted to.

The Samurai in *The Unknown Industrial Prisoner* is an anarchist who can never bring himself to act: like the workers he represents, he too is divided against himself. The narrator of Ireland's first novel, *The Chantic Bird* (1968), is also an anarchist, living on the fringes of society, against authority and yet oddly paternal, protective and sentimental. Several other novels from the late 1960s and early 1970s also present anarchist figures who are certainly (to recall the remark from Cappiello's *Oh Lucky Country*) 'not part of the gang', committing solitary acts of violence against the establishment. In Peter Mathers' *Trap* (1966) the narrator, the right-wing but increasingly schizophrenic David David, is asked to investigate a part-Aboriginal, Jack Trap. As the novel goes on, David David surrenders to the influence of his radical subject:

> You go to him a reasonable conservative sort, a defender of established things, and you leave fermenting with ideas of—wait for it—anarchism, nihilism, Buddhism, all isms and wild, general revolt.

Jack Trap mounts an assault not only on the present-day establishment but also on established views of Australian history—and the very structure of the novel, with its many wild digressions and diversions, supports this anarchist vision. The presentation of two contradictory characters in the novel, Jack Trap and David David, perhaps recalls that earlier classic, George Johnston's *My Brother Jack* (1964), with protagonists also named Jack and David (Meredith). Mathers' second novel, *The Wort Papers* (1972), which contains a discreet allusion to *My Brother Jack*, is also about two brothers, the conservative Thomas Wort and the radical, unhinged Percy. Percy's motives are less directly political than Trap's; the novel is concerned with mining and undermining, parodying conventional Australian scenarios such as the trip into the outback (to 'Orebul Downs'), and representing Percy's anti-progress in a satiric and picaresque way that ends with Percy and his memoirs buried in 'the terrible below'. Like Ireland's Samurai, both Jack Trap and Percy Wort, for all their anti-establishment intentions, are nevertheless 'unable to co-operate with people': Australian fiction has yet to imagine revolution in its collective form.

Like Mathers' *Trap*—and in a not dissimilar picaresque way—novels such as David Malouf's *Johnno*, Thea Astley's *The Acolyte* (1972) and Barry Oakley's *Let's Hear it for Prendergast* (1970) have also looked into the dynamics of a relationship between the conventional and stable narrator and an unconventional and unstable or quixotic subject, with the narrator being destabilised along the way. Oakley's novel neatly expresses these dynamics when the narrator Morley remarks of his subject, 'whenever I'm tired Prendergast glows like a filament'. Morley's 'balance' and 'clear eye' contrast with the cartoon-anarchist behaviour of the mad, stork-like Prendergast, a character killed off in a spectacular climax (taking Melbourne's Exhibition Building with him) when his madness becomes too threatening. In a more elegiac way, Frank Hardy has explored a similar kind of relationship in *But the Dead are Many* (1975), with the narrator Jack becoming almost mystically involved with his subject, Communist Party member and suicide John Morel. In the more recent *The Obsession of Oscar Oswald* (1983), an American narrator finds himself obsessed with an introverted character who, it turns out, commits solitary acts of violence against capitalist oppressors in the tradition of (as the novel has it) Ned Kelly.

In Mathers' *Trap*, the anarchist is part-Aborigine. The Aborigine especially is 'not part of the gang', a marginalised voice, and in novels like David Ireland's *Burn* (1974) and Thomas Keneally's *The Chant of Jimmie Blacksmith* (1972), the Aborigine or part-Aborigine, alone and exploited, becomes a site for the manifestation of violence specifically directed against oppressors who are both capitalist and white. In Keneally's novel (drawing on a real incident in 1900), Jimmie begins by using his axe to build boundary fences for his white employers, endorsing their notions of property and ownership. As the novel goes on, however, that same axe takes on a very different role in a graphic assault on a white family that forms a mid-point climax. But Jimmie's vengeance is double-edged, both necessary and 'a yawning lie', an illusion. Afterwards, his 'brain heaving in contrary directions', Jimmie's character is split in a way that possibly reflects the nature of the novel itself with (to quote the Aboriginal novelist Colin Johnson) its 'white forms, Aboriginal content'. For Jimmie, those 'white forms' extend well beyond the boundary fences his white employers pay him to construct: they include even the form of the novel that contains him.

Several Aboriginal writers have themselves used the novel form, again often taking the Aborigine as a site of violence against white racism and white laws: Johnson's *Wild Cat Falling* (1965) and *Long Live Sandawara* (1979) and Archie Weller's *The Day of the Dog* (1981) are examples. The first novel of a 'nuclear trilogy', *Walg: A Novel of Australia* (1983) by 'B. Wongar' (in fact, the Yugoslav immigrant Sreten Bozic), places white violence against the Aborigines in the context of male violence against women: the narrator Djumala is a black woman and the title *Walg* means 'womb', linking Australia itself with the female. Colin Johnson has also written an historical novel, *Doctor Wooreddy's Prescription for Enduring the End of the World* (1983), about one of the last Tasmanian Aborigines who were, as a race, rendered extinct by the whites ('the end of the world')—this history, however, runs counter to the histories offered up by white Australia. The genocide of the Tasmanian Aborigines is also the subject of white writer Robert Drewe's novel *The Savage Crows* (1976). Drewe's protagonist Stephen Crisp, writing a thesis about the genocide to be published in 1976 ('in time for the centenary of the death of the last Tasmanian', the woman Truganini), is disturbed by his subject-matter. Crisp looks at the journals of George Augustus Robinson, a minister who came to Tasmania in the 1820s—and who also appears in Johnson's novel, presented (not surprisingly) somewhat less sympathetically. Robinson's project, the 'amelioration of the native race', is questioned, as Drewe's novel suggests, when he sees how natives are mistreated by the whites. Robinson is split by an ideological crisis, and his helplessness and the Aborigines' deterioration parallel the helplessness and deterioration in the present of Crisp himself, who makes a final desperate pilgrimage to Flinders Island, the last habitat for the first Tasmanians. Thea Astley's *A Kindness Cup* (1974) also uses a historical incident to explore racist attitudes towards Aborigines and the complexities of white guilt: set in the 1920s, it looks back to murders that took place some decades earlier, basing them around a real event that occurred at a place in Queensland known locally as The Leap.

Like Drewe's novel, Astley's dialogue with specific historical moments amounts to a representation of the past in the present: these novels assess the nature of white guilt, then and now, produced through the white Australians' treatment of the Aborigines. A number of novels have engaged in other dialogues with history by turning to other historical moments: for example, the turbulent and often unpleasant origins of white settlement in Australia. Thomas Keneally's *Bring Larks and Heroes* (1967), set as Keneally says in his opening note in 'the late eighteenth century', and Jessica Anderson's *The Commandant* (1975), set in Moreton Bay in 1830, both look into the harsh, authoritarian world of the penal colony. White's *A Fringe of Leaves* is set around Hobart Town and Moreton Bay in the 1830s, with Ellen Roxburgh frequently recalling her life in England before emigration and before marriage. In David Foster's *Moonlite*, set initially on a remote Scottish island, emigration to Australia in the early nineteenth century corrupts some people and purifies others. In this detailed, partly picaresque novel, the protagonist, leaving his 'pristine' origins and planning at the end to become 'a future premier' of New South Wales, belongs to the former category.

World War I provides another historical moment for contemporary novelists: Malouf's *Fly Away Peter* (1982) is an example. The defeat at Gallipoli still seems to be a significant event for fiction: Roger McDonald's *1915* (1979) and Jack Bennett's *Gallipoli* (1981), a rendering of the film of the same name by Peter Weir, have made sure of the event's place in white Australian mythology. In semi-autobiographical or retrospective novels like Keneally's *The Fear* (1965), Randolph Stow's *The Merry-Go-Round in the Sea* (1965) and Malouf's *Johnno*, World War II has less of a presence, not least because the protagonists are at the time young children. Stow's novel is another kind of family saga, set in Geraldton in Western Australia. At one point, Rick, a soldier himself, says that 'War is a different country': it happens elsewhere, not here in what C. J. Koch in *The Doubleman* has called 'the safe side of the world'. There have, incidentally, been few novels written about the Vietnam War, probably because few novelists have explored that particular 'different country' at first hand: Kenneth Cook's *The Wine of God's Anger* (1968), Hugh Atkinson's *The Most Savage Animal* (1972) and William Nagle's popular *The Odd Angry Shot* (1975) are examples. For a much fuller discussion of war novels, see chapter 21, 'War Literature 1890s to 1980s'.

A novelist's dialogue with history may take place on a more personal level, looking back not to major events in history but to the lives of obscure individuals. In Tim Winton's *Shallows* (1984), set on the Western Australian coast, Cleve Cookson finds himself involved in the whaling journals of Nathaniel Coupar written in the 1830s. In Janine Burke's *Second Sight* (1986), the protagonist Lucida writes a history of Lydia O'Shea, 'a woman of the turn of the century', a utopian socialist: like the protagonist in Drewe's *The Savage Crows*, Lucida is profoundly affected by her subject. Recent writing by women especially has looked back to obscure(d) *female* lives, lives often made obscure by the dominant presence of the male. Jean Bedford's *Sister Kate* (1982) is a good example. It turns to the sister of Ned Kelly, a woman marginalised in a household full of men and later ignored altogether in a legend about men for men. Bedford has said of the novel, 'I've tried to show . . . how women, then and now, have always been left out of history': Kate, a character with great possibilities, is finally crushed by the legend of the Kelly gang as it grinds into motion, leaving her behind. Novels like Barbara Hanrahan's *Annie Magdalene* (1982) and Margaret Barbalet's *Blood in the Rain* (1986)—both set in Adelaide—focus specifically on women obscured by (or in) history. Hanrahan's novel takes its epigraph from Virginia Woolf's *A Room of One's Own*:

> For all the dinners are cooked; the plates and cups washed; the children sent to school and gone out into the world. Nothing remains of it all. All has vanished. No biography or history has a word to say about it. And the novels, without meaning to, inevitably lie . . . All these infinitely obscure lives remain to be recorded.

Blood in the Rain is set during World War I and the Depression years; other novels which take up the obscure(d) life of the woman around or just after the Depression include Glen Tomasetti's *Thoroughly Decent People* (1976) and Nene Gare's *A House with Verandahs* (1980).

Women's writing in recent years has often rigorously addressed women's issues and analysed the female position. In an early example, Elizabeth Harrower's *The Watch Tower* (1966), marriage is represented as imprisonment for the woman in a man's world. The protagonist, Clare, is offered security in the 'beautiful house' of her husband and employer Mr Shaw, a petty capitalist who runs a factory in Sydney. Shaw's 'power to inflict punishments' on women is consistent with his role in capitalism with the woman as employee: unable to see outside that role, Shaw imposes his petty vision onto Clare and her sister, 'to have us see everything as he sees it'. In Jessica Anderson's lyrical and melancholy novel *Tirra Lirra by the River* (1978), the central character Nora Porteous, returning to live in Queensland, looks back to her own imprisoning marriage in the Depression years. Like Clare, she responds with 'passive resistance' ('Beneath my . . . submission a sour rebellion lay'), but eventually she leaves her husband and goes to London: 'nobody could stop me'. Nora's life after marriage is buoyed up by a support network of women which she recollects, ageing and alone at last in her Queensland home.

As Sara Dowse has noted in her novel exploring women's issues in the male-dominated political arena in Canberra, *West Block* (1983), there are always two worlds, 'His world, and hers'. There are also two stories, his story and her story. In Kate Grenville's novel *Lilian's Story* (1985), the focus is on that other world of women: the novel tells the story of Lilian Una (based on the real figure of Sydneyite Bea Miles), born on 'a wild night in the year of Federation'. Lilian is also 'not part of the gang': her difference is signified by her size and her eccentricities, which get her institutionalised for a while. But Lilian's 'madness' is a cause for celebration: 'her remarkable story' shows that 'utter liberation', if impossible, can at least be dreamed about. In this novel, a woman tells *her* story; and yet, to paraphrase Clare in *The Watch Tower*, men still want women to see everything as they see it. As Ellen Roxburgh realises in White's *A Fringe of Leaves*, 'the whole of her uneventful life had been spent listening to men telling stories': her own story is obscured, while his story (that is, *history*) remains the dominant mode.

Notes

For survey articles on recent Austral-Asian novels, see Helen Tiffin, 'Asia and the Contemporary Australian Novel', *Australian Literary Studies*, 11 (1984) and Robert Drewe, '*A Cry in the Jungle Bar*: Australians in Asia', *Meridian*, 5 (1986). Other relevant survey articles are Margaret Smith, 'Australian Woman Novelists of the 1970s: A Survey' in Carole Ferrier (ed.), *Gender, Politics and Fiction: Twentieth-Century Australian Women's Novels* (1985); Kerryn Goldsworthy, 'Feminist Writings, Feminist Readings: Recent Australian Writing by Women', *Meanjin*, 44 (1985); and Laurie Hergenhan, 'War in Post-1960s Fiction: Johnston, Stow, McDonald, Malouf and Les Murray', *Australian Literary Studies*, 12 (1985).

Critical studies of recent novels include D. R. Burns, *The Directions of Australian Fiction, 1920-1974* (1975); Nancy Keesing (ed.), *Australian Postwar Novelists: Selected Critical Essays* (1975); K. G. Hamilton (ed.), *Studies in the Recent Australian Novel* (1978); and Helen Daniel, *Liars: Australian New Novelists* (1988). There have been a number of book-length studies of Patrick White, too numerous to list here. Other book-length studies of contemporary novelists include Helen Daniel, *Double Agent: David Ireland and His Work* (1982) and Anthony J. Hassall, *Strange Country: A Study of Randolph Stow* (1986).

The novel can certainly be popularised through film. Novels written since 1965 which have been filmed include Thomas Keneally's *The*

Chant of Jimmie Blacksmith, C. J. Koch's *The Year of Living Danger-
ously* and Joan Lindsay's *Picnic at Hanging Rock* (both filmed by Peter
Weir), William Nagle's *The Odd Angry Shot*, Helen Garner's *Monkey
Grip*, Peter Carey's *Bliss*, Gabrielle Carey and Kathy Lette's *Puberty
Blues* and Peter Corris' *The Empty Beach* (1983). For a discussion of
the links between film and some contemporary novels, see Graeme
Turner, *National Fictions: Literature, Film and the Construction of
Australian Narrative* (1986).

Chapter 31

Mythmaking in modern drama

Peter Fitzpatrick

While the dedication and cussedness of a large number of writers, performers and theatre people through the preceding decades had attempted to give the lie to the popular impression that there was no such thing as an indigenous theatre tradition in Australia, it was not until the late 1960s that such efforts gathered real momentum. The reluctance of theatre managements to depart from the proven paths of period classics and English repertory, and of governments to accept a major responsibility for the funding of initiatives in the theatre, helped to ensure that even popular successes like Ray Lawler's *Summer of the Seventeenth Doll* (1955) and Alan Seymour's *The One Day of the Year* (1960) were remarkable more for their singularity and achievement against the odds than for any blazing of decisive new trails.

But whatever the strength of these practical inhibitions, there appear to have been other reasons for the pattern of promise and frustration that has characterised the development of Australian drama. Not surprisingly those playwrights who sought to establish the distinctiveness of their work from the imported models did so by creating images of the distinctiveness of their culture—its concerns, its rituals, its people, and their styles of talk. The available social stereotypes (in particular 'the shepherds going mad in lonely huts' which J. M. Synge had recommended to Esson as such promising material for drama) created some problems, however. In a dominant dramatic mode devoted to plausible conversations in seemingly real interiors, the elemental conflicts of the outback and the laconic solitariness of their protagonists proved awkward. *The Doll*, which brings its supposedly anti-sentimental males from North Queensland to deal with the emotional claims of four women in an inner suburb of Melbourne, and *The One Day of the Year*, where the male veterans of two wars preserve the rituals of Anzac Day incongruously in an inner suburb of Sydney, meet the problem in a similar way. Not only do they transpose the traditional systems of value into a context which the audience can accept as familiar; they are also able to suggest the reality of these received stereotypes by dramatising their obsolescence. Both are able to define patterns of psychological interaction in the way that most easily fits the conventions of the naturalistic proscenium stage—by the things that people say, and the subtextual implications of the things which they are unable or unwilling to say.

When the 'new wave' of the late 1960s began to gather momentum, it was not the result of generous government subsidy, nor of recognition by the commercial and establishment theatre, though these things of course became very important in sustaining it. The plays from the alternative 'rough-theatre' companies which created that momentum were characterised by an explosion of talk, in a rich and recognisable vernacular that vigorously proclaimed its difference from the models and decorums of the Anglophile theatre. Shows like Boddy and Ellis's *The Legend of King O'Malley* (1970), Hibberd and Romeril's *Marvellous Melbourne* (1970), and Barry Oakley's *The Feet of Daniel Mannix* (1971) and *Beware of Imitations* (1973) brought a boots-and-all style of political cartooning to the rogue's gallery of Australian history. There was little room for proscenium arches or classical unities; instead there was increasingly a fascination with language which was new in its assertive Australianness and its exploitation of a crumbling censorship, and yet traditional enough in its assumptions about the ways in which words can communicate. The playwrights' impulse was customarily satiric, but their delight in styles of talk most commonly ensured that they celebrated the culture at least as much as they castigated it. Even in plays like Alex Buzo's *Norm and Ahmed* (1969) and David Williamson's *The Removalists* (1971), where the crudity of the language is related directly to a capacity for horrifying violence, there is a generous measure of comic relish in its vitality.

Monk O'Neil's eulogy to his dead mate Mort in Jack Hibberd's *A Stretch of the Imagination* (1971) epitomises that pleasure in the way that words from very different orders of language can be made to dance together in joyful discord:

You're a tower of strength to me, Mort. Two minutes of silence for Mort, a man who was once the life of the party, who always did the right thing, a digger who has ceased to shovel, an Einstein of the stab pass and brindle chuck, a knuckler of pansies who always wore the pants, old silver-tongue, a man's man, the first off Gallipoli, one of nature's policemen. Mate.

The subjects of Monk's praise are ostensibly the doubtful virtues of the stereotypical Australian bonehead, but it is less Monk's mastery of the stab pass, stoush and spew that is celebrated here than his verbal agility, and the cultural pluralism that it implies. The play's layers of self-parody are underscored by an interplay of crude and formal language which seems to assert that it is possible, and rich, to be a larrikin intellectual; Monk seems anxious to assure us that, while he may be polysyllabic, he is most definitely no pansy.

Stretch is the most acclaimed of a surprising number of monologue plays which appeared in Australian theatres during the 1970s. The number is surprising, though, only by the measure of the stage tradit- ions of other cultures, where the one-man show, for all the attract- iveness to managements of its relative cheapness and portability, has normally been a very minor tributary of the dramatic mainstream. In Australia the vogue may be largely ascribed to the playwrights' fascination with styles of talk, and with the way in which a speaker's choice of register implies the cultural values which determine the preference for a particular social role. The virtuoso talkers include the brother haunted by received ideas in Ron Blair's *The Christian Brothers* (1976), the old trouper Noah Hope in Hibberd's *A Man of Many Parts* (1980), the transvestite elocutionist O'Brien in Steve J. Spears' *The Elocution of Benjamin Franklin* (1976) and Sylvia the drag queen in Peter Kenna's *Mates* (1975); they have in common a certain professional or stereotypical garrulousness, a defensive preoccupation with their sexuality, and the fact that they are male (the actress Jocasta Vaudeville-Smith in Hibberd's 1981 *Mothballs* is a rare exception among the monologuists). In all these respects they may fairly be said to represent the conversational emphases of a new wave which became the mainstream.

The dominant talker on the Australian stage in the 1970s, when the local product at last established its place in the repertoire of the establishment theatre, was the ocker. Male, characteristically young, and usually middle-class, the ocker was a violator of all decorums, big in his talk and his drinking, and (by his own graphic but mostly very suspect account) a pretty awesome sexual performer as well. The ocker was more than just a brash vulgarian, however. He customarily liked to show himself as more complicated, verbally and intellectually, than he seemed. Though his currency could be put down in part to that recurrent Australian cultural phenomenon 'the new nationalism'—he was, from the top of his head to the soles of his thongs, assertively and outrageously an Aussie—the ocker may be seen as epitomising the concern with cultural definition through conversational style which was so prevalent in Australian theatres during this period. Even Kenny Carter, the motor mechanic in *The Removalists* who defines himself as 'just a beer-swilling slob', makes it clear that he is crude by choice, and not by nature or necessity. The affluent professionals who parade their mid-life crises in Williamson's *Don's Party* (1971) are still more assertive about the degree of self-consciousness in their role-playing. The main focus of their interaction involves the rituals of male sexual proving; but when Simon, the Liberal-voting stooge and isolate at the party, expresses his disgust 'that university-educated people could be so bloody uncouth', he quickly finds that there are other areas of defensiveness and competitiveness as well:

> *Mal:* Well he is a fucking peabrain.
> *Simon:* Cut that out!
> *Mal:* What?
> *Simon:* If you have to resort to bad language to express yourself then you can't have much of a vocabulary!
> *Mal:* Vocabulary? I've forgotten more words than you've ever learned! What's the meaning of evanesce?
> *Simon:* Really.
> *Mal:* Pendulous, coruscate, ochlocracy, paplionaceous.
> *Simon:* I don't have to indulge in word games.
> *Mal:* What's the meaning of didactic?
> *Simon:* In the manner of a teacher.
> *Mal:* Aha! Teased you out with an easy one.

In the plays of Williamson, and in those of writers like Alex Buzo and Barry Oakley too, the ocker-figure aged with the playwright and moved up-market in educational terms. The habit of strategic role-playing developed into a capacity for irony and self-mockery of an increasingly sophisticated kind in accomplished performers like Paul, the English lecturer of Oakley's *Bedfellows* (1975), Frank, the writer-figure in Oakley's *Marsupials* (1979), Andrew, the novelist in Williamson's *What if You Died Tomorrow* (1973), Russell, the history professor in Williamson's *A Handful of Friends* (1976), and Edward in Buzo's *Martello Towers* (1976), to whom no profession would seem sufficiently challenging.

Such masters of the game of put-down and send-up set the tone, and the conversational agenda, of the plays they are in; their skill in being disarmingly wry ensures a degree of ingratiating comedy, even when the action exposes the moral vacuum which sometimes lies behind their cleverness. They exert a powerful influence, too, over the structure and scope of the action. The limits of their self-awareness tend to define the degree to which the plays can penetrate the surface patterns of manipulativeness and multiple role-playing. In the work of Buzo and Oakley the private self of men who have built their lives on defensive irony is understood to exist somewhere, but beyond the range of words and action; the playwright is subject to the same constraints as the character to avoid anything that cannot be squeezed into a joke, and to call no powerful emotion by its name. Williamson, with his great skill in charting the subtleties of social interaction, presents people who seem no more than the sum of the public roles they play; the horror for them is not that they can never be wholly themselves, but that there is no centre of self to be known.

Perhaps plays which are primarily about words are, by their very nature, predisposed towards a circular, or at least indeterminate plot; the concern for the reflection of a particular culture similarly reduced the importance of purposeful action. When the words reflect a culture as practised in deceptions and self-deceptions as the one we meet in these plays, the tendency is compounded. It has become a cliché of commentaries on the Australian cinema of the 1970s that in its delight in atmospherics and period reproductions it was inclined to be weak on plot; Australian plays, though their focus has characteristically been urban and contemporary, are liable for different reasons to a similar accusation.

David Williamson's phenomenal success has been built, in part, on what he has called his 'symbiotic relationship' with the educated middle-class who patronise the major subsidised theatres. His plays have mirrored for those audiences social rituals and personal anxieties which they recognise as their own, and his detractors have seen Williamson's sureness of touch in providing theatre that people really want to see as a mark of the artistically (and even morally) second-rate. The unfairness and inaccuracy of such disparagement is clear enough when one examines the premises from which it proceeds, and the substance of the plays themselves; it leaves out of account the strength of Williamson's craft as a comic writer, and the power of the images of contemporary Australian urban life which he has shaped into myth. Williamson largely defined the terms for what was perceived through the 1970s as the mainstream Australian play. It was a kind of art which reflected, in its satiric emphasis and its focus on the narrow but revealing situation, the theatre of rough-house revue in which it had its roots; the satire coexisted oddly but pleasurably with a celebration of cultural quirks and awfulness, the angle of interest primarily concerned the conversational interactions of the male, and the lines of significant action were inclined to lead backwards or nowhere.

The tendency to circularity or irresolution in the structure of Williamson's work is evident in those early plays which offer something that looks like a conventional denouement. In *The Removalists* the violence culminates in Kenny's death, while *Jugglers Three* takes a number of relationships to a point of conclusion or perilous restoration, but both plays end with very powerful images of stylised interaction—the ritual slugging-match between the two policemen in *The Removalists* and the obsessive ping-pong game in *Jugglers Three*—which fade slowly to blackout to leave the impression that the real conflicts defy resolution. That sense becomes a structural principle in *The Perfectionist* (1982), a play about marital negotiation which invites us all to share, with a mixture of joyful recognition and ruefulness, in the realisation that the balancing of personal claims to fulfilment against domestic obligations is a messy and finally pretty hopeless business. Barbara's introductory monologue sounds the note of comic failure before she guides us through the flashbacks which detail just how funny it was; at the end of the tale of role-playing and role-swapping, she anticipates the future in a speech to Stuart which makes it clear that unresolved conflict is the nature of the game:

> O.K. So it's going to be a bunfight! You're always going to think your career is suffering the most and I'm going to think it's mine and we're going to fight about that for the rest of our lives. There aren't any easy solutions—you just have to hope there are enough good moments to make the whole hassle worthwhile.

The vision is a singularly dispiriting one; but there is a quality of generosity in Williamson's mode of satire here, built on the audience's perception that the play is not merely mocking but self-mocking, which maintains a spirit of collaboration and reconciliation to the end.

Buzo's early work shows a similar potential for tension between the impulses to exposure and celebration, and between an essentially non-linear structure and the completion of the story-line. Despite the expulsion or death of the malcontent Jacko in *The Front Room Boys*, the barren rites of office life which the play depicts in its twelve monthly parts continue inexorably to be performed in the same way to a new calendar. The primary interest is in the patterns of cliché which deform all relationships; in *Rooted* (1969) Pinteresque litanies of triteness like the following are tokens of emptiness, and of the impenetrability of surfaces.

> *Richard:* You've got no charisma.
> *Diane:* You've got a complex.
> *Richard:* You need a rest.
> *Diane:* A complete break.
> *Richard:* Rejuvenation.
> *Diane:* Regeneration.
> *Richard:* Wake up to yourself.
> *Diane:* Wake up and live.
> *Richard:* You'll be all right.
> *Diane:* You see what we mean?
> *Bentley:* Yes.
> *Richard:* Take the bull by the horns.
> *Diane:* Grab the nettle.
> *Richard:* Face the facts.
> *Diane:* You'll be all right.
> *Bentley:* Yes, I'll be all right. I'll take action.

Language in such a context becomes a game that subsumes its players. Dead metaphor after dead metaphor ripples outward from a lame or dishonest idea, as Buzo focuses all attention on his retardation of the line of plot. Unlike Williamson's art that conceals art, Buzo's theatre offers the action directly as a symbolic structure; it also develops a more overtly moral dimension to its satire, by presenting perceptions of the culture in the form of comic nightmare.

There were exceptions during the 1970s to the preoccupation with cultural definition through talk, and its corollaries in terms of structure and the emphasis on male interaction, which represented the rule; the plays of Dorothy Hewett and Patrick White were the most conspicuous of them in the establishment theatre, while John Romeril's commitment to the principles of agit-prop with Melbourne's Australian Performing Group gave his work a distinctive direction and breadth of scope. White's strength in swimming against the theatrical tide had been demonstrated before, in plays like *The Ham Funeral* (1961) and *The Season at Sarsaparilla* (1962); two very potent parables of contemporary life, *Big Toys* (1977) and *Signal Driver* (1982), show similar disdain for the theatre of conventional illusions. Hewett's early plays focus on the figure of the exceptional woman. The passionate histories of her golden girls characteristically take the shape of the whole life, as in *The Chapel Perilous* (1972) and *The Tatty Hollow Story* (1974), or the experience of successive generations, as in *Bon-bons and Roses for Dolly* (1972) and *The Golden Oldies* (1977). The encompassing of a life as a dramatic subject suits Hewett's readiness to be adventurous in matters of form—devices like the cross-gender dressing and parodic effigies in *The Chapel Perilous* draw attention to the way the story is being told as well as to its substance.

By the late 1970s a number of writers expressed the view that the wave had passed, and that theatre in Australia was in a trough. Partly this feeling was a response to a general economic down-turn; reductions in subsidies appeared to produce a situation where the rich establishment theatre got bigger while the poor alternatives disappeared. But perhaps that was too simple an equation. The demise of the Australian Performing Group in Melbourne, for example, had at least as much to do with a loss of direction and energy (of which in its heyday it had had plenty) as a lack of funds (which had always been in very short supply). And the loss of impetus was also related to the kinds of plays that were being written, or at least those that were being fostered by the major companies. The concern for defining what was distinctive about the culture, and the middle-class white male figures who had been its principal vehicle, seemed rather to have run out of steam. Accordingly, the interest of the 'second wave' playwrights like Louis Nowra, Stephen Sewell and Ron Elisha in subjects that were conspicuously non-parochial was hailed as in itself the basis for another renaissance. The most significant development of the last decade, however, has not been internationalism at the level simply of locale, though initially that seemed the most striking point of departure from the mainstream. Nowra's *Inner*

Voices (1976), which took as its subject the education in language and power of Ivan VI of Russia, *Visions* (1978), set in turn-of-the-century Paraguay, and *The Precious Woman* (1980), located in a province of Northern China, established the pattern. Sewell's *Traitors* (1979), which dealt with factionalism in Stalinist Russia, and *Welcome the Bright World* (1982), set in Germany in the 1970s, were followed by Elisha's *Einstein* (1983) and *Pax Americana* (1984). The tendency seemed to be confirmed by the readiness of well-established writers like Buzo and Hibberd to deal in a little exotica themselves: Buzo in *Makassar Reef* (1978) and *Marginal Farm* (1984), where the conflicts are centred on an Indonesian port and a Fijian sugar plantation; and Hibberd in his adaptation of Gogol, *The Overcoat* (1977).

The apparent rejection of parochialism was less decisive than it seemed, however. Nowra's concern with pressure points of cultural transmission and interaction, for example, had clear metaphorical implications for Australian society which weakened the force of the contrast with the preceding wave; and for the other playwrights, too, the new preparedness to look outwards from the island could also be seen as a new tactic for looking within. In Buzo's excursions into foreign parts the primary focus is on the expatriate Australians anyway, as the unfamiliar culture throws into relief qualities of emotion which on home ground might be strategically disguised. As in those plays set in Australia which deal with the impact of people from other countries on aspects of the local culture, Buzo's 'foreign' outsiders tend to be confined to impenetrable stereotype, and to the functions of catalyst and contrast; a similar point could be made about John Romeril's *The Floating World* (1974), where Les Harding's nightmare memories of Changi are theatrically reinforced in ways which powerfully exploit the cliché of Asian inscrutability. The avoidance of parochialism may be seen in general as a modified form of the quest for definition of the local culture, rather than a rejection of those lines of interest. Nowra and Sewell, in their most recent work, have in fact focused on specific aspects of their own society, in the context of its relationship to wider patterns of political and cultural influence: Nowra in *Inside the Island* (1980), *Spellbound* (1982), *Sunrise* (1983) and *The Golden Age* (1985); and Sewell in *The Blind Giant is Dancing* (1983) and *Dreams in an Empty City* (1986).

The most significant characteristic shared by these plays of the 1980s—and indeed by the recent work of Williamson, Buzo and Hewett as well—is a new kind of concern with plot, and the mythic or ideological structures which might give it shape. At the same time there is a new concern, too, with the perspectives which were largely excluded from the plays based on the parody of verbal styles—the perspectives of the reflective, the emotionally open, and, in particular, the female. That proposition sounds like a value judgement. It need have no relation, though, to the quality, or the theatricality, or even the supposed worthiness, of the plays in themselves. Not only is there many a slip (and, in the theatre, many an unknown factor) between the ambition and its realisation; all plays are obviously the products of stringent conditions of choice in the writing and the performance which confer particular privileges and entail corresponding limits of scope. The relevant distinction between the published plays of the 1980s and those of the preceding decade is not between more or less conservative models of dramatic form, or even between different degrees of parochialism, but between different kinds of myth-making. Where the plays of the earlier period are characterised by a kind of mythologising which is concerned with the ways in which we perceive our culture, the recent work of Sewell, Nowra, Hewett and Williamson reflects a quest for myths which might help us to understand the forces which have produced that culture. This kind of mythic perspective is one which effectively imposes linear plot.

David Williamson's recent work has moved away from the model of sustained conversations within the unities of time and (usually) place which characterised his early work; while the fascination with the social strategies of role-playing remains, plays like *Travelling North* (1979), *The Perfectionist*, and *Emerald City* (1987) work episodically in ways that seem to reflect the playwright's experience in writing for the cinema. Instead of the specificity of location and solid naturalistic decor that visually amplified the class and interests of Kenny or Don or Andrew and their mates, Williamson develops an impressionistic sense of place based on particular cultural polarities. In *Travelling North* and *Emerald City* he contrasts the damp and sober south with the balmy north, where the living seems easy: in the first, Frank and Frances travel north into the tropics, in search of some space for the love they have found late in their lives; while in the latter play Colin, like Williamson, takes the yellow brick road to Sydney not only because it is warmer there but also to advance his flourishing career as a script-writer.

In neither case is the dichotomy as simple as it seems, however. The north has strong associations with death and decay in *Travelling North*, while at least in the oppressive Melbourne winter babies are born, and people confront critical choices about the ways they are to live their lives. The stereotype of Melbourne's staidness is balanced in *Emerald City* with Colin's view that Sydney's stereotypical hype and hedonism is a gaudy cover for hollowness and deceit. In both cases Williamson is able to find terms for a spiritual journey which are grounded in the substance of the plot and yet can sustain the moral complexity warranted by his subject. He also draws on some symbolic associations which lie deep in the mythology of popular culture; only in *Summer of the Seventeenth Doll* has the juxtaposition of north and south been handled with this sort of ironic suggestiveness. Both plays support the iconography of place in ways which further draw attention to the shaping of a structure: though *Emerald City* does little with its second-level mythic framework—as an Oz version of another Oz story—the systematic use of music in *Travelling North* gives further resonance to the quest of the play's people for order and romance. A recent development of the latter approach is evident in Michael Gow's *Away* (1985), where the north-south polarity is powerfully underscored by music, particularly in the play's final sequence set to the romantic sweep of Mendelssohn; like Williamson, Gow uses the suggestiveness of musical themes to move the play emotionally beyond the limits imposed by the language of caricature. Gow also establishes a secondary structure for the action in his play's network of references to Shakespeare, which very subtly shifts the emphasis from the roles people play in strategic conversation to those they dream and imagine.

Dorothy Hewett has increasingly turned to musical effects as a means of penetrating social and accountable surfaces, but in her work the presentation of the irrational is given a distinctive shape by her interest in folklore and the forms and rites of magic. *Joan* (1975), *Pandora's Cross* (1978) and *The Man from Mukinupin* (1979) attest to the way in which esoteric systems of knowledge underpin the richly theatrical flights of fancy. Alex Buzo's *Marginal Farm* draws on a different order of folklore when it makes its sudden late transition from a relatively straightforward play about the collision of cultures into a disorienting fable; the time-jump which depicts the consequences of Toby's decision to abandon her own culture for the Fijian exposes her as a 'crone' with a basket of apples, the epitome of a fairytale wicked queen. *Marginal Farm* offers an extreme, though not particularly coherent, instance of the imposition of a mythic superstructure on the ostensible action.

Though Nowra and Sewell shared from the beginning an articulate disdain for the comedy of bad manners, they represent quite different approaches to the new form of myth-making. Sewell is a Marxist, and his cultural perceptions are within a causal and historical framework; Nowra's interest is in primary oppositions of good and evil, innocence and experience, which resist all rational explanations and received structures. Location for Sewell is important, since there are networks of influence to be charted. *Traitors* and *Welcome the Bright World* establish their historical credentials in considerable detail; in the plays set in contemporary Australia, *The Blind Giant is Dancing* and *Dreams in an Empty City*, the factor of recognition is as crucial in an audience's response as it is in Williamson's work, since the convincingness of the analysis rests on the perceived authenticity of the sample. Nowra's plays, despite their varying degrees of cultural particularity, are all set, in one sense, in the place which he defined as the 'real' context of *Inner Voices*—'the country of the mind'.

Nowra's vision of the heart of darkness, while it makes its meanings metaphorically and deals in recognitions that undermine or mock the structures of civilised interaction, has characteristically depended on a historical or pseudo-historical framework to give it shape. His own sense of his work is that it consists of intersecting 'coils'; this seems in itself to reflect that need to frame potentially anarchic perceptions within a coherent system, and it corresponds to a dialectic which is felt as a dramatic tension in all his plays. The fascination with forms of oppression and processes of corruption which was evident in *Inner Voices* remains in *Inside the Island, The Precious Woman* and *The Golden Age,* but in those plays the emphasis is on the human capacity to survive intolerable knowledge. *Inside the Island* and *The Golden Age* develop this concern in peculiarly Australian images of suppression and denial, and offer a distinctive form of the myth of the great emptiness.

Sewell's ideological commitment provides its own system, and even contains its own dialectic. But the kind of myth-making which his theatre represents is considerably more complex than any routine demonstration of a political hypothesis. Both *Blind Giant* and *Dreams in an Empty City* present visions of reality that merge into nightmare; the super-real, manic quality of the world which Sewell depicts reflects his perception of the wild irrationality of the capitalist system itself. Through the multiplicity of scenes depicting power plays at all levels of public and private life, Sewell develops not only his case for the real indivisibility of the personal and the political, but also his own vision of the heart of darkness. It is that darkness which the crusading left-winger Allan Fitzgerald comes to acknowledge in *Blind Giant* as the only reality, and in which he finds a self-evident argument for self-hatred and a cynical quest for power; and it is that darkness which Wilson, the corrupt prototype of capitalist high civilisation in *Dreams*, tries to force the idealist Chris to see as they look together across the empty city at night. The Marxist ideology which affirms that the darkness is redeemable is not in itself much help in providing a structure to contain intuitions of that chaos. Accordingly Sewell draws in these two plays on myths which come from the traditional Christian culture, and places the war between the classes and between rival political models within a Manichean framework. In *Blind Giant* it is the Faust story, and Mephistopheles is (almost) everywhere; *Dreams in an Empty City* presents the temptation, triumph and sacrifice of Chris in terms of the story of Christ. It is a risky ploy, precisely because the myths invoked are so familiar; but it works, very powerfully. Both the panoramic nature of the political vision, and the acute sense that things fall apart, place the structure of the plays under enormous pressure. The centre holds, though only just.

Playwrights like these have in a sense been set free by the shift away from a preoccupation with the ways in which language may be culturally defining. Not only has the change opened the way for kinds of theatre which are impassioned, confrontational and metaphorically rich, it has also given some space to those who were verbally disenfranchised by the pre-emptive conversational rules imposed by the ocker. It is no coincidence that Nowra and Sewell have written some of the most rewarding roles for women in the mainstream theatre. The matriarch Lilian Dawson in *Inside the Island* is built on the lines of Bond's Mrs Rafi in *The Sea*, but transcends her in the power of what she can feel and refuse to feel. Su-Ling, whose sufferings in *The Precious Woman* still cannot extinguish her capacity to feel love, is a marvellously complex study, even though the mode of the play requires that all her complexity is expressed in symbolic action. Sewell has also written some very substantial roles for women, in particular his sceptical feminist Louise in *Blind Giant*, despite the general male dominance of the political struggles he depicts. It remains the case, though, that the experiences of women, blacks and people from other cultures have been, in a sense, marginalised in recent Australian drama by their relative lack of access to the repertoires of the establishment companies and the processes of publication which together determine what Australian drama is understood to be. Writers like Hannie Rayson, Sandra Shotlander, Tess Lysiotis and Jack Davis have not yet made significant inroads into those strongholds, though Davis' *The Dreamers* (1981) and *No Sugar* (1986) have been widely toured and enthusiastically received. Davis' powerful images of the conflicting perceptions of black and white point to the ways in which voices that seek to be newly heard call for distinctive theatrical structures. It may be in the alternative theatres, where the experiences that particularly concern those previously neglected groups are now finding expression, that the next wave is gathering. Certainly the rival mythologies which have developed in the last two decades demonstrate the society's continuing fascination with images which help to reveal us to ourselves, and there are a number of Australians still who await that revelation in the theatres of the dominant culture.

Notes

The dates given in parentheses in the text are those of the play's first professional production.

Australian playwrights have until quite recently been poorly served by publishers. The Hanger collection at the University of Queensland and the Campbell Howard Collection at the University of New England both have extensive manuscript holdings of mostly un-published material; the National Library in Canberra holds a large number of copies of playscripts from these two collections. Currency since 1972 has produced an impressive number of Australian plays; more recently, Yackandandah Press has been a very active contributor to the field.

The same long period of general neglect applied also to criticism and other secondary material relating to Australian theatre. Leslie Rees' two-volume *A History of Australian Drama* (1978; rev. 1987) is an idiosyncratic but valuable record at first-hand. Margaret Williams' *Drama* (1977) surveys the territory succinctly, and with greater critical astuteness. My *After 'The Doll': Australian Drama since 1955* (1979) is still the only extended critical discussion of that period and includes chapters on the work of Lawler, White, Buzo, Hibberd, Williamson and Hewett, as well as sections broader in scope. Peter Holloway's anthology of critical review material, *Contemporary Australian Drama: Perspectives Since 1955* (1981, rev. 1987) covers a similar period. Holloway has gathered a wide range of articles, some general, some concerned with particular writers, and the collection is an invaluable reference for students in this area. In 1987 both Methuen (in Sydney) and Rodopi Press (in Amsterdam) released the first titles in a projected series of monographs dealing with individual playwrights; that fact in itself suggests recognition of the very substantial achievements of the last twenty-five years.

Periodicals devoted to Australian theatre have come and gone through the period—the much-lamented *Theatre Australia* (1976-82) contains particularly important reviews and other material. Recently *Australasian Drama Studies* from the University of Queensland has provided a regular forum for critical studies in the area. The British magazine *Theatre Quarterly* (now *New Theatre Quarterly*) has published two interesting supplements on the state of Australian theatre—the first (7, 1977) includes an excellent survey by Katharine Brisbane, 'From Williamson to Williamson: Australia's Larrikin Theatre', while the second (11, 1986) deals with established playwrights in my own lengthy introduction, but also acknowledges the real pluralism of contemporary Australian theatre, particularly in two commentaries on community theatre by Malcolm Blaylock and Tom Burvill.

A number of the most significant critical articles may be found represented in Peter Holloway's book. More recent articles of importance include John McCallum's 'The World Outside: Cosmopolitanism in the Plays of Nowra and Sewell' in *Meanjin*, 43 (1984) and his survey of recent Williamson, 'A New Map of Australia: The Plays of David Williamson' in *Australian Literary Studies*, 11 (1984). Veronica Kelly's 'A Mirror for Australia: Louis Nowra's Emblematic Theatre' in *Southerly*, 41 (1981) demonstrates the metaphorical significance for Australia of Nowra's early plays with non-Australian locales. The question of the treatment of the racial outsider is developed in my article, 'Asian Stereotypes in Recent Australian Plays in *Australian Literary Studies*, 12 (1985). Among some useful interview material, Jim Davidson's interviews with John Romeril in *Meanjin*, 37 (1978) and David Williamson in *Meanjin*, 38 (1979) and Jeremy Ridgman's with Nowra and Sewell in *Australasian Drama Studies*, 1 (1983) are particularly interesting. Jennifer Palmer, in *Contemporary Australian Playwrights* (1979) has collected transcripts of her ABC interviews with Katharine Brisbane, Lawler, Seymour, Kenna, Hewett, Williamson, Buzo, de Groen and Compton, which are all well worth reading.

Chapter 32

SHORT FICTION

KERRYN GOLDSWORTHY

Rigby Limited, one of the large Australian publishers, welcome any type of manuscript. Careful consideration given to all kinds of literary work excepting short stories and poetry . . .

> (From an advertisement in *Australian Letters*, 1958)

But there was another change occurring which is obscured by the introduction of television and tangled with it. It was the change in taste for and development of the short story . . . By the early 60s the change which I've tried to identify was becoming visible. The new editor of the *Bulletin* told marketing guides: 'The Editor has recently tried to revitalise interest in the Australian short story and is anxious to secure short stories of Australian interest that break new ground . . .'

> (Frank Moorhouse, 1977)

It is apparent from these two quotations that interest in the Australian short story was rekindled, and that this was something that happened quite quickly. Moorhouse's passing comment about television is a tantalising one, opening up all kinds of questions and avenues for speculation about people's tastes in entertainment and leisure activities; about the relationship between 'serious' literature, popular culture, and market forces; about the reasons why people read fiction.

One wonders what might be the connections between the *Bulletin* editor's comment and the fact that two of Australia's 'master practitioners' of the short story published collections in the same year: John Morrison's *Twenty-Three* (his last collection) and Hal Porter's *A Bachelor's Children* (his first, not counting a limited edition of a short collection published earlier) both appeared in 1962.

What is most interesting about these two writers is that while they were near-contemporaries who have in common a distinguished reputation in Australian literary history, they could not be more different in their writing styles and subject matter. Morrison is a social realist, a writer whose stories are for the most part simple and straightforward in style, uncomplicated in structure, and clear and powerful in their implications. Morrison is concerned with social and economic injustices, but he is neither didactic nor polemical; he writes about money and work, about the exchanges of one for the other and the exercise of various kinds of power involved in these transactions, but his stories always focus on individual human lives, on the emotional responses and moral dilemmas of people who find themselves in situations outside their control. Morrison's work represented for many people the mid-century Australian short story at its best: widely accessible and not 'difficult' or obscure, but not facile or over-simple; conscious of what Christopher Brennan once called 'Australianity', but not preoccupied with nationalism; politically engaged, with a focus on various disadvantaged social groups, but not aggressively didactic; realist, but not drearily so. *Twenty-Three*, in hindsight, harks back rather than forward, summing up the best qualities of the short story over the previous few decades.

Hal Porter, however, is a solitary figure in the history of the Australian short story. Unlike Morrison, Porter appears to be concerned as much with style as with content; words like 'brilliance' and 'virtuosity' recur in critical discussions of his work. Given the consciousness demonstrated in his stories of writing *as writing* rather than primarily as representation of experience, it seems odd that he has rarely been seen as any kind of precursor of the 'new writing' of the 1970s. Much of his work is satirical, and some critics have identified him with Patrick White and Barry Humphries as a satirist of Australian suburban life in the 1950s and 1960s.

At least one critic has named Porter and White as the two dominating figures, as far as the short story is concerned, of the 1960s. White occupies a rather special place here, as a writer whose crusade against what he called the 'dreary . . . dun-coloured realism' of Australian fiction had begun in earnest in 1948 when he published *The Aunt's Story;* by 1964 when *The Burnt Ones*—his first collection of stories—appeared, earlier critical hostility to his novels was giving way to respect and a growing realisation of the importance of his work.

But Porter—also a novelist but better known for his stories—operated in the 1960s as a kind of fulcrum between the traditional realism of mid-century and the 'new writing' of the 1970s. The publication of Morrison's *Twenty-Three* and Porter's *A Bachelor's Children* in 1962, White's *The Burnt Ones* in 1964 and Frank Moorhouse's first collection, *Futility and Other Animals*, in 1969 provides a set of signposts showing where the short story had been and which way it was heading.

For the interesting thing about the 1960s is that both White and Porter, considered here as representative of the decade, defy any kind of classification or grouping with other writers of their time, unlike those who went before and those who came after. This chapter begins with the 1960s chiefly because it seems the most important period of transition in the history of the Australian short story; it marked the beginnings of a reaction away from what had until then been firmly constructed and reconstructed—in a self-perpetuating process whereby critics and editors went on demanding a certain kind of writing which writers went on supplying—as 'the Australian tradition', or 'the Lawson tradition'.

If Hal Porter's work represents a turning point in the history of Australian short fiction then so, and more so, does Henry Lawson's; the title of a recent book by Cecil Hadgraft, *The Australian Short Story Before Lawson* (1986), speaks for itself—or, rather, constitutes an argument in itself.

For almost everywhere in Australian literary history and criticism is manifested the conviction, stated or assumed, that the Australian short story really *began* with Lawson; that short fiction written before the 1890s is not worth much critical attention, but is rather a sort of throat-clearing before the short story begins to speak. In H. M. Green's *A History of Australian Literature* (1961), the section on the short story from 1850 to 1890 begins: 'The short stories of the period were many in number but poor in quality.' Much of the short fiction written before 1890 is regarded by him as 'sketches' rather than 'stories', although the distinction between the two is not really explained.

Cecil Hadgraft traces the development of short fiction in Australia from 1830 to 1893. His detailed and informative introduction to the pre-1893 stories he has collected in *The Australian Short Story Before Lawson*—as well as the stories themselves—makes clear the wide variety of writers and writing involved; this is a period about which it is difficult to generalise. There is widespread critical agreement that some of the best pre-Lawson short-story writers were those who were better known as novelists, like Marcus Clarke, Rosa Praed, and 'Tasma' (Jessie Couvreur), who, Green maintains, is the best of them. 'Price Warung' (William Astley) stands out as the writer whose stories deal predominantly with the subject of the convict system; other names which recur in discussions of their period are John Lang, whose *Botany Bay* was published in 1859, and Francis Adams, a writer of a later generation, an acute commentator on Australian culture and a contemporary of Lawson's.

It was Adams, writing in 1893, who described the *Bulletin* as the only mouthpiece of originality in the country. For the purposes of this account the two most significant events of the 1890s were the publication in 1894 of Lawson's first book, *Short Stories in Prose and Verse*, and the institution in 1896 of the *Bulletin*'s Red Page under the literary editorship of A. G. Stephens. It was from this point, John Barnes has argued, that 'the *Bulletin* saw itself as nurse and guardian of national literature'; this self-image is reflected in the writers it encouraged, with Lawson and his *Bulletin* companions engaged in writing that was, for the first time, consciously of, by and for the Australian people.

It is impossible to conjecture what the course of Australian literary history might have been if Henry Lawson's most productive period as a writer had not coincided with Stephens' literary editorship of the *Bulletin*—except to say that the history of Lawson's career in particular might have been radically different. Lawson and Barbara Baynton are the two short-story writers whose names are most often mentioned in connection with the *Bulletin* of the 1890s, along with Edward Dyson, Ernest Favenc, Price Warung and others—though only one story by Baynton ever appeared there, and that was heavily edited. The names of Lawson and Baynton have often been invoked together in a way which tends to obscure the differences between their work. Lawson's stories, though often bleak, celebrate certain positive human qualities—mateship, endurance, courage, honesty— which manifest themselves in his characters in spite of (or sometimes because of) harsh outback conditions; 'The Drover's Wife' is the best-known example of this. Baynton's stories are altogether blacker, their vision of human nature ranging from the stern to the hopeless; those of her characters who are not weak, dishonest, cowardly, cruel or downright evil are always at the mercy of those who are, and her evocation of the Australian outback frequently presents it not just as bleak and harsh but—as in her terrifying story 'The Dreamer'—as actively malign, the stuff of nightmare.

Henry Handel Richardson's stories were collected and published as *The End of a Childhood* in 1934, although some of them had appeared twenty years earlier or more. The title of the collection is both appropriate and revealing; some of her most powerful (and most frequently anthologised) stories—'And Women Must Weep', 'Two Hanged Women', the appropriately titled 'The Bathe: A Grotesque'— involve female characters with a fear sometimes amounting to horror of sexual maturity. Richardson is better known for her novels, especially *The Fortunes of Richard Mahony*; but until recently she has not been highly regarded as a writer of short fiction except by H. M. Green.

On first looking into the titles of collections and individual stories published from the 1920s through to the 1950s, one is immediately struck by the large number of titles to do with nature: landscape, weather, and especially animals. The best-known short-story writers of the period are—to list them in order of date of birth; they were all born within thirty years—Katharine Susannah Prichard, Vance Palmer, 'Brian James' (John Tierney), Frank Dalby Davison, Cecil Mann, Alan Marshall, Gavin Casey, Dal Stivens and Peter Cowan. And between them these nine writers produced a list of 'animal stories' of which the following is only a sample: 'The Dog', 'The Cow', 'The Bull Calf', 'The Jackass', 'The Dingo', 'The Donkey', 'The Galah', 'The Pelican', 'The Seahawk', 'Tell Us About the Turkey, Jo', 'The White Turkey', 'The Grey Kangaroo', 'The Grey Horse', 'The Black Mare', 'Wild Red Horses', 'The Red Bullock', 'The Red 'Roo', 'The Rainbow Bird', 'The Three-Legged Bitch', 'The New Australian Dog', 'Goldfish', 'The Mullet', 'The Snoring Cod', 'Hawkins' Pigs', 'My Bird', 'His Dog' and 'Nobody's Kelpie'.

But few of the stories named above, or of the other animal stories, are *simply* 'animal stories'; rather, they are stories which use birds and animals as metaphors or correlatives or totems for what is going on in the minds and hearts of their human characters—a sort of D. H. Lawrence mode, with more humour and less sex. And interestingly enough the writer of this period in whose work animals loom largest is precisely the one whose work does not fit these zoological general-isations; Dal Stivens is largely a fabulist rather than a realist, as the titles of his animal stories tend to indicate—'The Helpful Pink Elephant', 'The Scholarly Mouse'—and in this he was ahead of his time. Another exception is Margaret Trist, a comparatively undervalued writer of the period, who did not entitle one of her fifty-two stories with any animal reference whatever, unless you count 'Fishing'.

What these stories and their titles indicate is a preoccupation typical of the period with the external, physical world and the rural world at that. They use the exterior landscape of the natural world (for a similar list could be made of botanical and geographical titles) as a simple and straightforward parallel for the internal landscape of human dilemma. They are characterised by a small parcel of often-related qualities: a realist mode; a rural (or suburban) setting; an implicit moral stance which demonstrates or upholds—or mourns the lack of—various human virtues, more often than not the Lawson-ish ones of honesty, egalitarianism, kindliness and courage; and, allied to this, a political position more or less to the left of centre and more or less explicit.

Like that of Dal Stivens, the work of Ethel Anderson is atypical of its time and has found a kinder climate in the reading tastes of the 1980s. *At Parramatta* (1956) was reprinted in 1985, and reveals a writer who is a kind of combination of Elizabeth Jolley, Frank Moorhouse and Jane Austen. Another writer as yet unmentioned is Marjorie Barnard, one half of 'M. Barnard Eldershaw', who in 1943 published (under her own name) *The Persimmon Tree and Other Stories*; the title story is one of the most haunting and evocative pieces of writing in Australian literature.

The 1950s were notable for the appearance of Frank Hardy; his volume *The Man From Clinkapella and Other Prize-Winning Stories* was published in 1951 and he has been producing fictional and non-fictional prose pretty much ever since. Judah Waten's *Alien Son* (1952) anticipated by some thirty years the emergence of the category 'migrant writing'. What links these two writers is their overtly political motivation and their concentration on characters from disadvantaged social groups, and in this they are joined by their contemporary John Morrison.

The year 1972 brought the lifting of censorship restrictions (after decades of groundwork by such assorted characters as Brian Penton, Max Harris, Geoffrey Dutton and Don Chipp); the first issue of the peripatetic short-story magazine *Tabloid Story*; and the beginnings of a completely new kind of government support for the arts (see chapter 27).

Frank Moorhouse and Michael Wilding are the two names which

recur most frequently in discussions of the Australian short story in the 1970s, not only because of the quality and innovativeness of their own short fiction but also in connection with *Tabloid Story*, which Moorhouse has called 'a travelling exhibit'. *Tabloid Story* was produced not as a self-contained magazine but as a supplement to host journals.

The 'new' fiction of the 1970s was characterised by a break from realist stories and nationalist preoccupations, although it must be remembered that two of the dominating figures of the 1960s, Hal Porter and Patrick White, had already broken this ground to a considerable extent. So had Dal Stivens, who since the 1930s had been writing short fiction in the fabulist mode which now became predominant; and Peter Cowan, whose fourth and fifth volumes, *The Tins and Other Stories* (1973) and *Mobiles* (1979), showed a continuing interest in experimentation with the short-story form which he uses to expose frustration, bitterness and futility in contemporary living. Another writer to remember here is Christina Stead: of her story collection *The Salzburg Tales* (1934) Elizabeth Webby has written:

> The vitality and stylistic and formal variety of Stead's stories would, I think, be quite a revelation to younger Australian writers who would be staggered to discover her anticipation of the current fabulist mode.

The 'new' fiction, influenced largely by contemporary European and American writing, incorporated such elements as fantasy, surrealism, experiments with narrative chronology and narrative voice, a new awareness of the role and status of the author in the story, and a generally enlarged consciousness of fiction *as fiction*, of a story as an artefact rather than as a simple reflection of 'life'. Common to all of the Australian writers whose names recur in surveys of Australian short fiction of this period is an acute and articulated consciousness of there being no simple, uncomplicated relationship between language and experience.

In his anthology *The Most Beautiful Lies* (1977) Brian Kiernan assembled a selection of stories by five writers—Murray Bail, Peter Carey, Morris Lurie, Frank Moorhouse and Michael Wilding—whom he sees as sharing these preoccupations; there were many others, but Kiernan's selection of these five implies that he thinks they are the best of them, a perfectly justifiable and widely held view. Of the five, Carey is the one most concerned with fantasy and surrealism, Bail with the nature of language and writing, Moorhouse with narrative experimentation and ways of writing frankly about sex, while Wilding shares aspects of all these concerns. In his introduction to *The Most Beautiful Lies*, Kiernan observes that these five writers share

> a tendency for their stories to present themselves self-consciously as 'fictions', to be less mimetic, less concerned with character and social situation and more with style and form as part of the stories' 'content'; and a tendency to employ less realistic forms, such as the fable and the science-fiction tale.

Kiernan is careful in his introduction to disclaim any suggestion that these writers comprise any kind of 'school' or 'movement', but the very fact of their work having been juxtaposed and encapsulated in such a book inevitably suggests an image of them as a more or less homogeneous, and representative, group. *The Most Beautiful Lies* does not announce itself as an anthology of men's writing: the fact that these five stars in the 1970s heaven are all male seems to be regarded as too normal a fact to warrant comment—as, indeed, it was.

But women were writing in the 1970s too. Elizabeth Jolley has said that she was sending story after story to magazines and having them steadily rejected. The short-story collection by a woman that literary critics and commentators took most seriously during the 1970s was Thea Astley's *Hunting the Wild Pineapple* (1979); Astley already had a deserved and firmly established reputation as a novelist.

Numerous anthologies, general and specialised, have appeared since 1980, and most of them have sold well. Perhaps the best way to survey the scene is to fall back on statistics: to look at three anthologies of contemporary Australian writing published between 1983 and 1986 and see which names, themes and preoccupations recur.

Of the eighty-four writers represented in *The State of the Art: The Mood of Contemporary Australia in Short Stories* (ed. Frank Moorhouse, 1983), *Transgressions: Australian Writing Now* (ed. Don Anderson, 1986) and *Coast to Coast: Recent Australian Prose Writing* (ed. Kerryn Goldsworthy, 1986), only three appear in all three collections: Frank Moorhouse, Helen Garner and Gerard Windsor. The writers who appear in two out of three are Kate Grenville, Olga Masters, Elizabeth Jolley, Tim Winton, David Malouf, Marian

Eldridge, Angelo Loukakis, Michael Wilding, Ania Walwicz and David Brooks.

Of these thirteen names only Moorhouse, Wilding and Malouf have been well-known ones for more than ten years. The rest are relative newcomers, the most established of whom are Garner and Jolley, both better known as novelists. Jolley and Masters began winning prizes and recognition late in life. The list contains the names of six women, and of a Pole and a Greek.

These apparently random facts do tell us something about the drift of the Australian short story in the 1980s; their message is best summarised in the title of an article in *Meanjin* in 1983 by Elizabeth Webby. 'Short Fiction in the Eighties: White Anglo-Celtic Male No More?' traces the trend in Australian writing—and publishing—away from the dominance of people called John, Peter, Alan, Patrick, Hal and Frank and towards a more equitable representation of people with names like Serge and Angelo and Ania, and Marian and Elizabeth and Kate. There is a growing taste for 'women's writing' and 'migrant writing', and there are increasing numbers of people in these categories who *are* writing, now that there is a market for their work; this is to some extent a self-perpetuating phenomenon.

'White' is the uneasy word in Webby's title. Perhaps the best-known Aboriginal writers are Kath Walker, Jack Davis and Colin Johnson, but these three between them have produced poetry, drama and novels—no short stories, or at least no well-known ones. Archie Weller's collection of stories *Going Home* (1986) is the first by an Aborigine. The shape and language of Aboriginal storytelling, however, does not sit easily with traditional notions of 'the short story'. Some of the most valuable work in this area has been done by Stephen Muecke, Krim Benterrack and Paddy Roe, whose book *Reading the Country* (1984) demonstrates the differences; their story 'Mirdinan' is included in Don Anderson's *Transgressions* (1986).

There has been increasing interest in 'experimental' writing (although opinions differ as to what this word might actually mean). The title of and introduction to *Transgressions* reflect this, and the two short pieces in it by Ania Walwicz indicate a connection between these two newish developments: Walwicz's work demonstrates how the fact of being a woman *and* a migrant might, in its effects on one's use and perceptions of language, liberate a writer *into* an experimental mode.

Of the three writers who appear in all three anthologies, Gerard Windsor has been less well known, and known for a shorter time, than either Moorhouse or Garner; his first collection, *The Harlots Enter First* (1982), was received quietly but *Memories of the Assassination Attempt* (1985) gained critical notice. Helen Garner published *Postcards From Surfers* in 1985; this collection contains the much-quoted, much-discussed and much-reprinted story 'The Life of Art'. In Frank Moorhouse's three most recent collections—*The Everlasting Secret Family* (1980), *Room Service* (1985) and *Forty-Seventeen* (1988)—he has moved away from charting the moods and movements of a counter culture and towards a closer attention to individual experience, of travel and transgression; his concern (there from the beginning of his career) with narrative structure, narrative voice, and the relationship between experience and language is maintained, however, in these more recent collections.

Of the remaining ten names, the ones heard most often have been those of David Malouf (*Antipodes*, 1985), Elizabeth Jolley (*Five Acre Virgin*, 1976; *The Travelling Entertainer*, 1979; *Woman in a Lampshade*, 1983), Olga Masters (*The Home Girls*, 1982; *A Long Time Dying*, 1985), Kate Grenville (*Bearded Ladies*, 1984) and Tim Winton (*Scission*, 1985; *Minimum of Two*, 1987). They are all known equally well, or better, as novelists. Other noted practitioners of the form include Barry Hill; in his works *A Rim of Blue* (1978) and *Headlocks* (1983) the dominant themes are politics and family relations (or, sometimes, the politics of family relations). There is also Beverley Farmer, whose books *Milk* (1983) and *Home Time* (1985) are best known for their 'Greek stories'—stories which invert the migrant experience and reflect the cultural and social vertigo of Australians in Greece; and Joan London, whose first collection *Sister Ships* won the *Age* Book of the Year Award for 1986.

As well as the increasing interest in women's writing and migrant writing—both categories have produced anthologies, collections in which the short-story form, though not always adhered to, is used as a kind of generic basis—there have recently appeared several regional anthologies, mostly State-based. This is probably due to a shift over the last fifteen or twenty years in the literary community's focus of interest, away from 'Australianity' and towards a more locally based vision of 'place'.

One major contribution to this development can be found in various recent writings of David Malouf—fictional, autobiographical, theoretically speculative—in which, by way of writing about and as it were *through* his native Brisbane, he has arrived at an aesthetic of locale. In particular his *12 Edmondstone Street*, a collection of autobiographical essays published in 1985, presents a vision of the relation between place and the self, and of the ways in which that relation can be not only expressed but constructed, and re-created, through writing. Malouf's Brisbane, Garner's Melbourne, Astley's North Queensland, Jolley's Western Australian wheatfields and Winton's Western Australian south-west coast, as well as highlighting the relationship between character and place, also suggest new 'regional' ways of reading the fiction of earlier writers.

In addition, prizewinning novelist Jessica Anderson turned her hand to the short-story form in 1987 with a collection which raises questions about both regionalism and autobiography, a book suggestively entitled *Stories From the Warm Zone and Sydney Stories*. Like Malouf, Anderson is interested in the relationship between place and the self; the 'warm zone' of the title is a sometimes uncomfortably tropical childhood—part of which is literally a place, the prewar Brisbane in which that childhood is experienced. In the Brisbane stories Anderson explicitly addresses the distinctions between fiction and autobiography and thereby implicitly questions the validity of the all-too-common and over-simple opinion that 'excessive' autobiographical content somehow automatically diminishes the literary value of fiction. The grouping of Anderson's last three stories under the collective title 'Sydney Stories' again calls attention to the importance of location in the stories—although this may not have been the intention of Anderson herself.

As a whole the collection sets up some interesting resonances between images of the two cities, moving away from the traditional, now rather tired, and increasingly overdetermined contrast between Sydney and Melbourne to a newer and much more subtle implicit comparison between Sydney and Brisbane—a comparison not ready-made for us, but which we are invited by the structure of the book to make for ourselves.

In the meantime, regional anthologies proliferate: Queensland's *Latitudes* (ed. Susan Johnson and Mary Roberts, 1986), South Australia's *Unsettled Areas* (ed. Andrew Taylor, 1986), and several impressive Western Australian anthologies have helped alert us to the fact that what we call 'Australia' consists of a vast number of sometimes very different places. Regionalism considered as a category—like women's writing, migrant writing or experimental writing—has been another way of moving on from an over-simple preoccupation with 'nation'. It is another new way of classifying, thinking about, and—most importantly—*writing* short stories.

Notes

'The *Tabloid Story* Story' by Michael Wilding—the source of the quotation from Brian Kiernan in *The Most Beautiful Lies*—appeared as an afterword in *The Tabloid Story Pocket Book* (1978), and is reprinted in *Cross Currents: Magazines and Newspapers in Australian Literature* (1981), edited by Bruce Bennett.

Stephen Torre's *The Australian Short Story, 1940-1980: A Bibliography* is an invaluable reference book for scholars and curious others who want to know exactly who wrote what when during those four decades.

The quotation from Frank Moorhouse is from his article 'What Happened to the Short Story?' in *Australian Literary Studies*, 8 (1977).

The October 1981 issue of *Australian Literary Studies* is a special issue on 'The Contemporary Australian Short Story'. The quotation from Elizabeth Webby is from her article 'Australian Short Fiction: from *While the Billy Boils* to *The Everlasting Secret Family*' in this issue. It also contains an article by Bruce Clunies Ross on short fiction from 1960 to 1980 and one by Christina Stead, 'Ocean of Story', as well as statements by authors and editors and a selective bibliography.

Recent anthologies include Kerryn Goldsworthy (ed.), *Australian Short Stories* (1983); Suzanne Falkiner (ed.), *Room to Move: The Redress Anthology of Australian Women's Short Stories* (1985); Laurie Hergenhan (ed.), *The Australian Short Story: An Anthology from the 1890s to the 1980s* (1986); Geoffrey Dutton (ed.), *An Illustrated Treasury of Australian Short Stories* (1987); Lynn Harwood, Bruce Pascoe and Pamela White (eds), *The Babe is Wise: Contemporary Stories by Australian Women* (1987); and Murray Bail (ed.), *The Faber Book of Contemporary Short Stories* (1988).

Chapter 33

CHILDREN'S LITERATURE

BRENDA NIALL

Until the 1950s, Australian children's reading came from the same shelf as that of their English contemporaries. The experience of the writer Ivan Southall as a child in the 1930s was not unusual:

> Good things, which parents would buy for you, came from England . . . Australia rarely earned a mention except as the wilderness to which profligate cousins were sent and out of which lost uncles came.

Adventure stories and pioneering sagas, first devised by English writers for English children in the mid-nineteenth century were reworked by Australian writers in the early twentieth century. The result was, long after Australia was predominantly an urban nation, its literary images remained much the same: droughts, floods and bushfires, goldmines, lost children, Aborigines, squatters and swagmen. The transformation of a weedy new chum into a sun-bronzed settler was the most durable of New World plots. It is almost as though Kingsley's *Geoffry Hamlyn* (1859) had been endlessly recycled for children. There were few notable departures from the adventure mode. In the half century which produced, for adults, works as diverse as *Such is Life, The Fortunes of Richard Mahony, For Love Alone, Lucinda Brayford* and *The Aunt's Story*, children's literature had comparatively little to show. Ethel Turner's stories of suburban Sydney which began with *Seven Little Australians* (1894), Ethel Pedley's bushland fantasy *Dot and the Kangaroo* (1899) and Norman Lindsay's comic masterpiece *The Magic Pudding* (1918) are among the most important exceptions in a period of gradual development within a narrow range. Turner and Lindsay are still in print; so are Mary Grant Bruce's Billabong books, and the work of two very gifted artists, May Gibbs and Ida Rentoul Outhwaite. Yet even at a time when publishers are looking for Australian classics to reprint, very few of the Australian children's books of the early twentieth century have been reclaimed. In the history of what is now a strong and vital tradition the decade from the mid-1950s seems the crucial period, at least for fiction. Picture books, which are outside the scope of this essay, have a rather different chronology, as Marcie Muir has shown in her definitive *History of Australian Children's Book Illustration* (1982).

That the 1950s should have been a time of change in children's literature is not surprising. Postwar nationalism and the loosening of emotional ties with Britain, the heightened value placed on family life, and the postwar 'baby boom' combined to create a favorable climate of feeling for a renaissance in Australian children's books. The ideas that 'good books came from England' was tempered by a new assertiveness and a new value given to distinctively Australian settings and situations. Yet there was nothing so simple as a declaration of literary independence. The emergence of talented writers for children had at least as much to do with British publishing initiatives as with Australian literary nationalism. In several ways, the development of Australian children's books in the 1950s repeated the pattern of the 1890s when *Seven Little Australians* was published. In both periods, an English publishing house and the demands of a readership of English as well as Australian children were important shaping influences. It is illuminating to look at the success of the 1950s revolution against the background of the comparative failure of the 1890s.

In 1893, Ethel Turner sent the manuscript of *Seven Little Australians* to William Steele, the Melbourne representative of Ward Lock of London. It was Steele's ambition to discover an Australian counterpart of Louisa Alcott's *Little Women*, and in Turner's work he believed he had found it. As the first author of any talent to discard the outback adventure story and write about ordinary children in a Sydney suburban setting, Ethel Turner was in herself a revolution. Her book succeeded beyond her expectations or Steele's; within a few weeks of its first Australian reviews it was sold out in Sydney and a second edition was being printed in London. Turner was then only twenty-two; she was energetic and ambitous and she had already published a short story in the *Bulletin*. She was by no means committed to writing for children, and without the sudden fame brought by her first novel she might have become one of the *Bulletin* school. Steele, with English readers in mind, toned down the Australian local colour in her work, censored such colloquialisms as 'My oath!', and in 1895 tried to persuade her to leave Sydney for London:

> a little English experience would help to (excuse me so putting it) correct the free and easy, somewhat rowdy associations due to atmosphere, climate, environment and the influence of the *Bulletin* . . . To ensure your complete success, the English people must be reckoned with and that is why I advocate your staying for a time in their midst.

Although Turner stayed in Sydney, the rest of her long career shows a continuing tension between her wish to extend the boundaries of what was thought suitable for children and her London publishers' concern for more decorum and larger sales of Sunday-school prizes. Unwillingly, too, she yielded to pressure for sequels to *Seven Little Australians*; writing within a series did not suit her and the chronicles of the Woolcots trailed off feebly in the third volume, *Little Mother Meg* (1902). At the end of her career, Turner gave in to Ward Lock's demand for one more Woolcot book. Unable to move her family story forward in time, she took the extreme measure of resurrecting the heroine of her 1894 success. Judy Woolcot, killed by a falling tree in *Seven Little Australians*, is seen at an earlier stage in her life in Turner's last novel, *Judy and Punch* (1928).

William Steele's second major discovery was Mary Grant Bruce, whose fifteen Billabong books published between 1910 and 1942 were produced by Ward Lock in a format identical with that of the Turner novels. More tractable than Ethel Turner, Bruce accepted the limitations of writing to the formula of a series. She gave new life to the outdoor adventure story by creating a memorable family group against an idyllic background of pastoral Australian life. Billabong Station became a permanent part of the mythology of outback Australia, endlessly appealing to the city children who made up most of Bruce's readership. In an important sense, however, the creation of Billabong was a counter-revolution. Ethel Turner had opened up the possibilities of the urban domestic novel, with drama based on character rather than on outdoor adventure. The Bruce novels, which pleased Ward Lock by being distinctively Australian in a style equally suited to readers at home or abroad, were nostalgic celebrations of the 'vision splendid'; they led nowhere except back to Billabong.

Turner and Bruce, who between them published eighty-three books, were the dominant figures in Australian children's literature within the period from 1894 to 1942. They had some lacklustre imitators, but no successors. They both died in 1958. By that time, the early novels of Nan Chauncy, Patricia Wrightson and Joan Phipson had appeared and the renaissance in Australian children's literature was confirmed. The step from late Victorian-Edwardian confidence to modernist uncertainty was taken comparatively late in Australian children's writing: there are signs of change in Turner, but none in Bruce. Some of the gaps in the history of Australian children's literature are predictable; others are hard to explain. Not only did the new land lack smuggler's caves and haunted castles as well as the boarding-school tradition; its country towns were no substitute for English village life or for the small community in the United States in which the 'good bad boy' could flourish. One or two attempts to create an Australian Tom Sawyer failed, perhaps because of the self-consciousness of the enterprise, or because the authors' antipathy to the country-town atmosphere worked against the comedy. Apart from the comic-strip character Ginger Meggs, the larrikin spirit, allegedly so much part of the Australian tradition, scarcely finds expression in children's reading. There is no tradition of urban or country-town success stories; the city which beckons so enticingly to the Horatio Alger hero is seen in Australian children's books in almost wholly negative terms. Fantasy, time-travel stories and historical novels, which are all among the great strengths of the English tradition, met the obvious difficulties of a land without an accessible folklore and a past too recent to seem colourful.

Apart from the Lintons of Billabong and the Woolcots of Ethel Turner's Misrule, no major character or family group caught the popular imagination. From fantasy, one might add the Banksia Men, the Magic Pudding, and perhaps Blinky Bill. There is no match for Canada's Anne of Green Gables, America's Ragged Dick and other Horatio Alger heroes, Tom Sawyer, Jo March and Pollyanna, Britain's Tom Brown, Eric, Alice, Stalky, the Bastables . . . Australian writers, lost in the bush or misguidedly trying to adapt incongruous literary modes, missed the period in which childhood was most confidently affirmed and child characters were self-determining. To emerge in the 1950s was to face a time of transition in ideas about childhood's experience. In the United States the resilient loner Huckleberry Finn declined into Holden Caulfield, the first memorable drop-out, as early as 1951. In Australia (insulated by the censorship which kept out *The Catcher in the Rye* until 1957) the anxieties were controlled; panic and emptiness would come later. Although there are signs of anxiety in the work of the first major postwar writer, Nan Chauncy, it is not in the American style. Nothing comparable with the American *angst* of the 1950s appeared until the mid-1960s novels of Ivan Southall.

Nan Chauncy's career, like that of Ethel Turner more than half a century before, was linked from the beginning with an English publishing house. Her first book, *They Found a Cave*, was published by Oxford University Press in 1948. Two years later, Frank Eyre, the author of *Twentieth-Century Children's Books 1900-1950* (1952), who had worked as a children's book editor for Oxford immediately after the war, came to Melbourne as manager of the Australian branch of the firm. At a time when few Australians were experienced in children's book publishing, Eyre's prestige and enthusiasm were invaluable. He already knew Nan Chauncy's work; and she was to remain an Oxford author for the whole of her career. Hesba Brinsmead and Eleanor Spence were added to the Oxford list which between 1958 and 1969 included six winnners of the Australian Children's Book of the Year Award. Thus, Eyre set a record at Oxford University Press scarcely matched even by Beatrice Davis at Angus and Robertson who published the early work of Joan Phipson and Patricia Wrightson. Ivan Southall and the winner of the 1987 Children's Book of the Year Award, Simon French, are among the best-known contemporary children's writers on the Angus and Robertson list, which began with Louise Mack's *Teens* (1897) and included *The Magic Pudding* and the work of May Gibbs. That Ward Lock's enterprise in the 1890s led to *Teens* (which was produced in a format almost identical with that of *Seven Little Australians*) is less remarkable than the fact that sixty years later the role of the English publishing houses was still as important as that of any local firm.

Some aspects of the Anglo-Australian publishing relationship in the 1950s remained almost unchanged since the time when William Steele directed Ethel Turner's career. Although Eyre found and fostered some of the most talented Australian writers of the 1950s and 1960s, most of their books were edited, illustrated and printed in England just as those of Turner and Bruce had been. Moreover, as late as 1979, the Australian sales of Oxford's Australian authors counted as 'overseas', and drew only half the royalty paid in Britain. Yet the sense of writing for English as well as Australian children had its satisfactions to weigh against the remoteness from editor and illustrator and, sometimes, a disconcertingly English effect in illustrations and format. For Eleanor Spence, who began to publish with Oxford in 1958, the anomaly of the 'overseas' royalties was financially an advantage: until the 1970s her English sales were much larger than those in Australia. Although she was advised by Eyre to elaborate on the details of the Australian landscape for the benefit of English readers, she was not asked, as Ethel Turner had been, to trim or adapt her work in any significant way. The tyranny of the series had all but disappeared, and the local flavour of Spence's settings in Sydney or in New South Wales coastal towns was acknowledged as an advantage for English as well as Australian readers.

Whether they published with Angus and Robertson in Sydney, Rigby's of Adelaide, or with the Australian branch of one of the many English firms which became actively involved in Australian publishing in the postwar period, there is no evidence of editorial pressures on the writers of the 1950s to choose (or to avoid) specifically Australian themes and situations; Chauncy, Phipson, Wrightson, Thiele, Brinsmead, Spence and Southall show a marked individuality of voice and vision which declares that they wrote as they pleased. No publisher, English or Australian, could have created them or their successors. Yet the climate in which they wrote must be counted as a factor in their success. Such developments as the postwar Children's Book Council awards, better funding for school and municipal libraries and, more recently, writers' and publishers grants from the Literature Board and the Public Lending Right Scheme all had their effect in a period of steadily increasing confidence in Australian writing. Ivan Southall's Carnegie Medal for *Josh* (1971), and the Hans Christian Andersen Medals awarded in 1986 to Patricia Wrightson and the illustrator Robert Ingpen confirm the achievement of the 1950s. In the 1980s it is obvious that the days of dependence on English publishing houses have ended: sales within Australia are substantial, and there are notable 'all-Australian' publishing successes.

The bush tradition in Australian children's books was modified but not reversed in the mid-century revival. It was not a question of going back to the confident serenity of Billabong. The pastoral mode returned with some significant differences. Nan Chauncy's first books, set in a remote valley in south-western Tasmania, matched the feeling of the 1950s in their assertion of family solidarity against the threatening world her characters call 'Outside'. Home is a refuge in the wilderness, a fortress to be held against all comers. The capacity to survive in primitive surroundings is the mark of a Chauncy hero: he is as much a member of an endangered species as the wild creatures he protects. Joan Phipson moved from a rather conventional wish-fulfilment plot in *Good Luck to the Rider* (1953) to a group of family stories which affirm the values of the bush without denying its hardship. Colin Thiele's *The Sun on the Stubble* (1961) shared the postwar mood of qualified optimism: its celebration of family life in rural South Australia is a period piece which recalls the author's 1920s childhood. Thiele's lost world, lovingly re-created, Chauncy's endangered Eden and Phipson's sense of struggle belong to the first stage of the reshaping of Australian life in children's books. Family unity is guaranteed by the shared work of a not-too-prosperous farm; change is suspect, and urban ways are not only dreary but morally destructive.

In the early 1960s a rather different use of outback settings appeared. The natural world is not merely the harsh environment in which character is tested, it is a means of demonstrating the ultimate helplessness of human beings in a universe without meaning. Ivan Southall's novels of ordeal by flood, fire, and man-made disaster show children struggling against the odds. In the early *Hills End* (1962) and *Ash Road* (1965), there are qualified victories; the later works are bleak. There are no certainties; parents are useless and nature is arbitrarily cruel. Reginald Ottley's unnamed hero in *By the Sandhills of Yamboorah* (1965), a laconic battler in the literary tradition of Lawson, is better fitted for survival than Southall's confused, jittery children, but he cannot win. There are vulnerable children in Joan Phipson's adventure stories; and like Southall she moved from qualified optimism in *The Boundary Riders* (1962) to psychological terror in *The Way Home* (1973). Her work, however, asserts that there is a right relationship to nature which the city-dweller has lost. When the fact of human dependence is accepted, the earth will protect her children.

From practical stories of conservation crusades to the abstract moralities of the later Phipson novels, many of the mid-century Australian writers take up the environmental concerns of this period. The question of finding the right relationship with the land is linked with that of reconciliation with the Aborigines. Two books published in 1960 made an imaginative breakthrough: Nan Chauncy's *Tangara* and Patricia Wrightson's *The Rocks of Honey*. In these a white child's perspective on the Aboriginal tradition is managed with skill and subtlety. Until then the strength of Australian children's literature had been found in the realistic mode. The 1960s brought a sense of mystery. The minor tradition of fantasy, awkwardly handled in the early twentieth century in adaptations of English conventions, became a major one in the work of Patricia Wrightson. In *An Older Kind of Magic* (1972) and *The Nargun and the Stars* (1973) that threshold was crossed. The later work of Joan Phipson and the epic fantasies of Victor Kelleher helped to change the direction of Australian children's fiction away from the realism which had for so long been its major mode. The historical novel, developed in the 1960s by Eleanor Spence and others, merged with fantasy in Ruth Park's brilliant time-travel story of old and new Sydney, *Playing Beatie Bow* (1980).

One reason why the way to fantasy in Australian children's books was such a slow and difficult one is vividly illustrated in some comments on her Queensland childhood by P. L. Travers, author of that essentially English nursery fantasy *Mary Poppins* (1934):

> I was born in the sub-tropics of Australia. Not that I spent all my life there, only my young years, and most of it far from cities. I lived a life that was at once new and old. The country was new and the land itself very old— the oldest in the world geologists say, and in spite of the brash pioneering atmosphere that still existed even a child could sense the antiquity of it . . . My body ran about in the southern sunlight but my inner world had subtler colours, the greys and snows of England where little Joe swept all the crossings and the numberless greens of Ireland which seemed to me to be inhabited solely by poets plucking harps, heroes lordly cutting off each other's heads and veiled ladies sitting on the ground, keening.

Pamela Travers' family was Irish, and her literary imagination was nourished by English novels and Irish legends. Her perception of the ancient landscape of Australia as something quite separate from the images of her inner world is not unique; what makes it relevant here is the consciousness of division in someone who found fantasy the natural means of expression. She left Queensland in 1923, when she was seventeen, without having been culturally at home in her birthplace, and she created nothing directly from her early years. It was left to a later generation to discover through the exploration of Aboriginal myths and legends an authentic source of magic, appropriate to the land. In this achievement Patricia Wrightson is the central figure. The next stage, in which Aboriginal writers themselves interpret their past in children's books, is just beginning.

The family story presented no special difficulties or restrictions, once it was acknowledged that city life had at least as much to offer in literary terms as the bush. The happy families of the 1950s became troubled and divided in the 1960s. *The Racketty Street Gang* (1961) by L. H. Evers marks a transition: not only is it set in a Sydney slum but it refuses the conventional happy ending which removes the slum children to the middle class. *The Racketty Street Gang* was one of the first to reflect the contrast of cultures which came with Australia's postwar migration. Its representation of a German family is an early example of a tendency to idealise the newcomers: paternal gentleness and refinement, maternal warmth and good cooking are seen as European qualities. As the literary images of the city changed, so did those of country life. In Reginald Ottley's *The War on William Street* (1971) a gang of inner city boys is characterised in a style almost identical with the outback stereotype of an earlier period, by understated, stoic humour and mateship. Mavis Thorpe Clarke's *The Min-Min* (1966), set in a fettler's cottage near the railway line on the Nullarbor Plain, shows children for whom distance from the city is not safety, as it is in Nan Chauncy's novels, but deprivation.

In less than two decades the range of Australian children's books was immeasurably widened. In the 1960s, United States influences on Australian writers, and the sale of Australian books in this relatively new market helped to break down the exclusiveness of the Anglo-Australian literary relationship. In American editions of the works of Chauncy, Wrightson, Phipson, Southall and others, the ute turned into the pick-up truck and a weatherboard house became a clapboard. As well as these editorial adjustments, there were echoes of American speech patterns and a new style in disillusioned drop-out heroes. J. M. Couper's *The Thundering Good Today* (1970) a first-person narrative of the Vietnam War period, caught the edginess as well as the idiom of Holden Caulfield. A new stage in Australian-American literary relationship came in 1980 when Lee Harding's science fiction novel *Displaced Person* won the Australian Children's Book of the Year Award. Published in New York (as *Misplaced Person*) just before it appeared in Australia, it reflects a nightmare world of anonymity and lost connections. That Harding's literary affinities were more American than British is clear not only from the novel itself but from his view of the Australian scene in 1980. Commenting on the popularity among Australian children of 'the best American writers, people such as Paul Zindel, M. E. Kerr, Robert Cormier, S. E. Hinton and Judy Blume', Harding characterised his Australian contemporaries as evasive and backward-looking. Tendentiously he referred to the attempts by Patricia Wrightson and others to create a fantasy world appropriate to the Australian continent: 'some prefer to plunder Aboriginal mythology, perhaps preferring folklore and its comforts to the more telling fantasy of the modern world'.

While it is not necessarily a matter for regret, it is probably true that there is no Australian counterpart of Cormier or Zindel. Such 'problem novels' as Mavis Thorpe Clarke's *Solomon's Child* (1981) and Frank Wilmott's *Breaking Up* (1984) are harsh but neither brutal nor nihilistic; and they are comparatively few in number. The developments in Australian fantasy are much more impressive, with the novels of Patricia Wrightson being the most influential and original. Her most ambitious work, the Wirrun trilogy of the late 1970s, took her further into the controversial territory of Aboriginal life and legend. This work is much admired and justly so; and Wrightson has shown herself to be well aware of the skill and sensitivity needed in her enterprise. Nevertheless there has been some concern, not merely from those who, like Lee Harding, see the past as escape from the 'real', but from Aborigines who want their heritage of folklore to be interpreted from within their own tradition.

Until the 1980s the Aboriginal contribution to Australian children's reading had scarcely begun. Apart from Kath Walker's *Stradbroke Dreamtime* (1972) and the picture-book series of Dreaming legends by Dick Roughsey and Percy Tresize, there was little of significance until 1984. The 'Mindi' books by Maureen and Richard Simpson, and Maureen Watson's *Kaityu's Waiting* (all published in 1984) are unselfconscious and entertaining stories of Aboriginal children presented from an insider's perspective. Such works signal an end to a long line of stereotyped Aboriginal characters as seen by white writers. Even though such creations as the charmingly unreal Bett-Bett of Mrs Aeneas Gunn's *Little Black Princess* (1905) and the faithful or treacherous black 'boy' of countless adventure stories had yielded by the mid-twentieth century to more sensitive portrayals of Aboriginal children, there was still a sense of strain in many of the approaches from outside. Again, the writers who emerged in the 1960s made the most significant changes, with Patricia Wrightson's *The Rocks of Honey* and Nan Chauncy's *Tangara* outstanding for their easy and natural characterisation.

Children's books in Australia (and elsewhere for that matter) are usually discussed as though they were a self-contained branch of literature. There are writers and there are 'children's writers'. A few, like Ruth Park and David Martin, are both: but there is a tendency to give such writers two literary personas rather than to discuss the relationships between the two modes of writing. Except in the few specialist periodicals, or on that one day of the year on which the Children's Book Council awards are announced, it is rare to see any extended discussion of children's books; they seem to go to reviewers in parcels of a dozen or so, and to be reviewed in the same way. The general articles in *Australian Book Review* as well as its regular reviews are a welcome development. Literary histories tend to ignore children's books, or to give them a few unenlightening lines at the end of a chapter. Geoffrey Dutton's *Snow on the Saltbush* (1984) is unusual in looking at them, not in isolation, but as an important part of a literary tradition.

Because writing for children is seen as a small, separate area (a sandpit, perhaps, in the Aust. Lit. garden), some interesting questions remain unexplored. The sense of place in the novels of Nan Chauncy, Colin Thiele and Hesba Brinsmead might be considered as part of the growth of regionalism in Australian literature generally. Since many children's books have a strong autobiographical impulse, it may be significant that the 1960s, the decade in which Hal Porter, Donald Horne, Graham McInnes and others recreated their Australian past, also brought so many new writers for children. Some, like Southall in *What About Tomorrow?* (1977) and Thiele in *The Sun on the Stubble*, used the period of their own childhood in the Depression years; in these books, as in *The Education of Young Donald* (1967), the social context is almost as important as the central figure. The major writers for children in the postwar years were all late starters: Nan Chauncy was forty-eight when she published her first book and several of the others were in their early forties. Their versions of Australian childhood, written at a stage of life at which others were turning to autobiography, might make an interesting comparison if literary history did not so determinedly keep them apart. Similarly, at a time when so much attention is given to women writers, it is surprising that little has so far been said about the ways in which Australian women have written for and about children. This is a promising field for someone to explore.

The sense of place was a particular strength in many of the novels of the 1960s. Hesba Brinsmead's *Pastures of the Blue Crane* (1964), set in north-eastern New South Wales, and her Blue Mountains family chronicles, which began with *Longtime Passing* (1971), are outstanding examples. In the children's books of the 1980s, the setting is less likely to be so precisely individualised. Some of the most highly praised novels of 1986, like Simon French's *All We Know* and Donna Sharp's *Blue Days*, depend on characterisation rather than setting, and are recognisably Australian rather than regionally placed. Ruth Park's *My Sister Sif*, a fable of the future, creates an Edenic physical world on a

Pacific island in the twenty-first century. In *Taronga*, Victor Kelleher uses the Sydney Zoo for his nightmare of survival after the nuclear war has wiped out most of the world; although the place could hardly be more specific, the nature of the story transforms it. In Allan Baillie's *Riverman*, a journey into the past in the Tasmanian wilderness, there is a strong feeling for a particular region, but Gillian Rubinstein's *Space Demons*, a brilliant fantasy about children trapped in a computer game, could have been set anywhere. It was a shock as well as a victory in 1969, when Margaret Balderson's *When Jays Fly to Barbmo*, set in wartime Norway, won the Book of the Year Award; as the first prize-winner to use a European setting it marked a necessary stage. Nearly twenty years later it is not an issue to trouble the judges or anyone else. The question of Australianism as a moral imperative seems almost as remote as Ethel Turner's colonial oath of 1894. Today's writers, with an international readership and multinational publishers, need not think too much about 'the Australian child' or 'the English child'. Their real problem, as the twentieth century closes, is in knowing what childhood experience itself may be.

Notes

This discussion is based mainly on work done for my *Australia Through the Looking-Glass: Children's Fiction, 1830-1980* (1984). Ivan Southall's comment on his early reading comes from *A Journey of Discovery* (1975) and that of P. L. Travers from Egoff, Stubbs and Ashley (eds), *Only Connect* (1969). The Turner-Steele correspondence from which I quote is held in the Mitchell Library (State Library of New South Wales). Some of Mary Grant Bruce's papers, held in the La Trobe Library (State Library of Victoria), also shed light on the publishing history of the Billabong series. I have also looked at the role of Ward Lock in *Seven Little Billabongs: the World of Ethel Turner and Mary Grant Bruce* (1979). Frank Eyre's *Oxford in Australia, 1890-1978* (1978) is one source for the discussion of Oxford University Press in the 1950s and 1960s. The perspective of the authors themselves, in my own correspondence with Eleanor Spence and Hesba Brinsmead, supplements the official history. In 1981, while preparing to write *Australia Through the Looking-Glass*, I sent a questionnaire to forty Australian writers of children's books, asking about their publishing experience and their attitudes towards the use of Australian settings and idiom in their books; their replies have contributed to this discussion. A chapter in Geoffrey Dutton's *Snow on the Saltbush* (1984), 'What Some Writers Used To Read', is based on the replies of forty-five Australian writers to a questionnaire on their early Australian literary influences. 'What emerged most powerfully,' Dutton comments, 'was that the children's books these writers read were those that gave them the strongest sense of belonging to Australia. Mary Grant Bruce was the most popular writer (read by as many boys as girls), followed by Ethel Turner, May Gibbs, Mrs Aeneas Gunn (*We of the Never-Never*), Louise Mack, Norman Lindsay (*The Magic Pudding*) and Ethel Pedley (*Dot and the Kangaroo*). The only other writers to have anywhere near the same following were Henry Lawson, Marcus Clarke and Rolf Boldrewood, followed by Ion Idriess, C. J. Dennis and Steele Rudd.' Lee Harding's comments on the novels of the 1970s were published in *Reading Time* (76, July 1980).

The annual judges' reports on the Children's Book Council awards are published in the Council's journal *Reading Time*. Walter McVitty's 'The Effect of Children's Book Awards', *Reading Time*, 85 (October 1982), and Margaret Hamilton's 'Publishing of Australian Children's Books', *Reading Time*, 100 (July 1986) consider questions of sales as well as standards. 'Aboriginal Children's Literature: Continuing Resistance to Colonization', by Michael J. Singh (*Reading Time* 86, January 1983), looks at some of the problems of cultural integration.

Chapter 34

Autobiography

Chris Wallace-Crabbe

Autobiography seems to be a parody, or at least a black-and-white caricature, of other literary genres. It makes the same claim to refer to life as other genres do, but a good deal more crassly. It makes the same claims about truth and edification, but is more blatant about them. And it brings rapidly to the fore all those coarse, nagging questions about whether it is art—formal, aesthetic, beautiful and all that—or merely documentation. It is not surprising, then, that autobiographies have begun to receive a great deal more critical questioning at a time when the construction of all literary canons has become subject to radical questioning.

Culturally speaking, it is also the case that the subjective faceting of experience goes pressing on from fragmentation to fragmentation: that the romantic movement never stops regenerating itself. And this pressure makes its way from texts into social habits and into our very selves, irradiating our dailiness in ways that are scarcely noticeable any longer. As Rockwell Gray wrote in *Kenyon Review* in 1982, 'one sees the spider web of autobiography woven in myriad corners. Tentacular, boldly extended, imperialistic—the impulse presses into our writing, our speech, our taste in reading, our very patterns of self-perception.' Everything we experience is somehow saturated with subjectivity.

We are looking here at the admission of a new genre, that of autobiography and memoir, to the category of serious literature. How did it get in? Who left the gate open? How did autobiography disguise itself? Or were the rules of the game changed for some clutch of reasons? Like any serious question in literary history this problem leads out in different directions, fanning into the passive crystallisation of separate decisions which is historical process. Let us, since we have no option, come at the modern rise of auto-biography from several different angles.

In H. M. Green's *A History of Australian Literature* (1961) autobiographies are treated in chapters which bear the cross-generic title 'History, Biography, Description', which is to say that they are tucked away as one of the ancillary kinds of history. Green does, admittedly, air the question of how history may rise to being literature, but it does not emerge as a pressing issue in the case of the autobiographies he discusses.

Important books have a tendency to appear in exactly the right year. There are exceptions, of course, most notably Furphy's *Such is Life* (1903), which was published either ten years too late or sixty years too early. But serious works of literature have a tendency simultaneously to represent historical processes and to engender them, so that it appears in retrospect there was no other time at which they could have appeared.

Hal Porter's *The Watcher on the Cast-Iron Balcony* is probably the most widely studied and surely the most brilliant of all Australian autobiographies. Its publication in 1963 has exactly that implied rightness, and it initiates the decades in which autobiography and memoir in this country became a discernible artistic genre. Before that year autobiographies were merely the handmaidens of the 'real' modes: fiction, poetry, drama, even history. In 1963, to adapt a phrase of Virginia Woolf's, everything changed.

Let us pause over this. Nothing is harder to trace than historical causation, above all in literary history—above all in the short span of our own literary history. What is the nature of this particular histori-cal crux, and what the relation between cart, horse, stick and carrot?

To begin from chronological facts, how conveniently the year 1963 marks a climax and watershed in this matter of writing the self into a book. As well as Porter's *Watcher*, it saw the publication of Miles Franklin's *Childhood at Brindabella*—a deliberate auto-biography though very inferior to her fictional treatment of much the same materials in *My Brilliant Career*—Katharine Susannah Prichard's *Child of the Hurricane,* and Xavier Herbert's larrikinish *Disturbing Element.* Whatever their informative virtues, none of these three has been seen to encourage any complexity of aesthetic judgement. Jack Lindsay had completed his autobiographical trilogy with the appearance of *Fanfrolico and After* the previous year. In 1964 there would appear that stunningly successful autobiographical novel *My Brother Jack*, by George Johnston. It would be joined in 1965 by two more Melbourne autobiographies, Graham McInnes' *The Road to Gundagai* and Martin Boyd's *Day of My Delight*, the latter subtitled 'An Anglo-Australian Memoir' and filled with the same array of preoccupations as are to be found in Boyd's better novels, as well as in his first stab at autobiography, twenty-six years earlier. It was always characteristic of Boyd's stance to present himself as both eccentric and representative; thus he could suggest that, 'As far as I know I am the only one to put on record the kind of life led by these people, even if I have done it with a touch of levity.' It should be added that Boyd's memoir has a lot to say about religious belief, an area which seems to be taboo in most Australian life stories.

This bundle of broadly contemporary texts should immediately make clear what I mean by calling 1963 a watershed. The books by Franklin, Prichard and Herbert all lean backwards, not just because they abjure the formal procedures of modernism but also because all three quietly assume that an autobiography is merely secondary, merely the writing out of background information about the *real* person who wrote the novels. This is not to say that these books are factually truthful; they contain as much subjective swerving from crude fact as anybody else's life story; but they all treat the writing of the self-life as a low-pressure operation, not to be compared in imaginative density with the writing of actual novels. Even Prichard's book settles down to modest recollection after a catastrophist beginning in which the little girl's birth coincides with a hurricane hitting Suva.

But let us come back to the tangled question of historical causation. Why did Hal Porter's book come out in 1963 and why did our attitude to autobiographical writing change? It may only have been a matter of Australia responding to strong overseas influences. Such books as Edwin Muir's *Autobiography* (1954), Nabokov's *Speak, Memory* (1951) and Leonard Woolf's first volumes had helped to bring such writing overseas to a new level of self-conscious art. Such books may have done much to make possible the kind of writing Porter achieved, as well as that to be found in Maie Casey's modernist memoir, *An Australian Story* (1962) and in Donald Horne's *The Education of Young Donald* (1967). And whatever potent forces were in the air in the early part of the decade would lead in 1964 to Jean-Paul Sartre's elegantly ironic masterpiece, *Les Mots*.

Does a spate of Australian autobiographies represent our dependence on overseas cultural movements, then, or does it signify distinctive movements in our own culture? In chapter 17 Brian Kiernan suggests that the early 1960s in Australia was a period notable for cultural introspection, for reflection and analysis. There must be some correlation between this and the concurrent flurry of autobiographical writings. It is of interest to see that such writing falls away steeply in the late 1960s and early 1970s, only to bloom again in the 1980s. Without going as far as Brecht's hardhearted assertion that 'a deep need makes for a superficial grasp', the conflicts and pressures of the Vietnam War period did not favour personal reflection, but rather pushed the imagination outward, bringing it to bear on public issues and the definition of political stances. The poetry of Bruce Beaver and Vincent Buckley stood out against the current as, more obliquely, did Frank Moorhouse's diplomatically slippery stories, but in general the 1970s were a blank period for the writing of self-life stories, or at least for their publication. Surely the art of autobiography flourishes better when politics are vegetating. It should be added that some of the kinds of experimental writing which were being practised at this stage were performative or impersonal, marked by a mannerist disregard for subjectivity. The 'an-aesthetic' position espoused by John Tranter in his introduction to *The New Australian Poetry* (1979) was but one example of this cold swing against subjective utterance.

If we turn to the blooming of autobiographies and memoirs since 1980, a further point should be made. It is unfortunately true that academia exerts an influence on the progress of literature, and the universities which were expanding so fast a quarter of a century ago have kept up their literary offerings and diversified them, teaching more Australian writing and looking for new texts to study. As their courses became more adventurous and more inconoclastic, the universities and colleges moved on from the firm tradition of foregrounding three genres (fiction, poetry and drama) and opened their gates wide to autobiographies; radical theory also came willingly to the party, unpacking the supposed continuity of the first-person pronoun. (After the speculations of Barthes, Lacan and Kristeva, what author can write, 'I am', with impunity?) This broad development has also received a great deal of support from the committees who design the syllabuses for secondary schools. A recent favourite for discussion, at whatever level, has been A. B. Facey's *A Fortunate Life* (1981). A rattling good yarn, this has the paradoxical critical advantage of not even being 'good' writing, yet being full of common topics to which every bosom returns an Aussie echo. In its easy give and take between private memories and romantic expectations, between honesty and acquired cliché, Facey's book sits down well with Freud's insight in *The Psychopathology of Everyday Life* (1901) that

> Childhood memories come in general to acquire the significance of screen memories, and in doing so offer a remarkable analogy with childhood memories that a modern nation preserves in its store of legends and myths.

Like Lawson's stories and Alan Marshall's *I Can Jump Puddles,* Facey provides readers with the deepest of mimetic consolations, the assurance that they have come fully into contact with the real Australia: the text can be felt as utterly dinkum. It has already shown itself to be capable of bearing widely different readings. How it will weather is another question.

At this point we should turn to the possibility of reading subject and process, author and influences, quite differently. Hal Porter's verbally inventive talent had for years been expressing itself in short stories, and in one melodramatic historical novel. What the stories had revealed, by and large, was that he had 'one story, and one story only' to tell: the self-story, done in different facets and locations. According to this reading, we should take 1963 as signalling the point at which he had fully realised what had been implicit in most of those shorter narratives, the tug of past authorial experience, the challenge to come to plain terms with the trinity of author, narrator and protagonist in telling the wry tale of that young Hal Porter who grows from non-innocence to the bruised innocence of young manhood. All Porter's flair for evocation of locality, period, fabrics, furniture, foods and fads could at last be drawn upon for a book-length narrative. If he had never had any gusto for the invention of characters, he had a stunning theatrical gift for the development of conceivable selves, playing with the present tense, with pronouns and with readerly expectations. Throughout *The Watcher,* self is conceived not as stable ego but as a theatre in which all sorts of possibilities and processes act themselves out. We can hear this in the springing grammar of such sentences as 'What shocks me, then and now, is that, as a writer, I have been outraced before I begin to run and that, if I wish to outrace, I shall never be able to stop running' and 'Anyway, I am already the only mourner at one of my own funerals'. This is the most thespian of all our autobiographies, capering between three re-runs of the same death.

In the long run, a lot of the proof of the autobiographical pudding resides in its complexity of approach, its air of overdetermination in the told events. Our virtue rejoices in being able to read a book in several different ways. In the first volume—but not the latter two—of Porter's trilogy we find this. The text is as rich as a fruitcake. A similar multiplicity in the ways of envisaging a self distinguishes Bernard Smith's *The Boy Adeodatus* (1984), but in this case the shifts and tropes are cultural, political, even religious, rather than being deployed for aesthetic distancing. Smith's Marxism demands that his book should conduct an inquiry into the historical forces which shaped a particular Australian life, but like many autobiographers he also wants vivid epiphanies. For example, we may read his second chapter, 'Celtic Twilight', either as an attempt to explore the oral village culture of Co. Cavan or as a numinous celebration of Irish tales in the blood. Or as both, one feature of the book being its refusal to close off possibilities, its repeated framing of the life experiences—in St Augustine, in the legend of the Nuts of Knowledge, in Marxism, in oral history, in art history. Like Porter, but consistently, Smith writes in the third-person singular; this novelistic swerve allows both authors to write with some explicitness about sexual intercourse, a subject much neglected by auto-biographers.

The case of Smith also suggests how often the protagonist is portrayed with impact if shown leaning against an ideology. Or, to put it another way, ideological structures are part of the history which we welcome in an autobiography. In a surprising number of Australian books the ideology in question is Marxist (Jack Lindsay's dazzling trilogy being a curious exception, giving all its weight to re-creation and almost none to the authorial subject); in Donald Horne's two volumes and Vincent Buckley's *Cutting Green Hay* (1983) it is anti-communist and in Boyd, as we have noted, it is religious-pacifist.

Two political autobiographies of particular interest have appeared in the mid-1980s, both locking the dramatic self into historical process. Oriel Gray's *Exit Left* (1985) is in some ways the lighter of these, giving a racy account of a woman's restless life in New Theatre circles, its bohemian exchanges handled with the ease of a good novelist. However it offers an implicit feminist critique of the left-wing world within which Gray moved, not merely in its portrayal of the male-dominated Party machine but also in the priority her text gives to the private nexus of sexual relations. Roger Milliss writes a more publicly analytical book in *Serpent's Tooth* (1984), overloading his life story with so much political history that his focus sometimes seems uncertain. Twice as long as Gray's book, *Serpent's Tooth* concentrates particularly and with anguish on the Oedipal struggle between a loving Stalinist father and his 'softer' communist son; it simultaneously offers a treatment of Australian communism from the Depression through to 1970. Section three, 'Byzantium', is a compelling account of an outsider's life in the Soviet Union in the 1960s, its particularity interwoven with the story of a creaky marriage in which 'All we could do was tacitly agree to try to make the best of things and hope that what we sought from one another would emerge and grow in time.' Perhaps everybody's turning of life into a text has a prime emotional spur: in Milliss' case, as in Porter's very different *Watcher,* it is the attempt to expiate guilt. For some unexplained reason, *Serpent's Tooth* carries the sub-title 'An Autobiographical Novel'.

Of course, the line between autobiographies and novels is not only devious but frequently quite blurred. *My Brother Jack* proves itself to be a novel, at the very least by its use of fictitious names, however much it may have borrowed events from the author's own life; and like Henry Handel Richardson before him Johnston ran remembered people together to build composite characters. Nevertheless, readers tend to regard *My Brother Jack* as an autobiography. So they do David Malouf's slender, stylish, underpopulated *Johnno* (1975); this book resembles most of Malouf's successful fiction in being structured as a narrated memoir of novella length. The narrator's voice and tempo remain recognisable even in those books where he becomes Ovid or an Italian terrorist. *Johnno* has an additional interest, however, in that the same 'material' is used in an elegiac poem for a friend—'The Judas Touch', dedicated to J[ohn] M[illiner]—and in the title section of Malouf's own memoir, *12 Edmonstone Street* (1985), with its similarly eloquent fetishism of objects.

Texts learn from texts, even down to the umpteenth generation. Just as the eighteenth-century novel again and again learned from letters, voyages, memoirs and Tyburn confessions, so the auto-biography in our time has kept showing its willingness to imitate that powerful genre, the novel. Transactions between the 'true' and the 'fictive' mode have shown every possible blend of ingredients. We may glide from the extremely complicated novelistic adaptation of family memories in *The Fortunes of Richard Mahony* through Boyd's and Lawson's transactions with the self-life to *My Brilliant Career,* where autobiography was ever so slenderly decked out as romantic fiction, and to Waten's *Alien Son,* which seemed both thoroughly realist and a variant on all traditional Jewish storytelling. Again, Jack Lindsay's trilogy bears a strong resemblance to the typical English *Bildungsroman* of the early twentieth century: arty kid makes good, with lots of escapades and local colour.

Certain strains in nineteenth-century fiction stand behind a curious sub-genre in our writing: life stories of Melbourne toffs. This little tradition includes Maie Casey's *Tides and Eddies* (1966), Dame Mabel Brookes' *Memoirs* (1974), Kathleen Fitzpatrick's *Solid Bluestone Foundations* (1983) and Kathleen Mangan's *Daisy Chains, War, then Jazz* (1984), all of them much preoccupied with houses, sense-impressions and the easy movement of gentry to and fro. Fitzpatrick writes at length of her Buxton grandparents' waterfront mansion, Hughendon, to whose inhabitants 'South Melbourne did not represent trackless worlds, but the cradle of their race': the phrase could easily have come from Boyd. In *Afternoon Light* (1967) R. G. Menzies aspires to the company of the toffs, his text being glazed with literary allusions and stunningly external; his obsession with Winston Churchill neatly combines the cringe and the strut. Brookes' is the keenest and most wide-ranging of these books: her writing is packed with nouns, suggesting a life moving through a world of solid tangible objects. Her positivism reanimates a chain of historical moments.

On the whole, rentier and middle-class writers tend to pride themselves on their capacity for gathering perceptions and to rely on the eye, organ of separation, rather than on the ear, organ of community. At the one extreme we have McInnes, Maie Casey, Patrick White and Malouf, collecting memory's colour slides with their private, numinous glow; at the other, the writers whose memories seize on the way individuals gather, clash and interact to form successive social units. Alan Marshall's economical and very popular *I Can Jump Puddles* (1955) is an example of this latter kind; so too is *Exit Left.* Far from the left wing, we can also find it in Donald Horne's *The Education of Young Donald,* in which the protagonist's need for ego-integration leads him to keep attaching himself to groups, student cabals and incipient literary movements. ('Ostracism is a fearful thing ... Most don't understand, of course, or are too stupid to have the experience. A sense of injustice always surrounds it.') Horne's interest in social groupings and in the way they replace the family circle makes him one of the most interesting social historians among our autobiographers. The authorial subject also maintains a very quaint ironical distance from his earlier self, categorising him as both 'young Donald' and 'D. R. Horne', while sprinkling the text liberally with quotation marks most comically in the sentence, 'Several days later I fell in love with a different "woman".' In a sequel, *Confessions of a New Boy* (1985), such syntactical irony becomes so strong that the prose frequently has the tone of Anthony Powell's fiction. Horne is an author who leans towards *knowing* rather than towards openness, for all his social inquisitiveness.

Another point should be made about social class. Very few autobiographies give a voice to those who were not already vocal. The selves who are privileged in these texts have almost always been privileged already: most have made a reputation as writers, the self-story building its sandcastle on top of existing fiction, or poetry, or journalism. Among the few exceptions are Facey and 'Caddie', a Sydney barmaid who published her story in 1953. Another 'unliterary' work of some interest is Margaret Tucker's *If Everyone Cared* (1977), the anecdotal account of an Aboriginal woman who grew up in the Riverina and who distinguishes between Liliardia, her authentic self, and the woman who has been named by the dominant culture; also striking in this book is the casual counterpoint between textual and photographic evidence. All too little has been written about photographs as autobiography. *An Aboriginal Mother Tells of the Old and the New* (1984) is another stirring memoir by a writer divided between two cultural identities, Labumore and Elsie Roughsey; and Sally Morgan's *My Place* (1987) gradually reveals, in detective-story fashion, the suppressed Aboriginal past of a young woman.

Mention should also be made of two maverick autobiographies by particularly versatile writers. Patrick White's *Flaws in the Glass* (1981) is cobbled from three disparate parts: a vivid, tesselated personal exploration which occupies the first two-thirds of the book; a dull Aegean travel interlude; and 'Episodes and Epitaphs', a ferocious bunch of personal sketches which remind one of how judgementally timid our autobiographers commonly are. *Unreliable Memoirs* (1980), by the expatriate critic Clive James, is marked out by the liveliness with which it can metamorphose experience into one-liners and hilarious vignettes.

For the sake of some clarity of definition (definition being a commodity hard to come by in literary criticism) this discussion has kept its eye on works which might justly be called autobiographies rather than merely *memoirs,* the memoir as a rule lacking that drive to interpret a life which marks the larger genre. In this it follows the French critic, Philippe Lejeune, who insists that a proper auto-biography must 'try to show the profound unity of a life'. Accordingly, books like Ellen Newton's *This Bed My Centre* (1979) and Peter Ryan's *Fear Drive My Feet* (1959) have been left aside, since they dramatise one section of a lifetime, a phase which fate has marked with a particular accent.

Poetry is another cup of tea again. Most lyric poetry, however subjective and self-analytical in demeanour, cannot seriously be compared with autobiographical texts because it lacks length, factual fullness, causal chains, continuous traction. Some poets, certainly, tease us into believing that if sufficient of their lyrics are read in the right way the person 'behind' the poetry will emerge, dripping with real life. Gwen Harwood, for instance, is a writer whose poems gain much of their emotional power from such titillation; yet the games and melodramatic sleights of her poetry are so adroit that we can find no personal vantage point from which to interpret them. Dorothy Hewett's poetry raises similar questions, hinting at a raunchy life which is designed to eroticise the text. Bruce Beaver's *Letters to Live Poets* (1969), on the other hand, alludes directly, continuously to the dailiness of experience in the manner of a journal or of fragmentary memoirs, never seeking to impose a whole view on his successive immediacies.

What we can find in the period, however, are certain suites of poems which are organised—despite their lyrical mode—in such a way as to permit a fuller telling of the self-life. Most notably these include Vincent Buckley's 'Golden Builders' (1976), Robert Adamson's *Where I Come From* (1979) and the 'On the Western Line' sequence from James McAuley's *Surprises of the Sun* (1969), although this last is far more elliptical than the other two suites.

The twenty-seven poems in 'Golden Builders' offer glints of a life at different stages between young manhood and middle age; they also work on the atavistic assumption that places, parts of inner Melbourne, are somehow charged with the life that has been lived in them: landscape as palimpsest. The question which keeps accompanying Buckley's expressionist urban scenes is 'Will I find my soul here?' Echoes of Blake's mythological poems work as a tool with the aid of which Buckley attempts to evoke his own life in changing, intensely physical places. The numinous, even neurasthenic mimesis of these poems is absent from his prose autobiography, *Cutting Green Hay* (1983), which tends to concern itself with cultural movements and micropolitics.

Robert Adamson's poetry of self is artfully simple, almost Hemingwayan, in contrast to Buckley's highly coloured orchestration: it is also far more secular, so that the unity it finds is vitalistic diversity, successively framing moments of conflict, delinquency or sexual experience. Where Adamson's poems offer the endless prelude to a life, McAuley's hanker after closure and explicit significance. His re-creations from childhood, adolescence and marriage are pinched between the question, 'Why change the memory into metaphors / That solitary child would disavow?' and the blocking answer.

> It's my own judgement day that I draw near,
> Descending in the past, without a clue
> Down to that central deadness: the despair
> Older than any hope I ever knew.

There can be no doubt that the late twentieth century is a time which favours a diversity of autobiographical writing. Overseas at least, it is already sending up growths of autobiographical theory. There is a great deal to be written about the small print in the autobiographical contract. How, for instance, should one discuss fiction like that of Frank Moorhouse in which the fictive characters mingle with accurately named people in recognisable places? What kinds of lying do we allow autobiographers to practise? Are autobiographies really novels? And what difference will the present spread of oral history bring to the genre? Just as Emerson described *The Divine Comedy* as 'autobiography in colossal cipher', it does seem that an understanding of the role of the authorial subject in autobiographies sheds light on the construction and contractual obligations of all literature.

Notes

Three French works which have broadened the terms of reference for talking about self-texts and textual selves are Roland Barthes' *The Pleasure of the Text* (1975), Gaston Bachelard's *The Poetics of Space*

(1969) and Philippe Lejeune's *Le Pacte Autobiographique* (1975). *Roland Barthes* (1977) by Roland Barthes charmingly dismantles the genre while practising it, and Carolyn Steedman's *Landscape for a Good Woman: a Story of Two Lives* calls the middle-class assumptions of all such writing in question by focusing on the lives of working-class women. Important works of recent criticism include *Autobiographical Acts* (1976) by Elizabeth Bruss, Roy Pascal's *Design and Truth in Autobiography* (1960), W. C. Spengemann's *The Forms of Autobiography* (1980) and Paul Jay's *Being in the Text* (1984). Paul de Man's 'Autobiography as De-facement', *MLN*, 94 (1979) is an especially challenging article.

Any account of Australian autobiography should pay tribute to the boldness of Nettie Palmer's *Fourteen Years* (1948), a book which displays the editorial strokes which could transform journal entries into an intellectual history. Two theoretical works have been of particular value: Alan Davies' *Private Politics: a Study of Five Political Temperaments* (1962), for all that it is not a work of literary criticism, and Richard Coe's *When the Grass Was Taller: Autobiography and the Experience of Childhood* (1984), for all that it is omnivorously piecemeal. Garry Kinnane, in *George Johnston: a Biography* (1986) is interesting about the relations between life and invention in the works of an autobiographical novelist. There are some useful essays in *Autobiographical and Biographical Writing in the Commonwealth* (1984), edited by Doireann MacDermott, and the salutary life stories of 'sixteen modern Australian women' in *The Half-Open Door* (1982), edited by Patricia Grimshaw and Lynne Strahan. One volume of critical essays which displays a particular concern for the autobiographical impulse is Fay Zwicky's *The Lyre in the Pawnshop: Essays on Literature and Survival, 1974-1984* (1986). *The Penguin Book of Australian Autobiography* (1987) is a historical anthology edited by John and Dorothy Colmer.

APPENDIX: SOURCES FOR THE STUDY OF AUSTRALIAN LITERATURE

JOHN ARNOLD

Australian literature is well served by guides to its resources, and this appendix will survey the major reference works, bibliographies and sources for reading and research. The most up-to-date guide is the 'English language and literature' section in *Australians: A Guide to Sources* (1987), one of the volumes in the bicentenary series, *Australians: A Historical Library*. Compiled by Alan Lawson, D. Blair and Marcie Muir, it contains a survey of sources, followed by 108 annotated references. Lawson, along with Fred Lock, also compiled *Australian Literature: a Reference Guide* (1980). The Gale Research Company of Michigan has published three Australian volumes in its 'Guides to Literature in English' series. The best of these is Barry Andrews and William H. Wilde's *Australian Literature to 1900: A Guide to Information Sources* (1980). The section on 'Bibliographies and bibliographical guides' is particularly useful. Companion works in the series are *Modern Australian Prose, 1901-1975* compiled by A. Grove Day (1980) and Herbert Jaffa's *Modern Australian Poetry, 1920-1970* (1979).

There are several approaches to gaining an overview of Australian literature. The quickest is to scan the article on 'Literature' in volume 6 of the *Australian Encyclopaedia* (1983); the most ambitious is to read H. M. Green's *A History of Australian Literature: Pure and Applied* . . . 2 vols, (1961). This work of more than 1400 pages attempts to survey all forms of Australian writing, and a revised edition by Green's widow, the poet and critic Dorothy Green, was published in 1984.

The Oxford History of Australian Literature, edited by Leonie Kramer (1981), is a scholarly and formal study consisting of three long chapters on fiction, drama and poetry, plus an extensive bibliography compiled by Joy Hooton. Ken Goodwin's *A History of Australian Literature* (1986) has a useful chronology of Australian literature and related events. For ready reference one cannot do better than *The Oxford Companion to Australian Literature* (1985). This takes a wide view on what constitutes literature, and besides the entries on authors and their works, the *Companion* covers, via its many subject entries, the literary, historical and other cultural contexts within which these works can be placed. Also valuable in this area is H. Priessnitz, 'Australian literature: a preliminary subject checklist', *Australian Literary Studies*, 11 (1984).

Although there is no one comprehensive bibliography of Australian books, there are several sources which together give an adequate coverage of the country's publishing and literary output. Sir John Ferguson's seven-volume *Bibliography of Australia* (1941-69; facsimile, 1974-77) is the first of these. Its arrangement is chronological to 1850, and alphabetical thereafter. Ferguson included only creative literature in the chronological volumes and an addendum to these was published by the National Library in 1986. The library is also planning a three-volume addendum to the 1851-1900 volumes.

In 1936 the Commonwealth (now National) Library began publishing and *Annual Catalogue of Australian Publications*. This has grown into the *Australian National Bibliography*, which is a comprehensive listing with detailed indexes of what is published each year. Since 1972 its arrangement has been a classified one, enabling the user to go straight to the literature sections to see what books of, say, fiction or verse were published in any one year. The National Library, as part of its contribution to the bicentenary, plans to produce a *Retrospective National Bibliography*. This will cover monographs published in the period known as 'the Ferguson gap', that is, from 1901 to 1950, the year that the *Annual Catalogue . . .* is considered to have attained adequate coverage.

Two important sources for details and holdings of retrospective Australiana are *The Mitchell Library . . . Dictionary Catalog of Printed Books*, 38 vols plus supplement (1968-70) and the *National Union Catalogue of Monographs (NUCOM)*. The Mitchell Library, State Library of New South Wales, has one of the most comprehensive holdings of Australiana in the world, and its published catalogue complements Ferguson as a bibliography of Australiana. *NUCOM* is an alphabetical card index of the holdings of books in major libraries in Australia published both here and abroad. It has been published in microformat in three series, covering holdings reported to 1974, 1975-80 and 1981-84, but is no longer compiled, having been replaced by the on-line *Australian Bibliographic Network (ABN)*. An outline of this is given in the *Guide to the National Union Catalogue of Australia* (1985).

Ferguson, the Mitchell Library catalogue, *NUCOM* and *ABN* are all accessible in the major State and academic libraries in Australia, along with the following bibliographies devoted specifically to Australian literature. E. Morris Miller's *Australian Literature . . . a Descriptive and Bibliographical Survey . . . to 1938*, 2 vols (1940; facsimile 1973) includes critical and biographical information, bibliographical listings, an author index and a fiction subject index. It was rearranged into one straight alphabetical author listing and updated to 1950 by Frederick T. Macartney and published as *Australian Literature: a Bibliography to 1938 . . . Extended to 1950* (1956). This is often referred to as 'Miller and Macartney' and one of the serious gaps in Australian literary research is that there has been no update of it. Some of the major works are listed in Grahame Johnston's *Annals of Australian Literature* (1970) and G. V. Hubble's *Modern Australian Fiction, 1940-1965* (1969). However, for any degree of comprehensiveness, one has to consult the annual volumes of the *Australian National Bibliography* as well as *NUCOM* and *ABN*.

The State libraries throughout Australia have in-depth collections of Australian literature, while the major academic libraries have extensive collections. Public libraries hold stocks of contemporary and established writers, and all have access to other collections through the inter-library loan network. These resources and collections will be outlined in the Library Association of Australia's forthcoming *Encyclopaedia of Australian Archives, Information Services and Libraries*. For overseas readers, access to Australian books, especially out-of-print titles, can be difficult. The Australian High Commission at Australia House in London has a large Australiana library and the various Australian consulates throughout the world have libraries attached to them. These are listed as an appendix to the annual *Australian Books: A Select List of Recent Publications and Standard Works in Print* (1949-). There are also Australiana collections of varying sizes attached to the Australian studies centres and libraries at overseas universities which teach Australian studies. A list of these is available from the Cultural Section, Department of Foreign Affairs in Canberra. In the United

States, holdings of Australiana are included in the *National Union Catalog Pre-56 Imprints*, 754 vols (1968-81) and its successor, the *National Union Catalog (NUC)*.

Access to specific research material such as manuscripts and private papers is more selective. It usually involves a visit to the holding institution or obtaining microform copies. The National Library publishes the *Guide to Collections of Manuscripts Relating to Australia*, which is in effect a union catalogue and the fourth series, published in microfiche form in 1985, includes a name-index to all collections and sub-groups within collections detailed in the four series. *Our Heritage: A Directory to Archives and Manuscript Repositories in Australia* (1983) contains details on the National and State libraries, and other repositories relevant to Australian literary research, including the Baillieu Library, University of Melbourne and the Fryer Library, University of Queensland.

Australian Books in Print (1956-) is the standard guide to books available for purchase. It is arranged by author, title and key-word subject and is published quarterly on microfiche and annually in book form. Each issue also lists Australian publishers and local agents for overseas publishers. A recent offshoot is *Australian Books in Print by Subject* (1986-). Similar trade publications are available for British titles (*British Books in Print*) and American imprints (*Books in Print*). Booksellers, both new and secondhand, are listed in business and telephone directories.

Several series of reprints have helped to overcome the problem of the unavailability of texts. Both nineteenth and twentieth-century novels have been reprinted in facsimile form in the Angus and Robertson/Lloyd O'Neil 'Australian Classics' series, while Virago Press in London and Pandora Press in Melbourne are both reprinting novels by Australian women writers. A valuable series, especially for teaching purposes, is published by the University of Queensland Press as the 'Australian Authors' series, formerly 'Portable Australian Authors'. To date fifteen titles have been published; when devoted to a single author, they consist of a reprint of a major work plus a selection of other writings supported by an introduction, commentary and notes. The Department of English at the University College of the Australian Defence Force Academy, is planning a 'Colonial Text Series' of scholarly editions of select nineteenth-century Australian novels.

The new series of the *Australian Book Review* (1978-), published ten times a year, aims to review or at least notice every Australian book, whether published locally or overseas. The Footscray Institute of Technology Library has published two indexes to it, covering the first thirty seven numbers (October 1978-December 1981). However, there has been no national book review indexing service since the Libraries Board of South Australia suspended publication of its *Index to Australian Book Reviews*, which appeared quarterly with annual cumulations from March 1965 to June 1981. For recent reviews, one has to rely on the unpublished in-house indexes compiled by the major State libraries and the selective 'Annual Bibliography of Studies in Australian Literature' published in *Australian Literary Studies* (see below).

Reviews of Australian books can also be found in the *Index to the Argus* (Melbourne, 1910-49), the *Sydney Morning Herald Index* (1927-61) and the two volumes of the *Meanjin Quarterly Index* covering 1940-65 and 1966-76 respectively (1969; 1983). There are also in-house indexes in several major research libraries, the most important of which is the card 'Index to Selected Melbourne Magazines and Newspapers, 1880-1900' in the Fryer Library, University of Queensland. International reviews of books by Australian authors can be found in *The Times Literary Supplement Cumulative Index* (1902-39, 2 vols; 1940-80, 3 vols; and 1981-5, 1 vol.) and *The New York Times Book Review Index, 1896-1970*, 2 vols (1973). There is also the *Book Review Digest* (quarterly with annual cumulations and cumulative indexes, 1905-) and *Book Review Index* annual with master cumulation for 1965-84 (1965-).

Australian literary magazines, both past and present, are surveyed in *Cross Currents: Magazines and Newspapers in Australian Literature*, edited by Bruce Bennett (1981). Holdings of these and all other Australian serials are listed in the *National Union Catalogue of Serials* (*NUCOS*), issued twice-yearly in microfiche form with full cumulations by the National Library of Australia. Lurline Stuart's *Nineteenth Century Australian Periodicals: an Annotated Bibliography* (1979) gives full publication details of 449 periodicals which published creative literature in the nineteenth century, and includes an extensive index. Elizabeth Webby's *Early Australian Poetry . . .* (1982) is an annotated listing of original poetry published in Australian newspapers and magazines before 1850. John Tregenza's *Australian Little Magazines, 1923-1954: Their Role in Forming and Reflecting Literary Trends* (1964) includes a chronological bibliography. *Small Press Publishing in Australia: the Early 1970s* by Michael Denholm (1979) deals in part with the proliferation of little magazines published in the late 1960s and early 1970s. *The Australian Short Story: 1940-1980* (1980) compiled by Stephen Torre, is an extensive bibliography of short stories by Australian authors, and includes a list of periodicals publishing this medium.

The major scholarly journal is *Australian Literary Studies* (1963-). Published twice-yearly, it includes critical articles, reviews and interviews. Of particular importance is its 'Annual Bibliography of Studies in Australian Literature' published in the May number. As a companion to this book, Penguin intend to issue a cumulation of these annual bibliographies with added brief biographical details, to cover the first twenty-five years (1963-88) of their publication. *Australian Literary Studies* also publishes intermittently details of research in progress in Australian literature. *Notes and Furphies* (1978-), the bulletin and newsletter of the Association for the Study of Australian Literature, gives details of awards, current research including theses, forthcoming conferences and details of overseas courses in Australian studies. Other important periodicals include *Southerly* (Sydney, 1939-), *Meanjin* (Brisbane and Melbourne, 1940-), *Overland* (Melbourne, 1954-), *Quadrant* (Sydney, 1956-), *Westerly* (Perth, 1956-) and *Island Magazine* (Hobart 1979-).

The 'Australian Writers and their Work' booklets, first published by Lansdowne Press and later Oxford University Press, but now discontinued, were designed to provide a brief introduction to a number of Australian writers. Each of the thirty or so published gave a brief survey of the life and writings of the subjects, plus a select bibliography. The Australian volumes in the 'Twayne's World Authors' series published in Boston are similar in content, but longer, and likely to be more accessible to American readers than many of the other references cited in this survey. There have been several recent collections of interviews in which writers discuss their life and work. Amongst these are Jim Davidson's *Sideways from the Page* (1983), Jennifer Ellison's *Rooms of their Own* (1986) and the two compiled by Candida Baker, *Yacker: Australian Writers Talk About Their Work* and *Yacker 2 . . .* (1986; 1987).

Authors' professional journals, newsletters and directories often provide information on members' activities, literary awards and views on such questions as copyright and writers' earnings. The Australian Society of Authors publishes quarterly *The Australian Author* (1969-) while the State branches of the Fellowship of Australian Writers issue regular newsletters. The *Writers' and Photographers' Marketing Guide, Australia, New Zealand, Overseas,*

1982-83 (1982) is valuable for details of magazine markets, literary
agents and awards. *Bookmark* (1974-86) was an annual diary which
included a valuable directory for readers, writers and those involved
in the handling of books. It has ceased publication, but is likely to
reappear soon as a directory only. *The Writer's Directory: Writers for
Radio, Screen, Stage and Television in Australia* (1984) lists authors
working in the various media and includes their major credits and
awards.

Biographical information on Australian writers can be found
scattered throughout almost all the publications mentioned in this
appendix. A major reference is the multi-volume *Australian
Dictionary of Biography* (1966-). Readers who wish to know about
the environment which an author lived in and wrote about should
consult *The Oxford Literary Guide to Australia*, edited by Peter Pierce
(1987). There are also numerous regional guides and State histories.
Into this category come *The Literature of Western Australia* (1979);
Western Australian Literature: a Bibliography edited by Bruce Bennett,
Susan Ashford and John Hay (1981); Paul Depasquale's *A Critical
History of South Australian Literature, 1836-1970* ... (1978);
Queensland and Its Writers (100 Years—100 Writers) (1959) by Cecil
Hadgraft; and *Tasmanian Literary Landmarks* (1984) by Margaret
Giordano and Don Norman.

Graeme Kinross Smith's *Australian Writers* (1980) profiles some fifty
authors. *Australia Brought to Book: Responses to Australia by Visiting
Writers, 1836-1939* (1985), compiled by Kaye Harman, is a collection
of accounts and impressions of Australia by overseas writers.

The study of indigenous children's literature was given a
considerable boost in the 1970s by the publication of H. M. Saxby's *A
History of Australian Children's Literature*, 2 vols, (1969; 1971) and
Marcie Muir's *A Bibliography of Australian Children's Books*, 2 vols,
(1970; 1976). Saxby's work has been superseded somewhat by Brenda
Niall's *Australia Through the Looking Glass: Children's Fiction, 1830-
1980* (1984). Michael Dugan edited *The Early Dreaming: Australian
Children's Authors on Childhood* (1980), while in *Innocence and
Experience: Essays on Contemporary Australian Children's Writers*
(1981) Walter McVitty deals with the work of eight authors. Josie
Arnold and Tesha Piccinin's *A Practical Guide to Young Australian
Fiction* (1985) is a review of and commentary on more than 200
Australian children's books published between 1970 and 1982.
Marcie Muir in 1982 published *A History of Australian Children's
Book Illustration*.

The feminist movement and the resultant interest in women's studies has produced several studies of themes or particular periods, but not yet an overview. *Her Story: Australian Women in Print, 1788-1975* (1980), compiled by Margaret Bettison and Anne Summers, lists articles, chapters and books on all issues involving women. Arranged by subject, the section of 'The arts' and 'Individual biographies' is the most useful as regards Australian literature. Drusilla Modjeska's *Exiles at Home: Australian Women Writers, 1925-1945* (1981) is a pioneering study which includes a long bibliography. Two collections of essays on women's writings are *Who is She? Images of Women in Australian Fiction* (1983) edited by Shirley Walker; and *Gender, Politics and Fiction: Twentieth-Century Australian Women's Novels* (1985), edited by Carole Ferrier, which includes a checklist of Australian women's novels, 1900-83. The work of eighty-nine female writers, both past and present, is represented in *The Penguin Book of Australian Women Poets*, edited by Susan Hampton and Kate Llewellyn (1986).

The writing and depiction of minority groups in Australian literature is covered by various sources. J. J. Healy's *Literature and the Aborigine in Australia, 1770-1975* (1978) is a valuable overview and includes a select bibliography of perspectives on the Aborigines. There are two bibliographies that deal with ethnic literature. In 1983 Peter Lumb and Anne Heizell compiled *Diversity and Diversion: an Annotated Bibliography of Australian Ethnic Minority Literature*, which covers novels, short stories, biographies and autobiographies, and includes a thematic index. Lolo Houbein, *Ethnic Writings in English from Australia: a Bibliography* (1984) gives biographical information as well as details of authors' works. *Outrider* (Brisbane, 1984-) is a journal devoted to multicultural literature in Australia. An anthology of gay literature was published in 1983. Entitled *Edge City in Two Different Plans: a Collection of Lesbian and Gay Writings from Australia*, it includes the work of forty-two writers and gives brief biographical details.

NOTES ON CONTRIBUTORS

Barry Andrews was for many years a Senior Lecturer in English at the Australian Defence Force Academy before his death in 1987. He was one of the founders, and a President, of ASAL (the Association for the Study of Australian Literature). As well as many journal articles his publications include a monograph on *Price Warung* (1976) and an edition of his stories (1975); *Australian Literature to 1900* (1980) a bibliography compiled with W. H. Wilde; and, with W. H. Wilde & Joy Hooton, *The Oxford Companion to Australian Literature* (1985).

John Arnold is the La Trobe Research Librarian at the State Library of Victoria. He has published widely in Australian studies and has a particular interest in the life and work of Jack Lindsay. He is currently working on a history and bibliography of the Fanfrolico Press.

Bruce Bennett is an Associate Professor of English and Director of the Centre for Studies in Australian Literature at the University of Western Australia, where he edits *Westerly*. His publications include: *The Literature of Western Australia* (1979), *Cross Currents: Magazines and Newspapers in Australian Literature* (1981) and *Place, Region and Community* (1985). He is co-author, with Kay Daniels and Humphrey McQueen, of *Windows Onto Worlds: Studying Australia at Tertiary Level* (1987), the report of the Committee to Review Australian Studies in Tertiary Education.

Veronica Brady is a Senior Lecturer in English at the University of Western Australia. She is author of *Crucible of Prophets: Australians and the Question of God* (1981) and has published widely in Australian literature, culture and theology in journals in Australia and overseas. She was a member of the board of the Australian Broadcasting Corporation from 1983-1986.

Judith Brett was the editor of *Meanjin* from 1982-1986 and Chairman of the Literature Committee of the Victorian Ministry for the Arts, 1985-1987. She is writing a book on Robert Menzies and conservative ideology.

David Carter is a Lecturer in Australian Studies at Griffith University,

Brisbane. He is currently writing a study of the literary and political careers of Judah Waten.

Bruce Clunies Ross was educated at the Elder Conservatorium and the University of Adelaide, and later at Balliol College, Oxford. He has taught at Macquarie University, New South Wales, and Tufts University, USA, and is currently Associate Professor of English at Copenhagen University. He has published essays on Australian literature and music, and is editing the writings on music of the composer Percy Grainger.

Julian Croft is a Senior Lecturer in English at the University of New England. He has published a volume of poems, *Breakfasts in Shanghai* (1984), and a novel, *Their Solitary Way* (1985), and was the editor of Kenneth Slessor's collection of light verse, *Backless Betty from Bondi* (1984). He wrote a study of the Anglo-Welsh poet T. H. Jones in 1975 and co-edited that poet's *Collected Poems* in 1976. He was editor of *R. D. FitzGerald* (1987) and is currently writing with Ken Stewart *A History of Australian Poetry: 1788-1988*.

Jack Davis is an award winning Aboriginal playwright and poet. He has been joint editor of the Aboriginal magazine *Identity* (1973-1979). In 1976 he was awarded the BEM for services to the Aborigines and for his writings. His books of poetry are: *The First-born and Other Poems* (1970), *Jagardoo: Poems from Aboriginal Australia* (1978); his plays include: *Kullark* and *The Dreamers* (1982), *No Sugar* (1986), *Honeyspot* (1987) and *Barungin: Smell the Wind* (1988). In 1988 he was awarded the BHP Bicentennial Award of Excellence For Literature and the Arts.

Arthur Delbridge is the Director of the Dictionary Research Centre, Macquarie University, having retired from his position as foundation professor of linguistics in that university. Editor-in-chief of the *Macquarie Dictionary*, he pursues an interest in Australian lexicography and in the specification of an Australian style in publication.

Robert Dixon is a Lecturer in English at James Cook University, and author of *The Course of Empire: Neo-Classical Culture in New South Wales 1788-1860* (1986). He is currently writing on narrative form and ideology in Australian popular fiction, 1870-1914.

Martin Duwell is a Lecturer in the English Department of the University of Queensland where he teaches Old Norse, Rhetoric and Australian Literature. He was the editor of the journal *Makar* during the 1970s and ran Makar Press. He is assistant editor of *Australian Literary Studies* and the author of *A Possible Contemporary Poetry* (1982).

Peter Fitzpatrick is a Senior Lecturer in English at Monash University. His principal research interest is in recent Australian drama, and he is the author of *After 'The Doll': Australian Drama Since 1955* (1979), *Williamson* (1987), and of a number of articles in the area.

Alan Frost is a Reader in History at La Trobe University. He is the author of *Arthur Phillip, 1738-1814: His Voyaging* (1987) and, with Glyndwr Williams, the editor of *Terra Australis to Australia* (1988).

Ken Gelder is Senior Tutor in English at La Trobe University, Melbourne. He has published articles on Australian fiction and has been associate editor of the *Australian Book Review* and co-editor of the *CRNLE* [Centre for Research in New Literatures in English] *Reviews Journal.* He is currently co-writing with Paul Salzman a book on contemporary Australian fiction 1970-1988.

Robin Gerster teaches Australian literature at Monash University. He wrote his doctoral thesis on Australian war writing; this formed the basis of his critical study *Big-noting* (1987). At present he is co-writing a book on Australian cultural and political life in the 1960s.

Fiona Giles is a graduate of the Universities of Western Australia and Melbourne who is currently studying nineteenth century Australian fiction for her doctorate at Oxford. She has collected a volume of nineteenth century Australian women's short stories, *From the Verandah* (1988) and worked as a consultant to the British Library for its Australian Bicentennial Exhibition.

Kerryn Goldsworthy is a Lecturer in Australian Literature at the University of Melbourne. She edited *Australian Short Stories* (1983) and *Coast to Coast: Recent Australian Prose Writing* (1986), and edited *Australian Book Review* in 1986-7.

Cliff Hanna is a Senior Lecturer in the Department of English at the University of Newcastle, New South Wales. At present he is compiling a three volume collection of ballads relating to Australia.

Anthony J. Hassall is a Professor of English at James Cook University of North Queensland and Executive Director of the Foundation for Australian Literary Studies. He is the author of *Strange Country: A Study of Randolph Stow* (1986), and is editing a Randolph Stow volume for the University of Queensland Press Australian Authors series. He is General Editor of the UQP Studies in Australian Literature series.

Laurie Hergenhan is a Reader in English at the University of Queensland. He is foundation editor of *Australian Literary Studies* (1963 to the present, including a period as co-editor, 1971-1975, with E. Stokes) and general editor of the University of Queensland Press

Australian Authors series (formerly Portable Australian Authors series). From 1979-1982 he was foundation Director of the Australian Studies Centre, University of Queensland. His publications include: *A Colonial City: Selected Journalism of Marcus Clarke; Unnatural Lives: A Study of Australian Convict Fiction* (1983); *The Australian Short Story: An Anthology from the 1890s to the 1980s* (1986); an edition of George Meredith's *Harry Richmond* (1970).

Van Ikin is a Lecturer in English at the University of Western Australia. He is editor of *Australian Science Fiction* (1982), and is editor/publisher of the journal *Science Fiction: A Review of Speculative Literature* (1977-). He is currently writing *A History of Australian Science Fiction* with Russell Blackford.

Ivor Indyk is a Lecturer in Australian Literature at the University of Sydney and has published on a variety of topics in the field.

Dorothy Jones is a Senior Lecturer in English at the University of Wollongong. Her principal research interests are in post-colonial literatures, especially Australian and Canadian, with a particular emphasis on women's writing.

Brian Kiernan is an Associate Professor of English at the University of Sydney. His books include *Patrick White* (1980). He has edited collections of Henry Lawson, contemporary fiction, and criticism. He is currently writing a book on the playwright David Williamson.

Brian Matthews is a Reader in English at the Flinders University of South Australia. He is the author of *The Receding Wave: Henry Lawson's Prose* (1972), *Romantics and Mavericks: The Australian Short Story* (1986) and *Louisa* (1987); and editor of *Henry Lawson Selected Stories* (1971).

Patrick Morgan taught Australian literature at Monash University and is a Senior Lecturer at the Gippsland Institute of Advanced Education. He has published articles on the subject in magazines such as *Quadrant, Meanjin,* the *Bulletin, Kunapipi, Westerly,* and *Australian Book Review.* He was an Associate Editor of *The Oxford Literary Guide to Australia* (1987), and is currently completing a Bicentennial project on the literature of Gippsland.

Stephen Muecke is a lecturer in communications at the University of Technology, Sydney. He writes widely on cultural production, especially in relation to Aboriginal issues. He edited *Gularabulu* (1983) for Paddy Roe, and in 1984 co-authored *Reading the Country* with Roe and Krim Benterrak.

Brenda Niall is a Senior Lecturer in English at Monash University. She is the author of *Seven Little Billabongs: the World of Ethel Turner* *and Mary Grant Bruce* (1979) and *Australia Through the Looking Glass: Children's Fiction 1830-1980* (1984). Her biography of Martin Boyd will be published in 1988.

Richard Nile has taught history at the University of New South Wales, where he has completed a PhD thesis on 'The Rise of the Australian Novel'. He is currently a Lecturer at the University of Western Australia. His speciality is Australian culture. He edited J. M. Harcourt's banned novel *Upsurge* (1934; 1987) and co-edited (with Robert Darby) Lesbia Harford's lost novel, *The Invaluable Mystery* (1987). He is co-author, with Ffion Murphy, of the forthcoming, *Seduced Again: That Western City*, and is currently editing a collection of essays on Australia, *Making Way for Australian History.*

Elizabeth Perkins is an Associate Professor in English at the James Cook University of North Queensland. She has edited Charles Harpur, *The Poetical Works* (1984) and Charles Harpur, *Stalwart the Bushranger* (1987).

Peter Pierce is a graduate of the universities of Tasmania and Oxford and has lectured in English at the Australian Defence Force Academy. Co-author of a best-selling pasta cookbook, he was co-editor, with Chris Wallace-Crabbe, of *Clubbing of the Gunfire: 101 Australian War Poems* (1984) and was general editor of *The Oxford Literary Guide to Australia* (1987).

Susan Sheridan is a Lecturer in Women's Studies at the Flinders University of South Australia, and has taught literary studies at Deakin and Adelaide universities and the South Australian College of Advanced Education. Her book on Christina Stead will appear in 1988 in the Harvester Key Women Writers series. She is Review Editor of *Australian Feminist Studies.*

Adam Shoemaker is a Canadian-Australian who works for the Commission of the European Community, Brussels. He is the author of *Black Words, White Page: Aboriginal Literature, 1929-1988* (1988) and a co-editor, with Jack Davis, Colin Johnson and Stephen Muecke, of the first national anthology of Black Australian writing (in preparation).

Ken Stewart is a senior Lecturer in English at the University of New England. A founding member of the Association for the Study of Australian Literature, he has been co-editor of its magazine, *Notes and Furphies,* since 1978. He has published widely on nineteenth century Australian literary culture, and is currently writing a history of Australian poetry with Julian Croft.

James Tulip is an Associate Professor of English Literature at Sydney

University. He has widely reviewed contemporary Australian poetry in *Southerly* and is a contributing Editor to *Poetry Australia.*

David Walker teaches history at the University of New South Wales. He is author of *Dream and Disillusion: A Search for Australian Cultural Identity* (1976) and has since written widely on Australian social and cultural history. He is currently writing *Australian Perceptions of Asia* with John Ingleson.

Shirley Walker is a Senior Lecturer in English at the University of New England. She has published two books (one critical, one bibliographical) on Judith Wright's poetry and has edited a book of essays entitled *Who Is She? Images of Woman in Australian Fiction* (1983). She is currently writing a *History of Women's Writing in Australia.*

Chris Wallace-Crabbe, poet and critic, holds a Personal Chair in English at the University of Melbourne. His most recent collections of poetry are *I'm Deadly Serious* (1988) and a volume of prose poems, *Action Shots* (1988). In 1987-1988 he was Visiting Professor of Australian Studies at Harvard.

Elizabeth Webby is an Associate Professor in English at Sydney University. Her publications include *Early Australian Poetry* (1982) and *Happy Endings* (edited with Lydia Wevers, 1987). From 1988 she has been the editor of the literary magazine *Southerly.*

INDEX

Bold type indicates major discussion of a topic.